D0085947

MIS Cases
Decision Making with Application Software

MIS Cases
Decision Making with Application Software

Fourth Edition

M. Lisa Miller
University of Central Oklahoma

Pearson Prentice Hall
Upper Saddle River, NJ 07458

Editorial Director: Sally Yagan
Editor-in-Chief: Eric Svendsen
Acquisitions Editor: Bob Horan
Product Development Manager: Ashley Santora
Assistant Editor: Kelly Loftus
Editorial Assistant: Mauricio Escoto
Marketing Manager: Anne Fahlgren
Marketing Assistant: Susan Osterlitz
Associate Managing Editor: Suzanne DeWorken
Project Manager, Production: Ann Pulido
Senior Operations Supervisor: Arnold Vila
Operations Specialist: Michelle Klein
Cover Design: Suzanne Behnke
Cover Photo: Getty Images, Inc.
Printer/Binder: Courier/Westford
Printer/Cover: Lehigh Lithographers

Credits and acknowledgments borrowed from other sources and reproduced, with permission, in this textbook appear on appropriate page within text.

Pearson Education Ltd., London
Pearson Education Singapore, Pte. Ltd
Pearson Education, Canada, Inc.
Pearson Education–Japan
Pearson Education Australia PTY, Limited
Pearson Education North Asia Ltd., Hong Kong
Pearson Educación de Mexico, S.A. de C.V.
Pearson Education Malaysia, Pte. Ltd.
Pearson Education Upper Saddle River, New Jersey

PEARSON
Prentice Hall

10 9 8 7 6 5 4 3 2 1
ISBN-13: 978-0-13-238105-5
ISBN-10: 0-13-238105-2

Dedication

To Mom and Dad: As a child, you taught me many things. As an adult, you have taught me even more. Your love, support, and encouragement are constant and unwavering.

To Mark: You have shown me that life is a journey best shared by two. I am so thankful to have the opportunity to spend my journey with you.

Table of Contents

Part I: Spreadsheet

Part II: Database

Preface

Introduction

MIS Cases: Decision Making with Application Software, Fourth Edition serves as a supplementary textbook for any business course where students are encouraged to use application software to solve managerial problems. This casebook is especially useful for introductory management information systems, personal productivity, end user systems, and graduate, foundation-level management information systems courses. This casebook provides students with different case scenarios, emphasizes different software packages and their integration, emphasizes managerial problem solving, and provides varying levels of difficulty. By providing a variety of cases with different difficulty levels, the instructor can use this casebook as a leveling or teaching tool.

MIS Cases: Decision Making with Application Software, Fourth Edition contains numerous cases, reflecting human resource, production, accounting, financial, and marketing managerial decision-making situations. The cases present students with managerial decision-making activities, ranging from basic problem-solving situations to more advanced problem-solving situations. The number and variety of cases enable the instructor to select the most appropriate cases for his class, as well as vary the cases between semesters.

To prepare each case, students use spreadsheet, database, or Web page development software. Each case encourages students to use their knowledge, creativity, and software skills to solve realistic managerial problems. Fourteen cases require students to use varying levels of database development skills, and fourteen cases require students to use varying levels of spreadsheet skills. Two of the cases require students to apply basic Web development skills. Several of the cases are integration cases, requiring students to apply their knowledge of more than one software package to solve managerial problems. In particular, two integration cases require students to use intermediate to advanced spreadsheet and database skills. The integration cases are given a five star difficulty rating and may require extra time to complete.

Organization

MIS Cases: Decision Making with Application Software, Fourth Edition uses a standard format for each case. Each case uses a fictitious company and characters to present each case's requirements. Each case has difficulty rating, skills check, case background, case scenario, information specification, implementation concerns, test your design, and case deliverable sections. To facilitate the preparation of the database and integration cases, the database and integration case format includes storage specification and input specification sections. Likewise, the spreadsheet and Web page development cases have a design specification section.

Each case is given a difficulty rating. The difficulty rating is intended to help the instructor determine the appropriateness of the case for his students. At the beginning of the case, one or more stars designate the difficulty rating. Cases with a one star rating are the easiest cases in the casebook, while cases with a five star rating are the more rigorous cases.

The skills check feature provides both the instructor and students with a list of the primary skills required to complete the case. The instructor may use the skills check list to determine the appropriateness of the case for his students and whether the case should be used as a leveling or a teaching tool. Students can use the skills check list to determine whether they need further study before attempting the case.

The case background section provides the instructor and student with a quick summary of the case. Again, this enables the instructor to determine the appropriateness of the case for his students. The case scenario section sets the stage for the application and decision-making activities, provides insights into how the case's main character will use the application, and briefly identifies several of the case character's information requirements. The information specification section outlines additional information requirements for the case. The implementation concerns section provides final comments about the design and development of the application. This section also points out areas that may cause the student some concern and provides helpful hints about which tools or techniques the student can use to avoid potential trouble spots.

Once a student has developed the application, the test your design section requires the student to make modifications to his application. This section encourages the student to develop a flexible application that is adaptable to a manager's changing information needs. For instance, this section may require the student to generate a new query, add new records to a database, insert additional columns and formulas into a spreadsheet, or add additional content to a Web page.

The case deliverables section specifies what deliverables are to be submitted to the instructor. Each case requires the student to prepare both written and oral presentations for his case solution. This section also requires the student to provide working, electronic copies of his solution, hard copies, and results for the information requested by the case's character. The instructor, at his discretion, may require the student to submit one or all of the deliverables.

The fourth edition includes spreadsheet, database, and Web page tutorials and glossaries. The tutorials take the student step by step through the creation of a spreadsheet, database, and Web page for Timeka's Tanning Salon. The glossaries provide students with a brief explanation and screen shots for many of the skills identified in each case's skills check feature.

Support Material

Student data files, solution files, and an instructor's manual are the primary support materials for this casebook. To facilitate the preparation of most cases, student data files are available. Once the database or spreadsheet is created, students can use the data file to populate the database or spreadsheet. Solution files for many of the cases and an instructor's manual are available for casebook adopters. The instructor's manual contains teaching tips, additional comments about the cases, and suggested case solutions for many of the cases.

Acknowledgments

As is true in most business settings, the accomplishment of a goal is a team effort. The fourth edition of *MIS Cases: Decision Making with Application Software* would not be possible without the dedication and numerous contributions from my Pearson Prentice Hall team, students, colleagues, and family.

Although many individuals at Pearson Prentice Hall are instrumental to the fourth edition, Robert Horan and Kelly Loftus are keys to its success. I would especially like to thank Robert Horan. Robert's wealth of knowledge, motivational e-mails, encouragement, and dedication to this fourth edition are obvious. Kelly's professionalism, guidance, support, and attention to detail definitely enhanced the quality of the fourth edition.

My students and colleagues continue to provide valuable comments and suggestions. While I am fortunate to work with a talented group of individuals at the University of Central Oklahoma, I would like to offer a special thank you to Dr. Saba Bahouth, Dr. David Noel, Dr. Hassan Pourbabaee, Dr. Randall Ice, Dr. Robert Terrell, Dr. Bambi Hora, and Dr. Katherene Terrell for their feedback. My sincerest appreciation goes to both Dr. Bambi Hora and Dr. Katherene Terrell. From the first edition to the fourth edition, both Dr. Hora and Dr. Terrell have gone the extra mile to help a colleague and friend.

During the preparation of the fourth edition, my family's understanding and support were a constant source of encouragement. Mark, James, Joan, Tracy, Jacob, Danette, Baylee, Caedee, and Jacob Hash are my greatest inspirations. A special thank you goes to my husband, Mark, for his helpfulness, insights, recommendations, and comments during the preparation of this fourth edition.

CASE 1 Milligan's Backyard Storage Kits

Spreadsheet Case **Difficulty Rating:** ★

SKILLS CHECK
You should review the following areas:

SPREADSHEET SKILLS

- ✓ AVERAGE Function
- ✓ Cell Formatting
- ✓ Chart
- ✓ MAX Function
- ✓ MIN Function
- ✓ NOW Function
- ✓ Sort
- ✓ SUM Function
- ✓ Worksheet Formatting

CASE BACKGROUND

Milligan's Backyard Storage Kits, a mail order company, sells a variety of backyard storage unit kits and landscaping decorations to its customers. Although the company makes a profit, David Milligan, the company's owner, realizes that he can improve his company's operations if he better manages his inventory. Mr. Milligan requests your help in preparing an Inventory Analysis worksheet. The Inventory Analysis worksheet provides Mr. Milligan with information about his annual sales, cost of goods sold, gross profit, markup, inventory turnover, and days in inventory for his products. Preparing the worksheet for Mr. Milligan requires you to insert columns, use several functions, and apply proper formatting to the worksheet and cells.

CASE SCENARIO

Ten years ago, David Milligan was short on storage space. After shopping around for a backyard storage unit and not finding one that met his specifications, Mr. Milligan built his own storage unit for his backyard. Realizing that many homeowners had similar storage needs, Mr. Milligan began selling a backyard storage unit kit via mail order. He felt that given good instructions, precut lumber, and the necessary hardware, just about anyone could assemble a storage unit. His idea proved popular, and he now stocks and sells 35 different items, including storage barn, gazebo, and landscaping decoration kits.

Mr. Milligan does not use a formal, consistent inventory tracking system. Periodically, Mr. Milligan or his staff visually checks to see which kits are in stock. Although he does try to keep a certain level of each kit in stock, the lack of a formal inventory tracking system has led to the overstocking of some items and understocking of still other items. In fact, on occasion, a customer will request a particular kit, and it is only then that Mr. Milligan realizes that the kit is out of stock. If a kit is not available, Mr. Milligan must tell the customer that he is currently out of stock, and then hope that the customer will wait for a kit to become available.

Lately, Mr. Milligan has become concerned with his inventory management methods. He now wants to better manage his inventory. As a starting point, he wants to examine costs, sales, markup percentages, gross profits, inventory levels, inventory turnover, and days in inventory for his products. He asks you to review his inventory and make suggestions for improvement. He provides you with the data contained in Figure 1 and asks you to prepare an Inventory Analysis worksheet.

Figure 1: Inventory Data

Milligan's Backyard Storage Units Inventory Data					
Item No.	**Description**	**Unit Cost**	**Unit Sales Price**	**Average on Hand**	**Average Unit Sales/Year**
A00100	8' x 6' Aluminum Shed	$148.14	$199.99	48	475
A00110	10' x 8' Aluminum Shed	$185.17	$249.99	50	400
A00120	12' x 20' Aluminum Shed	$1,393.56	$1,950.99	32	65
A00130	6' x 4' Aluminum Shed	$346.36	$519.59	50	241
A00140	8' x 4' Aluminum Shed	$424.58	$620.75	50	215
A00150	10' x 14' Aluminum Shed	$650.99	$1,200.00	20	250
A00210	8' x 10' Aluminum Barn	$840.47	$1,050.59	75	202
A00310	12' x 8' Double Door Aluminum Shed	$1,043.57	$1,304.47	80	302
A00320	16' x 10' Double Door Aluminum Shed	$1,141.84	$1,507.24	12	50
A00410	8' x 10' Wood Barn	$541.33	$804.49	50	700
A00420	8' x 12' Wood Barn	$751.87	$999.99	48	140
A00430	10' x 16' Wood Barn	$808.26	$1,074.99	10	67
A00510	8' x 10' Picnic Table	$269.28	$399.99	26	299
A00520	3' x 7' Picnic Table	$207.42	$299.99	77	850
A00530	8' Child's Picnic Table	$210.59	$350.99	44	157
A00610	10' Octagon Cedar Gazebo	$2,499.99	$2,999.99	71	144
A00620	12' Cedar Octagon Gazebo	$2,963.99	$3,430.99	15	39
A00710	4' x 6' Cedar Shed	$333.33	$500.00	80	200
A00720	8' x 10' Cedar Shed	$1,135.32	$1,702.99	72	75
A00730	6' x 10' Cedar Garden Hut	$1,135.00	$1,350.00	80	175
A00740	8' x 10' Cedar Cabana Shed	$1,148.56	$1,607.99	75	136
A00750	6' x 6' Cedar Garden Hut	$879.99	$950.78	114	325
A00810	6' x 20' Covered Bridge	$1,250.00	$1,400.99	42	75
A00820	8' x 40' Covered Bridge	$2,509.72	$4,700.00	2	2
A00910	Wagon Planter	$11.42	$15.99	237	702

A00920	Mailbox Planter	$21.02	$27.99	230	845
A00930	4' Windmill	$30.66	$45.99	275	201
A00940	6' Windmill	$43.99	$65.99	300	278
A00950	6' Wishing Well	$53.32	$79.99	300	780
A00960	12' Wishing Well	$130.66	$195.99	25	147
A01100	Monroe Wooden Trellis	202.30	$252.87	10	25
A01110	Majesty Copper Trellis	379.29	$505.72	14	35
A01120	Boston Folding Trellis	145.92	$207.56	12	42
A01130	Miniature Folding Trellis	48.00	$54.87	20	100
A01140	Milligan's Superior Trellis	764.81	$899.78	1	7

Design Specifications

Mr. Milligan asks you to determine the cost of average inventory, annual sales, cost of goods sold, annual gross profit, gross margin ratio, markup percentage, inventory turnover, and days in inventory for each inventory item. The determination of these values requires you to add columns to the Inventory Analysis worksheet. Mr. Milligan asks you to use the formulas shown in Figure 2.

As Mr. Milligan will use the Inventory Analysis worksheet during a presentation, he wants the worksheet to have a professional appearance. To enhance the worksheet's appearance, you include an appropriate header and format to the worksheet, column, and row labels. The header should display the name of the business, the name of the worksheet, and the current date. As you construct the worksheet, you use the currency format for all columns containing dollar values. Also, for any column that contains a percentage, you use the percentage format and format the data to two decimal places.

Figure 2: Inventory Analysis Worksheet Formulas

Inventory Analysis Worksheet Formulas	
Annual Gross Profit	Annual Sales - Cost of Goods Sold
Annual Sales	Unit Sales Price * Average Unit Sales Per Year
Cost of Average Inventory	Unit Cost * Average Units on Hand
Cost of Goods Sold	Unit Cost * Average Unit Sales Per Year
Gross Margin Ratio	$\frac{\text{Annual Gross Profit}}{\text{Annual Sales Per Unit}}$
Markup Based on Cost	$\frac{\text{Unit Sales Price - Unit Cost}}{\text{Unit Cost}}$

Inventory Turnover	$\frac{\text{Cost of Goods Sold}}{\text{Cost of Average Inventory}}$
Days in Inventory	$\frac{365}{\text{Inventory Turnover}}$

Information Specifications

For the cost of average inventory, annual sales, cost of goods sold, annual gross profit, gross margin ratio, and markup percentage values, Mr. Milligan wants the average, minimum, and maximum value for each. Mr. Milligan wants to know the maximum unit cost, unit sales price, inventory turnover, and days in inventory values, as well as the minimum unit cost, unit sales price, inventory turnover, and days in inventory values. He also wants to know the total cost of average inventory, total annual gross profit, total cost of goods sold, and the total annual sales.

Mr. Milligan also needs answers to the following questions. Using your newly designed Inventory Analysis worksheet, provide Mr. Milligan with answers to his questions.

1. Mr. Milligan wants a markup of at least 30 percent on all items. Which items have markups less than 30 percent?
2. In terms of annual sales, which item has the lowest annual sales?
3. In terms of annual sales, what were Mr. Milligan's biggest selling items last year? Identify the top five.
4. What are the company's total annual sales?
5. What is the company's annual gross profit?
6. Based on average unit sales, which five items had the lowest sales? Based on average unit sales, which five items had the highest sales?
7. Mr. Milligan wants a column chart that compares the top five selling items. Based on annual sales, prepare the column chart for Mr. Milligan.
8. Which items have an inventory turnover greater than 12?
9. Which items have days in inventory values greater than 150 days?

Implementation Concerns

Although you are free to work with the design of your worksheet, the worksheet should have a consistent, professional appearance. Also, you should use appropriate formatting for the cells and worksheet. For instance, dollar values should display a dollar sign and be formatted to two decimal places.

Test Your Design

After creating the Inventory Analysis worksheet, you should test your design. Perform the following steps. Keep in mind that you may need to insert additional rows and columns to provide Mr. Milligan with this information.

1. Add the following six items to the Inventory Analysis worksheet.

Item No.	Description	Unit Cost	Unit Sales Price	Average on Hand	Average Unit Sales/Year
A01020	10' x 20' Aluminum Carport	$999.99	$1,789.95	27	45
A01030	12' x 24' Aluminum Carport	$1,199.99	$1,888.72	25	50
A01040	14' x 20' Aluminum Carport	$1,307.84	$2,500.99	15	27
A02010	8' x 12' Arbor Roof	$1,326.42	$1,550.42	4	10
A02020	12' x 20' Arbor Roof	$2,787.96	$4,100.00	10	12
A00160	6' x 6' Aluminum Shed	$370.11	$458.93	75	150

2. For each inventory item, Mr. Milligan wants to know what percentage of the company's total annual sales the item generated.

3. What is the gross margin per unit for each inventory item? Which inventory item(s) has (have) the largest gross margin per unit? Least?

4. Prepare a bar chart that compares the age of inventory for the trellis items.

5. Based on inventory turnover, which five items are held the longest in inventory?

6. Mr. Milligan wants to reduce his inventory by $200,000. Which items would you recommend that he remove from his inventory? Why?

CASE DELIVERABLES

In order to satisfactorily complete this case, you should build the worksheet(s) as described in the case scenario and then prepare both written and oral presentations. Unless otherwise specified, submit the following deliverables to your professor.

1. A written report discussing any assumptions you have made about the case and the key elements of the case. Additionally, what features did you add to make the worksheet(s) more functional? User friendly? (Please note that these assumptions cannot violate any of the requirements specified above and must be approved by your professor.)

2. A printout of the worksheet(s).
3. A printout of each worksheet's formulas.

4. An electronic, working copy of your worksheet(s) that meet the criteria mentioned in the case scenario and specifications sections.

5. Results for each question posed above. (A memo to your instructor discussing these results should also be provided.)

6. As mentioned above, you should prepare an oral presentation. (Your instructor will establish the time allocated for your presentation.) You should use a presentation package and discuss the key features of your worksheet(s). Also, discuss how the worksheet(s) is(are) beneficial for Mr. Milligan. What additional information should be included in the worksheet(s) to make it more useful?

CASE 2 Piedmont Trailer Manufacturing Company

Spreadsheet Case **Difficulty Rating:** ★

SKILLS CHECK
You should review the following areas:

SPREADSHEET SKILLS

- ✓ Cell Formatting
- ✓ Cell Reference
- ✓ Chart
- ✓ Consolidating Worksheets
- ✓ Formula
- ✓ IRR Function
- ✓ Protecting Cells
- ✓ Range Name
- ✓ SUM Function
- ✓ Worksheet Formatting

CASE BACKGROUND

Piedmont Trailer Manufacturing Company, a nationally recognized trailer manufacturer, produces a wide range of quality standard and custom-built trailers, ranging from gooseneck to bumper pull trailers. Although the Piedmont Trailer Manufacturing Company uses state-of-the-art information systems for most of its business processes, its custom order-tracking process is primarily manual-based and requires major renovations. In an effort to improve the custom order-tracking process, a systems analysis and design project is currently underway. As part of the systems development team, one of your responsibilities is to prepare an economic feasibility analysis for an upcoming presentation to management.

Ms. Geraldine Pablo, the project manager, asks you to construct an Economic Feasibility workbook. The purpose of this workbook is to summarize and analyze the benefits and costs associated with the proposed custom order-tracking project. The preparation of an Economic Feasibility workbook requires you to design five worksheets, use several formulas and functions, use basic cell and worksheet formatting, and consolidate data from multiple worksheets into a summary worksheet.

CASE SCENARIO

Quality trailers and excellent customer service are the two primary reasons why the Piedmont Trailer Manufacturing Company is the nation's largest manufacturer of standard and custom-built trailers. Although the majority of the company's income is derived from the sale of standard trailers, the number of custom orders is on the rise. When a custom order is placed, the request is captured on several paper forms and then routed to the production department. Often it takes three months before a custom order is released to production. This is due in part to the careful attention given to the customer by helping him select the right finishes, fixtures, trailer size, and other amenities. Management has decided that the custom ordering process is inefficient, time-consuming, and costly. In an effort to improve the custom order-tracking process, your project team is assigned the task of developing a custom order-tracking system.

During the planning phase, your project team identified several tangible benefits and costs. The new custom order-tracking system will save the company money by decreasing storage, staff, and order rework expenses. Additionally, the proposed system should increase sales, improve order processing speed, provide better data management, and streamline activities. Table 1 summarizes these benefits and their respective savings.

The proposed custom order-tracking system will incur both one-time and recurring costs. From one of your business courses, you recall that one-time costs often occur during the start up and development of a project, and recurring costs occur throughout the useful life of the new system. The one-time costs for this project currently include development personnel, training, project-related technology purchases, site-preparation, and miscellaneous costs. Table 2 lists the one-time costs and their estimated dollar values. Recurring costs include software maintenance, hardware, supplies, new information technology positions, and site rental costs. Table 3 summarizes these recurring costs.

Table 1: Yearly Recurring Benefits

Benefit	Approximate Dollar Value
Storage Savings	$30,000
Staff Reduction (2 people)	$45,000
Reduced Order Rework	$14,000
Increased Sales	$100,000
Faster Order Processing	$40,000
Better Data Management	$125,000
Streamline Activities	$80,000

Table 2: One-Time Costs

One-Time Cost	Approximate Dollar Value
Development Personnel	$142,000
Training	$45,000
Project-Related Technology Purchases	$65,000
Site Preparation	$105,250
Miscellaneous	
Conference-Related	$7,500
Supplies	$2,704
Duplication	$3,249

Table 3: Yearly Recurring Costs

Cost	Approximate Dollar Value
Software Maintenance	$55,000
Hardware	$30,000
Supplies	$35,000
IT Positions (3 people)	$160,000
Site Rental	$38,000

Design Specifications

Since the project is in the early stages of development, you want your workbook to be as flexible as possible, so that additional costs and benefits, when identified, are easily added to the Economic Feasibility workbook. You decide that the Economic Feasibility workbook should contain at least five worksheets: Documentation, One-Time Cost, Recurring Cost, Tangible Benefit, and Economic Feasibility Summary. The Documentation worksheet provides information about the creator, each individual worksheet, and the date created. (Your professor will provide additional guidelines for the Documentation worksheet.)

You decide to construct the One-Time Cost, Recurring Cost, and Tangible Benefit worksheets first, because these worksheets have a simple design. These worksheets each contain two columns, with the first column identifying the items in the category, and the second column containing the dollar values associated with the items. Each worksheet totals the dollar values; these totals are then used in the Economic Feasibility Summary worksheet.

As Figure 1 shows, the Economic Feasibility Summary worksheet has a more complex design. Since the Economic Feasibility Summary worksheet is a summary worksheet, it consolidates data from the One-Time Cost, Recurring Cost, and Tangible Benefit worksheets, requiring you to reference specific cells on these worksheets.

As part of the Economic Feasibility Summary worksheet design, you must discount the recurring benefits and costs to their present values. Although several ways exist to determine the present value of the benefits, you decide to multiply the recurring benefit (or cost) by a present value factor. Since each year requires a different present value factor, the worksheet must compute the present value factor for each year. You decide to use the formula provided below to determine each year's present value factor. (In the following formula, "i" refers to the discount rate, and "n" refers to the year. The worksheet shown in Figure 1 assumes that the project's useful life is five years.) To determine the present value of a benefit or cost for a particular year, you multiply the recurring value of the benefit or cost for that year by the present value factor for that year. The net present value of all benefits (or costs) is a summation of the benefits (or costs) up to and including the current year. The overall net present value is the difference between the net present value of all benefits and the net present value of all costs. The cash flow section provides a summary of the cash flows on a yearly basis, as well as a summation of the overall cash flows.

$$\mathbf{PVF = 1/(1+i)^{\wedge n}}$$

Figure 1: Economic Feasibility Summary Worksheet*

Piedmont Trailer Manufacturing Company
Custom Order-Tracking Project
(Current Date)

Discount Rate	**.14**						**Totals**
Year	**0**	**1**	**2**	**3**	**4**	**5**	
Benefits							
Recurring Value of Benefits	$0.00	$434,000.00	$434,000.00	$434,000.00	$434,000.00	$434,000.00	
Present Value Factor	1.000000	.877193	.769468	.674972	.592080	.519369	
Present Value of Benefits	**$0.00**	**$380,701.75**	**$333,948.91**	**$292,937.64**	**$256,962.84**	**$225,406.00**	
Net Present Value of All Benefits	**$0.00**	**$380,701.75**	**$714,650.66**	**$1,007,588.30**	**$1,264,551.14**	**$1,489,957.14**	**$1,489,957.14**
Costs							
One-Time Costs	($370,703.00)						
Recurring Costs		($318,000.00)	($318,000.00)	($318,000.00)	($318,000.00)	($318,000.00)	
Present Value Factor		.877193	.769468	.674972	.592080	.519369	
Present Value of Recurring Costs		($278,947.37)	($244,690.67)	($214,640.94)	($188,281.53)	($165,159.24)	
Net Present Value of All Costs	($370,703.00)	($649,650.37)	($894,341.04)	($1,108,981.98)	($1,297,263.51)	($1,462,422.75)	**($1,462,422.75)**
Overall Net Present Value							**$27.534.39**

Cash Flow Analysis							
Yearly NPV Cash Flow	($370,703.00)	$101,754.39	$89,258.23	$78,296.70	$68,681.31	$60,246.77	
Overall NPV Cash Flow	($370,703.00)	($268,948.61)	($179,690.38)	($101,393.68)	($32,712.37)	$27,534.39	

*Adapted from Modern Systems Analysis and Design, fifth edition, Jeffrey A. Hoffer, Joey F. George, and Joseph S. Valacich

Although Ms. Pablo is the primary user of the Economic Feasibility workbook, other project team members will have access to this workbook. Therefore, you decide that all cells, other than input cells, should be protected. (You may wish to use your system's online help feature to review worksheet protection.)

Information Specifications

Ms. Pablo wants to generate optimistic, realistic, and pessimistic views of the data, so she requests the ability to quickly change the discount rate. To satisfy this requirement, you include a cell on your Economic Feasibility Summary worksheet to hold the discount rate. Figure 1 shows that the discount rate is placed at the top of the worksheet. The discount rate is used in several formulas, so referencing this cell in a formula facilitates the economic feasibility analysis.

The Economic Feasibility Summary worksheet summarizes the costs and benefits, shows the present values of the costs and benefits, calculates the overall net present value, and shows the yearly and overall cash flows for the project. Although not shown in Figure 1, Ms. Pablo requests that the project's breakeven point and internal rate of return be determined. During her presentation to management, Ms. Pablo will use the breakeven point to help justify the project's viability and show how quickly management will recover its investment in the project. Since the internal rate of return provides an indication of the project's profitability, Ms. Pablo will use the internal rate of return to help justify management's investment in the project.

Ms. Pablo needs answers to the following questions. Using your newly designed Economic Feasibility workbook, provide Ms. Pablo with answers to her questions.

1. How will discount rates of 8, 10, 12, 14, and 16 percent affect the project's feasibility?

2. Reset the discount rate to 14 percent. Prepare a breakeven chart that compares the net present value of all benefits to the net present value of all costs.

3. If management stipulates that the internal rate of return must be equal to or greater than the discount rate, is this project still justifiable?

4. Assuming the discount rate is 14 percent, how will eliminating an additional staff position of $32,500 affect the economic feasibility assessment?

5. Assume that the staff position mentioned in Step 3 is eliminated, the site preparation cost increases to $120,000, and the discount rate is 14 percent. What impact will these changes have on the project's feasibility?

6. Assume that management has enough money to fund two development projects. After you determine this project's internal rate of return, compare its internal rate of return to the internal rate of returns for the proposed development projects listed in the following table. Based on the projects' internal rate of returns, do you think management will fund the custom order-tracking system?

Proposed Project	IRR
Delivery System	15.7 percent
Human Resources System	27.8 percent
Inventory Tracking System	18.9 percent
Forecasting System	23.7 percent

Implementation Concerns

To design the Economic Feasibility workbook described in the case scenario, you will create a workbook consisting of five worksheets. You should create separate worksheets for the documentation, one-time costs, recurring costs, recurring benefits, and economic feasibility summary. Since the Economic Feasibility Summary worksheet consolidates data from three of the worksheets, you should create this worksheet last.

Although you are free to work with the design of your worksheets, each worksheet should have a consistent, professional appearance. You should also use proper formatting for the cells. For instance, dollar values should display with a dollar sign and be formatted to two decimal places.

Test Your Design

After creating the Economic Feasibility workbook described in the case scenario, you should test the design of your worksheets. Perform the following operations.

1. What recommendations would you make if the useful life of the project is three years instead of five years? Six years? (Use the original case values and assume a discount rate of 14 percent.)

2. Identify at least three additional benefits that might be derived from this project. Estimate their value and include the values in your analysis. What impact do these new benefits have on your economic feasibility?

3. Identify at least one additional one-time cost and at least three additional recurring costs. Estimate their values and include these values in your analysis. What impact do these new costs have on your economic feasibility? Is the project still justifiable? Why or why not?

CASE DELIVERABLES

In order to satisfactorily complete this case, you should build the workbook as described in the case scenario and then prepare both written and oral presentations. Unless otherwise specified, submit the following deliverables to your professor.

1. A written report discussing any assumptions you have made about the case and the key elements of the case. Additionally, what features did you add to make the worksheets more functional? User friendly? (Please note that these assumptions cannot violate any of the requirements specified above and must be approved by your professor.)

2. A printout of each worksheet.

3. A printout of each worksheet's formulas.

4. An electronic, working copy of your workbook that meets the criteria mentioned in the case scenario and specifications sections.

5. Results for each question posed above. (A memo to your instructor discussing these results should also be provided.)

6. As mentioned above, you should prepare an oral presentation. (Your instructor will establish the time allocated for your presentation.) You should use a presentation package and discuss the key features of your worksheets. Also, discuss how the workbook is beneficial for Ms. Pablo. What additional information should be included in the workbook to make it more useful?

CASE 3 Francisco's Lawn Care

Spreadsheet Case **Difficulty Rating:** ★

SKILLS CHECK
You should review the following areas:

SPREADSHEET SKILLS

- ✓ **Cell Formatting**
- ✓ **Cell Reference**
- ✓ **Chart**
- ✓ **COUNTA Function**
- ✓ **COUNTIF Function**
- ✓ **Formula**
- ✓ **PMT Function**
- ✓ **Sort**
- ✓ **SUM Function**
- ✓ **SUMIF Function**
- ✓ **VLOOKUP Function**
- ✓ **Worksheet Formatting**

CASE BACKGROUND

Fernando Francisco owns and operates a small, growing lawn care business called Francisco's Lawn Care. Record keeping for the business has reached a point where Mr. Francisco needs a better system for tracking his customers, service dates, customer payments, and revenue. After considering several options for improving his record keeping system, Mr. Fernando decided that a Microsoft Excel workbook will be beneficial for him. The Lawn Care workbook contains several worksheets, including Customer, Payment, and Amortization worksheets. The preparation of this workbook requires you to create and format multiple worksheets, create several formulas, use several functions, and prepare charts.

CASE SCENARIO

As Mr. Francisco's client base continues to grow, he does not want to rely on his memory for price quotes, service dates, payments, and business revenue. Instead he will use Microsoft Excel to track this information. As you are familiar with Microsoft Excel, you agree to develop Mr. Francisco's Lawn Care workbook.

Currently, Mr. Francisco keeps basic information about his lawn care customers in a spiral notebook. In the notebook, he records the customer's first and last names, standard fee, additional weekly charges, total weekly charges, service day, lawn size, and start date. When a customer requests an estimate, Mr. Francisco provides an initial price quote based on the standard fees shown in Figure 1. The standard fee is the minimum price charged for a certain lawn size. Before giving a final quote, Mr. Francisco visits the customer's site and may adjust the initial quote based on his site visit. Any additional weekly charges are determined after Mr. Francisco visits the customer's site. Additional charges include such things as extra weed eating, yard fertilization, or cleaning a flower bed. For each customer, the total weekly charges include the standard fee plus additional weekly charges.

Figure 1: Pricing Guide

Francisco's Lawn Care Standard Pricing Guide	
Lawn Size	**Standard Price**
Small	$25.00
Medium	$35.00
Large	$50.00
Commercial	$75.00

After Mr. Francisco's site visit, the customer is given a final quote for the total weekly charges. If the customer agrees to the final quote, a weekly lawn maintenance schedule is arranged. Mr. Francisco wants a quote sheet developed, summing the weekly charges. After he returns to his office, he will prepare the quote sheet and mail it to the customer.

In one of your conversations with Mr. Francisco, he mentions that he needs to purchase new lawn care equipment, and he will purchase the lawn care equipment on credit. Before purchasing the lawn care equipment, he will evaluate different payment scenarios. As part of the workbook's design, he asks you to build an amortization schedule for him.

Design Specifications

The Lawn Care workbook will store the customer, service, and payment information that is currently kept in the spiral notebook. In the Lawn Care workbook, a worksheet should be created and named Customers. The Customers worksheet will store customer information. The Customers worksheet should have columns for customer first and last names, standard fee, additional weekly charges, total weekly charges, service day, lawn size, start date, and comments. Mr. Francisco will use the Comments column to record relevant comments about the customer's service, such as why additional charges were applied. When viewing the Customers worksheet, Mr. Francisco wants to see a total count of his customers, anticipated total revenue by day, anticipated total weekly revenue, and anticipated total monthly revenue. As the standard fee is based on lawn size, Mr. Francisco recommends that you recreate the standard pricing guide in the Customers worksheet, and then use the VLOOKUP function to retrieve the standard lawn size price. (If you are unfamiliar with the VLOOKUP function, consider using your system's online help feature to learn more about it.) The customer entries should be sorted alphabetically by last name.

Mr. Francisco asks you to create a Payment worksheet for him. The Payment worksheet enables Mr. Francisco to track customer payments. The Payment worksheet should include the payment date, customer's first and last name, total weekly charges, one-time fees, this week's total charges, amount paid, remaining balance, and comments columns.

Periodically, a customer will ask Mr. Francisco if he can remove a tree limb or trim a hedge. As this one-time fee is not reflected in the established total weekly charges, Mr. Francisco wants a one-time fee column included in the Payment worksheet. Sometimes a customer does not pay the correct amount, so Mr. Francisco wants a column to track the remaining balance. The Comments column enables Mr. Francisco to enter any comments about the transaction for later reference. For the total weekly charges column, Mr. Francisco recommends that you look up this value from the Customer worksheet.

Mr. Francisco asks you to prepare a quote sheet for him. After the initial site visit, Mr. Francisco will use the quote sheet to prepare a summary of the quoted charges. The quote sheet should show the standard fee, any additional weekly charges and the total weekly charges. Mr. Francisco wants the business name, current date and start date provided on the quote sheet.

Mr. Francisco will purchase new lawn care equipment on credit. To help him manage his payments, he asks you to create an amortization schedule. For each month, the schedule shows how much of the payment applies to interest, how much of the payment applies to the principle, and the remaining loan balance. Mr. Francisco will periodically make additional monthly payments of differing amounts, so he wants this capability built into the schedule.

Information Specifications

In addition to the information requirements specified above, Mr. Francisco requests answers to the following questions.

1. Mr. Francisco wants a list of his customers based on service day. Provide Mr. Francisco with this list.

2. Mr. Francisco wants to compare the business's anticipated revenue by week day. Prepare a chart that compares the anticipated revenue by week day. (You select the chart.)

3. Mr. Francisco wants to compare the business's weekly revenue by lawn size. Prepare a chart that compares weekly revenue by lawn size. (You select the chart.)

4. A local hardware store is advertising zero percent interest on all purchases, as long as the balance is paid within one year of the purchase date. If Mr. Francisco takes advantage of this offer, what will his monthly payments be? (Assume he spends $12,000 on new equipment and makes monthly payments.)

5. If the interest rate is 5 percent and the loan period is for two years, what are Mr. Francisco's monthly payments?

Implementation Concerns

Although you are free to work with the design of your workbook, it should have a consistent, professional appearance. You should apply appropriate formatting to the cells and worksheets. For instance, all cells containing dollar values should use a currency format and be formatted to two decimal places. Your worksheets should have appropriate headers, as well as appropriate column and row headings.

To prepare the Lawn Care workbook according to the specifications provided above, you will design several worksheets, construct formulas, may use the IF, COUNTIF, COUNTA, SUM, SUMIF, and VLOOKUP functions, and create charts. If you are not familiar with any of these skills, use your system's online help feature to learn more about the skill.)

Test Your Design

After creating your workbook, you should test your design. Perform the following steps.

1. If the lawn care business operates seven months out of the year, what is the projected revenue for the year? (Assume no new clients are added.)

2. Mr. Francisco has five new clients. Add the following new clients to your Lawn Care workbook. (Make any additional assumptions that you feel are necessary.)

Last Name	First Name	Additional Weekly Charges	Scheduled Day	Lawn Size	Start Date
Your Last Name	Your First Name	$10.00	Tuesday	Small	5/6/2008
Malcom	Loretta	$15.00	Tuesday	Large	5/6/2008
Orosco	Amilso		Tuesday	Commercial	5/6/2008
Popoola	Rajesh		Wednesday	Medium	5/7/2008
Rishel	Ravi	$25.00	Wednesday	Medium	5/7/2008

3. Mr. Francisco may raise his prices for next year. Using his current customer data for analysis, what impact will these prices have on next year's revenue?

New Lawn Care Prices	
Commercial	$90.00
Large	$60.00
Medium	$45.00
Small	$35.00

CASE DELIVERABLES

In order to satisfactorily complete this case, you should build the worksheet as described in the case scenario and then prepare both written and oral presentations. Unless otherwise specified, submit the following deliverables to your professor.

1. A written report discussing any assumptions you have made about the case and the key elements of the case. Additionally, what features did you add to make the worksheet(s) more functional? User friendly? (Please note that these assumptions cannot violate any of the requirements specified above and must be approved by your professor.)

2. A printout of each worksheet and chart.

3. A printout of each worksheet's formulas.

4. An electronic, working copy of your workbook that meets the criteria mentioned in the case scenario and specifications sections.

5. Results for each question posed above. (A memo to your instructor discussing these results should also be provided.)

6. As mentioned above, you should prepare an oral presentation. (Your instructor will establish the time allocated for your presentation.) You should use a presentation package and discuss the key features of your workbook. Also, discuss how the workbook is beneficial for Mr. Francisco. What additional information should be included in the workbook to make it more useful?

CASE

4

Maxi's Grocery Mart

Spreadsheet Case **Difficulty Rating:** ★★

SKILLS CHECK
You should review the following areas:

SPREADSHEET SKILLS

- ✓ **Absolute Cell Reference**
- ✓ **Cell Formatting**
- ✓ **Chart**
- ✓ **Formula**
- ✓ **IF Function**
- ✓ **Page Break**
- ✓ **Protecting Cells**
- ✓ **Relative Cell Reference**
- ✓ **SUM Function**
- ✓ **Worksheet Formatting**

CASE BACKGROUND

Since its opening almost 50 years ago, Maxi's Grocery Mart has continued to grow and evolve with the times. The family-owned business has survived many ups and downs and is currently experiencing a modest growth in business. Leroy Feronti, the current owner, wants to expand his family's business by renovating the grocery mart building. While Mr. Feronti has some personal funds available, he will need to procure a loan from the local bank. Before approaching the local bank, he would like to prepare and review several pro forma financial statements. If Mr. Feronti decides to go forward with the renovation, he will use the pro forma financial statements as part of his loan application. Mr. Feronti wants the pro forma income statement prepared first, and he asks you to prepare it for him. Preparation of the pro forma income statement requires you to design a worksheet with input and information sections, properly format the worksheet, construct simple formulas, perform what-if analysis, and generate a chart.

CASE SCENARIO

Maxi's Grocery Mart is a family-owned business that has been in operation since the 1950s. Although Leroy Feronti is very active with his business, he does employ a store manager, assistant manager, and 17 full-time employees. The store manager and assistant manager are paid a salary, and the employees are paid an hourly wage. Each employee works 40 hours a week, 50 weeks a year.

CASE 4: Maxi's Grocery Mart

Figure 1: Maxi's Food Mart Income Statement Outline

Maxi's Food Mart Pro Forma Income Statement				
	2008	2009	2010	2011
Sales				
Deli	Assume 5 percent of total sales each year.			
Dairy	Assume 19 percent of total sales each year.			
Canned Goods	Assume 10 percent of total sales each year.			
Frozen Foods	Assume 22 percent of total sales each year.			
Meats	Assume 21 percent of total sales each year.			
Produce	Assume 12.5 percent of total sales each year.			
Dry Goods	Assume 9 percent of total sales each year.			
Video Sales	Assume 1.5 percent of total sales each year.			
Total Sales	Assume $3,750,000.00 in total sales for 2008.			
Cost of Goods Sold				
Deli	Assume 50 percent of deli sales each year.			
Dairy	Assume 50 percent of dairy sales each year.			
Canned Goods	Assume 75 percent of canned good sales each year.			
Frozen Foods	Assume 65 percent of frozen food sales each year.			
Meats	Assume 50 percent of meat sales each year.			
Produce	Assume 65 percent of produce sales each year.			
Dry Goods	Assume 66 percent of dry good sales each year.			
Video Sales	Assume 30 percent of video sales each year.			
Total Cost of Goods Sold				
Gross Profit				
Operating Expenses				
Sales and Marketing	Assume 5.5 percent of total sales each year.			
General and Administrative	Assume 8.75 percent of total sales each year.			
Depreciation	Assume $20,000 per year.			
Wages	Includes the employees' wages, store manager's salary, and assistant manager's salary.			
Common Costs	Mr. Feronti's salary.			
Total Operating Expenses				
Income Before Taxes				
Income Taxes				
Net Income				

Figure 2: Assumptions and Additional Information

Maxi's Food Mart **Assumptions and Additional Information**	
Growth and Tax Rates	**Salary**
2009 Growth: 6.25 percent	Mr. Feronti: 12 percent of gross profit
2010 Growth: 7.75 percent	Store Manager: $57,000
2011 Growth: 8.25 percent	Assistant Manager: $42,000
Tax Rate: 35 percent	Employee Hourly Wage: $13.00

Having recently assumed ownership of the business from his parents, Mr. Feronti feels that one of the keys to the business's continued success is the renovation of the grocery mart building. Renovating the existing building will cost approximately $450,000. Mr. Feronti must borrow $300,000 from the local bank and will use income generated from the grocery mart to repay the loan. Mr. Feronti asks you to prepare a set of pro forma financial statements for him. He will use these statements to analyze his business. If he decides to pursue the renovation project, he will use the pro forma statements as part of his loan application.

Mr. Feronti asks you to use the income statement outline shown in Figure 1 and use the grocery mart's 2008 sales as the base period. You will use the 2008 sales to estimate Mr. Feronti's sales, cost of goods sold, expenses, taxes, and net income for the next three years. When preparing the pro forma income statement, several assumptions and additional information are necessary. Figure 2 provides these assumptions and additional information.

Design Specifications

As Mr. Feronti will use the pro forma income statement as part of his loan application, he requests that it have a consistent, professional, and well-organized appearance. Mr. Feronti specifically requests that you include an appropriate header and apply proper formatting to the cells and worksheet.

Using Figures 1 and 2 as guides, you decide that the worksheet requires both input and information sections. Figure 1 provides an outline and guidelines for constructing the information section and Figure 2 provides the necessary data for the input section. By creating separate sections, it is easy for Mr. Feronti to not only view the input data to his income statement, but also, if necessary, change the parameters, thus facilitating his decision-making activities.

The information section contains the pro forma income statement, and this section provides Mr. Feronti with information about his projected sales, cost of goods sold, operating expenses, and net income for years 2009 - 2011. The information section uses the grocery mart's 2008 sales as the basis for these projections. You make sure that, where appropriate, the information section formulas reference the cell values contained in the input section.

As you study Figure 1, you realize that Mr. Feronti wants his store item sales, cost of goods sold, and operating expenses expressed as a percentage of total sales. To facilitate Mr. Feronti's analysis, you place the total sales value in the input section, along with the other assumptions. By doing this, your formulas in the information section can reference the actual total sales figure. As you study Figure 2, you notice that Mr. Feronti's salary is 12 percent of gross profit. Since Mr. Feronti only draws his salary if the grocery mart makes a profit, you must build this logic into the income statement. You do so by using the IF function. To keep the information section's formulas from accidentally being updated, you protect the cells in the information section.

Mr. Feronti wants the input and information sections printed on separate pages. For each section's printout, he wants the results printed on a single page. The printouts should utilize a portrait orientation and be centered horizontally and vertically.

Information Specifications

Mr. Feronti needs information to support his decision making about the upcoming renovation to Maxi's Grocery Mart. Using the newly constructed pro forma income statement, provide Mr. Feronti with the information that he needs. (Before answering each of the following questions, reset your worksheet to its original values.)

1. What impact will sales growths of 9 percent in 2009, 9.5 percent in 2010, and 10 percent in 2011 have on the grocery mart's net income?

2. What impact will sales growths of 4 percent in 2009, 5 percent in 2010, and 5.5 in 2011 have on Mr. Feronti's net income?

3. Mr. Feronti wants a chart that compares the store items based on their 2008 sales. He asks you to select an appropriate chart type and then prepare the chart.

4. If Mr. Feronti decreases his salary to 8 percent and increases the employees' hourly wages to $15, what impact will this have on the grocery mart's net income?

5. Assume Mr. Feronti has 19 employees instead of 17. What impact will two additional employees have on the business's net income?

Implementation Concerns

The preparation of this case requires you to apply basic spreadsheet construction concepts. Since Mr. Feronti will change the input values during his decision-making activities, you should have a separate input section for the input values. Keep in mind that the formulas in the information section will reference the input cells. You should use absolute and relative cell references, as opposed to constant values.

Test Your Design

After creating the pro forma income statement worksheet, you should test your design. Perform the following steps.

1. Assume sales in 2008 were $2.5 million, instead of $3.75 million. Now, assume sales in 2008 were $7 million. What impact, if any, do these changes have? Are there any significant changes in the sales, expenses, or net income? (Other than the changes specified in this question, use the original case values.)

2. Make the following changes to the percent of sales for the following items. The deli accounts for 4 percent of sales; dairy items account for 18 percent of sales; canned goods account for 18 percent; frozen food items account for 20 percent; and meats account for 17 percent.

3. Make the following salary changes. Mr. Feronti takes home 16 percent of the gross profit, the store manager makes $60,000, and the assistant manager makes $48,000. How will these changes impact the grocery mart's net income?

4. Reset your sales percentages and salaries back to their original values and then make the following changes. Assume a discount chain is opening a grocery store in a neighboring town. Mr. Feronti thinks this may cause his sales to decrease. He thinks his growth may decrease in 2009 by 12 percent, 2010 by 10 percent and 2011 by 5 percent. Would you still recommend renovating the grocery mart? Why or why not?

CASE DELIVERABLES

In order to satisfactorily complete this case, you should build the worksheet as described in the case scenario and then prepare both written and oral presentations. Unless otherwise specified, submit the following deliverables to your professor.

1. A written report discussing any assumptions you have made about the case and the key elements of the case. Additionally, what features did you add to make the worksheet more functional? User friendly? (Please note that these assumptions cannot violate any of the requirements specified above and must be approved by your professor.)

2. A printout of each worksheet and chart.

3. A printout of the worksheet's formulas.

4. An electronic, working copy of your worksheet that meets the criteria mentioned in the case scenario and specifications sections.

5. Results for each question posed above. (A memo to your instructor discussing these results should also be provided.)

6. As mentioned above, you should prepare an oral presentation. (Your instructor will establish the time allocated for your presentation.) You should use a presentation package and discuss the key features of your worksheet. Also, discuss how the worksheet is beneficial for Mr. Feronti. What additional information should be included in the worksheet to make it more useful?

CASE 5 Klein Technology Seminars

Worksheet Case **Difficulty Rating:** ★★

SKILLS CHECK
You should review the following areas:

WORKSHEET SKILLS

- ✓ **AVERAGE Function**
- ✓ **Cell Formatting**
- ✓ **Chart**
- ✓ **COUNTIF Function**
- ✓ **MEDIAN Function**
- ✓ **MODE Function**
- ✓ **PivotChart**
- ✓ **PivotTable**
- ✓ **SUM Function**
- ✓ **Worksheet Formatting**

CASE BACKGROUND

Klein Technology Seminars provides information technology seminars to local corporations and continuously strives to provide its corporate clients with quality, timely instruction. As part of its quality-first strategy, seminar students are asked to complete customer satisfaction surveys. These satisfaction surveys are then reviewed by Dr. Klein, the company's founder. Based on the survey results, Dr. Klein makes adjustments to the company's courses.

To facilitate his analysis of the customer satisfaction surveys, Dr. Klein asks you to develop a Survey Results workbook. The preparation of this workbook requires you to design worksheets, use formulas, use several functions, use basic cell and worksheet formatting techniques, and prepare PivotTable and PivotChart reports.

CASE SCENARIO

Dr. Earl Klein is the founder and president of Klein Technology Seminars. As a former university vice president, Dr. Klein came into contact with many corporate executives. Frequently, the corporate executives would remark about the necessity of keeping their employees up-to-date in their field. Dr. Klein took this message to heart, and when he retired a few years ago, he formed Klein Technology Seminars.

Since its beginning, Klein Technology Seminars has seen a steady growth in its business and has a reputation for providing quality instruction to its clients. The company's reputation is due in part to its 10 full-time, highly qualified instructors. The instructors teach a variety of courses, ranging from productivity to certification courses. The courses are one-week courses, last from 8 a.m. to 5 p.m. each day, and are limited to 24 students. The company offers its courses on its campus, at the client's site, and at other off-site locations.

Once seminar attendees finish a course, they complete satisfaction surveys. The surveys help Dr. Klein judge the quality of the courses, as well as the instructors. Figure 1 shows a copy of the survey.

Until now, Dr. Klein has just read through the surveys and has not had time to analyze the survey data. Dr. Klein realizes the surveys contain a wealth of information, and he wants to analyze the data with a spreadsheet application. Dr. Klein assigns you the task of developing a Survey Results workbook that will enable him to enter and track the results of the satisfaction surveys.

Once the surveys are collected, Dr. Klein or his secretary will code each survey respondent's answers. For each question, the possible responses are given a unique number. For instance, if a respondent answers "no" for Question 1, then Dr. Klein will record "1" in the worksheet cell. If the respondent answers "yes" for Question 1, then Dr. Klein will record "2" in the worksheet cell. Figure 2 shows how the questionnaire responses are coded.

Figure 1: Customer Satisfaction Survey

Klein Technology Seminars
Satisfaction Survey

1. **Have you previously attended a technology seminar offered by Klein Technology Seminars?**

   a. No
   b. Yes

2. **Have you attended a technology seminar offered by another company?**

   a. No
   b. Yes

3. **Overall, I am satisfied with the course.**

   Strongly Agree Agree Neutral Disagree Strongly Disagree

4. **I will take another course with Klein Technology Seminars.**

   Strongly Agree Agree Neutral Disagree Strongly Disagree

5. **The information presented will be useful on my job.**

   Strongly Agree Agree Neutral Disagree Strongly Disagree

6. **The instructor was knowledgeable about the subject matter.**

   Strongly Agree Agree Neutral Disagree Strongly Disagree

7. **The seminar's content is timely.**

   Strongly Agree Agree Neutral Disagree Strongly Disagree

8. **The instructor met the stated course objectives.**

   Strongly Agree Agree Neutral Disagree Strongly Disagree

Figure 2: Customer Satisfaction Survey Codes

If Response Is:	Code
No	1
Yes	2
Strongly Agree	5
Agree	4
Neutral	3
Disagree	2
Strongly Disagree	1

Design Specifications

Dr. Klein hands you a copy of an incomplete workbook called Klein Survey. The Klein Survey workbook currently contains sample survey data in the Response worksheet. Dr. Klein asks you to use the data from the Response worksheet when designing the Survey Results workbook. Figures 3 and 4 show how the survey data are currently organized in the Response worksheet. Columns A through E provide general information about the course. As the general information is readily available, it is not necessary to collect this information from the survey respondent. Instead, Dr. Klein will enter the general course information as he enters the respondent's answers into the worksheet. Figure 5 explains the codes for Columns A through E.

Columns F - M display data that have been captured on the survey forms. The data displayed in these columns have been coded, meaning the survey responses have been coded using the codes displayed in Figure 2. For instance, if a student circled "no" as her answer for Question 1 on the survey form, then a "1" is displayed in Column F. Likewise, if a student circled "yes" as her answer for Question 1, then a "2" is displayed in Column F. (The codes help facilitate the analysis of the data.)

Figure 3: Survey Results Sample Data

Columns A - E

	A	B	C	D	E
1	Course No.	Location	Instructor ID	Class Size	Seminar Start Date
2	RTS1	2	2	10	10/6/2008
3	RTS1	2	2	10	10/6/2008
4	RTS1	2	2	10	10/6/2008
5	RTS1	2	2	10	10/6/2008
6	RTS3	3	5	12	10/6/2008
7	RTS3	3	5	12	10/6/2008
8	RTS3	3	5	12	10/6/2008

Figure 4: Survey Results Sample Data
Columns F - M

	F	G	H	I	J	K	L	M
1	Question 1	Question 2	Question 3	Question 4	Question 5	Question 6	Question 7	Question 8
2	1	2	4	3	4	4	4	4
3	2	2	5	4	4	5	4	5
4	1	2	1	2	5	1	2	5
5	2	1	1	2	4	4	4	4
6	2	2	4	4	2	5	4	5
7	2	1	4	2	1	5	5	2
8	2	1	5	5	5	4	5	2

The Response worksheet contains survey responses for a two-week period. Dr. Klein wants you to add a Summary worksheet to the Klein Survey workbook and then save the workbook as Survey Results. The purpose of the Summary worksheet is to summarize the survey response data contained in the Response worksheet. For each worksheet, you should include a worksheet title. Dr. Klein wants the title to reflect the contents of the worksheet, as well as the date range for the data the worksheet covers. Dr. Klein wants descriptive names for the column headings.

Figure 5: General Course Information Codes

Column	Codes	Explanation
A	Uses the actual course number.	Contains the course number.
B	1 = Client's Site 2 = Klein Technology Seminars 3 = Another Location	Indicates where the course was offered. The course can be offered at the client's site, at Klein Technology Seminars or at another location.
C	Uses the instructor's identification number.	Contains the instructor's identification number.
D	Uses the number of students enrolled in the class.	Indicates the number of students enrolled in the class. (Not all students submit a survey.)
E	Uses the start date of the seminar.	Indicates the starting date of the seminar.

When the survey forms are returned, Dr. Klein or his assistant will code and then enter the individual survey results into the Response worksheet. When entering survey data into the Response worksheet, Dr. Klein wants the results for each survey assigned a respondent number. This request requires the insertion of a new column. This column should be the leftmost column in the worksheet, and should include a unique number for each row that contains survey results. So, if you have 20 surveys, the surveys would be numbered 1 through 20, respectively.

As previously mentioned, the purpose of the Summary worksheet is to summarize the data contained in the Response worksheet. For each question, the Summary worksheet should provide a count for each possible response. The count should reflect the number of times a particular response for the question was given. For instance, the Summary worksheet should show how many "1" entries, "2" entries, and "3" entries appear in the Location column for the Response worksheet. For Questions 3 - 8, Dr. Klein wants to see their averages, modes, and medians displayed in the Summary worksheet. The Summary worksheet should also provide the average, mode, and median class size.

Where possible, Dr. Klein wants the Summary worksheet information displayed in a graphic format. Specifically, he asks you to prepare several charts, including a column chart comparing the user satisfaction ratings for each course, a column chart comparing the satisfaction ratings by instructor, and a bar chart showing the number of respondents who strongly agreed that the courses were useful.

Information Specifications

Dr. Klein will analyze the survey data at varying levels of detail. As mentioned above, Dr. Klein wants the survey results entered into a Response worksheet, and in the Summary worksheet he wants to see summarized results. Dr. Klein also wants to view data based on multiple conditions (such as satisfaction ratings for instructors by course). You suggest to Dr. Klein that the PivotTable and PivotChart reports are excellent tools for this type of analysis. Dr. Klein will use these tools to view the overall satisfaction ratings for each of his instructors by course, as well as the objectives met ratings for each course by instructor.

In addition to the information requests specified above, Dr. Klein wants answers for the following questions.

1. For each course, what is its average class size?

2. What percentage of respondents has attended a seminar before? Use a pie chart to summarize the results.

3. How many respondents who have taken a seminar course with another company agreed or strongly agreed that they would take another course with Klein Technology Seminars?

4. How many students strongly agreed that their instructor was knowledgeable about the subject matter? Display this information on a separate page for each course.

5. How did the students rate their instructor on the instructor's ability to meet course objectives? For each instructor, provide a count for each response. If possible, Dr. Klein wants this information summarized in a chart. (You select the chart.)

6. Which instructor had the highest percent of strongly agreed responses for Question 6?

Implementation Concerns

Although you are free to work with the design of your workbook, the worksheets should have a consistent, professional appearance. Also, you should use appropriate formatting for the cells and worksheets.

This case requires you to insert columns into worksheets, consolidate information into a summary worksheet, use formulas, use several functions, and use the PivotTable and PivotChart report tools. Although it depends on how you design the Summary worksheet, the COUNTIF function can be used in a formula to determine the response counts.

Test Your Design

After creating the Survey Results workbook, you should test your design. Perform the following steps.

1. Copy the survey results from the TYD Data worksheet located in the Klein Survey workbook and then paste these results immediately below the row containing the last October 13, 2008 entry.

2. Figures 6, 7, and 8 provide the results for three surveys. Enter the results for each survey into the Response worksheet. (You will need to code the response data.) For the survey results shown in Figure 6, the course was offered during the week of October 13th; the course number is RTS4; the location is 3; the Instructor ID is 2, and the course was conducted with 15 students. For the survey results shown in Figure 7, the course was offered during the week of October 20th; the course number is RTS4; the location is 2; the Instructor ID is 3, and the course was conducted with 23 students. For the survey results shown in Figure 8, the course was offered during the week of October 27th; the course number is RTS2; the location is 1; the Instructor ID is 4, and the course was conducted with 10 students.

3. Provide counts of the satisfaction ratings by class size for each instructor. Summarize this information in a PivotTable.

4. Which instructor had the highest percent of strongly disagree responses for Question 8?

5. Of those students who attended a seminar provided by another company, how did they rate Klein Technology Seminars? How do these results compare to students who have not attended a seminar offered by another company? Use a PivotTable to summarize this information. Also, prepare a chart that summarizes this information. (You select the chart.)

6. By class, how many students strongly agreed that the class provided useful information for their jobs? Summarize your results in a bar chart.

Figure 6: Survey Results

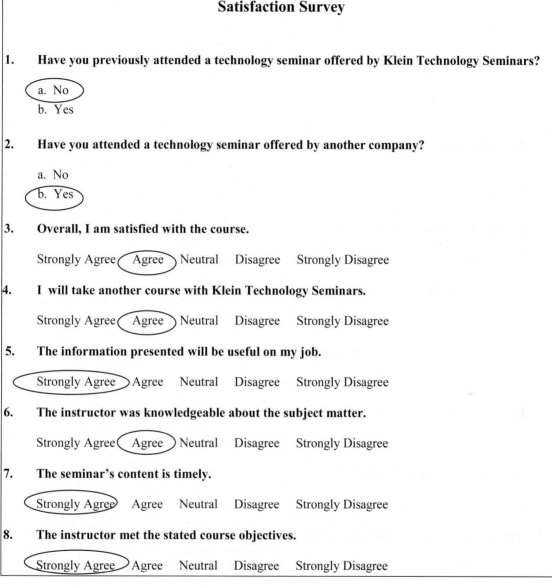

Klein Technology Seminars
Satisfaction Survey

1. **Have you previously attended a technology seminar offered by Klein Technology Seminars?**

   a. No (circled)
   b. Yes

2. **Have you attended a technology seminar offered by another company?**

   a. No
   b. Yes (circled)

3. **Overall, I am satisfied with the course.**

   Strongly Agree   Agree (circled)   Neutral   Disagree   Strongly Disagree

4. **I will take another course with Klein Technology Seminars.**

   Strongly Agree   Agree (circled)   Neutral   Disagree   Strongly Disagree

5. **The information presented will be useful on my job.**

   Strongly Agree (circled)   Agree   Neutral   Disagree   Strongly Disagree

6. **The instructor was knowledgeable about the subject matter.**

   Strongly Agree   Agree (circled)   Neutral   Disagree   Strongly Disagree

7. **The seminar's content is timely.**

   Strongly Agree (circled)   Agree   Neutral   Disagree   Strongly Disagree

8. **The instructor met the stated course objectives.**

   Strongly Agree (circled)   Agree   Neutral   Disagree   Strongly Disagree

Figure 7: Second Survey Results

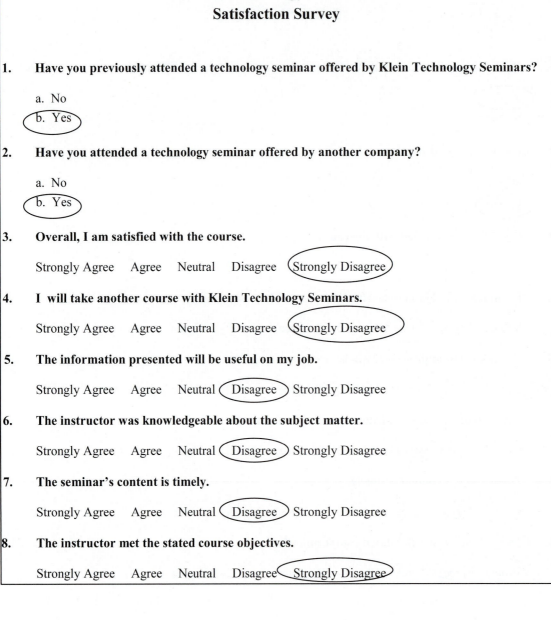

Klein Technology Seminars

Satisfaction Survey

1. Have you previously attended a technology seminar offered by Klein Technology Seminars?

a. No
b. Yes

2. Have you attended a technology seminar offered by another company?

a. No
b. Yes

3. Overall, I am satisfied with the course.

Strongly Agree   Agree   Neutral   Disagree   Strongly Disagree

4. I will take another course with Klein Technology Seminars.

Strongly Agree   Agree   Neutral   Disagree   Strongly Disagree

5. The information presented will be useful on my job.

Strongly Agree   Agree   Neutral   Disagree   Strongly Disagree

6. The instructor was knowledgeable about the subject matter.

Strongly Agree   Agree   Neutral   Disagree   Strongly Disagree

7. The seminar's content is timely.

Strongly Agree   Agree   Neutral   Disagree   Strongly Disagree

8. The instructor met the stated course objectives.

Strongly Agree   Agree   Neutral   Disagree   Strongly Disagree

Figure 8: Third Survey Results

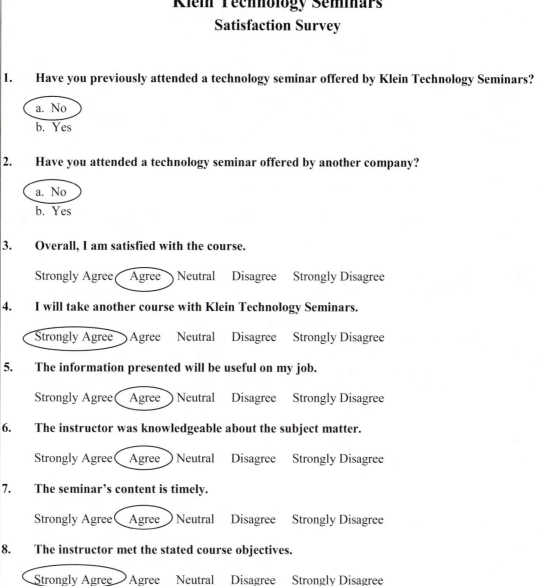

Klein Technology Seminars
Satisfaction Survey

1. **Have you previously attended a technology seminar offered by Klein Technology Seminars?**

   a. No (circled)
   b. Yes

2. **Have you attended a technology seminar offered by another company?**

   a. No (circled)
   b. Yes

3. **Overall, I am satisfied with the course.**

   Strongly Agree | Agree (circled) | Neutral | Disagree | Strongly Disagree

4. **I will take another course with Klein Technology Seminars.**

   Strongly Agree (circled) | Agree | Neutral | Disagree | Strongly Disagree

5. **The information presented will be useful on my job.**

   Strongly Agree | Agree (circled) | Neutral | Disagree | Strongly Disagree

6. **The instructor was knowledgeable about the subject matter.**

   Strongly Agree | Agree (circled) | Neutral | Disagree | Strongly Disagree

7. **The seminar's content is timely.**

   Strongly Agree | Agree (circled) | Neutral | Disagree | Strongly Disagree

8. **The instructor met the stated course objectives.**

   Strongly Agree (circled) | Agree | Neutral | Disagree | Strongly Disagree

CASE DELIVERABLES

In order to satisfactorily complete this case, you should build the workbook as described in the case scenario and then prepare both written and oral presentations. Unless otherwise specified, submit the following deliverables to your professor.

1. A written report discussing any assumptions you have made about the case and the key elements of the case. Additionally, what features did you add to make the worksheets more functional? User friendly? (Please note that these assumptions cannot violate any of the requirements specified above and must be approved by your professor.)
2. A printout of each worksheet.
3. A printout of each worksheet's formulas.
4. An electronic, working copy of your workbook that meets the criteria mentioned in the case scenario and specifications sections.
5. Results for each question posed above. (A memo to your instructor discussing these results should also be provided.)
6. As mentioned above, you should prepare an oral presentation. (Your instructor will establish the time allocated for your presentation.) You should use a presentation package and discuss the key features of your workbook. Also, discuss how the workbook is beneficial for Dr. Klein. What additional information should be included in the workbook to make it more useful?

CASE 6 Terrell & Terrell Property Management, Inc.

Spreadsheet Case **Difficulty Rating:** ★★

SKILLS CHECK
You should review the following areas:

SPREADSHEET SKILLS

- ✓ **AVERAGE Function**
- ✓ **Cell Formatting**
- ✓ **Chart**
- ✓ **External Cell Reference**
- ✓ **MAX Function**
- ✓ **MIN Function**
- ✓ **SUM Function**
- ✓ **Template**
- ✓ **Worksheet Formatting**

CASE BACKGROUND

Reyna and Rupert Terrell own a small property management business, consisting of four duplex units, three rent houses, and three commercial buildings. As part of their property management business, the Terrells track each unit's income and expenses, as well as the overall income and expenses for their business. Although their existing file management system is adequate, the Terrells want a more flexible property management system that will enable them to monitor and analyze their business's cash flows at varying levels of detail.

The Terrells ask you to prepare a standard cash flow worksheet template that summarizes each rental property's income and expenses, a summary worksheet that summarizes the business's income and expenses from all the rental properties, and several workbooks that will be used to organize the cash flow worksheets. Designing the cash flow worksheets requires you to format cells and worksheets appropriately, use several functions, use external workbook references, and work with multiple workbooks.

CASE SCENARIO

Last year Reyna and Rupert Terrell were looking for ways to earn additional retirement income. After locating, purchasing, and renovating several properties in the Crater Lake area, they began renting their properties to the public. The Terrells currently own four duplex units, three rent houses, and three commercial buildings. Although the rental properties generate a modest income for the Terrells, maintaining the properties can be expensive at times, because all units have appliance, property tax, insurance, advertisement, routine maintenance, materials, cable, utility, labor, and miscellaneous expenses.

The duplexes, rent houses, and commercial buildings are equipped with major appliances, such as dishwashers, washers, dryers, and refrigerators. When an appliance is no longer repairable, the Terrells replace the appliance and charge the expense to the unit. The Terrells must also pay property tax and insurance for each unit. The property tax is paid once a year, usually in December, and insurance is paid twice a year, generally in June and December. Routine maintenance includes such things as mowing, general landscaping, replacing air filters, cleaning empty rental units, and hauling off trash. When a rental unit requires repairs or routine maintenance, the Terrells record the labor charges, as well as the cost of the materials. Materials include any necessary items used to repair or clean a unit. As an enticement for potential renters, the Terrells pay for basic cable, even for the commercial buildings. When a unit is vacant, the Terrells place an advertisement in the local newspaper and run the advertisement until the unit is rented.

The Terrells use a simple filing system to track each rental unit's income and expenses. Although the filing system provides the Terrells with the necessary income and expense data, analyzing the income and expense data is cumbersome at best. The Terrells realize that using a spreadsheet application will make their property management activities much easier, more efficient, and more accurate. The Terrells ask you to organize their income and expense data into electronic workbooks, so that they can better manage their rental properties.

Design Specifications

The Terrells ask you to create a cash flow worksheet for each rental unit and a summary cash flow worksheet. As the Terrells want each cash flow worksheet to have a similar look and feel and will use the cash flow worksheet for future properties that they purchase, you decide that a standard cash flow template is necessary. Once you create the standard cash flow template, the Terrells can use the template to enter income and expense data for each rental unit. Figure 1 provides a sketch of a partially completed cash flow worksheet. (Figure 1 shows a cash flow worksheet for six months. Your cash flow worksheet should accommodate 12 months.)

As Figure 1 shows, the cash flow worksheet records the monthly income and expenses for a particular rental unit. Although not shown in Figure 1, the Terrells want to know each month's total expenses, monthly cash flow, overall cash flow, year-to-date total for each expense, and year-to-date total income. The monthly cash flow is the difference between the monthly income and total monthly expenses, and the overall cash flow is a summation of the monthly cash flow up to and including the current month. The year-to-date total for each expense sums the expenses incurred so far that year. The year-to-date total income displays the total income received so far in a given year.

Figure 1: Cash Flow Worksheet

Terrell and Terrell Property Management, Inc. Cash Flow Worksheet (Current Date)						
	1/1/08	**2/1/08**	**3/1/08**	**4/1/08**	**5/1/08**	**6/1/08**
Rent						
Expenses						
Advertising						
Appliances						
Cable						
Insurance						
Labor						
Material						
Miscellaneous						
Property						
Routine Maintenance						
Utilities						

The Terrells want the individual cash flow worksheets grouped according to property type. Since they have three main types of rental properties, you create Duplex, House, and Commercial workbooks. After the cash flow worksheets and workbooks are created, you prepare a Summary worksheet and place the Summary worksheet in its own Summary workbook. The Summary worksheet summarizes the income and expense data contained in the other workbooks. The Summary worksheet should show the name of the rental unit, as well as the rental unit's year-to-date income and year-to-date total for each expense category. The Summary worksheet should also show the total expenses and overall cash flow for each property type (commercial, duplex, and house). As the Summary worksheet must reference data contained in multiple workbooks, you use external cell references in the Summary worksheet to retrieve the necessary data from the other workbooks. (At this point, you may wish to review your system's online help feature to review external cell references.) The Terrells also request that the Summary worksheet resemble the individual cash flow worksheets.

Information Specifications

The Terrells will use the cash flow worksheets to better manage the income and expenses for their rental units. Each individual cash flow worksheet provides information specific to a particular rental unit's monthly income and expenses, year-to-date income and expenses, monthly cash flow, and overall cash flow. In addition to this information, the Terrells request average, minimum, and maximum values for each expense category in the individual cash flow worksheets, as well as the summary worksheet. The Terrells ask you to use data from the Summary worksheet to prepare two charts. The first chart compares the income for each unit, and the second chart compares the overall expenses for each unit. (You may select the chart types.)

In addition to the information requirements specified above, Mr. and Mrs. Terrell request answers to the following questions. Using the newly designed worksheets, provide Mr. and Mrs. Terrell with answers to these questions.

1. What was the rental income from all units last year?

2. On average, how much was spent in each expense category this past year?

3. Based on data contained in the Summary worksheet, where did the Terrells incur the largest expense?

4. What are the total revenues by property type?

5. What are the total expenses by property type?

6. What is the operating income by property type?

7. Should the Terrells raise the rent on any of their properties? Why?

Implementation Concerns

Although you are free to work with the design of your worksheets, each worksheet should have a consistent, professional appearance. Also, you should use appropriate formatting for the cells and worksheets. For instance, dollar values should display a dollar sign and be formatted to two decimal places. Since the worksheets have similar categories and contain similar data, you should strive to keep the worksheets' appearances similar.

The Terrells will use the individual cash flow worksheets to maintain the income and expense data for their individual rental property units. The Summary worksheet summarizes the data contained in the individual cash flow worksheets. As the Summary worksheet references external data, you will use external workbook references. Although you can manually enter an external workbook reference into a Summary worksheet cell, it is easier and less error-prone, if you use the point-and-click method. (For more information about external workbook references, use your system's online help feature.)

Test Your Design

After creating the Commercial, Duplex, House, and Summary workbooks, you should test your design. Perform the following steps.

1. Prepare a cash flow worksheet and update the Summary worksheet for the following property.

   The Terrells purchased a third duplex and currently rent one of the duplex units. (The second unit is undergoing renovations.) The duplex unit is located at 1412 Mockingbird and rents for $1,950.00 a month. The duplex unit was rented in November and December. October expenses include $2,500.00 in labor, $705.00 in materials, $25.00 in advertising, $98.00 in utilities, $1,050.72 in appliances, and $50.00 in routine maintenance. November expenses include $84.48 in cable, $98.00 in utilities, and $50.00 in routine maintenance. December expenses include $84.48 in cable, $98.00 in utilities, and $50.00 in routine maintenance. Property taxes and an insurance premium are paid in December. The property taxes are $1,050.00, and the insurance premium is $600.00.

2. The Terrells want a chart comparing the year-to-date income for each rental unit category. (You may choose which chart type to use.)

3. What is the overall cash flow for the rental properties?

CASE DELIVERABLES

In order to satisfactorily complete this case, you should build the workbooks as described in the case scenario and then prepare both written and oral presentations. Unless otherwise specified, submit the following deliverables to your professor.

1. A written report discussing any assumptions you have made about the case and the key elements of the case. Additionally, what features did you add to make the worksheets and workbooks more functional? User friendly? (Please note that these assumptions cannot violate any of the requirements specified above and must be approved by your professor.)

2. A printout of each worksheet and chart.

3. A printout of each worksheet's formulas.

4. Electronic, working copies of your workbooks that meet the criteria mentioned in the case scenario and specifications sections.

5. Results for each question posed above. (A memo to your instructor discussing these results should also be provided.)

6. As mentioned above, you should prepare an oral presentation. (Your instructor will establish the time allocated for your presentation.) You should use a presentation package and discuss the key features of your worksheets and workbooks. Also, discuss how the worksheets and workbooks are beneficial for Mr. and Mrs. Terrell. What additional information should be included in the worksheets and workbooks to make them more useful?

CASE 7 Mark's Collectibles, Inc.

Spreadsheet Case **Difficulty Rating:** ★★★

SKILLS CHECK
You should review the following areas:

SPREADSHEET SKILLS

- ✓ **AVERAGE Function**
- ✓ **Cell Formatting**
- ✓ **Chart**
- ✓ **COUNTA Function**
- ✓ **COUNTIF Function**
- ✓ **Import External Data (optional)**
- ✓ **Insert Sheet Columns**
- ✓ **MAX Function**
- ✓ **MEDIAN Function**
- ✓ **MIN Function**
- ✓ **MODE Function**
- ✓ **PivotTable**
- ✓ **Sort**
- ✓ **SUM Function**
- ✓ **Worksheet Formatting**

CASE BACKGROUND

Mark's Collectibles is a newly established online reseller of the very popular Tree Point Babies stuffed animals. Periodically, Mark Allan, the owner of the small, online business, downloads his Web site's traffic statistics from his Web hosting service. As the downloaded data are not in a useful format, Mr. Allan hires you to prepare a Site Statistics Analysis worksheet. The Site Statistics Analysis worksheet provides Mr. Allan with information about his Web site's visitors, including the number of visited pages, types of operating systems, browsers, visit durations, and used bandwidth. Preparing the worksheet requires you to properly format and design the Site Statistics Analysis worksheet, determine the visit duration for each visitor, the most popular operating systems, most popular browsers, most popular site connections, and amount of used bandwidth.

CASE SCENARIO

A few years ago, small, stuffed animals called Tree Point Babies became very popular with collectors, and demand for retired Tree Point Babies has continued to grow. Each month

Tree Point Babies issues several new stuffed animals. Collectors, like Mark Allan, purchase many of these stuffed animals in the hopes that the stuffed animals can be resold at a later date for a profit.

Mark's Collectibles is a newly formed, small, online reseller of the popular Tree Point Babies. In an effort to widen his market, Mr. Allan has built a small Web site, showing high-quality images of his available Tree Point Babies. Mr. Allan pays a nominal fee to a Web hosting service to host his Web site. As part of its service, the Web hosting service provides Mr. Allan with a text file containing traffic statistics for his Web site. Figure 1 shows a sample of this data. (The bandwidth is shown in kilobytes.) Currently, Mr. Allan purchases 10GB of bandwidth each month from the Web hosting service. If he uses more than his allotted amount, he is charged for the extra bandwidth.

Figure 1: Sample Data from Web Site Statistics Text File

IP Address	Operating System	Browser	Site Connection	Add To Favorites	Entry	Exit	Bandwidth	Viewed Page
999.010.210.133	Windows	Internet Explorer	HotBot	Yes	39731.47638	39731.49344	400	4
999.250.150.140	Linux	Firefox	Yahoo	No	39724.47352	39724.48189	1	3
999.111.233.190	Windows	Netscape	Lycos	Yes	39724.58203	39724.60697	250	2
999.140.152.160	Windows	Internet Explorer	AltaVista	No	39726.4299	39726.44541	750	15
999.180.007.222	Macintosh	Internet Explorer	Dogpile	No	39726.61228	39726.62361	255	4

Design Specifications

As previously mentioned, Mr. Allan periodically downloads a text file that contains the Web site's traffic data. As Figure 1 shows, the text file is not in a useful format, and the data must be formatted in order to provide useful information to Mr. Allan.

Mr. Allan gives you the most recent text file containing his Web site's traffic data and asks you to import the data into a worksheet. To improve the appearance of the data, Mr. Allan asks you to properly format the data. For instance, you can apply a time format that will more easily display the dates and times of visitor entries and exits. He also asks you to include a header in the worksheet. He specifically requests that a worksheet title and date range indicating the time series for the data be placed at the top of the worksheet.

Mr. Allan wants each row of data to be assigned a visitor number. The visitor number is intended to help him quickly determine the number of visits his Web site has received and is not intended to uniquely identify each visitor. Including a visitor number for each record requires the addition of a new column. Mr. Allan wants the Visitor Number column to be the leftmost column in the worksheet.

For each visit, Mr. Allan wants to know the visit duration. As you study the imported data, you notice that the entry and exit times for each visit are included. You decide to insert a Visit Duration column. You determine the visit duration values for this column by taking the difference between the exit and entry times.

Information Specifications

For the Visit Duration, Bandwidth, and Viewed Pages columns, Mr. Allan wants the worksheet to display the median and mean for each of these columns. Mr. Allan wants the worksheet to display the mode for the Bandwidth and Viewed Pages columns. The median identifies the middle numbers from the visit duration, bandwidth, and viewed pages values. The mode indicates the most frequently occurring bandwidth and number of viewed pages values. The mean provides averages for the visit duration, bandwidth, and viewed pages columns. Mr. Allan also wants the worksheet to show the maximum and minimum values for the Visit Duration, Bandwidth, and Viewed Pages columns.

Mr. Allan needs answers to the following questions. Using your newly designed Site Statistics Analysis worksheet, provide Mr. Allan with answers to his questions.

1. What is the average daily bandwidth used?

2. How many pages were viewed in October? November? December? Assume Mr. Allan wants a chart that compares the number of viewed pages for each month. What type of chart would be appropriate? Prepare the chart.

3. What is the average stay for each visitor? What is the longest time a visitor stayed at the Web site? What is the shortest visit?

4. Mr. Allan wants a chart that compares the site connections used to link to his Web site and the number of times the site connection was used. The chart should display the site connection data by month.

5. What percentage of visitors added the Web site to their list of favorite links? The chart should compare the visitor percentages by month.

6. Mr. Allan wants to know the average stay by operating system, connection, and browser. Mr. Allan wants this information displayed in pivot tables. Based on the results, what conclusions might you draw?

Implementation Concerns

Although you are free to work with the design of your worksheet, the worksheet should have a consistent, professional appearance. Also, you should use appropriate formatting for the cells and worksheet. Your instructor will provide you with either the text file containing the Web site statistics data referenced in the case scenario or with instructions on how to obtain the necessary Web site statistics data.

Test Your Design

After creating the Site Statistics Analysis worksheet, you should test your design. Perform the following steps.

1. Add the following data for January 2009 to your worksheet.

IP Address	Operating System	Browser	Site Connection	Add To Favorites	Entry	Exit	Bandwidth	Viewed Pages
999.010.210.133	Windows	Internet Explorer	Google	Yes	39814.48	39814.5	420	4
999.244.150.140	Windows	Firefox	Yahoo	No	39815.59	39815.63	100	3
999.107.233.190	Windows	Firefox	Lycos	Yes	39816.92139	39817.02	250	2
999.144.152.163	Windows	Firefox	AltaVista	No	39814.05	39814.12	950	15
999.182.007.219	Macintosh	Internet Explorer	HotBot	No	39818.48	39818.5	450	7

2. Which operating system is most popular? Prepare a chart comparing the operating systems and their percentages. The chart should display the operating system percentages by month.

3. Which browser is most popular? Prepare a chart comparing the browsers and their percentages. Prepare a chart comparing the browsers and their overall counts by month.

4. How much bandwidth was used for each month? Prepare a chart that compares the bandwidth usages by month. Should Mr. Allan consider raising or lowering his bandwidth?

5. Mr. Allan wants to know the average bandwidth by operating system, connection, and browser. Mr. Allan wants this information displayed in pivot tables. Based on the results, what conclusions might you draw?

6. Mr. Allan performs daily maintenance on his Web site, including backups and updates. The maintenance process usually takes between 30 minutes to 1 hour to complete. Using the site visit data, how can he determine the best time to maintain his Web site with the least disruption to his visitors? What is the best time?

CASE DELIVERABLES

In order to satisfactorily complete this case, you should build the worksheet as described in the case scenario and then prepare both written and oral presentations. Unless otherwise specified, submit the following deliverables to your professor.

1. A written report discussing any assumptions you have made about the case and the key elements of the case. Additionally, what features did you add to make the worksheet more functional? User friendly? (Please note that these assumptions cannot violate any of the requirements specified above and must be approved by your professor.)

2. A printout of the worksheet.

3. A printout of the worksheet formulas.

4. An electronic, working copy of your worksheet that meets the criteria mentioned in the case scenario and specifications sections.

5. Results for each question posed above. (A memo to your instructor discussing these results should also be provided.)

6. As mentioned above, you should prepare an oral presentation. (Your instructor will establish the time allocated for your presentation.) You should use a presentation package and discuss the key features of your worksheet. Also, discuss how the worksheet is beneficial for Mr. Allan. What additional information should be included in the worksheet to make it more useful?

CASE 8 Megan Davis Convention Center

Spreadsheet Case **Difficulty Rating:** ★★★

SKILLS CHECK
You should review the following areas:

SPREADSHEET SKILLS

- ✓ AVERAGE Function
- ✓ Cell Formatting
- ✓ Chart
- ✓ Date Calculations
- ✓ Filter
- ✓ Get External Data From Access
- ✓ IF Function
- ✓ Microsoft Query
- ✓ Nesting Functions
- ✓ PivotTable
- ✓ Subtotal
- ✓ VLOOKUP Function
- ✓ Worksheet Formatting

CASE BACKGROUND

The Megan Davis Convention Center, located on the outskirts of a metropolitan area, is a popular attraction for corporate meetings, special events, and educational seminars. The convention center's location, view, facilities, and outstanding reputation attract individuals and corporations from all over the United States. To ensure a reservation, the convention center's clients will often book rooms a year or more in advance.

Mavis Billingsley, the convention center's events coordinator, is responsible for scheduling the meeting rooms and helping the center's clients plan their special events. Ms. Billingsley currently uses the MDCC Reservations database to track the convention center's meeting room reservations. She would like to import the reservation data into a spreadsheet application for analysis. She asks you to import the reservation data into a worksheet, enhance the worksheet by inserting columns, and use the Subtotal, Chart, PivotTable, and Filter tools to analyze the reservation data.

CASE SCENARIO

As the events coordinator for the Megan Davis Convention Center, Ms. Billingsley is responsible for managing the meeting room reservations. The Megan Davis Convention

Center currently has five standard meeting rooms, a conference center, a boardroom, and an auditorium. A client may book one or all of the rooms. Although the conference center is primarily used for larger meetings, the center can be converted into four smaller meeting rooms, thus providing the convention center with extra meeting rooms. When booking a meeting room, the client may request a particular seating arrangement, such as circular, classroom, lecture, or U-shape. The number of available seats within a given meeting room is dependent upon the seating arrangement. Figure 1 shows the types of seating arrangements and their codes.

Figure 1: Available Seating Arrangements

Megan Davis Convention Center Available Seating Arrangements	
Seating Arrangement	**Code**
Circular	CI
Classroom	CL
Lecture	LE
U-Shape	US

Each day, Ms. Billingsley fields calls from potential clients, requesting information about room availability, room capacity, and charges. Convention center clients are quoted either a standard, advanced, or special rate. The standard rate applies to all bookings that are made less than six months in advance. The advanced rate applies to clients who book six months or more in advance, and the special rate is a negotiating tool used to attract large, highly recognizable companies or organizations to the Megan Davis Convention Center. Figure 2 summarizes the meeting room rates.

Figure 2: Meeting Room Rates

Megan Davis Convention Center Daily Meeting Room Rates				
Room Code	**Meeting Room**	**Advance Rate**	**Standard Rate**	**Special Rate**
AU	Auditorium	$2,418.75	$2,925.00	$1,735.00
BD	Boardroom	$1,912.50	$2,550.00	$1,330.00
CF	Conference Center	$2,475.00	$3,200.00	$1,900.00
AL	Alabama	$1,950.00	$2,300.00	$1,390.00
CA	California	$1,987.50	$2,350.00	$1,422.50
CO	Colorado	$1,968.75	$2,325.00	$1,375.00
FL	Florida	$1,950.00	$2,300.00	$1,390.00
GA	Georgia	$1,931.12	$2,275.00	$1,431.25

Design Specifications

The reservation data that Ms. Billingsley needs are currently stored in the Reservation Details table in the MDCC Reservations database. As Ms. Billingsley will use a spreadsheet application to analyze the reservation data, you import the data into a worksheet for her. As you recall, importing data into a worksheet is easily accomplished by using either Microsoft Query or Get External Data From Access.

Ms. Billingsley requests that you retrieve all fields from the Reservation Details table. Once you import the reservation data into the worksheet, you realize that the imported reservation data do not include the daily room charge, number of reserved days, or total charges for the clients. Ms. Billingsley explains that these data are not stored in the database because these values can be looked up or derived from the contents of other database fields. Therefore, it is not necessary for the database to store the daily room charges, number of reserved days, and total charges for each record. As Ms. Billingsley needs this information for her analysis, you insert the necessary columns into your worksheet.

The Daily Room Charge column specifies the daily meeting room rate that the customer is charged for a particular meeting room. To determine the daily room charge, you must use the room code and assigned rate code to look up how much a client is charged. Determining the value for this column requires using the imported room code and rate code to look up the appropriate rate in a lookup table. As a lookup table is necessary, you use Figure 2's data to construct your lookup table. You decide that the lookup table may need to be modified in the future, so you decide to place the lookup table in its own worksheet.

The Number of Reserved Days column specifies the number of days that the client reserved the meeting room. Determining the values for this column requires a formula that works with dates. Subtracting the reservation start date from the reservation end date does not give you the correct number of days that the client reserved the room, so you must modify your formula to implement the necessary logic to determine the correct number of reserved days.

The Total Charges column shows the total charges for the meeting room, based on the number of days that the room is reserved by the client. For instance, if a room is rented at $1,735.00 per day and the client rents the room for 2 days, then the total charges amount is $3,470.00.

Information Specifications

When a client books a meeting room, Ms. Billingsley enters the reservation data into the MDCC Reservations database for processing. Ms. Billingsley knows that the MDCC Reservations database contains important details about her clients' reservations, and she now wants to use a spreadsheet application to analyze the reservation data. Specifically, Ms. Billingsley wants to know how frequently the standard rate is charged, as opposed to the advanced or special rates. She wants a pivot table and chart that compares the count for each rate. (You should select an appropriate chart type.) She wants a count of the seating styles used in each room. She also wants to see the total charges by room.

Ms. Billingsley wants to review the booking habits of the convention center's clients. For instance, she wants to know how far in advance, on average, the center's clients book the meeting rooms. She also wants to know the number of rooms her clients book, as well as the total charges for each client. Additionally, Ms. Billingsley requests that you prepare a chart comparing the revenue by room.

In addition to the information requirements specified above, Ms. Billingsley requests answers to the following questions. Where appropriate, use the PivotTable, Subtotal, Chart, and Filter tools to provide Ms. Billingsley with answers to her questions.

1. On average, what is the length of time that a client books a room?
2. Using a reservation start date of August 5, 2008, what are the total charges for each client?
3. Overall, what is the average daily room charge?
4. Which seating arrangement is most popular?
5. Which reservations were made on February 15, 2008? What are the total charges for the reservations?
6. Based on the total charges for each customer, identify the five customers with the highest total charges.
7. Display each room's total charges as a percentage of the total charges for all rooms.

Implementation Concerns

Although you are free to work with the design of your worksheet, it should have a consistent, professional appearance. You should also apply appropriate formatting to the cells and worksheet. For instance, all cells containing dollar values should use a currency format and be formatted to two decimal places. Also, your worksheet should have an appropriate header, as well as appropriate column and row headings.

To prepare your worksheet according to the specifications provided above, you will import external data, insert columns, construct formulas that may include the IF and VLOOKUP functions, work with dates, and use several tools, such as PivotTable, Filter, Chart, Microsoft Query, and Subtotal.

You can use the Get External Data from Access command or Microsoft Query to import reservation data. The Microsoft Query Wizard guides you through the process of retrieving external data from the Reservation Details table in the MDCC Reservations database. Keep in mind the Test Your Design section requires you to retrieve external data that meet specific criteria. (You may wish to use your system's online help feature to review how to use Microsoft Query and the Microsoft Query Wizard.)

Test Your Design

After creating your worksheet, you should test your design. Perform the following steps.

1. Ms. Billingsley requests that you retrieve **only** the reservation data with a start date of August 12, 2008, from the Reservation Details table.

2. When retrieving data from the Reservation Details table, Ms. Billingsley wants the query to prompt her for a reservation start date. Create a new query that prompts Ms. Billingsley for a specific reservation date. Run the query several times and enter different reservation start dates.

3. When retrieving data from the Reservations Details table, Ms. Billingsley wants to retrieve reservation information for a given customer. Create a query that will prompt Ms. Billingsley for a given customer number. Run the query several times and enter different customer numbers.

CASE DELIVERABLES

In order to satisfactorily complete this case, you should build the worksheet as described in the case scenario and then prepare both written and oral presentations. Unless otherwise specified, submit the following deliverables to your professor. When preparing the following documentation, use all of the data contained in the Reservation Details table.

1. A written report discussing any assumptions you have made about the case and the key elements of the case. Additionally, what features did you add to make the worksheet(s) more functional? User friendly? (Please note that these assumptions cannot violate any of the requirements specified above and must be approved by your professor.)

2. A printout of each worksheet. (This includes your charts and pivot tables.)

3. A printout of each worksheet's formulas.

4. An electronic, working copy of your workbook that meets the criteria mentioned in the case scenario and specifications sections.

5. Results for each question posed above. (A memo to your instructor discussing these results should also be provided.)

6. As mentioned above, you should prepare an oral presentation. (Your instructor will establish the time allocated for your presentation.) You should use a presentation package and discuss the key features of your workbook. Also, discuss how the workbook is beneficial for Ms. Billingsley. What additional information should be included in the workbook to make it more useful?

CASE 9 BJR Investments, Inc.

Spreadsheet Case **Difficulty Rating:** ★★★

SKILLS CHECK
You should review the following areas:

SPREADSHEET SKILLS

- ✓ **Advanced Filter**
- ✓ **DAVERAGE Function**
- ✓ **DMAX Function**
- ✓ **DMIN Function**
- ✓ **DSUM Function**
- ✓ **Excel Table**
- ✓ **Filter**
- ✓ **IF Function**
- ✓ **PivotChart**
- ✓ **PivotTable**
- ✓ **Range Name**
- ✓ **Web Query**
- ✓ **Worksheet Formatting**

CASE BACKGROUND

BJR Investments, Inc., is a full-service brokerage firm, providing a variety of financial planning services to its current and prospective clients. Bradley J. Reynolds, the owner of BJR Investments, Inc., and his staff provide investment advice in such areas as tax advantage planning, retirement and estate planning, mutual funds, pensions, stocks, and risk management. Mr. Reynolds enjoys helping his clients manage their portfolios, which range in size from $1,000 to well over $3,000,000. His clients appreciate his advice, personal touch, and 15 years of investment experience. However, it is his attention to detail that keeps the business growing.

Mr. Reynolds wants to develop a Portfolio worksheet for each client. He feels that the Portfolio worksheet can provide him with current data about his client's investments, thus helping him keep better track of the client's investments. The Portfolio worksheet organizes the client's stock information into an Excel table and requires the retrieval of up-to-date stock information from the Web. Once current stock information is retrieved, Mr. Reynolds will analyze the information by using the Filter, Advanced Filter, PivotChart, and PivotTable tools.

CASE SCENARIO

Mr. Reynolds asks you to develop a Portfolio worksheet that he will use for each client. For each stock, the Portfolio worksheet provides Mr. Reynolds with the stock symbol, company name, industry, market capitalization, and capitalization level, as well as the number of shares, purchase date, purchase price, commission, total cost, portfolio percentage, current value of the shares, last price, previous close, return, and price-earning (P/E) and earnings-per-share (EPS) ratios for the stock. As the Portfolio worksheet is organized around the client's investments, Mr. Reynolds can carefully monitor a client's investment activity and provide timely, more accurate advice to the client. Mr. Reynolds thinks his clients will appreciate this special attention to detail.

Once the Portfolio worksheet is developed, Mr. Reynolds will use the PivotChart, PivotTable, Filter and Advanced Filter tools to analyze the client's portfolio and provide the best possible advice to the client. Mr. Reynolds will also print a copy of the worksheet, charts and pivot tables for the client.

Mr. Reynolds is anxious to begin using the worksheet at his firm, and he provides you with a partially completed worksheet for one of his clients. He asks you to complete the Portfolio worksheet for him.

Design Specifications

The partially completed Portfolio worksheet includes symbol, company, industry, number of shares, purchase date, and purchase price columns. The worksheet needs a descriptive title, appropriate column headings, and proper formatting for the cells. You supply a descriptive worksheet title and column headings for the worksheet. As this worksheet deals with stock information, you decide that the header should show the date, as well as the current time. For cells involving dollar values, you specify a currency format with two decimal places.

For each stock, Mr. Reynolds wants to see the symbol, company name, industry, market capitalization, market capitalization level, exchange, number of shares, purchase date, purchase price, commission, total cost, portfolio percentage, current value of the shares, last price, previous close, return, P/E ratio, and EPS ratio. Figure 1 provides a sketch of the proposed worksheet. As you study the worksheet, you realize that Mr. Reynolds must enter values for the symbol, industry, number of shares, purchase date, and purchase price. The values for the remaining columns are retrieved or computed based on the contents of the entered values. The company name, market capitalization, exchange, last price, previous close, and EPS values are retrieved from the Web.

Figure 1: Current Portfolio Worksheet

BJR Investments, Inc. Portfolio Worksheet (Current Date and Time)																			
Symbol	Company	Industry	Capitalization Level	Market Capitalization	Exchange	No. of Shares	Purchase Date	Purchase Price	Commission	Total Cost	Portfolio Percentage	Current Share Value	Last Price	Previous Close	Return	PE Ratio	EPS

The total cost, portfolio percentage, current share value, return, commission, and P/E ratio are computed, thus requiring formulas. Figure 2 provides formulas for computing the total cost, portfolio percentage, current value, P/E ratio, and return. You ask Mr. Reynolds to explain how to derive the commission. Mr. Reynolds explains that he charges either 2 percent of the purchase price or a $25 flat fee, whichever is greater. Based on this explanation, you decide that the commission cells must determine what fee to charge. The determination of what commission to charge requires the use of the IF function. Although the P/E ratio is retrievable from the Web, Mr. Reynolds wants this value computed based on data contained in the worksheet. The P/E ratio computation is easy to make, because a stock's P/E ratio is determined by dividing the stock's last price by the stock's EPS.

Figure 1 includes a capitalization level column. As Mr. Reynolds explains, this column specifies whether the stock's market capitalization is large-cap, mid-cap, small-cap, or micro-cap. Figure 3 shows the capitalization classifications. The IF function can be used to determine the company's capitalization level.

Figure 2: Required Portfolio Worksheet Formulas

Portfolio Worksheet Formulas	
Current Value	Last Price * Number of Shares
P/E Ratio	$\frac{\text{Last Price}}{\text{EPS}}$
Portfolio Percentage	$\frac{\text{Current Value of the Stock}}{\text{Total Current Value of All Stock}}$
Return	$\frac{\text{(Current Value of the Stock - Cost of the Stock)}}{\text{Cost of the Stock}}$
Total Cost	(Purchase Price * Number of Shares) + Commission

Figure 3: Capitalization Classifications

Portfolio Worksheet Formulas	
Large-Cap	Greater than $5 billion
Mid-Cap	Between $500 million and $5 billion
Small-Cap	Between $150 million and $500 million
Micro-Cap	Below $150 million

As you study the requirements for the new worksheet, you realize that the capitalization, last price, previous close, and EPS ratio require current stock market information. Luckily, you recall that the MSNStockQuote function makes retrieval of this information easy. When the MSNStockQuote function is refreshed, it returns the latest available stock market information to the cell. You decide to use the MSNStockQuote function to retrieve the company name, capitalization, last price, previous close, and EPS values. Once you obtain the most recent stock market information, you can use formulas to calculate the current value and return. (In addition to the MSNStockQuote function, the MSN MoneyCentral Investor Stock Quotes Web query retrieves current stock information. Your instructor will specify which feature to use. At this point, you may wish to use your system's online help function to review Web queries.)

Mr. Reynolds requests the averages, minimums, and maximums for the commission, purchase price, current share value, return, and P/E ratio columns. Mr. Reynolds wants the minimums and maximums for the portfolio percentages, previous close, and EPS columns. As he will work with this data as a table, he requests that you use database functions, where applicable, to determine the values for these columns.

Information Specifications

Mr. Reynolds will analyze the stock data at varying levels of detail. For instance, he wants to see the return by industry, and he wants a chart comparing the return by industry. Next, he wants to see the return, P/E, and EPS for each stock. He wants this information categorized by industry, and he does not wish to see grand totals. You suggest that he use the PivotTable and PivotChart tools for this purpose.

In addition to the information requirements specified above, Mr. Reynolds requests that you perform the following operations. Where appropriate, you should use the Advanced Filter, Filter, and PivotTable tools.

1. Identify the most expensive stock.

2. Identify which stock has the highest return. Lowest return.

3. Identify which stock has the largest P/E ratio. Lowest P/E ratio.

4. Identify which stock had the highest previous close. Lowest.

5. Identify which trades the client pays a $25 flat fee. Identify which trades the client pays a 2 percent commission.

6. Identify which stocks have a purchase price greater than $50 and a negative return.

7. Identify which stocks have a purchase price less than $50 and a positive return.

8. Identify the purchase price, last price and previous close for each stock. Mr. Reynolds wants to view this information on a separate "page" for each industry.

9. Identify which stocks are traded on NASDAQ. Identify which stocks are traded on NYSE.

Implementation Concerns

Although you are free to work with the design of your worksheet, the worksheet should have a consistent, professional appearance. You should also use proper formatting for the cells. For instance, dollar values should display with a dollar sign and be formatted to two decimal places.

To complete the case scenario, your worksheet must retrieve current stock information. Although the case scenario suggests using the MSNStockQuote function, you can also use the MSN MoneyCentral Investor Stock Quotes Web query. As the MSNStockQuote function provides more control over the information that is returned, it is the preferred method. However, the MSNStockQuote function requires the MSN MoneyCentral Stock Quotes add-in. Although this add-in is available on Microsoft's Web site, you may, for a variety of reasons, not have immediate access to the add-in. (Your professor will specify which method to use.) If you elect to use the MoneyCentral Investor Stock Quotes Web query, you will need to modify your worksheet to accommodate the information that the Web query returns.

The case scenario mentions that the commission fee is based on the purchase price. For each trade, Mr. Reynolds wants to charge either a 2 percent commission or a $25 flat fee, depending on which rate results in a higher commission. Building this logic into the commission cells requires using the IF function. (At this point, you may wish to use your system's online help feature to review the IF function.)

You will need to use the Advanced Filter tool to provide Mr. Reynolds with the information that he needs. The Advanced Filter tool requires a criteria range. As a general rule the criteria range should be placed above or below the Excel table. When filtering data in a table, you should use the DAVERAGE, DMIN, DMAX, and DSUM functions, as opposed to the AVERAGE, MINIMUM, MAXIMUM, and SUM functions. The database functions will accurately reflect the correct average, minimum, maximum, and total values for a filtered table. However, other Microsoft Excel functions may not. In order for your database functions to work properly, you should create your criteria range before using the database functions.

Test Your Design

After creating the Portfolio worksheet described in the case scenario, you should test your worksheet design. Perform the following operations.

1. Add the following stocks to the Portfolio worksheet. For the purchase date, use today's date. For the purchase price, use the stock's Previous Close value.

New Stocks			
Symbol	**Company**	**Industry**	**Number of Shares**
HOG	Harley-Davidson, Inc.	Leisure Time	100
HNZ	H. J. Heinz Company	Foods	200
NBR	Nabors Industries Ltd.	Oil & Gas	50
NCR	NCR Corporation	Computers	200
HSY	The Hershey Company	Foods	100
HES	Hess Corporation	Oil	50
BBT	BB&T Corporation	Banks	50
BMS	Bemis Company, Inc.	Containers and Packaging	50
CCU	Clear Channel Communications Inc.	Broadcasting	50

2. What is the average commission for all stocks? Average P/E ratio for all stocks?

3. For the new stocks that were just purchased, which has the highest return? Lowest? For the new stocks, provide averages for the commission, current value, and P/E ratio. Now, provide the minimums and maximums for the new stocks.

4. Of the large capitalization firms, which has the highest return? P/E ratio? EPS?

5. Which mid-capitalization firm has the highest current value for its stock? Lowest?

6. Based on portfolio percentage, identify the top five firms with which the client is invested.

7. Based on the information provided in the Portfolio worksheet, which stock(s) would you recommended eliminating from the portfolio?

8. Mr. Reynolds wants a count of the companies by capitalization size. He also wants to view this information on a separate "page" for each industry.

CASE DELIVERABLES

In order to satisfactorily complete this case, you should build the worksheet(s) as described in the case scenario and then prepare both written and oral presentations. Unless otherwise specified, submit the following deliverables to your professor.

1. A written report discussing any assumptions you have made about the case and the key elements of the case. Additionally, what features did you add to make the worksheet(s) more functional? User friendly? (Please note that these assumptions cannot violate any of the requirements specified above and must be approved by your professor.)

2. A printout of each worksheet. (This includes your chart and pivot tables.)

3. A printout of each worksheet's formulas.

4. An electronic, working copy of your workbook that meets the criteria mentioned in the case scenario and specifications sections.

5. Results for each question posed above. (A memo to your instructor discussing these results should also be provided.)

6. As mentioned above, you should prepare an oral presentation. (Your instructor will establish the time allocated for your presentation.) You should use a presentation package and discuss the key features of your workbook. Also, discuss how the workbook is beneficial for Mr. Reynolds. What additional information should be included in the workbook to make it more useful?

CASE 10 Madison's Department Store

Spreadsheet Case **Difficulty Rating:** ★★★★

SKILLS CHECK
You should review the following areas:

SPREADSHEET SKILLS

- ✓ Advanced Filter
- ✓ Average Function
- ✓ Cell Reference
- ✓ Chart
- ✓ Consolidating Worksheets
- ✓ DAVERAGE Function
- ✓ DMAX Function
- ✓ DMIN Function
- ✓ DSUM Function
- ✓ Excel Table
- ✓ Filter
- ✓ Grouping Worksheets
- ✓ IF Function
- ✓ MAX Function
- ✓ MIN Function
- ✓ Nesting Functions
- ✓ PivotTable
- ✓ Range Name
- ✓ SUM Function
- ✓ VLOOKUP Function

CASE BACKGROUND

Sylvester Tarkio understands the importance of a department store's sales force, especially when it comes to the sales force of a premiere, upscale department store like Madison's. Customers have long enjoyed the expert knowledge, attention to detail, and service that Madison's sales staff provides. Maintaining the quality sales force is a daily job for Mr. Tarkio. He carefully evaluates the performance of his sales staff and makes adjustments when needed. Currently, Mr. Tarkio monitors the performance of his sales staff by reading daily and weekly sales productivity reports. The problem is that these reports are prepared on a word processor. Mr. Tarkio has no efficient way of analyzing the data in detail. As a new intern at Madison's, you have impressed Mr. Tarkio with your work. Mr. Tarkio asks you to prepare a Productivity workbook for him. You will prepare seven daily productivity worksheets and a weekly productivity summary worksheet, analyze the sales data by using the PivotTable, Advanced Filter and Filter tools, and generate several charts.

CASE SCENARIO

Madison's Department Store is a prestigious, upscale department store located in one of the metropolitan area malls. The store has specialty departments for women, men, children, cosmetics, cologne, linen, furniture, and housewares. One of the reasons why Madison's has such a fine reputation is because of its highly trained sales staff. Madison's management believes in rewarding its sales staff for its hard work, so in addition to an hourly wage, sales representatives are paid a commission on sales above an established quota.

Sales representatives are classified as either part-time or full-time. Part-time representatives are then subcategorized as sales assistants or sales partners. Full-time representatives are subcategorized as assistant managers, sales consultants, or sales associates. Part-time representatives work 20 hours a week, while full-time representatives work 40 hours a week. Sales representatives have input into how many hours a day they work; however, they cannot work overtime. Within the company, sales representatives are ranked and paid according to their experience and tenure with the company. Sales representatives are paid a commission on all sales exceeding their established quota. As members of the sales staff may work a different number of hours on a given day, the sales quota is based on the hours worked. For instance, if a sales representative has an hourly quota of $100 in sales and he works 5 hours, then his daily sales quota is $500. For any sales above the $500 quota, the sales representative receives a commission. Figure 1 summarizes the hourly wages and established quotas.

Figure 1: Hourly Wages and Quotas

Sales Code	Sales Title	Hourly Wage	Quota	Commission Rate
AM	Assistant Manager	$23.50	$200.00	.030
PT1	Sales Assistant	$10.50	$100.00	.010
PT2	Sales Partner	$11.75	$125.00	.015
S1	Sales Associate	$13.50	$150.00	.020
S2	Sales Consultant	$15.00	$175.00	.025

At the end of each business day, Mr. Tarkio prepares a Daily Productivity Report. As Figure 2 shows, the Daily Productivity Report summarizes each employee's sales activity for the day. (The data shown in Figure 2 are for illustrative purposes only. Your report format and data may vary.) This report specifies the employee's name, rank, assigned department, daily sales, hours, base pay, commission, and gross pay. At the end of each week, Mr. Tarkio uses the Daily Productivity Reports to prepare a Weekly Productivity Report. The Weekly Productivity Report summarizes the Daily Productivity Reports. Mr. Tarkio currently uses a word processor to prepare the reports. However, he realizes that a spreadsheet application is a much better tool for the summarization and analysis work that he needs. Mr.

Tarkio asks you to develop a Productivity workbook for him.

Figure 2: Daily Productivity Report

Madison's Department Store

Daily Productivity Report

(Current Date)

Employee	Rank	Department	Sales	Hours Worked	Base Pay	Commission	Gross Pay
Allbaugh, Joshua	AM	Men's	$4,000.00	8.0	$188.00	$72.00	$260.00
				. . .			
Blake, Barney	S2	Cosmetics	$456.76	2.5	$37.50	$0.48	$37.98
Bolyard, Pat	S2	Housewares	$450.98	3.0	$45.00	$0	$45.00
				. . .			
Stanton, Catrina	S1	Women's	$821.36	7.0	$94.50	$0.00	$94.50
				. . .			

Design Specifications

Each day, Mr. Tarkio will enter each salesperson's sales and hours into a Daily Productivity worksheet. He then expects the worksheet to determine each salesperson's base pay, commission, and gross pay. While the gross pay involves adding the base pay to the commission, calculating the base pay and commission requires referencing values in a lookup table. As you want the lookup table to be easily accessible and updateable, you place the lookup table in its own worksheet.

The base pay and commission are dependent upon the salesperson's rank in the company. For instance, an assistant manager is paid $23.50 per hour and receives a 3 percent commission. In contrast, a sales associate is paid $13.50 per hour and receives a 2 percent commission. You use the VLOOKUP function to build this logic into the base pay, and you use the IF and VLOOKUP functions to build the logic into the commission cells. The base pay formula uses the salesperson's rank to retrieve the correct hourly wage and then multiplies the hourly wage by the number of hours. The determination of the appropriate commission requires more complicated logic than the base pay. For instance, the commission formula must determine if a commission is to be paid, the applicable commission rate, and the portion of sales on which to base the commission. As the commission formula involves several lookups and decisions, you realize that nesting the IF and VLOOKUP functions is required. (At this point, you may wish to review your system's online help feature to review the IF and VLOOKUP functions, as well as how to nest functions.)

As previously mentioned, Mr. Tarkio wants the Daily Productivity Reports summarized into a Weekly Productivity Report. The Weekly Productivity Report provides weekly sales, hours, base pay, commission, and gross pay totals for each salesperson. For instance, the sales column will reference and sum the individual sales for Sunday through Saturday.

After showing Mr. Tarkio the workbook prototype, he asks if you can determine the number of times each salesperson made his quota that week. You assure him that the worksheet can be modified to provide this information. On each worksheet, Mr. Tarkio requires grand totals, averages, minimums and maximums for the sales, base pay, commission, and gross pay columns. Also on each worksheet Mr. Tarkio wants to see the total quotas met and the percentage of quotas met.

Information Specifications

Mr. Tarkio wants to use the Productivity workbook to analyze the performance of his sales staff. He specifically requests that you show him how to use the PivotTable to analyze the sales data. Mr. Tarkio wants to compare the commissions and sales by department, view the commissions by individuals within each department, prepare a pie chart showing the commissions by department, and prepare pie charts for each department, comparing the department's sales representatives' sales.

In addition to the information requirements specified above, Mr. Tarkio wants answers to the following questions. Using the PivotTable, Advanced Filter and Filter tools, provide Mr. Tarkio with answers to these questions.

1. Which five sales representatives received the highest commissions last week?
2. Which sales representatives received commissions above average last week?
3. Excluding the Furniture Department and its employees, which sales representatives received commissions above average last week?
4. If sales staff must make their quotas at least 60 percent of the time, which sales staff did not achieve this goal?
5. For each department, which salesperson had the highest sales?
6. On average, how frequently will the sales staff make their quota?
7. What are the commissions and total sales for each sales position by department?
8. What are the base pay, commission, and gross pay categorized by sales position?

9. What are the total salaries and hours worked by department?

10. Which department's staff met their quotas more often than other departments? Least?

Implementation Concerns

Although you are free to work with the design of your workbook, each worksheet should have a consistent, professional appearance. You should use appropriate formatting for the cells and worksheets.

This case requires you to group worksheets, insert columns into worksheets, consolidate information into a summary worksheet, nest functions, use several functions, reference a lookup table, and use the retrieved value in a formula, work with an Excel table, prepare charts, and use several analytical tools to analyze the sales data.

In several instances, you can use the Advanced Filter tool to filter data contained in the summary worksheet. To provide Mr. Tarkio with correct answers, you should use the DAVERAGE, DMIN, and DMAX functions in the summary worksheet, as opposed to the AVERAGE, MIN, and MAX functions. When the Advanced Filter is used, the DAVERAGE, DMIN, and DMAX functions adjust their values based on the filtered data. The AVERAGE, MIN, and MAX functions do not.

The determination of each salesperson's commission requires nesting the VLOOKUP function within the IF function. The commission formula must look up the hourly sales quota, determine the daily sales quota, take the difference between the daily sales quota and the daily sales, and then multiply the applicable commission rate by the amount of sales above the quota.

Test Your Design

After creating the Productivity workbook described in the case scenario, you should test your design. Perform the following steps.

1. Mr. Tarkio hired four new sales personnel. Enter their data into the worksheets.

   Leandra Shekel is classified as a PT1 and works in the Men's Clothing Department. She worked 4 hours each day, Sunday through Thursday. Her sales Sunday through Thursday were $1,400.98, $1,500.42, $750.32, $550.08, and $900.78, respectively.

   Darise Ferrer was hired as an S1 and works in the Linen Department. She worked 8-hour shifts, Tuesday through Saturday. Her sales were $2,500.98, $878.23, $1,503.28, $602.98, and $1,304.17, respectively.

   Paulina Renfro is classified as an S1 and works in the Children's Department. She worked 8-hour shifts, Tuesday through Saturday. Her sales were $1,500.56, $402.22, $1,090.80, $908.43, and $350.98.
   Sethana Aynes is classified as a PT1 and works in the Women's Clothing Department. She worked 8 hours on Monday and her sales were $502.88. She worked 6 hours on

Tuesday, and her sales were $608.12.

2. Which salespersons received more than $1,500 in commissions last week? Which salespersons did not receive a commission last week?

3. Based on past performance, what would happen if Mr. Tarkio increased the sales quota for each position by $75 per hour? What would happen if Mr. Tarkio decreased the sales quota for each position by $75 per hour?

4. What would happen if Mr. Tarkio increased each sales position's commission by a half of a percent?

5. For the week, what are the average sales for the S1 employees working in the Children's Department? For the Children's Department S1 employees, which employee had the lowest sales for the week? For the Children's Department S1 employees, which employee had the maximum sales for the week?

6. For the week, what are the average sales for the PT1 employees working in the Women's Department? For the Women's Department PT1 employees, which employee had the lowest sales for the week? For the Women's Department PT1 employees, which employee had the most sales for the week?

7. For the week, Mr. Tarkio wants to see the total commissions paid by each department, each department's percentage of the total commissions paid for all departments, and the total sales for each department.

8. Based on your observations of the sales, sales quotas, and commissions, how might the sales quota system be improved?

CASE DELIVERABLES

In order to satisfactorily complete this case, you should build the workbook as described in the case scenario and then prepare both written and oral presentations. Unless otherwise specified, submit the following deliverables to your professor.

1. A written report discussing any assumptions you have made about the case and the key elements of the case. Additionally, what features did you add to make the worksheet(s) more functional? User friendly? (Please note that these assumptions cannot violate any of the requirements specified above and must be approved by your professor.)

2. A printout of each worksheet. (This includes your charts and PivotTables.)

3. A printout of each worksheet's formulas.

4. An electronic, working copy of your workbook that meets the criteria mentioned in the case scenario and specifications sections.

5. Results for each question posed above. (A memo to your instructor discussing these

results should also be provided.)

6. As mentioned above, you should prepare an oral presentation. (Your instructor will establish the time allocated for your presentation.) You should use a presentation package and discuss the key features of your workbook. Also, discuss how the workbook is beneficial for Mr. Tarkio. What additional information should be included in the workbook to make it more useful?

CASE 11 Lake West University

Worksheet Case **Difficulty Rating:** ★★★★

SKILLS CHECK
You should review the following areas:

WORKSHEET SKILLS

- ✓ **Chart**
- ✓ **Conditional Formatting**
- ✓ **COUNTA Function**
- ✓ **COUNTIF Function**
- ✓ **COUNTIFS Function**
- ✓ **Filter (Optional)**
- ✓ **IF Function**
- ✓ **Nesting Functions**
- ✓ **PivotChart**
- ✓ **PivotTable**
- ✓ **Template**
- ✓ **Worksheet Formatting**

CASE BACKGROUND

Lake West University places a major emphasis on helping its students learn. To accomplish this mission, departments are strongly encouraged to assess their programs, majors, and courses. To better assess their courses, the Lake West University's Economics faculty include standard questions on final exams given in core Economics courses. Once exams are graded, Dr. Hash Haddock, the Economics Department chairperson, reviews student responses to the standard exam questions to determine how well course objectives are met.

Dr. Haddock asks you to finish designing a Lake West Assessment workbook for him. The workbook should provide a convenient way to analyze student responses for the ECON 2103 final exam's standard questions. This workbook will eventually serve as a template for other economics courses. When designing the workbook, the COUNTA, COUNTIF, COUNTIFS, and IF functions will prove useful. Conditional formatting should be used to highlight all questions with responses below a set minimum. To facilitate his analysis, Dr. Haddock will use the Filter command, PivotTable, PivotChart, and charting tools.

CASE SCENARIO

Lake West University is a four-year university located in the Midwestern United States. As part of a campus-wide initiative, Lake West University's Economics Department recently updated its assessment plan. As part of its updated assessment plan, the Economics Department includes a standard set of questions on all ECON 2103 final exams. ECON 2103 is an introductory economics course, and all business majors take this course as part of their degree plan. As the ECON 2103 course does not have prerequisite courses, freshmen, sophomores, juniors, and seniors enroll in the course. Each semester several ECON 2103 sections are offered.

Dr. Haddock needs a system that enables him to analyze results for the standard questions across all ECON 2103 sections, as well as the individual sections of the course. Dr. Haddock envisions using this system to compare responses between various semesters as well. He wants a standard template developed, so he can use the same format for other Economics Department course offerings. As you are Dr. Haddock's assistant, you are tasked with developing a Microsoft Excel workbook to track student responses for the ECON 2103 final exam standard questions.

Design Specifications

At the end of the semester, all ECON 2103 section instructors give Dr. Haddock their student responses for the final exams. No standardized reporting format has been implemented, so Dr. Haddock wants a standard workbook developed so all instructors will use the same reporting format. He feels that a standard workbook format enables him to easily consolidate section data into the Lake View Assessment workbook, allowing him to analyze results across all sections.

Dr. Haddock hands you a copy of an incomplete workbook called Lake West Assessment. Although Dr. Haddock has begun incorporating each section's student responses into the workbook, he has not had time to format the workbook or complete its design. Figure 1 shows how data are currently organized for one of the sections.

Figure 1: Sample Worksheet

Section 1: Instructor Jones												
Student	Major	Classification	Q1	Q2	Q3	Q4	Q5	Q6	Q7	Q8	Q9	Q10
1	ACCT	Freshman	b	b	d	b	b	d	c	b	e	a
2	MIS	Senior	a	c	d	b	a	d	c	c	d	a
3	ACCT	Sophomore	a	c	d	b	a	b	c	c	e	a
4	ECON	Junior	a	c	e	b	a	b	c	c	e	a
5	MRKT	Sophomore	a	c	c	e	a	b	c	c	e	a
Correct Answer			a	c	d	b	a	b	c	c	e	a

As you study the workbook, you notice that the workbook contains several worksheets. Although Dr. Haddock initially created a separate worksheet for each section, he mentions that he would now like all student responses included on a single worksheet called Response. In the Response worksheet, Dr. Haddock wants counts of the correct and incorrect responses for each question. He also wants to see correct and incorrect counts by major and by classification.

As you study the student response data, you notice that student names are not included. Dr. Haddock indicates that he wants a number assigned to each student and does not want to include student names. He does want the student's major, classification, and response to each of the 10 standard questions included.

Dr. Haddock asks you to create a summary worksheet. For each section, the summary worksheet should show the correct response counts, incorrect response counts, and correct response percentages for each question by section. He also would like to see a correct response percentage for each question for all sections.

Dr. Haddock considers a correct response rate of 70 percent as acceptable. Response percentages lower than 70 percent are unacceptable and are marked for further analysis. Correct response percentages lower than 70 percent should display with a light red fill and dark red text. Dr. Haddock wants to see a count for correct responses, a count for incorrect responses, and the percentage of correct responses for each major. He also would like the same information organized by classification.

To facilitate his analysis, Dr. Haddock asks you to prepare Correct Response, Major Comparison, and Classification charts. You are free to select the chart format. The Correct Response chart compares each major's correct response percentages for each question. Dr. Haddock wants to know the majors of the students enrolled in the ECON 2103 sections. He will use the Major Comparison chart to view a breakdown by major. He asks that the Major Comparison chart provide both a count and a percentage for each major. Dr. Haddock wants to know how many seniors, juniors, sophomores, and freshmen took the ECON 2103 course. The Classification chart provides counts and percentages for the freshmen, sophomores, juniors, and seniors taking ECON 2103.

As Dr. Haddock is the department chairperson, he manages several economics classes. He wants to use this workbook for other classes, and requests that you create a template based on your newly created workbook.

Information Specifications

In addition to the information requests specified above, Dr. Haddock requests answers for the following questions.

1. Overall, which major's students answered the most questions correctly?
2. Which major's students answered the least number of questions correctly?
3. Which student(s) answered the most questions correctly?
4. Which section's students answered the most questions correctly?
5. Overall, which classification answered the most questions correctly?

6. How do freshmen economics majors compare to freshmen MIS majors?

7. For final exam Question 10, prepare a chart that compares the correct responses given by the different classifications across all sections. (You select the chart.)

Implementation Concerns

Although you are free to work with the design of your workbook, the worksheets should have a consistent, professional appearance. When designing the worksheets, you should apply basic cell and worksheet formatting principles.

Depending on how you choose to design the workbook, this case may require you to create new worksheets, modify existing worksheets, and consolidate information into a summary worksheet. To prepare this workbook according to Dr. Haddock's specifications, you will create formulas, use several functions, and use the PivotTable and PivotChart report tools. Your worksheet's design may require you to use the COUNTIFS function to determine response counts. The COUNTIFS function allows you to use multiple criteria to evaluate multiple cell ranges and count when the multiple criteria are met. You should use your system's online help feature to learn more about the COUNTIFS function.

When designing the workbook, cells containing a correct response percentage less than 70 percent use a light red fill with dark text. The conditional formatting command can accomplish this task. If you are unfamiliar with conditional formatting, use your system's online help feature to learn more about conditional formatting.

Flexibility is one of the key aspects of this case. Dr. Haddock will use this workbook as a template for other classes. When designing the workbook, you should design a workbook that is easily adaptable as Dr. Haddock's information needs change. For instance, the Test Your Design section asks you to modify the workbook's design to match the standard questions to their objective.

Test Your Design

After creating the Lake View Assessment workbook, you should test your design. Perform the following steps.

1. Professor Jones submitted responses for two addition students from Section 1. Please enter the following information into the appropriate worksheet(s).

Section 1: Instructor Jones												
Student	Student Major	Classification	Q1	Q2	Q3	Q4	Q5	Q6	Q7	Q8	Q9	Q10
Assign Next Available Number	MIS	Junior	c	e	d	e	e	d	c	d	e	c
Assign Next Available Number	FIN	Sophomore	c	d	d	b	b	d	c	d	c	c

2. Based on the following table, identify the sections achieving course objectives.

Objectives and Matching Questions	
Objective 1	Questions 1, 4, and 10
Objective 2	Questions 2, 5, and 7
Objective 3	Questions 3 and 8
Objective 4	Questions 6 and 9

3. Based on the acceptable percentage rate, which section did not meet at least 4 of its objectives?

4. Based on the acceptable percentage rate, did any section meet all of its objectives?

CASE DELIVERABLES

In order to satisfactorily complete this case, you should build the workbook as described in the case scenario and then prepare both written and oral presentations. Unless otherwise specified, submit the following deliverables to your professor.

1. A written report discussing any assumptions you have made about the case and the key elements of the case. Additionally, what features did you add to make the worksheets more functional? User friendly? (Please note that these assumptions cannot violate any of the requirements specified above and must be approved by your professor.)

2. A printout of each worksheet. (This includes your charts and PivotTables.)

3. A printout of each worksheet's formulas.

4. An electronic, working copy of your workbook that meets the criteria mentioned in the case scenario and specifications sections.

5. Results for each question posed above. (A memo to your instructor discussing these results should also be provided.)

6. As mentioned above, you should prepare an oral presentation. (Your instructor will establish the time allocated for your presentation.) You should use a presentation package and discuss the key features of your workbook. Also, discuss how the workbook is beneficial for Dr. Haddock. What additional information should be included in the workbook to make it more useful?

CASE 12 Baylee Byrd Playsets, Inc.

Spreadsheet Case **Difficulty Rating:** ★★★★★

SKILLS CHECK
You should review the following areas:

SPREADSHEET SKILLS

- ✓ **Chart**
- ✓ **Data Table**
- ✓ **Goal Seek**
- ✓ **Scenario Manager**
- ✓ **Solver**
- ✓ **Worksheet Formatting**

CASE BACKGROUND

A weekend, backyard project that began two years ago has now become a thriving, growing business for Jacob Byrd. Jacob Byrd is the owner and operator of Baylee Byrd Playsets, Inc., a small, part-time business, specializing in the production of quality, custom-built playsets. After friends and neighbors convinced him that he should custom build playsets for their children, Mr. Byrd began his part-time business. Although Mr. Byrd realizes a modest profit from his business, he wants to evaluate the business's operating performance, so that he can determine the best pricing and marketing strategies for his playsets.

Although last year's sales were good, the net income for the business was only $4,183.50. Mr. Byrd feels that his net income should be much higher and has requested your help in evaluating his business's operating performance. To assist Mr. Byrd with the analysis of his business, you will create an income statement, perform breakeven analysis, use several financial ratios, prepare one-variable data tables, use Goal Seek and Solver to perform what-if analysis, prepare a chart, and use the Scenario Manager to prepare different scenarios.

CASE SCENARIO

Two years ago, Jacob Byrd searched for a playset for his four-year-old daughter, Baylee. After spending several months visiting toy and discount stores looking for just the right playset and not finding the perfect one, he decided to custom build a playset for Baylee. The custom-built playset soon became the talk of the town, and Mr. Byrd found himself building playsets for friends and neighbors.

The custom-built playsets are widely recognized throughout the community and in neighboring towns and are an impressive sight. The playsets are made of redwood and equipped with a wave slide, fort, fireman's pole, chin-up bar, safety step ladder, tube slide, bridge, 6' by 6' platform, and two swings.

Last year, Baylee Byrd Playsets, Inc., sold 85 units at $999.99 per unit and generated $84,999.15 in revenue. However, after expenses and taxes were deducted, the business's net income was only $4,183.50. Mr. Byrd would like to improve his net income, and he wonders what he needs to do to achieve this objective. Mr. Byrd needs to evaluate his cash flow to determine areas for improvement and has requested your help.

Design Specifications

After speaking with Mr. Byrd and evaluating his information needs, you decide that an Income Analysis worksheet will help him with his decision-making activities. The Income Analysis worksheet provides Mr. Byrd with several tools for analyzing his business's operating performance. The Income Analysis worksheet enables Mr. Byrd to input the number of units sold, revenue per unit, desired target income, and costs. Once the data are entered, the Income Analysis worksheet provides Mr. Byrd with an income statement, computes financial ratios, performs breakeven analysis, and updates the one-variable data tables.

You determine that the Income Analysis worksheet needs both input and results sections. Figure 1 shows a tentative sketch for the input section. The input section enables Mr. Byrd to input data about the number of units sold, revenue per unit, desired target income, and costs. Table 1 summarizes the company's sales and costs for the previous year. As you study Table 1's contents, you notice that the costs are separated into two categories: fixed and variable. From a previous business course, you recall that fixed costs remain constant and do not vary with sales volume. Fixed costs for Baylee Byrd Playsets, Inc., include such items as fixed overhead, selling expenses, administrative expenses, and depreciation. In contrast, variable costs change in direct proportion to the sales volume. Variable costs include such items as marketing and sales, labor, variable overhead, variable selling, and variable administrative.

Figure 1: Input Section Sketch

Input Section For Income Analysis Worksheet	
Sales and Cost Summary	
Number of Units Sold	
Revenue Per Unit	
Desired Target Income	
Variable Costs (per unit)	
Marketing and Sales	
Labor	
Variable Overhead	
Variable Selling	
Variable Administrative	
Fixed Costs	
Fixed Overhead	
Selling Expenses	
Administrative Expenses	
Depreciation	

Table 1: Sales and Costs for Previous Year

Income		**Fixed Costs**	
Units Sold	85	Fixed Overhead	$4,652.11
Price Per Unit	$999.99	Selling Expenses	$2,500.00
Desired Target Income	$30,000.00	Administrative Expenses	$2,399.99
		Depreciation	$7,000.00
Variable Costs (Per Unit)			
Marketing and Sales	$15.24		
Labor	$150.00		
Variable Overhead	$514.72		
Variable Selling	$25.83		
Variable Administrative	$23.75		

The results section uses the data from the input section to produce an income statement, compute financial ratios, and perform breakeven analysis. The results section will also display your one-variable data tables. (Descriptions for the one-variable data tables are provided in subsequent sections.) Figures 2 and 3 provide sketches for the income statement and ratios.

Figure 2: Income Statement

Baylee Byrd Playsets, Inc. Income Statement (Current Date)	
Sales	
Variable Expenses	
Marketing and Sales	
Labor	
Variable Overhead	
Variable Selling	
Variable Administrative	
Total Variable Expenses	
Contribution Margin	
Fixed Expenses	
Fixed Overhead	
Selling Expenses	
Administrative Expenses	
Depreciation	
Total Fixed Expenses	
Operating Income	
Income Taxes	
Net Income	

Figure 3: Ratios

Ratios	
BEP	
BEP with Target Income	
Contribution Margin Ratio	
Operating Margin Ratio	
Net Margin Ratio	

Information Specifications

The Income Analysis worksheet provides Mr. Byrd with information about his business's income, calculates several financial ratios, performs breakeven analysis, and displays one-variable data tables. Therefore, the Results section of the Income Analysis worksheet will have income statement, ratio, and data table result areas.

As Figure 2 shows, the income statement section of the worksheet summarizes the business's revenues and expenses, allowing Mr. Byrd to examine the company's overall operating performance. As you study the income statement outline, you realize that many of your calculations will reference the data contained in the Input section of the worksheet, requiring Mr. Byrd to input the data only once. Mr. Byrd provides you with the formulas shown in Figure 4.

Mr. Byrd wants to examine the impact that various target income levels have on the breakeven point. For instance, Mr. Byrd knows that a target income of $15,000 requires 117 playsets in order to break even. He would like to see what impact $20,000, $25,000, $30,000, $35,000, and $40,000 target incomes have on the breakeven point. Although he can change the target income cell value for each of the desired target income levels, you recommend that he use a one-variable data table. By creating a one-variable data table, the target income values and their associated breakeven points are arranged in a table, enabling Mr. Byrd to view and compare all the target income values and their associated breakeven points at the same time. (You may wish to use your system's online help feature to review one-variable data tables at this point.)

Figure 4: Required Formulas

Income Analysis Worksheet Formulas	
Breakeven Point	Fixed Costs / (Revenue Per Unit – Variable Cost Per Unit)
Breakeven Point with Target Income	(Fixed Costs + Target Income) / (Revenue Per Unit – Variable Cost Per Unit)
Contribution Margin	Sales – Total Variable Expenses
Contribution Margin Ratio	(Sales – Variable Cost) / Sales
Income Taxes (Assume a 35 percent tax rate)	Operating Income * Income Tax Rate
Net Income	Operating Income – Income Taxes
Net Margin	Net Income / Net Sales
Operating Income	Contribution Margin – Total Fixed Expenses
Operating Margin	Operating Income / Net Sales
Variable Cost Per Unit	Total Variable Costs / Number of Units Sold

Mr. Byrd wants to see how different scenarios impact the business's net income. In addition to the current scenario, Mr. Byrd wants to evaluate two other possible scenarios. In the first scenario, he wants to increase the number of units sold to 150, decrease revenue per unit to $950, and decrease variable costs per unit by $20. (You can choose which variable cost to reduce.) In the second scenario, he wants to increase the number of units sold to 100, increase revenue to $1,650 per unit, and increase labor by $50. Using Scenario Manager, you prepare the three scenarios. The first scenario uses the original values, and the remaining two scenarios use the data that Mr. Byrd has just given you. After you create the three scenarios, you generate a scenario summary report based on the three scenarios.

Mr. Byrd needs answers to the following questions. Using your newly designed Income Analysis worksheet, provide Mr. Byrd with answers to his questions.

1. Mr. Byrd wants a net margin ratio of 15 percent. Using Solver, adjust the values for the revenue and number of units sold. Revenue per unit cannot exceed $1,100, the number of units sold cannot exceed 250, and total variable expenses cannot exceed $110,000. In order to have a net margin of 15 percent, how many playsets will Mr. Byrd need to sell? What price should he charge? Generate an answer report. (As a starting point for this answer, reset your worksheet's values back to the original values in Table 1, and then make the changes requested in this question.)

2. Assume that fixed overhead costs are $7,500, variable overhead is $375, labor is $200, and depreciation is $8,500. If Mr. Byrd wants a net income of $30,000, what price should Mr. Byrd charge for his playsets? How many playsets should Mr. Byrd sell? (As a starting point for this answer, reset your worksheet's values back to the original values in Table 1, and then make the changes requested in this question.)

3. Mr. Byrd wants a net income of $55,000. How many playsets should Mr. Byrd sell? What price should he charge? (As a starting point for this answer, reset your worksheet's values back to the original values in Table 1, and then make the changes requested in this question.)

4. Mr. Byrd needs a 3-D pie chart that compares the business's fixed costs.

Implementation Concerns

For this case, you will design a worksheet to facilitate Mr. Byrd's analysis of his business. When designing the worksheet, you will apply basic cell and worksheet formatting principles, create formulas, perform what-if analysis by using Goal Seek and Solver, create several scenarios, generate a chart, and create two one-variable data tables. Based on your what-if analysis, you will prepare several reports, including an answer report and a scenario summary report.

Although you are free to work with the design of your worksheet, the worksheet should have a consistent, professional appearance. You should use proper formatting for the cells. For instance, dollar values should display with a dollar sign and be formatted to two decimal places.

In several locations, the case references target income. Keep in mind that the target income does not reflect income taxes. Therefore, as it is used in this case, the target income is a better reflection of operating income, as opposed to net income.

Test Your Design

1. Assume that fixed overhead is $5,000, selling expenses are $4,500, administrative expenses are $3,000, and labor costs are $250. What is Mr. Byrd's net income? (As a starting point for this answer, reset your worksheet's values back to the original values in Table 1, and then make the changes requested in this question.)

2. In order to have a net income of $50,000, how many playsets must Mr. Byrd sell? What price should he charge for the playsets? (As a starting point for this answer, reset your worksheet's values back to the original values in Table 1, and then make the changes requested in this question.)

3. Mr. Byrd wants to identify the breakeven point and breakeven point with target income for varying pricing levels. Prepare a one-variable data table that shows this information. The pricing levels range from $1,000 to $2,500 in $50 increments. If Mr. Byrd does not want to sell more than 120 playsets and wants to have a $60,000 target income, how many units must he sell? What price should he charge? (As a starting point for this answer, reset your worksheet's values back to the original values in Table 1, and then make the changes requested in this question.)

CASE DELIVERABLES

In order to satisfactorily complete this case, you should build the workbook as described in the case scenario and then prepare both written and oral presentations. Unless otherwise specified, submit the following deliverables to your professor.

1. A written report discussing any assumptions you have made about the case and the key elements of the case. Additionally, what features did you add to make the worksheet more functional? User friendly? (Please note that these assumptions cannot violate any of the requirements specified above and must be approved by your professor.)

2. A printout of each worksheet and report.

3. An electronic, working copy of your workbook that meets the criteria mentioned in the case scenario and specifications sections.

4. Results for each question posed above. (A memo to your instructor discussing these results should also be provided.)

5. As mentioned above, you should prepare an oral presentation. (Your instructor will establish the time allocated for your presentation.) You should use a presentation package and discuss the key features of your worksheet. Also, discuss how the worksheet is beneficial for Mr. Byrd. What additional information should be included in the worksheet to make it more useful?

CASE 13 Edmund Grant Pharmaceutical Company

Spreadsheet Case **Difficulty Rating:** ★★★★★

SKILLS CHECK
You should review the following areas:

SPREADSHEET SKILLS

- ✓ **Advanced Filter**
- ✓ **Button**
- ✓ **Conditional Formatting**
- ✓ **DAVERAGE Function**
- ✓ **DMAX Function**
- ✓ **DMIN Function**
- ✓ **DSUM Function**
- ✓ **Excel Table**
- ✓ **Filter**
- ✓ **IF Function**
- ✓ **Macro**
- ✓ **Nesting Functions**
- ✓ **PivotChart**
- ✓ **PivotTable**
- ✓ **Template**
- ✓ **VLOOKUP Function**

CASE BACKGROUND

Keiko Lapeer is a district sales manager for the Edmund Grant Pharmaceutical Company. Ms. Lapeer has many responsibilities, including traveling, visiting with current and potential customers, supervising a growing sales staff, preparing numerous reports, and tracking her sales region's expenses. Each week, members of Ms. Lapeer's sales staff submit weekly expense claim forms. Currently, she scans through the expense forms, checks for anything out of the ordinary, and then authorizes reimbursement checks. Ms. Lapeer needs to become more organized about tracking her sales staff's expenses, and asks you to design an Expense worksheet for her. Specifically, she requests you to organize the expense data into an Excel table. To design the worksheet according to Ms. Lapeer's specifications, you are required to use database functions, other Microsoft Excel functions, and nest functions. You will then use the Filter, Advanced Filter, PivotTable, and PivotChart tools to analyze the data.

CASE SCENARIO

The Edmund Grant Pharmaceutical Company (EGPC) is a multinational company, well known in the United States for its anti-infective, wound care, and pain management products. The Edmund Grant Pharmaceutical Company's sales force is responsible for promoting EGPC products to doctors, pharmacists, and opticians around the globe. Keiko Lapeer is one of EGPC's many district sales managers and is responsible for supervising four sales areas.

As a district sales manager, Ms. Lapeer stays very busy. She often travels, attends several meetings a month, visits with customers, supervises a 23-member sales force, and performs managerial duties. As a manager, Ms. Lapeer's paperwork is often overwhelming, and she is looking for avenues of improvement. One area for improvement is the expense tracking of her sales force. She can easily spend an entire day just processing budget and expense reports. By using a spreadsheet application to analyze her sales force's expenses, she feels that she will save time and make better decisions.

Sales representatives are reimbursed for business meals and calls, gas, hotel, airfare, and other miscellaneous expenses. Each week, sales representatives complete expense claim forms and submit these forms to Ms. Lapeer. Figure 1 provides an example of the expense claim form. Ms. Lapeer summarizes the expense data contained on these forms and prepares several weekly reports. Report preparation is a tedious, time-consuming task, often requiring her to wade through the expense claim forms numerous times.

Figure 1: Expense Claim Form

Edmund Grant Pharmaceutical Company

Expense Claim Form

Employee Name: ____________ **For Week Ending:** ____________
Division Number: ____________

Expense

Meals: ____________
Phone: ____________
Gas: ____________
Hotel: ____________
Airfare: ____________
Miscellaneous: ____________
____
____
____
Total Expenses Claimed: ____________

Mileage

Beginning Mileage: ____________
Ending Mileage: ____________

Comments: ____________
____
____
____
____

Notice: All expense claims must be accompanied by receipts.

When a sales representative is hired, he is issued a company car. The sales representative may use his car for both business and personal travel, and he is given a weekly mileage limit. Each week, the sales representative reports the number of miles that he has driven that week. For any miles over the mileage limit, the employee is charged an overage fee. The allowable mileage and charge rate vary by sales position within the company. Table 1 summarizes the allowable mileage and charge rates. Ms. Lapeer wants the new Expense worksheet to determine the mileage overage amount and applicable charges for each sales representative.

Table 1: Allowable Mileage and Rates

Edmund Grant Pharmaceutical Company Allowable Mileage and Rates		
Position	**Allowable Miles**	**Rate**
MN	700	0.20
SU	600	0.22
S2	550	0.25
S1	500	0.32

When a car has 60,000 miles, the sales representative can request a new car. Ms. Lapeer wonders if there is some way that she can quickly determine when a car is reaching its end-of-service date. You recommend using conditional formatting to highlight ending mileage readings that are greater than 55,000 miles. If a sales representative has a car that is approaching its end-of-service date, Ms. Lapeer can remind the sales representative that it is time to request a new car.

Ms. Lapeer has used a spreadsheet application before and would like to organize the weekly expense data into a worksheet. She asks you to create an Expense worksheet for her. She specifically requests that you prepare an Excel table, establish a criteria range to support Advanced Filtering, include several database functions, insert four new columns, prepare pivot tables, and prepare several charts. Ms. Lapeer also requests that the new worksheet be saved as a template, so she can reuse it each week.

Design Specifications

As you examine the Expense worksheet, you realize that the worksheet columns need formatting. After formatting the columns, you decide that a mileage lookup table and four additional columns are necessary. Before inserting the four columns, you build the mileage lookup table. As you want to keep the mileage lookup table separate from the expense data, you place the table in its own worksheet. After creating the mileage lookup table, you insert the actual mileage, overage, overage charge, and total expense columns into the Expense worksheet. The actual mileage column calculates the actual miles that each employee drove during the week. Actual mileage is the difference between the week's ending mileage and the week's beginning mileage. You want the overage column to reference the mileage lookup table and then determine how many miles over the limit, if any, the employee has driven. (Performing this operation requires nesting IF and VLOOKUP functions. At this point, you may wish to use your system's online help feature to review how to nest functions.) The overage charge column uses the VLOOKUP function as well. This column multiplies the overage by the rate specified in the mileage table. The total expenses column is a summation of the expenses for that week.

Ms. Lapeer will use the Advanced Filter capability. Using the Advanced Filter requires the inclusion of a criteria range. For Ms. Lapeer's purposes, you decide the best place for the criteria range is above the Excel table. (At this point, you may wish to use your system's online help feature to review the Advanced Filter topic.) As Ms. Lapeer uses the criteria range, she needs to clear the range of the current conditions and enter new conditions in the criteria range. You decide to create a macro that will clear the criteria range and position the pointer in the upper left-hand cell of the criteria range. Once you have created the macro, you then assign it to a button named "Clear Criteria."

As you study the contents of the Expense worksheet, you realize that the contents are in a format suitable for creating an Excel table. You recall from one of your business courses that an Excel table is a collection of data, similar in concept to a database table. The data in this Excel table can be filtered, sorted, and manipulated in a variety of ways, thus facilitating Ms. Lapeer's decision-making activities. In fact, several database functions are available for usage with an Excel table, and you decide to use these functions in the Expense worksheet. Ms. Lapeer wants average, minimum, maximum, and total values for the meal, actual mileage, phone, gas, hotel, miscellaneous, airfare, overage, overage charge, and total expense columns in the table. Since Ms. Lapeer will manipulate the data in the Excel table, you use the DAVERAGE, DMIN, DMAX, and DSUM functions. (At this point, you may wish to use your system's online help feature to review list creation and usage.)

After you design the worksheet, Ms. Lapeer wants a template created. Then each week, she can use the template to create a worksheet for that week.

Information Specifications

Ms. Lapeer asks if it is possible to view the expense data at varying levels of detail and from different perspectives. She specifically requests a summary of all expenses categorized by division, the total expenses displayed by sales position and the total expenses for the meals, phone and gas expense categories by division and position. As the PivotTable tool can quickly change the way data are displayed and the level of summarization, you recommend that Ms. Lapeer use a pivot table.

As mentioned previously, Ms. Lapeer wants to know when a salesperson's car is approaching 60,000 miles. For any vehicle that has more than 55,000 miles, the spreadsheet application should highlight the ending mileage for that vehicle.

In addition to the information requirements specified above, Ms. Lapeer requests that you perform the following operations.

1. Identify which managers claimed airfare expenses totaling more than $1,700 and which supervisors claimed airfare expenses totaling more than $750.

2. Identify which sales representative(s) did not submit an expense claim form.

3. Identify hotel and airfare expenses by position.
4. Identify which managers traveled via airplane during the week.

5. Identify sales positions by division.

6. Identify which division had the lowest expenses for the week.

7. Identify which S1 sales representative(s) submitted hotel and airfare expenses this past week.

8. Identify which individuals went over their mileage limits.

Implementation Concerns

Although you are free to work with the design of your worksheet, it should have a consistent, professional appearance. You should also use proper formatting for the cells. For instance, dollar values should display with a dollar sign and be formatted to two decimal places.

This case scenario requires you to use an Excel table. Extracting the data requires you to prepare charts; use the DAVERAGE, DSUM, DMIN, DMAX, IF, and VLOOKUP functions; nest functions; establish a criteria range; prepare PivotTables and charts; and use the Filter and Advanced Filter tools. (You may wish to use your system's online help feature to review each of these areas.)

The determination of the overage amount for each salesperson requires the spreadsheet application to look up the mileage allowance, determine if the mileage is greater than the allowance, and then compute the actual overage amount, if any. Performance of this task requires nesting the VLOOKUP function inside the IF function. (At this point, you may wish to use your system's online help feature to review nesting functions.) Keep in mind that Ms. Lapeer wants the mileage overage amount to display in one column.

You should carefully consider the placement of the criteria range and the mileage table. It is generally recommended that the criteria range be placed above or below the Excel table. Placement of the criteria range in either of these locations facilitates the viewing of the criteria and filter results. Although your mileage lookup table may be placed in the Expense worksheet, consider placing the lookup table in its own worksheet. Using a separate worksheet for the mileage lookup table facilitates table maintenance and accessibility.

Test Your Design

After creating the Expense worksheet described in the case scenario, you should test your worksheet design. Perform the following operations.

1. Add the following three new employees to your Excel table.

Employee 1	Employee 2	Employee 3
Last Name: Ruokangas **First Name**: Leota **Division**: 1 **Position**: MN **Meals**: $376.89 **Phone**: $79.86 **Hotel**: $478.78 **Miscellaneous**: $2,987.42 **Airfare**: $894.87 **Beginning Mileage**: 101 **Ending Mileage**: 372	**Last Name**: Saghafi **First Name**: Abduellah **Division**: 3 **Position**: S1 **Meals**: $102.78 **Phone**: $10.07 **Hotel** $0.00 **Miscellaneous**: $0.00 **Airfare**: $0.00 **Beginning Mileage**: 904 **Ending Mileage**: 1,150	**Last Name**: Omari **First Name**: Kyleena **Division**: 4 **Position**: S2 **Meals**: $257.88 **Phone**: $58.77 **Hotel**: $509.78 **Miscellaneous**: $877.89 **Airfare**: $250.75 **Beginning Mileage**: 67 **Ending Mileage**: 803

2. Make the following changes to your mileage table.

Allowable Mileage Table

Position	Allowable Miles	Rate
MN	700	0.25
SU	600	0.28
S2	550	0.30
S1	500	0.32

3. Within each division, Ms. Lapeer wants to examine the expenses incurred by each employee. She would like to view the divisions one "page" at a time.

4. Prepare a column chart that compares the gas, hotel, airfare, and meal expenses for each division.

5. For each division, Ms. Lapeer wants to see the person's last name and the number of miles she/he drove last week. She would like to see a grand total for each division. Prepare a pivot table and also prepare a chart for Division 1. (Choose an appropriate chart.)

CASE DELIVERABLES

In order to satisfactorily complete this case, you should build the workbook as described in the case scenario and then prepare both written and oral presentations. Unless otherwise specified, submit the following deliverables to your professor.

1. A written report discussing any assumptions you have made about the case and the key elements of the case. Additionally, what features did you add to make the worksheets more functional? User friendly? (Please note that these assumptions cannot violate any of the requirements specified above and must be approved by your professor.)

2. A printout of each worksheet. (This includes your charts and pivot tables.)

3. A printout of each worksheet's formulas.

4. An electronic, working copy of your workbook that meets the criteria mentioned in the case scenario and specifications sections.

5. Results for each question posed above. (A memo to your instructor discussing these results should also be provided.)

6. As mentioned above, you should prepare an oral presentation. (Your instructor will establish the time allocated for your presentation.) You should use a presentation package and discuss the key features of your workbook. Also, discuss how the workbook is beneficial for Ms. Lapeer. What additional information should be included in the workbook to make it more useful?

CASE 14 Molly Mackenzie Boat Marina

Integration Case **Difficulty Rating:** ★★★★★

SKILLS CHECK
You should review the following areas:

DATABASE SKILLS	SPREADSHEET SKILLS
✓ AutoLookup Query	✓ Filter (optional)
✓ Calculated Control	✓ Chart
✓ Calculated Field	✓ Microsoft Query
✓ Command Button	✓ PivotTable
✓ Form Design	✓ Solver
✓ Lookup Wizard	✓ Subtotal
✓ Report Design	✓ SUM Function
✓ Subform	
✓ Switchboard	
✓ Tab Control	

CASE BACKGROUND

Marvin and Dena Mackenzie own and operate the Molly Mackenzie Marina. Currently, data about the marina's daily operating activities are manually captured and processed. When necessary, reports are created using a word processing package. As the marina continues to grow, Mr. and Mrs. Mackenzie recognize the necessity of using information technology to capture details about the marina's daily operations, as well as facilitate decision-making activities. Mr. and Mrs. Mackenzie need a database to track information about customer reservations, customer payments, and the marina's rental properties. Mr. and Mrs. Mackenzie hire you to build the database. Building the database requires you to develop forms and subforms, reports, queries, and a switchboard. The forms will utilize buttons to facilitate data navigation. Once the database is developed, Mr. Mackenzie will export selected data from the marina database to a spreadsheet for further analysis. Mr. Mackenzie will use the Subtotals function, PivotTable, Solver, and charting tools to analyze the data.

CASE SCENARIO

The Molly Mackenzie Marina and its surrounding property are located on Lake Merewether in the Midwest. Lake Merewether is a popular tourist spot, attracting visitors year round. The lake's notoriety is due to its beautiful surroundings, camping facilities, excellent fishing, and ability to handle large boats. Lake visitors are primarily local, but many visitors come from across the nation. Lake Merewether is situated between two large cities, serving as a weekend getaway for many of its visitors.

Mr. Mackenzie uses a manual-based information system to manage the marina's rental property. However, he realizes that automating the marina's daily operations will make his management activities more efficient. Mr. and Mrs. Mackenzie spend numerous hours keeping the marina's paperwork up to date. The marina's popularity continues to grow, and Mr. Mackenzie is quickly realizing the necessity of using information technology to ease the marina's paperwork burden. In an effort to run the office in a more efficient manner, Mr. Mackenzie hires you to design a marina database and worksheet for him. Since you have worked as a part-time marina employee, you are familiar with the marina's daily operations and are eager to help.

The Molly Mackenzie Marina rents cabins, a variety of watercraft, and boat slips to its customers. When a customer requests a watercraft or a cabin, a price quote is given. The price quote is based on a daily rate. If a customer wants to rent a jet ski for a half day, then the daily rate is adjusted. Likewise, if a customer rents a cabin or boat slip for more than a day, Mr. Mackenzie will discount the daily rate, making a longer stay more attractive. Cabins can be rented for a weekend, week, or month at a reduced rate. Table 1 shows the discount codes and their associated percentage discounts. If a customer rents a jet ski for a half day, Mr. Mackenzie will charge the person 65 percent of the daily rate. If a person rents a boat slip for 180 days, Mr. Mackenzie will reduce the daily rate by 15 percent.

Table 1: Rate Codes and Discounts

Rate Code	Rate Description	Percentage
D	Daily	100.00%
HD	Half Day	65.00%
SD	Special Discount	25.00%
SM	Six Months	85.00%
Y	12 Months	80.00%
W	Weekend	90.00%

When a property is reserved, the customer places a deposit on the rental property. The deposit is applied to the rental fees for the property or is forfeited if the customer cancels the reservation. Mr. Mackenzie is flexible on the deposit amount. Mr. Mackenzie requires a minimum deposit from frequent customers, but does charge a hefty deposit for new customers. When a customer picks up the watercraft or checks into a cabin, he is required to pay the entire balance for the property, minus any deposit. If an advanced reservation was not made, the customer pays the entire balance when he rents the property.

When a customer requests a particular property, Mr. Mackenzie or an employee checks to see if the property is available for the dates requested by the customer. If the requested dates are available, reservation data are captured on a reservation form. Based on the length of stay, Mr. Mackenzie determines which rate is applicable. For a typical reservation, customer contact information (name, phone number, and mailing address), reservation dates, and property information (rental property number and rate), are recorded. When a reservation is made, the customer is given a reservation number. The customer uses the reservation number if he needs to cancel the reservation or when he checks in. When a payment is made, the payment date, payment amount, and any comments are recorded. When the customer returns the watercraft or checks out of the cabin, he stops by the office and is given an invoice showing his rental transactions.

Storage Specifications

To build the marina database, you decide Customer, Rate, Property, Payment, and Reservation tables are necessary. The Customer table stores basic customer information, such as customer identification number (CID), last name, first name, street address, city, state, zip, and phone number. As the customer identification number is unique for each customer, it serves as the primary key for the Customer table. Table 2 shows the Customer table structure.

The Rate table stores information about the rate codes, rate descriptions, and discount percentages. As the rate code value is unique for each rate code, the Rate Code field serves as the primary key. The rate description provides additional information about the rate code, such as daily, weekend, six-month, special discount, half price, or twelve-month. Where applicable, the discount percentage is multiplied by the daily rate to provide a reduced rate for the customer for a given rental property. Table 3 shows the Rate table structure.

The Property table stores information about each of the marina's rental properties. The property identification number (PID) is unique for each property. Therefore, the PID serves as the primary key. The Property table also includes rental price, description, and property category fields. The rental price field stores the daily rental price for the property. The description field further clarifies the type of property. The PCategory field classifies the type of property, such as cabin, jet ski, powerboat, boat slip, or fishing boat. Table 4 shows the Property table structure.

The Payment table stores information about each payment made by a marina customer. The Payment table includes PaymentID, customer identification number (CID), PaymentDate, PaymentAmount, Comment, and Deposit? fields. The PaymentID field stores a unique value for each payment record; therefore, it serves as the primary key for the Payment table. The CID field associates a given payment record with the customer making the payment. The PaymentDate stores the date the payment was made. The PaymentAmount field stores the amount paid. The Comment field stores any necessary comments about the payment. The Deposit? field indicates whether this payment is a deposit. Table 5 shows the Payment table structure.

The Reservation table stores information about each of the marina's rental property reservations. The Reservation table's fields include ResID, customer identification number

(CID), ResDate, BookingDate, EndDate, PickUpTime, RateCode, and property identification number (PID). The ResID field contains a unique value for each reservation and serves as the table's primary key. The CID value associates a given customer with the reservation. The ResDate field indicates the starting date of the reservation. The BookingDate indicates when the reservation was made. The EndDate indicates the last day of the reservation. The PickUpTime field indicates the time that the rental property will be picked up. The RateCode field identifies the applicable rate code for the reservation. The PID field identifies the property associated with this reservation. Table 6 shows the Reservation table structure.

As part of the design process, relationships among tables are necessary. Where applicable, you should enforce referential integrity.

Table 2: Customer Table Structure

Field Name	Data Type	Field Description	Field Size	Comments
CID	AutoNumber	Uniquely identifies the customer. Serves as the primary key.	Long Integer	Is required.
Last Name	Text	Stores the customer's last name.	50	Is required.
First Name	Text	Stores the customer's first name.	25	Is required.
Street Address	Text	Stores the customer's street address.	50	
City	Text	Stores the name of the customer's city.	25	
State	Text	Stores the name of the customer's state.	2	
Zip	Text	Stores the customer's zip code. Use an input mask.	10	
Phone	Text	Stores the customer's phone number. Use an input mask.	10	

Table 3: Rate Table Structure

Field Name	Data Type	Field Description	Field Size	Comments
Rate Code	Text	Stores a unique identification number for each rate code. Serves as the primary key.	10	Is required.
Rate Description	Text	Stores the description for the rate code.	25	Is required.
Percentage	Number	Stores the discount percentage. Multiply this amount times the daily rate to get the adjusted price. Use percent format. Display 2 digits to the right of the decimal separator.	Single	Is required.

Table 4: Property Table Structure

Field Name	Data Type	Field Description	Field Size	Comments
PID	Text	Uniquely identifies the property. Serves as the primary key.	10	Is required.
RentalPrice	Number	Identifies the daily rental rate. Use currency format.	Long Integer	Is required.
Description	Text	Describes the rental property.	50	
PCategory	Text	Classifies the property.	2	

Table 5: Payment Table Structure

Field Name	Data Type	Field Description	Field Size	Comments
PaymentID	AutoNumber	Stores a unique value. Serves as primary key.	Long Integer	Is required.
CID	Number	Stores the customer's identification number. Consider using the Lookup Wizard.	Long Integer	Is required.
PaymentDate	Date/Time	Stores the date that the payment was made.		
PaymentAmount	Currency	Stores the amount paid.		Is required.
Deposit?	Yes/No	Indicates if this is a deposit.		
Comment	Text	Stores a comment about the transaction.	50	

Table 6: Reservation Table Structure

Field Name	Data Type	Field Description	Field Size	Comments
ResID	AutoNumber	Uniquely identifies each reservation. Serves as the primary key.	Long Integer	Is required.
CID	Number	Uniquely identifies the customer.	Long Integer	Is required.
ResDate	Date/Time	Identifies the start date of the reservation for the rental property.		Is required.
BookingDate	Date/Time	Identifies the date the reservation was made.		Is required.
EndDate	Date/Time	Identifies the final day of the reservation.		Is required.
PickUpTime	Date/Time	Identifies the time the property will be picked up or the check in time.		
RateCode	Text	Identifies the applied rate code. Use the Lookup Wizard.	50	Is required.
PID	Text	Identifies the rental property. Use the Lookup Wizard.	10	Is required.

Input Specifications

From your conversations with Mr. Mackenzie, you realize that the database must capture and store information about the marina's customers, rental property, rental reservations, and rental payments. Capturing this information requires you to build several forms and subforms. For instance, a customer form with reservation and payment history subforms is necessary. A sketch of the customer form is provided below.

The customer form captures and displays the customer's name, address, and phone number. Additionally, the customer form shows the customer identification number, total charges, the amount he has paid, and the balance due. The total charges field shows the total amount owed for the customer's current reservations. Likewise, the Amount Paid field shows the total paid toward the current reservations, and the Remaining Balance field indicates how much is still due.

When using the customer form, Mr. Mackenzie would like to view or enter information about the customer's current reservations and payments. You decide to use a tab control to organize each customer's reservation and payment information, as well as make the information easily accessible to Mr. Mackenzie as he views a customer's record.

On the reservation subform, Mr. Mackenzie wants to see, at a minimum, the reservation dates, booking date, property identification number, rate code, discount percentage, daily rental rate, discounted daily rental rate, total usage cost, and comments. When using the Reservation subform, Mr. Mackenzie wants to select the rental property number from a list of his rental properties and have the rental property's description and rental fee displayed. On the payment subform, Mr. Mackenzie wants to see the payment date, payment amount, and comments.

Figure 1: Customer Form

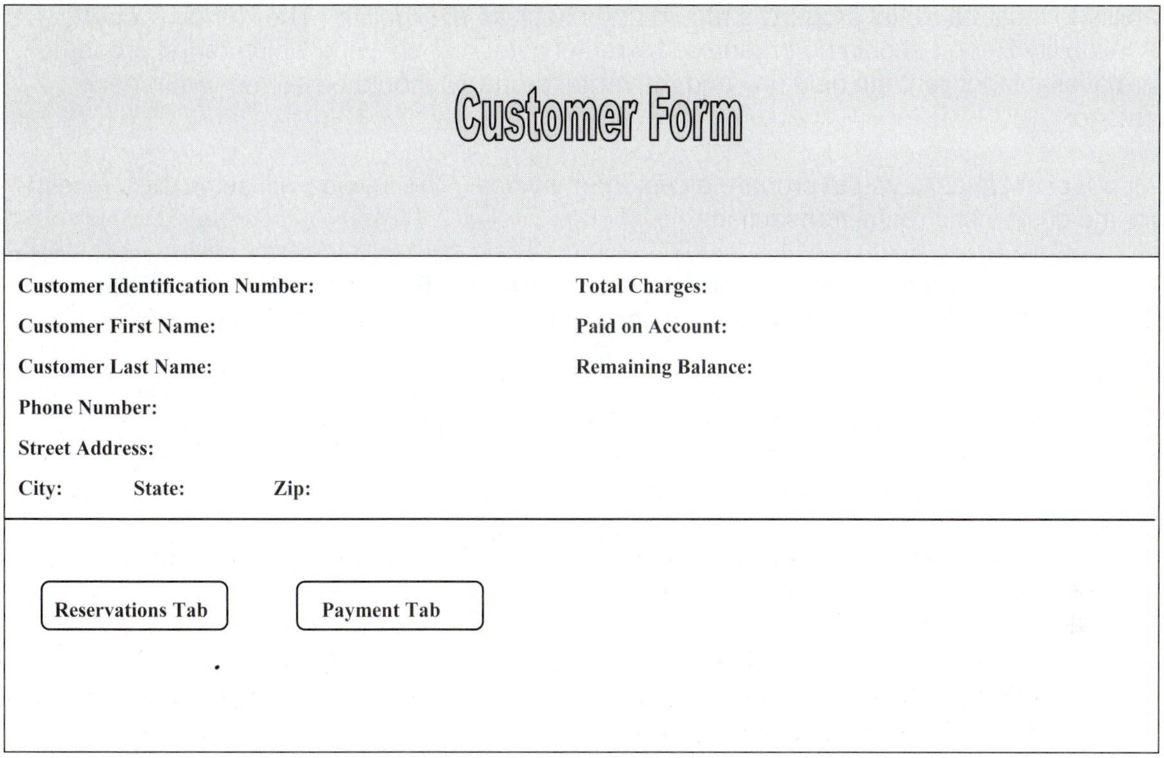

Although Mr. Mackenzie encourages you to be creative with your form design, he requests that the forms have a consistent, professional appearance, be easy to use, and show the business name and logo. Additionally, each form must include buttons that allow Mr. Mackenzie to add, delete, find, and print records. To facilitate data entry, Mr. Mackenzie would like to use AutoLookup, combo boxes, and control tips for fields where these features can (or should) be used. Where possible, you should use validation rules, default values, input masks, and proper formatting.

When the Molly Mackenzie Marina database is first opened, Mr. Mackenzie wants a switchboard to automatically display. The switchboard allows Mr. Mackenzie to access his forms, reports, and queries from a common location. When Mr. Mackenzie finishes with the database, he wants the option of exiting the application from the main menu.

Information Specifications

Mr. Mackenzie requires a Daily Rental Property Reservation Report, a Rental Availability Report, and a customer invoice. He asks you to design and build these reports for him. Each evening a Daily Rental Property Reservation Report is printed. This report shows which properties are reserved for the next day. This report sorts the properties by rental property category, then by rental property number within each category. Employees use this reservation report to make sure that the reserved watercraft and cabins are in working order.

CASE 14: Molly Mackenzie Boat Marina

Often customers will ask when a rental property is available. Mr. Mackenzie requires the ability to locate a rental property's record and check its availability. The Rental Property Availability Report should be organized by rental category, showing which rental properties are available for rent the next day and the rental property should be sorted within each category.

Mr. Mackenzie asks you to prepare a customer invoice. The invoice will serve as a receipt for the customer's rental transactions.

Mr. Mackenzie wants answers to the following questions. Prepare queries to retrieve the information for Mr. Mackenzie. If you choose, you may generate reports based on your queries.

1. For cabin rental customers, what is the average length of stay?

2. How frequently are watercrafts rented? On average, what is the length of rental time?

3. Which boat slip rental option is the most popular? What is the rental revenue by rate code?

4. How much revenue did Mr. Mackenzie receive on fishing boat rental fees last week? Last month? Jet skis? (Use the last week in July for the weekly analysis.)

5. On average, how much does a customer spend on each visit?

6. If customers rent a cabin from the marina, are they also likely to rent a watercraft from us? What is the percentage?

Mr. Mackenzie wants to export data from the marina database to Microsoft Excel for further analysis. He would like answers to the following questions. Using Microsoft Excel, provide answers to his questions.

7. For the month of June, what are the average sales for each product category and product within each category? For the month of June, what are the total sales for each product category and product within each category?

8. For the first seven days of June, prepare a bar chart comparing rental revenues by category by day.

9. For the month of June, prepare a pie chart comparing the revenue by property category.

10. What is the average revenue for each cabin? Which cabin is rented most often?

11. Which rate code is used most often?

12. Mr. Mackenzie has $75,000 to spend on new jet skis. He is evaluating one-person, two-person, and four-person jet skis. The one-person jet ski costs $8,700; the two-person jet ski costs $11,000, and the four-person jet ski costs $15,000. For each jet ski, maintenance costs are $150 per hour. Mr. Mackenzie estimates that each one-person jet ski requires 1 hour of weekly maintenance; each two-person jet ski requires 1.5 hours of weekly maintenance, and each four-person jet ski requires 2 hours of weekly maintenance. Mr. Mackenzie does not want the total number of weekly maintenance hours for the new jet skis to total more than 40 hours. He wants to purchase a maximum of 3 four-person jet skis. The rental season lasts for 100 days.

    If Mr. Mackenzie's main goal is to maximize his seasonal jet ski rental profit, how many jet skis should he purchase? Which jet skis should he purchase? Use Solver to help Mr. Mackenzie figure out how many one-person, two-person, and four-person jet skis he should buy. (You are free to make assumptions; however, these assumptions must be clearly stated in your analysis.)

Implementation Concerns

In order to build the Molly Mackenzie Marina database, you will construct several queries; design forms and subforms; design reports; construct tables; and establish relationships among tables. You are encouraged to be creative; however, your database should function properly and have a professional appearance.

To satisfy the spreadsheet requirements, you will export selected data from the marina database into a worksheet. To perform the required analysis, you will use several spreadsheet features, including Filter, PivotTable, Solver, Subtotal, and Microsoft Query.

As mentioned above, you are free to work with the design of the forms, reports, and worksheets. You are also free to make additional assumptions about this case. However, the assumptions should not violate any of the requirements and should be approved by your professor. To satisfy your assumptions, you may need to create additional forms or collect information that has not been previously specified.

Test Your Design

After creating your database and workbook, you should test your design. Perform the following steps.

1. Enter the following information into the marina database.

    Randall Petra rented a jet ski and cabin for July 4, 2008 – July 7, 2008. He made his reservations on May 1, 2008. He paid a 20 percent deposit and was given a weekend discount for the cabin. He was not given a discount for his jet ski rental. (You select the jet ski and the cabin. Make any other necessary assumptions).

Pauline Bishop rented two cabins for July 4, 2008 – July 6, 2008. She made her reservations on May 12, 2008. She paid a 30 percent deposit and was given a weekend discount for the cabins. (You select the cabins. Make any other necessary assumptions).

Frances Thomas rented a ski boat for July 4, 2008 – July 9, 2008. She made her reservations on June 25, 2008. She paid a 30 percent deposit and was not given a discount on the ski boat rental. (You select the ski boat. Make any other necessary assumptions).

2. On average, how far in advance do customers book their rentals?

3. Using Microsoft Excel's Subtotal function, identify the total discount in dollars given by rate code category.

4. On average, what is the daily, weekly, and monthly revenue by rental property category?

CASE DELIVERABLES

In order to satisfactorily complete this case, you should build the database and workbook as described in the case scenario and then prepare both written and oral presentations. Unless otherwise specified, submit the following deliverables to your professor.

1. A written report discussing any assumptions you have made about the case and the key elements of the case. Additionally, what features did you add to make the database and workbook more functional? User friendly? (Please note that these assumptions cannot violate any of the requirements specified above and must be approved by your professor.)

2. A printout of each worksheet.

3. A printout of the worksheet's formulas.

4. An electronic, working copy of your database that meets the criteria mentioned in the case scenario and specifications sections.

5. An electronic, working copy of your workbook that meets the criteria mentioned in the case scenario and specifications sections.

6. Results for each question posed above. (A memo to your instructor discussing these results should also be provided.)

7. As mentioned above, you should prepare an oral presentation. (Your instructor will establish the time allocated for your presentation.) You should use a presentation package and discuss the key features of your database and workbook. Also, discuss how the database and workbook are beneficial for Mr. Mackenzie. What additional information should be included in the database and workbook to make it more useful?

CASE 15 KoKo's Canine Pet Club

Database Case **Difficulty Rating:** ★

SKILLS CHECK
You should review the following areas:

DATABASE SKILLS

- ✓ **Aggregate Function**
- ✓ **Calculated Field**
- ✓ **Form Design**
- ✓ **Form Wizard**
- ✓ **Lookup Wizard**
- ✓ **Relationship**
- ✓ **Report Design**
- ✓ **Report Wizard**
- ✓ **Select Query**
- ✓ **Table Design**

CASE BACKGROUND

Six months ago, Caedee Hannah found herself facing a dilemma. As a result of a chronic illness, KoKo, her beloved schnauzer, required medication, a special diet, and daily exercise. While the medication and special diet were easy to accommodate into a busy life style, ensuring that KoKo received daily exercise was another matter. Although KoKo's daily exercise usually took the form of a walk around the neighborhood, Ms. Hannah, as a busy executive, had trouble scheduling KoKo's daily walks. Ms. Hannah's friend, Ian, would walk KoKo on the days when Ms. Hannah was extremely busy. Ms. Hannah's friends and neighbors liked the pet walking idea so much that they approached Ms. Hannah and Ian about walking their dogs as well. What began as a neighborhood walking service has now become a fledgling, yet growing, metropolitan area business. Ms. Hannah has hired you to build a simple, yet effective, database for her business. She needs you to build Client and Pet forms, Client and Pet tables, Walker Schedule and Client List reports, and several queries.

CASE SCENARIO

KoKo's Canine Pet Club is a dog-walking service, catering to caring, yet busy, pet owners. The service proves very popular with pet lovers who recognize the value of providing their pets with daily exercise. Although the service was only started six months ago, it currently provides pet walking services for 50 pets and is registering, on average, 5 pets per week. Paperwork is increasing, and Caedee Hannah, the service's owner, needs a better record-keeping system.

During a meeting with Ms. Hannah, she explains to you that a new client must register with the service. During the registration process, the new client provides basic information about his pet(s), chooses a preferred walk time for his pet(s) and specifies a walker preference. During this time, a dog-walking fee is determined and recorded on the pet registration form. The dog-walking fee varies by pet and is based on the pet's size, temperament, and the number of pets the owner has. The pet owner can request that his pet be walked in the early morning, late morning, early afternoon, late afternoon, or early evening hours. Available walk times are currently kept on a clipboard by the phone. However, Ms. Hannah wants the available walk times, as well as walker, client, and pet information, kept in the database that you are building.

Ms. Hannah's record-keeping needs are simple. She requires a database that tracks her clients, their pets, available walk times, and the pet walkers. Ms. Hannah gives you a partially completed database and requests that you build and populate Client and Pet tables, create several relationships, design Client and Pet forms, design Walker Schedule and Client List reports, and construct several queries.

Storage Specifications

After reviewing the partially completed KoKo's Canine Pet Club database, you notice that the database currently contains Walker and Walk tables. The Walker table stores basic information about each walker and the WalkerNo field serves as the table's primary key. The Walk table stores a set of walk time codes. When a client registers a pet, a walk time code is assigned to each pet. This walk time code indicates the pet owner's preference for the time of day when the pet should be walked.

KoKo's Canine Pet Club database requires both Client and Pet tables. You decide the Client table should store contact information for each client and that the client identification number should serve as the primary key. Table 1 shows the structure for the Client table. (Your instructor will provide you with the data to populate the Client table.)

The Pet table stores information about each pet, including the pet number, pet name, client identification number, walker identification number, quoted price, preferred walk time, enrollment date, and any relevant comments. Table 2 shows the structure for the Pet table. (Your instructor will provide you with the data to populate the Pet table.) As you study this structure, you notice that the WalkerNo and WalkTimeCode fields are part of the Pet table structure. As the WalkerNo and WalkTimeCode fields already exist in other tables, you use the Lookup Wizard to create these fields in the Pet table. By using the Lookup Wizard, you can facilitate data entry and ensure accuracy for both fields. (The Lookup Wizard is invoked when you select the Lookup Wizard as the data type for the field.)

Table 1: Client Table Structure

Field Name	Data Type	Field Description	Field Size	Comments
ClientNo	AutoNumber	Is a unique, identifying number assigned to each client. Serves as primary key.	Long Integer	Is required.
CLastName	Text	Is the customer's last name.	50	Is required.
CFirstName	Text	Is the customer's first name.	25	Is required.
CAddress	Text	Is the customer's street address.	25	Is required.
CCity	Text	Is the customer's city.	25	Is required.
CState	Text	Is the customer's state abbreviation. The default is OK.	2	Is required.
CZip	Text	Is the customer's zip code. Use an input mask.	10	Is required.
CPhone	Text	Is the customer's home phone number. Use for non-emergency contact. Use an input mask.	8	Is required.
EPhone	Text	Is the customer's emergency phone number. Use for emergency contact. Use an input mask.	8	Is required.

Table 2: Pet Table Structure

Field Name	Data Type	Field Description	Field Size	Comments
PetNo	Text	Is a unique identification number assigned to each pet. Serves as primary key.	10	Is required.
PetName	Text	Stores the pet's name.	25	Is required.
ClientNo	Number	Is the client identification number. Must match a client number from the Client table. Use the Lookup Wizard.	Long Integer	Is required.
WalkerNo	Text	Is the walker identification number. Must match a walker identification number from the Walker table. Use the Lookup Wizard.	4	Is required.
QuotedPrice	Currency	Stores the daily walk fee. Ms. Hannah determines the actual price per pet.		Is required.
WalkTimeCode	Text	Is the code designating the preferred time for walking the pet. Use the Lookup Wizard.	2	Is required.
EnrollmentDate	Date/Time	Indicates when the client enrolled the pet. Use the short date format.		Is required.
Comments	Memo	Contains any additional information that is necessary.		

After studying your notes, you decide three relationships are necessary. First, a relationship between the Pet and Client tables is needed. Since each table contains a ClientNo field, you use the ClientNo field to create the relationship. Second, a relationship between the Walker and Pet tables is necessary. The Walker and Pet tables have a WalkerNo field, and you use this field to create a relationship between the Walker and Pet tables. Third, both the Walk and Pet tables have a WalkTimeCode field. You use the WalkTimeCode field to create the relationship between the Walk and Pet tables. You decide each relationship should enforce referential integrity. (Note: The Lookup Wizard will create relationships for you. However, you need to edit these relationships to enforce referential integrity.)

Input Specifications

Figure 1 provides a tentative sketch for the Client form that Ms. Hannah wants to use. When a new client enrolls his pet with the walking service, Ms. Hannah uses this form to capture contact information about the client, such as his name, address, and phone number. As the tentative sketch shows, the form header includes the service's name and the form's name. After studying the tentative sketch, you use the Form Wizard to build an initial Client form. Once the form is built, you edit the form in Design view.

Figure 1: Client Form

KoKo's Canine Pet Club

Client

Client No:	**Street Address:**
Client Last Name:	**City:**
Client First Name:	**State:** **Zip:**
Client Phone:	
Emergency Phone:	

After a client registers, Ms. Hannah enrolls his pet(s). The pet enrollment process is simple and captures basic information about the pet, such as the pet's name, walk time, and walker preference. You use the Form Wizard to build the initial Pet form. Once the initial form is built, you edit the form in Design View. Figure 2 shows the initial Pet form sketch.

Figure 2: Pet Form

KoKo's Canine Pet Club

Pet

Client No:	**Walker No:**
Pet No:	**Walk Time Code:**
Pet Name:	
Enrollment Date:	**Quoted Price:**
Comments:	

Information Specifications

Ms. Hannah requests Walker Schedule and Client List reports. The Walker Schedule report is generated on a weekly basis and tells Ms. Hannah when her walkers are scheduled to walk the pets. As the Walker Schedule report uses data from four tables, you build a select query, and then base the report on the select query. As the tentative sketch in Figure 3 shows, the Walker Schedule report header contains the service's name, a report title, and the current date. The information in the report body lists the walkers in ascending order based on the walker's last name. A secondary sort is performed on the walk time code, and within the walk time code category, the information is sorted based on the client's last name. Ms. Hannah also mentions that she wants the Walker Schedule report to utilize a landscape orientation.

Figure 4 shows a tentative sketch for the Client List report. The Client List report provides a listing of the service's current clients. You use the Report Wizard to speed initial report development, and then edit this report in Design view. The Client List report's header contains the service's name, report name, and current date. To maintain a consistent appearance with the Walker Schedule report, you use a report style similar to the Walker Schedule report.

Figure 3: Walker Schedule

KoKo's Canine Pet Club

Walker Schedule

(Current Date)

Last Name	Code	Client	Pet Name	Address	City	Phone	E-Phone
Jordan	3	Monac	Bear	303 Northridge	Edmond	899-2395	909-8679
	3	Stone	Bruno	1408 Peter Pan Drive	Yukon	899-8182	606-3402
				.			
				.			
				.			
Morgan	1	Ruaz	Molly	1701 Memorial Road	Oklahoma City	905-8440	606-4102
				.			
				.			
				.			

Figure 4: Client List Report

KoKo's Canine Pet Club

Client List

(Current Date)

Client Name	Address	City	Phone
Blake, Barney	101 Sunnyville Lane	Edmond	606-8975
		.	
		.	
		.	
Stone, David	1408 Peter Pan Drive	Yukon	899-8182
		.	
		.	
		.	

Ms. Hannah needs answers to the following questions. Build queries to help Ms. Hannah answer these questions. If you choose, you may generate reports based on these queries.

1. How many pets does each pet walker currently walk? Show the walker's first and last name and the pet count for each pet walker. Sort the information in ascending order based on the pet walker's last name.
2. Which clients are located in Edmond? Provide their last and first names.
3. Which clients have three or more pets? Show each client's first and last name and the number of pets he currently has.
4. What are the total pet walking fees charged to each client? Show the client's first and last name and the total fees charged to him.
5. Which pets does Bob walk in the early morning? For each pet, show the pet's name, his owner's last name, and his owner's phone number.

Implementation Concerns

Although you are free to work with the design of the forms and reports, each form and report should have a consistent, professional appearance. Consider using the wizards to prepare the initial forms and reports. Once you have prepared the initial forms and reports, you can edit them in Design view.

A lookup field enables the end user to select a value from a list, thus facilitating data entry and promoting data accuracy. You should define the ClientNo, WalkerNo, and WalkTimeCode fields in the Pet table as lookup fields. When defining the data type for each field, select the Lookup Wizard in the Data Type column and follow the directions in the Lookup Wizard dialogue boxes.

Test Your Design

After creating the forms, tables, relationships, queries, and reports, you should test your database design. Perform the following steps.

1. In addition to the pet walker's base pay, Ms. Hannah wants to give each pet walker a 10 percent commission for each pet that he walks. The commission is based on the fee charged to walk the pet. What is the total commission for each pet walker? Provide the walker's first and last name and his total commission.

2. Ms. Hannah wants to know the number of clients she has in each town. Provide the name of the town and the number of clients for each town.

3. Ms. Hannah is considering raising her fees. She would like to raise the fee for the most popular time. Which walk time is most popular? Provide the walk time description and a count of the number of pets walked at that time.

4. On average, how much does Ms. Hannah charge her clients for walking their pets? Show only the average.

5. Two new clients have enrolled with the pet walking service. Enter their information, along with the information about their pets, into the database. For each client, assign the next available client identification number. For each pet, assign the next available pet identification number and add any comments that you feel are necessary.

   Fancy Tibbs lives at 48473 Roosevelt Drive in Luther, Oklahoma. The zip code is 73002; her phone number is 943-8789, and her emergency number is 910-5746. Mickey, Precious, Prancer, and Spot are her four pets. Mickey is a Yorkshire terrier, Precious is a poodle, Prancer is a Daschund, and Spot is a Dalmatian. The three small dogs cost $6.50 to walk, and the larger dog costs $8.50 to walk. Ms. Tibbs wants Bob Legier to walk each dog in the early morning. Use today's date as the enrollment date.

   Thunder Dumont lives at 84739 Park Lane in Guthrie, OK. The zip code is 73250; his phone number is 748-0098, and his emergency number is 748-9876. Mr. Dumont has two pets. Lightning is a poodle and costs $6.50 to walk. Sunshine is a Great Dane and costs $10.50 to walk. Mr. Dumont requests that Kelly Lamont walk his dogs in the late afternoon. Use today's date as the enrollment date.

CASE DELIVERABLES

In order to satisfactorily complete this case, you should build the database and then prepare both written and oral presentations. Unless otherwise specified, submit the following deliverables to your professor.

1. A written report discussing any assumptions you have made about the case and the key elements of the case. Additionally, what features did you add to make the database more functional? User friendly? (Please note that these assumptions cannot violate any of the requirements specified above and must be approved by your professor.)

2. A printout of each form.

3. A printout of each report.

4. An electronic, working copy of your database that meets the criteria mentioned in the case scenario and specifications sections.

5. Results for each query. (A memo to your instructor discussing these results should also be provided.)

6. As mentioned above, you should prepare an oral presentation. (Your instructor will establish the time allocated for your presentation.) You should use a presentation package and discuss the key features of your database. Also, discuss how this database is beneficial for Ms. Hannah. What additional data could be stored in the database?

CASE 16 Susan's Special Sauces

Database Case **Difficulty Rating:** ★

SKILLS CHECK
You should review the following areas:

DATABASE SKILLS

- ✓ **Calculated Control**
- ✓ **Form Design**
- ✓ **Relationship**
- ✓ **Report Design**
- ✓ **Select Query**
- ✓ **Table Design**

CASE BACKGROUND

Susan's Special Sauces is a small company that produces a variety of salad dressings and sauces. Joy Giovanni, the company's owner, recently purchased a building on the outskirts of town and now wishes to become more organized with her record keeping, especially as it relates to inventory tracking. Initially, Ms. Giovanni wants you to build a database that allows her to monitor the inventory levels of the company's products. For instance, she would like to know current inventory levels, maximum inventory levels, minimum inventory levels, production costs, and selling prices for the company's products. She needs simple, effective forms for entering data about her products. She needs reports that identify low-in-stock items and items that are currently in inventory. She also needs to extract specific information about the company's products and product categories from the database.

CASE SCENARIO

Ms. Giovanni owns and operates a small, Texas-based company called Susan's Special Sauces. Ms. Giovanni named the company after her grandmother and one of her daughters. Susan's Special Sauces produces and sells a variety of salad dressings and sauces, ranging from Creamy Italian Salad Dressing to Extra Spicy Barbecue Sauce. In the early years of her business, Ms. Giovanni prepared, packaged, and sold a variety of spaghetti sauces at local and state fairs, conventions, and flea markets. Over the years, Ms. Giovanni increased her company's product offerings to include gourmet salad dressings, pasta sauces, barbecue sauces, and steak sauces. Susan's Special Sauces currently offers 20 products in five product categories. Table 1 shows the company's current product list.

Randolph Restaurants, a small restaurant chain, uses and also sells many of the sauce company's products. In fact, Randolph Restaurants is the primary customer for Susan's Special Sauces. When the restaurant chain runs low on one of the sauce company's products, Mr. Randolph calls Ms. Giovanni and tells her which product he needs to replenish. The lead-time has been sufficient, so if Ms. Giovanni does not have the product already bottled, she prepares the product after the order is placed.

To date, Ms. Giovanni does not have a formalized method for tracking inventory. When Mr. Randolph calls, she writes the order down on any available scrap of paper or just relies on her memory. If she has the products already bottled, she boxes the order and then delivers the order to Mr. Randolph at one of his restaurants. If a new batch is required, Ms. Giovanni gives the order to her cooks. Sometimes, this method leads to problems with having too much or too little of a particular item on hand.

The growing popularity of the company's sauces has recently required the sauce company to move to a larger building. Customers can now purchase Susan's Special Sauces products from a small shop located in the front of the building.

Now that she has opened a shop, Ms. Giovanni recognizes the need to implement lead times and utilize safety stock. The lead-time to prepare new batches of dressings or special sauces is two days. In general, lead-time is the time it takes Ms. Giovanni to replenish her stock. To avoid stockouts, Ms. Giovanni also utilizes safety stock. Safety stock is extra bottles of the products that are kept on hand. Safety stock acts as a cushion, guarding against running out of a given product. Ms. Giovanni feels that each product's safety stock should be two days of expected daily demand.

As Ms. Giovanni needs a more formalized method for tracking inventory, she asks you to build a simple inventory tracking system. During your first meeting with her, she mentions that she wants to track each product's selling price, quantity on hand, and production cost. Additionally, the inventory tracking system should store the maximum and minimum inventory levels for each product. Ms. Giovanni provides you with a sheet, listing the maximum inventory levels for her products. However, she has not had time to determine the minimum inventory levels for all of her products. She asks you to determine the minimum inventory levels for each product and then insert this information into the database. (A formula is provided in the next section.) Initially, you will build the portion of the database that provides Ms. Giovanni with this information.

Storage Specifications

As you review your notes from your meeting with Ms. Giovanni, you realize that Product and Category tables are needed. The Product table contains nine fields, and its structure is shown in Table 2. (Once you have created the table, use the records provided in Table 1 to populate the table.) As you are constructing the Product table, you recall that Ms. Giovanni asked you to determine each product's minimum inventory level. After you determine each product's minimum inventory level, you create the MinInvLev field for the Product table, and then insert the minimum inventory level data into this field. During your meeting with Ms.

Giovanni, she recommended that you use the following formula for calculating a product's minimum inventory level.

Minimum Inventory Level = (Demand During Lead Time + Safety Stock).

As the Category table contains four fields, it is easy to construct. Table 3 shows the Category table's structure, and Table 4 contains the records for the Category table.

Since Ms. Giovanni has requested information that requires data from two tables, you establish a relationship between the Product and Category tables. As each table contains a PFamilyCode field, you use this common field to join the two tables.

Table 1: Product Records

Product No	Product Name	Product Family Code	Quantity on Hand	Selling Price	Production Cost	Expected Daily Demand	Maximum Inventory Level
1	Extra Creamy Ranch Dressing	DR	140	$3.50	$2.00	25	150
2	Extra Creamy Italian Dressing	DR	100	$3.50	$2.00	35	210
3	Italian Dressing	DR	100	$3.00	$1.50	40	240
4	Superior Caesar Salad Dressing	DR	150	$3.25	$1.25	40	240
5	Susan's French Dressing	DR	119	$3.25	$1.25	42	252
6	Susan's Thousand Island Dressing	DR	125	$3.25	$1.25	55	330
7	Susan's Creamy Blue Cheese Dressing	DR	330	$3.25	$1.25	55	330
8	Sensational Steak Sauce	SA	202	$4.50	$2.50	45	270
9	Thick and Hearty Sensational Steak Sauce	SA	40	$4.75	$2.75	30	180
10	Meatball Express	PS	180	$4.35	$2.85	30	180
11	Vegetarian's Delight	PS	150	$4.50	$2.90	30	180
12	Garlic, Onion, and Mushrooms	PS	30	$4.50	$3.00	5	30
13	More Cheese, Please	PS	4	$4.75	$3.50	15	90
14	Mild Picante	SL	149	$3.10	$1.55	25	150
15	Medium Picante	SL	130	$3.10	$1.55	25	150
16	Jumpin' Hot Picante	SL	115	$3.10	$1.55	20	120
17	Hickory Smoke Barbecue Sauce	BS	130	$4.90	$2.95	25	150

18	Uncle Steve's Best Ever Barbecue Sauce	BS	164	$5.90	$3.45	30	180
19	Magnificent Mesquite Flavored Barbecue Sauce	BS	110	$4.75	$2.75	20	120
20	Extra Spicy Barbecue Sauce	BS	101	$4.50	$2.25	25	150

Table 2: Product Table Structure

Field Name	Data Type	Field Description	Field Size	Comments
PNo	Number	Serves as the primary key. Is unique.	Long Integer	Is required.
PName	Text	Identifies the product.	45	Is required.
PFamilyCode	Text	Identifies the category to which the product belongs.	4	Is required.
QOH	Number	Identifies the number of units currently on hand.	Long Integer	Is required.
SellingPrice	Currency	Identifies the selling price of the product.		Is required.
PCost	Currency	Identifies how much it costs us per unit to produce this product.		Is required.
MinInvLev	Number	Identifies the amount we should keep on hand. New batches are made when we reach this level.	Long Integer	
DailyDemand	Number	Identifies the average daily demand.	Long Integer	
MaxInvLev	Number	Identifies the maximum level of inventory.	Long Integer	

Table 3: Category Table Structure

Field Name	Data Type	Field Description	Field Size	Comments
PFamilyCode	Text	Is a unique number. Use as the primary key.	4	Is required.
Description	Text	Contains the product family name.	15	Is required.
NoInFamily	Number	Contains the number of products in this category.	Long Integer	
Comments	Memo	Contains comments about this category.		

Table 4: Category Records

PFamilyCode	Description	NoInFamily	Comments
BS	Barbecue Sauce	4	
DR	Dressing	7	
PS	Pasta Sauce	4	
SA	Steak Sauce	2	
SL	Salsa	3	

Input Specifications

You prepare sketches of the Product and Category forms and schedule a meeting with Ms. Giovanni. Figures 1 and 2 show these sketches. During the meeting, Ms. Giovanni expresses her delight with the sketches; however, she encourages you to be creative with the design. She also requests that the forms use a consistent format, be user friendly, include the business name, and have a picture of a sauce bottle in the header. (You will need to locate a picture to include on each form.)

After your meeting with Ms. Giovanni, you begin working on the forms. As you study the sketch for the Product form, you decide the main purpose of the form is to enable Ms. Giovanni to add, modify, or delete products from the database. You also decide the form should include all fields from the Product table. As you study the Category form sketch, you recognize the simplicity of this form. This form contains only four fields and is used by Ms. Giovanni to add, modify, and delete information about each product family category.

Figure 1: Product Form

Susan's Special Sauces Product Form	
Product No:	Quantity on Hand:
Product Name:	Expected Daily Demand:
Product Family Code:	Minimum Inventory Level:
	Maximum Inventory Level:
Selling Price:	
Production Cost:	

Figure 2: Category Form

Susan's Special Sauces Category Form	
Family Code:	Description:
Products In Family:	Comments:

Information Specifications

Ms. Giovanni needs a Weekly Inventory Report and Low-In-Stock Report. She has developed sketches for these reports. Figures 3 and 4 show these preliminary sketches. As Ms. Giovanni hands you the sketches, she mentions that you are free to modify each report's overall appearance; however, each report should provide the required information and have a professional appearance.

The Weekly Inventory Report is prepared each Friday afternoon and provides Ms. Giovanni with detailed information about each product. She would like the Weekly Inventory Report format to resemble Figure 3. The report header includes the report's title and current date. Ms. Giovanni wants the Weekly Inventory Report to group the products by product category. The product categories should be sorted in ascending order. Ms. Giovanni would like the products within each category sorted in ascending order. For each product, Ms. Giovanni wants to see the product's name, number, quantity on hand, minimum inventory level, and current selling price. Use the column headings shown in Figure 3. As this is a multi-page report, Ms. Giovanni wants the column headings to appear on each page. She also would like a page number to appear in each page's footer. She also wants each report field to be formatted appropriately. For instance, make sure the current selling price uses a currency format. Ms. Giovanni would like the product category headings to stand out, so she requests that you bold these headings on the report. Keep in mind that this report is based on a select query, and the query uses data from the Product and Category tables.

Ms. Giovanni wants the Low-In-Stock Report to identify all products whose current quantity on hand is equal to or below the minimum inventory level. If a product's quantity on hand is equal to or below the minimum inventory level, Ms. Giovanni will then request that the recommended batch amount be produced to replenish each low-in-stock product. The Recommended Batch Amount is determined by subtracting the Quantity on Hand from the Maximum Inventory Level.

Figure 4 shows a sketch of the Low-In-Stock Report. As you review the sketch, you notice that the report header displays the report's title and current date. Ms. Giovanni has said that this report must contain product name, number, quantity on hand, minimum inventory level, and recommended batch amount columns. Ms. Giovanni wants the products listed in ascending order. In order to build this report, you decide to construct a select query based on the Product table and then base the report on the select query. To enhance the report, you place a page number in the page footer.

Figure 3: Weekly Inventory Report

Susan's Special Sauces

Weekly Inventory Report

(Current Date)

Product Name	Product Number	Quantity on Hand	Minimum Inventory Level	Current Selling Price
Barbecue Sauce				
Extra Spicy Barbecue Sauce				
Hickory Smoke Barbecue Sauce				
.				
.				
.				
Dressing				
Extra Creamy Italian Dressing				
Italian Dressing				
.				
.				
.				

Figure 4: Low-in-Stock Report

Susan's Special Sauces

Low-in-Stock Report

(Current Date)

Product Name	Product Number	Quantity on Hand	Minimum Inventory Level	Recommended Batch Amount
Extra Spicy Barbecue Sauce				
Hickory Smoke Barbecue Sauce				
.				
.				
.				
.				

Ms. Giovanni needs answers for the following questions. Build queries to help Ms. Giovanni answer these questions. If you choose, you may generate reports based on these queries.

1. Which products have a unit profit margin less than $2.00? For each product, include the product's name, number, and unit profit margin. (No other fields should be included.)

2. Which products have a unit profit margin equal to or greater than $2.00? For each product, include the product's name, number, and unit profit margin. (No other fields should be included.)

3. Which products cost Ms. Giovanni less than $2.50 per unit to produce? For each product, include the product's name, number, and production cost. (No other fields should be included.)

4. Which products cost Ms. Giovanni more than $3.00 per unit to produce? For each product, include the product's name, number, and production cost. (No other fields should be included.)

5. Which products have a minimum inventory level greater than 150? For each product, include the product's name and minimum inventory level. (No other fields should be included.)

Implementation Concerns

In order to build the inventory tracking system described in the case scenario, you will build two tables, two forms, two reports, and several select queries. You will also establish a relationship between the Product and Category tables. The forms require you to insert a picture. You will need to locate a picture to insert. Several of the select queries require you to sort, specify criteria, create expressions, and use data from two tables. In order to design the reports, you will base the reports on queries, specify sort orders, and work with report headers, footers, and page headers.

Test Your Design

After creating the tables, forms, queries, relationships, and reports, you should test your database design. Perform the following transactions.

1. Ms. Giovanni wishes to add a new product category to the database. The new product family is cocktail sauce; the product family code is CS, and the number of products currently in the family is 1.

2. Ms. Giovanni has developed several new products and wishes to offer them for sale. Enter the following products into the database.

Product No	Product Name	Product Family Code	Quantity on Hand	Selling Price	Production Cost	Expected Daily Demand	Maximum Inventory Level
21	Lite Italian Dressing	DR	100	$3.50	$2.00	25	150
22	Lite Superior Caesar Salad Dressing	DR	100	$3.50	$2.00	5	30
23	Traditional Meat Spaghetti Sauce	PS	150	$5.00	$3.50	25	150
24	Southern Barbecue Sauce	BS	150	$5.00	$3.00	25	150
25	Grandma's Cocktail Sauce	CS	150	$2.00	$.75	15	90

3. Ms. Giovanni no longer wishes to sell the Garlic, Onion, and Mushrooms pasta sauce. Delete this product from the Product table.

4. The daily demand for the Superior Caesar Salad Dressing has increased to 75 units. Update your database to reflect this change.

5. Identify the five products that have the highest expected daily demand. List only the product name and expected daily demand fields.

CASE DELIVERABLES

In order to satisfactorily complete this case, you should build the database and then prepare both written and oral presentations. Unless otherwise specified, submit the following deliverables to your professor.

1. A written report discussing any assumptions you have made about the case and the key elements of the case. Additionally, what features did you add to make the database more functional? User friendly? (Please note that these assumptions cannot violate any of the requirements specified above and must be approved by your professor.)

2. A printout of each form.

3. A printout of each report.

4. An electronic, working copy of your database that meets the criteria mentioned in the case scenario and specifications sections.

5. Results for each query. (A memo to your instructor discussing these results should also be provided.)

6. As mentioned above, you should prepare an oral presentation. (Your instructor will establish the time allocated for your presentation.) You should use a presentation package and discuss the key features of your database. Also, discuss how this database is beneficial for Ms. Giovanni.

CASE 17 Granny Joan's Cookies

Database Case **Difficulty Rating:** ★

SKILLS CHECK
You should review the following areas:

DATABASE SKILLS

- ✓ **Aggregate Function**
- ✓ **Calculated Field**
- ✓ **Form Design**
- ✓ **Form Wizard**
- ✓ **IIF Function**
- ✓ **Lookup Wizard**
- ✓ **Relationship**
- ✓ **Report Design**
- ✓ **Report Wizard**
- ✓ **Select Query**
- ✓ **Table Design**

CASE BACKGROUND

In the past several years, Fillmore school system students have sold Granny Joan's Cookies to the community and earned extra funds for their school. The fund-raising proceeds are often used to fund class trips, classroom equipment, band uniforms, and playground equipment. Next month, Fillmore students will begin selling Granny Joan's Cookies again. Fillmore's superintendent, Mr. Neely, hires you to design a Cookie database. The Cookie database will track the cookies available for sale, the students who are selling the cookies, and the income from the cookie sales. To build the Cookie database, you will design and populate five tables, create relationships among the tables, design four forms, design several reports, and create several queries.

CASE SCENARIO

Granny Joan's Cookies are very popular, attractively packaged cookies that nonprofit organizations often sell to their communities in an effort to help raise funds for various activities. Several cookie packages are available for sale. Cookies are packaged in tins, gift sets, and baskets. The Fillmore school system will purchase cookie packages from Granny Joan's Cookies, and then mark the packages up by 100 percent.

Although last year's fund-raising efforts were a success, Mr. Neely, Fillmore's superintendent, feels that a more organized approach to tracking the cookie sales is needed. By utilizing a database, Mr. Neely knows he can more accurately track the cookie sales and profits generated from the cookie sales.

Mr. Neely envisions the cookie selling process as follows. Mr. Neely's administrative assistant, Ms. Kelly, is responsible for checking out the cookies to the students and collecting the money from the students for their cookie sales. When a student wants to sell cookies, he will go to Ms. Kelly's office and request the cookie packages. Ms. Kelly will enter the number of packages checked out by the student into the database. When the student has cookie money to turn in, he will go to Ms. Kelly's office and give her the money. Ms. Kelly will update the database to reflect the amount of money turned in, as well as the number of cookie packages the student has sold. Beginning this year, students are only allowed to checkout and turn in money once a day.

Mr. Neely hires you to design a Cookie database. According to Mr. Neely's specifications, the Cookie database will store information about the students, cookie packages, cookie categories, cookie checkouts, and cookie sales. To create the Cookie database, you will build Category, Cookie, Seller, CheckOut, and Sales tables; design Seller, Cookie, Checkout, and Sales forms; design Daily Cookie Income and Cumulative Cookie Income reports, create relationships among tables, and create several queries.

Storage Specifications

To build the Cookie database according to Mr. Neely's specifications, you will create five tables. The required tables are Category, Cookie, Seller, CheckOut, and Sales. (Your professor will provide you with the necessary data to populate these tables.) Table 1 shows the Category table's structure. The CatID field contains a unique value for each cookie category. The CatDesc field provides a description for the cookie category.

Table 1: Category Table Structure

Field Name	Data Type	Field Description	Field Size	Comments
CatID	Text	Is a value that uniquely identifies each cookie category.	5	Is required.
CatDesc	Text	Provides a description for the category.	50	Is required.

The Cookie table stores information about the cookies that are available for sale. Table 2 shows the Cookie table's structure. The CID field contains a unique number for each cookie and serves as the primary key for the table. The CookieName field stores the cookie's name. The CatID field categorizes the type of package, such as tin, gift set or basket. As you study the CatID field, you notice that the CatID field is also included in the Category table. As the CatID field already exists in the Category table, you use the Lookup Wizard to create this field in the Cookie table. The OurCost field shows how much Fillmore pays for each cookie package.

Table 2: Cookie Table Structure

Field Name	Data Type	Field Description	Field Size	Comments
CID	Number	Is a number that uniquely identifies each cookie package.	Long Integer	Is required. Set format property to 0000.
CookieName	Text	Is the name of the cookie package.	50	Is required.
CatID	Text	Is the name of the cookie package type. Use the Lookup Wizard.	25	Is required.
OurCost	Currency	Identifies how much Fillmore pays for the cookie package.	Single	Is required.

The Seller table stores information about the students who are selling the cookies. Table 3 shows the Seller table's structure. As Table 3 shows, the SellerID field uniquely identifies each student and serves as the primary key. The SellerFirstName and SellerLastName fields store the student's first and last names, respectively. The Grade field identifies the student's grade level.

Table 3: Seller Table Structure

Field Name	Data Type	Field Description	Field Size	Comments
SellerID	Number	Identifies the student. Serves as primary key.	Long Integer	Is required.
SellerFirstName	Text	Stores the student's first name.	25	Is required.
SellerLastName	Text	Stores the student's last name.	50	Is required.
Grade	Number	Identifies the student's grade level.	Byte	Is required.

As students will check out a variety of cookie packages (cookie tins, cookie gift sets, and cookie baskets), a CheckOut table is needed to track the cookies checked out by each student. On any given date, one entry for each type of cookie package that a student checks out is made in the CheckOut table. If a student checks out five one-pound tins of butter cookies and two one-pound tins of sugar cookies, then two entries are made in the CheckOut table. One entry is made for the butter cookies, and the second entry is made for the sugar cookies.

Table 4 shows the CheckOut table's structure. As Table 4 shows, the CheckOut table has five fields. These fields are CheckOutID, CookieID, SellerID, CheckOutDate, and CheckOutQuantity. The CheckOutID field contains a unique number for each record and serves as the primary key. The CheckOutID value for each record will be used by the Sales table's RefNo field to associate collected money with a previously checked out cookie package. The CookieID field stores the cookie identification number. The SellerID field stores the seller identification number, identifying the student checking out the cookie package(s). As the CookieID and SellerID fields exist in other tables, you decide to use the Lookup Wizard to create these fields. The CheckOutDate field indicates when the student checked out the cookies, and the CheckOutQuantity field indicates the number of units that the student checked out.

Table 4: CheckOut Table Structure

Field Name	Data Type	Field Description	Field Size	Comments
CheckOutID	AutoNumber	Is a unique reference number assigned to each checkout transaction. Serves as the primary key.	Long Integer	Is required.
CookieID	Number	Identifies the cookie package. Use Lookup Wizard.	Long Integer	Is required.
SellerID	Number	Identifies the student checking out the cookie package. Use Lookup Wizard.	Long Integer	Is required.
CheckOutDate	Date/Time	Identifies the date the cookie package was checked out. Use the Short Date format.		Is required.
CheckOutQuantity	Number	Identifies the number of cookie packages that were checked out on a given date.	Byte	Is required.

The Sales table stores information about each student's cookie sales. Table 5 shows the Sales table's structure. The Sales table has six fields, including SalesID, RefNo, SellerID, SaleDate, QuantitySold, and AmountCheckedIn. The SalesID uniquely identifies each record in the Sales table. This number is assigned by the database management system.

When money is collected from a student, you need to associate the collected money with a record stored in the CheckOut table. One way to do this is to include a RefNo field in the Sales table. For each Sales table record, the RefNo field will have a matching CheckOutID value in the CheckOut table.

The SellerID field identifies the student who sold the cookie package. As the SellerID field also exists in the Seller table, you decide to use the Lookup Wizard to create this field. When a student turns in money to Ms. Kelly, the date the money was turned in is stored in the SaleDate field. The QuantitySold field indicates how many units of a particular cookie package were sold by the student. The AmountCheckedIn field stores the amount of money the student turned in to Ms. Kelly. (Depending upon the assumptions made about this case, it is possible that your professor will ask you to treat the AmountCheckedIn field as a computed field. Therefore, the actual inclusion of this field in the Sales table may not be necessary.)

Table 5: Sales Table Structure

Field Name	Data Type	Field Description	Field Size	Comments
SalesID	AutoNumber	Is a unique number assigned to each sales transaction. Serves as the primary key.	Long Integer	Is required.
RefNo	Number	Matches the CheckOutID from the CheckOut table.	Long Integer	Is required.
SellerID	Number	Identifies the student checking out the cookie package. Use Lookup Wizard.	Long Integer	Is required.
SaleDate	Date/Time	Identifies when the student turned in the money collected from his sales activities. Use the Short Date format.		Is required.
QuantitySold	Number	Identifies how many units the student sold.	Byte	Is required.
AmountCheckedIn	Currency	Stores the amount collected from a student on a particular date for a particular cookie package(s) sale.	Single	Is required.

Input Specifications

Mr. Neely asks you to design Seller, Cookie, CheckOut, and Sales forms. The Seller form allows Ms. Kelly, his assistant, to enter data about each student who will be selling cookies. The Cookie form allows Ms. Kelly to enter data about the different cookie packages. The CheckOut form allows Ms. Kelly to track the cookie packages checked out by each student. When a student comes into Ms. Kelly's office to turn in money, Ms. Kelly will use the Sales form to enter data about the sales and collected money. Figures 1 – 4 provide tentative sketches for these forms.

Figure 1: Seller Form

Seller Form

Seller Identification Number:

Seller First Name:

Seller Last Name:

Grade:

Figure 2: Cookie Form

Cookie Form

Cookie Identification Number:

Cookie Package Name:

Cookie Category:

Our Cost:

Figure 3: CheckOut Form

CheckOut Form

Seller Identification Number:

Seller's First Name:

Seller's Last Name:

Grade:

CheckOut ID	Cookie ID	CheckOut Date	CheckOut Quantity

Figure 4: Sales Form

Sales Form

Seller Identification Number:

Seller's First Name:

Seller's Last Name:

Grade:

Reference Number	Sale Date	Quantity Sold	Amount Checked In

Information Specifications

Mr. Neely needs Daily Cookie Income and Cumulative Cookie Income reports. Figures 5 and 6 show tentative sketches for these reports. (The information shown in the reports is for illustrative purposes only. Your report contents will vary.) Although you are free to work with the design of the reports, Mr. Neely requests that the reports have a standard, professional appearance.

Figure 5 shows the tentative sketch for the Daily Cookie Income report. Mr. Neely will use the Daily Cookie Income report to monitor the daily income from cookie sales. On the Daily Cookie Income report, the Packages Sold column indicates how many packages have been sold by the students and for which money has been collected.

Mr. Neely will use the Cumulative Cookie Income report to see how close the school is to reaching its fund-raising goals. The Cumulative Cookie Income report alphabetically lists each cookie package. For each cookie package, the report indicates the number of packages that have been sold to date, as well as the sales and gross income generated to date by the cookie package. Figure 6 provides a tentative sketch for the Cumulative Cookie Income report.

Figure 5: Daily Cookie Income

Daily Cookie Income

(Current Date)

Cookie Name	Packages Sold	Sales	Gross Income
A Lot of Chocolate Chip 1lb Tin	2	$10.00	$5.00
	. . .		
Sweet Dreams Gift Set 5 lbs	4	$104.00	$52.00

Figure 6: Cumulative Income

Cumulative Cookie Income

(Current Date)

Cookie Name	Packages Sold	Sales	Gross Income
A Lot of Chocolate Chip 1lb Tin	6	$30.00	$15.00
	.		
	.		
	.		
Sweet Dreams Gift Set 5 lbs	5	$130.00	$65.00

Mr. Neely needs answers to the following questions. Build queries to help Mr. Neely answer these questions. If you choose, you may generate reports based on these queries.

1. Based on gross sales, which grade has sold the most cookies? Identify the grade level and the gross sales.

2. Based on gross sales, which student has sold the most cookies?

3. Based on gross income, what is the most popular cookie?

4. Which students have sold all the cookies that they have checked out?

5. Which students have cookies checked out, but have not turned in any money?

6. What are the gross sales by category?

7. Which student has sold the most gift baskets? Least?

8. Mr. Neely now needs a Reference List report. This report will allow Mr. Neely or Ms. Kelly to look up a reference number associated with cookie packages checked out by a student. The Reference List report should alphabetically list each student. For each student, the report should provide the student's first and last names, as well as grade. This report should also show which cookie packages were checked out by the student, along with the cookie package name, checkout date, checkout quantity, and reference number.

9. Mr. Neely needs a Price List report. The Price List report alphabetically lists each cookie package. For each cookie package, the report should show the cookie package's name, identification number, cost, selling price, and gross income.

10. Mr. Neely wants Cookie CheckOut reports for each grade. At a minimum, each report should provide the student's name, cookie package name, and the checkout quantity for the cookie package. For each report, the information should be sorted in alphabetical

order by student last name.

Implementation Concerns

To prepare this database according to Mr. Neely's specifications, you will create several queries, establish relationships among tables, and design forms and reports.
Several of the select queries require you to sort, specify criteria, create expressions, and use data from multiple tables. When you create the relationships, make sure to enforce referential integrity. Although you are free to work with the design of the forms and reports, each form and report should have a consistent, professional appearance. Consider using the wizards to prepare the initial forms and reports. Once you have prepared the initial forms and reports, you can edit them in Design view.

At least one of the queries and a report may require the use of the IIF function. The IIF function allows you to check for a certain condition, such as a field that contains a null value. You can use your system's online help feature to learn more about the IIF function's syntax.

Test Your Design

After creating the forms, tables, relationships, queries, and reports, you should test your database design. Perform the following steps.

1. Add the following cookie categories to your database.

CatID	CatDesc
TP001	Two-Pack
MX001	Mix

2. Add the following cookies to your database.

CID	CookieName	Category	Our Cost
0020	Snickerdoodles	Two-Pack	$1.00
0021	Oatmeal Raisin	Two-Pack	$1.00
0022	Banana Pie Cookie	Mix	$1.50
0023	Coconut Delicious	Two-Pack	$1.00
0024	Mint Brownie	Mix	$1.50

3. The following students want to check out cookies. Enter their information into the database.

Seller First Name	Seller Last Name	Grade Level
Darrel	Jenel	6
Jared	Mounce	7
Mack	Fridley	4
Natalie	Perrot	5
Dominick	Rendley	3

4. Several students have checked out cookie packages. Enter the following information into the Cookie database. Assume the checkout date is October 6, 2008.

Seller	Cookie Package	Quantity
Darrel Jenel	A Lot of Chocolate Chip 1lb Tin Sugar Cookies 1lb Tin Butter Cookies 1lb Tin Snickerdoodles Two Pack	4 3 2 7
Jared Mounce	Butter Cookies 1lb Tin Peppermint Cookies 1lb Tin Cookies Galore Basket 2.5lbs Banana Pie Cookie Mix	2 1 2 2
Mack Fridley	Sweet Dreams Gift Set 5lbs A Lot of Chocolate Chip 1lb Tin Coconut Delicious Two Pack	2 11 3
Natalie Perrot	Butter Cookies 2lb Tin Sugar Cookies 2lb Tin Oatmeal Raisin Two Pack	6 1 10
Dominick Rendley	Sweet Dreams Gift Set 2.5lbs Cookies Galore Basket 2.5lbs Mint Brownie Mix	2 2 4

5. The following students turned in money. Enter the following information into the database. Assume the money was turned in on October 13, 2008.

Seller	Cookie Package	Quantity Sold	Amount Turned In
Darrel Jenel	A Lot of Chocolate Chip 1lb Tin	2	$10.00
Jared Mounce	Butter Cookies 1lb Tin Peppermint Cookies 1lb Tin Cookies Gallore Basket 2.5lbs	1 1 1	$6.00 $5.00 $8.00
Mack Fridley	Sweet Dreams Gift Set 5lbs A Lot of Chocolate Chip 1lb Tin	1 6	$26.00 $30.00
Micah Ernsberger	A Lot of Chocolate Chip 1lb Tin Butter Cookies 2lb Tin Sugar Cookies 1lb Tin	2 4 2	$10.00 $36.00 $10.00
Annette O'Mally	Sugar Cookies 2lb Tin	5	$45.00
Dominick Rendley	Sweet Dreams Gift Set 2.5lbs Cookies Galore Basket 2.5 lbs Mint Brownie Mix	1 1 2	$15.00 $8.00 $6.00
Cedrick Jerideau	Butter Cookies 1lb Tin	1	$6.00

6. Mr. Neely asks you to create an Income Sales Summary Report. Mr. Neely wants the report to list the sales dates in ascending order. For each sales date, he wants to see the total income received on that date.

7. Mr. Neely asks you to create a Student Cookie Sales Activity Report, summarizing each student's cookie checkout and sales activities. When you design the report, the report should alphabetically list each student, and then list each cookie package checked out by the student. For each cookie package checked out by the student, Mr. Neely wants to know the total units checked out, the total units sold, and the remaining number of cookie package units that are still checked out by the student.

8. Mr. Neely asks you to create a Cookie by Category Sales Report. The report should list each category alphabetically. For each category, Mr. Neely wants to see the total sales and gross income for each category.

CASE DELIVERABLES

In order to satisfactorily complete this case, you should build the database and then prepare both written and oral presentations. Unless otherwise specified, submit the following deliverables to your professor.

1. A written report discussing any assumptions you have made about the case and the key elements of the case. Additionally, what features did you add to make the database more functional? User friendly? (Please note that these assumptions cannot violate any of the requirements specified above and must be approved by your professor.)

2. A printout of each form.

3. A printout of each report.

4. An electronic, working copy of your database that meets the criteria mentioned in the case scenario and specifications sections.

5. Results for each query. (A memo to your instructor discussing these results should also be provided.)

6. As mentioned above, you should prepare an oral presentation. (Your instructor will establish the time allocated for your presentation.) You should use a presentation package and discuss the key features of your database. Also, discuss how this database is beneficial for Mr. Neely. What additional data could be stored in the database?

CASE 18 Friends In Need

Database Case **Difficulty Rating:** ★★

SKILLS CHECK
You should review the following areas:

DATABASE SKILLS

- ✓ **Aggregate Function**
- ✓ **AutoLookup Query**
- ✓ **Combo Box**
- ✓ **Command Button**
- ✓ **Form Design**
- ✓ **Form Wizard**
- ✓ **Label Wizard**
- ✓ **Relationship**
- ✓ **Report Design**
- ✓ **Report Wizard**
- ✓ **Select Query**
- ✓ **Table Design**

CASE BACKGROUND

Friends in Need is a well-respected charitable organization, often mentioned in the press for providing outstanding charitable services to local families. Currently, Friends in Need has a staff of 10 volunteers, including Roman Kieffer, who serves as the organization's director. Since the charitable organization's founding five years ago, the number and type of donations have continued to increase, necessitating changes in the way donations are currently tracked and distributed.

Although the donation and distribution processes are simple in concept, paperwork is mounting. Currently, Mr. Kieffer keeps the charity's records in spiral notebooks, and he needs a better method for tracking donors and distributing donations to qualifying families. Recently the Byrd Corporation donated the necessary hardware and software needed to create a computerized information system for Friends in Need. Mr. Kieffer asks you to organize and automate the charity's record-keeping activities. You will build and populate Donor, Donation, and Type tables; create New Donor and New Donation forms; prepare mailing labels and a Weekly Donations report; create relationships; and construct several queries.

CASE SCENARIO

One evening five years ago, Roman Kieffer watched a news program that discussed how several local families were having difficult times and unable to give their children Christmas presents. In an effort to help these families, Mr. Kieffer and several friends organized a charity drive, collecting toys, clothing, monetary gifts, and food items. The donations were then distributed to deserving families. The charity drive was so successful that Mr. Kieffer founded the Friends in Need charitable organization.

Since the charity's founding five years ago, the donation process has remained simple. When a donor makes a contribution, he either mails a check or drops by the Friends in Need Center. When a donation is made, a staff member records the donor's name, address, and phone number on a donation form, along with details about the donation. A receipt is then given to the donor. If the donor wishes to remain anonymous, the word "anonymous" is written across the donation form. Monetary donations are deposited in a local bank, while non-monetary donations are sorted according to type. Each week, the Friends in Need committee evaluates assistance requests. Donations are then distributed to qualifying families, based on type of need.

Currently, all record keeping is tedious, inefficient, time consuming, and manually performed. The manual, paper-based system is no longer adequate. As the newest Friends in Need volunteer, Mr. Kieffer asks you to build the Friends database. In order to construct the Friends database to Mr. Kieffer's specifications, you will build and populate Donor, Donation, and Type tables; design New Donor and New Donation forms; prepare mailing labels and a Weekly Donations report; create several relationships; and construct several queries.

Storage Specifications

After meeting with Mr. Kieffer and reviewing the forms and reports currently used by the charity, you decide the Friends database should have three tables: Donor, Donation, and Type. (Your professor will provide you with the data to populate the Donor and Donation tables.) The Donor table stores the donor's identification number, type, first and last name, company name, address, and phone number. The DonorType field indicates whether or not the donor is a company or individual. When a company makes a donation, the DonorType field is checked, indicating that the donor is a company. Information about the company's contact person is then entered into the LastName and FirstName fields. If an individual makes a donation, the company name field is left blank, and all other fields are completed. The DonorID field serves as the primary key. Table 1 shows the structure for the Donor table.

The Donation table stores data about each donation. After studying your notes about the donation process, you decide the Donation table should use the structure shown in Table 2. Since a donor can make several donations on any given day, you decide to create a field called DonationID. This field serves as the primary key. For each donation, Mr. Kieffer wants to record the donation's approximate worth. You create an AppWorth field to hold this data.

Table 3 shows the structure for the Type table. The Type table stores type codes and brief descriptions about the kinds of donations accepted by the organization. Once the Type table is created, you use the data from Table 4 to populate the table.

Two relationships are necessary. First, you create a relationship between the Donor and Donation tables. Since the Donor and Donation tables have a DonorID field, you decide to use this common field to create a relationship between these two tables. Second, a relationship between the Donation and Type tables is required. As you study the Donation and Type tables, you notice that these tables both have a TCode field. You use this common field to create a relationship between the Donation and Type tables. For each relationship, you enforce referential integrity.

Table 1: Donor Table Structure

Field Name	Data Type	Field Description	Field Size	Comments
DonorID	AutoNumber	Is a unique number assigned to each donor. Serves as primary key.	Long Integer	Is required.
DonorType	Yes/No	Indicates whether the donor is a company or individual. "Yes" represents a company. Set the default value to "No."	Yes/No	Is required.
LastName	Text	Stores the donor's last name or the contact person's last name.	50	Is required.
FirstName	Text	Stores the donor's first name or the contact person's first name.	25	Is required.
CompanyName	Text	Stores the company's name.	50	
SAddress	Text	Stores the street address for the individual or company.	50	Is required.
City	Text	Stores the city for the individual or company. Set the default value to "Chicago."	25	Is required.
State	Text	Stores the state abbreviation for the individual or company. Set the default value to "IL."	2	Is required.
Zip	Text	Stores the zip code for the individual or company.	10	Is required.
Phone	Text	Stores the donor's phone number. Uses an input mask.	10	

Table 2: Donation Table Structure

Field Name	Data Type	Field Description	Field Size	Comments
DonationID	AutoNumber	Serves as the primary key.	Long Integer	Is required.
DonorID	Number	Is the donor identification number of the individual or company making the donation.	Long Integer	Is required.
DDate	Date/Time	Stores the date the donation was made. Uses Short Date as the format.		Is required.
TCode	Text	Stores the donation type code.	4	
AppWorth	Currency	Stores the approximate worth of the donation. Uses a standard format.		
Comments	Memo	Stores comments about the donation.		

Table 3: Type Table Structure

Field Name	Data Type	Field Description	Field Size	Comments
TCode	Text	Serves as the primary key.	4	Is required.
TDescription	Text	Provides a brief description of the type.	25	Is required.

Table 4: Type Table Records

TCode	TDescription
T1	Monetary
T2	Food
T3	Clothing
T4	Toys
T5	Other

Input Specifications

When a new donor makes a contribution, the New Donor form captures contact information; this information is then stored in the Donor table. The contact information enables the charity to contact the donor about upcoming events and send out thank you letters for current and future donations. Figure 1 shows a sketch of the New Donor form. As you examine the sketch, you decide to use the Form Wizard to create an initial form. Once the initial form is created, you modify the form's appearance in Design view. To enhance the form's appearance, you include graphics on the form.

Mr. Kieffer wants information about each donation captured and stored in the database. The New Donation form captures the donor's identification number, donation date, donation type, the donation's approximate worth, and comments. Mr. Kieffer wants to select a donor's identification number from a Combo box and then have the system look up the donor's first and last name. He also wants to select the donation type from a Combo box. Since a donor can make more than one donation at a time, you decide to include a command button on the form. This button, when pressed, allows a staff member to add information about a new donation, thus facilitating data entry. Figure 2 shows a tentative sketch of the New Donation form. As this form uses data from multiple tables, you decide to first create a select query. You use the Form Wizard to create an initial New Donation form based on the query and then edit the form in Design view. You decide that this form should also include graphics.

Mr. Kieffer mentions that you are free to modify each form's design. However, the design must have a professional appearance, be consistent, and capture, at a minimum, the data as shown.

Figure 1: New Donor Form

Friends in Need

New Donor

Donor Identification Number:	Last Name:	First Name:
Donor Type:		
Company Name:	Street Address:	
	City:	State: Zip:

Figure 2: New Donation Form

Friends in Need

New Donation

(Donation Date)

Donor Identification Number:

Donor Name:

Donation Type:

Approximate Worth:

Comments:

Include a command button → Add Donation

Information Specifications

Each Monday, Mr. Kieffer sends thank you letters to the individuals and companies who made donations the previous week. As donor addresses are now stored in the database, you decide to generate mailing labels for him. You prepare a select query that retrieves contact information for the previous week's donors and sorts the donor last names in ascending order. You then use the Report Wizard to prepare mailing labels. Figure 3 shows a sketch of the mailing labels. (The actual data for the mailing labels may differ from what is shown below.)

Figure 3: Mailing Labels

Jwang Buyung
5010 Jackson Drive
Chicago, IL 60611

Woody Huang
777 Kelley Avenue
Chicago, IL 60612

Rayna Reyes
1801 Sandhurst
Chicago, IL 60601

.
.
.

Johnny Richards
1020 Beagle Drive
Chicago, IL 60612

Catrina Stanton
Betty's Interior Designs
4651 Asheville Lane
Chicago, IL 60613

Mr. Kieffer wants a report showing the types of donations that were made last week and their approximate values. Figure 4 shows a tentative sketch of the Weekly Donations report. The report header includes the report title and the current date. The report body shows the donation types, donor identification numbers, and the approximate worth of the donations. Mr. Kieffer wants this information sorted in ascending order by donation type. Within the donor identification number category, he wants the information sorted in ascending order based on the donor identification number. As this report requires data from multiple tables, you build a select query, and then base the report on the query.

Figure 4: Weekly Donations Report

Friends in Need

Weekly Donations

(Current Date)

Donation Type	Donor ID	Approximate Worth
Clothing	2	$30.00
	5	$15.00
	13	$5.00
	.	
	.	
	.	
Food	3	$50.00
	12	$10.00
	.	
	.	
	.	

Mr. Kieffer requires answers for the following questions. Build queries to help Mr. Kieffer answer these questions. If you choose, you may generate reports based on these queries.

1. Which donation type is most popular? Mr. Kieffer wants a count for each donation type. Show only the type descriptions (TDescription) and their counts. No other fields should be shown.

2. How many companies made donations last week? (Use October 13, 2008, as the beginning date for the previous week.)

3. Which of the charity's donors made contributions worth more than $500.00? For each donor, show the first and last name, company name (if applicable), and approximate worth of the contribution.

4. Who are the contact persons for the companies that have contributed to the charity? Show the company name and then the first and last name of the contact person. Sort the information in ascending order based on company name.

5. On average, what is the approximate worth of the donations made last week? (Use October 13, 2008, as the beginning date for the previous week.)

6. Mr. Kieffer wants a Daily Donor Report. The Daily Donor Report should alphabetically list the daily donors and identify the type of donation that was made by the donor. Mr. Kieffer requests that information about anonymous donors and donations be left out of the report. (Use October 16, 2008, as the report date.)

Implementation Concerns

For this case, you design and populate Donor, Donation, and Type tables; design New Donor and New Donation forms; prepare mailing labels, a Weekly Donations report and a Daily Donor report; create several queries; and establish relationships between tables.

As mentioned in the Storage Specifications section, you create relationships between the Donor and Donation tables and the Donation and Type tables. For each relationship, you should enforce referential integrity.

As previously mentioned, New Donor and New Donation forms are necessary. A simple way to create the New Donor form is to use the Form Wizard. Once you have created an initial form, edit the form in Design view. Several options are available for creating the New Donation Form. One option is to create a select query and then use the Form Wizard to create an initial form. Once the form is created, the form's appearance can be edited in Design view. The New Donation form in Figure 2 includes an Add Donation button. The Command Button Wizard enables you to easily include this record operation feature.

Since thank you letters are sent to donors for the previous week, you need a select query to identify these donors. Once the donors are identified, you can use the Label Wizard to create mailing labels. For the Weekly Donations report, you should construct a select query to retrieve the necessary data, and then use the Report Wizard to create the report.

Test Your Design

After creating the forms, tables, relationships, queries, and reports, you should test your database design. Perform the following transactions:

1. The charity has several new donors. Enter their contact information and contributions into the database.
   - Bobak Nazar donated $450.00 on October 20, 2008. His contact information is 1220 Hemingway Drive, Chicago, IL 60661. Also, enter the following comment: "A check for $247 was provided, along with $203 in cash." Bobak's phone number is (312) 337-2552.
   - Kwai Chang donated approximately $100 in food items on October 20, 2008. His contact information is 17493 Kelley Drive, Chicago, IL 60664. His phone number is (312) 337-9988.
   - Carmelo Pereles donated approximately $250 in baby clothes on October 21, 2008. Her contact information is 3321 Beverly Drive, Chicago, IL 60667. Also, enter the following comment: "The clothes range in size from newborn to toddler." Carmelo's phone number is (312) 335-1801.

2. Enter the following contributions for existing donors into the Friends database:
   - On behalf of Lancaster Paints, Robin Bibb donated $5,000 in cash, $3,000 in food items, and $2,500 in clothing to the charity on October 20, 2008.

- On behalf of Betty's Interior Designs, Catrina Stanton donated $1,557.74 in cash, $750.00 in toys, and $32.30 in clothing to the charity on October 21, 2008. Also, enter the following comment: "The toys are most appropriate for children over the age of three."

3. Prepare a Generous Donations report for Mr. Kieffer. The Generous Donations report should list all of the donations greater than $1,000 received during the past month. List the donations in descending order, along with the donor's name and phone number. (Use October as the past month.)

CASE DELIVERABLES

In order to satisfactorily complete this case, you should build the database and then prepare both written and oral presentations. Unless otherwise specified, submit the following deliverables to your professor.

1. A written report discussing any assumptions you have made about the case and the key elements of the case. Additionally, what features did you add to make the database more functional? User friendly? (Please note that these assumptions cannot violate any of the requirements specified above and must be approved by your professor.)

2. A printout of each form.

3. A printout of each report. (Where applicable, use the week of October 13, 2008 as the beginning date for the previous week.)

4. An electronic, working copy of your database that meets the criteria mentioned in the case scenario and specifications sections.

5. Results for each query. (A memo to your instructor discussing these results should also be provided.)

6. As mentioned above, you should prepare an oral presentation. (Your instructor will establish the time allocated for your presentation.) You should use a presentation package and discuss the key features of your database. Also, discuss how this database is beneficial for Mr. Kieffer. What changes to this database would you recommend? What additional data could be stored in the database?

CASE 19 Second Time Around Movies

Database Case **Difficulty Rating:** ★★

SKILLS CHECK
You should review the following areas:

DATABASE SKILLS

- ✓ **Aggregate Function**
- ✓ **Calculated Field**
- ✓ **Chart Wizard**
- ✓ **Crosstab Query**
- ✓ **Form Design**
- ✓ **Relationship**
- ✓ **Report Design**
- ✓ **Select Query**
- ✓ **Table Design**

CASE BACKGROUND

Sharrie Daniels owns and operates a local chain of video rental stores. Although business is steady, competition is forcing her to find new, innovative ways to market her business. Taylor and Berkley Daniels, having inherited their grandmother's entrepreneurial spirit, recognize the significance of using the Web to strengthen the family business. A few years ago the twins approached their grandmother about creating an online movie rental business. Although the new business's primary target market is the avid Web surfer, the twins think the online movie rental business will prove popular with individuals seeking convenience or living in rural areas.

After initial test marketing, Ms. Daniels gave the project a green light. With their grandmother's blessing and a significant advance on their inheritance, the twins opened Second Time Around Movies. Currently, Second Time Around Movies is doing well and serves five states: Arkansas, Kansas, Louisiana, Oklahoma, and Texas. If the business continues to do well, it will expand to other states.

The Second Time Around Movies database contains data about current movie club members, membership plans and the advertisement sources used to attract members. To make several marketing decisions, the twins need to extract and use data currently stored in this database. Taylor and Berkley Daniels are interested in learning more about their movie club members, investigating potential marketing opportunities and identifying the various advertisement sources that are currently attracting movie club members. The twins ask you to extract specific data and prepare several reports. As you examine the database, you realize that a Plans form, an Enrollment form, and minor table modifications are also necessary.

CASE SCENARIO

Second Time Around Movies, the brainchild of Taylor and Berkley Daniels, is a new type of movie rental business. Rather than a traditional brick-and-mortar business, Second Time Around Movies is an online movie rental store. Second Time Around Movies offers its movie club members a wide selection of both new releases and classic movies on DVDs. In fact, Second Time Around Movies has over 9,000 titles available for rental.

Second Time Around Movies offers its movie club members the convenience of renting movies from the comfort of their homes. Movie club members rent DVDs online, saving the time and expense of running to the local video store to check out or return videos.

To take advantage of the online movie store, a Web site visitor must subscribe and pay a monthly membership fee. The monthly membership fee is based on the size of the movie package. Until the membership subscription is cancelled, the movie club member's credit card is billed a monthly membership fee. A member is free to change or cancel his membership plan at anytime.

The online subscription form collects basic customer information, including credit card number, shipping address, e-mail address, and monthly newspaper request. At the time of enrollment, a subscriber selects a membership plan that is suitable to his viewing needs. During the subscription process, a new member indicates whether or not he would like to receive the Second Time Around Movies newspaper. This newspaper provides movie reviews, offers promotions, identifies upcoming releases, and is a good way for the twins to keep in touch with current movie club members.

Once a customer completes the subscription process and is approved, the customer builds his Movie Request List. A customer creates this list by selecting the movies he wishes to view. He will also rank these movies in order of viewing preference. The Movie Request List tells the Second Time Around Movies staff which movies the club member wishes to view or check out. Movie packages are then assembled based on the member's Movie Request List. Movie package refers to the number of DVDs shipped at one time to a movie club member.

While five plans are currently available, avid movie buffs can select the Seymour Movies plan, enabling them to receive as many as six DVDs at a time. In contrast, the occasional movie viewer may choose a more economical plan, such as the Blue Moon plan. The Blue Moon plan ships a single DVD at a time. Table 1 identifies the available membership plans, along with pricing for each plan.

CASE 19: Second Time Around Movies

Table 1: Available Membership Plans

PlanID	Description	Cost
001	Blue Moon	$12.99
002	Sharrie's Special	$17.99
003	Popcorn and More	$22.99
004	Couch Potato Special	$27.99
005	Seymour Movies	$34.99

At Second Time Around Movies, a current movie club member visits the company's Web site and adds movie names to his Movie Request List. If the movie is available, it is shipped as part of the member's next movie package. The number of DVDs contained within a movie package is determined by the selected membership plan. If a member is on the Just Released List, newly released movie DVDs are included as part of the next movie package being shipped to the customer.

Before receiving a new movie package, a club member must return all currently checked out DVDs. Returning DVDs is a simple process. After watching the DVDs, the customer places the DVDs in a specially marked, prepaid postage envelope and drops the envelope in the mail. When the Second Time Around Movies staff receives the envelope, a new movie package is mailed to the member. Usually, the member receives his new movie package within a few days.

Potential movie club members are discovering Second Time Around Movies in a variety of ways. Friends, television and print advertisements, other Web sites, and search engines are contributing to the new online store's success. Taylor and Berkley Daniels want to know how new movie club members learn about Second Time Around Movies. When subscribing, a new member is asked how he learned about the store. This information is then stored in the movie club member's record. Taylor and Berkley Daniels will use this information to better market their store in the future.

Taylor and Berkley Daniels want to modify the store's available membership plans. In order to do this, they need to know which plans are most popular. They also want to know how members are attracted to their online store. For instance, which advertisement source encouraged the member to visit the online store's Web site?

As Taylor and Berkley Daniels are very busy managing the online movie rental store, they ask you to retrieve information from and make modifications to the Second Time Around Movies database. The following sections describe the information and the modifications that are needed.

Storage Specifications

Your database copy contains Member, Plan, and Source tables. (Your instructor will provide you with a copy of the database. Your copy contains the tables and test data that you need for this case.) After examining the tables, you realize that a few modifications to the Member and Plan table structures are necessary. The Source table structure does not require modifications.

As you study the Member table, you notice that it contains a Newspaper field. This field indicates whether or not the member wishes to receive an electronic copy of the Second Time Around Movies monthly newspaper. You decide to set the Newspaper field's default value to "Yes" and use an input mask for the member's phone number.

Currently, the Plan table contains PlanID, Description, and Cost fields. However, the Plan table is missing a MaxMovies field. When included, the MaxMovies field identifies the maximum number of movies available for checkout according to a particular plan. You modify the Plan table to include this field. Table 2's fourth column contains the data that should be added to the Plan table.

Table 2: Plan Table

PlanID	Description	Cost	MaxMovies
001	Blue Moon	$12.99	1
002	Sharrie's Special	$17.99	2
003	Popcorn and More	$22.99	3
004	Couch Potato Special	$27.99	4
005	Seymour Movies	$34.99	6

Input Specifications

In the future, Taylor and Berkley Daniels will add, modify, and delete several membership plans. To facilitate changes to the Plan table, you design a simple form that accommodates the addition, modification, and deletion of membership plans. Taylor and Berkley Daniels provide you with a tentative sketch for the Membership Plan form. Figure 1 shows this tentative sketch. As you study the sketch, you realize that using the Form tool or Form Wizard is an easy way to begin the form's development. As you continue to study the sketch, you decide that a picture is needed. Locate a picture and include this picture on the form. While you are free to work with the form's design, the form must contain, at a minimum, all fields from the Plan table, have a professional appearance, and be easy to use.

Taylor and Berkley Daniels decide that an Enrollment form is necessary. When a new customer subscribes to the online movie club, Taylor and Berkley Daniels want to capture certain data about their new client. Figure 2 shows a tentative sketch for the Enrollment form. As with the Membership Plan form, you can use either the Form tool or Form Wizard to create a simple form, and then modify the form in Design view.

Figure 1: Membership Plan Form

Second Time Around Movies

Membership Plan

Plan ID:	**Cost:**
Description:	**Max Number:**

Figure 2: Enrollment Form

Second Time Around Movies

Enrollment

Member No:	**Phone Number:**
First Name:	**Credit Card:**
Last Name:	**ICC:**
City:	**Plan ID:**
State:	**Email Address:**
Zip:	**Newspaper:**

Information Specifications

Taylor and Berkley Daniels wonder which membership plan is the best seller. They also wonder how the plans compare with each other. As charts provide a good way of summarizing and visually presenting information, you decide a pie chart will prove useful for comparing and contrasting the membership plans. You decide to use the Chart Wizard to construct a pie chart that summarizes the information requested by the twins. Figure 3 shows a representation of how this pie chart might look. (Your chart values will vary from the values shown in Figure 3. You may wish to use the system's online help feature to review chart creation.)

As you examine Figure 3, you notice that the report's title is "Membership Plan Comparison Chart" and a current date is included. Also, each pie slice represents one of the available membership plans, and a data label and percentage are shown above each pie slice.

Taylor and Berkley Daniels are interested in examining the relationship between advertisement sources and states. Prepare a report similar to the one in Figure 4. Although you realize several methods for obtaining the report information exist, you construct a Crosstab query and base the Count By State report on this query. (Your counts will differ from the counts shown in Figure 4.)

The twins want to know which movie club members have requested a monthly newspaper. As mentioned previously, a new member specifies whether or not he wants to receive a monthly newspaper during the subscription process. Prepare a Newspaper Recipients report for the twins. Figure 5 provides a sketch of this report.

Figure 3: Membership Plan Comparison Chart

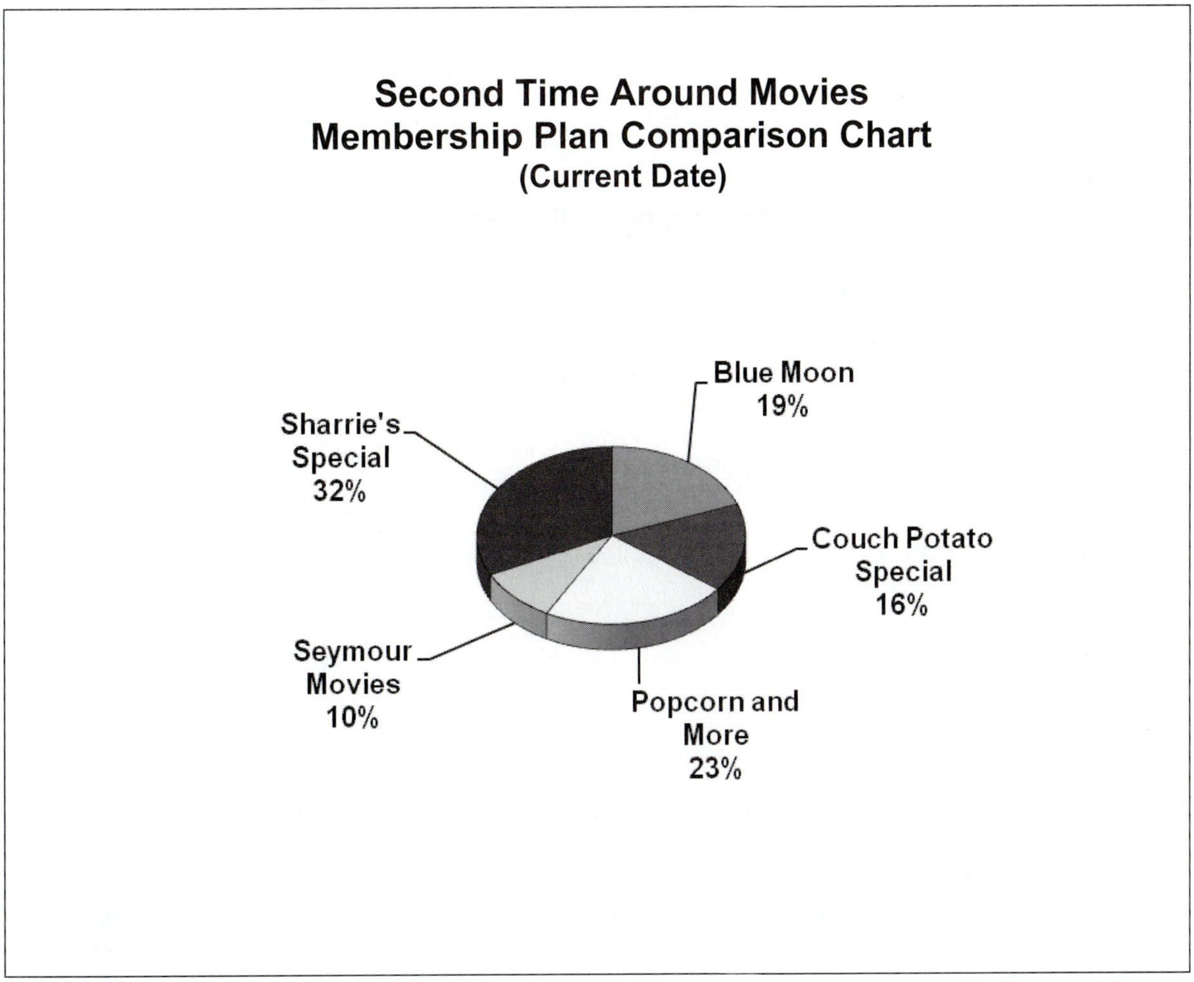

Figure 4: Count By State

Second Time Around Movies
Count By State
(Current Date)

Source Description	Arkansas	Kansas	Louisiana	Oklahoma	Texas	Count
Another Web Site	52	49	89	97	101	388
Friend						
Magazine						
.						
.						
.						
					Total Count:	

Figure 5: Newspaper Recipient Report

Second Time Around Movies
Newspaper Recipients
(Current Date)

Last Name	First Name	E-Mail Address
Kelly	Lisa	panda@pandasforever.com
Kelly	Val	imafriend@friendsaroundtheworld.com
Lansing	Peter	plansing@lansinghome.com
		.
		.
		.

Taylor and Berkley Daniels need answers to the following questions. If you choose, you may generate reports based on these queries.

1. The twins want to approach one or two major credit card companies about possible promotional opportunities. Which credit cards are movie club members using? Which credit card company is used most frequently? (Your answer should identify the credit card company and indicate a member count by state for that credit card company.)

2. Which current members have Hotmail accounts? (Show the member's name, state, and e-mail address.)

3. How many current members live in Texas towns? (Your results should list the town, a count for each town and an overall count.)

4. Taylor and Berkley Daniels want to know the total revenue generated by their membership plans for each Texas town. Your results should show the name of the Texas town and the total membership revenue for that town.

5. How did current movie club members from Kansas learn about the online movie store? (Show the results for the source description (not the source) and provide a count for each source description.)

6. Three new members have joined the online movie club. Using the Enrollment form, enter their information into the database. For the membership numbers, assign the next available numbers. For the e-mail addresses, enter your e-mail address. For the enrollment date, use the current date. The three new members want to receive the newspaper.

Last Name	First Name	Street	City	State	Zip	Phone	Credit Card	ICC	Plan ID
Melvin	David	104 Northridge	Waco	TX	76701	(254) 753-9933	MC	002	004
Livingston	Kirk	111 King's Way	Emporia	KS	66801	(620) 243-1111	DI	003	003
Moriamo	Tan	107 Northridge	Waco	TX	76701	(254) 753-9944	MC	002	004

7. Which members enrolled during October 2008? Prepare a New Membership Report.

8. Which members have been enrolled for two or more years?

9. Bonnie Hendrix has decided not to renew her membership. Locate and then delete her record from the database.

Implementation Concerns

This case requires you to modify tables, create forms, construct several queries, and prepare several reports. The table modification requires setting a default value for the Newspaper field and creating an input mask for the Phone Number field. To facilitate data entry to the Plans table, you will build a simple data entry form. This form will allow the twins to add, modify, or delete membership plans. As this is a simple form, you can use the Form tool or Form Wizard to build an initial form and then modify this form in Design view. To facilitate data entry to the Member table, you will create a data entry form. You can also use the Form tool or Form Wizard to build an initial form and then modify the form in Design view.

To construct the Membership Plan Comparison Chart, which is a type of report, you should first build a select query to retrieve the necessary data. Keep in mind that this select query retrieves data from two tables and uses the Count function. Once you have created your select query, use the Chart Wizard to build your pie chart. The chart may require editing, so use the system's online help feature to learn more about editing charts. The chart should include the current date, have an appropriate header, and be rotated to enhance its readability. Also, you should show a data label and percentage for each slice. As the Newspaper Recipients report is based only on the Customer table, you can use the Report tool or Report Wizard to create this report. The Count by State report requires data from two tables. Construct a select query to retrieve the information, and then use the Report tool or Report Wizard to build the report. Once the report is built, you can edit the design of the report.

Test Your Design

After making the requested changes specified in the case scenario, you should test your database design. Perform the following transactions.

1. Using your newly created Membership Plan form, change the price of each plan. Use the information provided in the following table. When the new plan costs are implemented, how much will revenue increase for the business?

PlanID	Description	Cost
001	Blue Moon	$15.99
002	Sharrie's Special	$19.99
003	Popcorn and More	$24.99
004	Couch Potato Special	$29.99
005	Seymour Movies	$37.99

2. The twins are interested in comparing the membership plans by state. Prepare plan comparison charts for both Texas and Louisiana. Your charts will be similar to the Plan Comparison Chart discussed previously and shown in Figure 3.

CASE DELIVERABLES

In order to satisfactorily complete this case, you should make the requested table modifications and then build the forms, queries, and reports. You should also prepare both written and oral presentations. Unless otherwise specified, submit the following deliverables to your professor.

1. A written report discussing any assumptions you have made about the case and the key elements of the case. Additionally, what features did you add to make the database more functional? User friendly? (Please note that these assumptions cannot violate any of the requirements specified above and must be approved by your professor.)

2. A printout of the form.

3. A printout of each report.

4. An electronic, working copy of your database that meets the criteria mentioned in the case scenario and specifications sections.

5. Results for each query. (A memo to your instructor discussing these results should also be provided.)

6. As mentioned above, you should prepare an oral presentation. (Your instructor will establish the time allocated for your presentation.) Instead of the queries and reports mentioned above, what other helpful information might Taylor and Berkley Daniels retrieve from the database? How could this information help them make better marketing decisions?

CASE 20 Elusive Moose RV Park

Database Case **Difficulty Rating:** ★★

SKILLS CHECK
You should review the following areas:

DATABASE SKILLS

- ✓ **Aggregate Function**
- ✓ **AutoLookup Query**
- ✓ **Calculated Control**
- ✓ **Calculated Field**
- ✓ **Form Design**
- ✓ **IIF Function**
- ✓ **Relationship**
- ✓ **Report Design**
- ✓ **Select Query**
- ✓ **Table Design**

CASE BACKGROUND

Alaska is described as one of the most beautiful places on earth. Its breath-taking beauty attracts tourists to its rivers, wilderness, and glaciers. Each year thousands of RVers travel to Alaska in search of adventure and a change of pace. Alex and Amber Malaski are RV enthusiasts and have just opened their Elusive Moose RV Park in Alaska.

Although the Elusive Moose RV Park has been open for just a few months, the Malaskis are quickly discovering that their manual reservation tracking system is not working. In an effort to fix their problematic system, they ask you to develop their Moose Reservations database. Building the Moose Reservations database requires you to develop Customer and Reservation forms; construct several queries; and prepare Daily RV Check-In, RV Station List, and Month-Long Customer reports.

CASE SCENARIO

Alex and Amber Malaski are avid RVers, and have driven their RV all over the United States and Canada. During their many RV travels, they spoke frequently about one day opening an RV park. It was on their recent trip to Alaska that they found the perfect location to make their dream come true. The Malaski's Elusive Moose RV Park has just opened, and business is brisk. To cater to the most discerning RVer, all stations provide customers with electricity, water and sewer hookups, cable and Internet access, and pull-through capability.

While Mr. Malaski maintains the RV park, Mrs. Malaski manages the reservations. Because the park has just opened, Mrs. Malaski has not had time to develop the Moose Reservations database. Instead she relies on a pen and paper method to track the park's reservations. Currently, Mrs. Malaski uses a three-ring binder with a separate page for each reservation day.

When a customer calls and requests a specific check-in day, such as June 1, Mrs. Malaski flips to the June 1 page in the notebook and records the customer's reservation. While making the reservation, the customer can select from Denali, wilderness or river views.

Currently, Mrs. Malaski records the customer's contact information, requested reservation dates, and view preference. When a customer checks-in, the customer is assigned an RV station. Mrs. Malaski records the assigned station number beside the customer's reservation details in the notebook.

The Malaskis are in need of a better, more efficient system and ask you to develop the Moose Reservations database for them. The specifications for the Moose Reservations database are provided below.

Storage Specifications

Mrs. Malaski asks you to design the Moose Reservations database for the Elusive Moose RV Park. The Moose Reservations database includes Customer, Type, Station, and Reservation tables. (Your instructor will provide you with the data to populate these tables.) Tables 1, 2, 3, and 4 provide the table structures.

Table 1 outlines the Customer table's structure. The Customer table stores basic customer information such as name, address, and phone number. As the CustomerID field is unique for each customer record, it serves as the primary key.

The Type table stores information about the different view types. As explained above, the Elusive Moose RV Park provides a selection of views for its customers. When making a reservation, the customer specifies the type of view he wants, such as wilderness, Denali, or river. Table 2 shows the Type table's structure. As the TypeID field is unique for each record, it serves as the primary key.

Table 3 shows the Station table's structure. The Station table stores information about the Elusive Moose RV Park's available stations and contains three fields. As the StationID field is unique for each record, it serves as the primary key.

Table 4 provides the Reservation table's structure. The Reservation table stores information about the Elusive Moose RV Park's current reservations. As the ResID field is unique for each record, it serves as the primary key for the Reservation table.

Table 1: Customer Table Structure

Field Name	Data Type	Field Description	Field Size	Comments
CustomerID	AutoNumber	Serves as primary key.	Long Integer	Is required.
CFirstName	Text	Stores the customer's first name.	50	Is required.
CLastName	Text	Stores the customer's last name.	50	Is required.
CStreet	Text	Stores the customer's street address.	50	
CCity	Text	Stores the city where the customer lives.	50	
CState	Text	Stores the state where the customer lives.	2	
CZipCode	Text	Stores the customer's zip code. Use an input mask.	10	
CPhNo	Text	Stores the customer's phone number. Use an input mask.	10	

Table 2: Type Table Structure

Field Name	Data Type	Field Description	Field Size	Comments
TypeID	Text	Serves as primary key.	2	Is required.
TypeDesc	Text	Provides a short description about the station type.	50	
DailyRate	Currency	Identifies the standard daily fee.		

Table 3: Station Table Structure

Field Name	Data Type	Field Description	Field Size	Comments
StationID	Text	Serves as primary key.	5	Is required.
StationType	Text	Identifies the station type.	2	
StationDesc	Text	Provides a description of the station.	255	

Table 4: Reservation Table Structure

Field Name	Data Type	Field Description	Field Size	Comments
ResID	AutoNumber	Serves as primary key.	Long Integer	Is required.
CustomerID	Number	Identifies the customer making the reservation. Use the Lookup Wizard.	Long Integer	Is required.
Check-In Date	Date/Time	Identifies when the customer is checking in. Use the Short Date format.		
Check-Out Date	Date/Time	Identifies when the customer is checking out. Use the Short Date format.		
StationRequestType	Text	Identifies the type of station requested by the customer. Request is granted based on availability. Use Lookup Wizard.	2	
StationAssigned	Text	Stores the station identification number for the station assigned to the customer. Use the Lookup Wizard.	5	

Input Specifications

For the Moose Reservations database, Customer and Reservation forms are required. Figures 1 and 2 provide sketches of the forms. Although you are free to modify each form's design, the forms should have a consistent, professional appearance. As requested by Mrs. Malaski, each form should use the Elusive Moose logo and include a picture of a moose. (You should design the logo and locate a picture of a moose.)

As Figure 1 shows, the Customer form captures basic information about the Elusive Moose

RV Park's customers, such as their name and address. As the form uses fields from the Customer table, you can use the Form tool to create the initial Customer form. After creating the initial form, you can easily modify the form's appearance in design view.

As you study the Reservation form sketch, you notice that the Reservation form uses data from multiple tables, including the Customer, Reservation, and Type tables. While the check-in date, check-out date, station request type, assigned station, and comments fields are stored in the Reservation table, the customer fields are stored in the Customer table, and the daily rate is stored in the Type table. The stay length, applicable discount, amount owed before discount, and amount owed fields are computed and require calculated controls.

On the Reservation form, Mrs. Malaski wants to select the Customer ID from a combo box, and then have the system look up the customer's name, address, and phone number. When determining how much a customer owes, the applicable discount is used. If a customer stays for a week, he is given a 10 percent discount. However, if the customer stays for 30 days or longer, he is given a 15 percent discount. Mrs. Malaski wants the Reservation form to display the amount owed before discount, any applicable discount, and then the final amount owed.

Figure 1: Customer Form

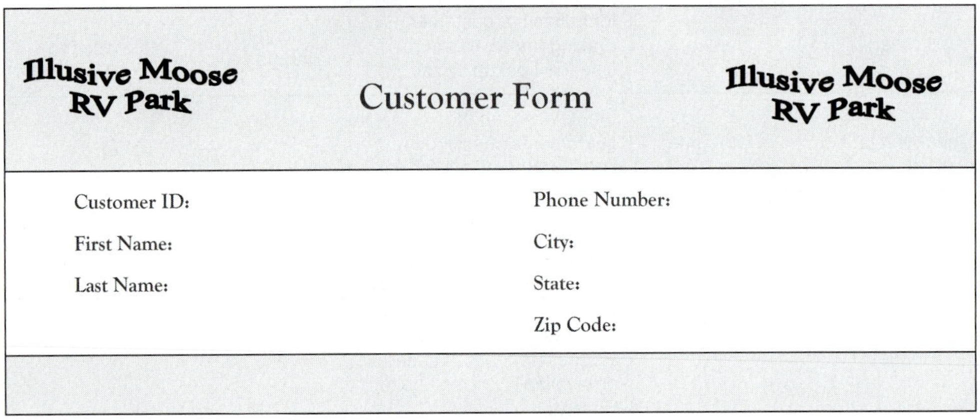

Figure 2: Reservation Form

Illusive Moose RV Park | Reservation Form | Illusive Moose RV Park

Customer ID:
First Name:
Last Name:
Phone Number:
City:
State: Zip Code:

Check-In Date:
Check-Out Date:
Stay Length:
Station Request Type:
Assigned Station:

Daily Rate:
Amount Owed Before Discount:
Applicable Discount:
Amount Owed:
Comments:

Information Specifications

Although you will build several reports for Mrs. Malaski, she asks you to first build RV Station List, Daily RV Check-In, and Month-Long Customer List reports. Figures 3, 4, and 5 provide sketches of these reports. At Mrs. Malaski's request, each report includes the company logo and a picture of a moose. (The data shown in the reports is for illustrative purposes. Actual data may differ.)

Figure 3 shows the RV Station List sketch. As the sketch shows, the report includes the station types, Station IDs, and station descriptions. The RV stations are sorted by type and then by Station ID.

At the close of each business day, Mrs. Malaski will print a Daily RV Check-In report. The Daily RV Check-In report identifies the customer, assigned station, and check-out date. Mrs. Malaski wants the customer names sorted in alphabetical order on last name and wants the total number of RVs checked-in that day displayed. Figure 4 provides a sketch for the Daily RV Check-In report.

Mrs. Malaski is especially appreciative of the Elusive Moose RV Park's month-long customers. She wants to know who they are so she can give them a small moose stuffed animal. Therefore, she needs a Month-Long Customer List report. As Figure 5 shows, the Month-Long Customer List report identifies all customers whose stay at the Elusive Moose RV Park has been for at least 30 days. As the sketch shows, Mrs. Malaski wants to know the customer's first and last names, Station ID, check-in date, check-out date, and length of stay. Mrs. Malaski wants the Month-Long Customer List report sorted in alphabetical order by customer last name.

Figure 3: RV Station List

Illusive Moose RV Park

RV Station List
(Current Date)

Station Type	Station ID	Station Description
Denali		
	D1	
	D2	
	D3	
		. . .
River		
	R1	
	R2	
	R3	
		. . .
Wilderness		
	W1	
	W2	
	W3	
		. . .

Figure 4: Daily RV Check-In

Illusive Moose
RV Park

Daily RV Check-In
(Current Date)

Last Name	First Name	Station ID	Check-Out
Belanger	Tillie	R2	7/31/2008
Gilsdorf	Malara	D4	8/3/2008
Rebbaj	Quinn	W3	8/1/2008

.
.
.

New Check-Ins: XXXX

Figure 5: Month-Long Customer List

Illusive Moose
RV Park

Month-Long Customer List
(Current Date)

Last Name	First Name	Station ID	Check-In	Check-Out	Length of Stay
Belanger	Tillie	R2	7/31/2008	8/31/2008	31
Gilsdorf	Malara	D4	6/1/2008	7/15/2008	44
Rebbaj	Quinn	W3	6/1/2008	7/1/2008	30

.
.
.

Mrs. Malaski needs answers to the following questions. If you choose, you may generate reports based on these queries.

1. How many customers were not assigned their requested station type?
2. What is the average length of stay for the RV park customers?
3. On June 12, 2008, how many stations are currently occupied?
4. What is the RV park's revenue for June 1, 2008? Mrs. Malaski wants the information organized by station type. The report should also show the total discount that was given.

Implementation Concerns

This case requires you to build and populate Customer, Type, Station, and Reservation tables, create Customer and Reservation forms, construct several queries, and prepare RV Station List, Daily RV Check-In, and Month-Long Customer List reports.

When designing the tables, consider designing them in the order as presented. You should consider using the Lookup Wizard to create the CustomerID field in the Reservation table and the StationAssigned and StationRequestType fields in the Station table. After designing the four tables, you should review the table relationships and ensure that referential integrity is enforced.

You can easily create the Customer form by using the Form tool. As the Reservation form requires data from three tables, you should consider building an AutoLookup query and then basing the form on the query. After the query is created, you can use the Form Wizard to create the initial Reservation form. The Customer and Reservation forms can then be modified in Design view.

Test Your Design

After making the requested changes specified in the case scenario, you should test your database design. Perform the following transactions.

1. Enter customer data for you and four of your friends.

2. Enter reservations for you and your four friends.

3. Mrs. Malaski only wants current reservation data kept in the RV Park database. She asks you to delete reservation data for the month of May.

CASE DELIVERABLES

In order to satisfactorily complete this case, you should build the database and then prepare both written and oral presentations. Unless otherwise specified, submit the following deliverables to your professor.

1. A written report discussing any assumptions you have made about the case and the key elements of the case. Additionally, what features did you add to make the database more functional? User friendly? (Please note that these assumptions cannot violate any of the requirements specified above and must be approved by your professor.)

2. A printout of each form.

3. A printout of each report.

4. An electronic, working copy of your database that meets the criteria mentioned in the case scenario and specifications sections.

5. Results for each query. (A memo to your instructor discussing these results should also be provided.)

6. As mentioned above, you should prepare an oral presentation. (Your instructor will establish the time allocated for your presentation.) You should use a presentation package and discuss the key features of your database. Also, discuss how this database is beneficial for Mrs. Malaski. What additional information from the database might Mrs. Malaski find useful?

CASE 21 Tyrone's Arcade Games

Database Case **Difficulty Rating:** ★★★

SKILLS CHECK
You should review the following areas:

DATABASE SKILLS

- ✓ **Aggregate Function**
- ✓ **Calculated Field**
- ✓ **Form Design**
- ✓ **Lookup Wizard**
- ✓ **Parameter Query**
- ✓ **Relationship**
- ✓ **Report Design**
- ✓ **Select Query**
- ✓ **Subform**
- ✓ **Tab Control**
- ✓ **Table Design**

CASE BACKGROUND

Tyrone Skalicky owns and operates Tyrone's Arcade Games. This small, yet growing business rents a variety of arcade games to local businesses, including video, novelty, pinball, photo, and bowling. To encourage game rentals, Mr. Skalicky shares a percentage of each game's income with the business owner. As Mr. Skalicky's arcade rental business continues to grow, so does his mounting paper work. Mr. Skalicky's current paper-based record-keeping system is inconvenient, time consuming, and unorganized. Mr. Skalicky hires you to complete an Arcade database for him. The Arcade database will enable Mr. Skalicky to track his customers, game rentals, and rental income. Completing the Arcade database requires you to design forms and reports, modify relationships, and create several queries.

CASE SCENARIO

As a teenager, Tyrone Skalicky was fascinated with arcade games and often spent his entire weekly allowance at the local arcade. As an adult, Mr. Skalicky's love of arcade games continued. So, after receiving his business degree from the local university, Mr. Skalicky decided to use his newly acquired business degree and knowledge of arcade games to start an arcade game rental business. When Mr. Skalicky first began his business, he purchased used arcade games, fixed them up, and then rented the games to local businesses. As his income increased, Mr. Skalicky invested in the latest and newest arcade games for his customers.

Arcade game rental is an attractive alternative to many business owners. Rather than owning an arcade game outright, the business owner can rent the equipment, receive a modest income from the game, and not have the headaches associated with maintaining and being stuck with outdated equipment.

During the arcade game rental process, Mr. Skalicky visits with the business owner, and they determine which game(s) will prove profitable for the business. During the visit, Mr. Skalicky and the business owner negotiate how to share the income from the game. Once Mr. Skalicky and the business owner agree on the income percentages, Mr. Skalicky jots down the agreed-upon percentages in a notebook. Needless to say, these percentages are currently not recorded in a timely manner.

Mr. Skalicky tries to visit each of his customers and service the machines on a regular basis. Servicing a game involves collecting the money from the game and providing any necessary maintenance. As the number of Mr. Skalicky's clients continues to increase, the frequency with which he visits his clients continues to decline, and he has not been diligent in tracking his income from the game rentals.

In order to remain successful, Mr. Skalicky must better organize and manage his business. As a starting point, he hires you to complete his Arcade database. When finished, the Arcade database will track Mr. Skalicky's customers, game rentals, and rental income. Initially, Mr. Skalicky asks you to design and populate Rental and Collection tables, prepare Machine and Customer forms, design Game List and Customer Rental reports, modify relationships between tables, and prepare several queries.

Storage Specifications

The partially completed Arcade database currently has Customer and Machine tables. The Customer table stores basic information about each of Mr. Skalicky's customers. For each customer, the Customer table stores a customer identification number, customer last name, customer first name, business name, street address, city, state, zip, and phone number. The field names in the Customer table are CID, CLastName, CFirstName, BusinessName, StreetAddress, City, State, Zip, and Phone. For each machine, the Machine table stores a machine identification number, machine name, and category. The field names in the Machine table are MID, MName, and MCategory. The CID field serves as the primary key for the Customer table, and the MID field serves as the primary key for the Machine table.

As Mr. Skalicky must store information about each machine's rental and income, you will add Rental and Collection tables to the Arcade database. The Rental table stores information about the machines rented by each customer and each machine's rental income percentage. Table 1 shows the Rental table's structure. The Collection table stores information about the income collected from each machine, as well as the date the income was collected. Table 2 shows the structure for the Collection table. (Your instructor will provide you with the data to populate both tables.)

As you examine the Rental and Collection table structures, you notice that the CID and MID fields also exist in the Customer and Machine tables. When creating the CID and MID fields for the Rental and Collection tables, you decide to use the Lookup Wizard. (When selecting the data type for the CID and MID fields, you select the Lookup Wizard option. When you select the Lookup Wizard as the data type, the Lookup Wizard is invoked. At this point, you enter the necessary information into the Lookup Wizard dialogue boxes.)

Although the Lookup Wizard created relationships between the Customer and Rental tables, Machine and Rental tables, Customer and Collection tables, and Machine and Collection tables, these relationships do not enforce referential integrity. You decide to modify the relationships to enforce referential integrity.

Table 1: Rental Table Structure

Field Name	Data Type	Field Description	Field Size	Comments
CID	Number	Serves with the MID and RentalDate as the primary key. Use the Lookup Wizard.	Long Integer	Is required.
MID	Number	Serves with the CID and the RentalDate as the primary key. Use the Lookup Wizard.	Long Integer	Is required.
RentalDate	Date/Time	Serves with the CID and MID as the primary key. Provides the date identifying when the arcade game was rented. Use an input mask.		Is required.
RotationDate	Date/Time	Identifies when the customer should be contacted about game rotation. Use an input mask.		Is required.
TheirPercentage	Number	Indicates the customer's percentage of the game's income.	Single	Is required.

Table 2: Collection Table Structure

Field Name	Data Type	Field Description	Field Size	Comments
CID	Number	Serves with the MID and CollectionDate as the primary key. Use the Lookup Wizard.	Long Integer	Is required.
MID	Number	Serves with the CID and CollectionDate as the primary key. Use the Lookup Wizard.	Long Integer	Is required.
CollectionDate	Date/Time	Identifies the date when coins were removed from the game.		Is required.
Gross	Number	Identifies the gross dollar amount generated by the game.	Single	Is required.

Input Specifications

Mr. Skalicky wants Machine and Customer forms added to the Arcade database. Mr. Skalicky will use the Machine form to enter records about new machines into the Arcade database, as well as update records regarding existing machines. The Customer form allows Mr. Skalicky to enter data about a customer, the machines rented by the customer, and the income generated for each rented machine.

As Figure 1 shows, the Machine form is a simple form and can be designed quite easily with the Form tool or Form Wizard. Once the Machine form is created, you can select appropriate graphics to add to the form.

Figure 2 shows the initial design for the Customer form. As you study Figure 2, you notice that the initial design indicates that the Customer form is actually a multipage form. Information about the customer is contained on the main form, while information about machine rental and machine income is organized by using tab control pages. When Mr. Skalicky clicks the Machine Rental tab, a subform containing fields from the Rental table should display. Mr. Skalicky will use this subform to enter data about the machines rented by a particular customer. Likewise, when Mr. Skalicky clicks the Income tab, a subform containing fields from the Collection table should display. Mr. Skalicky will use the Income subform to enter data about the income collected from a particular customer on a particular date.

Figure 1: Machine Form

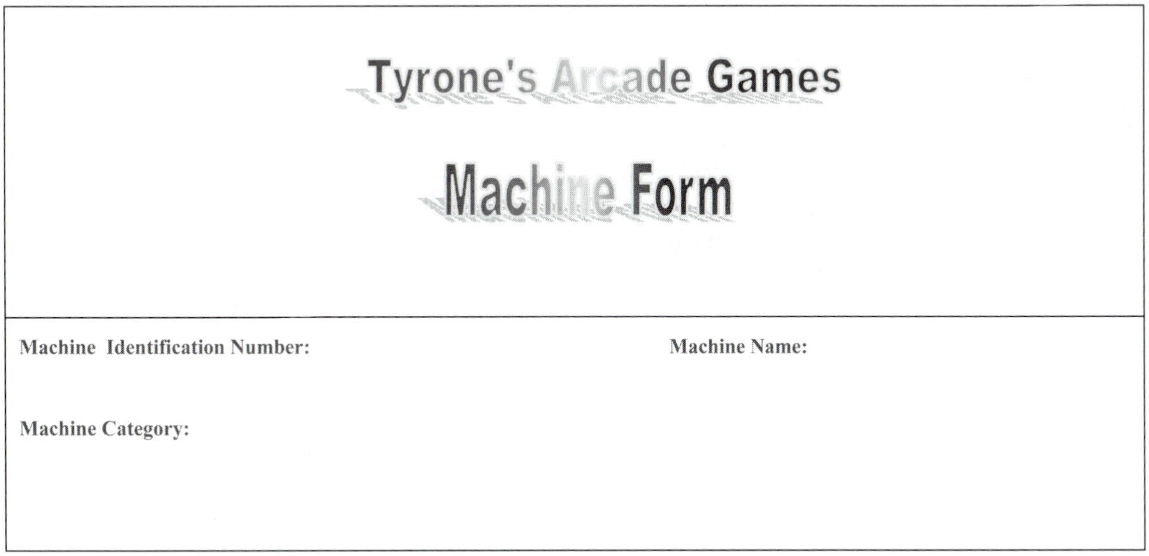

Figure 2: Customer Form

Tyrone's Arcade Games
Customer Form
Customer Identification Number:
Customer First Name:
Customer Last Name:
Business Name:
Street Address:
City:
State:
Zip:
Phone Number:
Machine Rental
Income

Information Specifications

Mr. Skalicky requests Customer Rental and Game List reports. As Figure 3 shows, the Customer Rental report provides Mr. Skalicky with a current alphabetical listing of his customers. The tentative sketch also shows that for each customer, the rented games and rental dates are also listed alphabetically. (Marvin Devon rented two Evil Empire games on February 5, 2008). The Game List report lists the games by category. The Game List report provides a count of how many games are rented and how many are still in stock and available for rent. Figure 4 provides a tentative sketch for this report.

Figure 3: Customer Rental Report

Tyrone's Arcade Games

Customer Rental Report

(Current Date)

Last Name	First Name	Business Name
Devon	Marvin	Marvin's Place
	Machine Name	Rental Date
	Evil Empire	2/5/2008
	Evil Empire	2/5/2008
Dipierro	Angelo	Angelo's Place
	Machine Name	Rental Date
	Fantasy Land	2/17/2008
	Last Man	2/17/2008
	Last Man	2/17/2008
	Millenium Fighter Jet	2/17/2008

.
.
.
.

Figure 4: Game List Report

Tyrone's Arcade Games

Game List Report

(Current Date)

Category	Name	Inventory	Rented	Available
Bowling	Extreme Bowling	3	2	1
		⋮		
Video	DayRider	2	2	0
	Deluxe Astroids	2	2	0
	Last Man	4	2	2
		⋮		

Mr. Skalicky needs answers to the following questions. Build queries to help Mr. Skalicky answer these questions. If you choose, you may generate reports based on these queries.

1. Which games have not been rented and are currently available? Mr. Skalicky needs each machine's name, identification number, and category.

2. Games that have been rented for six months or longer are eligible for upgrades or replacements. Which customers have games that have been rented for six months or longer? Mr. Skalicky wants to see each customer's last name, first name, business name, phone number, and rental date. The results should be displayed alphabetically by customer last name. Use the date of July 15, 2008, as the current date for this query.

3. Mr. Skalicky wants a query that prompts him for the name of a game, and then based on his input, will identify the customers who have rented that game. The results should display each customer's first name, last name, business name, phone number, and rental date.

4. Mr. Skalicky wants an Income Generation report. The Income Generation report should alphabetically list each customer. For each customer, Mr. Skalicky wants to see an alphabetical list of the customer's rented games, and for each game, he wants to see the gross income, client income, and his income. The report should provide group totals for each customer, as well as grand totals for the report.

5. Identify the game that has generated the most income for Mr. Skalicky.

6. Identify the customer who has generated the most income for Mr. Skalicky.

7. Identify the customers who have rented four or more games from Mr. Skalicky.

Implementation Concerns

Although you are free to work with the design of the forms and reports, each form and report should have a consistent, professional appearance. Consider using the form and report tools and wizards to prepare the initial forms and reports. Once you have prepared the initial forms and reports, you can edit them in Design view.

A lookup field enables the end user to select a value from a list, thus facilitating data entry and promoting data accuracy. You should define the CID and MID fields in the Rental and Collection tables as lookup fields. When defining the data type for each field, select the Lookup Wizard in the Data Type column and follow the directions in the Lookup Wizard dialogue boxes.

As Figure 2 shows, the Customer form has a Machine Rental tab and an Income tab. You will use a tab control to place these tabs on the Customer form. When Mr. Skalicky clicks the Machine Rental tab, he will access the Machine Rental page. This page enables Mr. Skalicky to enter data about a particular customer's rentals. When Mr. Skalicky clicks the Income tab, he will access the Income page. The Income page enables Mr. Skalicky to enter data about the income received for each machine rented by a particular customer. When creating the Customer form, you have several options. After creating the Customer form and using the tab control to place the tab pages on the Customer form, one option is to drag each newly created subform from the Database window onto its respective tab page. Use your system's online help feature to learn more about subforms and tab controls.

Test Your Design

After creating the forms, tables, queries, and reports, you should test your database design. Perform the following steps.

1. Mr. Skalicky has purchased five new arcade games. Enter the following information into the database. Mr. Skalicky purchased two games called Cruncher. The games are categorized as Video. He also purchased three Power Dunk games; these games are categorized as Basketball.

2. Enter the following rental information into the database. Marv Waxler owns Marv's Movie Rental. The store is located at 888 Pine Bluff, Bar Harbor, Maine. His phone number is (207) 288-5555. Benji Cullas owns Benji's Auto Shop. Benji's Auto Shop is located at 919 Brenham Way, Bar Harbor, Maine. The Phone number is (207) 288-6666. The zip code for both businesses is 04609. Mr. Waxler and Mr. Cullas rented the following games.

Customer	Machine Rented	Rental Date	TheirPercentage	RotationDate
Marvin Waxler	Cruncher	3/1/2008	45 percent	9/1/2008
Marvin Waxler	Power Dunk	3/1/2008	45 percent	9/1/2008
Marvin Waxler	MiniClaw (00027)	3/1/2008	45 percent	9/1/2008
Marvin Waxler	Last Man (00016)	3/1/2008	45 percent	9/1/2008
Marvin Waxler	MemoryMaker (00008)	3/1/2008	45 percent	9/1/2008
Benji Cullas	Power Dunk	3/6/2008	45 percent	9/6/2008
Benji Cullas	NightRaider (00032)	3/6/2008	50 percent	9/6/2008

3. Mr. Skalicky needs the following collection information entered into the database. The collection date is March 4, 2008.

Customer	Machine ID	Amount
Pauley Tien	4	$75.00
Marinello Pourchot	25	$178.00
Marinello Pourchot	29	$204.50
Angelo Dipierro	14	$132.50
Angelo Dipierro	17	$144.75
Angelo Dipierro	18	$199.50
Angelo Dipierro	20	$50.00

CASE DELIVERABLES

In order to satisfactorily complete this case, you should build the database and then prepare both written and oral presentations. Unless otherwise specified, submit the following deliverables to your professor.

1. A written report discussing any assumptions you have made about the case and the key elements of the case. Additionally, what features did you add to make the database more functional? User friendly? (Please note that these assumptions cannot violate any of the requirements specified above and must be approved by your professor.)

2. A printout of each form.

3. A printout of each report.

4. An electronic, working copy of your database that meets the criteria mentioned in the case scenario and specifications sections.

5. Results for each query. (A memo to your instructor discussing these results should also be provided.)

6. As mentioned above, you should prepare an oral presentation. (Your instructor will establish the time allocated for your presentation.) You should use a presentation package and discuss the key features of your database. Also, discuss how this database is beneficial for Mr. Skalicky. What additional data could be stored in the database?

CASE 22 Keller Industries

Database Case **Difficulty Rating:** ★★★

SKILLS CHECK
You should review the following areas:

DATABASE SKILLS

- ✓ **Aggregate Function**
- ✓ **AutoLookup Query**
- ✓ **Calculated Control**
- ✓ **Find Unmatched Query Wizard**
- ✓ **Form Design**
- ✓ **Lookup Wizard (optional)**
- ✓ **Parameter Query**
- ✓ **Relationship**
- ✓ **Report Design**
- ✓ **Select Query**
- ✓ **Table Design**

CASE BACKGROUND

Keller Industries is a company with a growing problem. As more of its employees are issued personal computers, the management of these personal computers and the installed software on them is creating massive headaches for the IT Department. Since no formal hardware/software tracking system is currently utilized, the IT Department has no way of knowing what hardware is currently assigned to Keller Industries employees, nor does the IT staff know whether all of the installed software is licensed.

In an effort to better manage its hardware and software, Keller Industries has decided to formally track all hardware and software currently assigned to its employees. Initially, the system will track personal computer and software assignments. Mica Meyers, the IT Department Director, provides you with a copy of a partially completed Tracking database. She then asks you to build forms and reports, design and populate a Hardware table, establish relationships between tables, and construct several queries.

CASE SCENARIO

When a Keller Industries employee needs to upgrade his computer system, he simply calls the IT Department and makes a verbal request. An IT staff member prepares a work order, and if the work order is approved, the request is filled as soon as possible. After the work order is completed, the work order is filed in a filing cabinet, never to be seen again. The lack of a formal hardware/software tracking system creates headaches for the IT Department staff, since the staff has only a general idea about what hardware and software are currently used by Keller Industries employees. Also, many problems currently exist, such as theft, use of illegal software, and incompatibility.

No one can say for certain how many personal computers are owned by Keller Industries or guarantee that only licensed software is on the personal computers. To gain control of the situation, Ms. Meyers asks you to inventory all personal computers and available software. She asks you to assign a unique hardware identification number to each personal computer and then finish building the Tracking database. Initially, the Tracking database will track all available personal computers, software, and hardware/software assignments. (For simplicity, operating systems are not included as part of the software list.)

When a new personal computer is purchased, Ms. Meyers wants the details about the newly acquired personal computer entered into the Tracking database. An IT staff member uses a Hardware form to capture details about the computer, such as the hardware identification number, processor type, processor speed, RAM amount, model, manufacturer, hard drive capacity, and serial number. After the personal computer is assigned to an employee, an assignment field in the table stores the employee's identification number.

When a work order is completed, Ms. Meyers wants the information entered immediately into the Tracking database, making a Hardware/Software Assignment form necessary. This form allows the IT staff member to add, modify, or delete current hardware/software assignments.

Ms. Meyers knows the Tracking database contains important details about the hardware, software, and current hardware/software assignments. By generating reports based on this data, she can make valuable decisions. For instance, the Software Assignment report helps Ms. Meyers determine how many copies of a particular software title are currently installed. The Hardware report tells Ms. Meyers about the current hardware and software configurations used by Keller Industries employees. The Employee Assignment report shows the current hardware/software configurations for each employee. While the Hardware report organizes this information by computer, the Employee Assignment report arranges the information by employee, thus facilitating the review of information.

Storage Specifications

The Tracking database contains populated Software, Employee, and Config tables. As you study these tables, you notice that the Software table contains SID, Publisher, Title, License, and Category fields. The SID field serves as the primary key, uniquely identifying a particular software package. The Publisher field identifies the company that publishes the software. The Title field includes the software package's name, and the License field indicates how many licenses the company has for that particular software package. The Category field classifies the software according to purpose. The Employee table contains EID, LName, and FName fields. The EID field stores the employee identification number and serves as the table's primary key. The LName and FName fields contain the employee's last name and first name, respectively. The Config table identifies the software that is currently stored on a particular computer. Currently, this table contains only two fields: HID and SID. The HID field identifies a particular computer, and the SID field identifies the software package. As you study this table, you realize that a particular computer can have more than one application program installed, so the HID and SID fields serve as a combination key.

Ms. Meyers gives you an electronic file containing data about each personal computer. As you study this file, you notice that the file contains data about the serial number, processor type, processor speed, RAM amount, hard drive capacity, model, and manufacturer for each computer. This file also contains an AssignedTo field, providing the identification number of the employee who is currently assigned the computer. You decide to use these fields for the Hardware table and design the table structure shown in Table 1. Once you build the Hardware table, you copy and paste the data from the electronic file into the Hardware table.

As you study your notes about the Tracking database, you realize at least three relationships are necessary and that these relationships should enforce referential integrity. First, you need a relationship between the Employee and Hardware tables. You join the tables on the EID field from the Employee table and the AssignedTo field from the Hardware table. Second, you need a relationship between the Hardware and Config tables. As both tables have an HID field, you join the tables on this field. Third, you must establish a relationship between the Config and Software tables. As both tables contain an SID field, you use the SID field to join the two tables.

Table 1: Hardware Table Structure

Field Name	Data Type	Field Description	Field Size	Comments
HID	Number	Stores the hardware identification number. Serves as primary key.	Integer	Is assigned by the IT staff and differs from the serial number. Is required.
PSpeed	Text	Identifies the processor's speed.	15	
PType	Text	Identifies the type of processor.	25	Is required.
SerialNo	Text	Identifies the computer's serial number and differs from the HID.	20	Is required.

HardDrive	Text	Identifies the hard drive capacity for this computer.	10	
RAM	Text	Identifies the amount of RAM currently installed on this computer.	10	
Manufacturer	Text	Contains the name of the company that manufactured the computer.	25	
Model	Text	Contains the model of the computer.	25	
Category	Text	Identifies the type (category) of computer.	10	
AssignedTo	Text	Stores the employee identification number for the employee who is currently assigned this computer.	4	

Input Specifications

Figures 1 and 2 provide sketches of the Hardware Entry and Hardware/Software Assignment forms. Although you are free to modify each form's design, the design must have a professional appearance and capture, at a minimum, the data as shown.

The IT staff needs a Hardware Entry form to capture data about newly purchased computers. Figure 1 shows a sketch of this form. As the data captured by this form are stored in the Hardware table, you decide to use the Form tool or Form Wizard to build this form. Once the form is created, you can modify its appearance in Design view.

The IT staff needs to know what software is installed on each personal computer. The Hardware/Software Assignment form enables the staff to add, modify, and delete the software installation data for each personal computer. Figure 2 shows a sketch of this form.

When using the Hardware/Software Assignment form, Ms. Meyers wants the data entry process to be as simple as possible. For instance, Ms. Meyers wants to select an HID number from a Combo box and then have the system look up the rest of the data shown in Figure 2, including any previously assigned software. You decide to use an AutoLookup query to automatically retrieve the data. When assigning software to a particular computer, Ms. Meyers wants to select an SID number, and then have the system look up the title and publisher information. You realize that the AutoLookup query also facilitates the lookup process for the software data.

Figure 1: Hardware Entry Form

Hardware Entry

Hardware ID: **EID:**

Serial No:
Category:

Manufacturer:
Model:
Processor Speed:
Processor Type:

RAM:
Hard Drive:

Figure 2: Hardware/Software Assignment Form

Hardware/Software Assignment

Hardware ID: **EID:**

Serial No:
Category:

Manufacturer:
Model:
Processor Speed:
Processor Type:

RAM:
Hard Drive:

Software On This Computer:

SID	Title	Publisher

Information Specifications

Ms. Meyers requires three reports, including Software Assignment, Hardware, and Employee Assignment reports. These reports organize the data from the Tracking database in different ways, providing Ms. Meyers with different views of the data. Figures 3 - 5 show sketches of these reports. Although Ms. Meyers encourages you to be creative with your report designs, she stresses that each report must provide the information shown in its sketch and have a professional appearance. She would like each report to have its name, current date, and a picture in the report header. Each report's page footer should contain a page number, as well as a count of the total number of pages in the report.

Ms. Meyers hands you a tentative sketch of the Software Assignment report. Figure 3 shows this sketch. As you examine the sketch, you notice that the Software Assignment report lists all currently licensed software packages, indicates on which machines the software packages are currently installed, and identifies the employees who are using the software packages. This report organizes the information alphabetically by software title. Within each software title category, the HIDs are sorted in ascending order. For each software title, a count of the number of installations is shown. Ms. Meyers uses this information to help verify that all software installations are licensed. You decide to build a select query to retrieve the data for this report, and then base the report on the select query.

Figure 4 shows a tentative sketch of the Hardware report. The Hardware report lists the company's personal computers in ascending order by HID. This report provides a description of each computer, listing the processor speed, processor type, RAM amount, and hard drive capacity. This report also shows what software is currently installed on the computer, as well as the employee who is assigned the computer.

Ms. Meyers wants to know what software and hardware are currently assigned to each Keller Industries employee. She would like this information organized by the employee's last name. Figure 5 shows a tentative sketch of the Employee Assignment report. As you study the sketch, you realize that an employee can have more than one computer assigned to him. You decide to perform a secondary sort based on the HID field.

Figure 3: Software Assignment Report

Software Assignment

(Current Date)

Software Title	Publisher	HID		Employee
		.		
		.		
		.		
IGRAFX Flowcharter 2007	Corel	20		Dancer, Robin
			Number Installed:	**XX**
		.		
		.		
		.		
Project 2007	Microsoft	1		Murphy, Agnes
		.		
		.		
		.		
			Number Installed:	**XX**

Page X of XX

Figure 4: Hardware Report

Hardware
(Current Date)

HID	Hardware Description	Software	Employee
1	3.6 GHz HP Intel Pentium 4 2 GB 80 GB	Symantec Norton Antivirus 2007 Microsoft Project Professional 2007 Corel WordPerfect Office X3 Professional . . .	Murphy, Agnes
2	3.6 GHz HP Intel Pentium 4 2 GB 80 GB	Microsoft Office Standard Edition 2007 . . .	Vorse, Barry

Page X of XX

Figure 5: Employee Assignment Report

Employee Assignment

(Current Date)

Employee	HID	Serial Number	Hardware Description	Software
Blatt, Renae	5	784569-58-2222	2.8 GHz Dell Intel Xeon	AntiVirus 2007
				WordPerfect Office X3 Professional
			. . .	
Vorse, Barry	2	746389-03-0098	3.6 GHz HP Intel Pentium 4	Office Standard Edition 2003
			. . .	

Page X of XX

Ms. Meyers requires answers for the following questions. Build queries to help Ms. Meyers answer these questions. If you choose, you may generate reports based on these queries.

1. What software is not currently installed on any computer? Ms. Meyers wants only the software title. She does not wish to view any other fields.

2. Which Keller Industries employees have not been assigned a computer? Ms. Meyers would like to know the first and last names of these employees. She does not require any other information.

3. Ms. Meyers needs a query that will prompt her for a software title. After entering the software title, the query should then list the first and last names of all employees who have the software installed on their computers. Prepare this query for Ms. Meyers. Sort the results in ascending order based on employee last name.

4. Three employees want a copy of Corel WordPerfect Office X3 Professional installed on their machines. How many copies of Corel WordPerfect Office X3 Professional are currently installed? Do we have enough licenses to accommodate these new requests?

5. Which employees have notebook computers? Provide the employee's first and last name, the manufacturer, model, processor type, and processor speed.

6. Ms. Meyers wants a query to prompt her for the name of an employee. When she provides the name of the employee, she would like information about the employee's hardware and software configuration to be displayed.

7. Ms. Meyers wants a Software Type report. The report should organize the software by category. Within each category, Ms. Meyers wants each software name listed and a count of how many copies of the software are currently installed. The categories should be sorted in alphabetical order. The software names within each category should also be sorted in alphabetical order.

Implementation Concerns

To make the modifications required in the case scenario, you will design a table, build two forms, prepare three reports, establish relationships between tables, and construct several queries. Once you have created the Hardware table, the data for this table is stored in an electronic file. You can then copy and paste the data into the Hardware table.

When constructing the Hardware Entry form, consider using the Form tool or Form Wizard. Once the basic form is created, you can easily make any necessary modifications to the form in Design view.

The Hardware/Software Assignment form is a main form with a subform. You should consider constructing an AutoLookup query and then use the Form tool or Form Wizard to create the Hardware/Software Assignment form. Once you have created an initial form, you can edit the form in Design view.

Each report uses data from multiple tables. For each report, you can construct a query to retrieve the necessary information from the underlying tables and then base your report on the query. The Hardware/Software Assignment report provides a count for each software package currently installed on the company's personal computers. One method for obtaining the count is to use a calculated control in your report.

Test Your Design

After creating your table, forms, queries, relationships, and reports, you should test your database design. Perform the following transactions:

1. The IT Department recently purchased five new computers. Using the Hardware Entry form, enter the following information about each new computer into the Tracking database. The computers have not been assigned to an employee, so the AssignedTo field is not included in the table below. You will also need to assign an HID to each computer.

PSpeed	PType	SerialNo	Hard Drive	Model	RAM	Manufacturer	Category
2.2 GHz	AMD Phenom 9500	684922-12-4944	500	M9100z	4 GB	HP	Desktop
3.6 GHz	AMD Phenom 9500	483203-98-4935	500	M9100z	4 GB	HP	Desktop
3.6 GHz	AMD Phenom 9500	483203-98-4936	500	M9100z	4 GB	HP	Desktop

2.2 GHz	Intel Core 2 Duo 4500	684922-12-4943	500	DX441X	4 GB	Gateway	Desktop
2.3 GHz	AMD Athlon	994847-90-0003	80 GB	OptiPlex 740	1 GB	Dell	Desktop

2. The IT Department made the following assignments.
   - Clint Zumwalt is assigned a personal computer; the HID is 22. He requests that copies of Microsoft Office Professional 2007 and Microsoft Project Professional 2007 be installed.
   - Marsha Leminsky is assigned a personal computer; the HID is 26. She requests that copies of Corel WordPerfect Office X3 Professional, Norton AntiVirus 2008, and SAS/STAT be installed.

3. Agnes Murphy wants to upgrade to Microsoft Office Professional Edition 2007. Make the appropriate entries in the database.

4. How many Pentium 4 computers does the company currently have? How many of these machines are desktop computers? How many Pentium D computers does the company have?

5. How many Dell notebook computers does the company currently own?

6. How many computers do not have Norton AntiVirus 2008 software installed? Do you think all the computers should have the latest antivirus software installed? If so, make the necessary updates.

7. How many computers have a hard drive with less than 500 GB?

CASE DELIVERABLES

In order to satisfactorily complete this case, you should build the database and then prepare both written and oral presentations. Unless otherwise specified, submit the following deliverables to your professor.

1. A written report discussing any assumptions you have made about the case and the key elements of the case. Additionally, what features did you add to make the database more functional? User friendly? (Please note that these assumptions cannot violate any of the requirements specified above and must be approved by your professor.)

2. A printout of each form.

3. A printout of each report.

4. An electronic, working copy of your database that meets the criteria mentioned in the case scenario and specifications sections.

5. Results for each query. (A memo to your instructor discussing these results should also be provided.)

6. As mentioned above, you should prepare an oral presentation. (Your instructor will establish the time allocated for your presentation.) You should use a presentation package and discuss the key features of your database. Also, discuss how this database is beneficial for Ms. Meyers. What changes would you recommend?

CASE 23

ABC Inc.'s Health Benefits

Database Case **Difficulty Rating:** ★★★

SKILLS CHECK
You should review the following areas:

DATABASE SKILLS

- ✓ **Advanced Report Design**
- ✓ **Aggregate Function**
- ✓ **AutoLookup Query**
- ✓ **Calculated Control**
- ✓ **Crosstab Query**
- ✓ **Filter By Form**
- ✓ **Form Design**
- ✓ **Form Wizard**
- ✓ **Lookup Wizard**
- ✓ **Word Mail Merge Wizard**
- ✓ **Relationship**
- ✓ **Select Query**
- ✓ **Subform**
- ✓ **Table Design**

CASE BACKGROUND

When it comes to health care, ABC Inc. recognizes that its employees have different health care needs. The company utilizes a flexible benefits plan, allowing company employees to customize their health benefit plans based on personal preferences. The health benefits enrollment process begins in two months, and Mr. Antonio Gonzalez, the Human Resources Director, is anxious to update the company's Benefits database. Mr. Gonzalez has hired you to manage the updates to the Benefits database. In Monday's meeting with Mr. Gonzalez, you were given a list of specifications for the database. These specifications require you to build an Employee Insurance Enrollment form, build and populate Employee and Select tables, construct several queries, prepare a form letter, prepare an Employees by Insurance report, and prepare a Personalized Employee Enrollment report for each ABC Inc. employee.

CASE SCENARIO

ABC Inc.'s Human Resources Department utilizes a "cafeteria-style" approach to providing its employees with health care benefits. Each fall, ABC Inc. employees review their current benefits, modify their elections, and then sign Section 125 forms. These changes must be entered into the Benefits database.

For medical insurance, an employee enrolls with a preferred provider organization (PPO) or a health maintenance organization (HMO). ABC Inc. currently pays the monthly medical premiums for its employees. However, if an employee enrolls in a dental plan or vision plan, the employee pays a modest monthly premium for the optional plan. An employee may carry medical, dental, and/or vision coverage for one or more of his family members. In order to carry insurance on a family member, the employee must carry the same coverage. For instance, to carry dental insurance on a spouse, the employee must also carry dental insurance on himself.

In a few weeks, an enrollment letter and an ABC Rates Change Schedule will be mailed to each employee. The enrollment letter notifies the employee about the upcoming enrollment period, providing time and location information. The ABC Rates Change Schedule lists the new health benefit rates, effective January 1. Table 1 shows the new ABC Rates Change Schedule.

After reviewing your notes from your meeting with Mr. Gonzalez, you realize that several modifications to the current Benefits database are necessary. These modifications require you to build an Employee Insurance Enrollment form, build and populate Employee and Select tables, construct several queries, prepare a form letter, prepare an Employees by Insurance report, and prepare a Personalized Employee Enrollment report for each ABC Inc. employee.

Table 1: ABC Rates Change Schedule (Effective January 1st)

	Rates					
Insurance Company	**E**	**S**	**S1**	**S2**	**C1**	**C2**
All American Life Care (AALC)--PPO	$00.00	$281.22	$462.06	$523.54	$180.84	$242.32
Best Health Care (BHC)--HMO	$00.00	$263.07	$405.64	$455.54	$142.57	$192.47
Midwest Dental (MD)	$15.89	$37.92	$67.96	$78.29	$30.04	$40.37
Perfect Vision (PV)	$18.44	$25.78	$48.64	$79.27	$22.86	$30.63

E = Employee Only
S = Spouse Only
S1 = Spouse and Only One Child
S2 = Spouse and Two or More Children
C1 = Only One Child
C2 = Two or More Children

Storage Specifications

The Benefits database includes populated Company, Dependent, and Rate tables. As you study these tables, you notice that the Company table currently contains information about each insurance company. For each insurance company, an insurance company code (InsCode), company name (InsName), and brief description (Comments) are stored. The Dependent table identifies the dependent codes (DepCode) and provides descriptions of these codes (DepDesc). The Rate table contains InsCode, DepCode, and Rate fields. The Rate table has a combination key, consisting of the InsCode and DepCode fields. The Rate table contains current insurance rate information and will be updated to reflect the changes outlined in Table 1.

During a meeting with Mr. Gonzalez, he gives you an electronic file containing the data that you need to populate the Employee and Select tables. After meeting with Mr. Gonzalez, you decide to use the structures shown in Tables 2 and 3 for the Employee and Select tables. For the Employee table, you decide that the EID field should serve as the primary key, and the State field should use a default value of "TX." You then build the Employee table.

As you study the Select table's design, you determine that the table's primary key is a combination key, consisting of the EID, DepCode, and InsCode fields. The EffectiveDate field contains the date the policy takes effect. While this date is usually January 1, it can differ. For instance, an employee hired in the middle of the year will have a different effective date. You realize that the data values for the EID, DepCode, and InsCode fields are already stored in the Employee, Dependent, and Company tables, respectively. To facilitate data entry, you decide to use the Lookup Wizard to create a list of values for these fields.

The Lookup Wizard creates relationships among the Select table and the Employee, Company, and Dependent tables. You decide these relationships should enforce referential integrity. You edit each relationship's join properties to enforce referential integrity.

Table 2: Employee Table Structure

Field Name	Data Type	Field Description	Field Size	Comments
EID	Number	Stores the employee's identification number. This number is unique. Serves as primary key.	Long Integer	Set the format property to 00000. This field is required.
DeptID	Number	Stores the department code. This number is unique.	Long Integer	Set the format property to 00. This field is required.
EFirstName	Text	Stores the employee's first name.	50	
ELastName	Text	Stores the employee's last name.	50	
StreetAddress	Text	Stores the employee's street address.	50	
City	Text	Stores the city where the employee lives.	50	
State	Text	Stores the state where the employee lives.	2	The state abbreviation should display in all caps. The default value is "TX."
ZipCode	Text	Stores the employee's zip code.	10	Use an input mask.
OfficeExt	Text	Stores the employee's office extension number.	4	

Table 3: Select Table Structure

Field Name	Data Type	Field Description	Field Size	Comments
EID	Number	Contains the employee's identification number. Serves as part of the combination key.	Long Integer	Set the format property to 00000. This field is required. This number is located in the Employee table.
DepCode	Text	Stores the dependent code. Serves as part of the combination key.	3	This code is taken from the Dependent table.
InsCode	Text	Stores the insurance company's code. Serves as part of the combination key.	4	This code is taken from the Insurance table.
EffectiveDate	Date/Time	Stores the date the policy becomes effective.		

Input Specifications

The Benefits database requires an Employee Insurance Enrollment form. Figure 1 shows a tentative sketch of this form. (The actual data may differ. The data displayed in the sketch is for illustrative purposes.) As the Employee Insurance Enrollment form uses data from three tables, you decide to construct a select query. Once you create the select query, you can use the Form Wizard to expedite the creation of the Employee Insurance Enrollment form. (You may wish to view your system's online help feature to review the Form Wizard and subforms.)

As you study the Employee Insurance Enrollment form sketch, you note that the Monthly Payroll Deduction field displays the sum of the employee's monthly health insurance premiums. The Monthly Payroll Deduction field appears on the main form and sums the rates from the Enrollment Options subform. Use your system's online help feature to research how to calculate a total on a subform and then display it on a main form.

Figure 1: Employee Insurance Enrollment Form

Employee Insurance Enrollment

Employee ID: 00005

Employee Name: Votaw, Jaque
Employee Address: 203 Chowning Avenue
Arlington, TX 76004

Monthly Payroll Deduction: $379.25

Department ID: 05
Office Extension: 3201

Enrollment Options:

Dependent Code	Insurance Code	Rate	Effective Date
S	AALC	$281.22	1/1/2009
S	PV	$25.78	1/1/2009
S	MD	$37.92	1/1/2009
E	PV	$15.89	1/1/2009
E	MD	$18.44	1/1/2009

Information Specifications

Mr. Gonzalez wants to send a form letter to all current employees announcing the upcoming enrollment period. Mr. Gonzalez wants the form letter to be personalized for each employee. At a minimum, the employee's address should appear in the letter address section, and the salutation line should use the employee's last name. The body of the letter should announce the upcoming enrollment period and provide the new rate schedule. He asks you to prepare the letter for him.

Mr. Gonzalez also requests an Employees by Insurance report and a Personalized Employee Enrollment report for each employee. Figures 2 and 3 show sketches of these reports. While you are free to work with the design of these reports, each report must provide the information shown in its sketch and have a professional appearance. The Employees by Insurance report associates employees with their chosen health insurance carriers. The Personalized Employee Enrollment report is a personalized report prepared for each employee. This report identifies the employee's current health benefits for a particular enrollment period.

The Employees by Insurance report sorts the information by insurance company and then sorts by employee name within the insurance company category. Each grouping is sorted in ascending order. For each employee, Mr. Gonzalez requests the employee's identification number, first and last name, and dependent code. As this report requires data from multiple tables, you decide to create a select query, and then base the report on the select query. As part of the report's header, you include the report's title and current date.

Figure 2: Employees by Insurance Report

Employees by Insurance

(Current Date)

Insurance Company	Employee Identification Number	Last Name	First Name	Dependent Code
All American Life Care Company				
	00013	Enriquez	Antonio	C2
	00020	Timanus	Deona	S
		. . .		
Best Health Care				
	00010	Chee	Akiko	S2
	00011	Lou	Chia-Yi	E
		. . .		

Mr. Gonzalez wants each employee to receive a Personalized Employee Enrollment report. This report will be printed in January after the new rates take effect. As this report requires data from multiple tables, you construct a select query, and then base the report on the select query. From the sketch in Figure 3, you notice that the header consists of a report title, current date, the employee's first and last names, department code, employee identification number, and monthly payroll deduction. You also notice that for each health benefit, the insurance company name, dependent code, and rate are printed. As you use the Force New Page property to cause each employee's report to print on a new page, you do not need to design separate reports for each individual employee. (You may wish to use the system's online help to review the Force New Page property.)

Figure 3: Personalized Employee Enrollment Report

Personalized Employee Enrollment

(Current Date)

Prepared for: Antonio Enriquez

Employee Identification No: 00013

Department Code: 01

Monthly Payroll Deduction: $284.45

Insurance Company	Dependent Code	Rate
Best Health Care	C2	$3.66
Midwest Dental	C2	$41.63
Perfect Vision	C2	$239.16

Mr. Gonzalez needs answers to the following questions. Build queries to help Mr. Gonzalez answer these questions. Where applicable, you may generate reports based on these queries.

1. How many ABC employees are currently signed with an HMO? PPO?
2. How many ABC employees carry medical insurance for two or more children, but do not cover a spouse?
3. If vision insurance for an employee's dependents increases, how many employees are impacted?
4. Mr. Gonzalez wants a count of employees by insurance company. He wants the insurance company name, a description of the insurance company, and the count displayed.
5. Mr. Gonzalez wants a count of dependent code by insurance company. He wants the insurance company name, the dependent code name, and the dependent code count displayed.
6. On average, how much does an ABC Inc. employee pay per month for insurance?

Implementation Concerns

To make the changes specified in the case scenario, you will design and populate Employee and Select tables, create an Employee Insurance Enrollment form, establish relationships between tables, prepare a form letter, prepare an Employees by Insurance report, and prepare a Personalized Employee Benefits report for each employee. When building the Select table, use the Lookup Wizard to specify a list of values for the EID, DepCode, and InsCode fields.

You will define several relationships, in addition to the three relationships described in the Storage Specifications section. For each relationship that you define, you should enforce referential integrity.

For the form letter, you should investigate the Microsoft Word Mail Merge Wizard. More information about the Microsoft Word Mail Merge Wizard can be obtained by using your system's online help feature.

Although several ways exist for creating the Employee Insurance Enrollment form, you can use the Form Wizard. Once you have created the main form and subform, you can then edit each form. For additional information on subforms, use your system's online help feature.

While the Employees by Insurance report's design is straightforward, the Personalized Employee Enrollment report requires extra care. You should first build a query to retrieve the necessary data for the report, and then base the report on this query. In order to prepare this report according to Mr. Gonzalez's specifications, you will use the Force New Page property. Use your system's online help feature to learn more about this property.

Test Your Design

After creating the form, tables, relationships, queries, form letter, and reports, you should test your database design. Perform the following transactions:

1. The following employees are requesting changes to their health plans. For the effective date, use the current date.

    - Mr. Ying Fang (00025) adds dental and vision insurance for his wife and two children.
    - Mrs. Donatica Angelo (00016) adds her spouse to her current coverage. He will be covered with Best Health Care and Perfect Vision.
    - Dr. Gayle Yates adds dental coverage for her spouse and five children. She does not recall her employee identification number.

2. ABC hired two new employees. Please enter the following information into the database. Assign the next available employee identification numbers.

Employee Name: Barbara Michaels
Employee Address: 1944 Calvin Boulevard
Dallas, TX 75261
EID: XXXXX

Department: 04
Office Extension: 4822

Dependent Code	Insurance Code	Rate	Effective Date
S	AALC	XXX	3/15/2009
S	PV	XXX	3/15/2009
E	AALC	XXX	3/15/2009
E	PV	XXX	3/15/2009

Employee Name: Fredrico Behar
Employee Address: 2204 Pigeon Nest
Garland, TX 75040
EID: XXXX

Department: 02
Office Extension: 2797

Dependent Code	Insurance Code	Rate	Effective Date
S1	AALC	XXX	5/1/2009
S1	PV	XXX	5/1/2009
S1	MD	XXX	5/1/2009
E	AALC	XXX	5/1/2009
E	PV	XXX	5/1/2009
E	MD	XXX	5/1/2009

3. Use the new rates in Table 1, and update the Rate table. You may wish to build a Rate form to help with data entry.

4. Which employees are impacted by an increase in their dental insurance? List the employee's first and last names.

CASE DELIVERABLES

In order to satisfactorily complete this case, you should build the database and then prepare both written and oral presentations. Unless otherwise specified, submit the following deliverables to your professor.

1. A written report discussing any assumptions you have made about the case and the key elements of the case. Additionally, what features did you add to make the database more functional? User friendly? (Please note that these assumptions cannot violate any of the requirements specified above and must be approved by your professor.)

2. A printout of each form.

3. A printout of each report.

4. An electronic, working copy of your database that meets the criteria mentioned in the case scenario and specifications sections.

5. Results for each query. (A memo to your instructor discussing these results should also be provided.)

6. As mentioned above, you should prepare an oral presentation. (Your instructor will establish the time allocated for your presentation.) You should use a presentation package and discuss the key features of your database. Also, discuss how this database is beneficial for Mr. Gonzalez. What additional information from the database might Mr. Gonzalez find useful?

CASE 24 Wright Brothers' Airport Shuttle Service

Database Case **Difficulty Rating:** ★★★★

SKILLS CHECK
You should review the following areas:

DATABASE SKILLS

- ✓ **Aggregate Function**
- ✓ **AutoLookup Query**
- ✓ **Calculated Control**
- ✓ **Calculated Field**
- ✓ **Combo Box**
- ✓ **Filter By Form**
- ✓ **Form Design**
- ✓ **LookUp Wizard**
- ✓ **Parameter Query**
- ✓ **Relationship**
- ✓ **Report Design**
- ✓ **Select Query**
- ✓ **Table Design**

CASE BACKGROUND

The Wright Brothers' Airport Shuttle Service provides economical off-airport parking and an airport shuttle service for its customers. Basil and Sage Wright, recognizing the advantage of offering these services to their customers, opened their off-airport parking and shuttle service two months ago. Since that time, they have watched demand for their business steadily increase. Basil Wright, overwhelmed with paperwork, began developing a simple reservation database. The intent of the database is to track current parking space reservations. As of today, Basil Wright has been unable to complete the database and has requested your help.

CASE SCENARIO

As a frequent traveler, Basil Wright recognizes the need for economical, off-airport parking. When an opportunity presented itself last year, Basil Wright and his brother, Sage Wright, purchased ten acres of land near the International Airport. The brothers have since converted a portion of their newly acquired land into a parking facility and provide a shuttle service for travelers. While Sage Wright is responsible for shuttling travelers to and from the airport, Basil Wright manages the business's daily paperwork activities.

Wright Brothers' Airport Shuttle Service offers valet parking, providing 200 covered valet parking spaces and 250 uncovered valet parking spaces. Covered parking is $12.00 per day, and uncovered parking is $10.50 per day.

When a customer arrives, he turns his car over to a parking attendant. The customer then walks into the office, provides necessary information to another attendant, requests covered or uncovered parking, receives a claim ticket, and then boards an airport shuttle. When a vehicle is checked in, the attendant uses a list of available parking spaces to determine where the car is to be parked. The vehicle is assigned a parking location, and a claim tag is hung from the vehicle's rearview mirror. When the valet parking customer returns, he calls the shuttle service, provides his claim ticket number, and then catches the next available shuttle to the parking facility. When he arrives at the parking facility, the parking attendant locates the customer's record by ticket number. The customer then pays his parking fees, picks up his car and leaves.

Basil Wright began building a database for the parking and shuttle service last month. However, the parking facility's popularity keeps Mr. Wright very busy with its daily operations, so he has been unable to complete the database. You are Mr. Wright's good friend, so you volunteer to continue working with the database. Initially, you will modify the database to track the company's current parking reservations.

Mr. Wright gives you a current reservation list and a copy of the incomplete database. After examining these items, you notice that the reservation list was created using a spreadsheet application and that the list contains basic, current reservation information. As the reservation list is in an electronic format, you can copy and paste the list's contents into the Parking table, once the table is created.

The current database contains several tables, including Airline, Car, Model, and Rate tables. These tables are populated with data. These tables require very little, if any, modifications. However, you realize that a Parking table is necessary, as well as a Parking Reservation form, Daily Check-In and Tentative Check-Out reports, a relationship between the Car and Model tables, and several queries. Mr. Wright stresses that the database should be simple in its design. He also mentions that he does not need to keep information about his past customers, previously parked vehicles, or past reservations.

Storage Specifications

As mentioned previously, Mr. Wright began working on the parking facility's database last month. However, his busy schedule prohibits him from completing the database. He gives you the incomplete database and requests that you continue working on its development. Mr. Wright has already designed and populated the Airline, Car, Model, and Rate tables. You must now design and populate the Parking table.

Table 1 shows the Parking table's structure. As mentioned above, the data to populate this table is stored in an electronic file. Once you have designed the table, you can copy and paste the data into the appropriate fields.

Since the ticket number serves as the primary key, the attendant will enter a unique number for each ticket. You can assume that the ticket number is obtained from a preprinted claim ticket. To facilitate data entry, the Car Make, Car Model, Airline Abbreviation, and Rate Code values are obtained from a list of values. During table design, use the LookUp Wizard to create a list of values for each of these fields. As Mr. Wright does not wish to keep historical information on his customers, information about customers who have claimed their vehicles will be deleted from the database. However, you are not required to develop a delete query for this exercise.

A relationship between the Car and Model tables is required. You should look for a common column between the two tables for which you are establishing a relationship. For instance, the Car and Model tables both have a MakeID column. You can use this field to establish a relationship between the two tables. Keep in mind that the columns are not required to have the same name, although in this instance they do.

Table 1: Parking Table Structure

Field Name	Data Type	Field Description	Field Size	Comments
Ticket Number	Number	Stores the claim ticket number. This number is unique.	Long Integer	Serves as primary key.
Customer Last Name	Text	Stores the customer's last name.	50	Is required.
Customer First Name	Text	Stores the customer's first name.	50	Is required.
Check-In Date	Date/Time	Stores the date the vehicle is checked in.		Is required.
Check-Out Date	Date/Time	Stores the actual date the vehicle is picked up. Can differ from tentative return date.		
Tag Number	Text	Stores the vehicle's tag number.	10	Is required.
Tag State	Text	Identifies the state where the car is registered.	2	Use a default value of "OK."
Parking Location	Text	Identifies where the vehicle is parked.	5	Is required.
MakeID	Number	Identifies the vehicle's make.	Long Integer	Is required.
ModelID	Number	Identifies the vehicle's model.	Long Integer	

Tentative Return Date	Date/Time	Is the expected return date.		
AAB	Text	Is the airline code.	3	
Rate Code	Text	Identifies the designated rate code for the vehicle.	3	Is required.
Comments	Memo	Used by the parking attendant to enter additional comments about the vehicle.		

Input Specifications

Figure 1 provides a sketch of the Parking Reservation form you will build. Although you are free to modify the form's design, the form must have a professional appearance and capture the data shown in Figure 1.

As the parking attendant completes the form, you would like him to select a rate code and then have the Rate and Description fields automatically filled in. To accomplish this, you construct an AutoLookup query that uses data from both the Parking and Rate tables. When constructing this query, add all the fields from the Parking table. From the Rate table, add the Rate and Description fields.

As you used the LookUp Wizard to create the Airline, Car Make, Car Model, and Rate Code fields in the Parking table, you realize that dropdown lists for these fields automatically appear on the Parking Reservation form. Using dropdown lists for these fields facilitates data entry, and you like this idea.

As you study the Current Charges field, you realize that Current Charges is a calculated field that works with date values. If a customer drops off his car on January 1 and picks the car up on January 2, he should pay for two days of parking, so your Current Charges formula should reflect this fact.

Figure 1: Parking Reservation Form

Wright Brothers' Airport Shuttle Service

Parking Reservation Form

Ticket No:	Check-In Date:
Customer Last Name:	Tentative Return Date:
Customer First Name:	Check-Out Date:
Airline:	
Car Make:	Parking Location:
Car Model:	
Tag:	
Tag State:	
	Rate Code: Rate Description:
	Rate:
	Current Charges:
Comments:	

Information Specifications

At the end of each day, Mr. Wright prepares two reports, a Daily Check-In Report and a Tentative Check-Out Report. The Daily Check-In Report lists each vehicle that was checked in that day. The Tentative Check-Out Report identifies vehicles scheduled for pickup the next day. Figures 2 and 3 provide sketches of these reports. Although you are free to work with the design of these reports, each report must provide the information shown in its sketch and have a professional appearance.

As mentioned above, the Daily Check-In Report identifies vehicles that have been dropped off that day. You decide to base this report on a parameter query. By using a parameter query, the end user is asked to supply a date. The Daily Check-In Report also specifies how many parking spaces were required for each type of valet parking. A grand total is provided at the end of the report. To enhance readability, the report contents are sorted by the rate description. As part of the report's header, you should include a report title, the current date, and a picture. You should locate an appropriate picture to include.

Figure 2: Daily Check-In Report

Wright Brothers' Airport Shuttle Service

Daily Check-In Report

(Current Date)

Covered/ Uncovered	Parking Location	Customer Last Name	Customer First Name	Ticket Number	Tag Number	Car Make	Car Model	Tentative Check-Out Date
Covered	C1	Bennett	Brooke	144	B7987	Mitsubishi	Montero	1/5/2009
	C3	Lansing	Larry	146	D4756	Lexus	ES250	1/7/2009
				. . .				
				Category Subtotal:				
Uncovered	U5	Farmer	David	145	IMOK4	Ford	Expo	1/4/2009
	U7	Yu	Samantha	148	IM47	Mazda	Miata	1/15/2009
				. . .				
				Category Subtotal:				
				Total Vehicles Checked In:				

At the end of each day, Mr. Wright prints a Tentative Check-Out Report. This report identifies the vehicles tentatively scheduled for pickup the next day. Mr. Wright wants this report sorted by rate code. He also wants to know how many vehicles are tentatively scheduled for pick up. Since the report is printed for a particular day, you will construct a parameter query. The parameter query requests the user to provide a specific date, and then a report is generated based on this date. This parameter query is similar to the one you constructed above. Figure 3 shows a sketch for the Tentative Check-Out Report.

Figure 3: Tentative Check-Out Report

Wright Brothers' Airport Shuttle Service

Tentative Check-Out Report
(Current Date)

Parking Location	Customer Last Name	Customer First Name	Ticket Number	Tag Number	Car Make	Car Model
C1	Adams	Audrey	144	B7987	Mitsubishi	Expo
C3	Lansing	Larry	146	D4756	Lexus	ES250
			. . .			
U5	Farmer	David	145	IMOK4	Ford	Expo
U7	Yu	Samantha	148	IM47	Mazda	Miata
			. . .			

Total Vehicles Scheduled for Pick Up:

Mr. Wright needs answers for the following questions. Build queries to help Mr. Wright answer these questions. If you choose, you may generate reports based on these queries. Also, base your answers on the data that are currently in the database. (Do not worry about whether a customer's record should have been deleted.)

1. What is the average length of stay for vehicles? What are the average earnings?

2. How many cars are utilizing covered parking? Uncovered?

3. How many cars were checked in today? Checked out? (Use 12/31/2008 as the current date.)

4. Which airline is used most frequently?

5. For 12/31/2008, what percentage of covered valet parking spaces is used? What percentage of uncovered valet parking spaces is used?

6. Assume the brothers want to increase their rates for uncovered parking to \$12 and for covered parking to \$16 per day. How will this increase impact their overall revenue?

7. Which airlines are the Wright Brothers' Airport Shuttle Service customers using on January 22, 2009? The results should identify the airline and provide a customer count for the airline.

8. To date, what are the total earnings for the shuttle service? How much revenue has been generated by covered valet parking? Uncovered valet parking?

9. How much revenue has already been received for the month of January?

Implementation Concerns

In order to build the portion of the database described in the case scenario, you will build a table, a form, two reports, and several queries, including select, parameter, and AutoLookup queries. Several of the queries require you to sort, specify criteria, create expressions, and use data from two or more tables. Keep in mind that the form and reports are based on queries, so you should construct your queries before building the form and reports.

In order to design the reports, you base the reports on queries, specify sort orders, and work with report headers, footers, and page headers. To enhance the appearance of the form and reports, you should locate a picture to insert in the form or report header. The form and reports require calculated controls.

You will establish a relationship between the Car and Model tables. You should establish this relationship before designing your queries.

Test Your Design

After creating the table, form, queries, and reports, you should test your database design. Perform the following transactions.

1. The following customers have dropped off their cars. Enter this information into the database. You do not need to enter data into the Check-Out Date and Comments fields, so these fields are not shown in the following table.

Ticket Number	Customer Last Name	Customer First Name	Car Make ID	Car Model	Tag No	Tag State	Parking Location	Check-In Date	Tentative Return Date	AAB	Rate Code
400	Jester	Eleanor	Mitsubishi	Montero	E7T89	OK	U21	Enter Current Date	Scheduled to return 1 week from current date.	AA	1
401	Pellegrino	Allan	GMC	Envoy	YT090	OK	U22	Enter Current Date	Scheduled to return 2 weeks from current date.	WN	1
402	Ho	Chen	Cadillac	Escalade	KYRJT	TX	C14	Enter Current Date	Scheduled to return the next day.	AA	2

403	Yeh	Ling	Infiniti	G20	HI9864	TX	C19	Enter Current Date	Scheduled to return the next day.	CO	2
404	Polito	Ralph	Jeep	Grand Cherokee	KL76H	KS	C20	Enter Current Date	Scheduled to return 4 days from current date.	WN	2
405	Arnett	Benny	Buick	LeSabre	TR3345	KS	C21	Enter Current Date	Scheduled to return 1 week from current date.	DL	1

2. The following customers have claimed their cars.

Ticket Number	Customer Last Name	Customer First Name	Check-Out Date
9	Wodraska	Lester	January 3, 2009
10	Longfellow	Tabitha	January 3, 2009

3. Locate ticket number 20. What are the customer's current charges? Which airline did she use?

CASE DELIVERABLES

In order to satisfactorily complete this case, you should make the necessary modifications to the database and then prepare both written and oral presentations. Unless otherwise specified, submit the following deliverables to your professor.

1. A written report discussing any assumptions you have made about the case and the key elements of the case. Additionally, what features did you add to make the database more functional? User friendly? (Please note that these assumptions cannot violate any of the requirements specified above and must be approved by your professor.)

2. A printout of each form.

3. A printout of each report. For the Tentative Check-Out Report, use January 3, 2009, as the current date. For the Check-In Report, use January 22, 2009, as the current date.

4. An electronic, working copy of your database that meets the criteria mentioned in the case scenario and specifications sections.

5. Results for each query. (A memo to your instructor discussing these results should also be provided.)

6. As mentioned above, you should prepare an oral presentation. (Your instructor will establish the time allocated for your presentation.) You should use a presentation package and discuss the key features of your database. Also, discuss how this database is beneficial for Mr. Wright. What modifications would make this database more beneficial for Mr. Wright?

CASE 25 Natalie's Tours

Database Case **Difficulty Rating:** ★★★★

SKILLS CHECK
You should review the following areas:

DATABASE SKILLS

- ✓ **Advanced Report Design**
- ✓ **Aggregate Function**
- ✓ **AutoLookup Query**
- ✓ **Calculated Control**
- ✓ **Calculated Field**
- ✓ **Command Button**
- ✓ **Form Design**
- ✓ **Relationship**
- ✓ **Parameter Query**
- ✓ **Select Query**
- ✓ **Subform**
- ✓ **Tab Control**
- ✓ **Table Design**

CASE BACKGROUND

Natalie Harper's hometown and its surrounding area are steeped in history and have long attracted tourists to their historical, beautiful sites. After graduating from college, Ms. Harper combined her love of hometown, history, and people to create Natalie's Tours. She opened Natalie's Tours a few years ago and has watched her business grow. Natalie's Tours offers a variety of informative, popular tours to local tourist attractions. Ms. Harper's current tour information system is outdated, and she asks you to develop a database for her tour company.

Building the Tours database requires you to design forms, build and populate tables, construct several queries, and prepare several reports. Several skills are necessary, including advanced report design, form and subform design, query design, use of aggregate functions, and knowledge of calculated controls and calculated fields.

CASE SCENARIO

Natalie's Tours is located in a popular tourist area. Natalie's Tours offers a variety of tours, such as haunted walk, bird watching, and local cuisine tours. Currently, each tour is offered once a day and at the same time each day. Although the high tourism season occurs during summer months, Natalie's Tours operates 12 months a year. Tourism has been increasing, and Ms. Harper is offering more tours and hiring more guides to keep up with demand. In the near future, Ms. Harper will add more tours to the list, so having a Tours database will definitely help her manage the growing tour list.

When a new guide is hired, his training involves learning about each tour offered by Natalie's tours. Training each guide for every tour makes it easier for Ms. Harper to schedule tours and also for her to find someone at the last minute to fill in should the need develop. Also, if guides are familiar with all the tours, they can recommend other Natalie's tours to the tourists.

When a customer requests information about a tour, Ms. Harper provides the customer with basic information about the tour, such as tour time, tour description, and price. When the customer selects a tour, a reservation is made and payment is received. When making the reservation, the customer is asked how many people are in his party. Ms. Harper records the reservation information, calculates a total price based on party size, and then provides the customer with the total price. Each customer is given an individualized scheduled tours report, listing the customer's reserved tours. Upon payment, the customer is given a receipt.

Ms. Harper realizes her tour business needs an updated Tours database to track her customers, tours, guides, reservations, and customer payments. As you are familiar with Microsoft Access, Ms. Harper asks you to custom develop the Tours database.

Storage Specifications

Ms. Harper hands you a partially completed Tours database and asks you to finish its design and development. The partially completed Tours database includes populated Tour, Guide, and ScheduledTour tables. As you study these tables, you notice that the Tour table contains information about each tour. For each tour, tour identification number (TourID), tour name (TourName), tour time (TourTime), tour description (TourDesc), and tour price (TourPrice) are stored. The TourID field is unique for each record and serves as the primary key.

The Guide table stores information about Ms. Harper's tour guides. This table contains a guide identification number (GuideID), guide first name (GFirstName), guide last name (GLastName), guide city (GCity), guide state (GState), guide zip code (GZipCode), and guide start date (GStartDate) fields. The GuideID field is a unique value for each guide and serves as the primary key.

As several tours are given on any given day, you realize that the ScheduledTour table is necessary because it identifies which guide is giving a particular tour on a given day. The ScheduledTour table contains scheduled tour identification (STID), tour identification number (TourID), guide identification number (GuideID), and schedule date (ScheduleDate) fields. The STID field serves as the primary key and is unique for each record.

Ms. Harper tracks customer reservations and payments, so she asks you to add Customer, Reservation, and Payment tables to the database. (Your instructor will provide you with the data to populate these tables.) The Customer table stores information about the tour company's customers. Table 1 shows the Customer table's structure. The Reservation table tracks each customer's tour reservation. Table 2 shows the Reservation table's structure. When a customer makes a payment, the Payment table stores information about the payment. Table 3 shows the Payment table's structure. Each table's relationship join properties should enforce referential integrity.

Table 1: Customer Table Structure

Field Name	Data Type	Field Description	Field Size	Comments
CustomerID	AutoNumber	Serves as primary key.	Long Integer	Is required.
CFirstName	Text	Stores the customer's first name.	50	Is required.
CLastName	Text	Stores the customer's last name.	50	Is required.
CStreet	Text	Stores the customer's street address.	50	
CCity	Text	Stores the city where the customer lives.	50	
CState	Text	Stores the state where the customer lives.	2	
CZipCode	Text	Stores the customer's zip code. Use an input mask.	10	
CPhNo	Text	Stores the customer's phone number. Use an input mask.	10	

Table 2: Reservation Table Structure

Field Name	Data Type	Field Description	Field Size	Comments
ResID	AutoNumber	Serves as primary key.	Long Integer	Is required.
TourID	Number	Stores the guide's first name.	Long Integer	Is required.
CustomerID	Number	Stores the customer's identification number.	Long Integer	Is required.

ResDate	Date/Time	Stores customer's requested reservation date. Use short date format.		
PartyNo	Number	Stores the party size.	Long Integer	

Table 3: Payment Table Structure

Field Name	Data Type	Field Description	Field Size	Comments
PID	AutoNumber	Serves as primary key.	Long Integer	Is required.
CustomerID	Number	Identifies the customer making the payment. Use Lookup Wizard.	Long Integer	Is required.
Amount	Currency	Identifies the amount the customer paid.		Is required.

Input Specifications

The Tours database requires several forms, including Tour, Guide, Scheduled Tour, and Customer forms. The Customer form also includes Reservation and Payment subforms. Although you are free to modify each form's design, the design must have a professional appearance and capture, at a minimum, the data as shown. For each form, Ms. Harper asks you to place the Natalie's Tours logo on the form. (Ms. Harper asks you to design the Natalie's Tours logo.)

The Tour form adds, modifies, and deletes records from the Tour table. Figure 1 provides a sketch of the Tour form. Like the Tour form, the Guide form adds, modifies, and deletes records from the Guide table. As Figure 2 shows, the Guide form is a simple form and easily created. (The data shown in Figures 1 and 2 are for illustrative purposes. Actual data may differ.)

Figure 1: Tour Form Sketch

Natalie's Tours Natalie's Tours

Tour Form

Tour ID: 0001
Tour Name: Haunted Walk
Tour Time: 9:00 PM
Tour Price: $15.00

Tour Description:

Takes tourists to haunted sites, including the famous Mary Winters cottage.

Figure 2: Guide Form Sketch

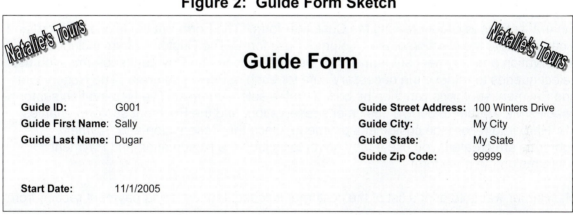

Natalie's Tours Natalie's Tours

Guide Form

Guide ID: G001
Guide First Name: Sally
Guide Last Name: Dugar

Guide Street Address: 100 Winters Drive
Guide City: My City
Guide State: My State
Guide Zip Code: 99999

Start Date: 11/1/2005

Using the Scheduled Tour form, Ms. Harper assigns a guide to lead a tour on a given date. Figure 3 provides a sketch of the Scheduled Tour form. (The data shown in Figure 4 are for illustrative purposes. Actual data may differ.) As you study the Scheduled Tour form, you notice that several fields are not stored in the Scheduled Tour table. As Ms. Harper specifically requests that these fields display, you decide the Scheduled Tour form should be based on a query.

Figure 3: Scheduled Tour Form Sketch

Natalie's Tours   Natalie's Tours

Scheduled Tour Form

Scheduled Tour ID:	000001	**Tour ID:**	0001
Scheduled Date:	11/3/2008	**Tour Name:**	Haunted Walk
		Tour Time:	9:00 PM
Guide Last Name:	Dugar		
Guide First Name:	Sally		

As the sketch in Figure 4 shows, the Customer form consists of a main form with two subforms. (The data shown in Figure 4 are for illustrative purposes. The actual data may differ.) The main form allows Ms. Harper to enter data about her customers, while the Reservations and Payments subforms allow her to enter data about the customer's reservations and payments.

Several options exist for creating the Customer form. The Form Wizard is one method, and it can expedite the creation of the Customer main form. The Customer form includes Reservation and Payment subforms. For the Reservation and Payment subforms, you use select queries to retrieve the necessary data for each of these subforms. The Reservation and Payment subforms can then be based on the select queries. The Reservation subform enables Ms. Harper to book a customer's reservation, and the Payment subform enables Ms. Harper to record the customer's payment. Once the Reservation and Payment subforms are created, you use a tab control to include the Reservation and Payment subforms on the main form.

Ms. Harper wants to print a list of the customer's scheduled tours and payment receipt from the Customer form. She asks you to include buttons on the Customer form to accommodate this request. (The customer's scheduled tours and payment receipt reports are described below.)

While studying the Customer form sketch, you notice that the Amount Owed field displays the total cost for the customer's reservations, and the Amount Paid field displays how much the customer has paid. The Amount Owed field appears on the main form and sums the costs of the customer's reservations from the reservations subform. The Amount Paid field appears on the main form and sums the customer's payments from the Payments subform. On the Customer form, the Balance field displays the difference between the Amount Owed and Amount Paid fields. (Use your system's online help feature to research how a main form control can reference a control located on a subform.)

Figure 4: Customer Form

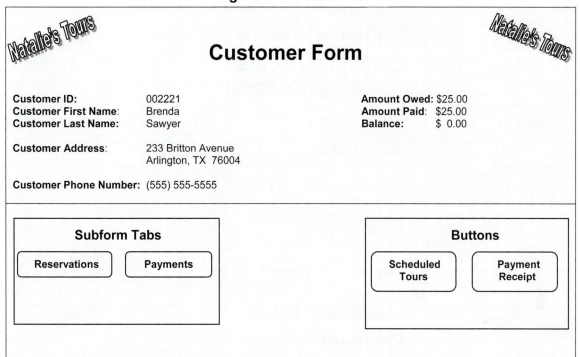

Customer Form

Customer ID:	002221	**Amount Owed:**	$25.00
Customer First Name:	Brenda	**Amount Paid:**	$25.00
Customer Last Name:	Sawyer	**Balance:**	$ 0.00
Customer Address:	233 Britton Avenue Arlington, TX 76004		
Customer Phone Number:	(555) 555-5555		

Subform Tabs

Reservations | Payments

Buttons

Scheduled Tours | Payment Receipt

Information Specifications

When a customer stops by the office and makes a reservation, Ms. Harper prints a list of the customer's scheduled tours and a payment receipt. Figure 5 shows a sketch of the customer's scheduled tours report. The customer's scheduled tours report identifies for the customer his scheduled tours, times, and tour dates. To further individualize the report for the customer, Ms. Harper wants the customer's name included as part of the report header. When a customer pays for his reservations, Ms. Harper will provide the customer with a payment receipt. Figure 6 shows a sketch of the payment receipt. As mentioned above, Ms. Harper wants the ability to print both of these reports from the Customer form. You mention that you can place buttons on the Customer form to accomplish these tasks. Ms. Harper needs a Scheduled Tours by Guide report. The Scheduled Tours By Guide report lists all tours scheduled for a given day and identifies the guide that will lead the tour. The report also identifies how many reservations were made for the tour. Figure 7 provides a sketch for the Scheduled Tours by Guide report.

Figure 5: Customer Scheduled Tours Report

Customer's Name
Scheduled Tours
Printed on: (Current Date)

Tour Name	Tour Time	Scheduled Date
River Walk	1:00 p.m.	11/3/2008
Haunted Walk	9:00 p.m.	11/3/2008

Please arrive 10 minutes before the scheduled tour time. All tours leave promptly at the scheduled time.

Figure 6: Payment Receipt

Natalie's Tours
Payment Receipt
Printed on: (Current Date)

Tour Name	Tour Time	Scheduled Date	Party Number	Cost Per Person	Total
River Walk	1:00 p.m.	11/3/2008	5	$20.00	$100.00
Haunted Walk	9:00 p.m.	11/3/2008	2	$15.00	$30.00

Total Cost: $130.00
Total Paid: $130.00
Balance: $0.00

We appreciate your business.

Figure 7: Scheduled Tours

Scheduled Tours by Guide
(Schedule Date)

Tour Name	Tour Time	Guide Name	Tour Size
River Walk	1:00 p.m.	Paul Winfield	10
Haunted Walk	9:00 p.m.	Sally Dungar	6

In addition to the requirements identified above, Ms. Harper needs answers for the following questions, and she asks you to obtain the information from the Tours database. Build queries to help Ms. Harper answer these questions. Where applicable, you may generate reports based on the queries.

1. What times are the tours currently offered? Ms. Harper needs the tours sorted in ascending order by tour time. The results should display both the tour name and tour time.

2. Who is the tour guide for each tour given during November? Sort the results by tour date, then by tour name and then by guide.

3. What is each guide's tour schedule for the week of November 3, 2008? Ms. Harper wants each guide's results printed separately. For each guide, Ms. Harper needs to see the tour name, tour date, tour time, and tour size.

4. What is the most popular tour? Base your answer on the total number of people having participated in each tour.

5. Which tours are offered in the afternoon? Which tours are offered in the morning?

6. What is the average tour size?

Implementation Concerns

To design the Tours database according to Ms. Harper's specifications, you will design and populate Customer, Reservation, and Payment tables, create Tour, Guide, Scheduled Tour, and Customer forms, design Reservation and Payment subforms for the Customer form, create several queries, establish relationships between tables, prepare scheduled tours and payment receipt reports for customers, and prepare a Scheduled Tours by Guide report.

When a form or report uses data from multiple tables, consider constructing a query to retrieve the data, and then basing the form or report on the query. The Customer form is a main form with two subforms. When designing the Customer form, one option is to use a tab control to organize the subforms. (For additional information on subforms, use your system's online help feature.)

For each customer, Ms. Harper wants a report showing the customer's scheduled tours, as well as a payment receipt. She asks that buttons be placed on the Customer form so she can print the customer's scheduled tours report and payment receipt. The scheduled tours report and payment receipt should print for the current customer displayed in the Customer form.

When creating forms that require data from multiple tables, an auto lookup query can prove useful. Use your system's online help feature to investigate how to use auto lookup.

While you are encouraged to be creative with your form and report designs, remember to use a consistent, professional format. The forms and reports should include the Natalie's

Tours logo. Before designing the forms and reports, you should design a logo for Natalie's Tours and then use the logo on the forms and reports that you create.

Test Your Design

After creating the tables, relationships, forms, queries, and reports, you should test your database design. Perform the following steps.

1. During the week of November 3, 2008, which tours did not have reservations?

2. Beginning January 1, 2009, two new tours will be offered. Enter the following information into the Tours database. (Assign the next available TourID and make any other necessary assumptions.)

Tour Name	Tour Description	Tour Time	Tour Price
Waterfall ATV Tour	Takes tourists on a three-hour ATV tour.	1:00 p.m.	$75.00
Burgin-McKay Mansion Tour	Takes tourists on a tour of the Burgin-McKay mansion.	11:00 a.m.	$25.00

3. The following customers have made reservations. Enter their reservation data into the Tours database.

   - Mike Jones made a reservation for the Waterfall ATV tour on January 9, 2009. Mr. Jones made the reservation for three people. (Include any other necessary data.)
   - Signora Mogseth made a reservation for the Burgin-McKay Mansion Tour on January 9, 2009. The reservation was made for 10 people. (Include any other necessary data.)

4. Sally Dungar cannot give the Cemetery Walk 2 tour on November 3, 2008. Which guides are not scheduled for any tours on November 3, 2008? Prepare a list.

CASE DELIVERABLES

In order to satisfactorily complete this case, you should make the necessary modifications to the database and then prepare both written and oral presentations. Unless otherwise specified, submit the following deliverables to your professor.

1. A written report discussing any assumptions you have made about the case and the key elements of the case. Additionally, what features did you add to make the database more functional? User friendly? (Please note that these assumptions cannot violate any of the requirements specified above and must be approved by your professor.)

2. A printout of each form.

3. A printout of each report.

4. An electronic, working copy of your database that meets the criteria mentioned in the case scenario and specifications sections.

5. Results for each query. (A memo to your instructor discussing these results should also be provided.)

6. As mentioned above, you should prepare an oral presentation. (Your instructor will establish the time allocated for your presentation.) You should use a presentation package and discuss the key features of your database. Also, discuss how this database is beneficial for Ms. Harper. What modifications would make this database more beneficial for Ms. Harper?

CASE 26

Healthy Plant and Tree Nursery

Database Case **Difficulty Rating:** ★★★★★

SKILLS CHECK
You should review the following areas:

DATABASE SKILLS

- ✓ Calculated Field
- ✓ Chart (Microsoft Excel)
- ✓ Command Button
- ✓ Export Data to Microsoft Excel
- ✓ Export Report to HTML Document
- ✓ Filter (Microsoft Excel)
- ✓ Form Design
- ✓ Macro
- ✓ PivotTable
- ✓ Relationship
- ✓ Report Design
- ✓ Select Query
- ✓ Table Design
- ✓ Update Query

CASE BACKGROUND

Having operated in the sunny, southern Florida area for over 100 years, Healthy Plant and Tree Nursery is well known for raising quality plants and fruit trees, especially tropical varieties. The nursery's primary customers are local landscaping companies, home and garden stores, and individuals. All paperwork is manually performed, creating a headache for Juan Regaldo, the nursery's current owner. Mr. Regaldo also has problems keeping his store managers and customers informed about the nursery's available inventory and product prices. In an effort to correct the mounting paperwork and communication problems, Mr. Regaldo hires you to build an inventory database for the nursery. After an initial meeting with Mr. Regaldo, you determine that a Product table, Product form, Low-in-Stock report, Current Inventory List report for the Web, and several select queries are necessary. Mr. Regaldo is especially interested in using the nursery's data to support decision-making activities. As the nursery's data will soon be stored in electronic form, Mr. Regaldo requests the ability export data to Microsoft Excel and also to an HTML document.

CASE SCENARIO

Healthy Plant and Tree Nursery provides its customers with a wide selection of quality plants and trees, particularly tropical varieties. The nursery's inventory list includes many types of fruit trees, including mandarin orange, guava, and mango. Trees are sold in containers, and the containers range in size from 7 to 25 gallons. The nursery also sells quality exotic plants, including Glorisa Superba, Yucca, and Medinilla. All nursery plants are sold in pots, ranging in size from 6- to 12-inch containers. Plant and tree prices are based on type and container size.

Currently, Healthy Plant and Tree Nursery has two stores and a nursery. The nursery location has several greenhouses where plants and trees are raised. When a plant or tree is ready for sale, it is moved to a special distribution greenhouse where all plants and trees ready for immediate distribution and sale are stored. Each evening, each store's inventory is checked, and a replenishment order is placed with the nursery. A replenishment order is filled from the distribution warehouse's current inventory and is usually delivered to the store the next day.

Customers frequently call the stores, requesting current inventory and pricing information. To reduce the number of phone calls, Mr. Regaldo will make the distribution warehouse's current inventory and pricing information available online for his customers and store managers. Mr. Regaldo feels this change will improve the efficiency and performance of the nursery's operations. After reflecting on this requirement, you decide that a Current Inventory List report can be generated and then exported to an HTML document. The HTML document can be made available on the nursery's Web site.

Besides fielding phone calls from store managers and customers, one of the most time-consuming activities for Mr. Regaldo is keeping the nursery's inventory records up to date. Mr. Regaldo requests the ability to identify which plants and trees in the distribution greenhouse are currently low in stock. He uses this information to restock the distribution greenhouse from the nursery's other greenhouses. A Low-in-Stock report satisfies this information request.

In addition to easing the data maintenance burden, Mr. Regaldo wants the capability to analyze the nursery's data with Microsoft Excel. In particular, Mr. Regaldo wants to determine his top selling items, gross margins, and inventory costs. He also wants the ability to prepare charts for presentations and analysis. This information will help him develop better marketing, pricing, and inventory stocking strategies. Mr. Regaldo asks you if it is possible to export the inventory data to a spreadsheet application, such as Microsoft Excel, for further analysis. Although several methods for moving data from a database to a spreadsheet exist, you recommend using the Export to Excel spreadsheet command. You explain to Mr. Regaldo that once the data are moved to Microsoft Excel, he can use Microsoft Excel to further support his decision-making needs.

Initially, Mr. Regaldo needs an inventory database to track the plants and trees currently housed in the distribution greenhouse. Later, he will include plants and trees from the nursery's other greenhouses in the inventory database. In order to build this database, you will design and populate a Product table; design a Product form; create a Current Inventory List report, design a Low-in-Stock report; and create several select queries.

Storage Specifications

After reviewing Mr. Regaldo's information requirements, you decide the Nursery database requires a Product table. The Product table stores important inventory data about the plants and trees available for immediate sale and distribution. For each product, its product number, name, category, cost, selling price, container size, and quantity on hand are stored. Table 1 shows the Product table's structure. (Your instructor will provide you with the data necessary to populate the Product table.) As the product number is unique for each product record, you decide this field should serve as the primary key. The category field indicates whether the item is a plant or tree. As plants and trees are available in a variety of sizes, the container size field indicates the size of the pot or container. If the nursery item is a tree, its container size is measured in gallons. However, if the nursery item is a plant, its pot size is measured in inches.

Table 1: Product Table Structure

Field Name	Data Type	Field Description	Field Size	Comments
PNo	Number	Contains the product number. Serves as the primary key.	Long Integer	Is required.
PName	Text	Contains the name of the product.	25	Is required.
PCategory	Text	Is a two-digit code, indicating the type of product. Currently is either a tropical plant or fruit tree. All characters should display in uppercase.	2	Is required.
ProductCost	Currency	Shows the product's cost.		Is required.
SellingPrice	Currency	Indicates the retail price of the product.		Is required.
ContainerSize	Number	Identifies the container size of the product.	Long Integer	Is required.
QOH	Number	Identifies the quantity on hand of a particular product that is ready for distribution.	Long Integer	Is required.

Input Specifications

In order to maintain the nursery's inventory, a Product form is necessary. Figure 1 shows a tentative sketch for this form. As you examine the sketch, you realize that the form's header includes the nursery's name and the form's name. You also decide to locate a suitable picture of a plant or tree to include. The form's body contains all the fields from the Product table, so you use the Form tool or Form Wizard to quickly build an initial Product form. Once the tentative Product form is created, you edit the form in Design view, providing the form with a more professional appearance.

During a recent conversation with Mr. Regaldo, he mentioned the need to simplify record navigation and operations. To satisfy this requirement, you decide the Product form should include Add, Find, Save, and Print buttons. The Command Button Wizard simplifies the inclusion of these buttons on the Product form, so you use the Command Button Wizard to place these buttons on the form.

Figure 1: Product Form

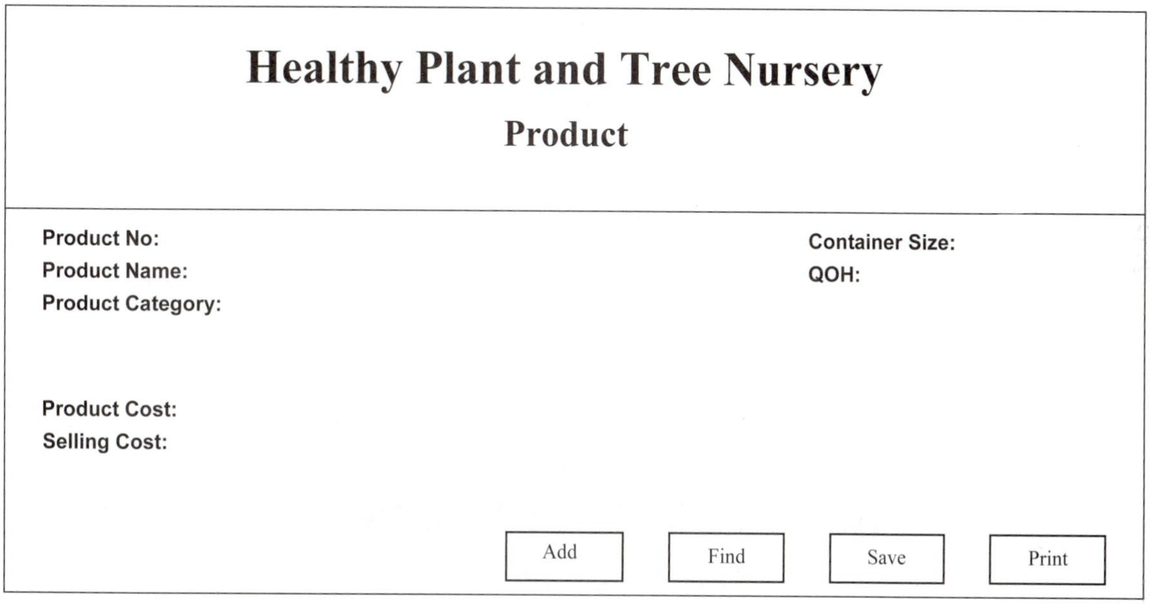

Information Specifications

After studying your notes from a meeting with Mr. Regaldo, you decide that Low-in-Stock and Current Inventory List reports are necessary. The Low-in-Stock report identifies which of the distribution warehouse's plants and trees have less than 75 units on hand. Figure 2 provides a tentative sketch of the Low-in-Stock report. Mr. Regaldo wants the nursery's name, report title, and current date displayed in the report header. The report body lists the product's category, name, product number, container size, and quantity on hand. Mr. Regaldo wants the nursery items grouped in ascending order by category and then sorted in ascending order by product name. Although not shown in the sketch, Mr. Regaldo wants the page number printed in the report's page footer.

Mr. Regaldo will make his distribution warehouse's current inventory and product pricing available via the nursery's Web site. To accomplish this, he asks you to prepare a Current Inventory List report and then export the report to an HTML document. He will then post the report on the nursery's Web site. Figure 3 shows a tentative sketch of the Current Inventory List report. As the nursery's customers will also view this report, Mr. Regaldo does not want product costs included in the report.

Figure 2: Low-In-Stock Report

Healthy Plant and Tree Nursery
Low-in-Stock
(Current Date)

Category Name	Product Name	Product Number	Container Size	Quantity on Hand
FT	Allspice	30	10	72
	Allspice	5	15	48
		.		
		.		
		.		
TP	Glorisa Superba	22	6	9
		.		
		.		
		.		

Figure 3: Current Inventory List Page

Healthy Plant and Tree Nursery
Current Inventory List

Category Name	Product Name	Product Number	Container Size	Quantity on Hand	Selling Price
FT	Allspice	5	15	50	$79.42
FT	Allspice	30	10	75	$54.17
			.		
			.		
			.		
TP	Bonsai	6	24	159	$22.75
TP	Calathea	6	20	199	$15.75
			.		
			.		
			.		

As Mr. Regaldo is familiar with spreadsheet applications, he asks if it is possible to export data from a database to a spreadsheet. He wants to use the spreadsheet's Filter command to analyze the nursery's data. Specifically, Mr. Regaldo wants to export the product's number, name, category, cost, selling price, container size, and quantity on hand to Microsoft Excel. In addition, he wants the gross margin and total inventory cost for each product included in the worksheet. As gross margin and total inventory cost are calculated fields, these data are not stored in the database. Although several methods for obtaining the gross margin and total inventory cost are available, you construct a select query that uses calculated fields to determine these values. Once the select query is constructed, you use the Export to Excel spreadsheet command to export the dynaset to a worksheet. Once the dynaset is exported to the worksheet, Mr. Regaldo can analyze the data using any of Microsoft Excel's features.

Mr. Regaldo needs answers to the following questions. Use Microsoft Excel's Filter command to answer these questions.

1. Which products have less than 20 units on hand?

2. What is the total cost of inventory? (You may find Microsoft Excel's Sum function beneficial.)

3. Which products have the highest gross margin? (Show the top ten.)

4. Which products have the lowest gross margin? (Show the lowest five.)

5. For which products does the nursery have more than 300 units on hand?

Implementation Concerns

To build the database according to Mr. Regaldo's specifications, you will design and populate a Product table; design a Product form and Low-in-Stock report; construct select queries; prepare and then export a Current Inventory List report to an HTML document, and analyze data using Microsoft Excel. Although you are free to work with the form and report designs, these objects must have a professional, consistent appearance.

Consider using the available form and report tools and wizards to create the initial form and reports. These objects can then be easily edited in Design view. After you have created the Current Inventory List report, you can use Microsoft Access's HTML Document command to export the report to an HTML document. (You may wish to use your system's online help feature to learn more about exporting Microsoft Access data.)

Although several methods for exporting data from a database to a spreadsheet application for further analysis exist, the Export to Excel spreadsheet command is a nice, easy tool to use. Before exporting the inventory data to Microsoft Excel, consider constructing a select query. The select query can retrieve the necessary data from the Product table and calculate the gross margin and inventory cost for each product. (You may wish to use your system's online help feature to review calculated fields.)

Test Your Design

After creating the table, form, report, HTML document, and queries, you should test your database design. Perform the following steps.

1. Insert the following five new products into the database.

PNo	PName	PCategory	PCost	SellingPrice	ContainerSize	QOH
41	Lemon	FT	$47.68	$65.95	10	155
42	Navel Orange	FT	$37.87	$55.25	10	102
43	Apricot	FT	$56.78	$79.95	10	274
44	Strelitzia	TP	$8.25	$18.95	10	487
45	Medinilla	TP	$8.25	$18.95	10	397

2. For each of the following nursery items, use the Product form to locate and then update its quantity on hand.

   The nursery's distribution warehouse now has 187 15-gallon lime trees (PNo = 2) on hand.
   The nursery's distribution warehouse now has 182 15-gallon cherry trees (PNo = 12) on hand.
   The nursery's distribution warehouse now has 12 6-inch Glorisa Superba (PNo = 22), plants on hand.

3. Using the Product form, locate the Croton plant record (PNo = 16). Print this record.

4. Using Microsoft Excel's Filter command, identify the ten nursery products that have the highest selling price. The products should be sorted in descending order by selling price.

5. Prepare a column chart showing the gross margin for each of the 15-gallon trees.

6. Mr. Regaldo wants to use a PivotTable to view the cost, selling price, and markup for each nursery product. He wants to filter the products based on product category.

7. Mr. Regaldo wants to increase the selling prices of his products by 15 percent. Use an update query to update the selling prices of his products.

CASE DELIVERABLES

In order to satisfactorily complete this case, you should build the database and then prepare both written and oral presentations. Unless otherwise specified, submit the following deliverables to your professor.

1. A written report discussing any assumptions you have made about the case and the key elements of the case. Additionally, what features did you add to make the database more functional? User friendly? (Please note that these assumptions cannot violate any of the requirements specified above and must be approved by your professor.)
2. A printout of each form, report, HTML document, and PivotTable.
3. An electronic, working copy of your database that meets the criteria mentioned in the case scenario and specifications sections.
4. An electronic working copy of your spreadsheet that meets the criteria mentioned in the case scenario.
5. Printouts showing the results for the questions asked in the Information Specifications Section. (A memo to your instructor discussing these results should also be provided.)
6. A printout of the Products table.
7. Printouts showing the results for Test Your Design Section Steps 3, 4, 5, and 7. (A memo to your instructor discussing these results should also be provided.)
8. As previously mentioned, you should prepare an oral presentation. (Your instructor will establish the time allocated for your presentation.) You should use a presentation package and discuss the key features of your database. Also, discuss how this database is beneficial for Mr. Regaldo. What additional data could be stored in the database?
9. What other types of decisions might Mr. Regaldo use Microsoft Excel to answer? You should identify at least two additional types of decisions. In addition to the chart mentioned above, identify at least one other chart that Mr. Regaldo might use.
10. What other formats are available for exporting the Current Inventory List report? Would you recommend using one of these formats? Why? Why not?

CASE 27 Franklin University: Student Scholarship Management

Database Case **Difficulty Rating:** ★★★★★

SKILLS CHECK
You should review the following areas:

DATABASE SKILLS

- ✓ **Aggregate Function**
- ✓ **Calculated Control**
- ✓ **Calculated Field**
- ✓ **Command Button**
- ✓ **Form Design**
- ✓ **IIF Function**
- ✓ **Macro**
- ✓ **Parameter Query**
- ✓ **PivotTable**
- ✓ **Relationship**
- ✓ **Report Design**
- ✓ **Select Query**
- ✓ **Subform**
- ✓ **Switchboard**
- ✓ **Table Design**

CASE BACKGROUND

Early each spring, Franklin University students apply for scholarships, tuition waivers, and various other awards for the next academic year by completing general scholarship applications. Students leave the completed general scholarship applications with their college dean's office. After the application deadline has passed, the applications are forwarded to the appropriate departments, based on student major. The departments review the general scholarship applications and make awards. While each department wants deserving students to receive the awards to which the students are entitled, the departments do not want to allocate money that cannot be used. Until recently, no central source could help the departments determine if a student already had most, if not all, of his college fees covered. One of the major tasks of the newly formed Franklin University Scholarship Office is to track all awards, scholarships, and tuition waivers that have been granted. Although the departments are still responsible for identifying award recipients, the departments will now work closely with the Franklin University Scholarship Office to avoid any overlap with awards. You are hired to develop a Scholarship database for the Franklin University Scholarship Office and to assist with the award distributions. Development entails designing and populating an Award table; designing Award and Applicant forms; preparing Award Availability, In-State Tuition Waiver Eligibility, Applicant by Major, and Award Recipient List reports; creating Main, Form, Query, and Report switchboards; constructing several queries; and creating macros.

CASE SCENARIO

Each spring semester, a Franklin University student interested in obtaining an award, tuition waiver, or scholarship completes a general scholarship application. The student then drops his completed application off at his college dean's office. From there, the dean's office forwards the application to the appropriate department for evaluation. Although this application process has merit, this decentralized approach to allocating awards to students has created numerous problems. The university often finds that a multiple-award winning student is unable to use all the money allocated to him. For instance, tuition waivers are only applicable to general enrollment fees and cannot be applied to other educational expenses, such as room, board, or technology fees. So, if a student receives multiple tuition waivers from various sources, these tuition waivers can only pay for the student's general enrollment fees. He cannot use the excess tuition waiver money to pay for any other educational expenses. The unused money is left in an account until the end of the semester or academic year, depending on how it was earmarked for distribution. Since this money is not reallocated in a timely fashion, other deserving students are unable to take advantage of the unused award money.

In an effort to better coordinate the award distribution process, the Franklin University Scholarship Office is now responsible for coordinating the award distribution activities. You are hired to assist Franklin University's Scholarship Director, Simona Xavier, in managing the award distributions.

Ms. Xavier explains that the new process works as follows. During March, an Awards Availability report, along with the general scholarship applications relevant to the particular college, are distributed to each college. The Awards Availability report reminds the college and departments about the awards available for each college and department and the amount allocated for each award. The departments then meet, evaluate applications, and make recommendations for awards. The departments submit Tentative Award Allocation reports to the Franklin University Scholarship Office. The Franklin University Scholarship Office staff enters the information from the Tentative Award Allocation reports into the Scholarship database and cross checks the award recipients to make sure that the recipients are only receiving awards that can be used. For instance, an applicant may receive a Merit Credit Scholarship and a tuition waiver from a department. As each of these awards provides tuition assistance, one of these awards could be reallocated to another deserving student.

Ms. Xavier hands you a partially completed Scholarship database and asks you to finish building the database. After reviewing the database contents, you decide the database requires Award and Applicant forms; Main, Form, Query, and Report switchboards; Award Availability, In-State Tuition Waiver Eligibility, Applicant by Major, and Award Recipient List reports; several queries; and macros. Ms. Xavier specifically asks that the Scholarship database be user friendly and provide "push of a button" access to the most frequently used forms, reports, and queries.

Storage Specifications

The current Scholarship database contains Applicant and Allocation tables. When a student submits a general scholarship application, data from this application are entered and stored in the Applicant table. As you study the Applicant table, you notice that this table has several fields, including fields for the student's basic contact information, current GPA, completed hours, expected hours for each semester, major, general comments, in-state tuition, and expected graduation date. The Completed Hours field indicates how many hours the student has on his transcript, and the Expected Hours field gives an indication about how many hours, on average, the student expects to carry each semester. The In-State Tuition field indicates whether or not the student pays in-state tuition fees. A student identification number serves as the primary key for the Applicant table. The Allocation table stores information about the awards a student receives. This table uses a combination key, consisting of award identification number and student identification number fields.

As you examine the Scholarship database, you realize that an Award table is necessary. This table stores information about each available award, including an award identification number, name, maximum available amount per student, total available amount, a designation indicating whether the award is an internal or external award, a designation indicating if the award is a departmental award, and general guidelines for administering the award. While a department or college gives an internal award, an external foundation or organization provides an external award. Also, an award is associated with a particular department or is given to a student who meets certain criteria, regardless of the student's college or major. For instance, the MIS Faculty Merit Scholarship is an internal award and is given each year to an outstanding MIS student. In contrast, the Bob Horan Foundation Scholarship is an external award and is available to any qualifying student, regardless of his college or major. Table 1 shows the Award table's structure. (Your instructor will provide you with the data to populate this table.)

As you study your notes, you decide two relationships are necessary. First, a relationship is necessary between the Award and Allocation tables. As the Award and Allocation tables each have an AwardNo field, you use the AwardNo field to establish a relationship between the two tables. Second, a relationship between the Allocation and Applicant tables is necessary. As the Allocation and Applicant tables have an SID field, you use the SID field to establish a relationship between these tables. You also enforce referential integrity for each relationship.

Table 1: Award Table Structure

Field Name	Data Type	Field Description	Field Size	Comments
AwardNo	Number	Serves as primary key.	Long Integer	For each award, assign the next available number. Is required.

Field Name	Data Type	Field Description	Field Size	Comments
AwardName	Text	Specifies the name of the award.	50	Is required.
Internal	Yes/No	Indicates whether the funding source is an organization outside the university.		Mark "No" only if it is a company or foundation. Government sources are considered internal.
Department	Yes/No	Indicates whether the award or scholarship is specific to a particular department.		
CollegeAffiliation	Text	Indicates the college for which this award is targeted.	4	The field values should display in all caps.
MajorCode	Text	Indicates the major code for which the award is targeted.	4	
MaxStudentAmount	Currency	Indicates the maximum amount that can be given to a single student.		Is required.
TotalAvailable	Currency	Indicates the total amount allocated for this award.		Is required.
TuitionOnly	Yes/No	Designates whether this award can only be used for tuition and general fees.		
Guidelines	Memo	Provides the criteria for this award.		

Input Specifications

The Scholarship database requires Award and Applicant forms. The Award form enables end users to update information about existing awards and also add new awards. While the Award form updates data in the Award table, the Applicant form updates data in two tables: the Applicant and Allocation tables. The Applicant form captures details about the applicant and details about any awards the applicant receives. As the Award form is the easier form to build, you decide to design it first and then work on the Applicant form.

Figure 1 shows a tentative sketch for the Award form. As Figure 1 indicates, the Award form includes all the fields from the Award table, so you use the Form tool or Form Wizard to quickly create an initial Award form. Once the initial form is created, you edit the Award form in Design view. The Award form's header section includes the Franklin University Scholarship Office's name and the form name. (You should also locate an acceptable graphic to include in the form's header.) Figure 1 shows that the Award form should also include buttons that will allow Ms. Xavier to add a new award, find an existing award, or print the current form.

Figure 1: Award

Franklin University Scholarship Office

Award

Award No:
Award Name:
Maximum Amount Per Student:
Total Amount Available:

Internal:
Department:
Tuition Only:

College Affiliation:
Major Code:

Guidelines:

Add | Find | Print

The Applicant form captures information about each applicant and any awards he receives. Figure 2 provides a tentative sketch for this form. The form header includes the Franklin University Scholarship Office name and the form's name. (You should also locate an acceptable graphic to include in the form's header.) The Applicant form includes all the fields from the underlying Applicant table and identifies, for each award, the award number, name, and award amount that a student received.

As the award number and award amount are stored in the Allocation table and the award name is stored in the Award table, a subform is necessary. (You may wish to use your system's online help feature to review subform design at this point.) Of special interest to Ms. Xavier is the ability to see, at a glance, the total dollar value of the awards a student received. You use a calculated field on the subform to sum the dollar amount of the received awards. You then reference the subform field on the main form.

Figure 2: Applicant

Franklin University Scholarship Office

Applicant

Student Identification No:
Student First Name:
Student Last Name:

City:
State:
Zip:

In-State:
Expected Hours:
Completed Hours:
Expected Graduation Date:

Major:
GPA:

Comments:

Add   Find

Allocated Awards:

Award No.	Award Name	Award Amount

Total Allocation: $XXX.XX

Ms. Xavier requests easy access to the database's various forms, reports, and queries. She literally wants to "push a button or two" and view the requested object. Since a switchboard provides a standard interface, you decide to create four switchboards: Main, Form, Query, and Report. The Main switchboard page serves as a main menu, providing access to the other switchboard pages. The Form switchboard provides access to the database's forms, the Query switchboard provides access to the database's queries, and the Report switchboard provides access to the database's reports.

Figures 3 and 4 show tentative sketches for the Main and Form switchboards. (The Query and Report switchboards should use a similar format to the Main and Form switchboards.) On the Main switchboard, the last switchboard item, Exit Franklin Database, enables the user to exit the Franklin Database. In order to perform this function, you create a macro and assign this macro to the Exit Franklin Database button. (You may wish to use your system's online help feature to review macro and switchboard creation at this point.) Figure 4 provides a tentative sketch for the Form switchboard. As Figure 4 shows, the Form switchboard provides access to the forms in the database. You also place an option that enables the user to return to the Main switchboard. The Report and Query switchboards also include buttons that return the user to the Main switchboard.

Figure 3: Main Switchboard

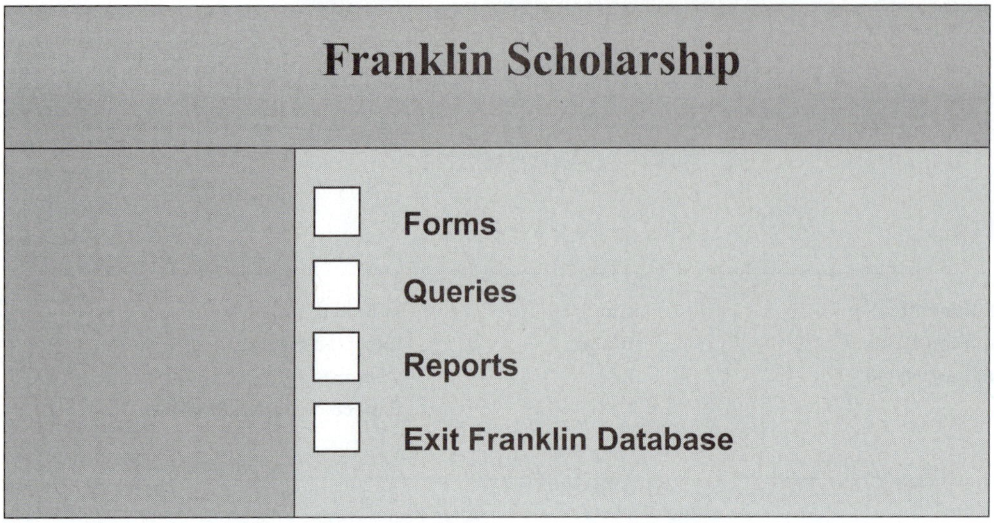

Figure 4: Form Switchboard

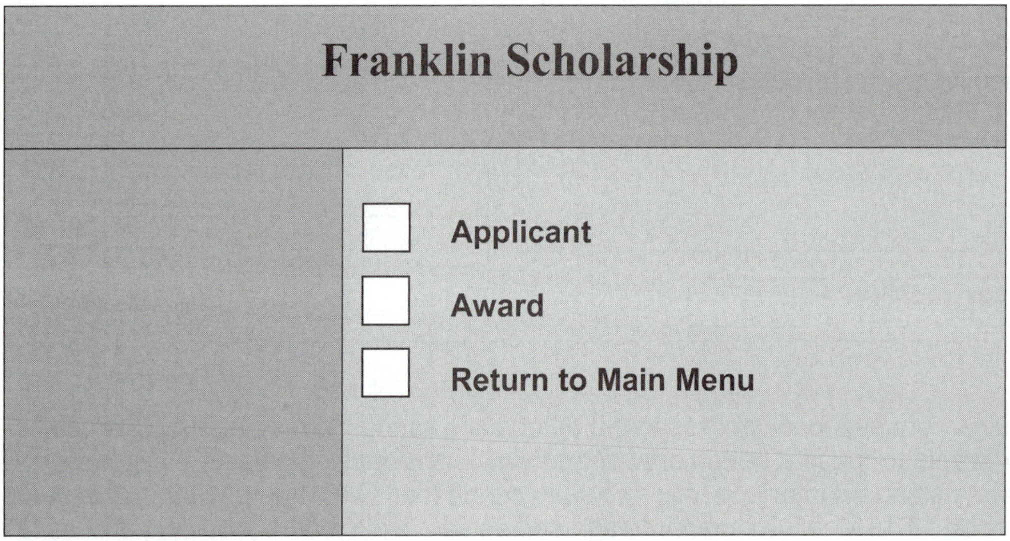

Information Specifications

Ms. Xavier requires Award Availability, In-State Tuition Waiver Eligibility, Applicant by Major, and Award Recipient List reports. Figure 5 provides a tentative sketch for the Award Availability report. This report identifies the available awards for the coming academic year. A designation of "UNIV" in the college affiliation or major code fields means that the award is not restricted to a particular college or department. Likewise, a designation of "CBA" means that the award is given to a particular college, but is not restricted to a particular department or major. The report header includes the scholarship office's name, the report's name, and a current date. The report information is sorted by college affiliation, then by major code and by award name within each major code category.

Figure 5: Award Availability

Franklin University Scholarship Office

Award Availability

(Current Date)

College Affiliation	Major Code	Award Name	Amount Per Student	Total Amount Available
CBA	411	Caedee Hannah Excellence Award	$3,500	$3,500
CBA	411	MIS Faculty Award	$800	$800
		.		
		.		
		.		
UNIV	UNIV	Merit Credit Award	$1,500	$20,000
		.		
		.		
		.		

The In-State Tuition Waiver Eligibility report, shown in Figure 6, identifies which students pay in-state tuition and are eligible for state tuition waivers. The report header includes the scholarship office's name, the report's name, and the current date. (Ms. Xavier requests that you locate suitable graphics for the reports.) As Figure 6 shows, the report body contains the student's last and first name, student identification number, major, expected hours, and expected graduation date. The information is sorted in ascending order by student last name. Although not shown in the sketch, Ms. Xavier requests that a page number be placed in the page footer.

Figure 6: In-State Tuition Waiver Eligibility

Franklin University Scholarship Office

In-State Tuition Waiver Eligibility

(Current Date)

Name	SID	Major	Expected Hours	Expected Graduate Date
Arenivar, Aaron	231717578	417	12	5/12/2009
Bernaldo, Delorise	652134881	411	12	5/12/2009
		. . .		
Lowe, Ruby	218392004	416	12	7/31/2012
		. . .		

Ms. Xavier periodically needs to view the applicants by major. She asks if it is possible to specify a major code and then generate a report. To satisfy this requirement, you build a parameter query and then base the Applicant by Major report on this query. Figure 7 shows a tentative sketch for this report. The report header includes the scholarship office's name and report name, specifies the major code, and shows the current date. The report body shows the first and last name, student identification number, GPA, completed hours, expected hours, and expected graduation date for each applicant. The report information is sorted in ascending order by last name.

Figure 7: Applicant By Major

Franklin University Scholarship Office

Applicant by Major

Major Code: 411

(Current Date)

Name	SID	GPA	Completed Hours	Expected Hours	Expected Graduation Date
Bernaldo, Delorise	652134881	3.64	94	12	5/12/2009
Chambers, James	660635664	3.12	99	12	5/12/2009
			. . .		
Noels, Frank	100496263	3.77	60	12	7/25/2011
			. . .		

The Award Recipient List identifies the applicants and the awards they received. This report is generated after all awards are given and is then distributed to the college deans and department chairpersons. Figure 8 shows a tentative sketch of the Award Recipient List. The Award Recipient List report header includes the scholarship office's name, the name of the report, and a current date. As Figure 8 illustrates, the report body alphabetically lists the students by last name, and then lists the awards each student received. For each student, the total dollar value of his awards is shown. Although not shown in Figure 8, a page number is included in the page footer.

Figure 8: Award Recipient List

Franklin University Scholarship Office

Award Recipient List

(Current Date)

Student Name	SID	Award Name	Award Amount
Dennington, Louise	012780183	Bob Horan Foundation Scholarship	$1,500.00
		MIS Department Tuition Waiver	$350.00
		Total Value:	**$1,850.00**
		.	
		.	
		.	
Ninemire, Guy	122388169	Marketing Department Tuition Waiver	$450.00
		Total Value:	**$450.00**

Ms. Xavier requires answers to the following questions. Build queries to help Ms. Xavier answer these questions. If you choose, you may generate reports based on these queries.

1. Which applicants are seniors? Provide the first and last names for these applicants. Do not show any other fields.
2. How many applicants have GPAs greater than 3.5? Show each applicant's first name, last name, and GPA. Do not show any other fields.
3. What is the average amount of award money that the applicants received?
4. What are the guidelines for the Bob Horan Foundation Scholarship award?
5. How much money is available for the CBA Outstanding Student award? What are the criteria for this award? Prepare a list of applicants that you feel meet the criteria for this award.
6. Which applicants did not receive an award? Why do you think the applicants did not receive an award?
7. Which applicants received more than one tuition waiver? Provide their names, the awards, and award amounts. Should any of the money be reallocated?

8. In terms of total award dollars allocated, which major's students has received the most award dollars?
9. What is the average dollar amount available for each award?

Implementation Concerns

The specifications presented in the case scenario require you to build and populate an Award table, create relationships among tables; design Award and Applicant forms; design Award Availability, In-State Tuition Waiver Eligibility, Applicant by Major, Award Recipient List reports; prepare Main, Form, Query, and Report switchboards; construct several queries; and create macros.

The Form tool easily creates the Award form. Once created, the Award form can be modified in Design view. The Applicant form consists of both a main form and a subform. Although several methods exist for creating the Applicant form and its subform, one method is to use the Form Wizard. Once you have created the main form and subform, you can then edit each form. (For additional information on subforms, use your system's online help feature.) The Total Allocation field on the Applicant form is a calculated field. Consider including on your subform a field that sums the dollar amount for each award a student receives. Then reference this field on your main form.

As part of this case, you are asked to create four switchboards. In essence, a switchboard is a menu. A switchboard presents the user with a standard interface or method for accessing database objects. Use the Main switchboard to branch to a Form switchboard, a Query switchboard and a Report switchboard.

You are asked to display the Main switchboard at startup. This is an easy feature to implement. To learn more about this feature, use the system's online help and request information about "bypassing startup options." Also, the last button on the Main switchboard page requires you to exit the database. To accomplish this task, you must create a macro and then assign the macro to the "Exit Franklin Database" button.

You are free to work with the design of the forms, reports and switchboards. However, each object should have a professional, consistent format. Also, at a minimum, the Query switchboard should provide access to at least five queries.

Test Your Design

After creating the forms, tables, relationships, queries, reports, and macros, you should test your database design. Perform the following transactions:

CASE 27: Franklin University: Student Scholarship Management

1. The following students have applied for scholarships:

Student Identification No: 63548780
Student Last Name: Zeytounian
Student First Name: Ossie
Street Address: 101 Mockingbird Lane
City: Los Angeles
State: CA
In-State: Yes
Major: 411
Expected Hours: 15
Completed Hours: 93
GPA: 3.22
Expected Graduation Date: 5/14/2009

Student Identification No: 25972225
Student Last Name: Yu
Student First Name: Linda
Street Address: 2874 Pippin Street
City: Los Angeles
State: CA
In-State: No
Major: 417
Expected Hours: 18
Completed Hours: 88
GPA: 3.57
Expected Graduation Date: 12/14/2010

Student Identification No: 48484329
Student Last Name: Abernathy
Student First Name: Lamont
Street Address: 7878 Baylee Way
City: Los Angeles
State: CA
In-State: Yes
Major: 411
Expected Hours: 12
Completed Hours: 36
GPA: 3.77
Expected Graduation Date: 5/14/2012

Student Identification No: 58485529
Student Last Name: Beaumont
Student First Name: Joan
Street Address: 7584 Harrison Street
City: Los Angeles
State: CA
In-State: No
Major: 413
Expected Hours: 15
Completed Hours: 80
GPA: 3.98
Expected Graduation Date: 7/31/2012

2. The Franklin University Scholarship Office has been notified about two new awards. Enter the following information into the database:

Award Number: Use next available number.
Award Name: Friends of Education Award
Total Amount: $750
Maximum Per Student: $750
Internal: Yes
Departmental: No
Tuition Only: No

Guidelines: Is given to a senior with an outstanding GPA. The student must have at least a 3.75 GPA. Must be active on campus.

Award Number: Use next available number.
Award Name: Mary Lou Memorial Fund
Total Amount: $1,000
Maximum Per Student: $1,000
Internal: No
Departmental: Yes
Tuition Only: No

Guidelines: Is given to an MIS major. The student should demonstrate need.

3. Which scholarships have not been awarded? Prepare a report.

4. Ms. Xavier wants to know each applicant's rank and the awards the applicant received. Display the applicant's last and first name, hours completed, rank, award name, and award amount. (Hint: Use the following table to determine the student's rank. Also, consider using the IIF function.)

Table 2: Student Classification

Rank	Hours Completed
Senior	90 or more
Junior	60 - 89
Sophomore	30 - 59
Freshman	0 - 29

5. Using a PivotTable, Ms. Xavier wants to see the award names and the total amount available for each award. She will filter the PivotTable on college affiliation and whether it is an internal or external award. Create the PivotTable for Ms. Xavier.

CASE DELIVERABLES

In order to satisfactorily complete this case, you should build the database and then prepare both written and oral presentations. Unless otherwise specified, submit the following deliverables to your professor.

1. A written report discussing any assumptions you have made about the case and the key elements of the case. Additionally, what features did you add to make the database more functional? User friendly? (Please note that these assumptions cannot violate any of the requirements specified above and must be approved by your professor.)

2. A printout of each form.

3. A printout of each report. (Where applicable, use a major code of 411.)

4. An electronic, working copy of your database that meets the criteria mentioned in the case scenario and specifications sections.

5. Results for each query. (A memo to your instructor discussing these results should also be provided.)

6. As mentioned above, you should prepare an oral presentation. (Your instructor will establish the time allocated for your presentation.) You should use a presentation package and discuss the key features of your database. Also, discuss how this database is beneficial for Ms. Xavier. What additional information from the database might Ms. Xavier find useful?

CASE 28 Letty's Costume Rentals

Integration Case **Difficulty Rating:** ★★★★★

SKILLS CHECK
You should review the following areas:

DATABASE SKILLS	SPREADSHEET SKILLS
✓ AutoLookup Query	✓ Advanced Filter
✓ Calculated Control	✓ Filter (optional)
✓ Calculated Field	✓ Chart
✓ Command Button	✓ DAVERAGE Function
✓ Form Design	✓ DMAX Function
✓ IIF Function	✓ DSUM Function
✓ Lookup Wizard	✓ PivotTable
✓ Macro (optional)	
✓ Report Design	
✓ Subform	
✓ Switchboard	
✓ Tab Control (optional)	
✓ Update Query	

CASE BACKGROUND

Letty's Costume Rentals is a newly opened costume rental business. Letty Scott opened the business this past summer and is pleased that her business continues to grow. Ms. Scott recognizes the importance of customer service and feels that a database will help track costume rentals, customers, customer payments, costumes, and past costume rentals. Ms. Scott hires you to build the database for her. Building the database requires you to develop several forms and subforms, reports, queries, and a switchboard. Additionally, Ms. Scott wants the ability to export data to Microsoft Excel for further analysis. When analyzing the data with Microsoft Excel, Ms. Scott will use Microsoft Excel's PivotTable, charting and filtering tools, and database functions.

CASE SCENARIO

This past summer, Letty Scott opened a costume rental business. The business is doing well, and Ms. Scott has hired two employees to help with the business. With the upcoming Halloween and holiday seasons, Ms. Scott realizes that a database can help her costume rental business be more efficient. Ms. Scott also realizes that the costume rental data can be further analyzed to help her make better, more informed business decisions. Currently, Letty's Costume Rentals rents costumes for adults, but in the future will add children's costumes to its inventory. Ms. Scott's current costume inventory consists of approximately 500 costumes. Once the database is computerized, she will begin adding new categories and new costumes to her inventory.

When a customer comes in to the store, he asks Ms. Scott, or one of her sales assistants, if a certain costume is available for rent. Ms. Scott reviews her costume rental notebook kept beside the cash register and determines if the costume is available on the requested date. If the costume is available for the requested date, she makes an entry in the notebook. The entry records the booking date, rental dates, and customer name and contact information. The customer is then asked to sign a customer rental contract and pay a deposit and rental fee.

If the costume is returned in good condition, the deposit is refunded. However, if the costume is damaged, penalties may be assessed. Generally, a customer picks up his costume the day before his event and then returns the costume the day after the event. For instance, a customer renting a pirate costume for a Friday event would pick up the costume on Thursday and then return the costume the next business day, in this case Saturday. Special arrangements can be made for a longer rental period, if necessary. If special arrangements are not made, a late penalty of $20 is assessed for each additional day.

Storage Specifications

After visiting with Ms. Scott, you decide that the costume database should include Category, Costume, Customer, Payment, Rental, and RentalHistory tables. (Your instructor will provide you with the data to populate these tables.) Ms. Scott wants her costumes categorized by type of costume. Types of costumes include such categories as medieval, food, and fictional character. To facilitate the categorization of her costumes, the costume database needs a Category table. The Category table includes a CategoryID field and a CategoryDescription field. The CategoryID field is unique for each record and serves as the primary key. The CategoryDescription field provides additional information about the specific costume category. Table 1 provides the structure for the Category table.

Table 1: Category Table Structure

Field Name	Data Type	Field Description	Field Size	Comments
CategoryID	Number	Serves as primary key.	Long Integer	Is required.

Field Name	Data Type	Field Description	Field Size	Comments
CategoryDescription	Text	Describes the category.	50	

The Costume table stores information about each costume in inventory. The Costume table includes CostumeID, Description, Size, RentalPrice, and CategoryID fields. The CostumeID field is unique for each costume and serves as the table's primary key. The Description field stores the name of the costume, such as pirate or toad. The Size field indicates the size of the costume, such as small, medium, or large. The RentalPrice field stores the costume's rental price, and the CategoryID field stores the category identification number. The CategoryID value is obtained from a list of values stored in the Category table. Table 2 shows the Costume table's structure.

Table 2: Costume Table Structure

Field Name	Data Type	Field Description	Field Size	Comments
CostumeID	Number	Serves as primary key.	Long Integer	Is required.
Description	Text	Describes the costume.	50	
Size	Text	Indicates the costume's size.	5	
RentalPrice	Currency	Stores the daily rental price.		
CategoryID	Number	Associates the costume with a certain category or group of costumes. Use the Lookup Wizard.	Long Integer	Is required.

The Customer table stores information about each customer. The Customer table includes CustomerID, LastName, FirstName, StreetAddress, City, State, Zip, and Phone fields. As the CustomerID field is unique for each customer, this field serves as the primary key for the Customer table. Table 3 shows the Customer table's structure.

Table 3: Customer Table Structure

Field Name	Data Type	Field Description	Field Size	Comments
CustomerID	AutoNumber	Uniquely identifies each customer. Serves as primary key.	Long Integer	Is required.
LastName	Text	Stores the customer's last name.	50	Is required.
FirstName	Text	Stores the customer's first name.	50	Is required.
StreetAddress	Text	Stores the customer's street address.	30	Is required.
City	Text	Stores the customer's city.	50	Is required.
State	Text	Stores the customer's state.	2	Is required.
Zip	Text	Stores the customer's zip code.	10	
Phone	Text	Stores the customer's phone number.	10	Is required.

The Payment table stores information about customer payments. The Payment table includes the fields shown in Table 4. These fields include PaymentID, CustomerID, PaymentDate, PaymentAmount, and Comment. The PaymentID field is unique for each payment and serves as the primary key. The CustomerID field associates a given payment with a particular customer. The PaymentDate field indicates when a payment was made. The PaymentAmount field indicates how much was paid, and the Comment field stores any necessary comments about the payment transaction.

Table 4: Payment Table Structure

Field Name	Data Type	Field Description	Field Size	Comments
PaymentID	AutoNumber	Is unique for each payment. Serves as the primary key.	Long Integer	Is required.
CustomerID	Number	Associates the payment with a particular customer. Use the Lookup Wizard.	Long Integer	Is required.
PaymentDate	Date/Time	Identifies the date the payment was made. Use the short date format.		Is required.

Field Name	Data Type	Field Description	Field Size	Comments
PaymentAmount	Currency	Indicates how much was paid.		Is required.
Comment	Text	Stores any necessary comments.		

The Rental table structure contains ResID, CustomerID, CostumeID, RentalDate, BookingDate, DueDate, ActualReturnDate, CheckedIn, and AdditionalPenalty fields. The ResID is unique for each record and serves as the primary key. The CustomerID field identifies which customer rented the costume. The CostumeID field indicates which costume was rented. The RentalDate indicates when the customer wants the costume. The BookingDate indicates when the customer made the rental reservation. The DueDate field indicates when the costume should be returned. The ActualReturnDate indicates when the customer did return the costume. The CheckedIn field indicates whether or not the customer has returned the costume. This field is checked only when the costume is returned. The CheckedIn field's default value is set to no. The AdditionalPenalty field stores any additional fees charged to the customer. Additional fees are charged for garment stains, rips and tears, and returning the costume late. Table 5 shows the Rental table's structure.

Table 5: Rental Table Structure

Field Name	Data Type	Field Description	Field Size	Comments
ResID	AutoNumber	Uniquely identifies each reservation. Serves as primary key.	Long Integer	Is required.
CustomerID	Number	Identifies the customer renting the costume. Use the LookUp Wizard.	Long Integer	Is required.
CostumeID	Number	Identifies the costume being rented. Use the LookUp Wizard.	Long Integer	Is required.
RentalDate	Date/Time	Identifies the date for which the costume is reserved. Use a short date format.		Is required.
BookingDate	Date/Time	Identifies when the reservation was made. Use a short date format.		Is required.
DueDate	Date/Time	Indicates when the costume is scheduled to be returned to the store. Use a short date format.		
ActualReturnDate	Date/Time	Indicates when the costume was actually returned to the store. Use a short date format.		

Field Name	Data Type	Field Description	Field Size	Comments
CheckedIn	Yes/No	Indicates if the costume has been checked in. Set default value to no.		
AdditionalPenalty	Currency	Stores any additional penalties associated with this costume rental.		

The RentalHistory table's structure is similar to the Rental table. The RentalHistory table's purpose is to store information about previous costume rentals. When a customer checks in his rented costume, the CheckedIn field of the Rental record is then checked. At the end of each day, reservations whose CheckedIn field is yes should be moved to the RentalHistory table and deleted from the Rental table. Moving these reservations requires a query that identifies the reservations to move, as well as an update query to append the reservations to the RentalHistory table.

As part of the design process, you realize that relationships among tables are necessary. After studying the tables, you create any necessary relationships and also modify, where necessary, relationships to enforce referential integrity.

Input Specifications

The costume database must capture and store information about the business's customers, costumes, rentals, and payments. The costume database requires Customer, Costume, and Costume Availability forms. Ms. Scott asks you to design the forms for her. She also asks you to create a logo for the business and use it on the forms.

The Customer form should, at a minimum, enable Ms. Scott to capture and view the customer's name, address, and phone number. Additionally, the customer form should show the amount owed by the customer, the amount he has paid, total deposit, any assessed penalties, and the balance due. While viewing a customer's record, Ms. Scott wants to access a customer's current costume rentals and payments made on the current rentals. For each costume rental, Ms. Scott wants to see the costume identification number, costume description, size, rental price, required deposit, rental date, booking date, due date, and penalties. She also wants to see if the costume has been checked in. For each customer's payment, Ms. Scott wants to enter a payment date, payment amount, and comments.

The Costume form should allow Ms. Scott to create, modify, or delete costume records. At a minimum, this form should use the fields from the Costume table.

The Costume Availability form provides information about costumes and allows Ms. Scott to check if a costume is available. This form should include, at a minimum, the fields from the Costume table. This form should also include a field that indicates if the costume is available. If the costume is not currently available, then this field should indicate the date when the costume is expected to be available. Ms. Scott will use Filter by Form to locate a particular costume.

When the costume database is first opened, Ms. Scott wants a switchboard to automatically display. The switchboard will allow Ms. Scott to access her forms, reports, and queries from a common location. When Ms. Scott finishes with the database, she wants the option of exiting the database from the main switchboard.

Information Specifications

Ms. Scott requests Costumes by Category and Late Customer reports. She asks you to design and build these reports for her.

The Costume by Category report serves as a detailed inventory report. Ms. Scott wants this report to organize the costumes by category. The categories should be sorted in ascending order. Within each category, Ms. Scott wants the costume descriptions sorted in ascending order. This report, at a minimum, should show the category name, the costume identification number, the costume description, costume size, and costume rental price. The report header should include an appropriate name, the date the report was prepared, the store name, and store logo.

The Late Customer report identifies the names, addresses, and phone numbers of customers who have not returned their costumes by the specified due date. This report should also identify the costumes that have been rented and not returned by the customer. The report information is arranged in ascending order by due date. For each due date, organize the information in ascending order by customer last name. If a customer has more than one costume rented, sort the costume descriptions in ascending order.

Ms. Scott wants answers to the following questions. Prepare queries to retrieve the information for Ms. Scott. If you choose, you may generate reports based on your queries.

1. Which costumes were rented today? Which customers rented these costumes? (Use October 15, 2008, as the date. At a minimum, your results should show the customer's first and last name, costume description, reservation date, costume size, and rental price.)

2. Based on rental history data, which costumes have never been rented? (Base your answer on rental history table data.)

3. How many dinosaur costumes are currently checked out? How many princess costumes are currently checked out?

4. Based on rental history data, what is the average rental amount spent by each customer? (Base your answer on rental history table data. Do not include penalties or deposits.)

5. Based on rental history data, which customers have paid penalties? For each customer, provide a total. (Base your answer on rental history table data.)

6. What percentage of our customers return their costumes late?

7. Where do the store's customers live? Provide a count by city.

8. Ms. Scott wants to identify the store's repeat customers. Provide Ms. Scott with the names and addresses of all repeat customers.

9. What costume size is most popular? Provide a count by size.

   Ms. Scott will export data from the costume database to a Microsoft Excel worksheet for further analysis. (You need to determine which data to export.) Ms. Scott needs answers to the following questions. Using Microsoft Excel, provide Ms. Scott with answers for her questions.

10. Based on rental history data, Ms. Scott wants to know which costume category has generated the most revenue. Based on description, which costume has generated the most revenue?

11. For each category, what is the revenue by costume? Ms. Scott wants to see the results for each category on a separate "page."

12. For the month of October, prepare a bar chart comparing revenue by category.

13. Create an Excel table using data from the customer and rental history tables. For a given customer and rental date, what are the average penalties assessed? What are the total penalties assessed to that customer on the specified rental date? For all customers on the specified date, what were the maximum penalties assessed to a customer?

14. For those customers returning a costume late, what is the average number of days between the due date and the actual return date? (Use the rental history table data.)

15. For a given rental date, what are the average rental fees and penalties? (Use the rental history table data.)

Implementation Concerns

In order to build the costume database, you will construct select, AutoLookup, parameter, and action queries; design forms and subforms; design reports; construct tables; create a macro (if necessary); and establish relationships among tables. Although Ms. Scott encourages you to be creative with your form design, she also requests that the forms have a consistent, professional appearance, be easy to use, and show the business name and logo. (Ms. Scott has asked you to create the logo.) Where applicable, include buttons to add, delete and print records. To facilitate data entry, Ms. Scott wants to use AutoLookup, combo boxes, and control tips for fields where these features can (or should) be used. Where possible, you should use validation rules, default values, input masks, and proper formatting.

To satisfy the spreadsheet requirements, you will export selected data from the costume database to a worksheet(s). To perform the required analysis, you will use several spreadsheet features, including PivotTable, Advanced Filter, and database functions.

As mentioned above, you are free to work with the design of the forms, reports, and worksheet(s). You are also free to make additional assumptions about this case. However, the assumptions should not violate any of the requirements and should be approved by your professor. You may need to create additional forms or collect information that has not been previously specified.

Test Your Design

After creating your database and workbook, you should test your design. Perform the following steps.

1. Enter the following information into the costume database.

   Kiritu Mohammed wants to rent pumpkin and dinosaur costumes. Locate available costumes for him. Use today's date for the rental and booking dates. For the return date, use tomorrow's date. (Select one pumpkin and one dinosaur costume for him. Make any other necessary assumptions.)

   Petronna Hogan wants to rent a Bo Peep costume and a wolf costume. Locate available costumes for her. Use today's date for the rental and booking dates. For the return date, use tomorrow's date. (Make any other necessary assumptions.)

   Imran Segura wants to rent one nun, one bishop, and one cardinal costume. Locate available costumes for him. Use today's date for the rental and booking dates. For the return date, use tomorrow's date. (Make any other necessary assumptions.)

2. Update the Rental table's records to show that all rentals due on October 17, 2008, have been returned.

3. Ms. Scott wants to view a customer's rental history. Modify the Customer form to enable Ms. Scott to view each customer's rental history. (You should determine which rental history fields are necessary.)

CASE DELIVERABLES

In order to satisfactorily complete this case, you should build the database and workbook as described in the case scenario and then prepare both written and oral presentations. Unless otherwise specified, submit the following deliverables to your professor.

1. A written report discussing any assumptions you have made about the case and the key elements of the case. Additionally, what features did you add to make the database and workbook more functional? User friendly? (Please note that these assumptions cannot violate any of the requirements specified above and must be approved by your professor.)

2. A printout of each worksheet.

3. A printout of each worksheet's formulas.

4. An electronic, working copy of your workbook that meets the criteria mentioned in the case scenario and specifications sections.

5. An electronic, working copy of your database that meets the criteria mentioned in the case scenario and specifications sections.

6. Results for each question posed above. (A memo to your instructor discussing these results should also be provided.)

7. As mentioned above, you should prepare an oral presentation. (Your instructor will establish the time allocated for your presentation.) You should use a presentation package and discuss the key features of your database and workbook. Also, discuss how the database and workbook are beneficial for Ms. Scott. What additional information should be included in the database and workbook to make it more useful?

CASE 29

Mountain View Dental Clinic

Web Case **Difficulty Rating:** ★★

SKILLS CHECK
You should review the following areas:

WEB SKILLS

- ✓ **Basic Web Page Design**
- ✓ **Header**
- ✓ **HTML (optional)**
- ✓ **Hyperlink**
- ✓ **Image Insertion**
- ✓ **List**
- ✓ **Paragraph**
- ✓ **Table**
- ✓ **Text Editing**
- ✓ **Web Page Editor**

CASE BACKGROUND

Dr. Joshi Michailoff owns a thriving, private dental practice in the northeastern United States. Dr. Michailoff and his staff provide a variety of dental services to both children and adults. Dr. Michailoff has noticed that many dental clinics have informative, useful Web pages for their patients. Since he is interested in attracting new patients and providing information for his current patients, he asks you to design a professional-looking Web page for his dental clinic.

CASE SCENARIO

The Mountain View Dental Clinic is a family-oriented dental practice, located in the northeastern United States. The dental clinic caters to both children and adults. Dr. Joshi Michailoff opened the clinic ten years ago, after graduating from the University of Texas Health Science Center, with a Doctor of Dental Surgery degree. Dr. Michailoff is a member of several organizations, including the American Dental Association, American Academy of Cosmetic Dentistry, Academy of General Dentistry, and American Association of Hospital Dentists. He recently was awarded the Fellowship in the Academy of General Dentistry, a very prestigious honor.

Dr. Michailoff has a wonderful support staff that includes Dianne Hamrick, Benita Jackson, Clyde McGill, and Corey Passey. Dianne is a dental assistant and has worked with Dr.

Michailoff for the last 6 years. Benita is also a dental assistant and has worked at the clinic for the last year. Clyde is a dental hygienist and has worked at the clinic for 2 years, and Corey is the office manager and has worked at the clinic for the last 6 months.

The dental clinic provides a variety of services, including teeth cleaning, fluoride treatments, crowns and bridges, extractions, oral examinations, fillings, cosmetic bonding, porcelain veneers, teeth whitening, sealants, gum treatment, root canals, and partial and complete dentures. Payment for any of these services is expected at the time the service is provided. Patients may pay by major credit card, cash, check, or approved insurance.

The clinic's hours are Monday through Friday, from 9:00 a.m. to 5:00 p.m. Dr. Michailoff may be paged after hours for emergency care. Same day care is provided for most emergencies.

Dr. Michailoff asks you to design a Web page for his dental practice. He wants the Web page to promote his practice, provide basic information about the clinic, and attract new patients.

Design Specifications

Dr. Michailoff asks you to create an informative, professional-looking Web page. When his patients visit the Web page, Dr. Michailoff wants them to find an attractive, easily navigated page. Dr. Michailoff wants the Web page to serve as an information source for both current and future patients. At a minimum, he wants the Web page to provide basic information about the dental clinic, such as office hours, contact information, services, and staff. He wants the Web page's visitors to easily move around the site, and he wants the page to load quickly and contain links to other places of interest. He asks you to locate several of these sites.

Information Specifications

Before publishing the Web page, you want Dr. Michailoff to view the Web page. Dr. Michailoff has specifically said that he wants to view the following information on his clinic's Web page.

1. Dr. Michailoff wants to see the clinic's emergency care information.

2. Dr. Michailoff wants to see brief profiles for the clinic's staff. He feels this will help the patients feel more comfortable. (You should provide brief profiles for the staff.)

3. Dr. Michailoff wants to see a listing of the services provided by the clinic.

4. Dr. Michailoff wants the Web page to provide links to Web sites that contain useful information for dental patients. (You will need to supply this information.)

Implementation Concerns

The case scenario provides you with a broad background for the dental clinic. In several instances, you will need to make assumptions about the dental clinic in order to design an appropriate Web page. One helpful way to locate this information is to visit other dental clinic Web sites to see what information they display. However, keep in mind that you should not violate any existing copyrights.

While you are free to work with the design of the dental clinic's Web page, the Web page must have a consistent, professional appearance. Also, you should locate suitable graphics for the Web page. Your instructor will provide you with additional requirements for the Web page.

Test Your Design

After creating the Web page, you should test your design. Perform the following steps.

1. Dr. Michailoff has recently hired a new dentist. Dr. Ashok Patmon recently graduated from a well-known dental school. Dr. Michailoff asks you to develop a short profile for Dr. Patmon and then add his profile to the dental clinic's Web page. (You will need to provide the necessary profile information.)

2. Often a patient's bill for his dental care can be substantial. As a way of alleviating the financial burden, Dr. Michailoff is instituting a new payment plan called the Dental Care Monthly Payment Plan. This plan provides established patients with a way to make monthly payments, rather than having to pay the entire fee at the time the services are rendered. Dr. Michailoff wants this information added to the clinic's Web page.

CASE DELIVERABLES

In order to satisfactorily complete this case, you should build the Web page and then prepare both written and oral presentations. Unless otherwise specified, submit the following deliverables to your professor. Also, unless otherwise specified, perform these steps after you have tested your design.

1. A written report discussing any assumptions you have made about the case and the key elements of the case. Additionally, what features did you add to make the Web page more functional? User friendly? (Please note that these assumptions cannot violate any of the requirements specified above and must be approved by your professor.)

2. A printout of the Web page. (If additional pages are created, you must submit these pages.)

3. An electronic, working copy of your Web page that meets the criteria mentioned in the case scenario and specifications sections.

4. As mentioned above, you should prepare an oral presentation. (Your instructor will establish the time allocated for your presentation.) You should use a presentation package and discuss the key features of your Web page. Also, discuss how the Web page is beneficial for Dr. Michailoff and his clinic. What additional information might Dr. Michailoff's patients find useful?

CASE 30

Family Veterinary Pet Care Clinic

Web Case **Difficulty Rating:** ★★

SKILLS CHECK
You should review the following areas:

WEB SKILLS

- ✓ **Basic Web Page Design**
- ✓ **Header**
- ✓ **HTML (optional)**
- ✓ **Hyperlink**
- ✓ **Image Insertion**
- ✓ **List**
- ✓ **Paragraph**
- ✓ **Table**
- ✓ **Text Editing**
- ✓ **Web Page Editor**

CASE BACKGROUND

Dr. Paul Tao owns a small veterinary practice in the southwest United States. Dr. Tao and his staff provide a variety of quality services and products to caring pet owners. Dr. Tao has noticed that several other veterinary clinics in the area have Web pages. In an effort to keep up with the times, he asks you to design a professional-looking Web page for his clinic.

CASE SCENARIO

The Family Veterinary Pet Care Clinic is a small veterinary clinic located in the southwest United States, specializing in the care of small animals. Dr. Paul Tao opened the clinic almost 20 years ago, after graduating with a doctor of veterinary medicine degree in 1983. Dr. Tao has received numerous national and community awards, including the prestigious AVMA Animal Welfare Award. Dr. Tao is a member of the American Veterinary Medical Association and American Animal Hospital Association and holds veterinary licenses in Texas, New Mexico, Arizona, and Oklahoma.

The veterinary clinic is well staffed by caring professionals, including a veterinary technician, office manager, and several veterinary assistants. Isla Meiring is a veterinary technician and has worked at the clinic for almost 15 years. Mario Schwermer is the office manager and has worked at the clinic for 5 years; Valerie Widick, Harriett Lafollette, Brian Hallett, and Bill

McKee are veterinary assistants at the clinic. Valerie has worked at the clinic for 10 years, Harriett has worked at the clinic for two years, Brian has worked at the clinic for 6 months, and Bill was hired last week. Gary Dromgoole and Jules Dubois are groomers and have worked at the clinic since it opened in the 1980s.

The Family Veterinary Pet Care Clinic offers a wide range of services, including routine exams, surgery, radiology, pharmacy, orthopedic, dental, vaccinations, grooming, boarding, intensive care, home visitations, delivery of medications and supplies, and emergency care. As a full care pet clinic, the veterinary clinic offers a variety of products, including such items as accessories, dental, diet, cleaning products, medications, skin care, and dietary supplements. Payment for services and supplies is due when the services are rendered or the supplies are purchased. Clients may pay by cash, check, or major credit card. When using a credit card, all purchases must be over $25.00.

The clinic's hours are Monday through Friday, from 8:00 a.m. to 6:00 p.m., and on Saturday, from 8:00 a.m. to 12:00 p.m. Dr. Tao may be paged after hours for emergency care. Clients are encouraged to call for appointments; however, walk-ins are accepted.

During a recent conversation with Dr. Tao, he asked you to build a Web page for the clinic. He wants the Web page to promote his clinic, as well as provide basic information about the clinic.

Design Specifications

Dr. Tao asks you to create an informative, professional-looking Web page. When his clients visit the Web page, Dr. Tao wants them to find an attractive, easily navigated page. Dr. Tao wants the Web page to target individuals in the community who have small animals. At a minimum, he wants the Web page to provide basic information about the clinic, such as office hours, services, staff, and products. He wants the Web page's visitors to easily move around the site, and he wants the page to load quickly and contain links to other places of interest. He asks you to locate several of these sites.

Information Specifications

Before publishing the Web page, you want Dr. Tao to view the Web page. Dr. Tao has specifically said that he wants to view the following information on his clinic's Web page.

1. Dr. Tao wants to see the clinic's hours, as well as its emergency care information.

2. Dr. Tao wants to see brief profiles for the clinic's staff. He feels this will help the clients feel more comfortable.

3. Dr. Tao wants to see the clinic's policy on boarding animals. (You will need to supply this information.)

4. Dr. Tao wants to see a listing of his products organized by category, along with pricing information. (You will need to supply this information.)

5. Dr. Tao wants the Web page to provide links to Web sites that contain useful information for pet owners. (You will need to supply this information.)

Implementation Concerns

The case scenario provides you with a broad background for the veterinary clinic. In several instances, you will need to make assumptions about the clinic in order to design an appropriate Web page. One helpful way to locate this information is to visit other veterinary Web sites to see what information they display. However, keep in mind that you should not violate any existing copyrights.

Although you are free to work with the design of the clinic's Web page, the Web page must have a consistent, professional appearance. Also, you should locate suitable graphics for the Web page. Your instructor will provide you with additional requirements for the Web page.

Test Your Design

After creating the Web page, you should test your design. Perform the following steps.

1. Dr. Tao recently hired a new veterinarian. Dr. Lawanda Fontaine recently graduated from a well-known veterinary school. Dr. Tao asks you to develop a short profile for her and then add her profile to the clinic's Web page. (You will need to provide the necessary profile information.)

2. Often a client's bill for his pet can be substantial. As a way of alleviating the financial burden, Dr. Tao is instituting a new payment plan called the Pet Care Extended Payment Plan. This plan provides established clients with a way to make monthly payments, rather than having to pay the entire fee at the time the services are rendered. Dr. Tao wants this information added to the clinic's Web page.

CASE DELIVERABLES

In order to satisfactorily complete this case, you should build the Web page and then prepare both written and oral presentations. Unless otherwise specified, submit the following deliverables to your professor. Also, unless otherwise specified, perform these steps after you have tested your design.

1. A written report discussing any assumptions you have made about the case and the key elements of the case. Additionally, what features did you add to make the Web page more functional? User friendly? (Please note that these assumptions cannot violate any of the requirements specified above and must be approved by your professor.)

2. A printout of the Web page. (If additional pages are created, you must submit these pages.)

3. An electronic, working copy of your Web page that meets the criteria mentioned in the case scenario and specifications sections.

4. As mentioned above, you should prepare an oral presentation. (Your instructor will establish the time allocated for your presentation.) You should use a presentation package and discuss the key features of your Web page. Also, discuss how the Web page is beneficial for Dr. Tao and his clinic. What additional information might Dr. Tao's clients find useful?

Spreadsheet Tutorial

Timeka's Tanning Salon, Inc.

Tutorial Introduction

Timeka's Tanning Salon, Inc. is a tutorial designed to accompany MIS Cases: Decision Making With Application Software, Fourth Edition published by Pearson Prentice Hall. This tutorial serves as a spreadsheet development review tool, and assumes that you have a basic, fundamental knowledge of spreadsheets, spreadsheet terminology, and Microsoft Excel 2007.

This tutorial is separated into two parts. Part I provides the tutorial's background, scenario, design specifications, information specifications, test your design requirements, and deliverables. Part II steps you through the tutorial's preparation. Since Part I introduces the case's main character and sets the stage for the required spreadsheet design work, you should read Part I before attempting Part II. In Part II, you will design and build a workbook that satisfies the tutorial's information requirements.

Part I: Setting the Scene

Tutorial Background

Timeka Lorenzo owns and operates Timeka's Tanning Salon which is located in San Francisco, California. The tanning salon has been in operation for several years, and the clientele for the business continues to grow. The tanning salon provides customers with access to the latest tanning beds, tan enhancing products, and a fitness center.

Since the salon's records are manually kept, Ms. Lorenzo spends numerous hours each week just tracking her salon's sales activity. Lately, Ms. Lorenzo has begun to realize the necessity of moving the salon's paper-based records to an electronic format. Ms. Lorenzo hires you to design a workbook that will track the salon's daily sales activity. To prepare this case, you will design six worksheets, use several functions, consolidate data into a summary worksheet, properly format cells and worksheets, prepare a PivotTable, prepare a chart, and use the Filter tool.

Tutorial Scenario

Four years ago, Timeka Lorenzo opened Timeka's Tanning Salon in the San Francisco area. The tanning salon is doing well, and Timeka's clientele list continues to grow. Because the salon's business is growing, the manual record keeping system that Ms. Lorenzo currently uses is no longer effective.

At the end of each business day, Ms. Lorenzo manual records the salon's daily sales activity on a Daily Sales Activity Report. Figure 1 shows the Daily Sales Activity Report. Whenever it is convenient, Ms. Lorenzo calculates the dollar sales by using the Price List, which is shown in Figure 2. Ms. Lorenzo then compares the information contained in the Daily Sales Activity Report with the actual cash register receipts and notes any discrepancies between the documents. At the end of each week, Ms. Lorenzo prepares a Weekly Sales Activity Report, summarizing the data contained in the seven Daily Sales Activity Reports.

Figure 1: Daily Sales Activity Report

Timeka's Tanning Salon Daily Sales Activity Report For Date of:__________________		
Item	**Unit Sales**	**Dollar Sales**
1 Session		
5 Sessions		
10 Sessions		
15 Sessions		
20 Sessions		
One Month Unlimited		
Monthly Special		
Loyal Customer		
Referral		
Yearly Enrollment		
Bronze 12 oz Lotion		
Golden 12 oz Lotion		
Bronze 12 oz Oil		
Golden 12 oz Oil		
Timeka's Tan Enhancer 12 oz Lotion		
Timeka's Tan Enhancer 16 oz Lotion		
6-Month Membership		
Yearly Membership		
Total Daily Sales		

Figure 2: Price List

Timeka's Tanning Salon Price List	
1 Session	$5.00
5 Sessions	$25.00
10 Sessions	$50.00
15 Sessions	$75.00
20 Sessions	$100.00
One Month Unlimited	$35.00
Monthly Special	$30.00
Loyal Customer	$29.99
Referral	$29.99
Yearly Enrollment	$350.00
Bronze 12 oz Lotion	$24.99
Golden 12 oz Lotion	$27.99
Bronze 12 oz Oil	$19.99
Golden 12 oz Oil	$21.99
Timeka's Tan Enhancer 12 oz Lotion	$27.99
Timeka's Tan Enhancer 16 oz Lotion	$34.99
6-Month Fitness Membership	$180.99
Yearly Fitness Membership	$280.99

Ms. Lorenzo realizes the process of manually recording and tallying the salon's sales data is tedious and time consuming. Ms. Lorenzo needs a more efficient system for tracking and analyzing her salon's daily sales activity. Ms. Lorenzo hires you to build a workbook that will enable her to more efficiently track and analyze the salon's sales activity.

Design Specifications

At the close of each business day, Ms. Lorenzo manually records the daily sales information on a Daily Sales Activity Report. Figure 1 shows a copy of this report. As Figure 1 shows, Ms. Lorenzo records both the units sold and dollar sales for each salon item. At the end of each week, Ms. Lorenzo uses the Daily Sales Activity Reports to prepare a Weekly Sales Activity Report. The Weekly Sales Activity Report format uses the Daily Sales Activity Report format, except it reflects weekly sales data.

Ms. Lorenzo wants the salon's daily sales activity information organized into a workbook, and she would like a workbook created for each month of the year. (For this tutorial, you will create a workbook for the month of October.) The Salon workbook contains four weekly worksheets, a summary worksheet, and a price list worksheet. A weekly worksheet will be created for each week in the month. The weekly worksheet summarizes the daily sales activities for the week. The Summary worksheet consolidates data for the month. The PriceList worksheet contains the current price list for the salon items and has a format similar to the price list shown in Figure 2.

Information Specifications

Ms. Lorenzo will use the new Salon workbook to analyze the tanning salon's sales activities. She is particularly interested in identifying the most popular tanning sessions, as well as reviewing salon sales by category. In addition to these information requirements, Ms. Lorenzo would like you to provide her with the following information.

1. Ms. Lorenzo wants a pie chart that compares the monthly sales for the tanning products.

2. Based on the monthly total dollar sales, identify the salon's top two selling items.

3. Based on the monthly total dollar sales, which salon item appears to be the least popular?

Test Your Design

After you create the Salon workbook, you should test your design. Make the following changes to the Salon workbook.

1. Ms. Lorenzo now offers two new fitness packages. Modify your worksheets to reflect the new fitness membership packages. Figure 3 provides the unit sales data for each new package. The one-month fitness membership package costs $35.99, and the three-month membership package costs $66.99. (Use this data for all four weeks.)

Figure 3: Fitness Package Unit Sales

Timeka's Tanning Salon
New Fitness Packages
Unit Sales

Fitness Package	Sunday	Monday	Tuesday	Wednesday	Thursday	Friday	Saturday
One-Month Fitness Membership	5	3	4	2	1	7	3
Three-Month Fitness Membership	1	2	0	4	2	3	5

2. Using Week 4 as a guide, prepare a PivotTable that compares each item's total dollar sales. Ms. Lorenzo wants to see each category on a separate page.

Deliverables

In order to satisfactorily complete this tutorial, you should build the workbook as described in the tutorial and then prepare both written and oral presentations. Unless otherwise specified, submit the following deliverables to your professor.

1. A written report discussing any assumptions you have made about the tutorial and the key elements of the tutorial. Additionally, what features did you add to make the workbook more functional? User friendly? (Please note that these assumptions cannot violate any of the requirements specified above and must be approved by your professor.)

2. A printout of each worksheet.

3. A printout of each worksheet's formulas.

4. An electronic, working copy of your workbook that meets the criteria mentioned in the case scenario and specifications sections.

5. Results for each question posed above. (A memo to your instructor discussing these results should also be provided.)

6. As mentioned above, you should prepare an oral presentation. (Your instructor will establish the time allocated to your presentation.) You should use a presentation package and discuss the key features of your workbook. Also, discuss how the workbook is beneficial for Ms. Lorenzo. What additional information should be included in the workbook to make it more useful?

Part II: Workbook Preparation

Design Preparation

If you have not already done so, please read Part I of this tutorial.

To satisfy Ms. Lorenzo's design specifications, you will develop a workbook that contains weekly, summary, and price list worksheets. You will prepare four weekly worksheets. Each weekly worksheet summarizes the daily sales activity for its week. The weekly worksheets will be named Week1, Week2, Week3, and Week4. The summary worksheet is named Summary and consolidates the data from the weekly worksheets. The price list worksheet is named PriceList and contains the current price list for the salon. The weekly worksheets use the price list worksheet's data to calculate the daily dollar sales.

The Salon workbook preparation can be broken into four primary activities. These activities involve preparing the initial workbook, creating the PriceList worksheet, creating the weekly worksheets, and creating a Summary worksheet. Each activity is described below. For reference purposes, Figure 2 shows the completed PriceList worksheet. Figure 46 shows the Week1 worksheet. Figure 47 shows the completed Summary worksheet. (The data shown in these figures do not reflect the updates required by the Test Your Design section.)

Activity 1: Initial Workbook Preparation

The initial workbook preparation involves three major tasks: creating and saving a new workbook, inserting three additional worksheets, and renaming the worksheets. Each task is reviewed below. (Please keep in mind that you should periodically save your work.)

Task 1: Create and Save a New Workbook

To perform the initial workbook preparation, perform the following steps:

1. Start Microsoft Excel.
2. Create a new workbook.
3. Save the new workbook as Salon.

Task 2: Insert Three New Worksheets

To insert a new worksheet, you can:

1. From the Cells group located on the Home tab, click the arrow on the Insert button.
2. Select the Insert Sheet command. See Figure 4.

3. Repeat this step 2 times.

Figure 4: Cells Group

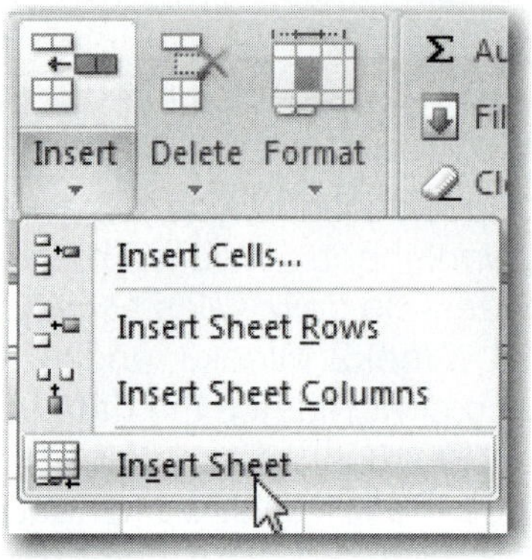

Task 3: Rename the Worksheets

To rename the worksheets, you can:

1. Right click the sheet tab name, and then select the Rename command. Type the worksheet's new name.

2. Repeat this process for each worksheet. Name the worksheets: PriceList, Summary, Week1, Week2, Week3, and Week4. (Hint: Keep the worksheets in this order.)

<u>Activity 2: Create the PriceList Worksheet</u>

The PriceList worksheet contains the current prices for the salon items, and serves as a price lookup table for the weekly worksheets. (The weekly worksheets use VLOOKUP functions to reference the prices contained in the PriceList worksheet.) Creating the PriceList worksheet involves designing and formatting the PriceList worksheet, entering data into the PriceList worksheet, and assigning a range name to the price list. As a point of reference, Figure 2 shows the completed PriceList worksheet.

Task 1: Design and Format the PriceList Worksheet

To prepare the PriceList worksheet, you should:

1. Make the PriceList worksheet your active worksheet.

2. Adjust row 1's height to 30. Adjust row 2's height to 21. To adjust the row height, you can:

   a. Select the row.

   b. From the Cells group located on the Home tab, click the Format button. Then, select the Row Height command. See Figure 5.

Figure 5: Format Options

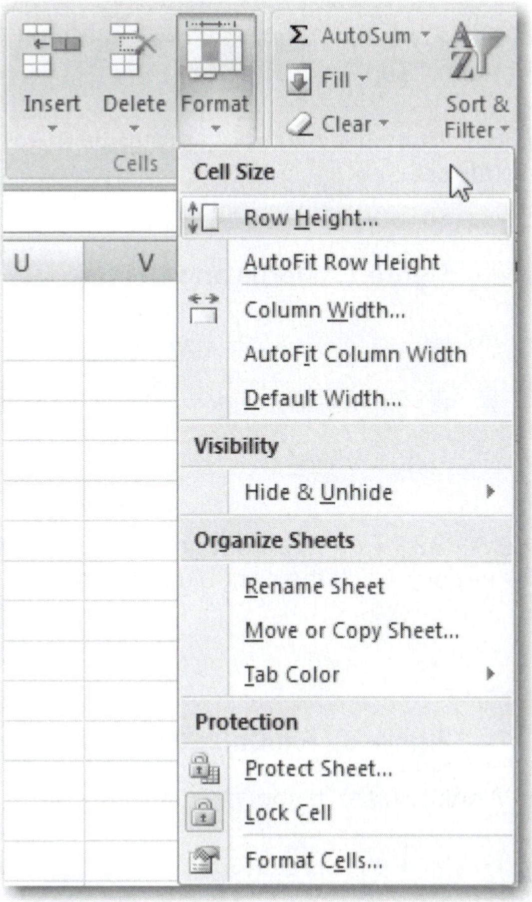

3. Adjust column A's width to 49. Adjust column B's width to 10. To set a column's width, you can:

    a. Select the column.

    b. From the Cells group located on the Home tab, click the Format button. Then, select the Column Width command.

4. Enter the text "Timeka's Tanning Salon" into cell A1. Set the font size for A1 to 26. Bold the text. See Figure 6.

Figure 6: Font Group

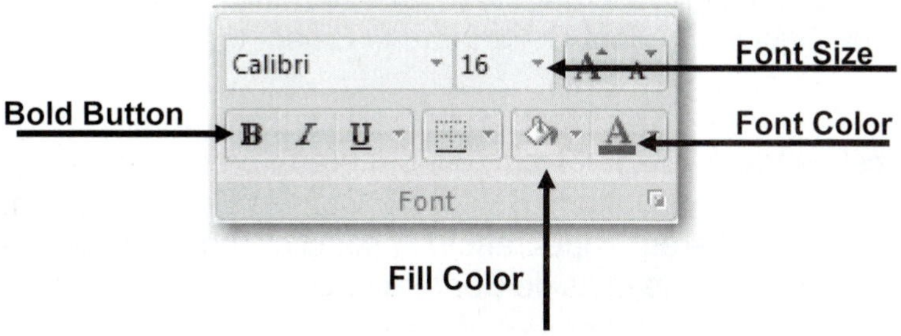

5. Enter the text "Price List" into cell A2. Set the font size for A2 to 16. Bold the text.

6. Select cells A1 and B1. From the Alignment group on the Home tab, click the Merge and Center button. See Figure 7.

7. Select cells A2 and B2. From the Alignment group on the Home tab, click the Merge and Center button.

Figure 7: Merge and Center

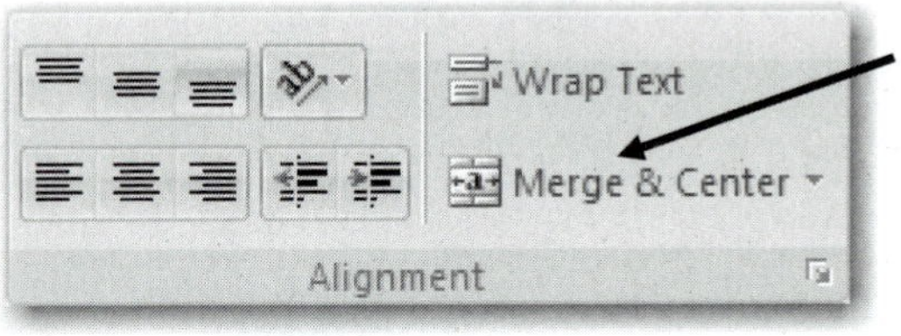

8. Select the cell range A1:B2. From the Font group on the Home tab, click the arrow beside the Fill Color button. Click the dark blue option (fourth column, fifth row). See Figure 8.

Figure 8: Fill Color Selection

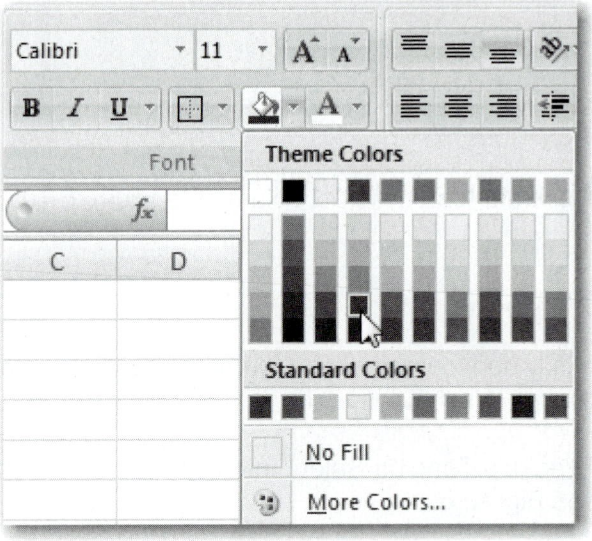

9. If necessary, reselect the cell range A1:B2. From the Font group on the Home tab, click the arrow beside the Font Color button. Select the white option. See Figure 9.

10. Select the cell range A1:B20. From the Font group on the Home tab, click the arrow beside the Borders button. Select the Outside Borders option. (Note: Your button may have a different appearance. If so, click the arrow beside the Borders button, and then select the Outside Borders option.) See Figure 10.

Figure 9: Font Color Selection

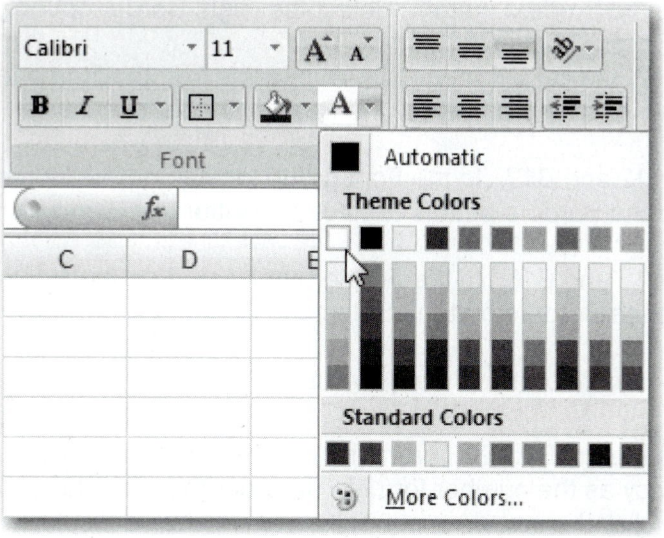

Figure 10: Border Options

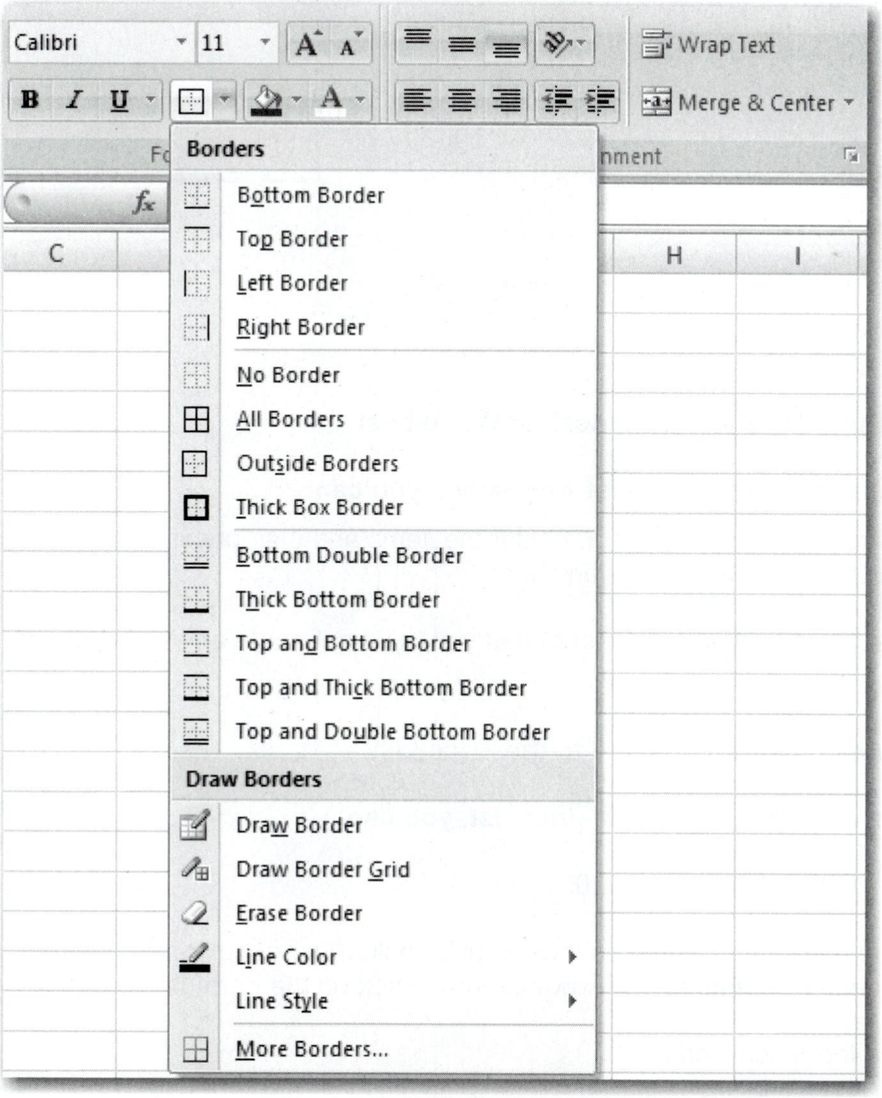

11. Select the cell range A3:A20. In the Font group located on the Home tab, click the arrow beside the Borders button. Select the Right Border option.

12. Select cells A7 and B7. In the Font group located on the Home tab, click the arrow beside the Borders button. Select the Bottom Border option.

13. Select cells A12 and B12. In the Font group located on the Home tab, click the arrow beside the Borders button. Select the Bottom Border option.

14. Select cells A18 and B18. In the Font group located on the Home tab, click the arrow beside the Borders button. Select the Bottom Border option.

15. Apply a bold format to the cell range A3:B20.

16. Select the cell range B3:B20. From the Number group located on the Home tab, select Currency as the number format. (In order to locate the currency format, you may need to click the arrow.) Your dollar values should display with two decimal places. See Figure 11.

17. Save your work.

Figure 11: Number Format

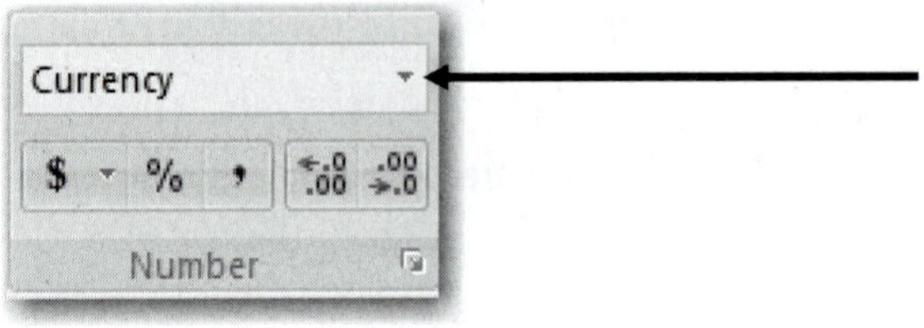

Task 2: Enter Data into the PriceList Worksheet

To enter data into the PriceList worksheet, you can:

1. Reference Figure 2, and then enter the items and their prices into the cell range A3:B20 of your PriceList worksheet.

2. Take a moment and make sure that you have not made any typing errors.

Task 3: Assign a Range Name to the Price List

To assign a range name to the price list, you can:

1. Select the cell range A3:B20.

2. In the name box located on the Formula toolbar, type the name “pricelist”. Press the enter key. Figure 12 shows the name box on the Formula bar.

3. Save the Salon workbook.

Figure 12: Name Box

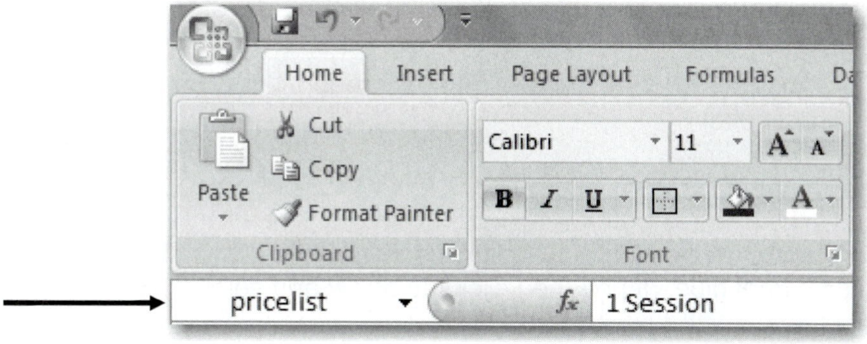

Activity 3: Create the Weekly Worksheets

Since the four weekly worksheets have the same design and formatting requirements, you can group the worksheets and then format and design their layout at the same time. To properly prepare the worksheets, you need to group the worksheets, format and design the worksheets, enter data into the worksheets, and enter formulas into the worksheets. When creating the formulas to calculate the daily sales, your formulas will reference data contained in the PriceList worksheet.

Task 1: Group the Week1, Week2, Week3, and Week4 Worksheets

To group the weekly worksheets, you can:

1. Click the Week1 sheet tab. While holding down the Shift key, click the Week4 sheet tab. (When a worksheet is part of a worksheet group, its sheet tab has a white background. Figure 13 shows that the Week1, Week2, Week3, and Week4 worksheets are grouped. In Figure 13, Week1 is the active sheet. Keep in mind that any changes made to the Week1 worksheet will also be made to the Week2, Week3, and Week4 worksheets.)

Figure 13: Grouped Worksheets

Task 2: Format and Design the Week1, Week2, Week3, and Week4 Worksheets

To format and design the weekly worksheets, you should:

1. Set row 1's height to 30; set row 2's height to 21, and set row 3's row height to 26.

2. Adjust column A's width to 38. Adjust column R's width to 16.

3. In cell A1, enter the text "Timeka's Tanning Salon".

4. Select the cell range A1:R1. From the Alignment group located on the Home tab, click the Merge and Center button. Set the font size to 26. Click the Bold button.

5. In cell A2, enter the text "Weekly Sales". Set the font size to 16. Click the Bold button.

6. Select the cell range A2:R2. From the Alignment group on the Home tab, click the Merge and Center button.

7. Select the cell range A1:R3.

8. From the Font group on the Home tab, click the Fill Color button. (The Fill Color button should be dark blue. If not, then click the arrow and select the dark blue option (fourth column, fifth row).

9. From the Font group on the Home tab, click the Font Color button. (If the Font Color button is not white, then click the arrow and select the white option.)

10. In cell A3, enter the words "Plan Type". In cell A4, enter the word "Item". In cell B4, enter the word "Category". Bold and center these text entries.

11. In cell C3, type the word "Sunday". Select the cell range C3:D3. From the Alignment group located on the Home tab, click the Merge and Center button.

12. In cell E3, type the word "Monday". Select the cell range E3:F3. From the Alignment group located on the Home tab, click the Merge and Center button.

13. In cell G3, type the word "Tuesday". Select the cell range G3:H3. From the Alignment group located on the Home tab, click the Merge and Center button.

14. In cell I3, type the word "Wednesday". Select the cell range I3:J3. From the Alignment group located on the Home tab, click the Merge and Center button.

15. In cell K3, type the word "Thursday". Select the cell range K3:L3. From the Alignment group located on the Home tab, click the Merge and Center button.

16. In cell M3, type the word "Friday". Select the cell range M3:N3. From the Alignment group located on the Home tab, click the Merge and Center button.

17. In cell O3, type the word "Saturday". Select the cell range O3:P3. From the Alignment group located on the Home tab, click the Merge and Center button.

18. In cell Q3, type the words "Total Weekly Sales". Select the cell range Q3:R3. From the Alignment group located on the Home tab, click the Merge and Center button.

19. Select the cell range C3:R3. From the Font group located on the Home tab, click the Bold button.

20. In cell C4, type "Sun Units". In cell D4, type "Sun Sales".

21. In cell E4, type "Mon Units". In cell F4, type "Mon Sales".

22. In cell G4, type "Tue Units". In cell H4, type "Tue Sales".

23. In cell I4, type "Wed Units". In cell J4, type "Wed Sales".

24. In cell K4, type "Thu Units". In cell L4, type "Thu Sales".

25. In cell M4, type "Fri Units". In cell N4, type "Fri Sales".

26. In cell O4, type "Sat Units". In cell P4, type "Sat Sales".

27. In Q4, type "Total Units". In Cell R4, type "Total Dollar Sales".

28. Select the cell range C4:R4. From the Alignment group located on the Home tab, click the Center button. Click the Bold button in the Font group.

29. Set the font size for cell range A4:R23 to 8.

30. Enter the data from Figure 14 into the cell range A5:B22 of your weekly worksheets. (As the data are used by the VLOOKUP function, you should make sure that you have not made typing errors.)

31. Select the cell range A5:A22. From the Font group located on the Home tab, click the Bold button.

32. Select the cell range B5:B22. From the Alignment group located on the Home tab, click the Center button. Click the Bold button.

33. Save your work.

Figure 14: Data for Cell Range A5:B22

Plan Type	
Item	Category
1 Session	SE
5 Sessions	SE
10 Sessions	SE
15 Sessions	SE
20 Sessions	SE
One Month Unlimited	SP
Monthly Special	SP
Loyal Customer	SP
Referral	SP
Yearly Enrollment	SP
Bronze 12 oz Lotion	PR
Golden 12 oz Lotion	PR
Bronze 12 oz Oil	PR
Golden 12 oz Oil	PR
Timeka's Tan Enhancer 12 oz Lotion	PR
Timeka's Tan Enhancer 16 oz Lotion	PR
6-Month Fitness Membership	FC
Yearly Fitness Membership	FC

Task 3: Enter Data into the Weekly Worksheets

To enter data into the weekly worksheets, you should:

1. Ungroup your worksheets. To ungroup your worksheets, you can:

    a. Right click the Week1 sheet tab.

    b. Select the Ungroup Sheets option from the shortcut menu.

2. If the Week1 sheet tab is not selected, click the Week1 sheet tab.

3. Enter the unit sales data for the Week1 worksheet. Figure 15 provides the sales data for the Week1 worksheet.

Figure 15: Week 1 Unit Sales

Week 1 Unit Sales							
	Sunday	Monday	Tuesday	Wednesday	Thursday	Friday	Saturday
Item	Units	Units	Units	Units	Units	Units	Units
1 Session	25	25	6	30	10	10	3
5 Sessions	10	10	5	10	9	2	2
10 Sessions	5	5	4	12	4	7	8
15 Sessions	5	5	13	5	5	9	10
20 Sessions	1	1	7	4	6	4	12
One Month Unlimited	25	25	10	10	5	4	6
Monthly Special	10	10	9	15	10	12	4
Loyal Customer	15	15	6	2	9	2	2
Referral	12	12	14	12	8	5	2
Yearly Enrollment	10	10	22	6	2	1	4
Bronze 12 oz Lotion	22	22	12	4	4	4	2
Golden 12 oz Lotion	10	10	4	3	5	3	5
Bronze 12 oz Oil	19	19	2	2	9	2	1
Golden 12 oz Oil	18	18	2	1	8	7	8
Timeka's Tan Enhancer 12 oz Lotion	14	14	4	5	7	1	9
Timeka's Tan Enhancer for 16 oz Lotion	2	2	0	5	12	1	0
6-Month Fitness Membership	12	12	1	0	2	5	2
Yearly Fitness Membership	19	19	2	0	10	2	1

4. Click the Week2 sheet tab.

5. Enter the unit sales data for the Week2 worksheet. Figure 16 provides the sales data for the Week2 worksheet.

Figure 16: Week 2 Unit Sales

Week 2 Unit Sales							
	Sunday	Monday	Tuesday	Wednesday	Thursday	Friday	Saturday
Item	Units	Units	Units	Units	Units	Units	Units
1 Session	12	1	1	1	5	8	10
5 Sessions	4	5	6	7	8	10	1
10 Sessions	5	1	2	3	4	7	8
15 Sessions	9	1	2	3	1	3	3
20 Sessions	5	1	2	4	7	8	10
One Month Unlimited	1	10	2	2	2	9	10
Monthly Special	4	7	1	10	15	1	12
Loyal Customer	5	2	3	1	0	4	1
Referral	1	5	4	9	1	0	5
Yearly Enrollment	1	2	3	8	0	1	2
Bronze 12 oz Lotion	5	7	1	1	2	10	12
Golden 12 oz Lotion	5	4	5	6	8	10	1
Bronze 12 oz Oil	3	8	9	10	1	1	8
Golden 12 oz Oil	0	4	5	5	5	6	7
Timeka's Tan Enhancer 12 oz Lotion	0	5	6	8	7	9	10
Timeka's Tan Enhancer for 16 oz Lotion	5	0	5	6	7	8	10
6-Month Fitness Membership	8	4	5	6	6	1	2
Yearly Fitness Membership	2	3	1	5	2	0	1

6. Click the Week3 sheet tab.

7. Enter the unit sales data for the Week3 worksheet. Figure 17 provides the sales data for the Week3 worksheet.

Figure 17: Week 3 Unit Sales

Week 3 Unit Sales							
	Sunday	Monday	Tuesday	Wednesday	Thursday	Friday	Saturday
Item	Units	Units	Units	Units	Units	Units	Units
1 Session	1	1	2	6	10	7	4
5 Sessions	3	2	0	7	2	5	4
10 Sessions	4	2	0	8	1	2	4
15 Sessions	7	2	0	2	2	2	6
20 Sessions	2	2	3	2	8	1	2
One Month Unlimited	2	5	3	1	0	5	5
Monthly Special	0	4	2	0	0	8	2
Loyal Customer	0	3	8	0	9	9	10
Referral	0	1	2	4	1	6	4
Yearly Enrollment	0	3	2	5	2	2	2
Bronze 12 oz Lotion	1	8	2	6	3	2	3
Golden 12 oz Lotion	1	5	4	1	4	2	8
Bronze 12 oz Oil	1	2	8	2	2	5	2
Golden 12 oz Oil	0	2	6	6	9	5	7
Timeka's Tan Enhancer 12 oz Lotion	0	0	7	4	2	1	2
Timeka's Tan Enhancer for 16 oz Lotion	5	1	2	2	1	1	2
6-Month Fitness Membership	1	2	2	8	1	5	2
Yearly Fitness Membership	1	2	1	1	1	4	2

8. Click the Week4 sheet tab.

9. Enter the unit sales data for the Week4 worksheet. Figure 18 provides the sales data for the Week4 worksheet.

Figure 18: Week 4 Unit Sales

Week 4 Unit Sales							
	Sunday	Monday	Tuesday	Wednesday	Thursday	Friday	Saturday
Item	Units	Units	Units	Units	Units	Units	Units
1 Session	2	4	2	7	7	1	0
5 Sessions	1	2	2	6	2	2	0
10 Sessions	1	5	2	5	2	1	0
15 Sessions	0	5	5	2	1	2	2
20 Sessions	1	6	2	6	3	1	2
One Month Unlimited	5	3	2	4	1	1	2
Monthly Special	2	1	2	1	1	1	2
Loyal Customer	2	1	1	1	4	1	1
Referral	2	1	2	1	2	1	1
Yearly Enrollment	1	1	12	1	1	3	1
Bronze 12 oz Lotion	3	1	3	2	1	3	1
Golden 12 oz Lotion	3	2	2	3	1	3	4
Bronze 12 oz Oil	3	5	3	5	1	1	4
Golden 12 oz Oil	4	6	2	4	1	2	4
Timeka's Tan Enhancer 12 oz Lotion	0	0	1	1	1	3	4
Timeka's Tan Enhancer for 16 oz Lotion	0	0	2	1	1	1	6
6-Month Fitness Membership	2	3	2	2	1	2	3
Yearly Fitness Membership	2	2	3	3	1	0	4

Task 4: Create Formulas for the Weekly Worksheets

To create the necessary formulas for the weekly worksheets, you can:

1. Group the Week1, Week2, Week3, and Week4 worksheets.
2. In cell D5, insert the following formula: =VLOOKUP($A5,pricelist,2,False)*C5. (In the formula, notice that the cell reference $A5 is a mixed cell reference. For cell D5, Microsoft Excel will use the value in A5 to look up the price of the item, which is found in column 2 of the lookup table. Excel will then multiply the return value by the contents of C5.)
3. Copy the formula from D5 to the cell ranges D6:D22, F5:F22, H5:H22, J5:J22, L5:L22, N5:N22, and P5:P22.
4. If necessary, format the cells containing dollar values to a currency format with 2 decimal places. If necessary, adjust the column widths so the dollar values show.
5. Insert the following formula into cell Q5: =C5+E5+G5+I5+K5+M5+O5.
6. Copy the formula from Q5 to the cell range Q6:Q22.
7. Insert the following formula into cell R5: =D5+F5+H5+J5+L5+N5+P5.
8. Copy the formula from R5 to the cell range R6:R22.

9. If necessary, apply the currency format with two decimal places to the cell range R5:R22.

10. Make cell A23 your active cell. In the Font group located on the Home tab, click the Bold button. In cell A23, type "Total Daily Sales".

11. Insert a formula that will sum the total dollar sales for each item. To sum the dollar sales for each item, you can:

    a. Make D23 your active cell.

    b. In the Editing group located on the Home tab, click the AutoSum button. See Figure 19.

Figure 19: AutoSum Button

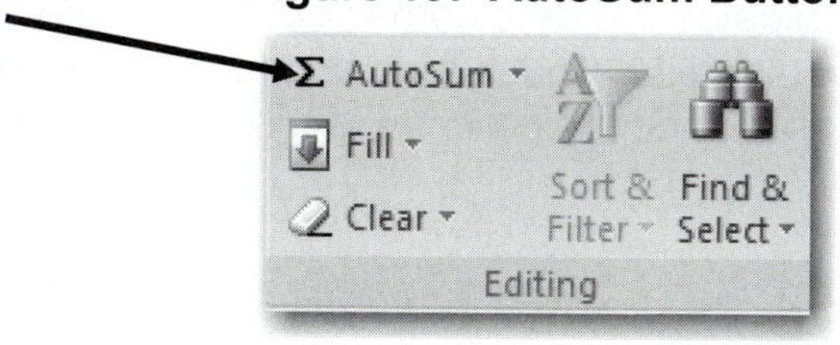

    c. Make sure the cell range is correct. If it is, press the enter key. If it is not, then edit the cell range.

    d. Repeat this process for cells F23, H23, J23, L23, N23, and P23.

12. In cell R23, include a grand total. To sum the dollar sales for each item, you can:

    a. Make R23 your active cell.

    b. In the Editing group located on the Home tab, click the AutoSum button.

    c. Make sure the cell range is correct. If it is, press the enter key. If it is not, then edit the cell range.

    d. If necessary, apply the currency format with two decimal places to cell R23.

13. If necessary, display all unit sales with a number format and no decimal points.

14. Select the cell range B23:R23. In the Font group located on the Home tab, click the Bold button. (You want the contents of row 23 to be bold.)

15. Select the cell range A22:R22. In the Font group, click the arrow beside the Borders button. Select the Bottom Border command.

16. Select the cell range A1:R23.

17. From the Font group on the Home tab, click the arrow beside the Border button. Select the Outside Borders command.

18. Select the cell range A3:R3. From the Font group on the Home tab, click the Border button arrow and then select the Bottom Border option.

19. Select the cell range A4:R4. From the Font group on the Home tab, click the Border button arrow and then select the Bottom Border option.

20. Ungroup the worksheets.

21. Save your work.

Activity 4: Summary Worksheet Preparation

The Summary worksheet consolidates the data contained in the four weekly worksheets. Preparation of the Summary worksheet involves formatting and designing the Summary worksheet and creating formulas with cell references to the weekly worksheets.

Task 1: Format and Design the Summary Worksheet

To format and design the Summary worksheet, perform the following steps.

1. Click the Summary sheet tab.

2. Set row 1's height to 30; set row 2's height to 20.25, and set row 3's row height to 26.

3. Adjust column A's width to 38. Adjust column L's width to 16.

4. In cell A1, enter "Timeka's Tanning Salon".

5. Select the cell range A1:L1. From the Alignment group located on the Home tab, click the Merge and Center button. Set the font size to 26. From the Font group located on the Home tab, click the Bold button.

6. In cell A2, enter the text "Monthly Sales Summary". (Enter the name of the current month before the word "monthly". If you prefer, you may use the month of October.) Set the font size to 16. Click the Bold button.

7. Select the cell range A2:L2. From the Alignment group located on the Home tab, click the Merge and Center button.

8. Select the cell range A1:L3.

9. In the Font group on the Home tab, click the Fill Color button. Click the Font Color button. (The fill color should be dark blue, and the font color should be white.)

10. In cell A3, enter the words “Plan Type”. In cell A4, enter the text “Item”. In cell B4, enter the word “Category”. Bold and center these text entries.

11. In cell C3, type the text “Week 1”. Select the cell range C3:D3, then click the Merge and Center button.

12. In cell E3, type the text “Week 2”. Select the cell range E3:F3, then click the Merge and Center button.

13. In cell G3, type the text “Week 3”. Select the cell range G3:H3, then click the Merge and Center button.

14. In cell I3, type “Week 4”. Select the cell range I3:J3, then click the Merge and Center button.

15. In cell K3, type the text “Total Weekly Product Sales”. Select the cell range K3:L3, then click the Merge and Center button.

16. Select the cell range C3:L3. Click the Bold button.

17. In cell C4, type “W1 Units”.

18. In cell D4, type “W1 Sales”.

19. In cell E4 type “W2 Units”.

20. In cell F4, type “W2 Sales”.

21. In cell G4, type “W3 Units”.

22. In cell H4, type “W3 Sales”.

23. In cell I4, type “W4 Units”.

24. In cell J4, type “W4 Sales”.

25. In cell K4, type “Total Units”.

26. In cell L4, type “Total Dollar Sales”.

27. Set the font size for the cell range A4:L4 to 8.

28. Click the Week1 sheet tab; copy the cell range A5:B22.

29. Click the Summary sheet tab; click cell A5. From the Clipboard group located on the Home tab, click the Paste button.

30. If necessary, select the cell range A5:L22. Set the font size for the range to 8.

Task 2: Create Formulas for the Summary Worksheet

To create formulas for the Summary worksheet, perform the following steps.

1. In cell C5, type the formula =Week1!Q5. Copy this formula to the cell range C6:C22.
2. In cell D5, type the formula =Week1!R5. Copy this formula to cell range D6:D22.
3. In cell E5, type the formula =Week2!Q5. Copy this formula to cell range E6:E22.
4. In cell F5, type the formula =Week2!R5. Copy this formula to cell range F6:F22.
5. In cell G5, type the formula =Week3!Q5. Copy this formula to cell range G6:G22.
6. In cell H5, type the formula =Week3!R5. Copy this formula to cell range H6:H22.
7. In cell I5, type the formula =Week4!Q5. Copy this formula to cell range I6:I22.
8. In cell J5, type the formula =Week4!R5. Copy this formula to cell range J6:J22.
9. In cell K5, insert the formula =C5+E5+G5+I5. Copy this formula to the cell range K6:K22. (If necessary, format cells K5:K22 to a general number format.)
10. In cell L5, insert the formula =D5+F5+H5+J5. Copy this formula to the cell range L6:L22.
11. Format the cell range L5:L22 to a currency format with two decimal places.
12. Bold the cell range L5:L22.
13. Apply the currency format to cell ranges D5:D22, F5:F22, H5:H22, and J5:J22.
14. Select the cell range A1:L22. From the Font group on the Home tab, click the Border button arrow and then select the Outside Borders option.
15. Select the cell range A3:L3. From the Font group on the Home tab, click the Border button arrow and then select the Bottom Border option.
16. Select the cell range A4:L4. From the Font group on the Home tab, click the Border button arrow and then select the Bottom Border option. Click the Bold button.
17. Select the cell range A4:L22. From the Tables group located on the Insert tab, click the Table button. See Figure 20.

Figure 20: Table Button

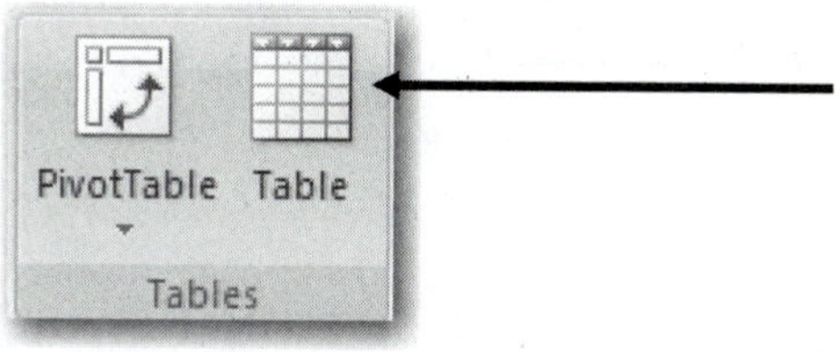

18. In the Create Table dialog box, make sure the cell range is correct and the My table has headers option is selected. Click the OK button. See Figure 21.

Figure 21: Create Table Dialog Box

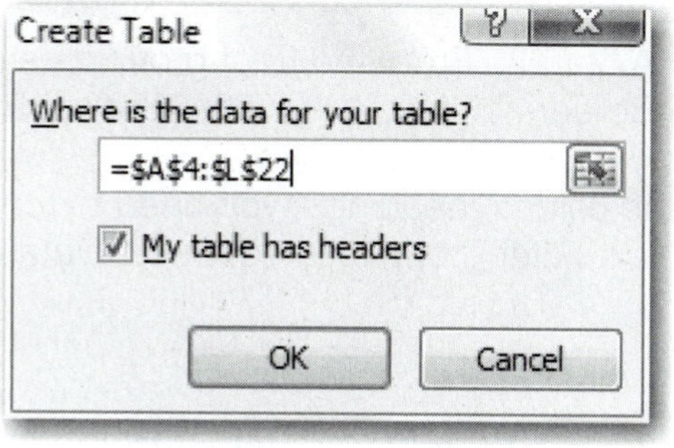

19. In the Table Style Options group located on the Design tab, click the Total Row option. See Figure 22.

Figure 22: Total Row Option

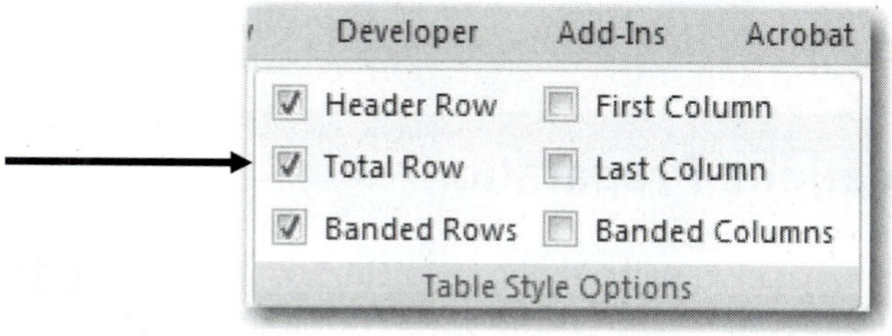

20. Select the cell range C23:L23. From the Editing group located on the Home tab, click the AutoSum button. See Figure 23.

Figure 23: AutoSum Button

21. If necessary, reselect the cell range C23:L23. From the Font group located on the Home tab, click the Bold button. Make sure the font size is set to 8.

22. Select the cell range A4:L23. From the Table Styles group located on the Design tab, select None as the table style.

23. Select the cell range A22:L22. From the Font group located on the Home tab, click the arrow beside the Borders button. Select the Bottom Border option.

24. If arrows appear by the column headings, you need to turn off the filter. To turn off the filter, from the Sort & Filter group located on the Data tab, click the Filter button. See Figure 24.

Figure 24: Filter Button

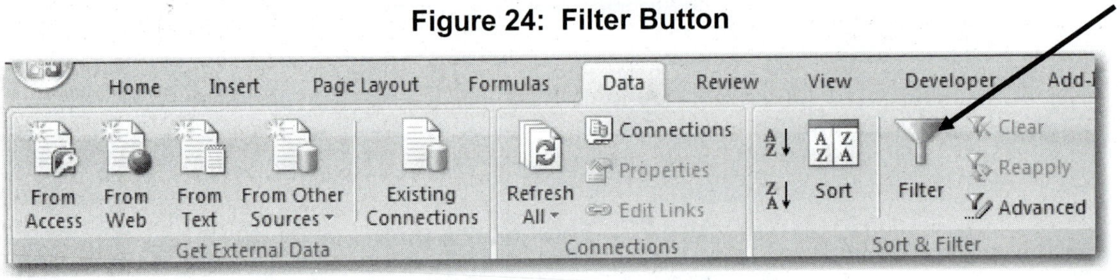

Information Specifications Preparation

In each MIS Cases: Decision Making with Application Software, Fourth Edition spreadsheet case, you will use your newly created workbook to provide the case's main character with information about his/her business. For this tutorial, you will use the Salon workbook to identify the most popular tanning sessions and the total sales by category. The Filter and PivotTable tools can satisfy these information requests. You can use the Filter tool to identify the most popular tanning sessions, and the PivotTable tool can show the total sales by category. Additionally, you are asked to prepare a pie chart that compares the monthly sales for the tanning products, identify the salon's top two selling items, and identify the least popular salon item. The chart tools can help prepare the pie chart, and the Filter tool can help identify the popular and unpopular items.

Task 1: Identify the Most Popular Tanning Sessions

To identify the most popular tanning sessions, you can:

1. Click the Summary worksheet tab.

2. From the Table Style Options group located on the Design tab, click the Total Row button. (The total row should not display in the worksheet.)

3. Click the arrow beside the Category field name. (If the arrows are not showing, you need to click the Filter button. The Filter button is located in the Sort & Filter group on the Data tab.) See Figure 25.

4. As Ms. Lorenzo wants to view the most popular tanning sessions, click the Select All option and then click the SE option in the category list. Click the OK button. The list is now filtered based on the SE option. Figure 26 shows the filtered results.

5. Click the Filter button. (This step turns off the Filter.)

Figure 25: Filter Example

	A	B	C	D	E	F	G	H	I	J	K	L
1	Timeka's Tanning Salon											
2	October Monthly Sales Summary											
3	Plan Type		Week 1		Week 2		Week 3		Week 4		Total Weekly Product Sales	
4	Item	Categor	W1 Uni	W1 Sale	W2 Uni	W2 Sale	W3 Uni	W3 Sale	W4 Uni	W4 Sale	Total Uni	Total Dollar Sales
5	1 Session	SE	109	$545.00	38	$190.00	31	$155.00	23	$115.00	201	$1,005.00
6	5 Sessions	SE	48	$1,200.00	41	$1,025.00	23	$575.00	15	$375.00	127	$3,175.00
7	10 Sessions	SE	45	$2,250.00	30	$1,500.00	21	$1,050.00	16	$800.00	112	$5,600.00
8	15 Sessions	SE	52	$3,900.00	22	$1,650.00	21	$1,575.00	17	$1,275.00	112	$8,400.00
9	20 Sessions	SE	35	$3,500.00	37	$3,700.00	20	$2,000.00	21	$2,100.00	113	$11,300.00
10	One Month Unlimited	SP	85	$2,975.00	36	$1,260.00	21	$735.00	18	$630.00	160	$5,600.00
11	Monthly Special	SP	70	$2,100.00	50	$1,500.00	16	$480.00	10	$300.00	146	$4,380.00
12	Loyal Customer	SP	51	$1,529.49	16	$479.84	39	$1,169.61	11	$329.89	117	$3,508.83
13	Referral	SP	65	$1,949.35	25	$749.75	18	$539.82	10	$299.90	118	$3,538.82
14	Yearly Enrollment	SP	55	$19,250.00	17	$5,950.00	16	$5,600.00	20	$7,000.00	108	$37,800.00
15	Bronze 12 oz Lotion	PR	70	$1,749.30	38	$949.62	25	$624.75	14	$349.86	147	$3,673.53
16	Golden 12 oz Lotion	PR	40	$1,119.60	39	$1,091.61	25	$699.75	18	$503.82	122	$3,414.78
17	Bronze 12 oz Oil	PR	54	$1,079.46	40	$799.60	22	$439.78	22	$439.78	138	$2,758.62
18	Golden 12 oz Oil	PR	62	$1,363.38	32	$703.68	35	$769.65	23	$505.77	152	$3,342.48
19	Timeka's Tan Enhancer 12 oz Lotion	PR	54	$1,511.46	45	$1,259.55	16	$447.84	10	$279.90	125	$3,498.75
20	Timeka's Tan Enhancer 16 oz Lotion	PR	22	$769.78	41	$1,434.59	14	$489.86	11	$384.89	88	$3,079.12
21	6-Month Fitness Membership	FC	34	$6,153.66	32	$5,791.68	21	$3,800.79	15	$2,714.85	102	$18,460.98
22	Yearly Fitness Membership	FC	53	$14,892.47	14	$3,933.86	12	$3,371.88	15	$4,214.85	94	$26,413.06

Figure 26: Filtered Results

	A	B	C	D	E	F	G	H	I	J	K	L
1	Timeka's Tanning Salon											
2	October Monthly Sales Summary											
3	Plan Type		Week 1		Week 2		Week 3		Week 4		Total Weekly Product Sales	
4	Item	Categor	W1 Uni	W1 Sale	W2 Uni	W2 Sale	W3 Uni	W3 Sale	W4 Uni	W4 Sale	Total Uni	Total Dollar Sales
5	1 Session	SE	109	$545.00	38	$190.00	31	$155.00	23	$115.00	201	$1,005.00
6	5 Sessions	SE	48	$1,200.00	41	$1,025.00	23	$575.00	15	$375.00	127	$3,175.00
7	10 Sessions	SE	45	$2,250.00	30	$1,500.00	21	$1,050.00	16	$800.00	112	$5,600.00
8	15 Sessions	SE	52	$3,900.00	22	$1,650.00	21	$1,575.00	17	$1,275.00	112	$8,400.00
9	20 Sessions	SE	35	$3,500.00	37	$3,700.00	20	$2,000.00	21	$2,100.00	113	$11,300.00

Task 2: Show Total Sales by Category

To view the total monthly sales by category, you can use the PivotTable tool. To prepare a PivotTable, you can:

1. In the Summary sheet, select the cell range A4:L22.

2. From the Tables group located on the Insert tab, click the PivotTable button. See Figure 27.

Figure 27: PivotTable Button

3. In the Create PivotTable dialog box, specify that your data are in a table or range, and you want the PivotTable placed in a new worksheet. See Figure 28. Click the OK button.

Figure 28: Create PivotTable Dialog Box

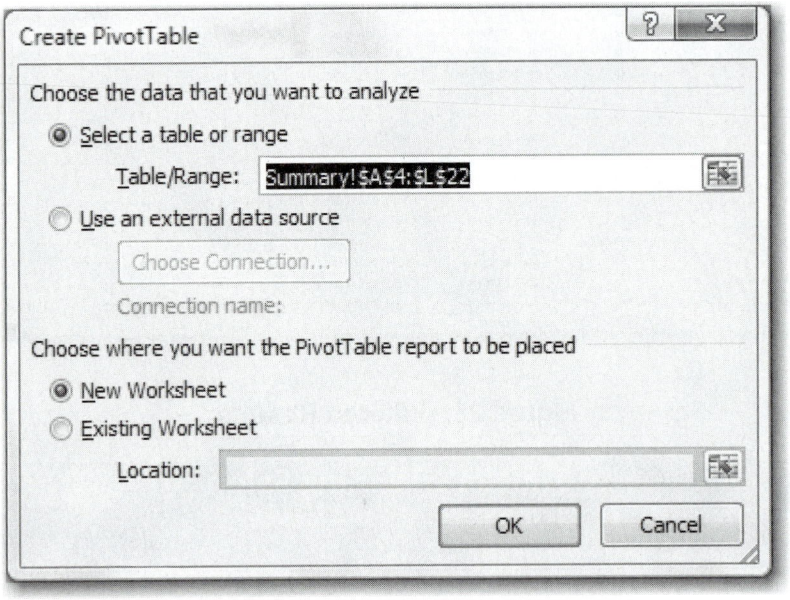

4. Specify the PivotTable's layout. Figure 29 shows the PivotTable's on screen report layout.

Figure 29: PivotTable Layout

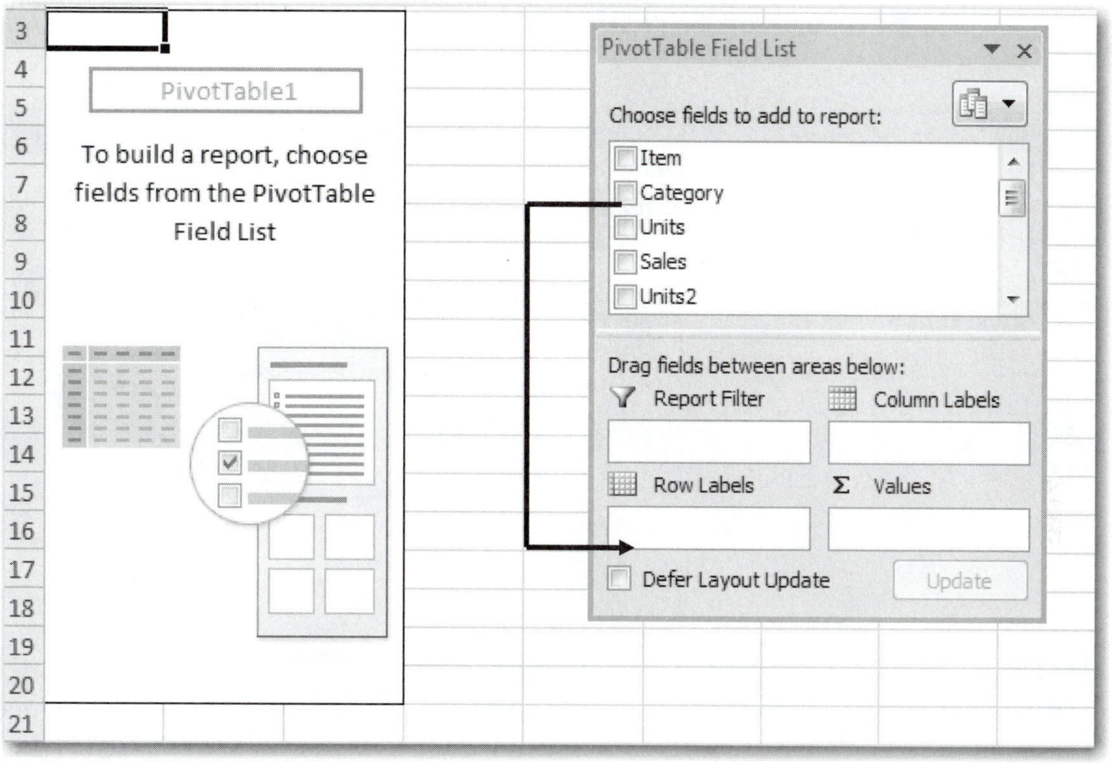

5. In the PivotTable Field List dialog box, drag the Category field name to the Row Labels box. Next, drag the Total Dollar Sales field to the Values box. (You will need to scroll down to locate the Total Dollar Sales field name.) See Figure 30.

6. In the PivotTable, right click on the field name "Sum of Total Dollar Sales". A shortcut menu will appear. See Figure 31. Select the Value Field Settings command.

7. In the Value Field Settings dialog box, type "Total Sales" as the custom name. See Figure 32.

8. Click the Number format button, and select the currency format. Click the OK button. Click the OK button. Your PivotTable should now resemble Figure 33.

9. Right click on the sheet tab. Rename the worksheet to "PivotTable".

10. Save your work.

Figure 30: PivotTable and PivotTable Field List

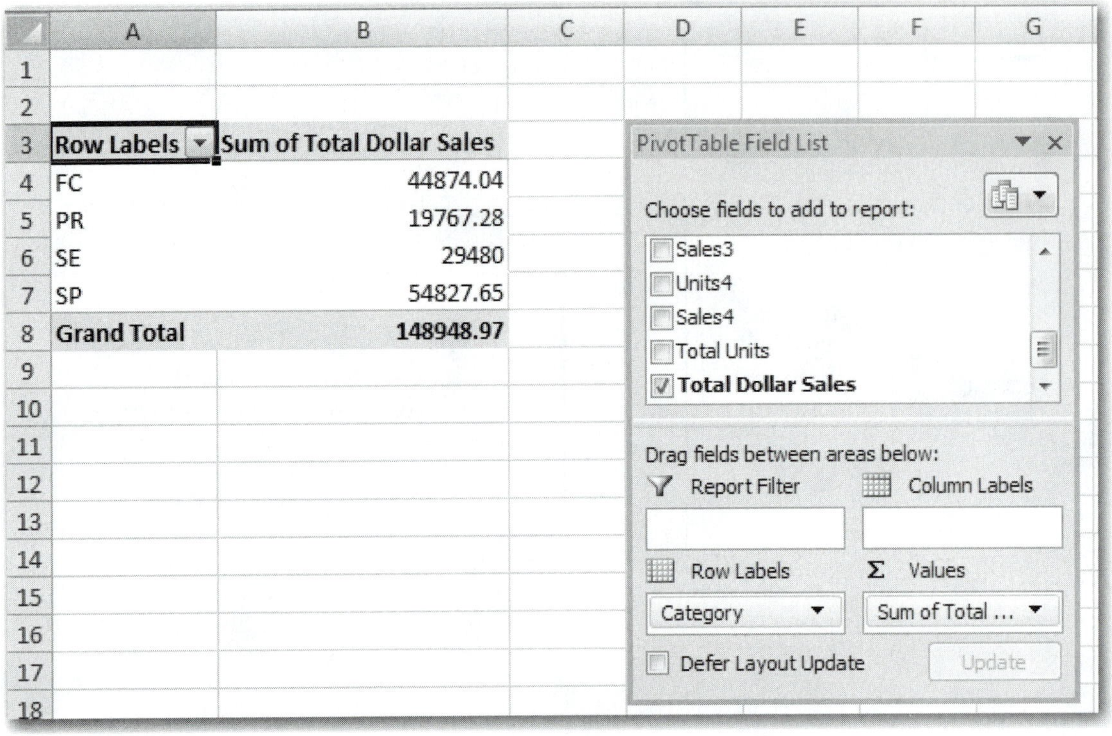

Figure 31: Value Field Settings

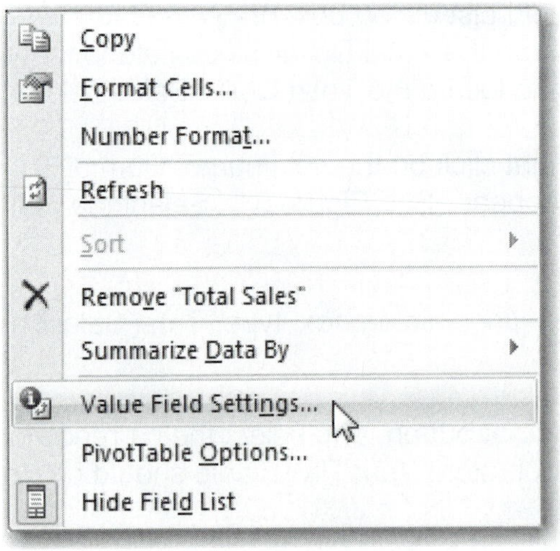

Figure 32: Value Field Settings Dialog Box

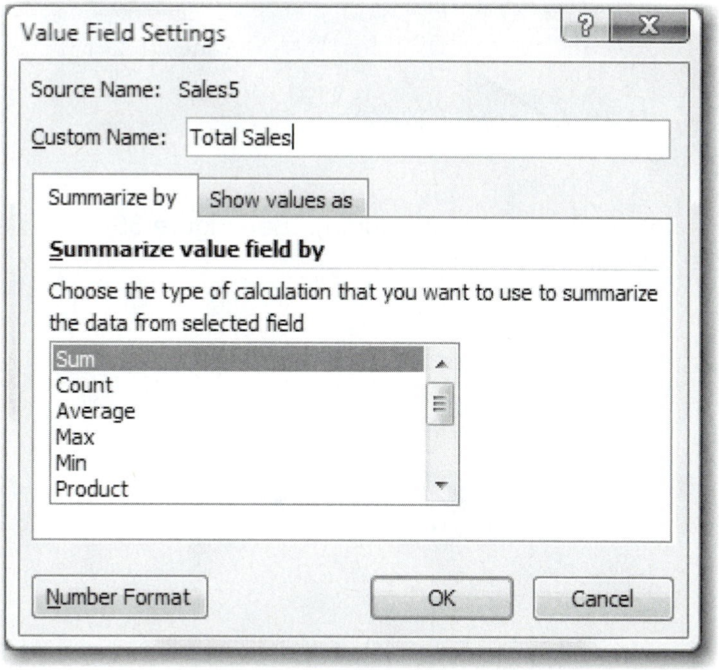

Figure 33: PivotTable Showing Total Sales by Category

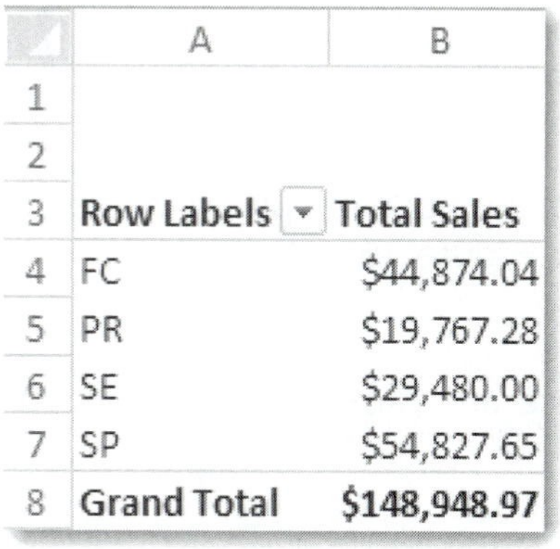

	A	B
1		
2		
3	**Row Labels**	**Total Sales**
4	FC	$44,874.04
5	PR	$19,767.28
6	SE	$29,480.00
7	SP	$54,827.65
8	**Grand Total**	**$148,948.97**

Task 3: Compare the Monthly Sales For Tanning Products

To prepare a pie chart, you can:

1. In the Summary sheet, select the cell range A15:A20; while holding down the CTRL key, select the cell range L15:L20.

2. From the Charts group located on the Insert tab, click the Pie button. See Figure 34.

Figure 34: Charts Group

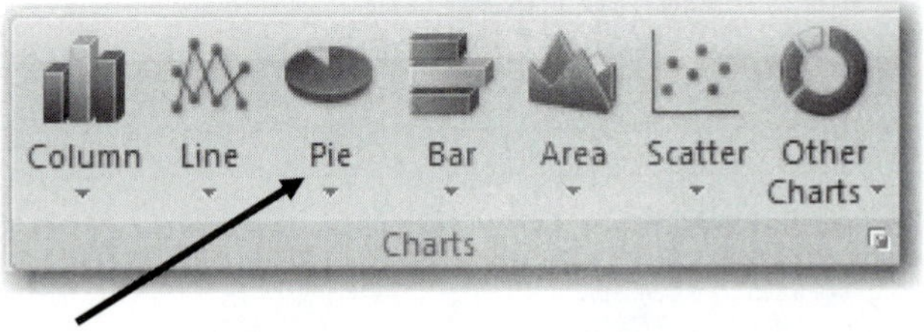

3. Click the Pie button (first row, first column). See Figure 35. The pie chart will be placed in the Summary worksheet.

Figure 35: Pie Chart Types

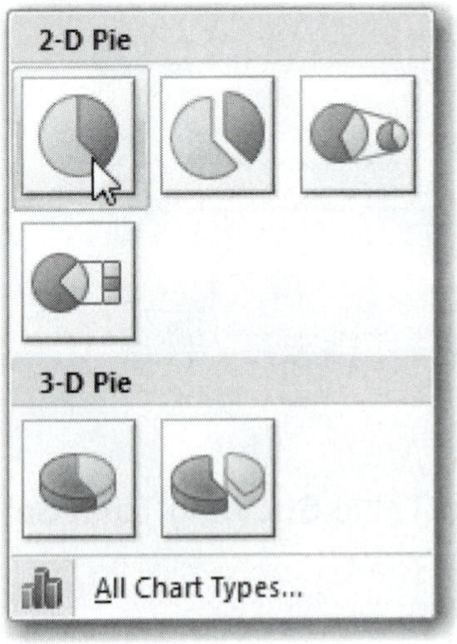

4. Click on the chart. From the Location group located on the Design tab, click the Move Chart button. See Figure 36.

Figure 36: Move Chart Location Button

5. In the Move Chart dialog box, select the New Sheet option, and type "Pie Chart" in the New Sheet box. Click the OK button. See Figure 37.

Figure 37: Move Chart Dialog Box

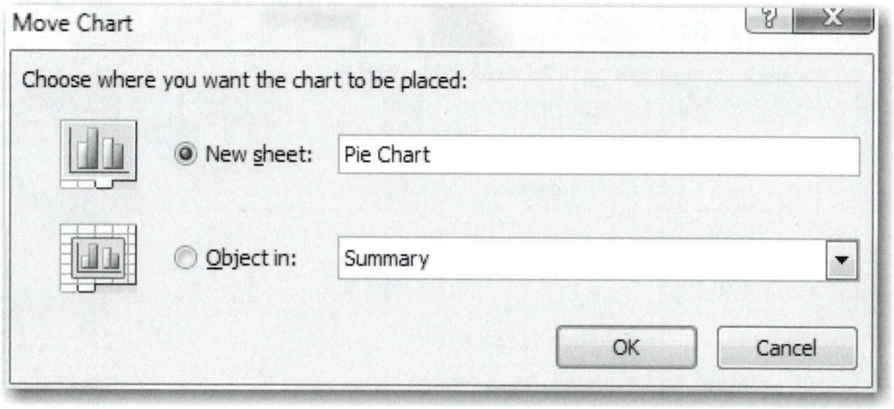

6. From the Chart Layouts group located on the Design tab, click the Layout 6 button. See Figure 38.

Figure 38: Chart Layouts Group

7. Right click on the pie chart. From the shortcut menu, select the Format Data Labels command. The Format Data Labels dialog box will appear. See Figure 39.

8. Select Outside End as the label position. Click the Close button.

9. Double click Chart Title. Select the words "Chart Title". Type "Monthly Product Sales Chart". Figure 40 shows the Monthly Product Sales Chart.

Figure 39: Format Data Labels Dialog Box

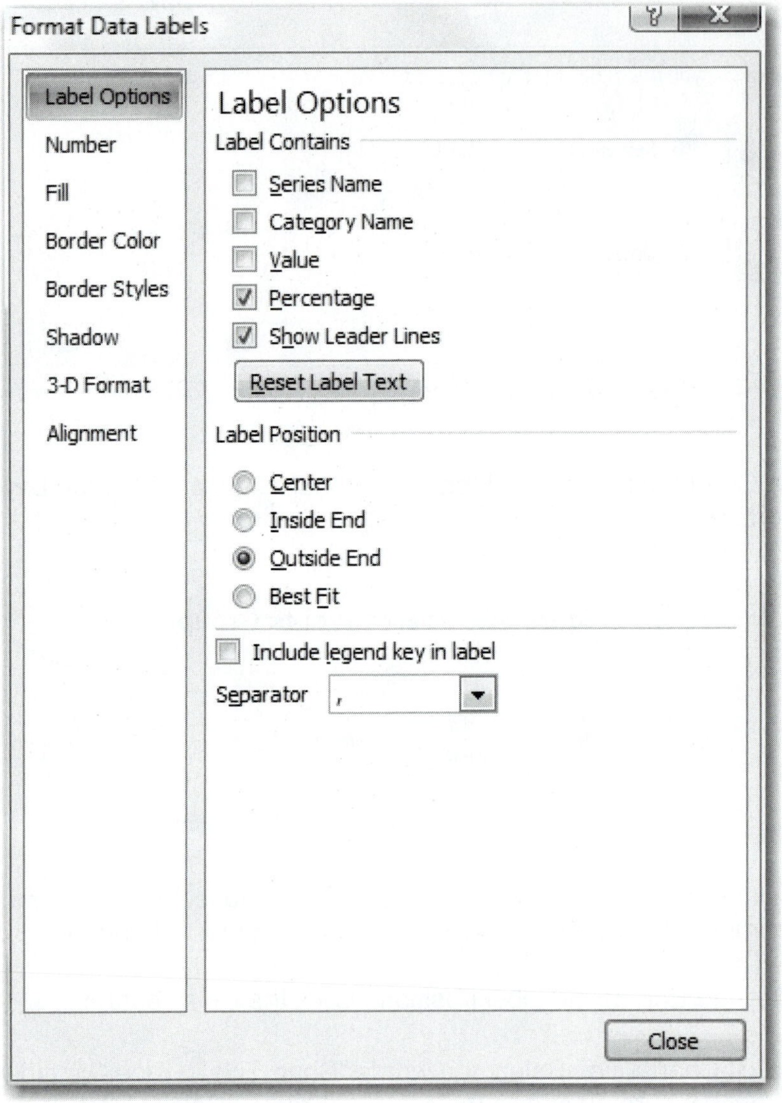

Figure 40: Monthly Product Sales Chart

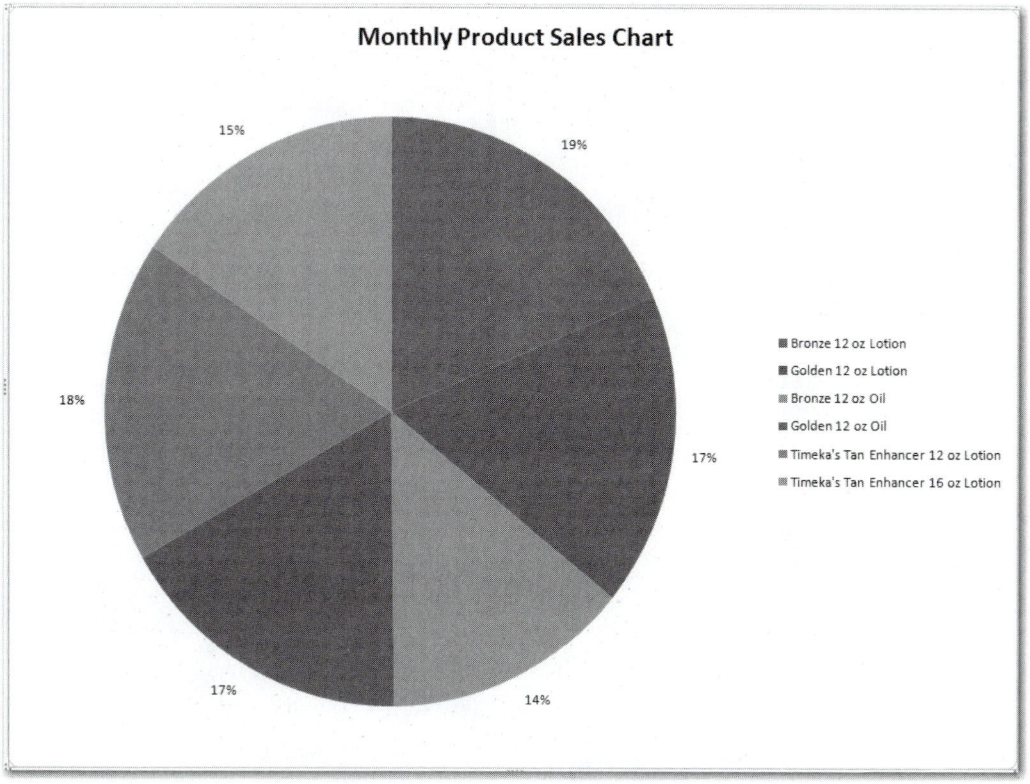

Task 4: Identify Top Two Selling Items

To identify the salon's top two selling items, you can use the Filter tool. To satisfy this information request, you can:

1. Click the Summary sheet tab.

2. If arrows are not displaying by the column names, click the Filter button located in the Sort and Filter group on the Data tab.

3. In cell L4, click the arrow beside the words "Total Dollar Sales". Select the Number Filters command and then select the Top 10 option. See Figure 41. The Top 10 AutoFilter dialog box appears. See Figure 42. In the middle box, insert the number 2. Click the OK button. As Figure 43 shows, the yearly enrollment and the yearly fitness membership plans are the top two selling items in terms of total dollar sales.

4. After you have prepared your answer, click the arrow again and then select the Select All option. Click the OK button. The entire list should now be displayed.

Figure 41: Top Ten Filter Command

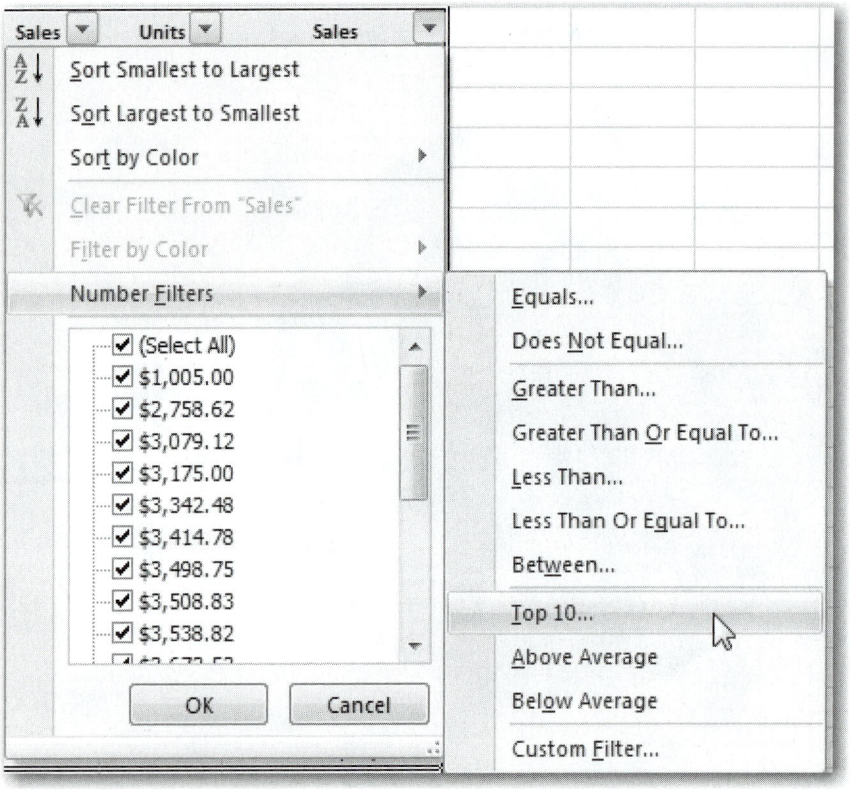

Figure 42: Top Ten Dialog Box

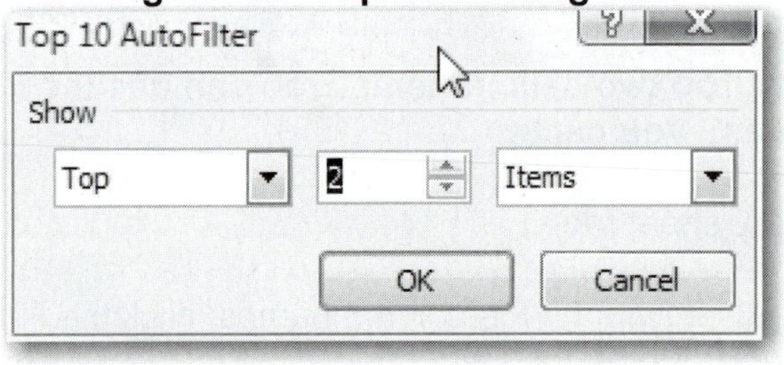

Figure 43: Top Two Selling Items

Task 5: Identify The Least Popular Item

To identify the least popular item, you can:

1. In the Summary sheet, make sure the filter is still active.

2. In cell L4, click the arrow beside the words "Total Dollar Sales". Select the Number Filters command, and then select the Top 10 option. The Top 10 dialog box appears. See Figure 44. Click the arrow beside the word Top, and then select the Bottom option. In the middle box, insert the number 1. Click the OK button. As Figure 45 shows, the single tanning session is the least popular item based on total dollar sales.

Figure 44: Criteria for Least Popular Item

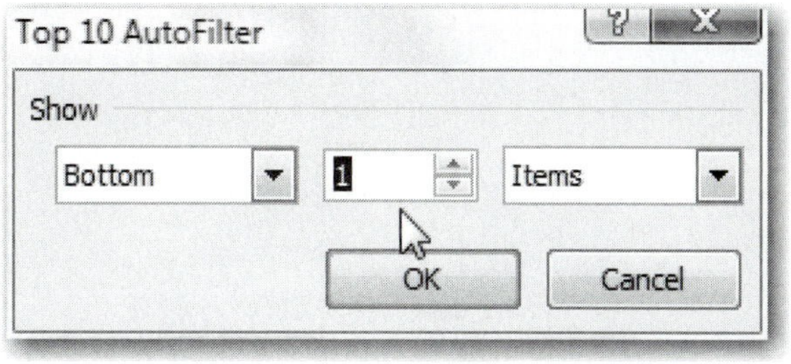

Figure 45: Least Popular Item

	A	B	C	D	E	F	G	H	I	J	K	L
1	Timeka's Tanning Salon											
2	October Monthly Sales Summary											
3	Plan Type		Week 1		Week 2		Week 3		Week 4		Total Weekly Product Sales	
4	Item	Categor	W1 Uni	W1 Sale	W2 Uni	W2 Sale	W3 Uni	W3 Sale	W4 Uni	W4 Sale	Total Uni	Total Dollar Sales
5	1 Session	SE	109	$545.00	38	$190.00	31	$155.00	23	$115.00	201	$1,005.00

Test Your Design Preparation

Each MIS Cases: Decision Making With Application Software, Fourth Edition spreadsheet case requires you to modify your worksheets or workbook. After you have modified the worksheet or workbook, you are asked to provide the case's main character with additional information about his business.

As the tutorial mentions, the salon now offers two new fitness packages. Figure 3 provides the new fitness package data. To include this new fitness package information, you need to insert two new rows in the PriceList, Summary, Week1, Week2, Week3, and Week4 worksheets. As you should be familiar with inserting rows and updating formulas, the process of inserting the two new rows is left as an exercise for you. In the PriceList worksheet, consider inserting the new rows between the current rows 18 and 19. For the Summary, Week1, Week2, Week3, and Week4 worksheets, consider inserting the new rows between the current rows 20 and 21.

The Test Your Design section requires you to prepare a PivotTable. The PivotTable compares each item's total dollar sales for week 4. As you should now be familiar with a PivotTable, the process of preparing the Test Your Design section's PivotTable is left as an exercise for you.

Case Deliverables Preparation

For each MIS Cases: Decision Making with Application Software, Fourth Edition spreadsheet case, you will prepare several deliverables. Your instructor will specify which deliverables you are to prepare.

The Test Your Design section often specifies that the workbook is to be modified and that new data are to be added. This request encourages you to prepare a flexible workbook that is adaptable to changing business needs.

Figure 46: Week 1 Worksheet

Timeka's Tanning Salon

Weekly Sales

	A	B	C	D	E	F	G	H	I	J	K	L	M	N	O	P	Q	R
3	Plan Type		Sunday		Monday		Tuesday		Wednesday		Thursday		Friday		Saturday		Total Weekly Sales	
4	Item	Category	Units	Sales	Units	Sales	Units	Sales	Units	Sales	Units	Sales	Units	Sales	Units	Sales	Total Units	Total Dollar Sales
5	1 Session	SE	25	$125.00	25	$125.00	6	$30.00	30	$150.00	10	$50.00	10	$50.00	3	$15.00	109	$545.00
6	5 Sessions	SE	10	$250.00	10	$250.00	5	$125.00	10	$250.00	9	$225.00	2	$50.00	2	$50.00	48	$1,200.00
7	10 Sessions	SE	5	$250.00	5	$250.00	4	$200.00	12	$600.00	4	$200.00	7	$350.00	8	$400.00	45	$2,250.00
8	15 Sessions	SE	5	$375.00	5	$375.00	13	$975.00	5	$375.00	5	$375.00	9	$675.00	10	$750.00	52	$3,900.00
9	20 Sessions	SE	1	$100.00	1	$100.00	7	$700.00	4	$400.00	6	$600.00	4	$400.00	12	$1,200.00	35	$3,500.00
10	One Month Unlimited	SP	25	$875.00	25	$875.00	10	$350.00	10	$350.00	5	$175.00	4	$140.00	6	$210.00	85	$2,975.00
11	Monthly Special	SP	10	$300.00	10	$300.00	9	$270.00	15	$450.00	10	$300.00	12	$360.00	4	$120.00	70	$2,100.00
12	Loyal Customer	SP	15	$449.85	15	$449.85	6	$179.94	2	$59.98	9	$269.91	2	$59.98	2	$59.98	51	$1,529.49
13	Referral	SP	12	$359.88	12	$359.88	14	$419.86	12	$359.88	8	$239.92	5	$149.95	2	$59.98	65	$1,949.35
14	Yearly Enrollment	SP	10	$3,500.00	10	$3,500.00	22	$7,700.00	6	$2,100.00	2	$700.00	1	$350.00	4	$1,400.00	55	$19,250.00
15	Bronze 12 oz Lotion	PR	22	$549.78	22	$549.78	12	$299.88	4	$99.96	4	$99.96	4	$99.96	2	$49.98	70	$1,749.30
16	Golden 12 oz Lotion	PR	10	$279.90	10	$279.90	4	$111.96	3	$83.97	5	$139.95	3	$83.97	5	$139.95	40	$1,119.60
17	Bronze 12 oz Oil	PR	19	$379.81	19	$379.81	2	$39.98	2	$39.98	9	$179.91	2	$39.98	1	$19.99	54	$1,079.46
18	Golden 12 oz Oil	PR	18	$395.82	18	$395.82	2	$43.98	1	$21.99	8	$175.92	7	$153.93	8	$175.92	62	$1,363.38
19	Timeka's Tan Enhancer 12 oz Lotion	PR	14	$391.86	14	$391.86	4	$111.96	5	$139.95	7	$195.93	1	$27.99	9	$251.91	54	$1,511.46
20	Timeka's Tan Enhaner 16 oz Lotion	PR	2	$69.98	2	$69.98	0	$0.00	5	$174.95	12	$419.88	1	$34.99	0	$0.00	22	$769.78
21	6-Month Fitness Membership	FC	12	$2,171.88	12	$2,171.88	1	$180.99	0	$0.00	2	$361.98	5	$904.95	2	$361.98	34	$6,153.66
22	Yearly Fitness Membership	FC	19	$5,338.81	19	$5,338.81	2	$561.98	0	$0.00	10	$2,809.90	2	$561.98	1	$280.99	53	$14,892.47
23	Total Daily Sales			$16,162.57		$16,162.57		$12,300.53		$5,655.66		$7,518.26		$4,492.68		$5,545.68		$67,837.95

Figure 47: Summary Worksheet

	A	B	C	D	E	F	G	H	I	J	K	L
1	Timeka's Tanning Salon											
2	October Monthly Sales Summary											
3	Plan Type		Week 1		Week 2		Week 3		Week 4		Total Weekly Product Sales	
4	Item	Category	W1 Units	W1 Sales	W2 Units	W2 Sales	W3 Units	W3 Sales	W4 Units	W4 Sales	Total Units	Total Dollar Sales
5	1 Session	SE	109	$545.00	38	$190.00	31	$155.00	23	$115.00	201	$1,005.00
6	5 Sessions	SE	48	$1,200.00	41	$1,025.00	23	$575.00	15	$375.00	127	$3,175.00
7	10 Sessions	SE	45	$2,250.00	30	$1,500.00	21	$1,050.00	16	$800.00	112	$5,600.00
8	15 Sessions	SE	52	$3,900.00	22	$1,650.00	21	$1,575.00	17	$1,275.00	112	$8,400.00
9	20 Sessions	SE	35	$3,500.00	37	$3,700.00	20	$2,000.00	21	$2,100.00	113	$11,300.00
10	One Month Unlimited	SP	85	$2,975.00	36	$1,260.00	21	$735.00	18	$630.00	160	$5,600.00
11	Monthly Special	SP	70	$2,100.00	50	$1,500.00	16	$480.00	10	$300.00	146	$4,380.00
12	Loyal Customer	SP	51	$1,529.49	16	$479.84	39	$1,169.61	11	$329.89	117	$3,508.83
13	Referral	SP	65	$1,949.35	25	$749.75	18	$539.82	10	$299.90	118	$3,538.82
14	Yearly Enrollment	SP	55	$19,250.00	17	$5,950.00	16	$5,600.00	20	$7,000.00	108	$37,800.00
15	Bronze 12 oz Lotion	PR	70	$1,749.30	38	$949.62	25	$624.75	14	$349.86	147	$3,673.53
16	Golden 12 oz Lotion	PR	40	$1,119.60	39	$1,091.61	25	$699.75	18	$503.82	122	$3,414.78
17	Bronze 12 oz Oil	PR	54	$1,079.46	40	$799.60	22	$439.78	22	$439.78	138	$2,758.62
18	Golden 12 oz Oil	PR	62	$1,363.38	32	$703.68	35	$769.65	23	$505.77	152	$3,342.48
19	Timeka's Tan Enhancer 12 oz Lotion	PR	54	$1,511.46	45	$1,259.55	16	$447.84	10	$279.90	125	$3,498.75
20	Timeka's Tan Enhancer 16 oz Lotion	PR	22	$769.78	41	$1,434.59	14	$489.86	11	$384.89	88	$3,079.12
21	6-Month Fitness Membership	FC	34	$6,153.66	32	$5,791.68	21	$3,800.79	15	$2,714.85	102	$18,460.98
22	Yearly Fitness Membership	FC	53	$14,892.47	14	$3,933.86	12	$3,371.88	15	$4,214.85	94	$26,413.06
23	Total		1004	$67,837.95	593	$33,968.78	396	$24,523.73	289	$22,618.51	2282	$148,948.97

Database Tutorial

Timeka's Tanning Salon, Inc.

Tutorial Introduction

Timeka's Tanning Salon, Inc., is a tutorial designed to accompany MIS Cases: Decision Making with Application Software, Fourth Edition, published by Pearson Prentice Hall. This tutorial serves as a database development review tool and assumes you have a basic, fundamental knowledge of databases, database terminology, and Microsoft Access 2007.

This tutorial is divided into two parts. Part I provides the tutorial's background, scenario, storage specifications, input specifications, information specifications, test your design requirements, and deliverables. Part II steps you through the tutorial's preparation. As Part I introduces the case's main character and sets the stage for the required database design work, you should read Part I before attempting Part II. In Part II, you will design and build a database that satisfies the tutorial's design and information requirements.

Part I: Setting the Scene

Tutorial Background

Timeka Lorenzo owns and operates Timeka's Tanning Salon, which is located in San Francisco, California. The tanning salon has been in operation for several years, and the clientele for the business continues to grow. The tanning salon provides customers with access to the latest tanning beds, tan enhancing products, and a fitness center.

Currently, the salon's customer records are manually kept, and Ms. Lorenzo spends numerous hours each week updating customer records. Ms. Lorenzo realizes the necessity for moving the salon's paper-based records to an electronic format. Ms. Lorenzo hires you to design a database that will track the salon's customers. Initially, the database will track the salon's customers, items for sale (such as membership plans), and customer enrollments. Later, the salon's tanning products will be added to the database. To prepare this tutorial, you will design three tables, three forms, three queries, and a report.

Tutorial Scenario

Four years ago, Timeka Lorenzo opened Timeka's Tanning Salon in the San Francisco area. Although the tanning salon is doing well, the salon is experiencing numerous problems. Customer complaints are on the rise, as customer records are often misplaced, lost, or incorrect. Additionally, Ms. Lorenzo has no efficient way of identifying which plans are most attractive to her customers. Ms. Lorenzo has decided it is time to correct the salon's problems, and she turns to you for help.

When a customer enrolls at the salon, a customer enrollment card is completed. The enrollment card contains the customer's name, address, phone number, plan type, enrollment date, and visits. Figure 1 shows the current Customer Enrollment card. When a customer purchases a new session, purchases a special plan, or the card is full, a new card is started and stapled to the front of the old card.

Currently, all past and present customer enrollment cards are kept in plastic tubs beneath the front counter. When a customer visits the salon, her card is pulled from one of the tubs, visit information is recorded on the card, and then the card is filed again in the tub. This manual process often leads to misplaced cards and erroneous information being recorded on the cards.

Figure 1: Customer Enrollment Card

Timeka's Tanning Salon Customer Enrollment			
Customer Name:			
Customer Address:			
Phone Number:			
Plan Type:			
Enrollment Date:			
	Visits		

Ms. Lorenzo needs a database to track the salon's customers. Specifically, Ms. Lorenzo wants the database to track the salon's customers, items, and enrollments. (This tutorial does not require you to track customer visits.) To build the database according to Ms. Lorenzo's requirements, you will design Customer, Item, and Enrollment tables, design Customer, Item, and Enrollment forms, construct qrySingleSession, qryInactive, and qryNewEnrollment queries, and prepare a Customer List report.

Storage Specifications

After meeting with Ms. Lorenzo on several occasions, you realize that the Salon database requires Customer, Item, and Enrollment tables. The Customer table stores the customer's identification number, last name, first name, phone number, street address, city, state, and zip code. The customer identification number will serve as the primary key. Table 1 shows the Customer table structure.

The Item table stores information about the salon's sessions, specials, and fitness memberships. The Item table stores each item's identification number, description, and price. The item's identification number will serve as the primary key. Table 2 shows the Item table's structure. In Table 2, the name IType is used to designate the item's identification number. Ms. Lorenzo requested that you use the field name IType.

The Enrollment table stores each customer's current enrollment information. For each enrollment, the table stores an enrollment identification number, customer identification number, item identification number, and enrollment date. Although the customer identification number and item identification number could serve as a combination key, you realize there are some instances when this combination would not prove unique, so you decide an enrollment identification number is necessary. The enrollment identification number will serve as the primary key. As the customer identification number is stored in the Customer table, you will use the Lookup Wizard to create the CID field for the Enrollment table. Likewise, the item identification number is stored in the Item table, so the Lookup Wizard can create the item identification number field in the Enrollment table. Table 3 shows the Enrollment table's structure.

As you study the three table structures, you realize that two relationships are necessary. Relationships between the Customer and Enrollment tables and between the Item and Enrollment tables are necessary. The relationship between the Customer and Enrollment tables should enforce referential integrity, allow cascade updates, and allow cascade deletes. The relationship between the Item and Enrollment tables should enforce referential integrity and allow cascade updates.

Table 1: Customer Table Structure

Field Name	Data Type	Field Description	Field Size	Comments
CID	AutoNumber	Serves as primary key.	Long Integer	Is required.
LastName	Text		50	
FirstName	Text		25	
PhoneNumber	Text		15	Use an input mask.
SAddress	Text		30	
City	Text		30	Default value is San Francisco.
State	Text		2	Default value is CA.
ZipCode	Text		5	

Table 2: Item Table Structure

Field Name	Data Type	Field Description	Field Size	Comments
IType	Text	Serves as primary key.	5	Is required.
Description	Text		50	
Price	Currency			Set decimal places to 2.

Table 3: Enrollment Table Structure

Field Name	Data Type	Field Description	Field Size	Comments
ENID	AutoNumber	Serves as primary key.	Long Integer	Is required.
CID	Number		Long Integer	Is required. Use the Lookup Wizard.
IType	Text		5	Use the Lookup Wizard.
EDate	Date/Time			Use the short date format.

Input Specifications

Ms. Lorenzo asks you to create Customer, Item, and Enrollment forms. Ms. Lorenzo will use the Customer form to enroll new customers and maintain existing customer data. As Figure 2 shows, the Customer form allows Ms. Lorenzo to capture the customer's name, address, and phone number. Ms. Lorenzo wants the system to automatically assign the customer an identification number.

Ms. Lorenzo will use the Item form to maintain data about her salon's items. Later, Ms. Lorenzo will add the salon's tanning products to the table. As Figure 3 shows, the Item form captures the item's identification number, description, and price.

When a customer purchases one of the sessions, specials, or fitness plans, Ms. Lorenzo will use the Enrollment form to capture the enrollment details. The enrollment details include the enrollment identification number, customer identification number, item identification number, and enrollment date. The enrollment identification number is automatically assigned by the system. Figure 4 provides a sketch of the Enrollment form.

To quickly generate the forms, you decide to use the Form Wizard to generate the initial forms. Then you will modify the forms in Design view. Once Ms. Lorenzo looks at the forms, you will make any requested design changes to the forms.

Figure 2: Customer Form Sketch

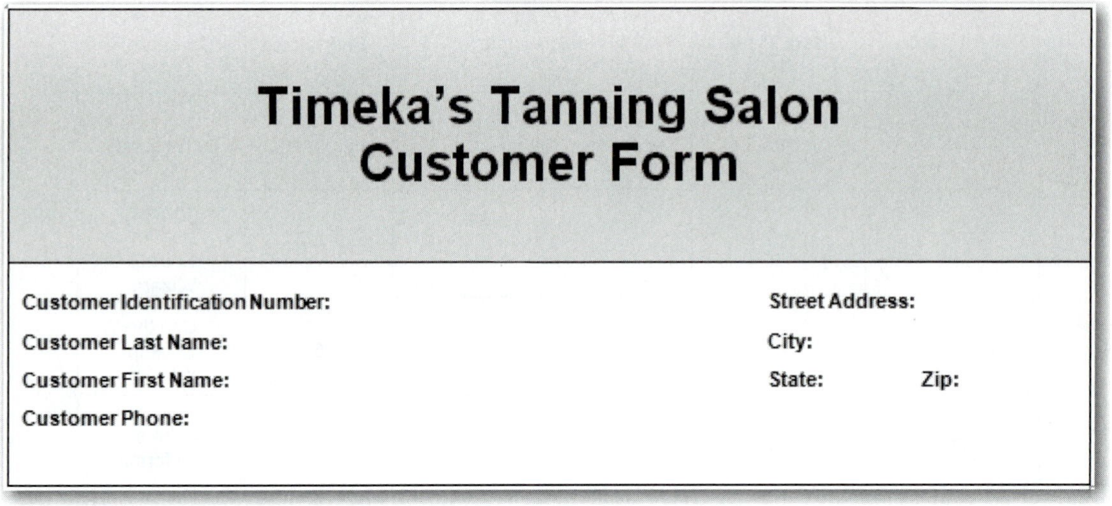

Timeka's Tanning Salon
Customer Form

Customer Identification Number:
Customer Last Name:
Customer First Name:
Customer Phone:
Street Address:
City:
State: Zip:

Figure 3: Item Form Sketch

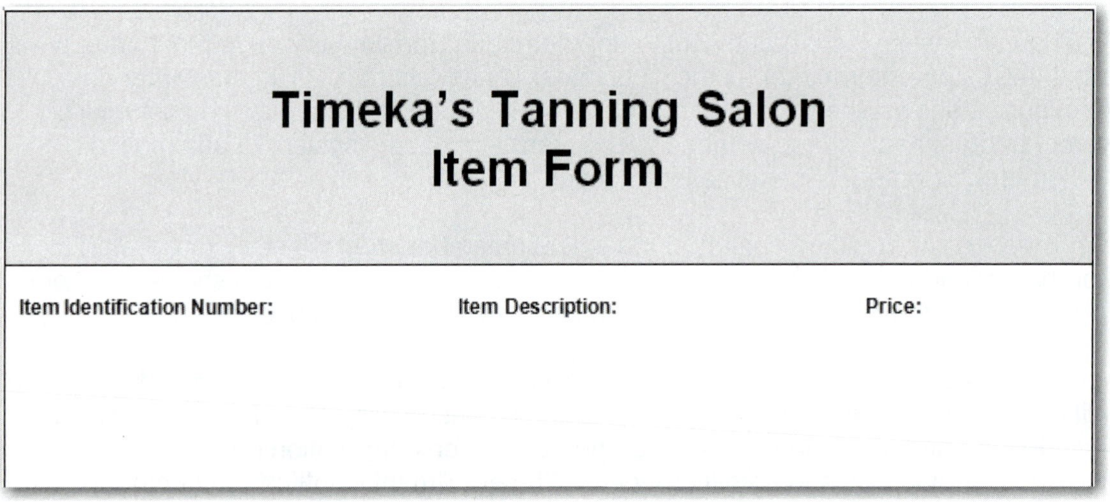

Timeka's Tanning Salon
Item Form

Item Identification Number: Item Description: Price:

Figure 4: Enrollment Form Sketch

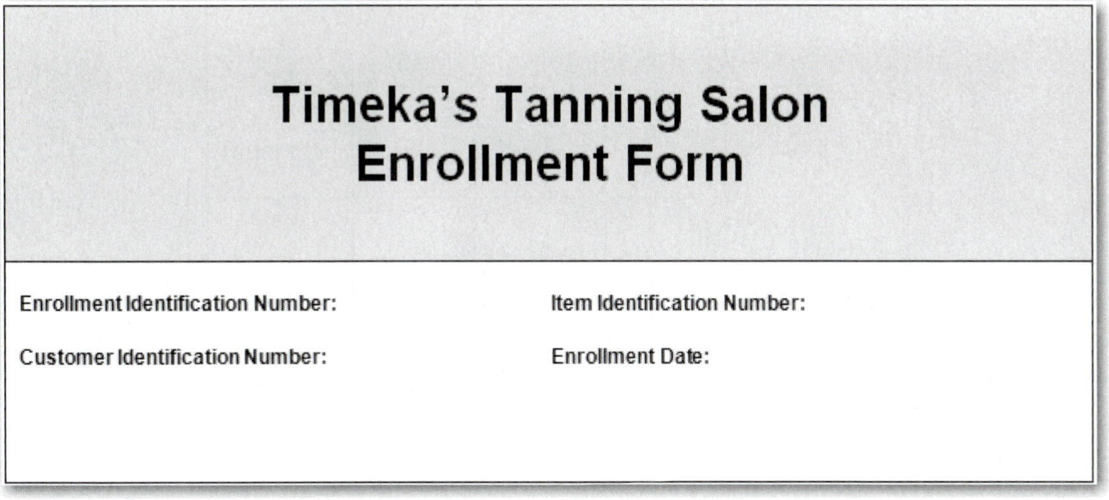

Timeka's Tanning Salon
Enrollment Form

Enrollment Identification Number:

Item Identification Number:

Customer Identification Number:

Enrollment Date:

Information Specifications

In an effort to learn more about her customers, Ms. Lorenzo asks you to prepare a Customer List report. The Customer List report provides Ms. Lorenzo with the customer's last and first name, address, and phone number. Ms. Lorenzo will use this information to call her customers and offer them special discounts for their loyalty to the salon.

In addition to the Customer List report, Ms. Lorenzo wants answers for the following questions. Provide Ms. Lorenzo with the requested information.

1. How many customers have purchased a single tanning session?

2. Which of the salon's customers are not currently enrolled?

3. Which customers enrolled after August 1, 2007?

Test Your Design

After you create the Salon database, you should test your design. Make the following changes to the Salon database.

1. Ms. Lorenzo wants the following fitness plans added to the Item table.

IType	Description	Price
FC001	One-Month Fitness Membership	$35.99

IType	Description	Price
FC002	Three-Month Fitness Membership	$66.99
FC003	Six-Month Fitness Membership	$180.99
FC004	Yearly Fitness Membership	$280.99

2. Enter data for you and two of your friends into the Customer table. Also, enter the following enrollment data for you and your friends.

CID	IType	EDate
Your CID.	FC004	8/1/2007
First Friend's CID.	FC003	8/1/2007
Second Friend's CID.	FC001	8/1/2007

Deliverables

In order to satisfactorily complete this tutorial, you should build the Salon database as described in the tutorial and then prepare both written and oral presentations. Unless otherwise specified, submit the following deliverables to your professor.

1. A written report discussing any assumptions you have made about the tutorial and the key elements of the tutorial. Additionally, what features did you add to make the database more functional? User friendly? (Please note that these assumptions cannot violate any of the requirements specified above and must be approved by your professor.)

2. A printout of each form.

3. A printout of each report.

4. An electronic, working copy of your database that meets the criteria mentioned in the scenario and specifications sections.

5. Results for each query. (A memo to your instructor discussing these results should also be provided.)

6. As mentioned above, you should prepare an oral presentation. (Your instructor will establish the time allocated to your presentation.) You should use a presentation package and discuss the key features of your database. Also, discuss how this database is beneficial for Ms. Lorenzo. What changes to this database would you recommend? What additional data could be stored in the database?

Part II: Workbook Preparation

Storage Preparation

If you have not already done so, please read Part I of this tutorial.

To satisfy Ms. Lorenzo's design specifications, you will develop a database that contains Customer, Item, and Enrollment tables; Customer, Item, and Enrollment forms; qrySingleSession, qryInactive, and qryNewEnrollment queries, and a Customer List report. Additionally, you must establish relationships between the Customer and Enrollment tables, as well as the Item and Enrollment tables.

The Salon database preparation is separated into four primary activities. These activities involve creating the database and designing the tables, creating the forms, creating the queries, and creating the report. Each activity is described below.

Activity 1: Database Creation and Table Design

Activity 1 involves five primary tasks. The first task creates the Salon database. The second task designs the Customer table. The third task creates the Item table. The fourth task designs the Enrollment table, and the fifth task creates the necessary relationships. (Please keep in mind that you should periodically save your work.)

Task 1: Create the Database

To create the Salon database, perform the following steps:

1. Start Microsoft Access 2007.

2. Click the Blank Database option in the Microsoft Access 2007 welcome screen.

3. In the Blank Database name box, type "Salon", and then click the Create button. The newly created Salon database will open. See Figure 5.

Task 2: Create the Customer Table

To create the Customer table, perform the following steps:

1. From the Views group, click the down arrow on the View button.

2. Select the Design view option. See Figure 6.

3. In the Save As dialog box, type "tblCustomer", and then click the OK button. See Figure 7. The Customer table opens in Design view. See Figure 8.

4. In the first row of the Field Name column, enter "CID" as the new field name. Click the tab key twice.

5. For the description, enter "Serves as primary key". See Figure 8.

Figure 5: Newly Created Salon Database

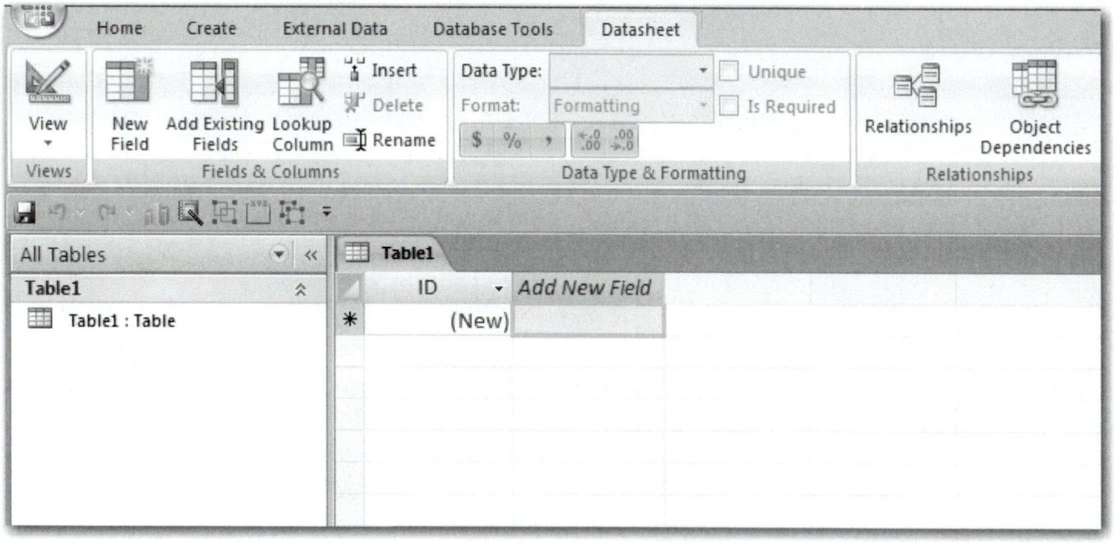

Figure 6: Design View Command

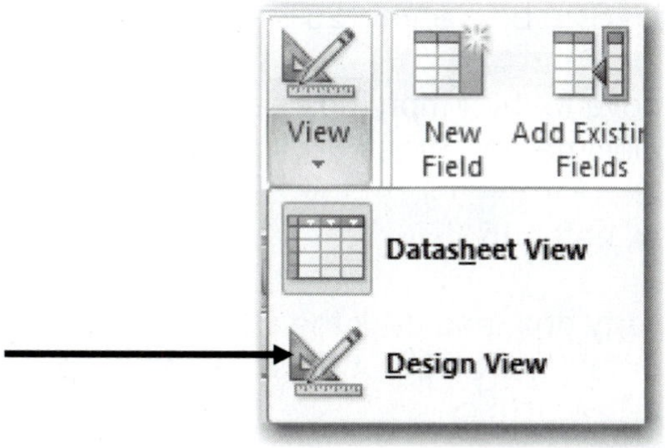

Figure 7: Save As Dialog Box

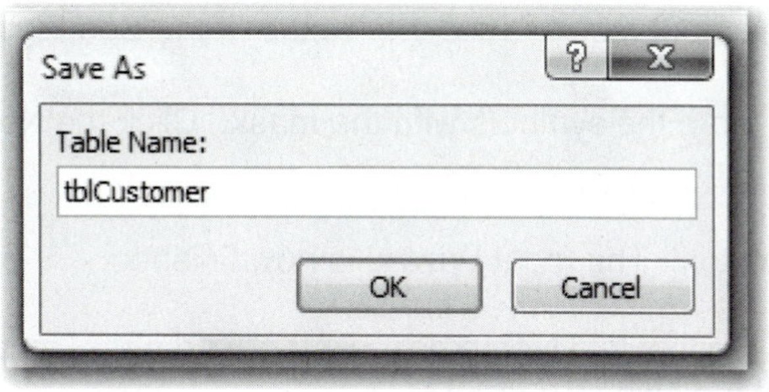

Figure 8: Customer Table Design View

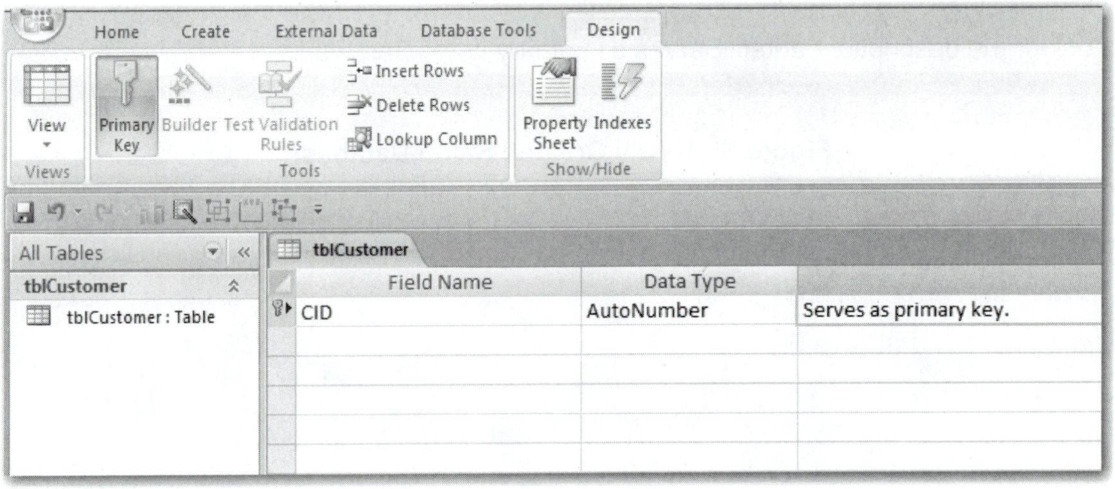

6. In the Field Name column, click in the Field Name box below the CID field. Enter "LastName" as the new field name.

7. Press the F6 key. In the Field Size property box, enter "50".

8. In the Field Name column, move to the empty box below the LastName field. Enter "FirstName" as the new field name.

9. Press the F6 key. In the Field Size box, enter "25".

10. In the Field Name column, move to the empty box below the FirstName field. Enter "PhoneNumber" as the new field name. Press F6.

11. In the Field Size property box, enter 15.

12. Move to the Input Mask property box, and click the Build button. When prompted, save the Customer table. The Input Mask Wizard appears. See Figure 9.

13. Select the Phone Number Input Mask, and then click the Next button.

14. Do not change the input mask. Click the Next button. See Figure 10.

15. When prompted, store the symbols with the mask. Click the Next button. See Figure 11.

16. Click the Finish button. The Input Wizard is now finished.

17. Move to the next empty Field Name box. Enter "SAddress" as the new field name. Press F6, and set the field size to 30.

18. Move to the next empty Field Name box. Enter "City" as the new field name. Press the F6 key, and set the field size to 30.
19. Move to the Default Value property box, and enter "San Francisco".

20. Move to the next empty Field Name box. Enter "State" as the new field name. Press the F6 key, and set the field size to 2.

21. Move to the Default Value property box, and enter "CA".

22. Move to the next empty Field Name box. Enter "ZipCode" as the new field name. Press the F6 key, and set the field size to 5.

23. Move to the Input Mask property box, and enter "00000;;_" . (Do not include the quotation marks and the period.)

24. Click the Save button on the Quick Access Toolbar. (If the Quick Access Toolbar is not showing, use your system's online help system to learn how to display the Quick Access Toolbar.)

25. Close the Design View window.

Figure 9: Input Mask Wizard Selection Dialog Box

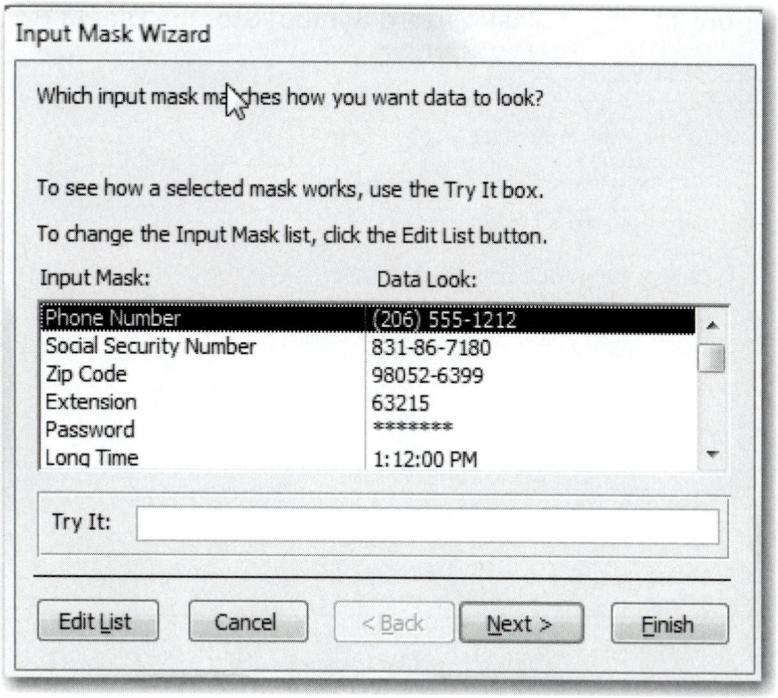

Figure 10: Input Mask Wizard Changes Dialog Box

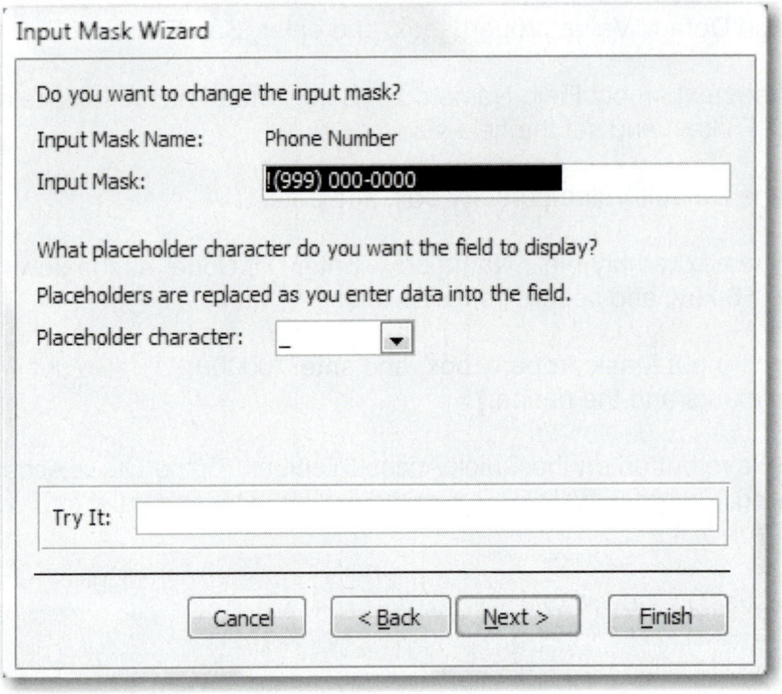

Figure 11: Input Mask Wizard Symbol Storage Dialog Box

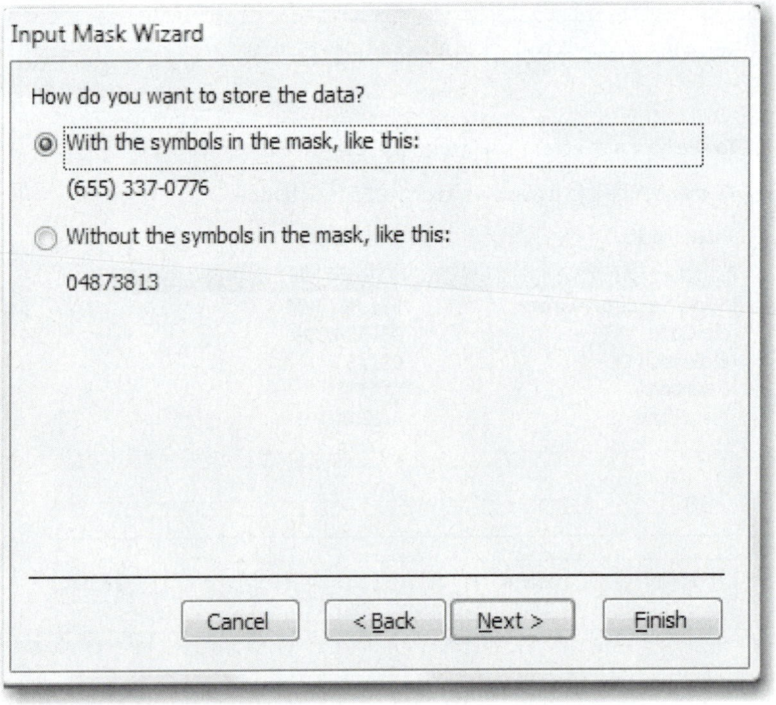

Task 3: Create the Item Table

1. From the Tables group located on the Create tab, click the Table button. See Figure 12.
2. From the Views group, click the down arrow on the View button.
3. Select the Design View option.
4. When prompted, save the table as “tblItem”. Click the OK button.
5. In the first row of the Field Name column, enter “IType” for the field name. Press the Tab key.
6. In the Data Type box, click the drop-down arrow, and then select Text. See Figure 13. Press the Tab key.
7. In the Description column, enter “Serves as primary key”.
8. Press the F6 key. Set the Field size to 5.
9. Click the Save button located on the Quick Access toolbar.
10. In the Field Name column, click in the Field Name box below the Itype field. Enter “Description” as the new field name.
11. Press the F6 key. Set the Field size to 50.
12. In the Field Name column, click the Field Name box below the Description field. Enter “Price” as the field name. In the Data Type box, click the drop-down arrow and then select Currency.
13. Press the F6 key, and then set the Decimal Places property to 2.
14. Click the Save button on the Quick Access Toolbar.
15. Close the Design View window

Figure 12: Table Button

Figure 13: Data Type Option

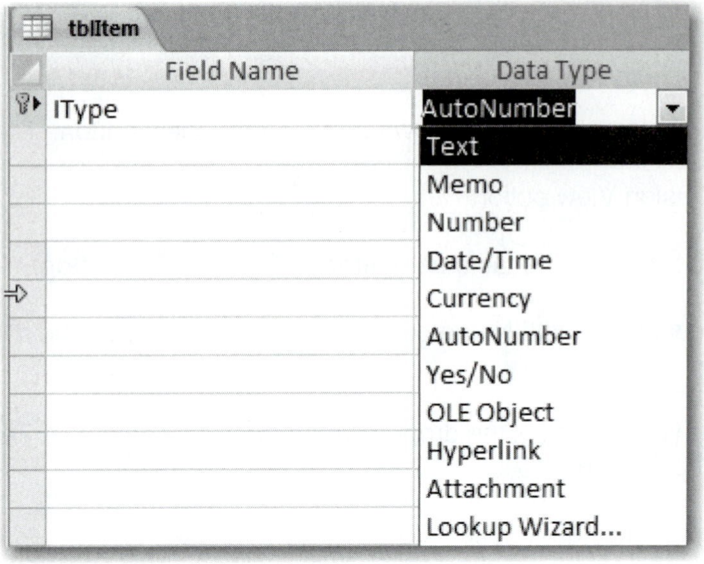

Task 4: Create the Enrollment Table

1. From the Tables group located on the Create tab, click the Table button.

2. From the Views group, click the down arrow on the View button.

3. Select the Design View option.

4. When prompted, save the table as "tblEnrollment". Click the OK button.

5. In the first empty row of the Field Name column, enter "ENID". Press the Tab key twice.

6. In the Description box, enter "Serves as primary key.".

7. In the empty Field Name box below the ENID field, enter "CID". Press the tab key.

8. In the Data Type column, click the drop-down arrow and select Lookup Wizard. The Lookup Wizard dialog box appears. Make sure the "I want the lookup column to lookup the values in a table or query" option is selected. Click the Next button. See Figure 14.

9. When prompted by the Lookup Wizard, specify tblCustomer as the table that provides the values for your lookup column. Click the Next button. See Figure 15.

10. When prompted by the Lookup Wizard, specify that the CID, LastName, and FirstName fields are the values that you want included in your lookup column. Click the Next button. See Figure 16.

Task 3: Create the Item Table

1. From the Tables group located on the Create tab, click the Table button. See Figure 12.
2. From the Views group, click the down arrow on the View button.
3. Select the Design View option.
4. When prompted, save the table as "tblItem". Click the OK button.
5. In the first row of the Field Name column, enter "IType" for the field name. Press the Tab key.
6. In the Data Type box, click the drop-down arrow, and then select Text. See Figure 13. Press the Tab key.
7. In the Description column, enter "Serves as primary key".
8. Press the F6 key. Set the Field size to 5.
9. Click the Save button located on the Quick Access toolbar.
10. In the Field Name column, click in the Field Name box below the Itype field. Enter "Description" as the new field name.
11. Press the F6 key. Set the Field size to 50.
12. In the Field Name column, click the Field Name box below the Description field. Enter "Price" as the field name. In the Data Type box, click the drop-down arrow and then select Currency.
13. Press the F6 key, and then set the Decimal Places property to 2.
14. Click the Save button on the Quick Access Toolbar.
15. Close the Design View window

Figure 12: Table Button

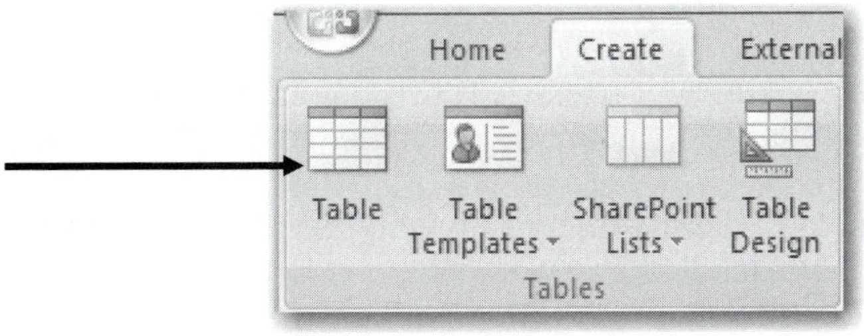

Figure 13: Data Type Option

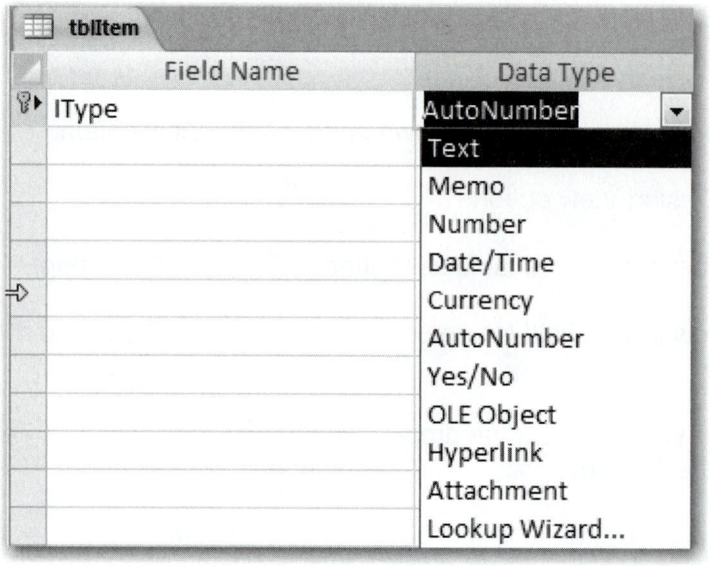

Task 4: Create the Enrollment Table

1. From the Tables group located on the Create tab, click the Table button.
2. From the Views group, click the down arrow on the View button.
3. Select the Design View option.
4. When prompted, save the table as “tblEnrollment”. Click the OK button.
5. In the first empty row of the Field Name column, enter “ENID”. Press the Tab key twice.
6. In the Description box, enter “Serves as primary key.”.
7. In the empty Field Name box below the ENID field, enter “CID”. Press the tab key.
8. In the Data Type column, click the drop-down arrow and select Lookup Wizard. The Lookup Wizard dialog box appears. Make sure the "I want the lookup column to lookup the values in a table or query" option is selected. Click the Next button. See Figure 14.
9. When prompted by the Lookup Wizard, specify tblCustomer as the table that provides the values for your lookup column. Click the Next button. See Figure 15.
10. When prompted by the Lookup Wizard, specify that the CID, LastName, and FirstName fields are the values that you want included in your lookup column. Click the Next button. See Figure 16.

11. When prompted by the Lookup Wizard, specify the sort order as shown in Figure 17. Click the Next button.
12. When prompted by the Lookup Wizard, adjust the column widths, if necessary. Make sure the Hide key column option is selected. Click the Next button. See Figure 18.
13. When the Lookup Wizard prompts you for a label name, name the field "CID". (CID is the default name displayed in the label name box. If not, then change the name to CID.) See Figure 19. Click the Finish button.
14. When prompted, save the table.
15. In the next empty Field Name box, enter "IType". For the data type, select the Lookup Wizard. You will perform the same steps as you did for the CID field.
16. When prompted by the Lookup Wizard, specify that the value should be looked up from a table.
17. When prompted by the Lookup Wizard, specify that the tblItem table provides the values.
18. When prompted by the Lookup Wizard, specify that IType and IDescription contain the values that you want included in your lookup column.
19. When prompted by the Lookup Wizard, do not specify a sort order. Click the Next button.
20. When prompted by the Lookup Wizard, adjust the column width, if necessary. Make sure the Hide key option is not selected.
21. When prompted by the Lookup Wizard, specify that the IType column contains the value that you want to store in your database.
22. When prompted, name the column "IType". Click the Finish button.
23. When prompted, save the table.
24. In the next empty Field Name box, enter "EDate" as the new field name. Set the data type to Date/Time.
25. Press the F6 key. In the Format box, click the drop-down arrow and select the Short Date format.
26. Save the Enrollment table.
27. Close the Design View window

Figure 14: Lookup Wizard Dialog Box

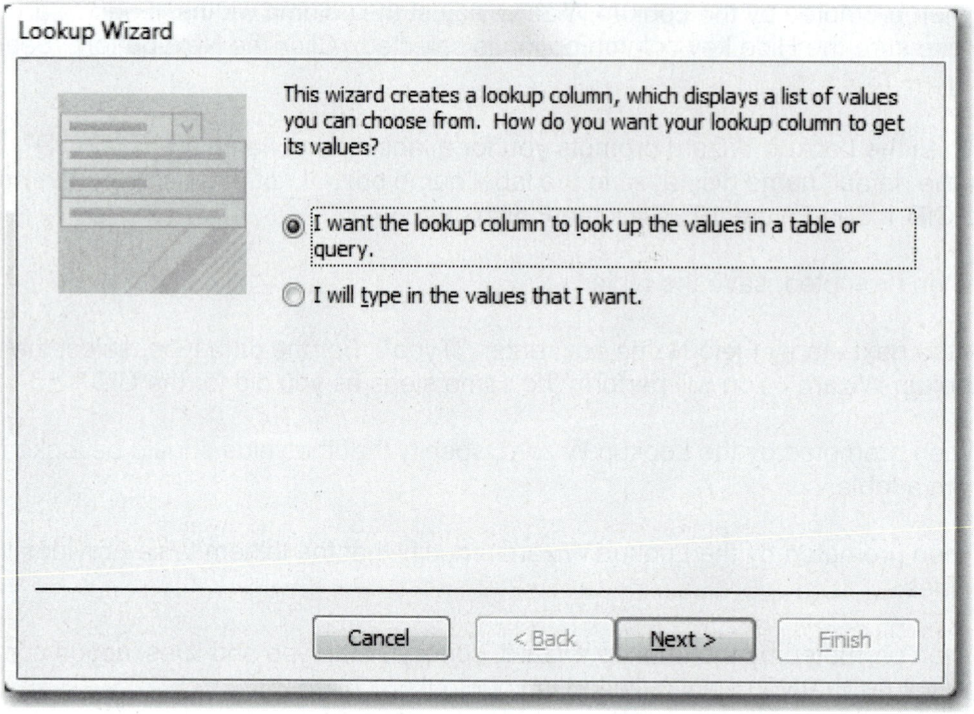

Figure 15: Lookup Wizard Table Values Dialog Box

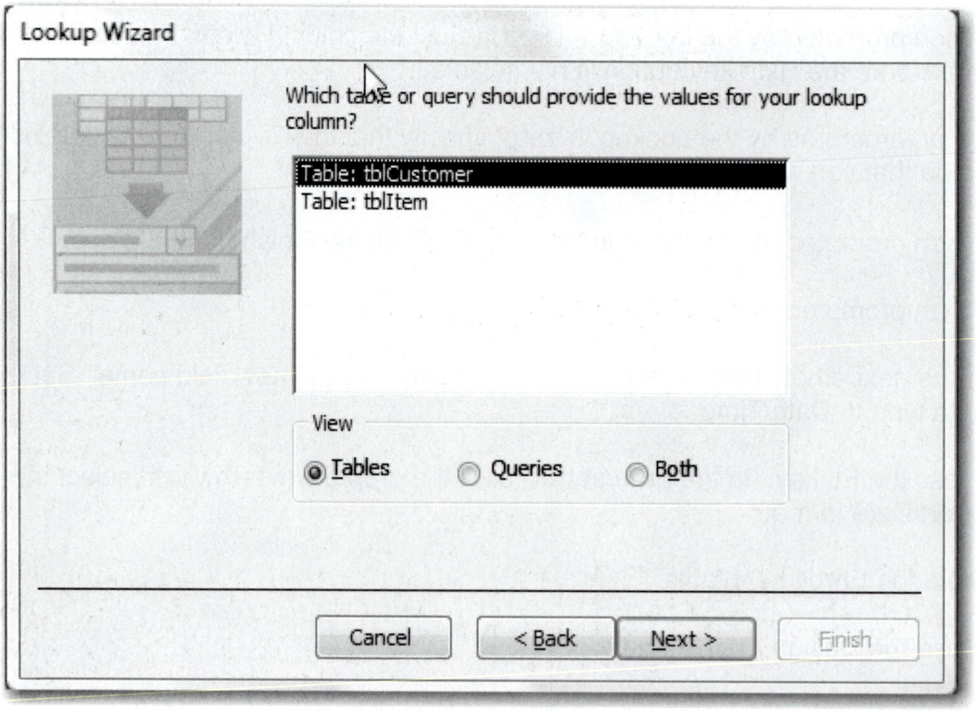

Figure 16: Lookup Wizard Lookup Column Fields Dialog Box

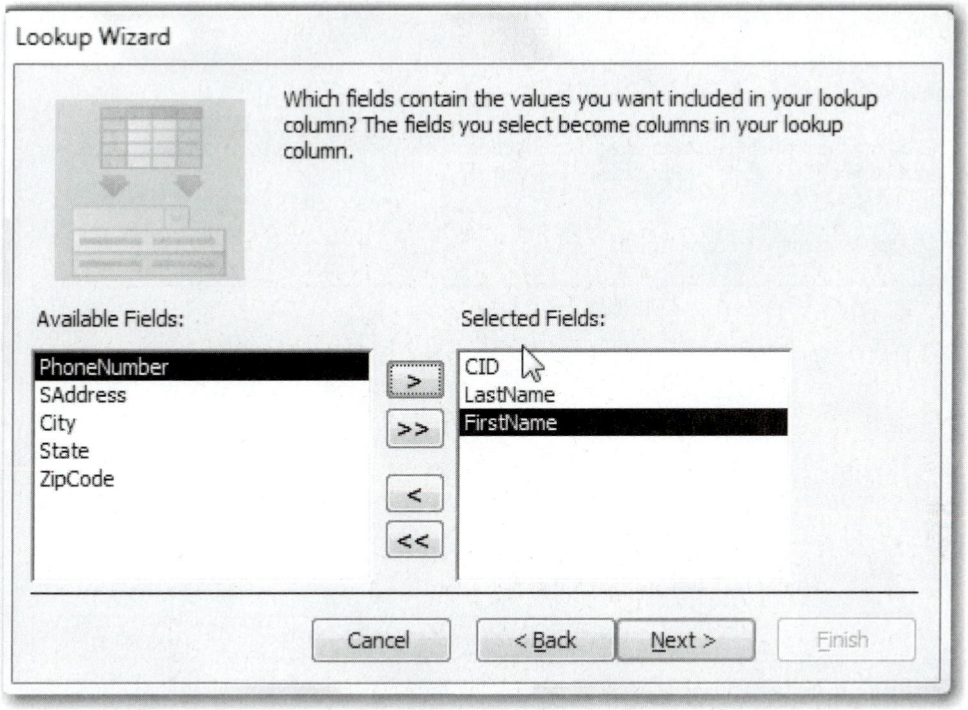

Figure 17: Lookup Wizard Sort Order Dialog Box

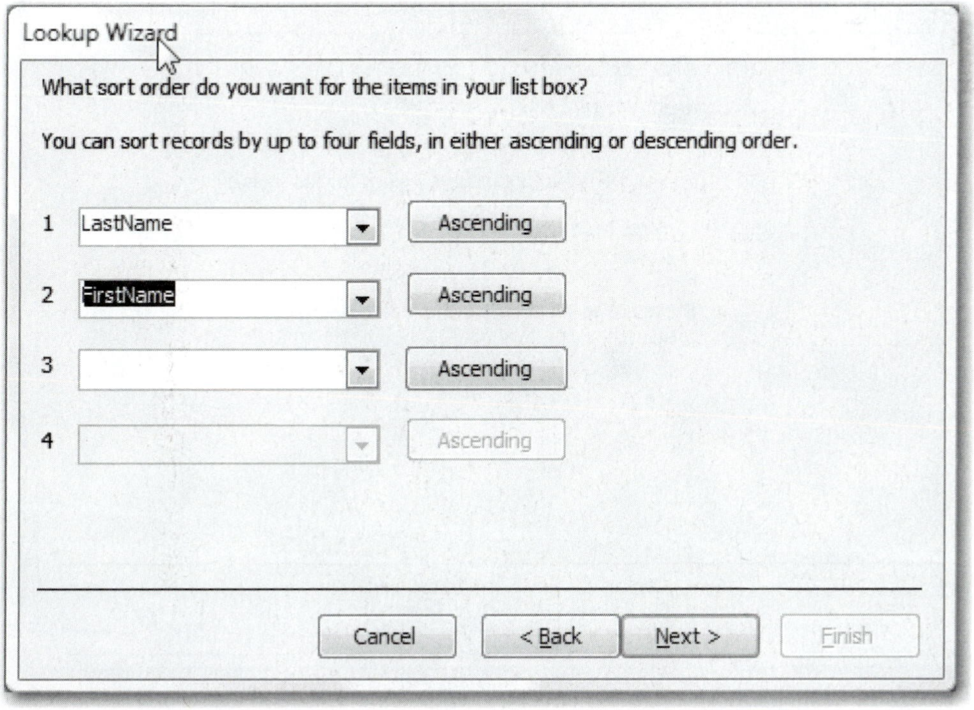

Figure 18: Lookup Wizard Column Width Dialog Box

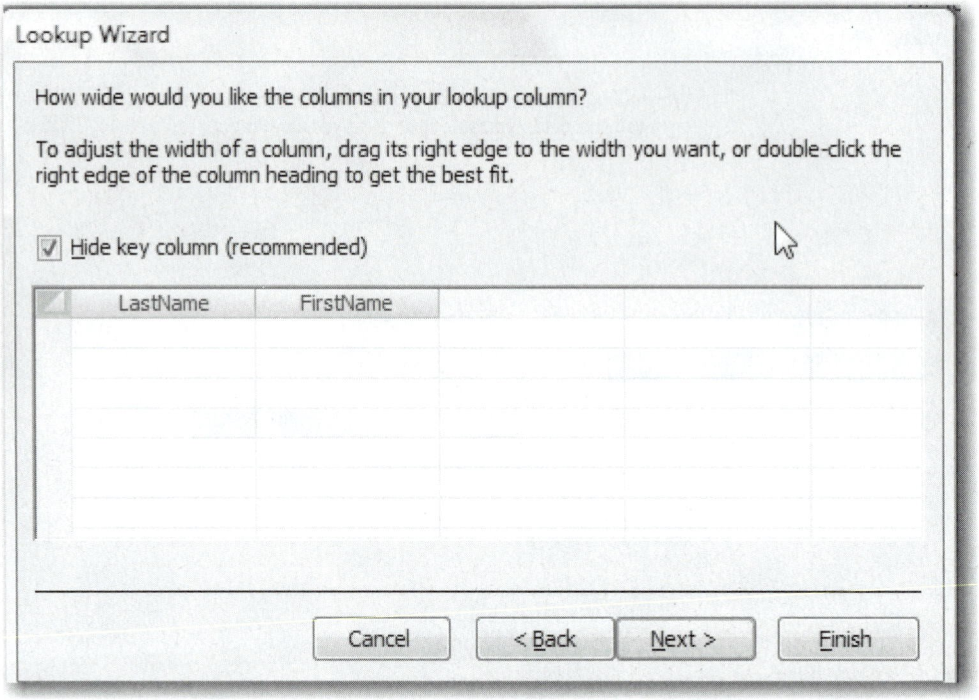

Figure 19: Lookup Wizard Label Dialog Box

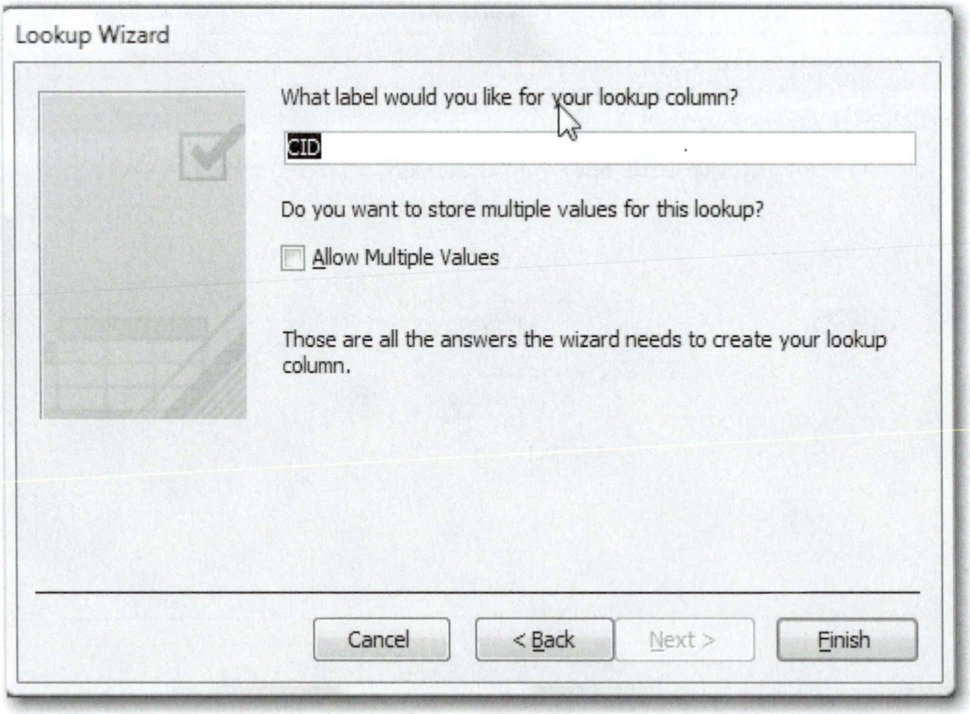

Task 5: Create Relationships

1. From the Show/Hide group located on the Database Tools tab, click the Relationships button. See Figure 20. The Relationships window will open. See Figure 21.

2. If a table is not showing, click the Show Table button located in the Relationships group. See Figure 22. (The Relationships group is located on the Design tab.) Double-click the table name in the Show Table dialog box. See Figure 23. Click the Close button.

3. Double click the line that connects the tblCustomer and tblEnrollment tables. The Edit Relationships dialog box opens.

4. Select the Enforce Referential Integrity, Cascade Update Related Fields, and Cascade Delete Related Records options. Click the OK button. See Figure 24.

5. Double click the line that connects the tblEnrollment and tblItem tables. The Edit Relationships dialog box opens.

6. Select the Enforce Referential Integrity and Cascade Update Related Fields options. Click the OK button.

7. Click the Save button located on the Quick Access Toolbar.

8. Close the Relationships window.

Figure 20: Relationships Button

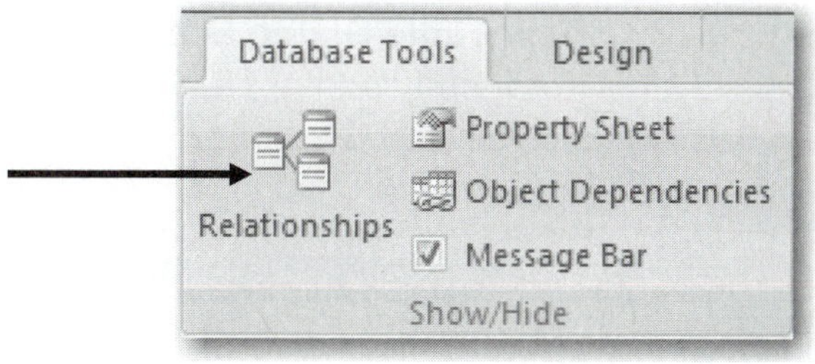

Figure 21: Relationship Window for Salon Database

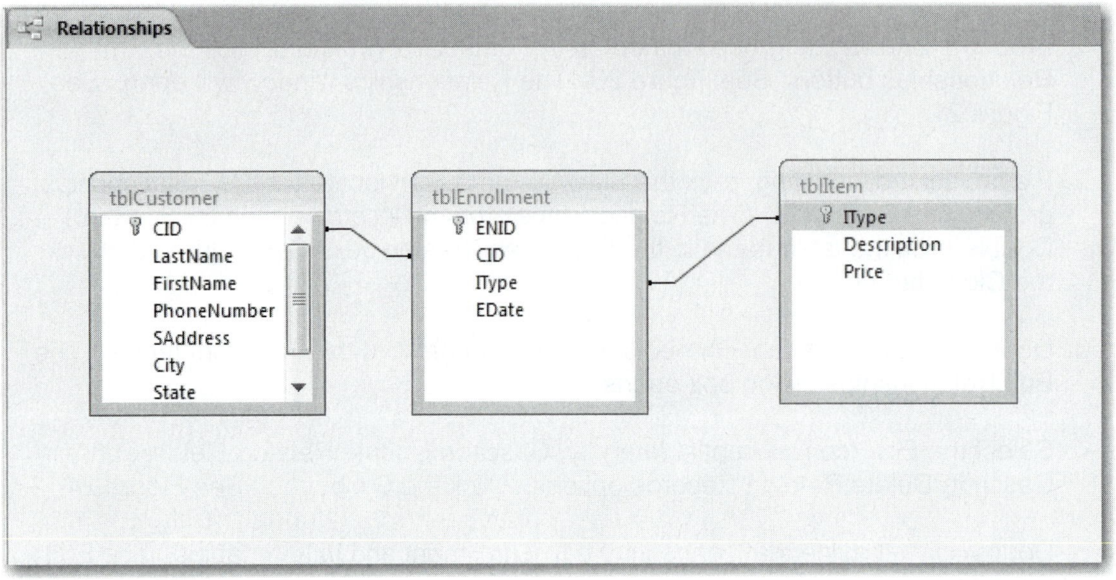

Figure 22: Show Table Button

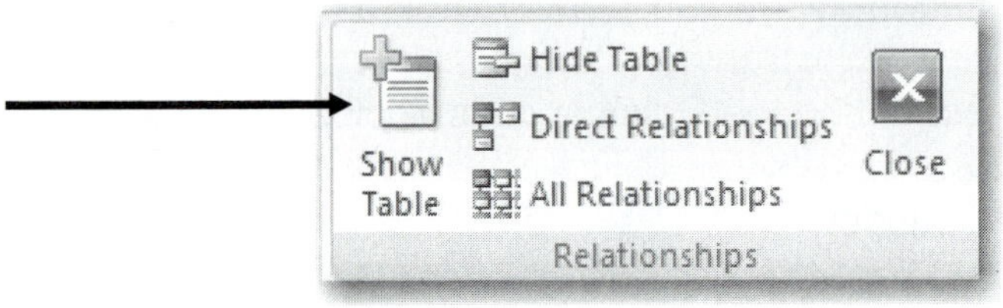

Figure 23: Show Table Dialog Box

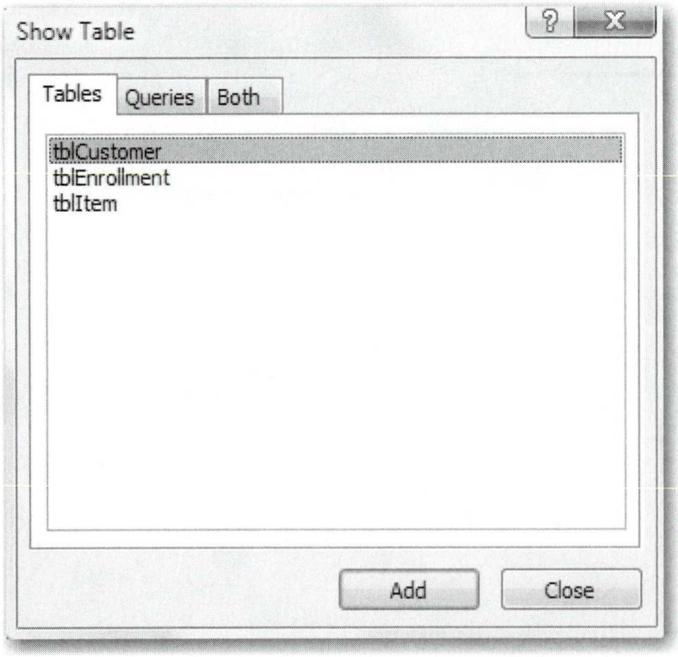

Figure 24: Edit Relationships Dialog Box

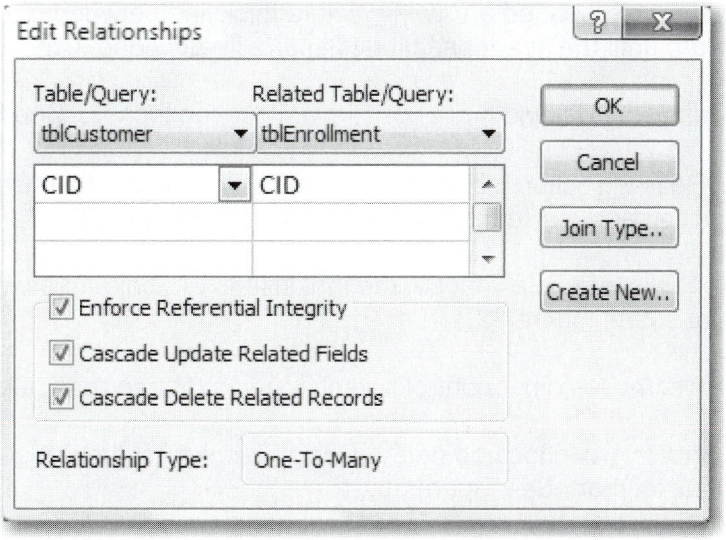

Activity 2: Form Creation and Test Data Entry

Activity 2 requires you to design Customer, Item, and Enrollment forms, as well as use the forms to enter test data. When designing these forms, you can use Figures 36, 39, and 42 as references. Once the forms are created, you can use the forms to enter the data shown in Figures 43 - 45.

Task 1: Create the Customer Form

To create the Customer form, you can:

1. From the Forms group located on the Create tab, click the More Forms button.
2. From the drop-down menu, select the Form Wizard option. See Figure 25.
3. Click the drop-down arrow, and select tblCustomer. Add all the tblCustomer fields to the form. See Figure 26. Click the Next button.
4. Select the columnar layout. See Figure 27. Click the Next button.
5. Select the Access 2007 style. See Figure 28. Click the Next button.
6. Name the form “frmCustomer”. See Figure 29. Click the Finish button. The initial Customer form is displayed. See Figure 30.
7. From the Views group, click the down arrow on the View button, and then select Design view. Figure 31 shows the initial Customer form in Design view.
8. If the Field List box is open, click the Close button on the Field List box.

9. Place the mouse pointer on top of the Detail Section Bar. When the mouse pointer changes to a double-headed arrow  with a thick line between the arrow heads, drag downward until the header section is approximately one inch.

10. Resize the form's border width to approximately seven inches. See Figure 32.

11. In the Form Header section, select the control containing the text “frmCustomer” and then position and resize the control as shown in Figure 32.

12. While the control is still selected, set the font size to 20; bold and center the text “frmCustomer”. See Figure 32.

13. Click inside the frmCustomer control and change the text to read “Customer Form”.

14. From the Controls group located on the Design tab, select the Label button located on the Toolbox toolbar. See Figure 33.

15. Place your mouse pointer in the Form Header section; then drag to size the control. Use Figure 34 as a guide.

16. Type the words “Timeka's Tanning Salon” inside the control. Set the font size to 26; set the font color to Access Theme 10. (Access Theme 10 is located in the Access Theme Colors group, and is in Column 10, Row 2.)

17. Bold and center the text inside the control.

18. Position the control so that its contents will appear centered on the form.

19. Move to the Detail section. Select the controls, and then right-click.

20. From the Shortcut Menu, select Layout, and then select the Remove command.

21. Using Figure 34 as a guide, reposition the field controls and their labels.

22. Double click the CID label. The Property Sheet window should appear. Click the Format tab. In the Caption box, type “Customer Identification Number:”. See Figure 35.

23. Close the Property Sheet window.

24. Bold and right justify the CID label.

25. Double click the LastName label. The Property Sheet window should appear. Click the Format tab. In the Caption box, type “Last Name:”. Close the Property Sheet window.

26. Bold and right justify the LastName label.

27. Double click the FirstName label. The Property Sheet window should appear. Click the Format tab. In the Caption box, type "First Name:". Close the Property Sheet window.

28. Bold and right justify the FirstName label.

29. Double click the PhoneNumber label. The Property Sheet window should appear. Click the Format tab. In the Caption box, type "Phone Number:". Close the Property Sheet window.

30. Bold and right justify the PhoneNumber label.

31. Double click the SAddress label. The Property Sheet window should appear. Click the Format tab. In the Caption box, type "Street Address:". Close the Property Sheet window.

32. Bold and right justify the SAddress label.

33. Double click the City label. The Property Sheet window should appear. Click the Format tab. In the Caption box, insert a colon after "City". Close the Property Sheet window.

34. Bold and right justify the City label.

35. Double click the State label. The Property Sheet window should appear. Click the Format tab. In the Caption box, insert a colon after "State". Close the Property Sheet window.

36. Bold and right justify the State label.

37. Double click the ZipCode label. The Property Sheet window should appear. Click the Format tab. In the Caption box, type "Zip Code:". Close the Property Sheet window.

38. Bold and right justify the ZipCode label.

39. While holding down the Shift key, click each control in the Detail Section (CID, LastName, FirstName, PhoneNumber, SAddress, City, State, and ZipCode).

40. Click the down arrow beside the Font Color button. From the Access Theme colors group, select Access Theme 9 (row 2, Column 9).

41. Make any other adjustments that you feel are necessary to improve the Customer form's appearance. See Figure 36.

42. Save the form.

Figure 25: Form Wizard Command

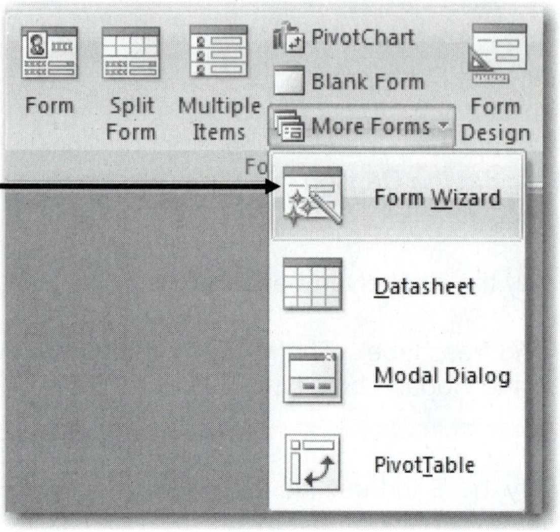

Figure 26: Form Wizard Field Selection

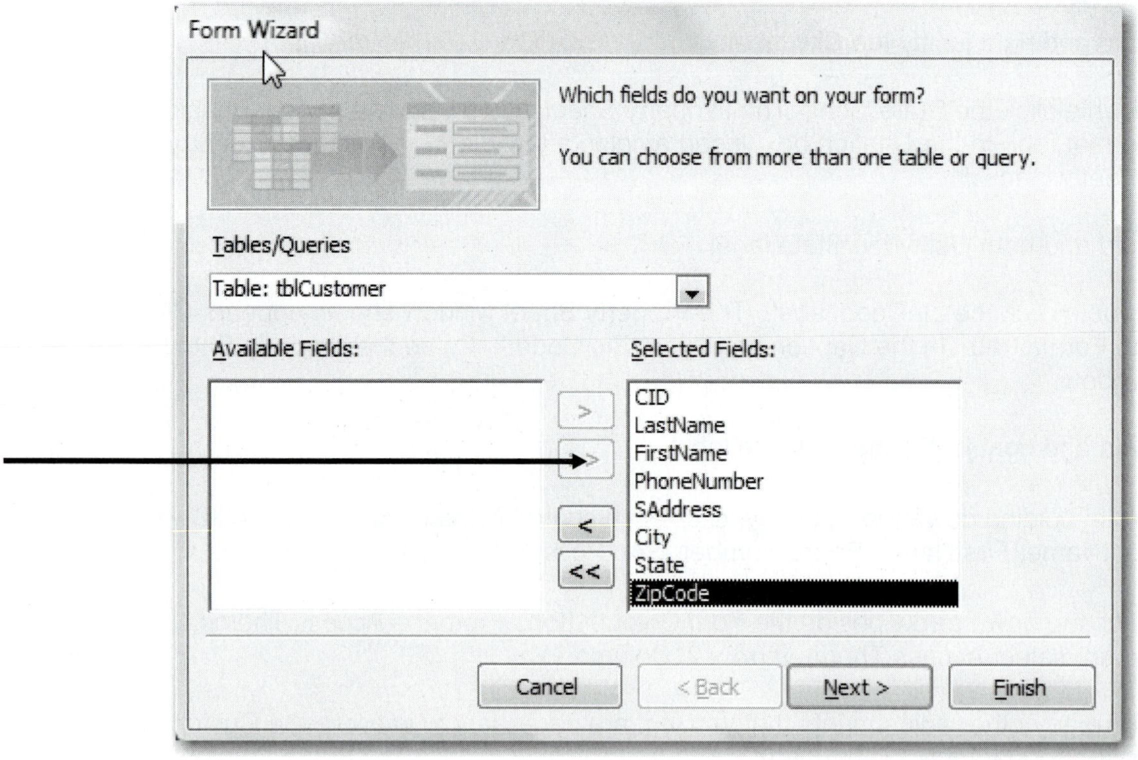

Figure 27: Form Wizard Layout Dialog Box

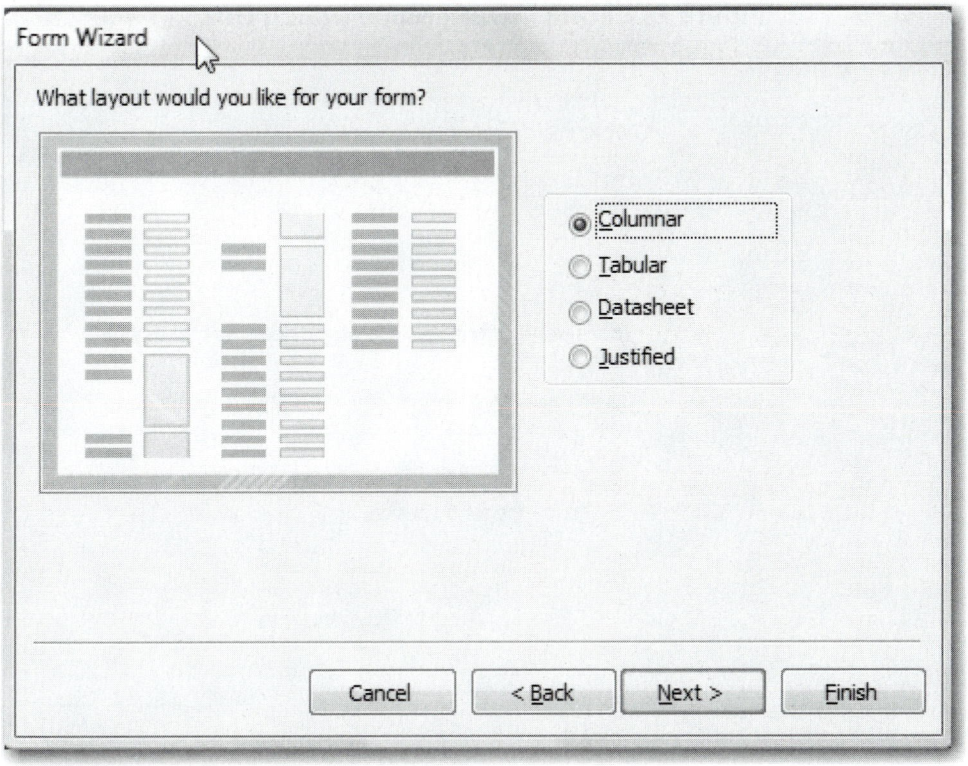

Figure 28: Form Wizard Style Dialog Box

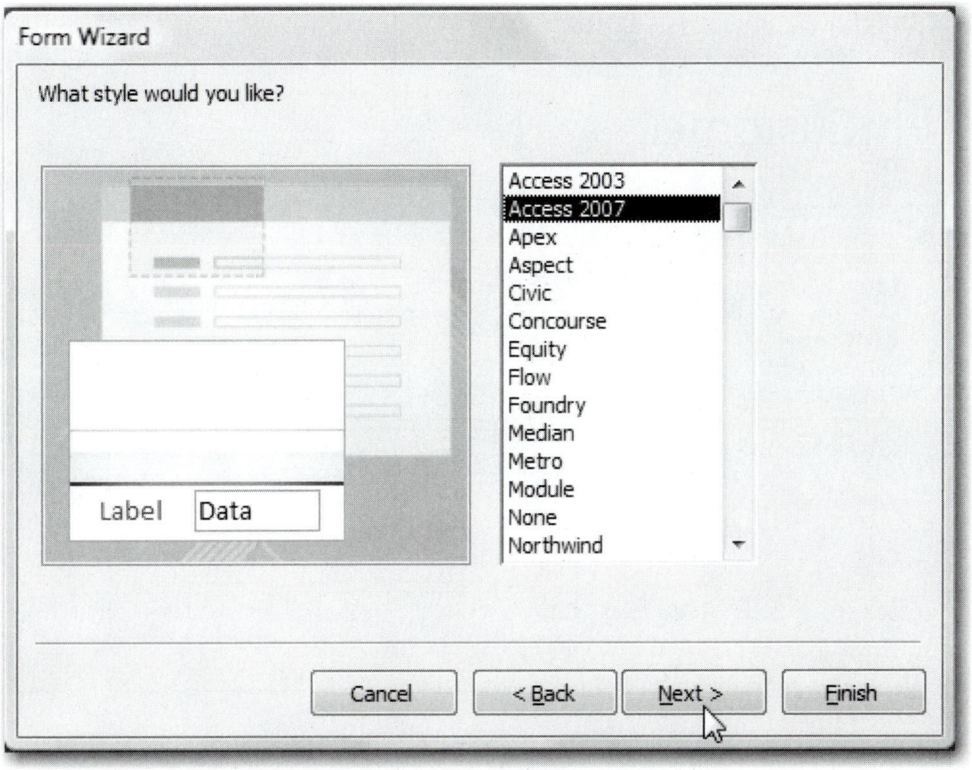

Figure 29: Form Wizard Name Dialog Box

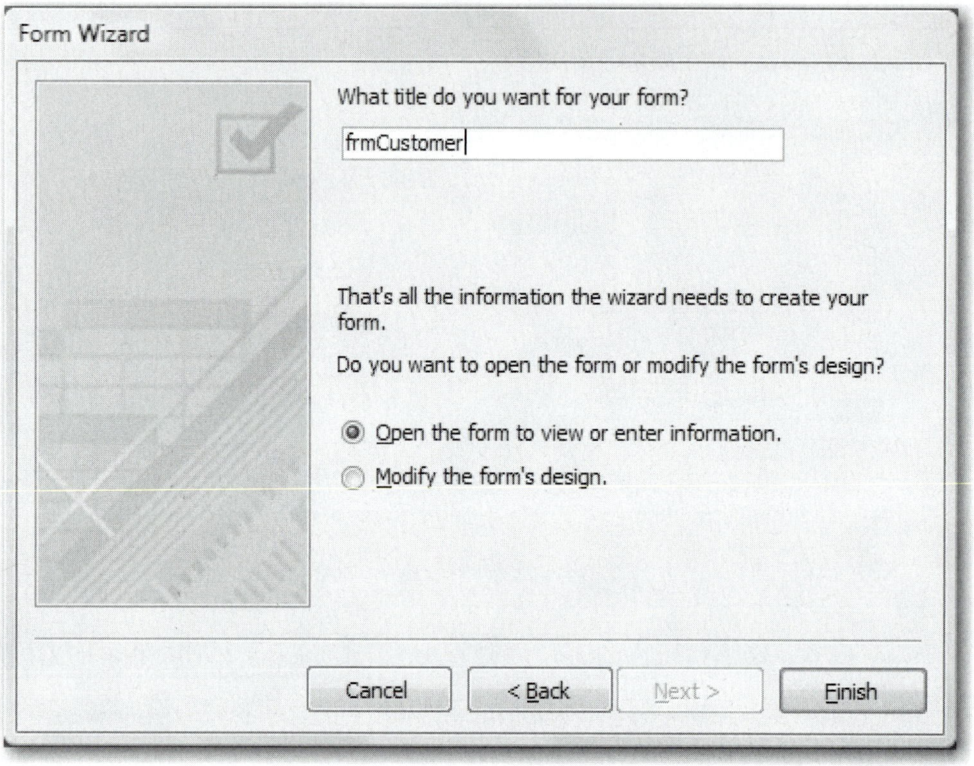

Figure 30: Initial Customer Form

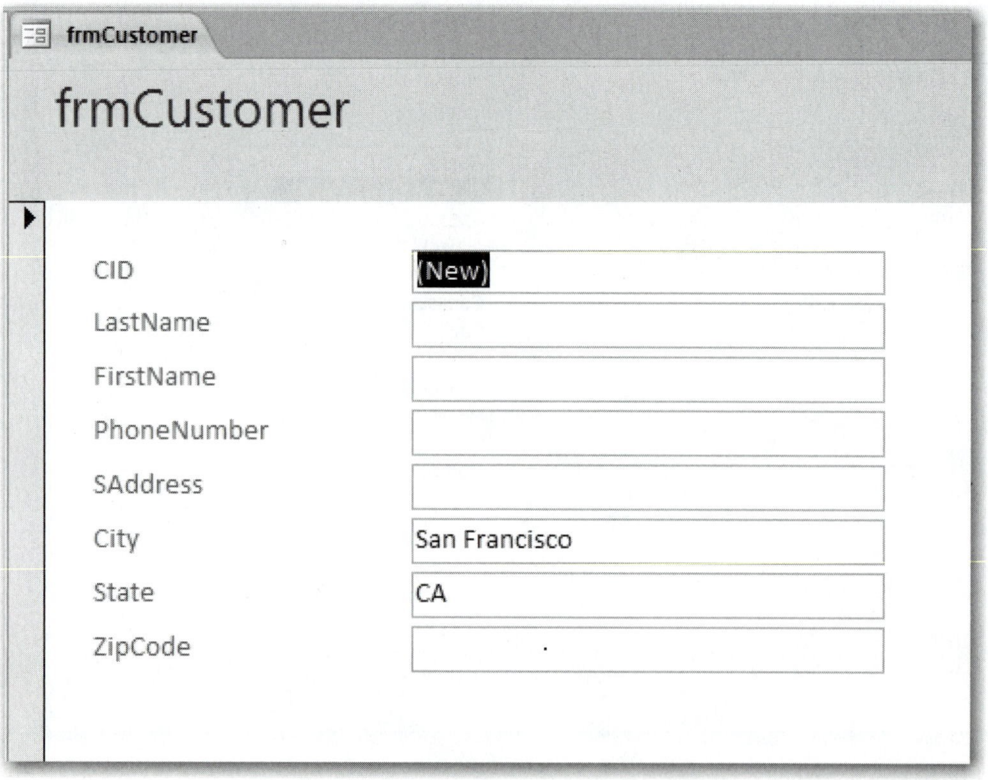

Figure 31: Initial Customer Form in Design View

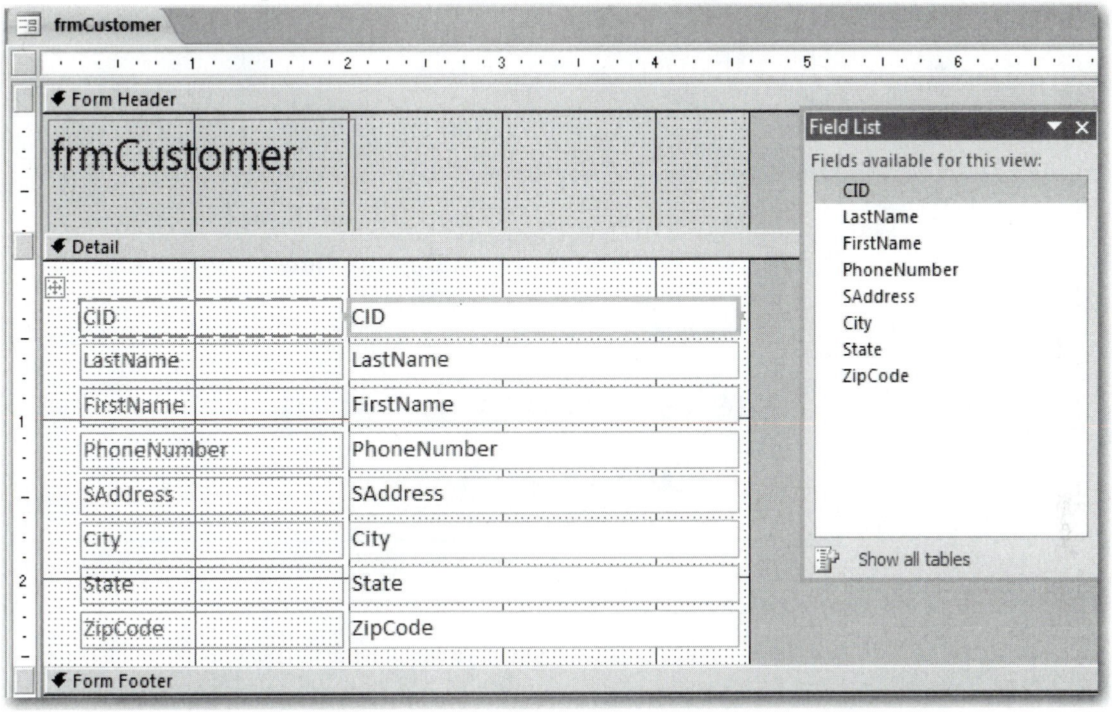

Figure 32: Customer Form with Increased Header Section and Border Width

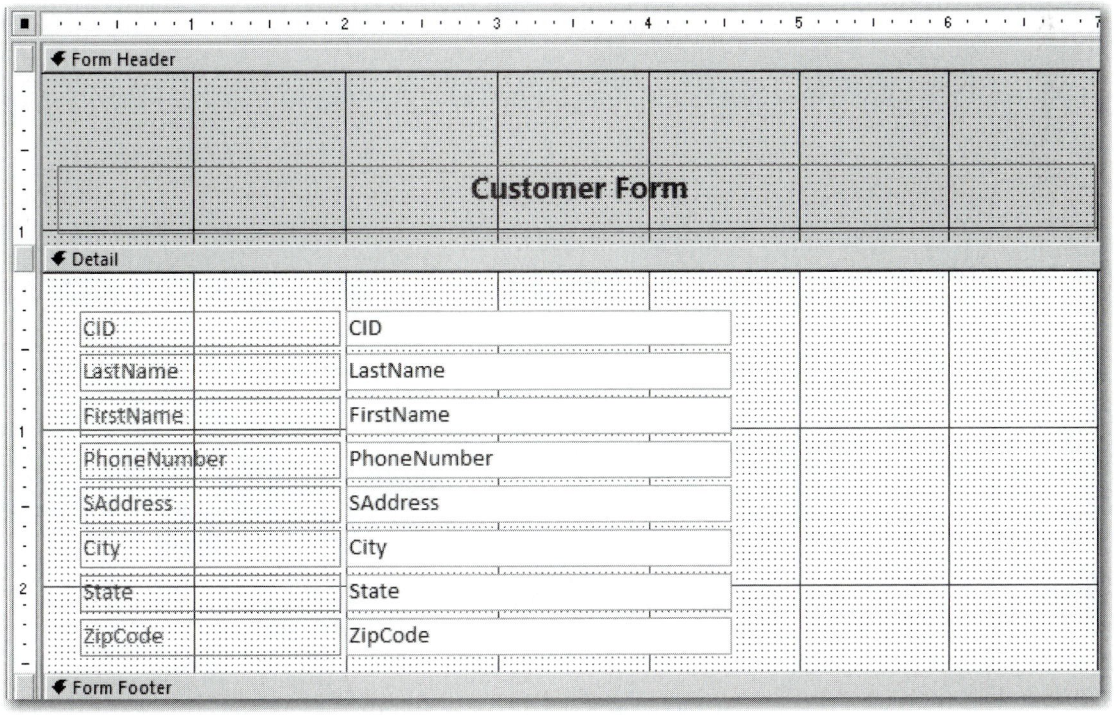

Figure 33: Controls Group

Figure 34: Customer Form in Design View

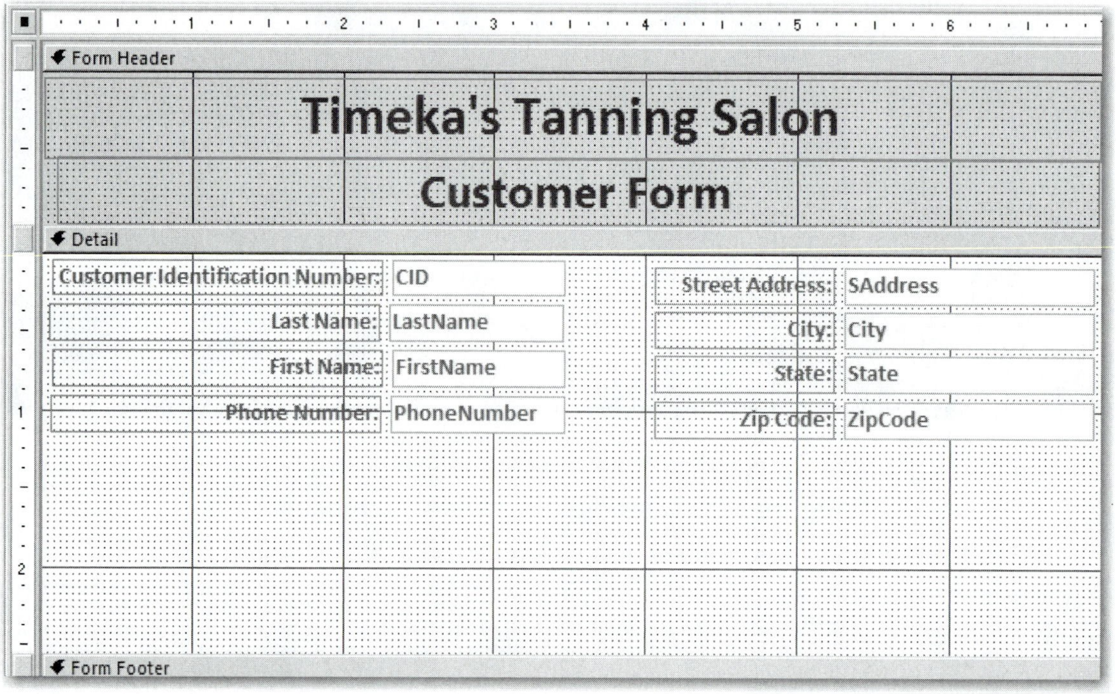

Figure 35: Property Sheet Window

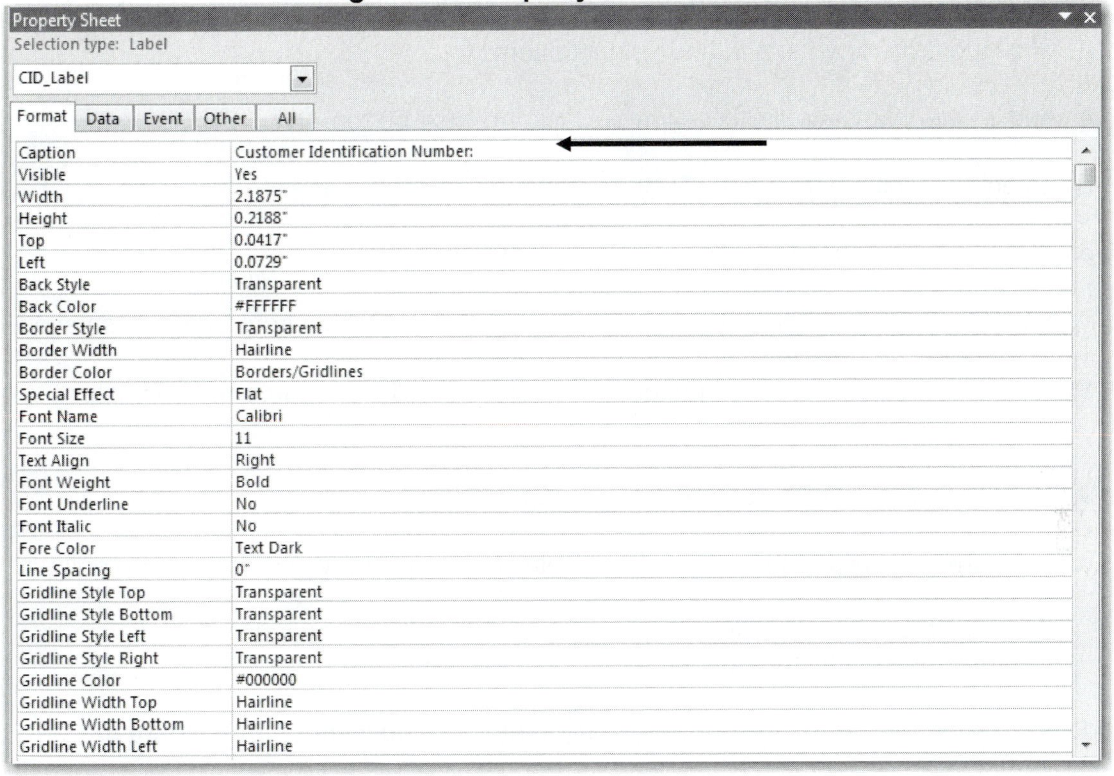

Figure 36: Customer Form in Form View

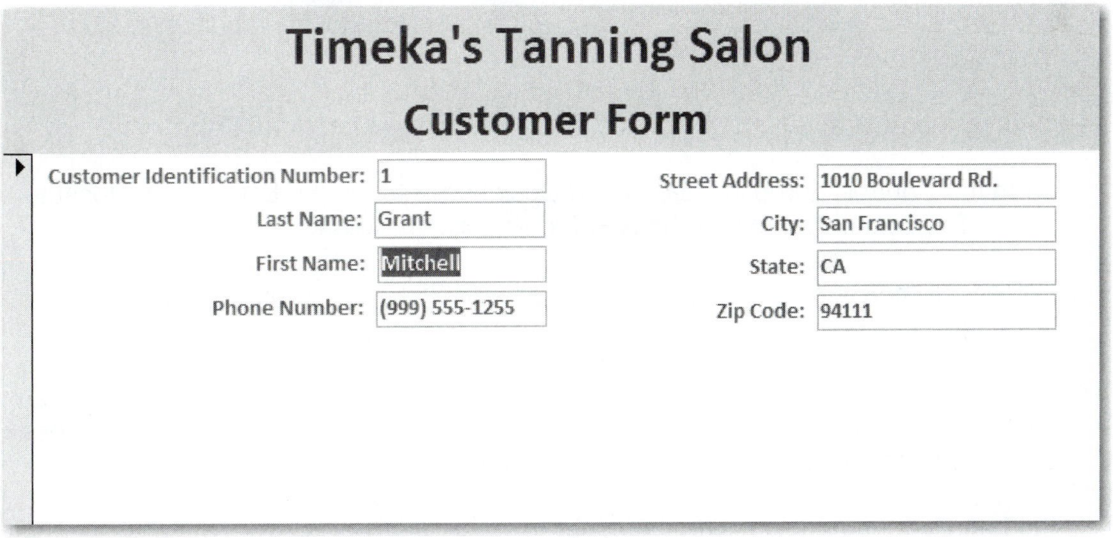

Task 2: Create the Item Form

To create the Item form, you can:

1. From the Forms group located on the Create tab, click the More Forms button.

2. From the drop-down menu, select the Form Wizard option.

3. Click the drop-down arrow, and select tblItem.

4. Add all the tblItem fields to the form. Click the Next button.

5. Select the Columnar layout. Click the Next button.

6. Select the Access 2007 style. Click the Next button.

7. Name the form "frmItem". Click the Finish button. The initial Item form is displayed.

8. From the Views group, click the down arrow on the View button, and then select Design view. See Figure 37.

9. If necessary, click the Close button on the Field List box.

10. Place the mouse pointer on top of the Detail Section Bar. When the mouse pointer changes to a double-headed arrow  with a thick line between the arrow heads, drag downward until the header section is approximately one inch.

11. Resize the form's border width to approximately seven inches. See Figure 38.

12. In the Form Header section, select the control containing the text "frmItem" and then position and resize the control as shown in Figure 38.

13. While the control is still selected, set the font size to 20; bold and center the text "frmItem".

14. Click inside the frmItem control and change the text to read "Item Form".

15. From the Controls group located on the Design tab, select the Label button located on the Toolbox toolbar. Refer back to Figure 33.

16. Place your mouse pointer in the Form Header section; then drag to size the control. Use Figure 38 as a guide.

17. Type the words "Timeka's Tanning Salon" inside the control. Set the font size to 26; set the font color to Access Theme 10. (Access Theme 10 is located in the Access Theme Colors group, and is in Column 10, Row 2.)

18. Bold and center the text inside the control.

19. Position the control so that its contents will appear centered on the form.

20. Move to the Detail section. Select the controls, and then right-click.

21. From the Shortcut Menu, select Layout, and then select the Remove command.

22. Using Figure 38 as a guide, reposition the field controls and their labels.

23. Double click the IType label. The Property Sheet window should appear. Click the Format tab. In the Caption box, type “Item Type:”. Close the Property Sheet window.

24. Bold and right justify the IType label.

25. Double click the Description label. The Property Sheet window should appear. Click the Format tab. In the Caption box, type a colon after Description. Close the Property Sheet window.

26. Bold and right justify the Description label.

27. Double click the Price label. The Property Sheet window should appear. Click the Format tab. In the Caption box, type a colon after Price. Close the Property Sheet window.

28. Bold and right justify the Price label.

29. While holding down the Shift key, click each control in the Detail section (IType, Description, and Price).

30. Click the down arrow beside the Font Color button. From the Access Theme colors group, select the Access Theme 9 (row 2, Column 9).

31. Make any other adjustments that you feel are necessary to improve the Item form's appearance. See Figure 39.

32. Save the form.

Figure 37: Initial Item Form

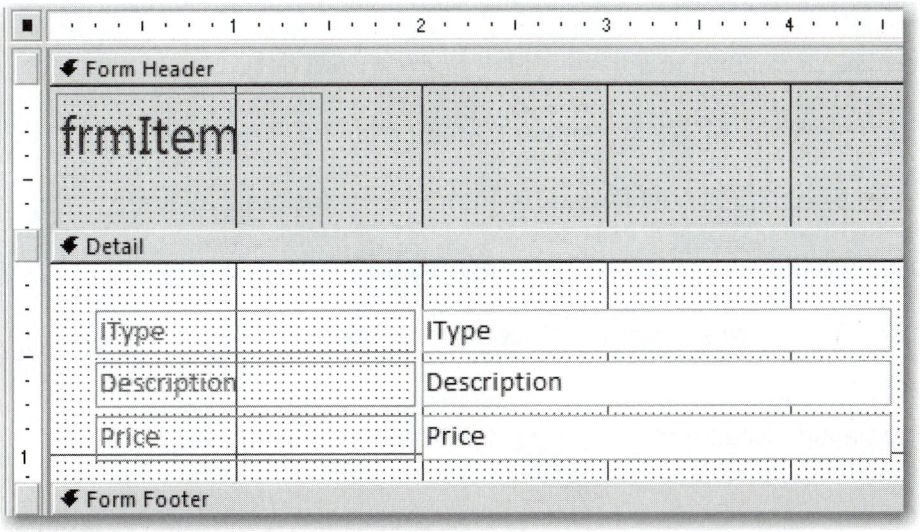

Figure 38: Final Item Form in Design View

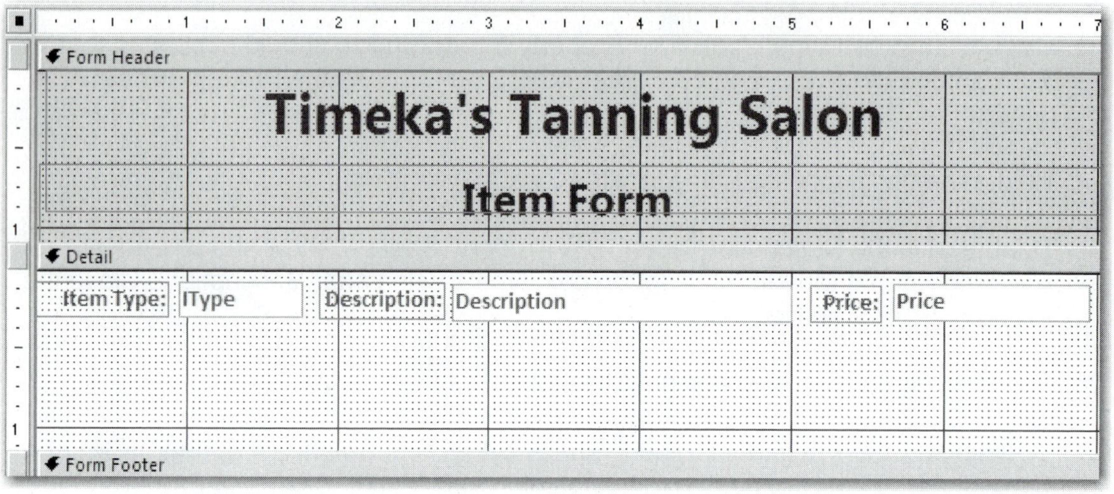

Figure 39: Item Form in Form View

Task 3: Create the Enrollment Form

To create the Enrollment form, you can:

1. From the Forms group located on the Create tab, click the More Forms button.
2. From the drop-down menu, select the Form Wizard option.
3. Click the drop-down arrow, and select tblEnrollment.
4. Add all the tblEnrollment fields to the form. Click the Next button.
5. Select the Columnar layout. Click the Next button.
6. Select the Access 2007 style. Click the Next button.
7. Name the form "frmEnrollment". Click the Finish button. The initial Enrollment form is displayed. See Figure 40.

8. From the Views group, click the down arrow on the View button, and then select Design view.
9. If necessary, click the Close button on the Field List box.

10. Place the mouse pointer on top of the Detail Section Bar. When the mouse pointer changes to a double-headed arrow  with a thick line between the arrow heads, drag downward until the header section is approximately one inch.

11. Resize the form's border width to approximately seven inches.

12. In the Form Header section, select the control containing the text "frmEnrollment" and then position and resize the control as shown in Figure 41.

13. While the control is still selected, set the font size to 20; bold and center the text "frmEnrollment". See Figure 41.

14. Click inside the frmEnrollment control and change the text to read "Enrollment Form".

15. From the Controls group located on the Design tab, select the Label button located on the Toolbox toolbar. Refer back to Figure 33.

16. Place your mouse pointer in the Form Header section; then drag to size the control. Use Figure 41 as a guide.

17. Type the words "Timeka's Tanning Salon" inside the control. Set the font size to 26; set the font color to Access Theme 10. (Access Theme 10 is located in the Access Theme Colors group, and is in Column 10, Row 2.)

18. Bold and center the text inside the control.

19. Position the control so that its contents will appear centered on the form.

20. Move to the Detail section. Select the controls, and then right-click.

21. From the Shortcut Menu, select Layout, and then select the Remove command.

22. Using Figure 41 as a guide, reposition the field controls and their labels.

23. Double click the ENID label. The Property Sheet window should appear. Click the Format tab. In the Caption box, type "Enrollment Identification Number:". Close the Property Sheet window.

24. Bold and right justify the ENID label.

25. Double click the CID label. The Property Sheet window should appear. Click the Format tab. In the Caption box, type "Customer Identification Number:". Close the Property Sheet window.

26. Bold and right justify the CID label.

27. Double click the IType label. The Property Sheet window should appear. Click the Format tab. In the Caption box, type "Item Type:". Close the Property Sheet window.

28. Bold and right justify the IType label.

29. Double click the EDate label. The Property Sheet window should appear. Click the Format tab. In the Caption box, type "Enrollment Date:". Close the Property Sheet window.

30. Bold and right justify the EDate label.

31. While holding down the Shift key, click each control in the Detail section (ENID, CID, IType, and EDate).

32. Click the down arrow beside the Font Color button. From the Access Theme colors group, select Access Theme 9 (row 2, Column 9).

33. While the controls are still selected, click the Property Sheets button located in the Tools group.

34. In the Border Width box, click the drop down arrow and select 1pt.

35. Make any other adjustments that you feel are necessary to improve the Item form's appearance. Figure 42 shows the final Enrollment form.

36. Save the form.

Figure 40: Initial Enrollment Form in Design View

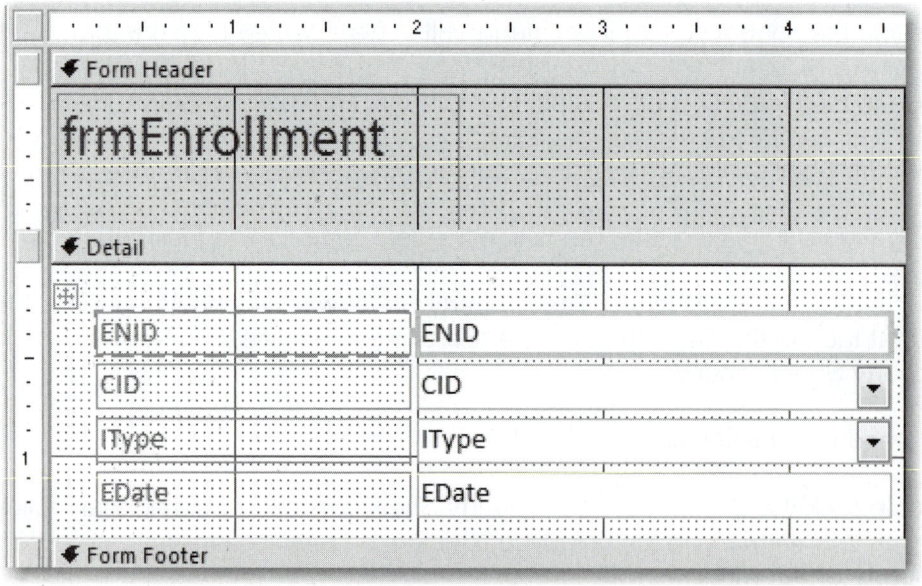

Figure 41: Enrollment Form in Design View After Changes

Figure 42: Enrollment Form in Form View

Task 4: Enter the Customer, Item, and Enrollment Data

1. Use your newly created Customer form to enter the customer data shown in Figure 43.
2. Use your newly created Item form to enter the item data shown in Figure 44.
3. Use your newly created Enrollment form to enter the enrollment data shown in Figure 45.

Figure 43: Customer Data

Customer Identification Number	Last Name	First Name	Phone Number	Street Address	City	State	Zip Code
1	Grant	Mitchell	(999)555-1255	1010 Boulevard Rd.	San Francisco	CA	94111
2	Sasser	Lexina	(999)555-6456	210 Rushing Meadows	San Francisco	CA	94112
3	Rother	Elwood	(999)555-6577	3001 Ripple Creek	San Francisco	CA	94113
4	Chen	Shibo	(999)555-4789	15712 Tanglewood Road	San Francisco	CA	94113
5	Elotmani	Damir	(999)555-3812	2121 Hyde Parke	San Francisco	CA	94115
6	Schoenhals	Eliah	(999)555-6058	1920 Pine Drive	San Francisco	CA	94111
7	Erbst	Troy	(999)555-1300	1780 Glacier Drive	San Francisco	CA	94112
8	Ottinger	Clarissa	(999)555-9351	11908 Coltrane	San Francisco	CA	94112
9	Blochowiak	Edith	(999)555-0202	1223 Ridgewood	San Francisco	CA	94115
10	Harley	Sasha	(999)555-5931	10625 Brighton	San Francisco	CA	94115

Figure 44: Item Data

Item Type	Description	Item Price
SE001	One Session	$5.00
SE002	5 Sessions	$25.00
SE003	10 Sessions	$50.00
SE004	15 Sessions	$75.00
SE005	20 Sessions	$100.00
SP001	One Month Unlimited	$35.00
SP002	Monthly Special	$30.00
SP003	Loyal Customer	$29.99
SP004	Referral	$29.99
SP005	Yearly Enrollment	$350.00

Figure 45: Enrollment Data

Customer Last Name	Description	Enrollment Date
Sasser	5 Sessions	1/17/2007
Rother	One Month Unlimited	1/18/2007
Chen	10 Sessions	1/15/2007
Elotmani	One Session	1/18/2007
Schoenhals	Loyal Customer	1/18/2007
Erbst	15 Sessions	1/18/2007
Ottinger	One Month Unlimited	8/15/2007
Blochowiak	10 Sessions	8/15/2007
Harley	5 Sessions	8/20/2007

Activity 3: Query Creation

Activity 3 creates three queries. The first query, qrySingleSession, identifies how many customers have purchased a single tanning session. The second query, qryInactive, identifies the salon's customers who are not currently enrolled. The third query, qryNewEnrollment, identifies the customers that enrolled after August 1, 2007.

Task 1: Create the qrySingleSession Query

1. From the Other group located on the Create tab, click the Query Design button. See Figure 46.

2. The Query Design view and the Show Table dialog box open. (If the Show Table dialog box is not open, click the Show Table button located in the Query Setup group.)

3. In the Show Table dialog box, double click tblEnrollment and tblItem. The field lists for both tables should now be added to the top pane of the Query Design window. Click the Close button.

4. Add the Description field from the tblItem table and the Itype field from the tblEnrollment table to the query design grid. (You can add a field by double clicking its name.)

5. From the Show/Hide group, click the Totals button. See Figure 47.

6. In the Total row for the IType field, click the drop-down arrow and select Count from the drop-down list. (If the drop-down arrow is not showing, just click by the word "By". The drop-down arrow should now appear.)

7. In the Sort row for the Description field, click the drop-down arrow and select Ascending from the drop-down list.

8. In the Criteria row for the Description field, enter "One Session".

9. Click the Save button located on the Quick Access Toolbar. When prompted, name the query "qrySingleSession". Figure 48 shows the query in Design View.

10. Click the Run button located in the Results group. Figure 49 shows the Run button, and Figure 50 shows the query results.

Figure 46: Query Design Button

Figure 47: Totals Button

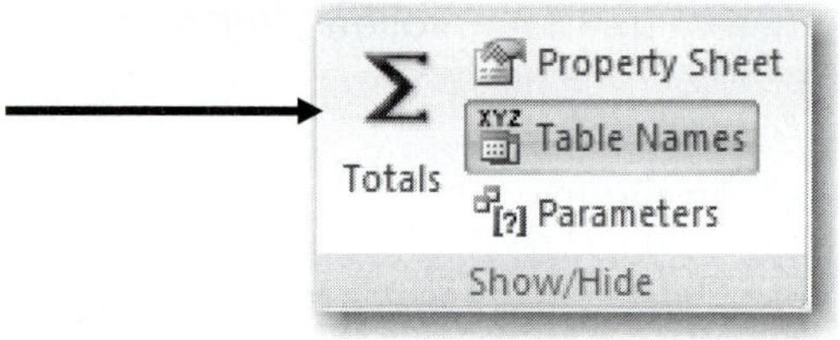

Figure 48: qrySingleSession Query in Design View

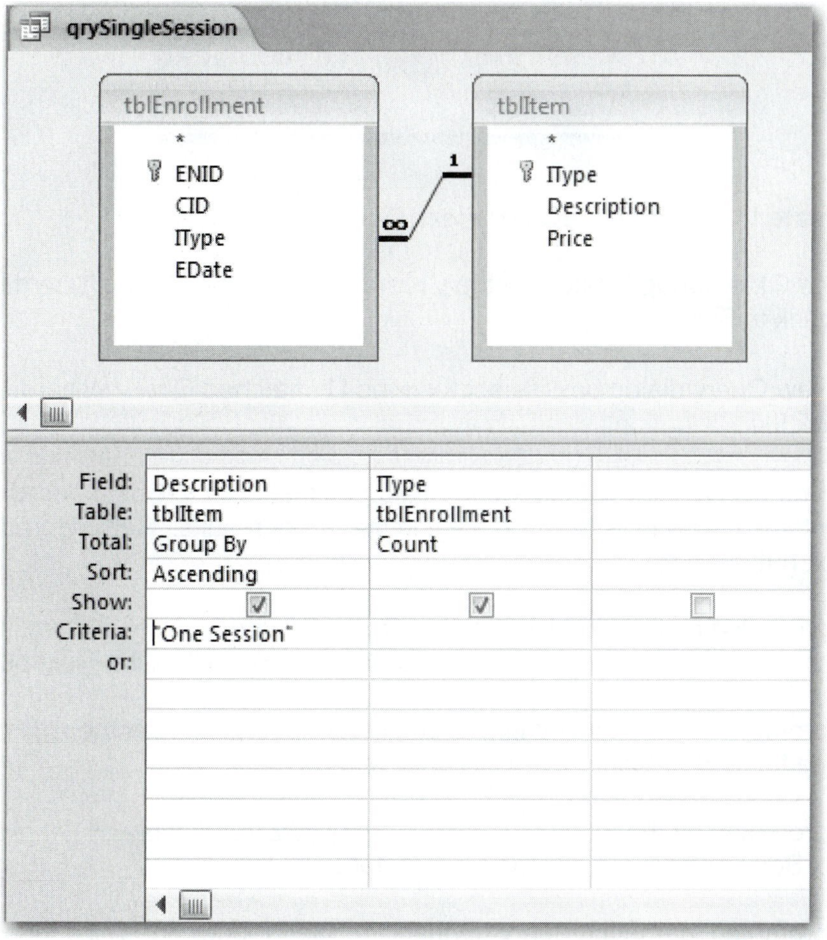

Figure 49: Run Button

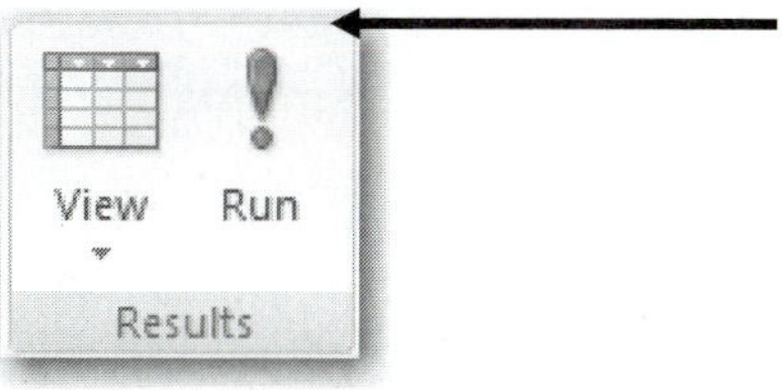

Figure 50: qrySingleSession Query Results

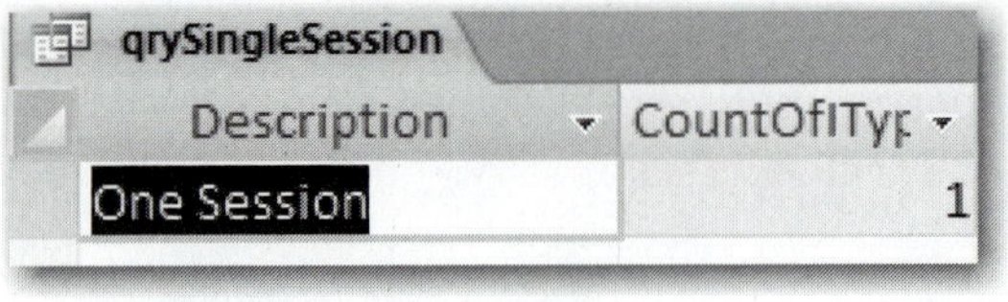

Task 2: Create the qryInactiveCustomers Query

1. From the Other group located on the Create tab, click the Query Wizard button. Refer back to Figure 46.

2. In the New Query dialog box, select the Find Unmatched Query Wizard. See Figure 51. Click the OK button.

3. In the Find Unmatched Query Wizard dialog box, specify tblCustomer as the table that contains the records that you want in the query results. See Figure 52. Click the Next button.

4. When prompted by the Find Unmatched Query Wizard, specify tblEnrollment as the table that contains the related records. See Figure 53. Click the Next button.

5. When prompted by the Find Unmatched Query Wizard, specify the CID field as the matching field. See Figure 54. Click the Next button.

6. When prompted by the Find Unmatched Query Wizard, display all fields in the results. See Figure 55. Click the Next button.

7. When prompted, name the query qryInactive. See Figure 56. Click the Finish button. Figure 57 shows that Mitchell Grant is an inactive customer.

Figure 51: New Query Dialog Box

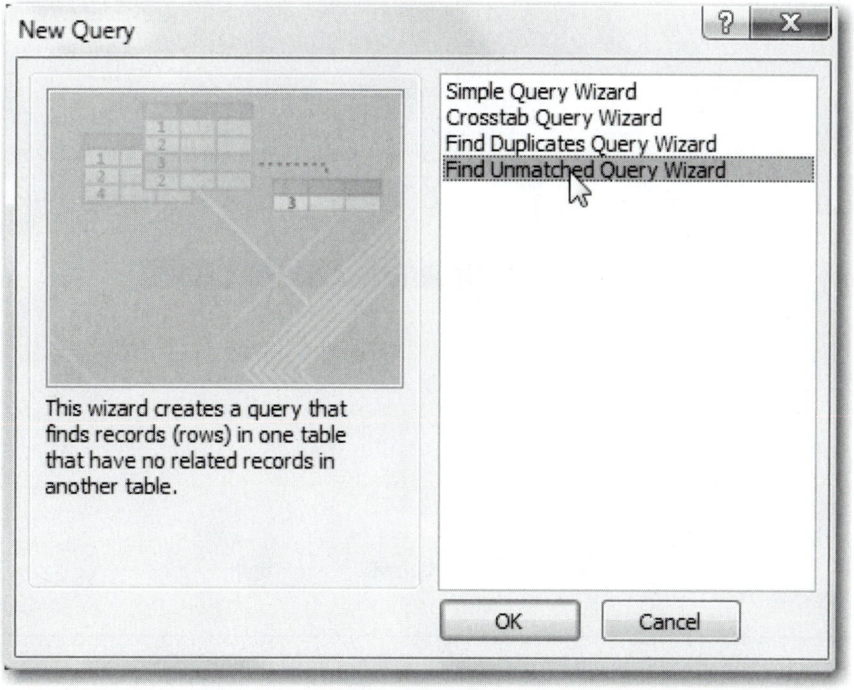

Figure 52: Find Unmatched Query Wizard Dialog Box

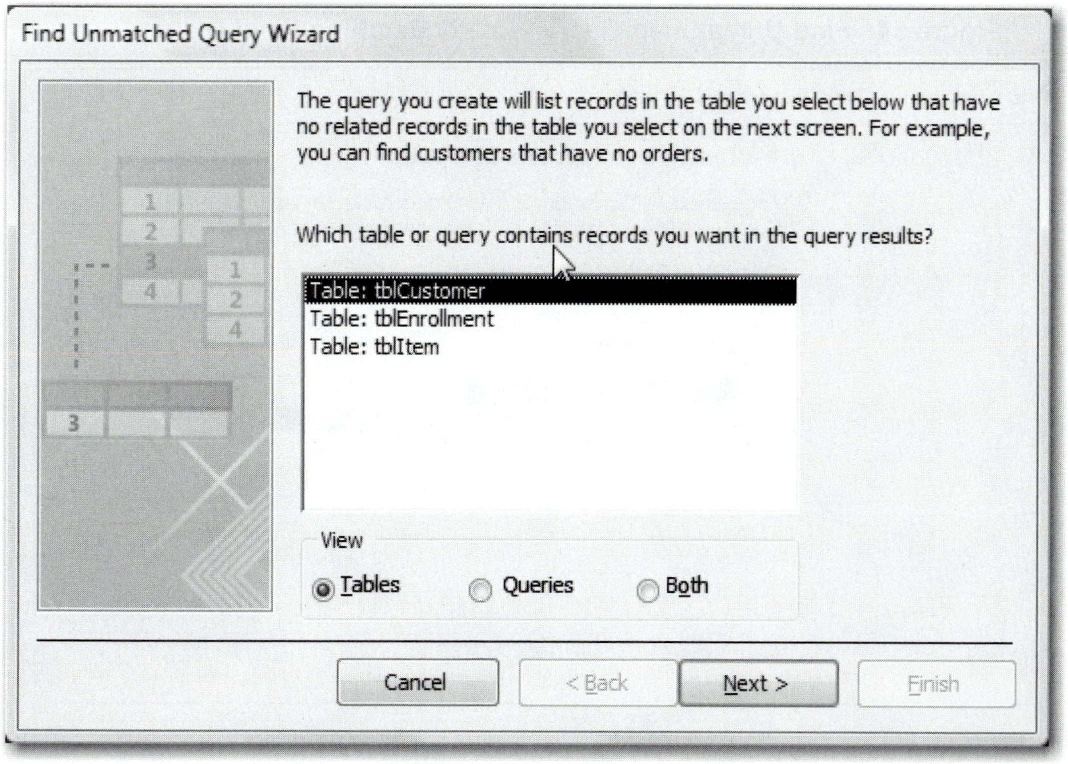

Figure 53: Find Unmatched Query Wizard Related Table Dialog Box

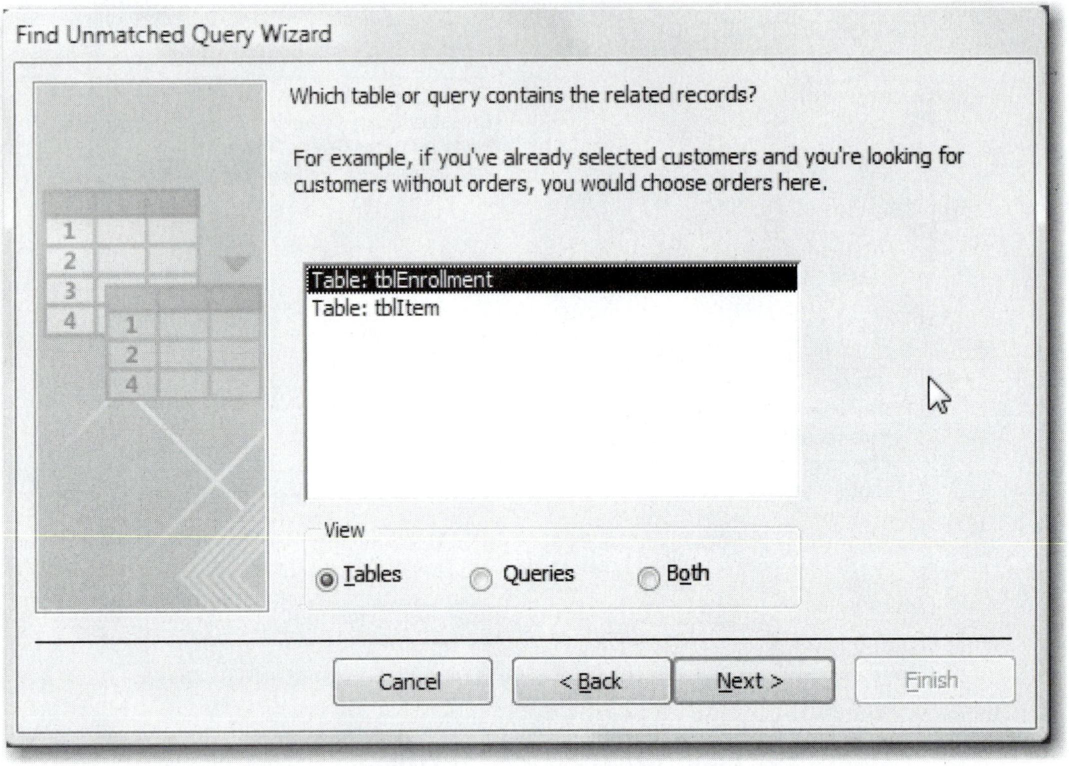

Figure 54: Find Unmatched Query Wizard Matching Field Dialog Box

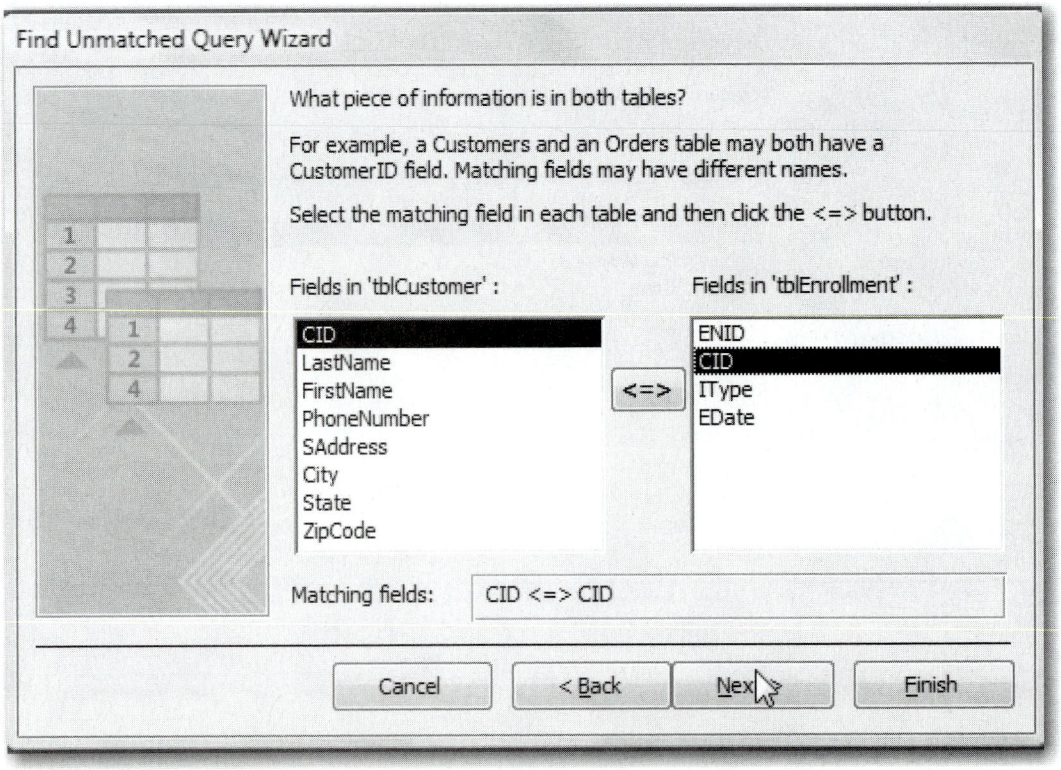

Figure 55: Find Unmatched Query Wizard Result Fields Dialog Box

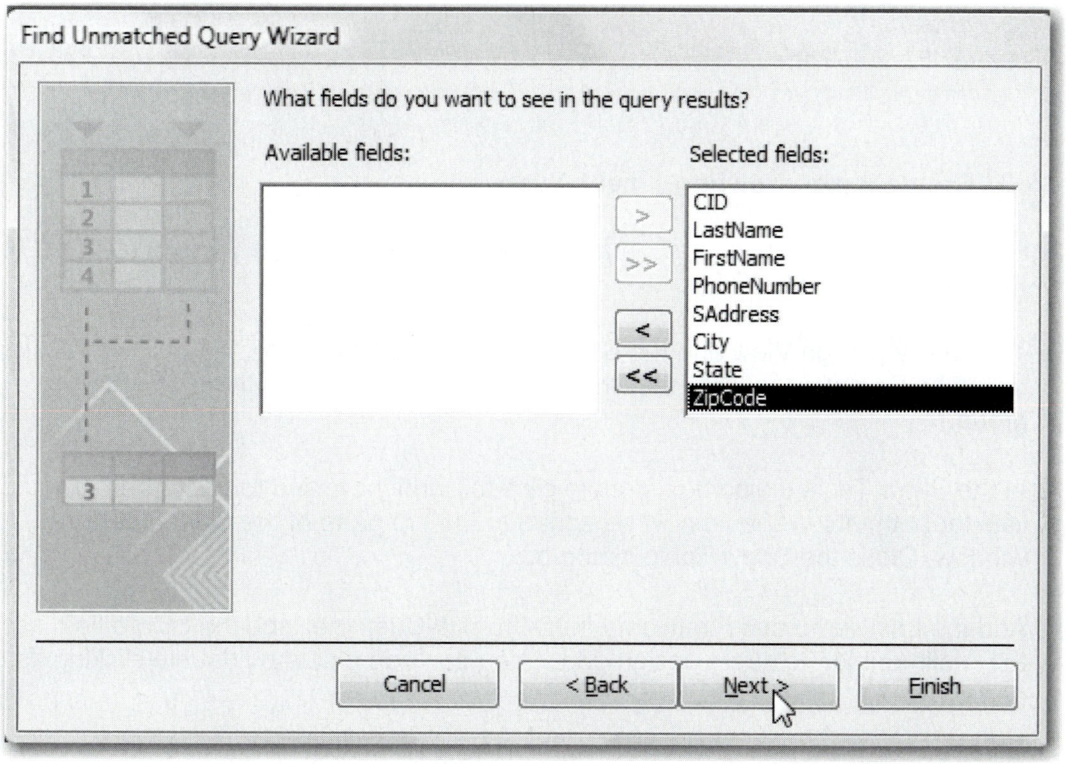

Figure 56: Find Unmatched Query Wizard Name Dialog Box

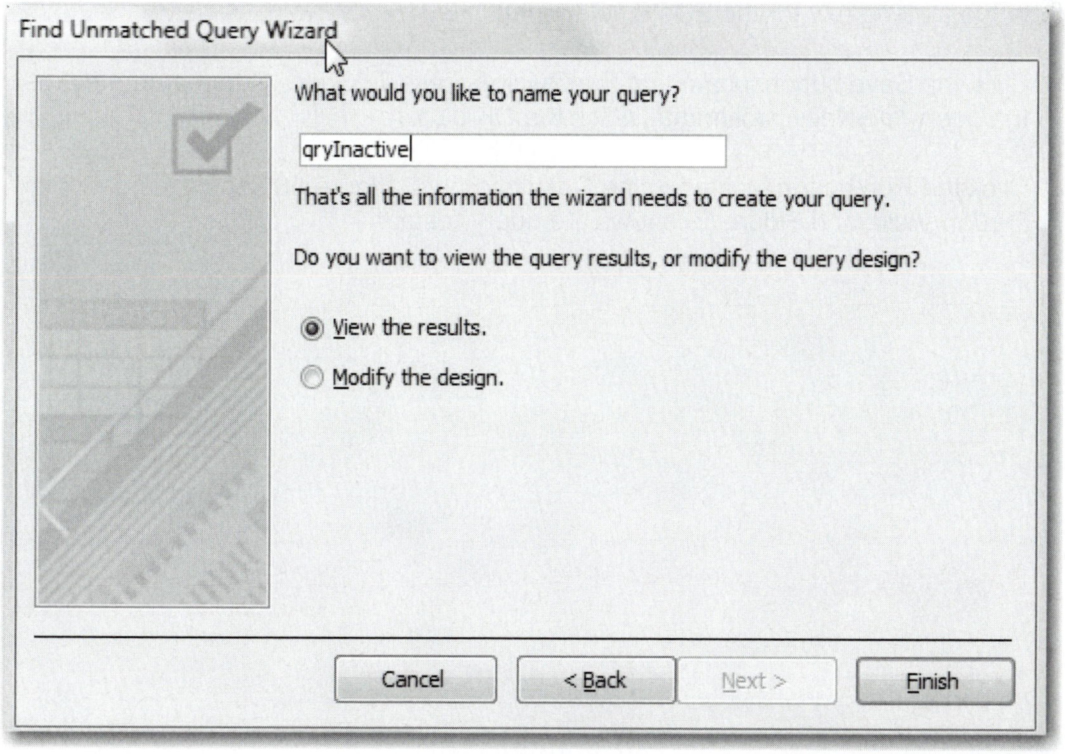

Figure 57: Inactive Query Results

CID	LastName	FirstName	PhoneNumber	SAddress	City	State	ZipCode
1	Grant	Mitchell	555-1255	1010 Boulevard Rd.	San Francisco	CA	94111
* (New)							

Task 3: Create the qryNewEnrollment Query

1. From the Other group located on the Create tab, click the Query Design button. Refer back to Figure 46.

2. The Query Design View and the Show Table dialog box open. (If the Show Table dialog box is not open, click the Show Table button located in the Query Setup group.)

3. In the Show Table dialog box, double click tblEnrollment and tblCustomer. The field lists for both tables should now be added to the top pane of the Query Design window. Close the Show Table dialog box.

4. Add the LastName and FirstName fields from tblCustomer and the EDate field from tblEnrollment to the query design grid. (You can add a field by double clicking its name.)

5. In the Sort row for the LastName field, click the drop-down arrow and select Ascending from the drop-down list.

6. In the Criteria row for the EDate field, enter “>8/01/2007”.

7. Click the Save button located on the Quick Access Toolbar. When prompted, name the query “qryNewEnrollment”. Click the OK button.

8. Click the Run button located in the Results group. Figure 58 shows the query in Design View, and Figure 59 shows the query results.

Figure 58: qryNewEnrollment Query in Design View

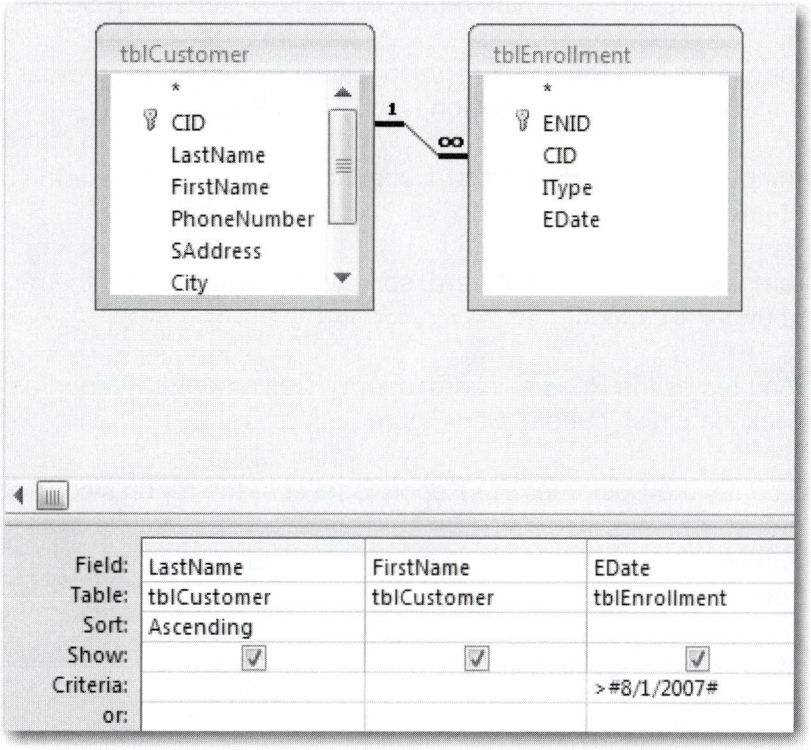

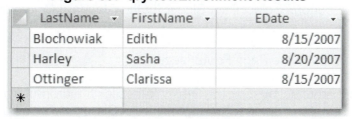

Figure 59: qryNewEnrollment Results

LastName	FirstName	EDate
Blochowiak	Edith	8/15/2007
Harley	Sasha	8/20/2007
Ottinger	Clarissa	8/15/2007

Activity 4: Prepare the Customer List Report

Activity 4 prepares the Customer List report according to Timeka's specifications. This activity is easy to perform, as the Report Wizard can be used.

Task 1: Create the Customer List Report

1. From the Reports group located on the Create tab, click the Report Wizard button. The first of several Report Wizard dialog boxes will appear.

2. In the Report Wizard dialog box, select tblCustomer as the data source.

3. Add all the fields from tblCustomer except the CID field. Click the Next button. See Figure 60.
4. Do not add a grouping level to the report; click the Next button. See Figure 61.
5. When prompted by the Report Wizard, specify an ascending sort order on the LastName field. Click the Next button. See Figure 62.
6. When prompted by the Report Wizard, specify a Tabular layout for the report. Click the Next button. See Figure 63.
7. When prompted by the Report Wizard, specify the Flow style for the report. Click the Next button. See Figure 64.
8. When prompted by the Report Wizard, specify Customer List Report as the report's name. Click the Finish button. See Figure 65.
9. Bold and center the Customer List Report label over the report's contents.
10. In the Page Header section, modify the labels so that they appear similar to the labels shown in Figure 66.
11. In the Detail section, reposition the controls so that they appear similar to Figure 66.
12. Select the controls in the Detail section.
13. From the Font group located on the Design tab, click the drop-down arrow beside the Font Color button. Select Dark Blue 4 (In the Standard Colors group, it is Row 5, Column 4).
14. Select the controls in the Page Footer section.
15. From the Font group located on the Design tab, click the drop-down arrow beside the Font Color button. Select Dark Blue 4 (In the Standard Colors group, it is Row 5, Column 4).
16. Save the report. Figure 67 shows the Customer List Report in Report view.

Figure 60: Report Wizard Table and Field Selection Dialog Box

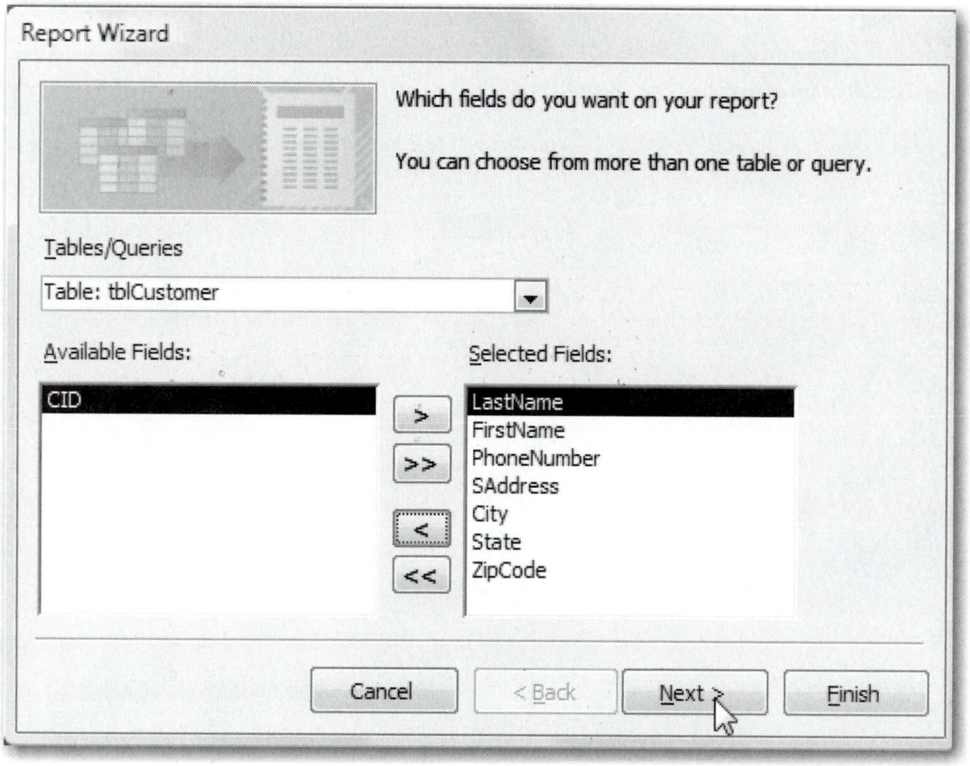

Figure 61: Report Wizard Grouping Dialog Box

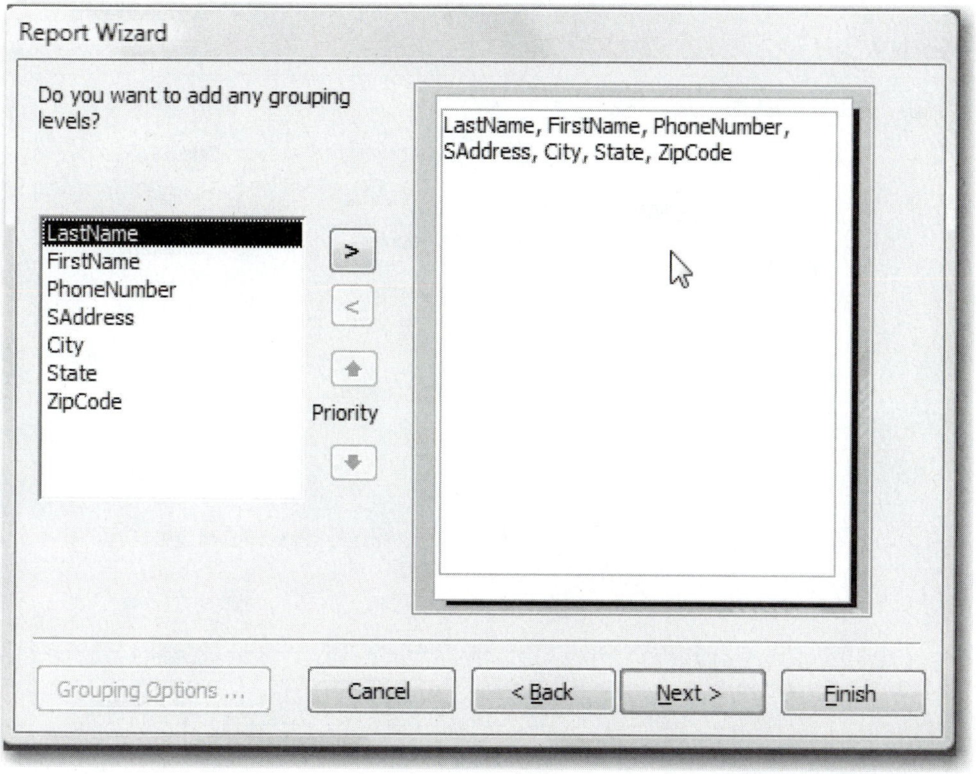

Figure 62: Report Wizard Sort Order Dialog Box

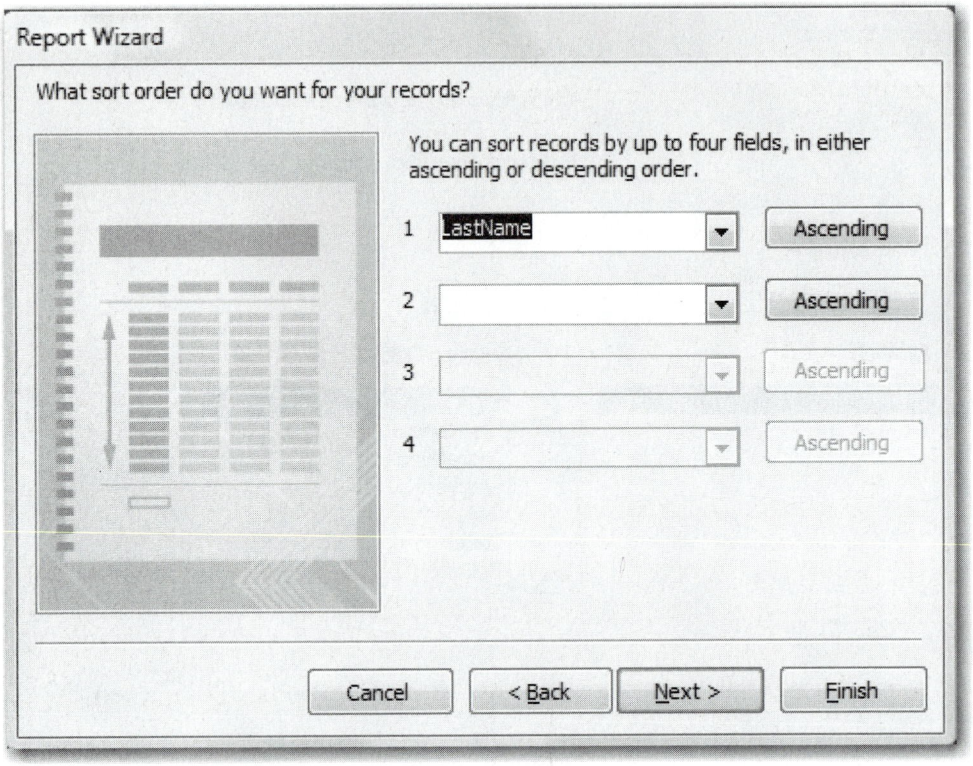

Figure 63: Report Wizard Layout Dialog Box

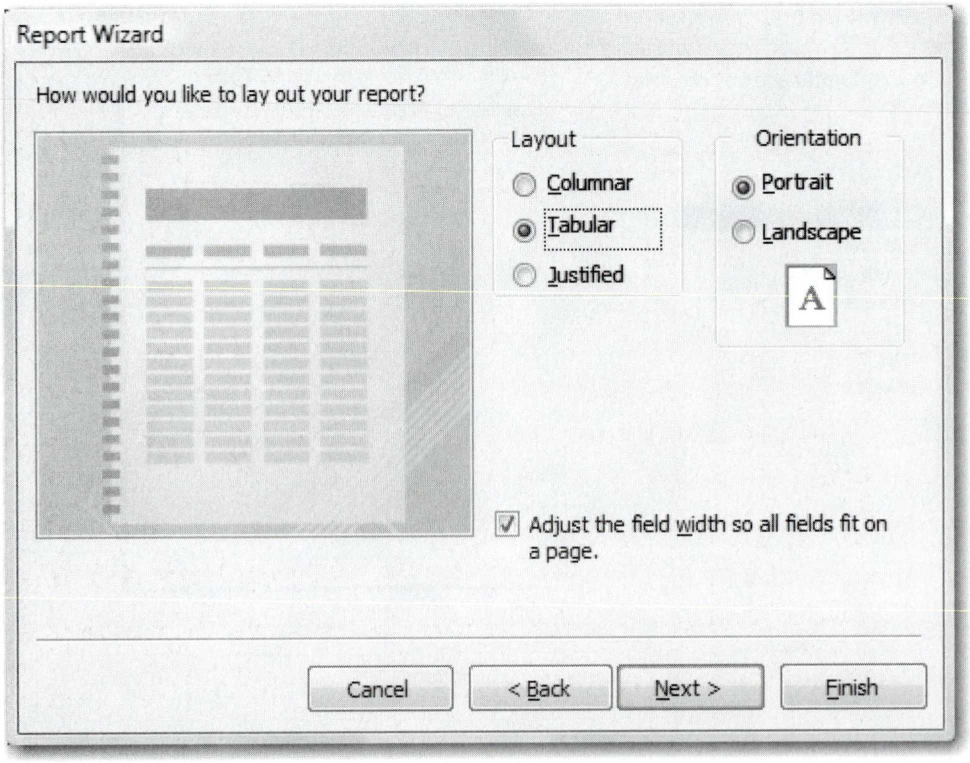

Figure 64: Report Wizard Style Dialog Box

Figure 65: Report Wizard Name Dialog Box

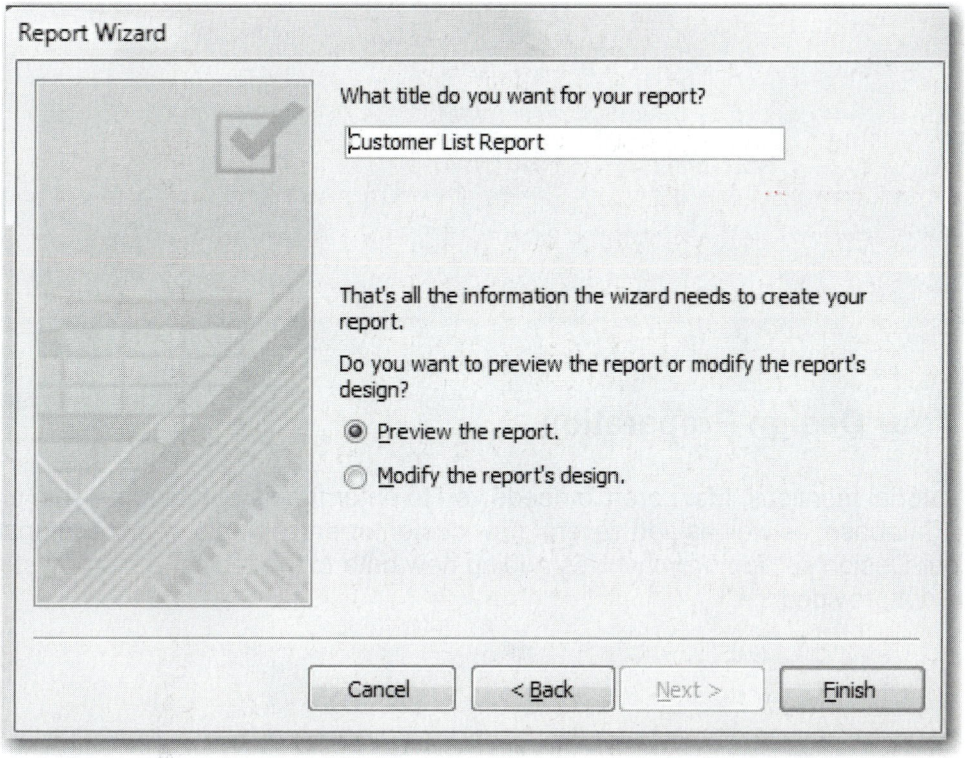

Figure 66: Customer List Report in Design View

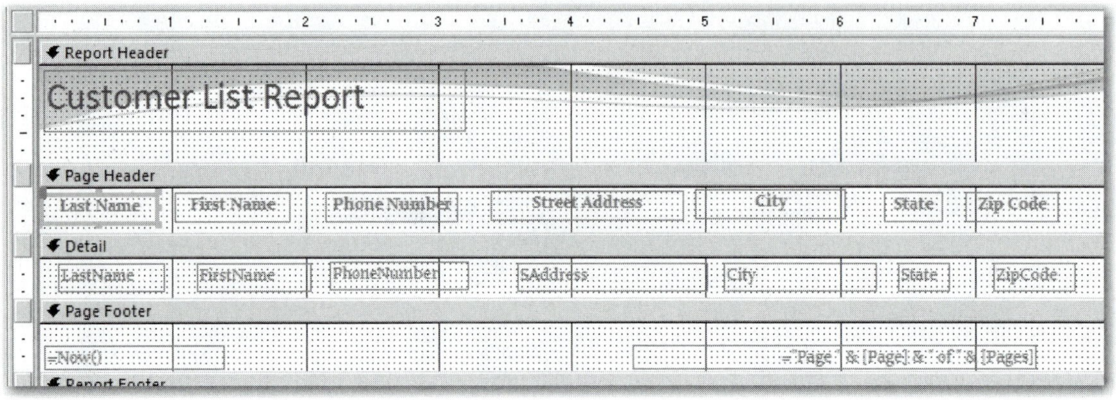

Figure 67: Customer List Report

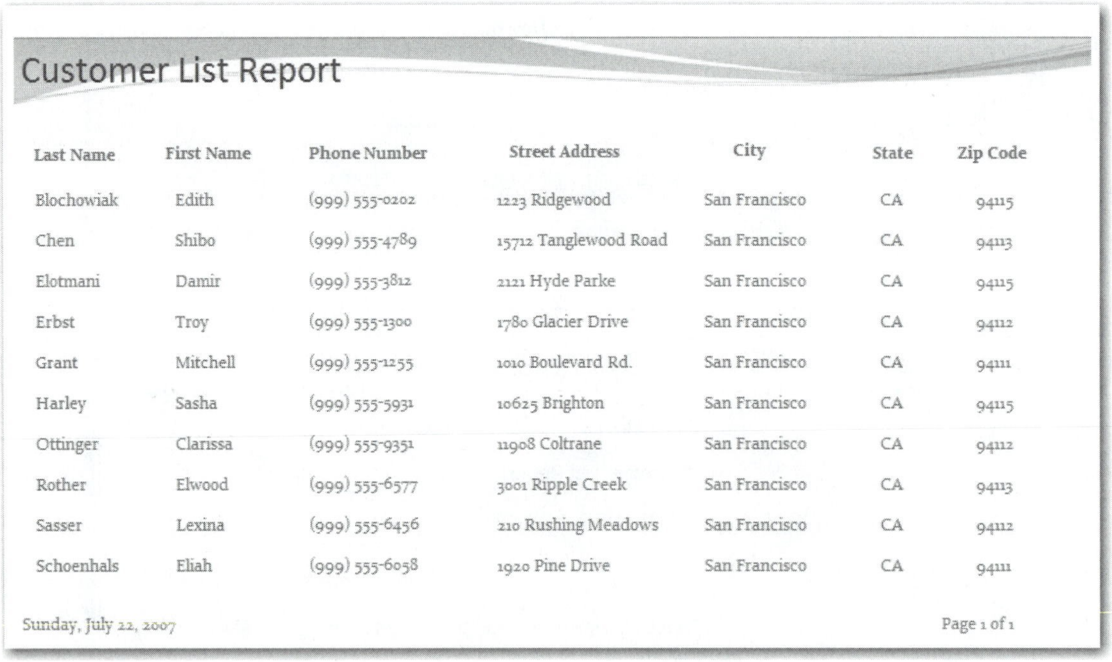

Customer List Report

Last Name	First Name	Phone Number	Street Address	City	State	Zip Code
Blochowiak	Edith	(999) 555-0202	1223 Ridgewood	San Francisco	CA	94115
Chen	Shibo	(999) 555-4789	15712 Tanglewood Road	San Francisco	CA	94113
Elotmani	Damir	(999) 555-3812	2121 Hyde Parke	San Francisco	CA	94115
Erbst	Troy	(999) 555-1300	1780 Glacier Drive	San Francisco	CA	94112
Grant	Mitchell	(999) 555-1255	1010 Boulevard Rd.	San Francisco	CA	94111
Harley	Sasha	(999) 555-5931	10625 Brighton	San Francisco	CA	94115
Ottinger	Clarissa	(999) 555-9351	11908 Coltrane	San Francisco	CA	94112
Rother	Elwood	(999) 555-6577	3001 Ripple Creek	San Francisco	CA	94113
Sasser	Lexina	(999) 555-6456	210 Rushing Meadows	San Francisco	CA	94112
Schoenhals	Eliah	(999) 555-6058	1920 Pine Drive	San Francisco	CA	94111

Sunday, July 22, 2007 Page 1 of 1

Test Your Design Preparation

As the tutorial mentions, Ms. Lorenzo needs you to enter the fitness membership plans into the database, as well as add several new customer enrollments. As the tutorial's Test Your Design section only involves adding new data to the tables, a step-by-step guide is not provided.

Case Deliverables Preparation

For each MIS Cases: Decision Making with Application Software, Fourth Edition database case, you will prepare several deliverables. Your instructor will specify which deliverables you are to prepare.

The Test Your Design section often specifies that the database is to be modified and that new data are to be added. This request encourages you to prepare a flexible database that is adaptable to changing business needs.

Web Page Tutorial

Timeka's Tanning Salon, Inc.

Tutorial Introduction

Timeka's Tanning Salon, Inc., is a tutorial designed to accompany MIS Cases: Decision Making with Application Software, Fourth Edition published by Prentice Hall. This tutorial serves as a Web page development review tool and assumes you have a basic, fundamental knowledge of Web pages. To complete this tutorial, you will use Microsoft Word 2007.

This tutorial is divided into two parts. Part I provides the tutorial's background, scenario, design and information specifications, test your design requirements, and deliverables. Part II steps you through the tutorial's preparation. Since Part I introduces the tutorial's main character and sets the stage for the required Web page design work, you should read Part I before attempting Part II. In Part II, you will design a Web page that satisfies the tutorial's design and information requirements.

Part I: Setting the Scene

Tutorial Background

Timeka Lorenzo owns and operates Timeka's Tanning Salon. The tanning salon is located at 555 Beach Haven Road in San Francisco, California. The tanning salon has been in operation for several years, and the clientele for the business continues to grow. Since its grand opening almost 4 years ago, the tanning salon has grown from 4 tanning beds to include 25 tanning beds and a fitness center.

Ms. Lorenzo realizes the power of the Web and wants to provide the salon's customers with information about the salon, fitness center, and tanning products via the Web. Ms. Lorenzo asks you to design a Web page for her salon.

Tutorial Scenario

Timeka Lorenzo, the salon's owner, opened Timeka's Tanning Salon almost 4 years ago in a popular, heavily trafficked San Francisco area. Today the tanning salon boasts 25 tanning beds, a fitness center, and an array of tan enhancing products. The salon is open daily from 6:00 a.m. to 10:00 p.m. Although walk-ins are appreciated, salon and fitness center appointments are made by calling (505) 555-5758.

Ms. Lorenzo wants to promote the salon's quality and professional service. To help meet this goal, Timeka's Tanning Salon is a member of the International Smart Tan Network.

The most recent addition to the tanning salon is a fitness center. The fitness center provides a jogging path, free weights, Stairmasters, treadmills, and exercise bicycles. In the near future, Ms. Lorenzo will add an indoor heated pool and aerobics classes for her customers. When a client joins the fitness center, she is given a complimentary fitness evaluation. Upon completion of the fitness evaluation, a fitness representative prepares a fitness program for the new client.

Figure 1 provides the salon's current price list. Clients may pay by cash, check, or credit card. Credit cards are only permitted for purchases greater than $50.00.

Figure 1: Current Price List

Timeka's Tanning Salon Price List	
1 Session	$5.00
5 Sessions	$25.00
10 Sessions	$50.00
15 Sessions	$75.00
20 Sessions	$100.00
One Month Unlimited	$35.00
Monthly Special	$30.00
Loyal Customer	$29.99
Referral	$29.99
Yearly Enrollment	$350.00
Bronze 12 oz Lotion	$24.99
Golden 12 oz Lotion	$27.99
Bronze 12 oz Oil	$19.99
Golden 12 oz Oil	$21.99
Timeka's Tan Enhancer 12 oz Lotion	$27.99
Timeka's Tan Enhancer for 16 oz Lotion	$34.99
6-Month Fitness Membership	$180.99
Yearly Fitness Membership	$280.99

Design Specifications

Ms. Lorenzo wants an informative, professional-looking Web page for the salon. The Web page should provide basic information about the salon and have a warm, sunny look and feel. The basic information should specify the salon's hours, identify the types of available tanning products, and provide information about the salon and fitness center. Ms. Lorenzo wants the salon's Web page visitors to easily navigate the Web page. Figures 2 and 3 show tentative sketches for the salon's Web pages.

Figure 2: Home Page Sketch

About Us	Email Us	Fitness Center	Home	Products	Salon

Timeka's Tanning Salon, Inc. Insert Image Here

555 Beach Haven Road
San Francisco, CA 94111
Phone Number: (505) 555-5758
Open Daily from 6:00 a.m. to 10:00 p.m.

Figure 3: Internal Web Page Sketch

About Us	Email Us	Fitness Center	Home	Products	Salon

Timeka's Tanning Salon, Inc. Insert Image Here

About Us

Insert Timeka's biography here.

Fitness Center

Insert brief description for the fitness center.
Include fitness membership price list.

Salon

Insert brief description for the tanning salon.
Include session price list.

Products

Insert introductory paragraph for the products.
Insert price list for the tanning products.

Information Specifications

Ms. Lorenzo wants the Web page to list the salon's hours, discuss the salon's origination, and contain links to other resources. Additionally, Ms. Lorenzo wants the salon's Web page to provide the following information:

1. Price list for the tanning products.

2. Available memberships for the fitness center.

3. Prices for the tanning sessions.

Test Your Design

After creating the Web page, you should test your design. Perform the following steps:

1. Ms. Lorenzo wants the aerobics class schedules placed on the Web page. Clients should call ahead for an appointment. (You should provide the aerobics class schedules.)

2. Timeka's Tanning Salon provides its customers with the opportunity to purchase special tanning session packages, such as the one-month unlimited, monthly special, loyal customer, referral, and yearly enrollment specials. Add a Monthly Specials section to the salon's Web page. (Besides the monthly special shown in Figure 1, include several additional monthly specials to this section.)

3. Timeka's Tanning Salon now offers one-month and three-month fitness membership plans. The one-month fitness membership plan costs $35.99, and the three-month fitness membership plan costs $99.99. Add this information to the salon's Web page.

Tutorial Deliverables

In order to satisfactorily complete this tutorial, you should build the Web page and then prepare both written and oral presentations. Unless otherwise specified, submit the following deliverables to your professor. Also, unless otherwise specified, perform these steps after you have tested your design.

1. A written report discussing any assumptions you have made about the tutorial and the key elements of the tutorial. Additionally, what features did you add to make the Web pages more functional? User friendly? (Please note that these assumptions cannot violate any of the requirements specified above and must be approved by your professor.)

2. A printout of the Web pages. (If additional pages were created, you must submit these pages.)

3. An electronic, working copy of your Web page that meets the criteria mentioned in the tutorial scenario and specifications sections.

As mentioned above, you should prepare an oral presentation. (Your instructor will establish the time allocated to your presentation.) You should use a presentation package and discuss the key features of your Web pages. Also, discuss how the Web pages are beneficial for Ms. Lorenzo and her tanning salon. What additional information might Ms. Lorenzo's clients find useful?

Part II: Web Page Preparation

Design Preparation

If you have not already done so, please read Part I of this tutorial.

To satisfy Ms. Lorenzo's design specifications, you will develop two Web pages for the salon. The first page is the home page. The home page is the first page that the salon's Web site visitors will see. The second page is an internal page that provides information about the specific salon areas.

The salon's Web page preparation is divided into three primary activities. These activities involve creating the home page, creating an internal page, and testing your Web pages. The home page should be saved as TimekasHomePage, and the internal page should be saved as TimekasDetailsPage. Each activity is described below. For reference purposes, Figures 32 and 33 show screen captures of the salon's Web pages.

Activity 1: Home Page Design

Designing the salon's home page involves creating a new Microsoft Word document, inserting a table, creating a navigation bar, entering text, and inserting an image. Each task is reviewed below. (Please keep in mind that you should periodically save your work.)

Task 1: Create and Save the Home Page

To create the salon's home page, perform the following steps:

1. Create a folder named Timeka. (Each page and related documents should be placed in this folder.)

2. Start Microsoft Word and create a new document.

3. From the Themes group located on the Page Layout tab, click the Themes button. Select the Solstice theme. See Figure 4.

4. Click the Office Button, and then select the Save As command. Select the Other Formats option. In the Save As dialog box, type "TimekasHomePage" as the name. For the File Type, select Web Page. Click the Change Title button. In the Page Title dialog box, type "Timeka's Tanning Salon" as the page title name. Click the OK button. Click the Save button.

Figure 4: Themes

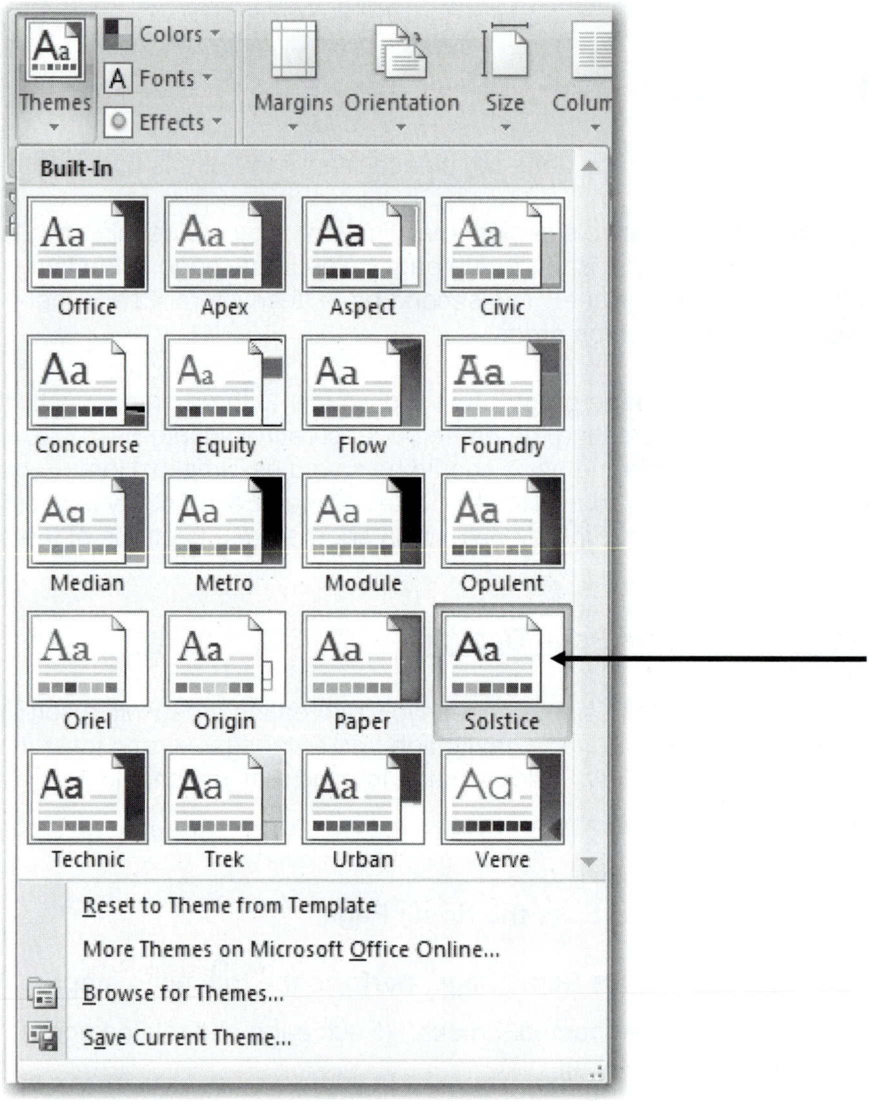

Task 2: Insert a Table

To insert a table, perform the following steps:

1. From the Tables group located on the Insert tab, click the Table button. From the drop-down menu, select the Insert Table command. See Figure 5. The Insert Table dialog box will appear.

2. In the Insert Table dialog box, specify 1 column and 2 rows. Select the AutoFit to Window option. See Figure 6. Click the OK button.

3. Select the table, and then right-click. A Shortcut menu appears. See Figure 7.

4. Select the Table Properties command. The Table Properties dialog box appears.

5. In the Table Properties dialog box, specify the row height as at least one inch. See Figure 8. Click the OK button.

Figure 5: Insert Table Command

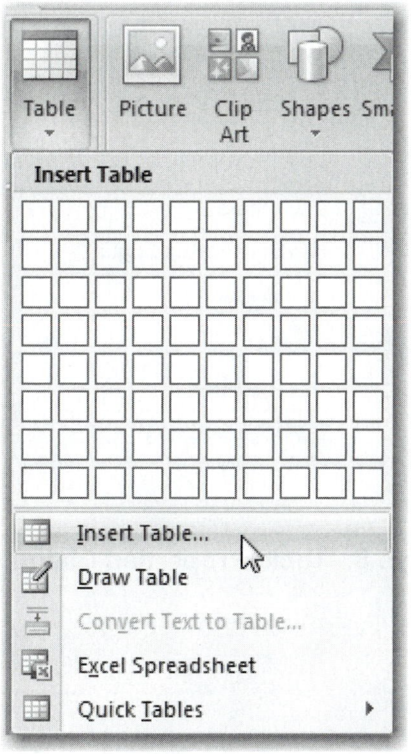

Figure 6: Insert Table Dialog Box

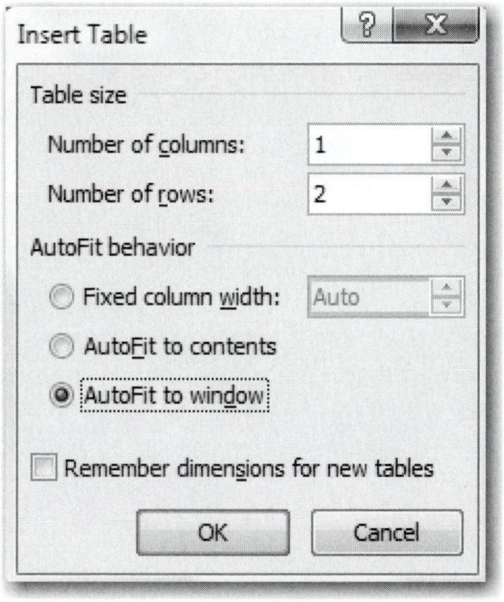

Figure 7: Table Properties on Shortcut Menu

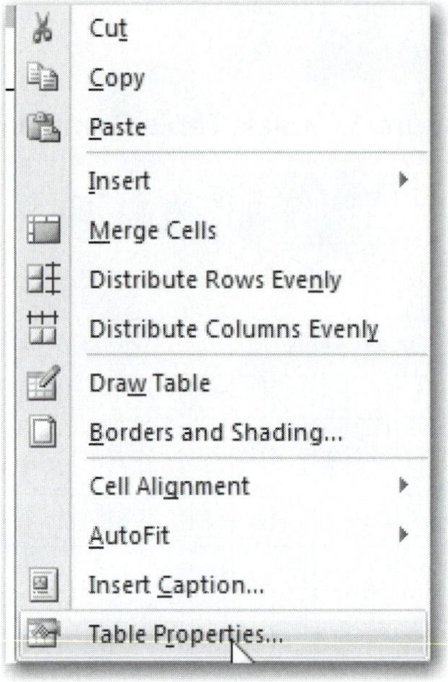

Figure 8: Table Properties Dialog Box

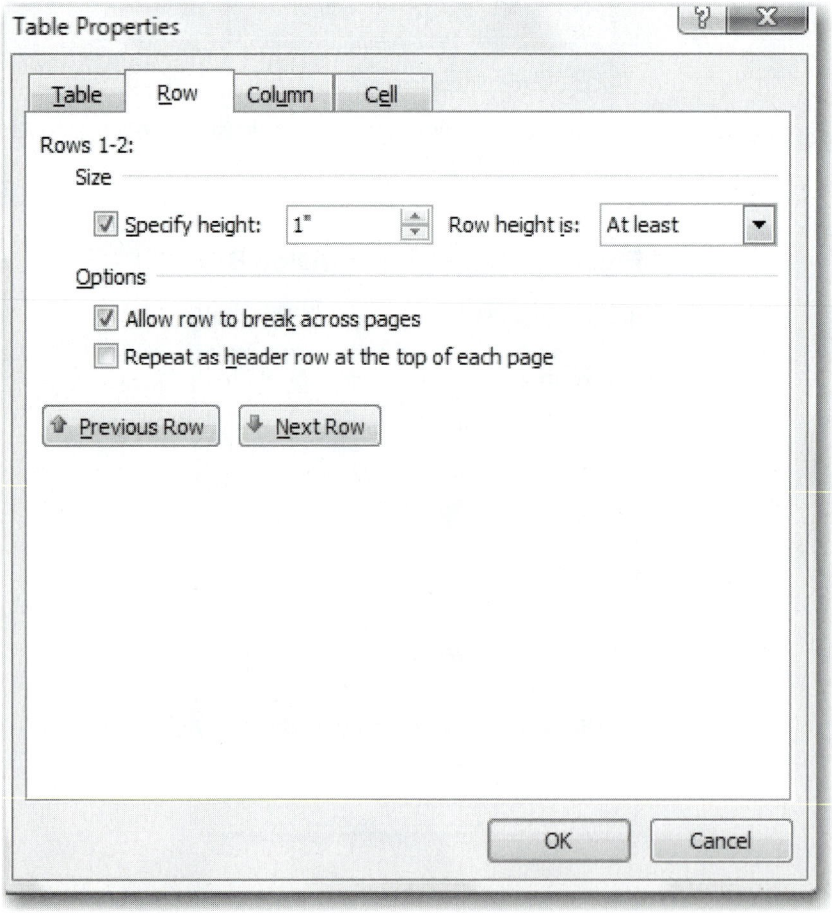

Task 3: Create the Navigation Bar

To create the navigation bar, perform the following steps:

1. Select the table. From the Font group located on the Home tab, set the font to Trebuchet MS and set the font size to 11. Set the font color to Gold Accent 2 Lighter 40% (Column 6, Row 4). Click the Bold button. See Figure 9.

2. Click in row 1 of the table. Click the Center button located in the Paragraph group.

3. Select row 1 of the table. Right click and then select Table Properties from the Shortcut menu.

4. In the Table Properties dialog box, click the Cell tab. In the Vertical Alignment section, click the Center button. Click the OK button.

5. Type "About Us". Press the spacebar 10 times, and then type "Email Us". Press the spacebar 10 times, and then type "Fitness Center". Press the spacebar 10 times, and then type "Home". Press the spacebar 10 times, and then type "Products". Press the spacebar 10 times, and then type "Salon".

Figure 9: Font Color

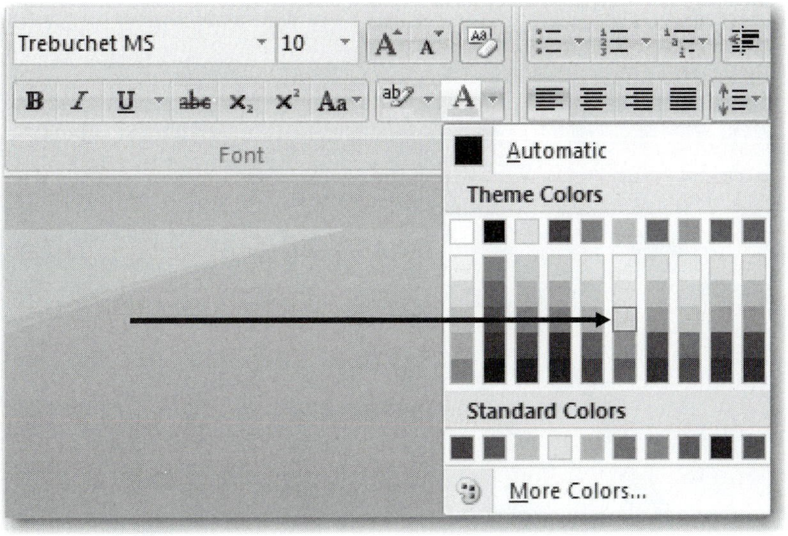

6. From the Illustrations group located on the Insert tab, click the Shapes button.

7. From the Basic Shapes category, select the Rounded Rectangle option. See Figure 10.

8. Drag the mouse pointer so that the rounded rectangle shape encompasses the words that you just typed. (Note: The entries that you just made are hidden by the rounded rectangle shape. The next step removes the fill, so that the entries can be seen.)

9. Right click the rounded rectangle shape, and select the Format AutoShape command that appears on the Shortcut menu. The Format AutoShape dialog box appears. See Figure 11.

10. Click the Colors and Lines tab. In the Fill section, click in the Color box, and select the No Color option. In the Line section, click the Color box and then select the color Gold Accent 2 Lighter 40% (Column 6, Row 4). Set the weight to 1 pt.

11. Click the Layout tab, and then click the Center button. See Figure 12. When finished, click the OK button.

12. Deselect the rounded rectangle AutoShape.

13. Click the Save button located on the Quick Access Toolbar.

14. Open TimekasHomePage with Microsoft Internet Explorer. Make sure the navigation bar appears centered and the rounded rectangle surrounds the text. If it does not, then close Microsoft Internet Explorer and open TimekasHomePage using Microsoft Word. Make any necessary adjustments. Save TimekasHomePage.

Figure 10: AutoShapes

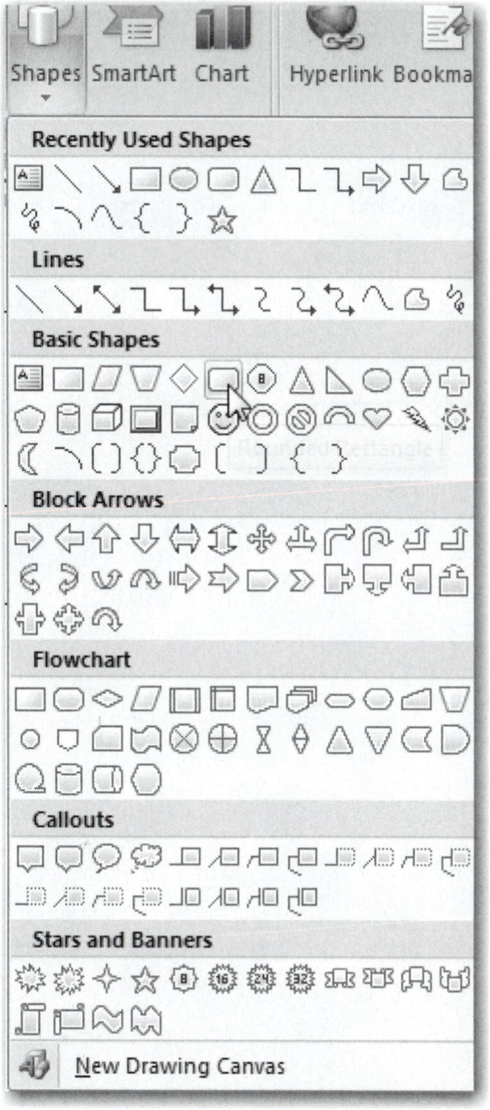

Figure 11: Format AutoShape Dialog Box

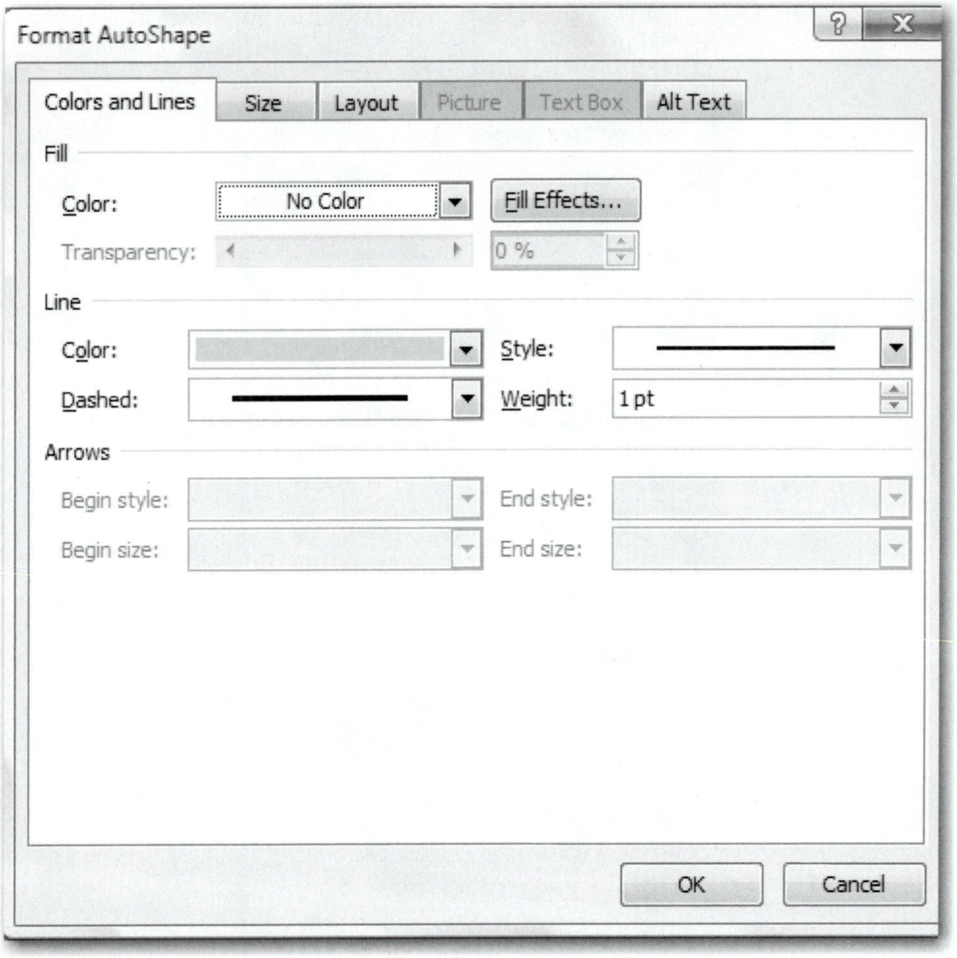

Figure 12: Format AutoShape

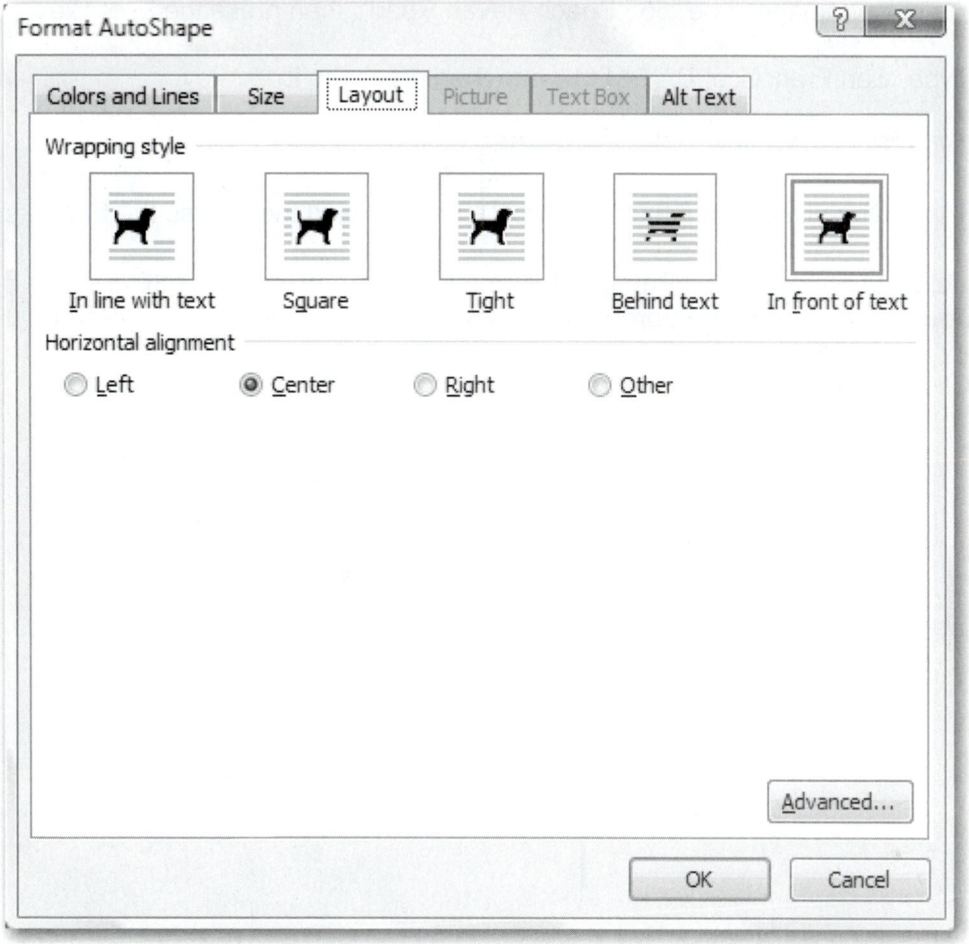

Task 4: Enter Text and Insert Image

To enter text and insert an image, perform the following steps:

1. Click in the second row of the table.

2. Click the Center button located in the Paragraph group. Set the font to Monotype Corsiva. Set the font size to 26. Set the font color to Gold Accent 2 Lighter 40% (Column 6, Row 4). Press the Enter key.

3. Type "Timeka's Tanning Salon, Inc." Do not press the Enter key.

4. From the Illustrations group located on the Insert tab, click the Clip Art button. See Figure 13. When prompted enter "sun" as the search text, and then locate a suitable clip art image. Click the clip art image to insert it into the document. Close the Clip Art Pane.

5. Right click the newly inserted clip art, and select Size from the Shortcut menu. The Size dialog box will appear. See Figure 14. If necessary, modify the height and width of your clip art image. Click the Close button.

6. Deselect the clip art image. On the line below Timeka's Tanning Salon, Inc. and the clip art image, type “555 Beach Haven Road”, then press the Enter key.

7. Type “San Francisco, CA 94111”, and then press the Enter key.

8. Type “Phone Number: (505) 555-5758”, then press the Enter key.

9. Type “Open Daily From 6:00 a.m. to 10:00 p.m.”, and then press the Enter key.

10. Select the table. In the Paragraph group located on the Home tab, click the drop-down arrow beside the Border button. Select the No Border option. See Figure 15.

11. Click the Save button located on the Quick Access Toolbar.

Figure 13: Clip Art Button

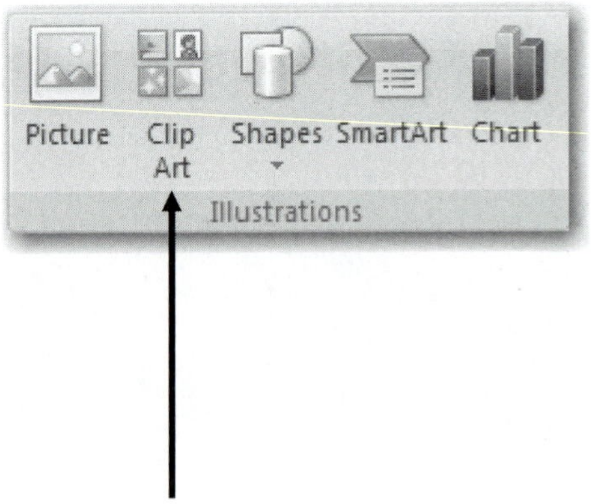

Figure 14: Size Dialog Box

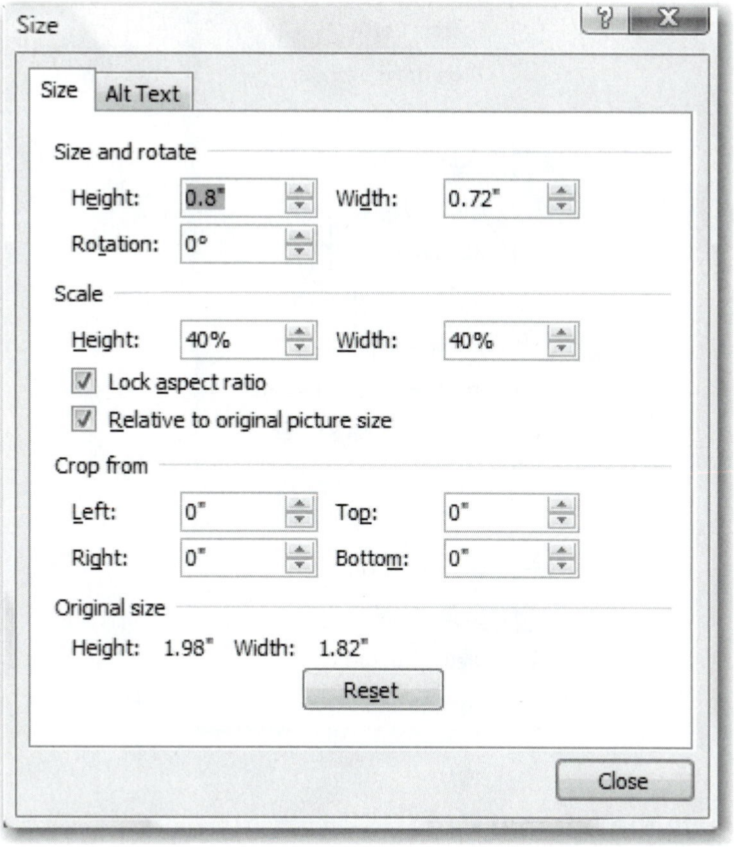

Figure 15: No Border Option

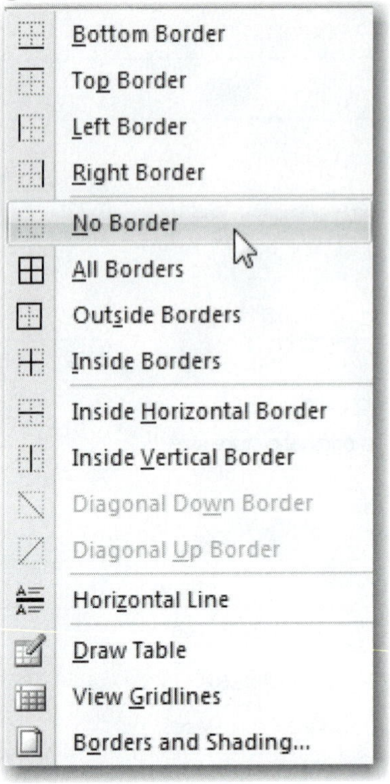

Activity 2: Create the Internal Page

Creating the internal page involves creating a new Microsoft Word document, inserting informational paragraphs, inserting tables, inserting bookmarks, and inserting hyperlinks into the pages.

Task 1: Create TimekasDetailsPage

To create TimekasDetailsPage, perform the following steps:

1. Create a new Microsoft Word document.

2. From the Themes group located on the Page Layout tab, click the Themes button. Select the Solstice theme.

3. Click the Office Button, and then select the Save As command. Select the Other Formats option. In the Save As dialog box, type “TimekasDetailsPage” as the name. For the File Type, select Web Page. Click the Change Title button. In the Page Title dialog box, type “Timeka’s Details Page” as the page title name. Click the Save button.

4. From the Tables group located on the Insert tab, click the Table button. From the drop-down menu, select the Insert Table command. The Insert Table dialog box will appear.

5. In the Insert Table dialog box, specify 1 column and 2 rows. Select the AutoFit to Window option. Click the OK button.

6. Select the table, and then right-click. A Shortcut menu appears.

7. Select the Table Properties command. The Table Properties dialog box appears.

8. In the Table Properties dialog box, specify the row height as at least one inch. Click the OK button.

9. Select row 1 in the table. Right click, and then select Table Properties.

10. Click the Cell tab, and then click the Center button in the Vertical Alignment section. Click the OK button.

11. Return to TimekasHomePage and select row 1 of the table.

12. From the Clipboard group located on the Home tab, click the Copy button.

13. Return to TimekasDetailsPage; select row one of the table.

14. From the Clipboard group located on the Home tab, click the Paste button.

15. Return to TimekasHomePage. In row 2 of the table, select Timeka's Tanning Salon, Inc. and the clipart.

16. From the Clipboard group located on the Home tab, click the Copy button.

17. Return to TimekasDetailsPage.

18. Click in row 2 of the table. From the Paragraph group located on the Home tab, click the Center button.

19. From the Clipboard group located on the Home tab, click the Paste button.

20. Press the Enter key twice.

21. From the Font group located on the Home tab, set the font size to 12; set the font to Trebuchet MS, and set the font color to Gold Accent 2 Lighter 40% (Column 6, Row 4). Click the Align Text Left button in the Paragraph group.

22. Type "About Us"; bold the text, and then press the Enter key twice.

23. Type the following paragraphs.

    Growing up in sunny California, Tamika always enjoyed the outdoors, especially any water-related activities. After graduating from college in 1994 with an accounting degree, Timeka accepted a job with Mervin Marshall Manufacturing. The new job required constant travel, and Timeka soon lost her marvelous tan.

After viewing her pasty reflection in a Chicago hotel room's mirror, Timeka realized what she must now do. She quit her job, borrowed money from her grandmother, and founded Timeka's Tanning Salon, Inc. Now, Timeka has a beautiful tan, and you can too.

In an effort to maintain quality and promote professionalism, Timeka's Tanning Salon is a member of the International Smart Tan Network. (Return to top of page.)

24. Press the Enter key twice.

25. Type "Fitness Center", and then press the Enter key twice.

26. Type the following paragraph:

    The fitness center provides a jogging path, free weights, treadmills, and exercise bicycles. In the near future, an indoor heated pool and aerobics classes will be added. Complimentary fitness evaluations are available upon request. Fitness membership plans are provided in the following table. (Return to top of page.)

27. When finished, press the Enter key twice.

28. Type "Salon", and then press the Enter key twice.

29. Type the following paragraph:

    The tanning salon provides 25 tanning beds. To enhance your tanning experience, a radio and complimentary goggles are made available. After each tanning session, the beds are sanitized. A variety of tanning session plans is available. The session plans and associated prices are provided in the following table. (Return to top of page.)

30. When finished, press the Enter key twice.

31. Type "Products", and then press the Enter key twice.

32. Type the following paragraph:

    To obtain a dark, glowing tan, Timeka's Tanning Salon offers its clients several tan enhancing products. The products and available prices are provided below. (Return to top of page.)

33. Press the Enter key twice.

34. Bold each occurrence of "(Return to top of page.)."

35. Bold the occurrence of "International Smart Tan Network."

36. Make sure the paragraphs are not bold. (Only the headings, the text identified in steps 34 and 35, and the navigation bar contents should be bold.)

Task 2: Insert the Fitness Center Table

1. Place the mouse pointer immediately after the right parenthesis at the end of the Fitness Center paragraph. Press the Enter key twice.

2. From the Tables group located on the Insert tab, click the Table button. From the drop-down menu, select the Insert Table command. The Insert Table dialog box will appear.

3. In the Insert Table dialog box, specify 2 columns and 4 rows. Select the AutoFit to Contents option.

4. Select the table, and then right-click. A Shortcut menu appears.

5. Select the Table Properties command. The Table Properties dialog box appears.

6. In the Table Properties dialog box, click the Row tab, and then specify the row height should be exactly .3. See Figure 16.

7. Click the Table tab, and then click the Center button located in the Alignment section of the Table Properties dialog box. See Figure 17. Click the OK button.

8. Select the first row in the Fitness Center table. Right click and then select the Borders and Shading command. See Figure 18.

9. Click the Shading tab. For Fill, select Gold Accent 2 Lighter 80% (Column 6, Row 2). Click the OK button. See Figure 19.

10. Make sure the first row in the table is still selected, and then make sure the Bold button located in the Font group on the Home tab is selected. (You want the text in the first row to appear bold.)

11. Select the last row in the table. From the Merge group located on the Layout tab, click the Merge Cells button.

12. Make sure the last row of the table is still selected. Right click and then select the Borders and Shading option.

13. Click the Shading tab. For Fill, select Gold Accent 2 Lighter 80% (Column 6, Row 2). Click the OK button.

14. Select the entire table. In the Paragraph group located on the Home tab, click the Center button.

15. If necessary, select rows 2 and 3 of the Fitness Center table. Click the Bold button located in the Font group on the Home tab to unbold the text. (The contents of rows 2 and 3 should not appear bold.)

16. Enter the data shown in Figure 20 into the table. (The table expands as you enter the data.)

Figure 16: Fitness Center Row Height in Table Properties

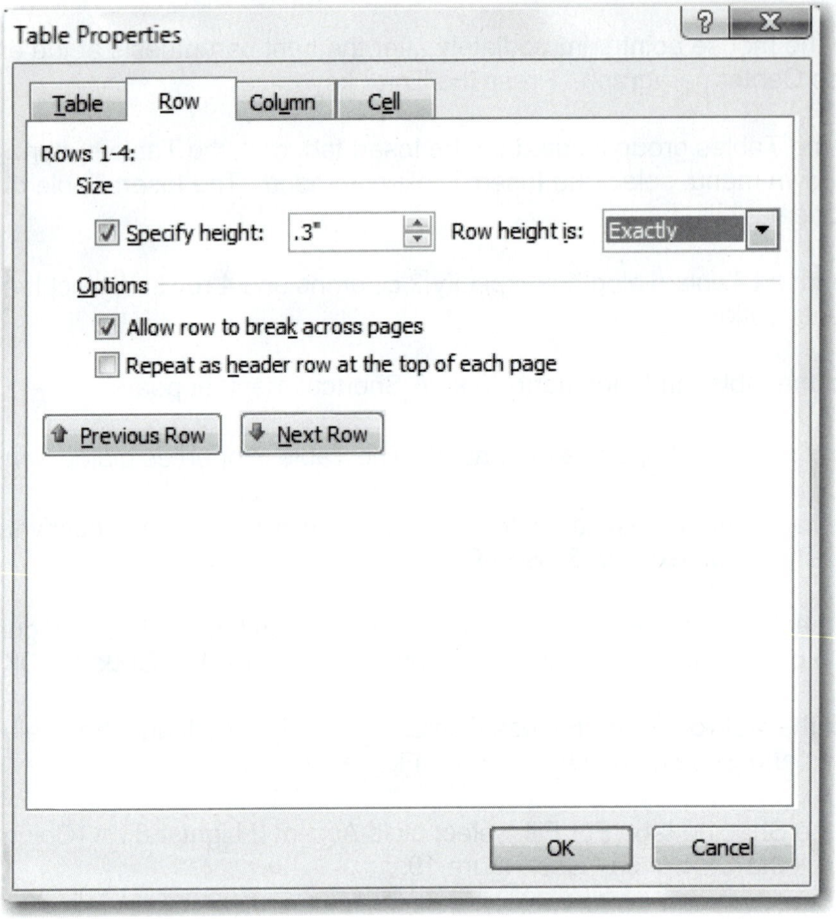

Figure 17: Table Tab in Table Properties Dialog Box

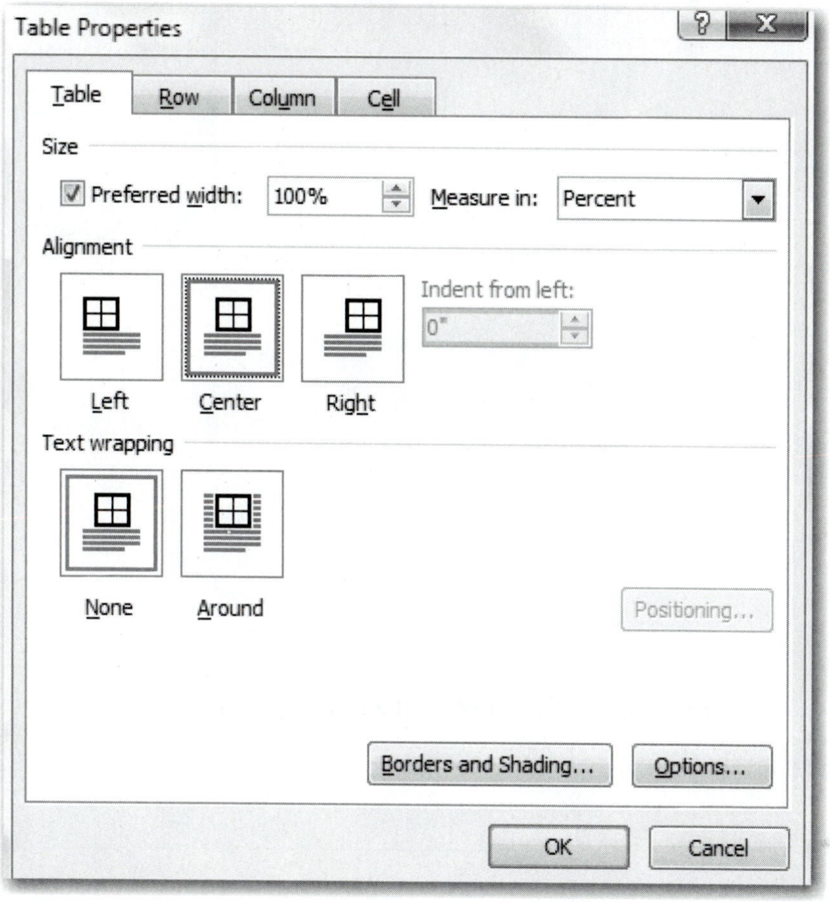

Figure 18: Borders and Shading Command

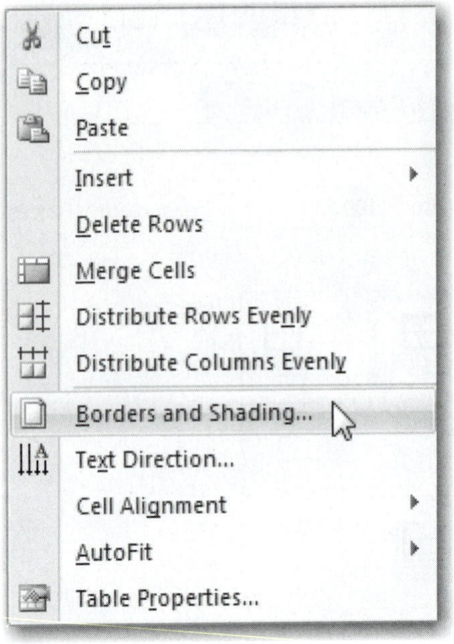

Figure 19: Borders and Shading Dialog Box

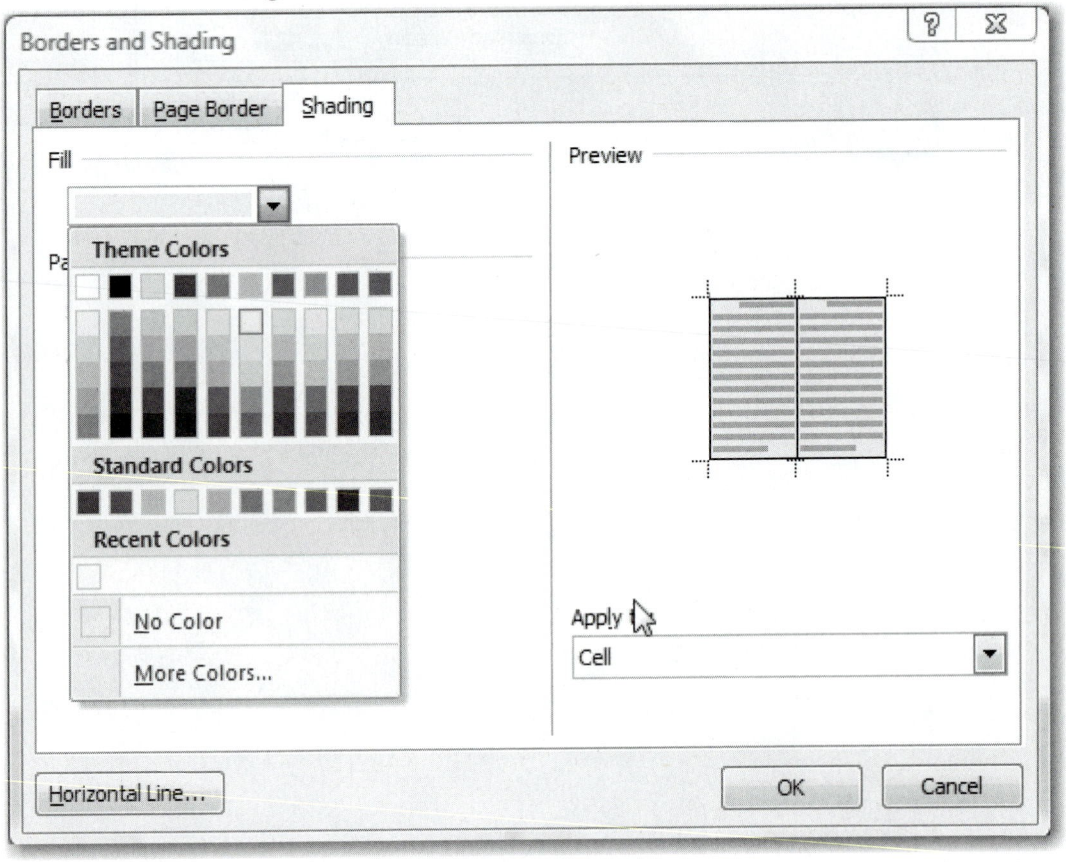

Figure 20: Fitness Membership Data

Fitness Membership List	Fitness Membership Prices
Six-Month Fitness Membership	$180.99
Yearly Fitness Membership	$280.99
Cash and checks are welcome. Credit cards can be used on purchases greater than $50.	

Task 3: Insert Salon Table

1. Place the mouse pointer immediately after the right parenthesis at the end of the Salon paragraph. Press the Enter key twice.

2. From the Tables group located on the Insert tab, click the Table button. From the drop-down menu, select the Insert Table command. The Insert Table dialog box will appear.

3. In the Insert Table dialog box, specify 2 columns and 7 rows. Select the AutoFit to Contents option. Click the OK button.

4. Select the table, and then right-click. A Shortcut menu appears.

5. Select the Table Properties command. The Table Properties dialog box appears.

6. In the Table Properties dialog box, click the Row tab, and then specify the row height should be exactly .3.

7. Click the Table tab, and then click the Center button located in the Alignment section of the Table Properties dialog box. Click the OK button.

8. Select the first row in the Salon table. Right click and then select the Borders and Shading option.

9. Click the Shading tab. For Fill, select Gold Accent 2 Lighter 80% (Column 6, Row 2). Click the OK button.

10. Make sure the first row in the table is still selected, and then make sure the Bold button located in the Font group on the Home tab is selected. (You want the text in the first row to appear bold.)

11. Select the last row in the table. From the Merge group located on the Layout tab, click the Merge Cells button.

12. Make sure the last row of the table is still selected. Right click and then select the Borders and Shading option.

13. Click the Shading tab. For Fill, select Gold Accent 2 Lighter 80% (Column 6, Row 2). Click the OK button.

14. Select the entire table. In the Paragraph group located on the Home tab, click the Center button.

15. If necessary, select rows 2 - 6 of the Salon table. Click the Bold button located in the Font group on the Home tab to unbold the text. (The contents of rows 2 – 6 should not appear bold.)

16. Enter the data shown in Figure 21 into the table. (The table expands as you enter data.)

Figure 21: Session Prices

Session List	Session Prices
1 Session	$5.00
5 Sessions	$25.00
10 Sessions	$50.00
15 Sessions	$75.00
20 Sessions	$100.00
Cash and checks are welcome. **Credit cards can be used on purchases greater than $50.**	

Task 4: Insert Products Table

1. Place the mouse pointer immediately after the right parenthesis at the end of the Products paragraph. Press the Enter key twice.

2. From the Tables group located on the Insert tab, click the Table button. From the drop-down menu, select the Insert Table command. The Insert Table dialog box will appear.

3. In the Insert Table dialog box, specify 2 columns and 8 rows. Select the AutoFit to Contents option. Click the OK button.

4. Select the table, and then right-click. A Shortcut menu appears.

5. Select the Table Properties command. The Table Properties dialog box appears.

6. In the Table Properties dialog box, click the Row tab, and then specify the row height should be exactly .3.

7. Click the Table tab, and then click the Center button located in the Alignment section of the Table Properties dialog box. Click the OK button.

8. Select the first row in the Products table. Right click and then select the Borders and Shading option.

9. Click the Shading tab. For Fill, select Gold Accent 2 Lighter 80% (Column 6, Row 2). Click the OK button.

10. Make sure the first row in the table is still selected, and then make sure the Bold button located in the Font group on the Home tab is selected. (You want the text in the first row to appear bold.)

11. Select the last row in the table. From the Merge group located on the Layout tab, click the Merge Cells button.

12. Make sure the last row of the table is still selected. Right click and then select the Borders and Shading option.

13. Click the Shading tab. For Fill, select Gold Accent 2 Lighter 80% (Column 6, Row 2). Click the OK button.

14. Select the entire table. In the Paragraph group located on the Home tab, click the Center button.

15. If necessary, select rows 2 - 7 of the Products table. Click the Bold button located in the Font group on the Home tab to unbold the text. (The contents of rows 2 – 7 should not appear bold.)

16. Enter the data shown in Figure 22 into the table. (The table expands as you enter data.)

Figure 22: Product Price List

Product List	Product Prices
Bronze 12 oz Lotion	$24.99
Golden 12 oz Lotion	$27.99
Bronze 12 oz Oil	$19.99
Golden 12 oz Oil	$21.99
Timeka's Tan Enhancer 12 oz Lotion	$27.99
Timeka's Tan Enhancer 16 oz Lotion	$34.99
Cash and checks are welcome. Credit cards can be used on purchases greater than $50.	

Task 5: Insert Bookmarks

1. Place the insertion pointer to the left of the About Us paragraph heading.
2. From the Links group located on the Insert tab, click the Bookmark button. See Figure 23.
3. In the Bookmark dialog box, type "AboutUs" as the bookmark name. Click the Add button. See Figure 24.
4. Place the insertion pointer to the left of the Fitness Center paragraph heading.
5. From the Links group located on the Insert tab, click the Bookmark button.
6. In the Bookmark dialog box, type "FitnessCenter" as the bookmark name. Click the Add button.
7. Place the insertion pointer to the left of the Salon paragraph heading.
8. From the Links group located on the Insert tab, click the Bookmark button.
9. In the Bookmark dialog box, type "TanningSalon" as the bookmark name. Click the Add button.
10. Place the insertion pointer to the left of the Products paragraph heading.
11. From the Links group located on the Insert tab, click the Bookmark button.
12. In the Bookmark dialog box, type "Products" as the bookmark name. Click the Add button.
13. Return to the top of the page, and place the insertion pointer to the left of the About Us text in the navigation bar.
14. From the Links group located on the Insert tab, click the Bookmark button.
15. In the Bookmark dialog box, type "PageTop" as the bookmark name. Click the Add button.
16. Return to the TimekasHomePage document.
17. At the top of the page, place the insertion pointer to the left of the About Us text in the navigation bar.
18. From the Links group located on the Insert tab, click the Bookmark button.
19. In the Bookmark dialog box, type "Home" as the bookmark name. Click the Add button.

Figure 23: Bookmark Button

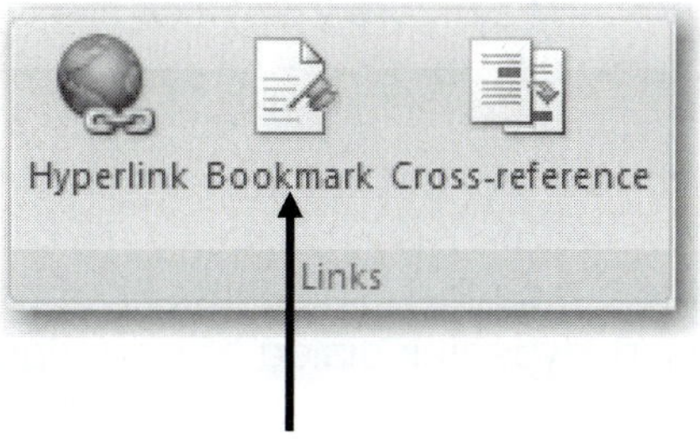

Figure 24: Bookmark Dialog Box

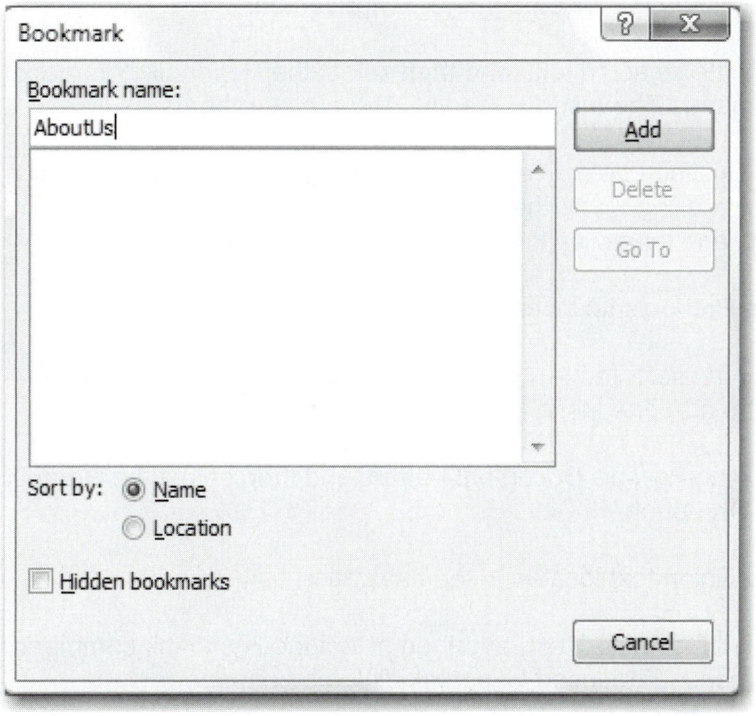

Task 6: Insert Hyperlinks in the TimekasDetailsPage Document

1. Return to the top of the TimekasDetailsPage document. Select the About Us text located in the navigation bar. See Figure 25.

2. Right click the selected text, and then select the Hyperlink command from the Shortcut menu. See Figure 26. The Insert Hyperlink dialog box appears.

3. Click the Place in This Document button, and then select the AboutUs bookmark. See Figure 27. Click the OK button.

4. Select the Email Us text located in the navigation bar.

5. Right click the selected text, and then select the Hyperlink command from the Shortcut menu. The Insert Hyperlink dialog box appears.

6. Click the Email Address button, and then type "timeka@timekastanningsalon.xxx" into the email address box. See Figure 28. Click the OK button. (Note: Microsoft Word automatically inserts mailto:.)

7. Select the Fitness Center text located in the navigation bar.

8. Right click the selected text, and then select the Hyperlink command from the Shortcut menu. The Insert Hyperlink dialog box appears.

9. Click the Place in This Document button, and then select the FitnessCenter bookmark. Click the OK button.

10. Select the Home text located in the navigation bar.

11. Right click the selected text, and then select the Hyperlink command from the Shortcut menu. The Insert Hyperlink dialog box appears.

12. Click the Existing File or Web Page button, click the Current Folder button, select TimekasHomePage, and then click the Bookmark button. Select the Home bookmark, and then click the OK button. Click the OK button.

13. Select the Products text located in the navigation bar.

14. Right click the selected text, and then select the Hyperlink command from the Shortcut menu. The Insert Hyperlink dialog box appears.

15. Click the Place in This Document button, and then select the Products bookmark. Click the OK button.

16. Select the Salon text located in the navigation bar.

17. Right click the selected text, and then select the Hyperlink command from the Shortcut menu. The Insert Hyperlink dialog box appears.

18. Click the Place in This Document button, and then select the TanningSalon bookmark. Click the OK button.

19. At the end of the third paragraph in the AboutUs section, select the text International Smart Tan Network.

20. Right click the selected text, and then select the Hyperlink command from the Shortcut menu. The Insert Hyperlink dialog box will appear.

21. Click the Existing File or Web Page button. In the Address box, type http://www.smarttan.com/. Click the OK button.

22. At the end of the third paragraph in the AboutUs section, select (Return to top of page.).

23. Right click, and then select the Hyperlink command from the Shortcut menu. The Insert Hyperlink dialog box appears.

24. Click the Place in This Document button, and then select the PageTop bookmark. Click the OK button.

25. Right click on the (Return to top of page) hyperlink, and then select the Copy Hyperlink command from the Shortcut menu.

26. At the end of the paragraph in the Fitness Center section, select (Return to top of page.).

27. Right click, and then select the Paste command from the Shortcut menu.

28. At the end of the paragraph in the Salon section, select the text (Return to top of page.).

29. Right click, and then select the Paste command from the Shortcut menu.

30. At the end of the paragraph in the Products section, select the text (Return to top of page.).

31. Right click, and then select the Paste command from the Shortcut menu.

32. From the Editing group located on the Home tab, click the Select button. From the drop-down menu, select the Select All command. See Figure 30.

33. From the Paragraph group located on the Home tab, click the arrow beside the Border button. From the drop-down menu, select the No Border option. (The gridlines from the outer table should be removed.)

Figure 25: About Us Hyperlink

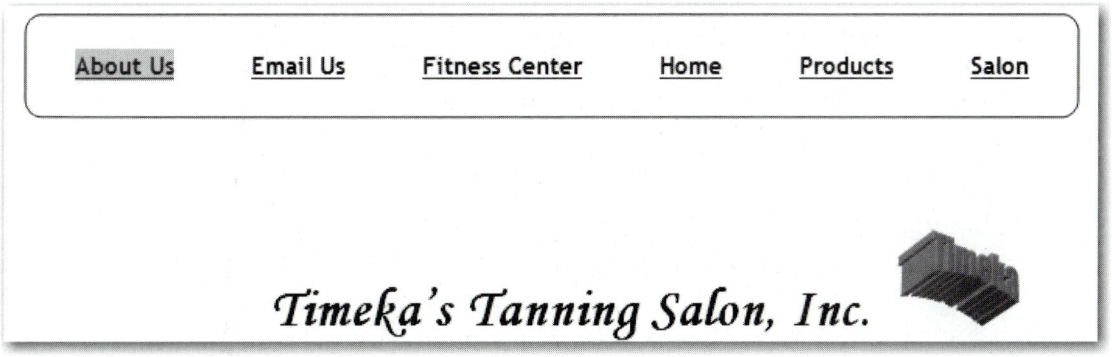

Figure 26: Hyperlink Command

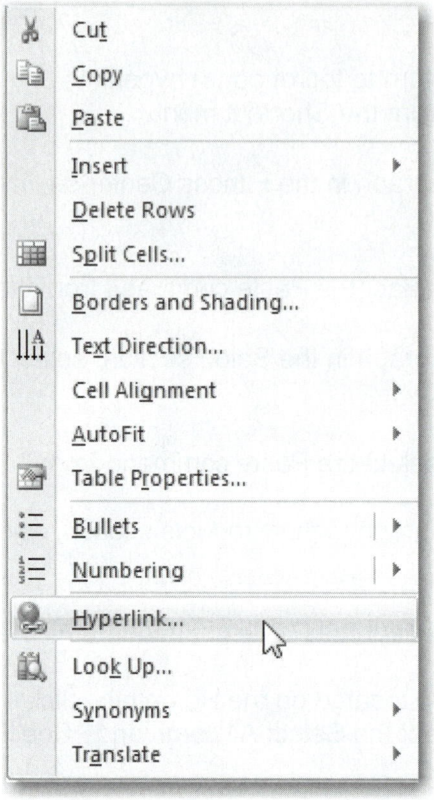

Figure 27: Insert Hyperlink Dialog Box

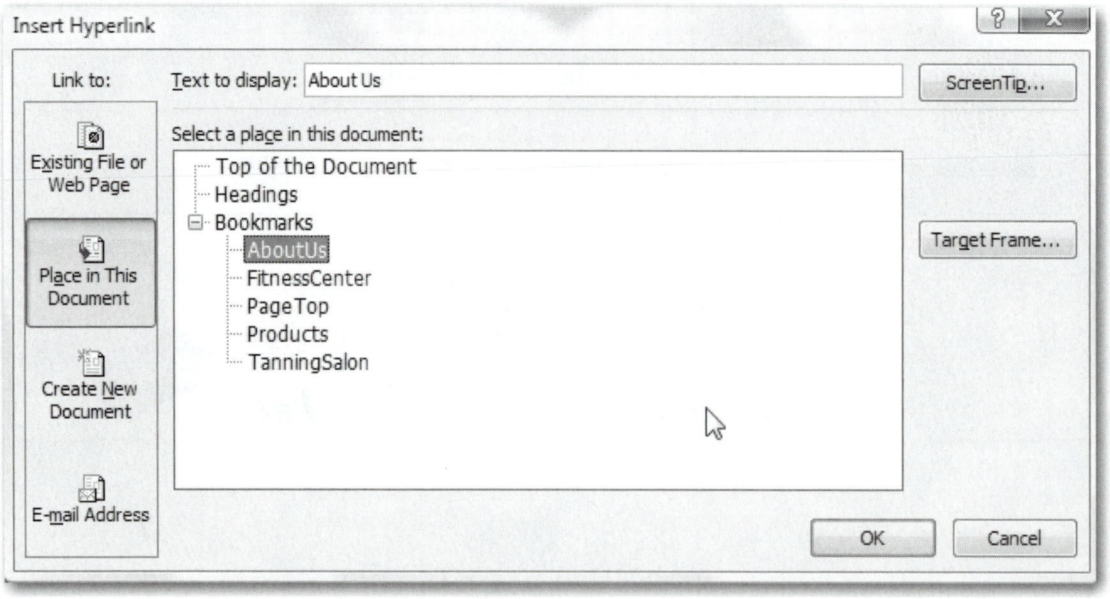

Figure 28: Email Address

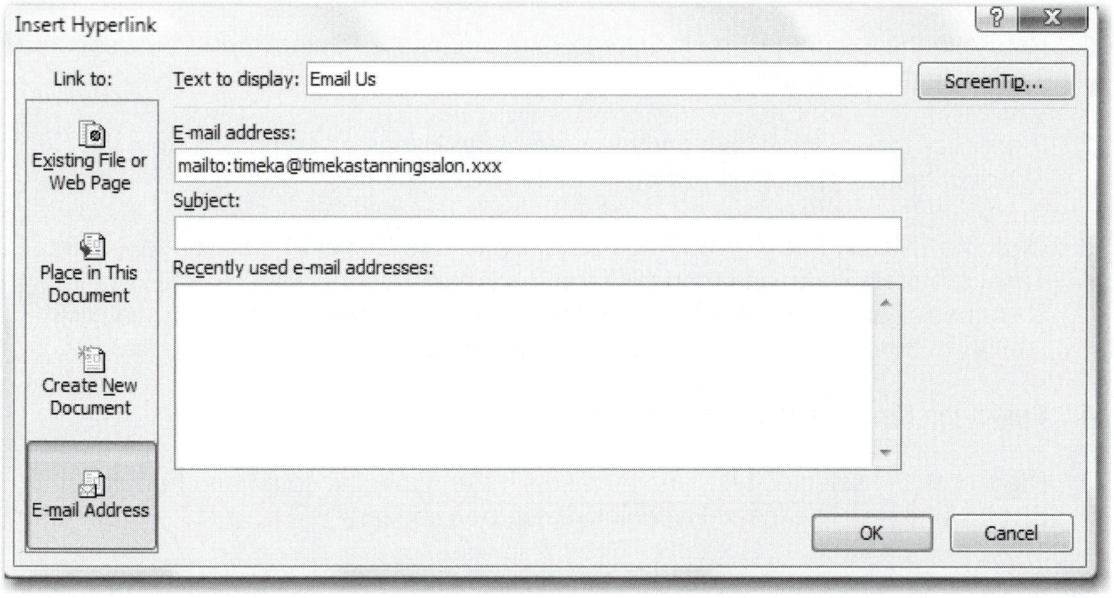

Figure 29: Linking to an Existing File

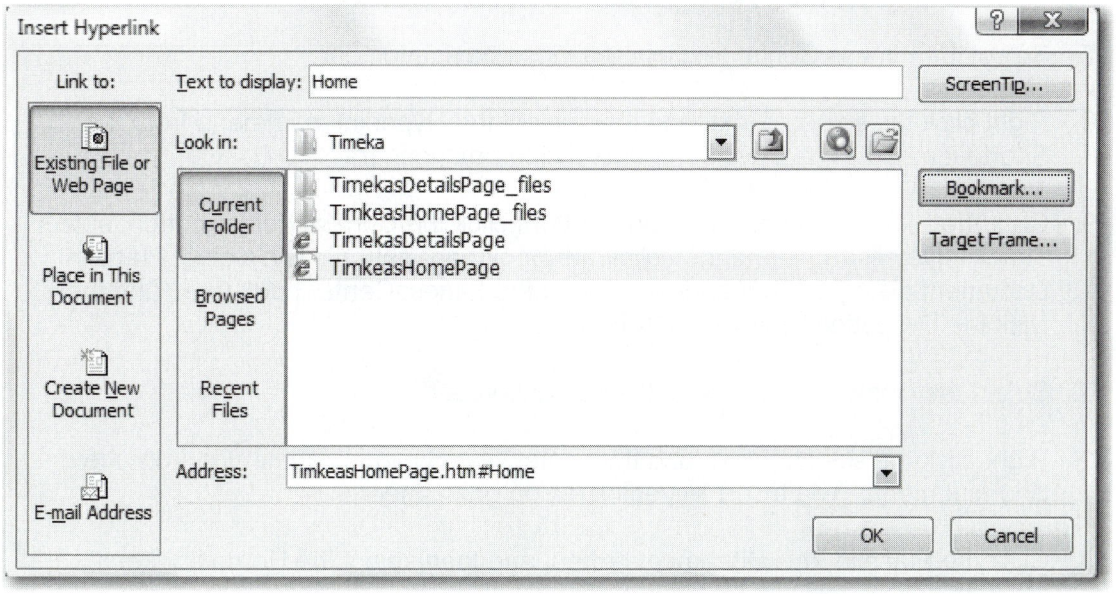

Figure 30: Select All Command

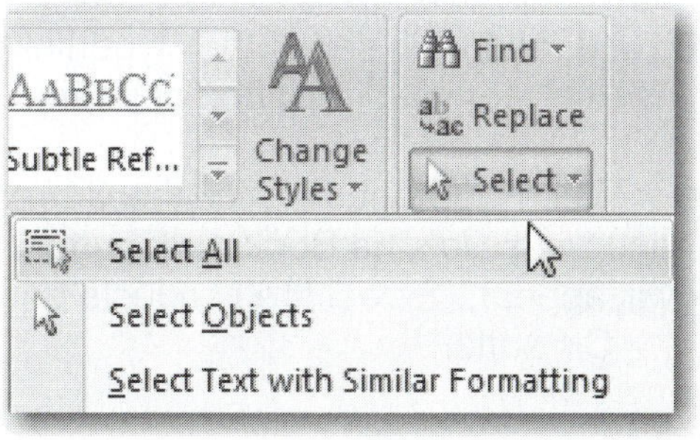

Task 7: Insert Hyperlinks in the TimekasHomePage Document

1. Return to the top of the TimekasHomePage document. Select the AboutUs text located in the navigation bar.

2. Right click the selected text, and then select the Hyperlink command from the Shortcut menu. The Insert Hyperlink dialog box appears.

3. Click the Existing File or Web Page button, click the Current Folder button, select TimekasDetailsPage, and then click the Bookmark button. The Select Place in Document dialog box will appear. Select the AboutUs bookmark, and then click the OK button. Click the OK button. See Figure 31.

4. Select the Email Us text located in the navigation bar.

5. Right click the selected text, and then select the Hyperlink command from the Shortcut menu. The Insert Hyperlink dialog box appears.

6. Click the Email Address button, and then click the timeka@timekastanningsalon.xxx address that is located in the recently used email addresses box. (If Timeka's email address does not appear, just retype it.) Click the OK button.

7. Select the Fitness Center text located in the navigation bar.

8. Right click the selected text, and then select the Hyperlink command from the Shortcut menu. The Insert Hyperlink dialog box appears.

9. Click the Existing File or Web Page button, click the Current Folder button, select TimekasDetailsPage, and then click the Bookmark button. The Select Place in Document dialog box will appear. Select the FitnessCenter bookmark, and then click the OK button. Click the OK button.

10. Select the Home text located in the navigation bar.

11. Right click the selected text, and then select the Hyperlink command from the Shortcut menu. The Insert Hyperlink dialog box appears.

12. Click the Place in This Document button, and then select the Home bookmark. Click the OK button.

13. Select the Products text located in the navigation bar.

14. Right click the selected text, and then select the Hyperlink command from the Shortcut menu. The Insert Hyperlink dialog box appears.

15. Click the Existing File or Web Page button, click the Current Folder button, select TimekasDetailsPage, and then click the Bookmark button. The Select Place in Document dialog box will appear. Select the Products bookmark, and then click the OK button. Click the OK button.

16. Select the Salon text located in the navigation bar.

17. Right click the selected text, and then select the Hyperlink command from the Shortcut menu. The Insert Hyperlink dialog box appears.

18. Click the Existing File or Web Page button, click the Current Folder button, select TimekasDetailsPage, and then click the Bookmark button. The Select Place in Document dialog box will appear. Select the TanningSalon bookmark, and then click the OK button. Click the OK button.

19. Click the Save button located on the Quick Access Toolbar.

Figure 31: Select Place in Document Dialog Box

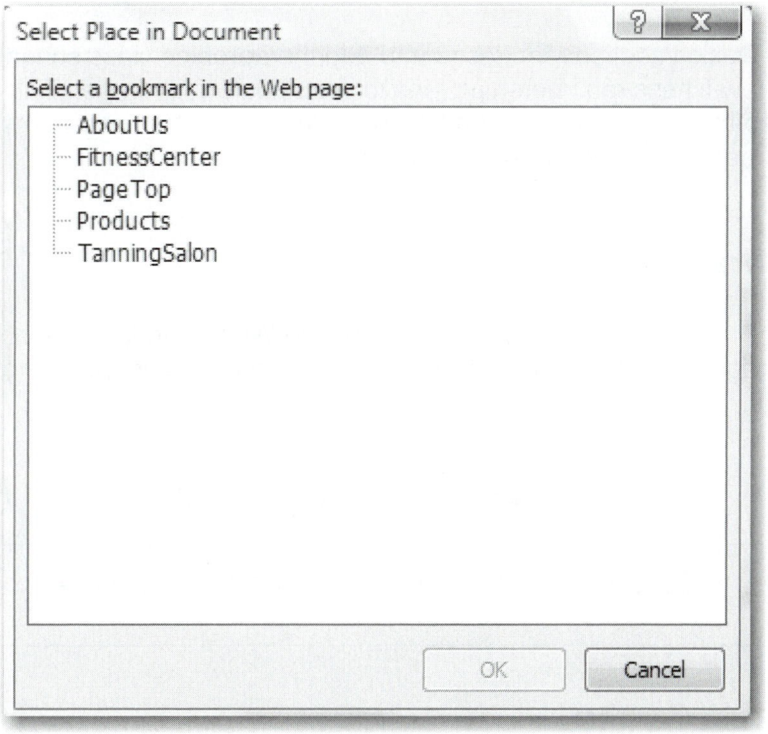

Activity 3: Saving, Viewing, and Testing the Web Pages

Performing the third activity involves viewing the pages as Web pages and testing the hyperlinks.

Task 1: View the Web Pages and Test the Hyperlinks

1. Open Microsoft Internet Explorer.

2. From the File menu located on the Menu Bar toolbar, select the Open option.

3. In the Open dialog box, click the Browse button and then locate TimekasHomePage. Figure 32 shows the completed home page.

4. Make sure that each hyperlink is working correctly. To do this, click on each hyperlink. (If the hyperlink is not working properly, then select the Edit with Microsoft Word option from the File menu. The document should now open in Microsoft Word. Make your corrections and then resave the document.)

5. After checking the links in TimekasHomePage, open TimekasDetailsPage in Microsoft Internet Explorer. Check the links in the TimekasDetailsPage. Figure 33 shows the salon's internal page.

Test Your Design Preparation

The Test Your Design section requires you to add the aerobics class schedules, session specials, and new fitness membership plans to the salon's Web page. This tutorial does not provide step-by-step instructions on how to include this information. Instead, this tutorial leaves these tasks as an exercise for you to complete.

Case Deliverables Preparation

The Test Your Design section often specifies that the Web page is to be modified. This request encourages you to prepare a flexible Web page that is adaptable to changing business needs.

Figure 32: Salon's Home Page

Figure 33: Salon's Internal Page

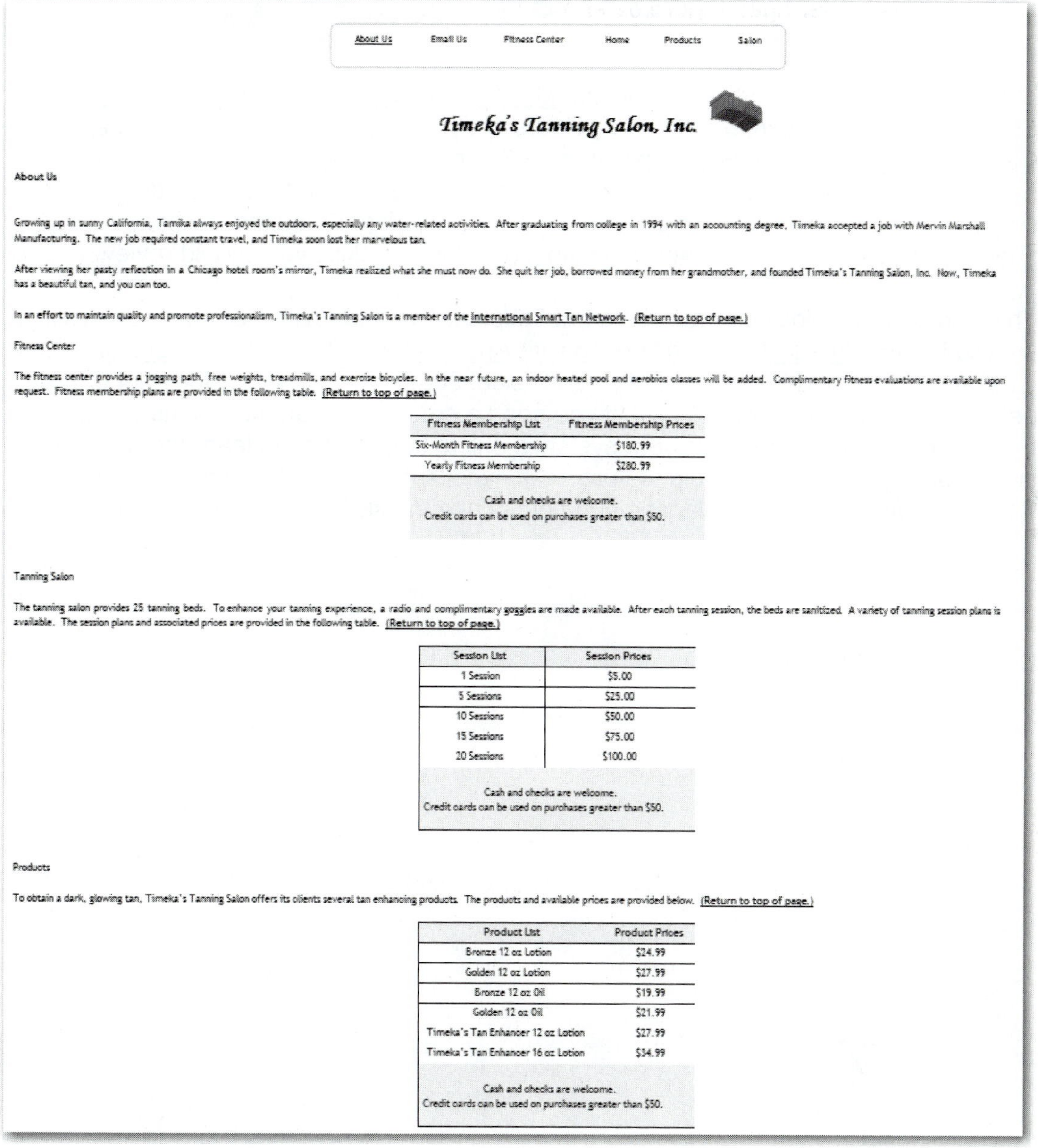

About Us   Email Us   Fitness Center   Home   Products   Salon

Timeka's Tanning Salon, Inc.

About Us

Growing up in sunny California, Tamika always enjoyed the outdoors, especially any water-related activities. After graduating from college in 1994 with an accounting degree, Timeka accepted a job with Mervin Marshall Manufacturing. The new job required constant travel, and Timeka soon lost her marvelous tan.

After viewing her pasty reflection in a Chicago hotel room's mirror, Timeka realized what she must now do. She quit her job, borrowed money from her grandmother, and founded Timeka's Tanning Salon, Inc. Now, Timeka has a beautiful tan, and you can too.

In an effort to maintain quality and promote professionalism, Timeka's Tanning Salon is a member of the International Smart Tan Network. (Return to top of page.)

Fitness Center

The fitness center provides a jogging path, free weights, treadmills, and exercise bicycles. In the near future, an indoor heated pool and aerobics classes will be added. Complimentary fitness evaluations are available upon request. Fitness membership plans are provided in the following table. (Return to top of page.)

Fitness Membership List	Fitness Membership Prices
Six-Month Fitness Membership	$180.99
Yearly Fitness Membership	$280.99
Cash and checks are welcome. Credit cards can be used on purchases greater than $50.	

Tanning Salon

The tanning salon provides 25 tanning beds. To enhance your tanning experience, a radio and complimentary goggles are made available. After each tanning session, the beds are sanitized. A variety of tanning session plans is available. The session plans and associated prices are provided in the following table. (Return to top of page.)

Session List	Session Prices
1 Session	$5.00
5 Sessions	$25.00
10 Sessions	$50.00
15 Sessions	$75.00
20 Sessions	$100.00
Cash and checks are welcome. Credit cards can be used on purchases greater than $50.	

Products

To obtain a dark, glowing tan, Timeka's Tanning Salon offers its clients several tan enhancing products. The products and available prices are provided below. (Return to top of page.)

Product List	Product Prices
Bronze 12 oz Lotion	$24.99
Golden 12 oz Lotion	$27.99
Bronze 12 oz Oil	$19.99
Golden 12 oz Oil	$21.99
Timeka's Tan Enhancer 12 oz Lotion	$27.99
Timeka's Tan Enhancer 16 oz Lotion	$34.99
Cash and checks are welcome. Credit cards can be used on purchases greater than $50.	

Spreadsheet Glossary

This spreadsheet glossary accompanies MIS Cases: Decision Making with Application Software, Fourth Edition, published by Pearson Prentice Hall. When preparing an MIS Cases: Decision Making with Application Software, Fourth Edition spreadsheet case, several spreadsheet skills are necessary. The case's skills check feature identifies the major skills that are required to complete the case. Before preparing the case, you should use the skills check feature to help identify which skills you should review.

This spreadsheet glossary provides a brief explanation and review for many of the skills utilized in MIS Cases: Decision Making with Application Software, Fourth Edition. This glossary is designed for users of Microsoft Excel 2007. This glossary does not provide detailed explanations for the skills. If you need a detailed explanation on how to use a particular skill, you should use your system's online help feature to learn more about the skill. Your system's online help feature is an excellent way to learn about the skill, as well as obtain a detailed explanation on how to use the skill in a spreadsheet application.

Spreadsheet Skills

Absolute Cell Reference: When you copy a formula to multiple cells, Microsoft Excel updates the formula's cell references to reflect the formula's new location. If you do not want the cell references updated, you should use absolute cell references. A cell reference is made absolute by placing dollar signs ($) before the column and row references. For instance, to make the cell reference A4 absolute, you would type the reference as $A$4.

Advanced Filter: The Advanced Filter command displays records from an Excel table that meet certain criteria. Records not meeting the criteria are temporarily hidden from view. The Advanced Filter command is similar to the Filter command, except the Advanced Filter command provides you with the ability to better customize your selection criteria. Before you use the Advanced Filter command, you must create a criteria range. Figure 1 shows a spreadsheet with a criteria range in rows 3 through 6. Row 3 contains the field names, and rows 4, 5 and 6 are where criteria can be entered. It is recommended that you include three rows for your criteria range and a blank row to separate the criteria range from your data values. In the Advance Filter example, only rows 3 and 4 are specified as the criteria range in the Advanced Filter Dialog box. This is because row 3 contains the column headings, and row 4 contains the criteria. Rows 5 and 6 do not contain criteria. You should also use your system's online help feature to learn more about the Advanced Filter command. (See Excel Table.)

To use the Advanced Filter command, you should:

1. Make sure you have created your Excel table.

2. Create the criteria range.

3. Insert your criteria into the criteria range.

4. On the Ribbon, click the Data tab. From the Sort and Filter group, click the Advanced button. The Advanced Filter dialog box will appear. Figure 2 shows the Advanced Filter dialog box. Notice that the dialog box asks for the table's location (list range), as well as the criteria range's location. As Figure 1's criteria range includes rows 3 and 4, the criteria range is designated as $A$3:$H$4.

Advanced Filter Example: Assume you want to know which information systems faculty members make more than $80,000 a year. Figure 3 shows the criteria and the Advanced Filter results. Figure 3 shows that only Larry Porter meets the criteria.

Figure 1: Advanced Filter with Criteria Range

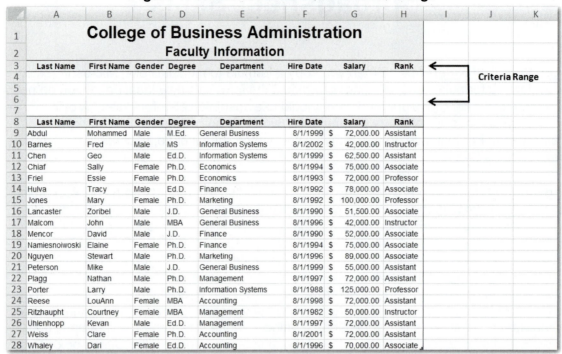

	A	B	C	D	E	F	G	H
1	College of Business Administration							
2	Faculty Information							
3	Last Name	First Name	Gender	Degree	Department	Hire Date	Salary	Rank
4								
5								
6								
7								
8	Last Name	First Name	Gender	Degree	Department	Hire Date	Salary	Rank
9	Abdul	Mohammed	Male	M.Ed.	General Business	8/1/1999	$ 72,000.00	Assistant
10	Barnes	Fred	Male	MS	Information Systems	8/1/2002	$ 42,000.00	Instructor
11	Chen	Geo	Male	Ed.D.	Information Systems	8/1/1999	$ 62,500.00	Assistant
12	Chiaf	Sally	Female	Ph.D.	Economics	8/1/1994	$ 75,000.00	Associate
13	Friel	Essie	Female	Ph.D.	Economics	8/1/1993	$ 72,000.00	Professor
14	Hulva	Tracy	Male	Ed.D.	Finance	8/1/1992	$ 78,000.00	Associate
15	Jones	Mary	Female	Ph.D.	Marketing	8/1/1992	$ 100,000.00	Professor
16	Lancaster	Zoribel	Male	J.D.	General Business	8/1/1990	$ 51,500.00	Associate
17	Malcom	John	Male	MBA	General Business	8/1/1996	$ 42,000.00	Instructor
18	Mencor	David	Male	J.D.	Finance	8/1/1990	$ 52,000.00	Associate
19	Namiesnoiwoski	Elaine	Female	Ph.D.	Finance	8/1/1994	$ 75,000.00	Associate
20	Nguyen	Stewart	Male	Ph.D.	Marketing	8/1/1996	$ 89,000.00	Associate
21	Peterson	Mike	Male	J.D.	General Business	8/1/1999	$ 55,000.00	Assistant
22	Plagg	Nathan	Male	Ph.D.	Management	8/1/1997	$ 72,000.00	Assistant
23	Porter	Larry	Male	Ph.D.	Information Systems	8/1/1988	$ 125,000.00	Professor
24	Reese	LouAnn	Female	MBA	Accounting	8/1/1998	$ 72,000.00	Assistant
25	Ritzhaupht	Courtney	Female	MBA	Management	8/1/1982	$ 50,000.00	Instructor
26	Uhlenhopp	Kevan	Male	Ed.D.	Management	8/1/1997	$ 72,000.00	Assistant
27	Weiss	Clare	Female	Ph.D.	Accounting	8/1/2001	$ 72,000.00	Assistant
28	Whaley	Dari	Female	Ed.D.	Accounting	8/1/1996	$ 70,000.00	Associate

Criteria Range (rows 3–6)

Figure 2: Advanced Filter Dialog Box

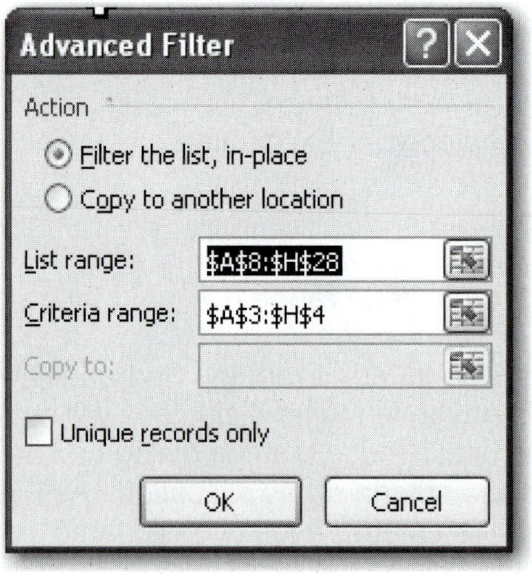

Figure 3: Advanced Filter Example

	A	B	C	D	E	F	G	H	I	J	K
1	College of Business Administration										
2	Faculty Information										
3	Last Name	First Name	Gender	Degree	Department	Hire Date	Salary	Rank	←		
4					Information Systems		>80000			Criteria Range	
5											
6									←		
7											
8	Last Name	First Name	Gender	Degree	Department	Hire Date	Salary	Rank			
23	Porter	Larry	Male	Ph.D.	Information Systems	8/1/1988	$ 125,000.00	Professor			

AVERAGE Function: The AVERAGE function returns an average for a specified range of cells. For instance, assume you want to calculate averages for the CSM students shown in Figure 4. Pauline Jeffrey's examination scores are contained in cells E4, F4, G4, and H4. To store the average in cell I4, you would type **=AVERAGE(E4:H4)** in cell I4.

Figure 4: Average Function

I4 | fx =AVERAGE(E4:H4)

	A	B	C	D	E	F	G	H	I
1	Computing Systems For Management								
2	Fall 2007								
3	First Name	Last Name	Days Absent		Exam I	Exam II	Exam III	Final	Average
4	Pauline	Jeffery	0		100	82	78	95	88.75
5	Margaret	Brady	1		87	89	77	92	86.25
6	Larry	Martin	3		65	78	89	94	81.50
7	Ti	Yee	5		43	81	96	97	79.25
8	Lester	LaMonte	0		94	92	56	98	85.00
9	Fred	Reed	6		78	97	98	100	93.25
10	Lawanda	Smith	1		75	56	85	100	79.00
11	Peter	Sands	9		62	75	88	89	78.50
12	Jewel	Rochat	2		90	94	88	89	90.25
13	Aubrey	Strunk	1		70	75	85	88	79.50

AutoFilter: In Microsoft Excel 2007, this command is called Filter. (See Filter.)

Button: A button is a small (or large) object that is added to your spreadsheet. The button can be assigned a macro, and when the button is clicked, the macro executes. Microsoft Excel provides you with the capability to add different types of buttons to your worksheet. For instance, you can add spin, command, toggle, and option buttons. A command button example is provided below.

To add a button to your worksheet, you can:

1. Click the Developer tab on the Ribbon. (If the Developer tab is not currently available, you will need to add it to the Ribbon. Use your system's online help system to learn more about adding commands to the Ribbon.)

2. From the Controls group, click the Insert command, and then click the Button (Form Control) command. See Figure 5.

Figure 5: Button Command

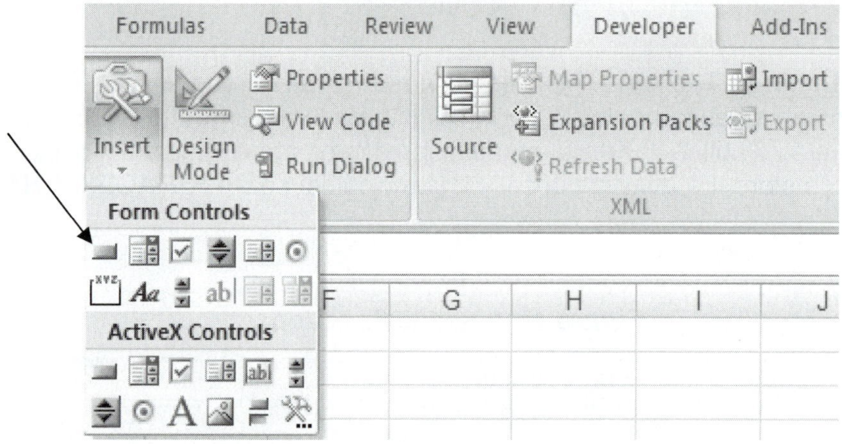

3. Draw the button on the worksheet. Once you have drawn the button, the Assign Macro dialog box appears. At this point, you can assign a macro to the button.

<u>Cell Formatting:</u> When you format a cell, you improve the appearance and readability of the cell's contents. From the Home tab, you can assign font, alignment, number, and style formats. Figure 6 shows the formatting options available from the Home tab.

Figure 6: Home Tab Cell Formatting Options

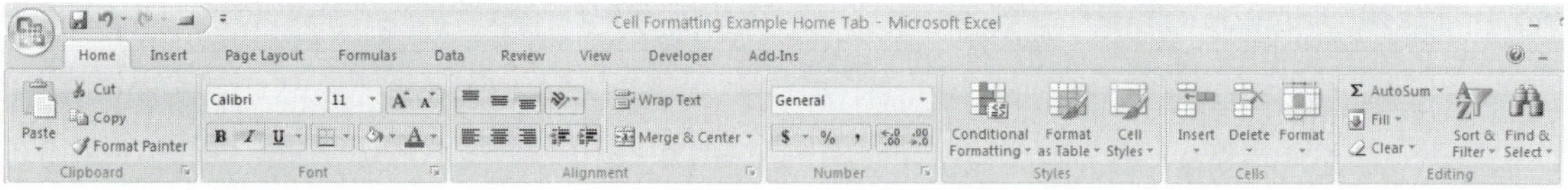

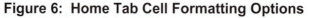

To apply a number format:

1. Click in the cell that you want formatted.

2. From the Number group located on the Home tab, click on the drop-down box for the number format that you want to apply.

Or:

1. Click in the cell that you want formatted.

2. Click the Dialog Box Launcher for the Number group. (See Figure 7.)

3. Select the formatting option that you want.

Figure 7: Format Cells Dialog Box

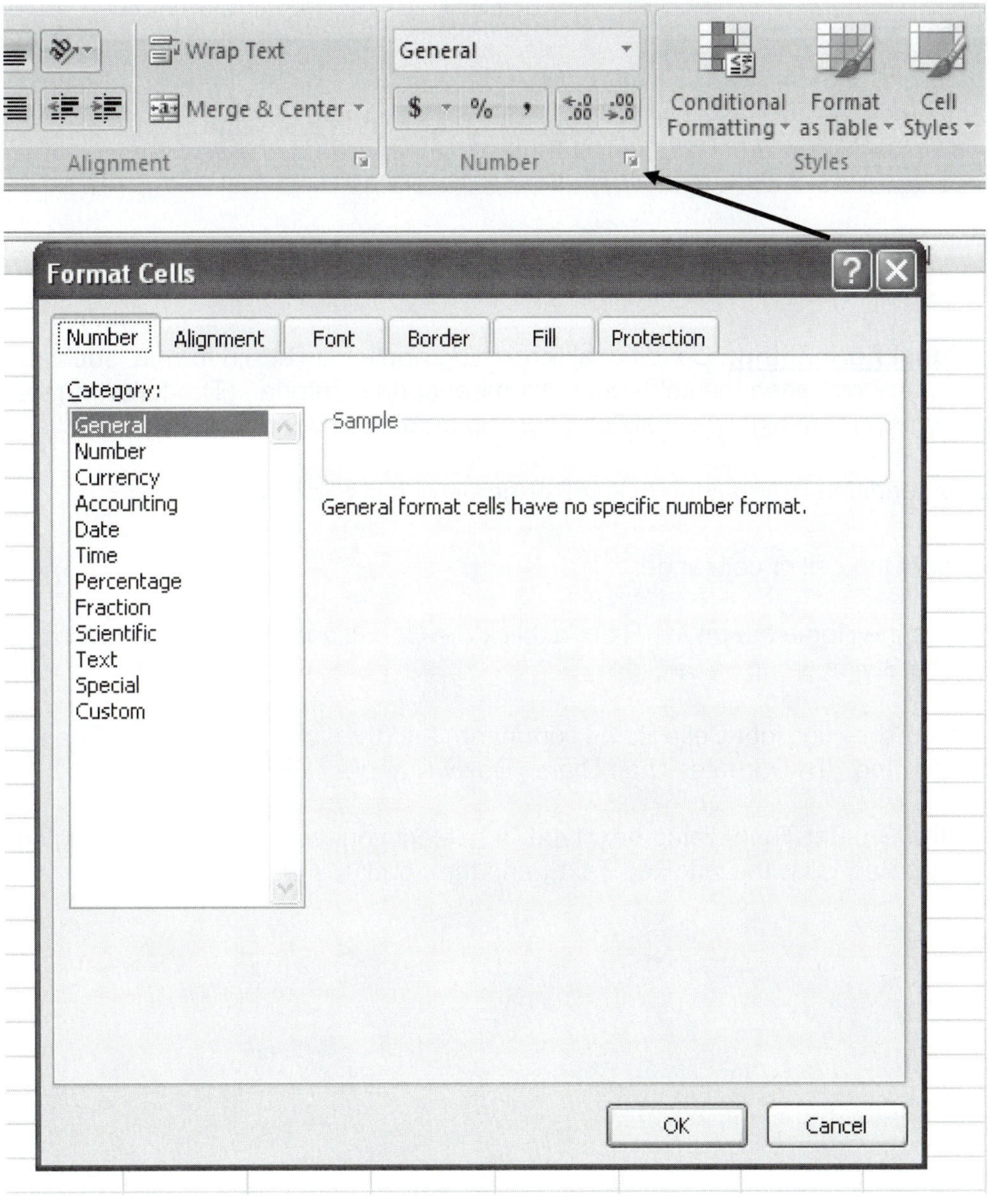

Cell Reference: See absolute cell reference and relative cell reference.

Chart: A chart is a graphical representation of selected data contained in the spreadsheet. Microsoft Excel provides you with several chart options.

To create a chart, perform the following steps:

1. Select the data that you want represented in the chart.
2. On the Ribbon, click the Insert tab.

3. From the Charts group, click one of the Chart buttons. See Figure 8.

Figure 8: Charts Group

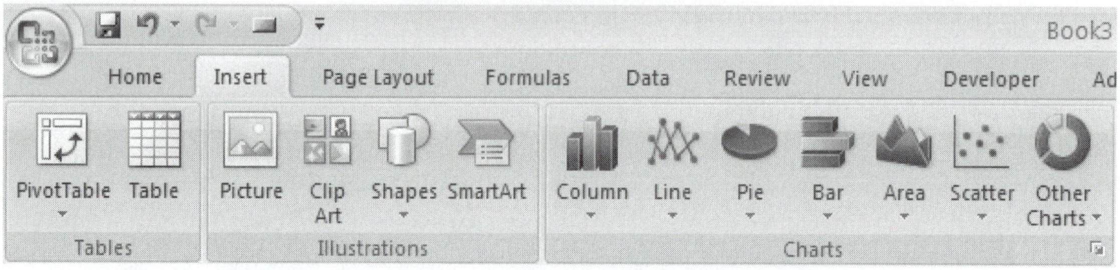

<u>Conditional Formatting:</u> Conditional formatting applies a certain format, such as the color red, to a cell when the cell's contents meet certain criteria. (The following steps assume you want to highlight cells that contain numbers larger than 5.)

To apply conditional formatting to a cell or group of cells, you would:

1. Select the cell or cell range.

2. From the Home tab on the Ribbon, click the Conditional Formatting button located in the Styles group. See Figure 9.

3. Select the Highlight Cells Rules command, and then click the Greater Than command. The Greater Than Dialog Box will appear. See Figure 10.

4. In the Greater Than dialog box, type "5"; select your conditional formatting criteria (Light Red Fill with Dark Red Text), and then click the OK button.

Figure 9: Conditional Formatting Options

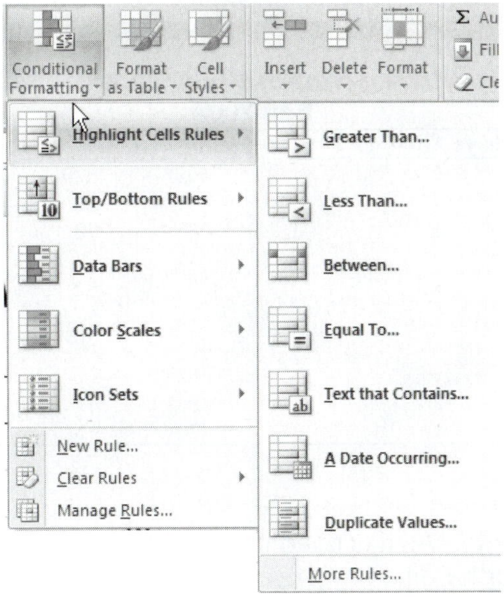

Figure 10: Greater Than Dialog Box

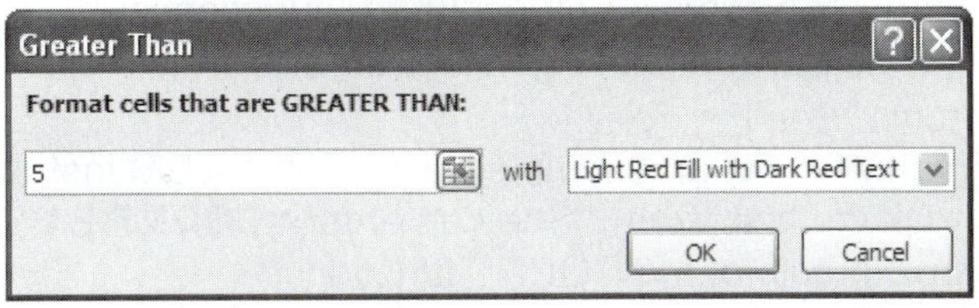

Conditional Formatting Example: Assume a Computing Systems for Management instructor wants to highlight a student's absences in red when the student has more than five absences. The instructor can apply conditional formatting to the cells appearing in the Days Absent column, so that the cells where the absences are more than five are highlighted in light red and the text is dark red. Figure 11 shows that conditional formatting has been applied to the Days Absent column.

Figure 11: Conditional Formatting Example

Computing Systems For Management
Fall 2007

First Name	Last Name	Days Absent		Exam I	Exam II	Exam III	Final	Average
Pauline	Jeffery	0		100	82	78	95	88.75
Margaret	Brady	1		87	89	77	92	86.25
Larry	Martin	3		65	78	89	94	81.50
Ti	Yee	5		43	81	96	97	79.25
Lester	LaMonte	0		94	92	56	98	85.00
Fred	Reed	6		78	97	98	100	93.25
Lawanda	Smith	1		75	56	85	100	79.00
Peter	Sands	9		62	75	88	89	78.50
Jewel	Rochat	2		90	94	88	89	90.25
Aubrey	Strunk	1		70	75	85	88	79.50

<u>Consolidating Worksheets</u>: As it is used in <u>MIS Cases: Decision Making with Application Software, Fourth Edition</u>, worksheet consolidation means summarizing the data contained in multiple worksheets into a summary worksheet.

<u>COUNT Function:</u> The COUNT function determines the number of numerical entries within a given cell range. The syntax for the COUNT function is: **=COUNT(BeginningCellAddress:EndingCellAddress)**.

<u>COUNT Function Example:</u> As an example, assume the CSM instructor wants to know how many students took the first exam. She can enter **=COUNT(E4:E13)** into cell E15. Figure 12 provides an example of the COUNT function.

Figure 12: COUNT Function Example

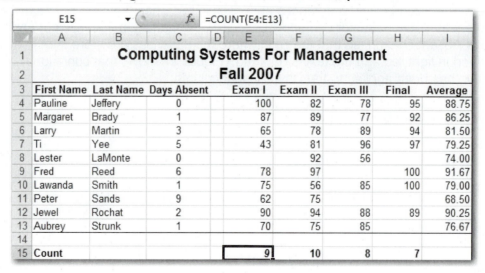

E15 =COUNT(E4:E13)

	A	B	C	D	E	F	G	H	I
1	Computing Systems For Management								
2	Fall 2007								
3	First Name	Last Name	Days Absent		Exam I	Exam II	Exam III	Final	Average
4	Pauline	Jeffery	0		100	82	78	95	88.75
5	Margaret	Brady	1		87	89	77	92	86.25
6	Larry	Martin	3		65	78	89	94	81.50
7	Ti	Yee	5		43	81	96	97	79.25
8	Lester	LaMonte	0			92	56		74.00
9	Fred	Reed	6		78	97		100	91.67
10	Lawanda	Smith	1		75	56	85	100	79.00
11	Peter	Sands	9		62	75			68.50
12	Jewel	Rochat	2		90	94	88	89	90.25
13	Aubrey	Strunk	1		70	75	85		76.67
14									
15	Count				9	10	8	7	

<u>COUNTA Function:</u> The COUNTA function is a statistical function that counts the number of nonempty cells in a cell range. The syntax for the COUNTA function is: **=COUNTA(BeginningCellAddress:EndingCellAddress)**.

<u>COUNTIF Function:</u> The COUNTIF function determines the number of cells in a range that meet certain criteria. For instance, you may want to know the number (count) of faculty members who earn more than $70,000 per year. Figure 13 demonstrates the use of the COUNTIF function.

Figure 13: COUNTIF Example

G24 fx =COUNTIF(G4:G23,">70,000")

	A	B	C	D	E	F	G	H
1	**College of Business Administration**							
2	**Faculty Information**							
3	**Last Name**	**First Name**	**Gender**	**Degree**	**Department**	**Hire Date**	**Salary**	**Rank**
4	Abdul	Mohammed	Male	M.Ed.	General Business	8/1/1999	$ 72,000.00	Assistant
5	Barnes	Fred	Male	MS	Information Systems	8/1/2002	$ 42,000.00	Instructor
6	Chen	Geo	Male	Ed.D.	Information Systems	8/1/1999	$ 62,500.00	Assistant
7	Chiaf	Sally	Female	Ph.D.	Economics	8/1/1994	$ 75,000.00	Associate
8	Friel	Essie	Female	Ph.D.	Economics	8/1/1993	$ 72,000.00	Professor
9	Hulva	Tracy	Male	Ed.D.	Finance	8/1/1992	$ 78,000.00	Associate
10	Jones	Mary	Female	Ph.D.	Marketing	8/1/1992	$ 100,000.00	Professor
11	Lancaster	Zoribel	Male	J.D.	General Business	8/1/1990	$ 51,500.00	Associate
12	Malcom	John	Male	MBA	General Business	8/1/1996	$ 42,000.00	Instructor
13	Mencor	David	Male	J.D.	Finance	8/1/1990	$ 52,000.00	Associate
14	Namiesnoiwoski	Elaine	Female	Ph.D.	Finance	8/1/1994	$ 75,000.00	Associate
15	Nguyen	Stewart	Male	Ph.D.	Marketing	8/1/1996	$ 89,000.00	Associate
16	Peterson	Mike	Male	J.D.	General Business	8/1/1999	$ 55,000.00	Assistant
17	Plagg	Nathan	Male	Ph.D.	Management	8/1/1997	$ 72,000.00	Assistant
18	Porter	Larry	Male	Ph.D.	Information Systems	8/1/1988	$ 125,000.00	Professor
19	Reese	LouAnn	Female	MBA	Accounting	8/1/1998	$ 72,000.00	Assistant
20	Ritzhaupht	Courtney	Female	MBA	Management	8/1/1982	$ 50,000.00	Instructor
21	Uhlenhopp	Kevan	Male	Ed.D.	Management	8/1/1997	$ 72,000.00	Assistant
22	Weiss	Clare	Female	Ph.D.	Accounting	8/1/2001	$ 72,000.00	Assistant
23	Whaley	Dari	Female	Ed.D.	Accounting	8/1/1996	$ 70,000.00	Associate
24					**Greater Than $70,000**		**12**	

<u>Data Table:</u> A data table summarizes the results of several what-if analyses. For instance, assume that you are purchasing a home and want to evaluate the impact that different down payments will have on your monthly payment. As Figure 14 shows, you can compare the results of several scenarios at once.

Microsoft Excel allows you to create one-variable and two-variable data tables. For a one-variable data table, you can specify one input cell and several result cells. The input cell references a cell in your worksheet that you want to modify as part of your analysis. The result cell references a cell in the worksheet that will change as a result of the change in the input cell's value. For a one-variable data table, you are limited to one input cell, but can have as many result cells as you want. With a two-variable data table, you may specify two input cells, but are limited to only one result cell.

To create a one-variable data table, you would:

1. List the input values that you want Microsoft Excel to substitute in the input cell. (Figure 14 shows the input values, which are the different down payments, placed in the leftmost column of the data table.) Keep in mind that the reference to the input cell must be placed in the upper leftmost cell of the data table. In Figure 14, the reference is placed in cell E4. In E4, you would insert the reference =B4.

2. Provide references to the result cells. A reference is provided by including a cell reference in the table that points to the result cell. For instance in cells F4 and G4, references are made to cells B8 and B10. Cell F4 contains the reference =B8, and cell G4 contains the reference =B10.

3. Select the table area. In Figure 14, the table area includes the cell range E4:G9.

4. On the Ribbon, select the Data tab.

5. From the Data Tools group, click the What-If Analysis button, and then select the Data Table command. See Figure 15.

6. Supply the location for the Row Input Cell or the Column Input Cell. Figure 16 shows the Data Table dialog box. (If your input values are arranged in a row, you would enter a reference to the input cell in the Row Input Cell box. If your input values are arranged in a column, you enter a reference to the input cell in the Column Input Cell box. (In Figure 16, the cell reference was typed in the Column Input Cell box, as the input values are arranged in a column.)

Figure 14: Data Table Example

	A	B	C	D	E	F	G	H
1	**Home Mortgage**							
2	**Payment Analysis**				**One-Variable Data Table**			
3	**Purchase Price**	100000			**Down Payment**	**Monthly Payment**	**Total Interest**	
4	**Down Payment**	5000			$5,000	($648.07)	($138,304.29)	
5	**Loan Amount**	95000			$6,000	($641.25)	($136,848.45)	
6	**Interest Rate**	0.0725			$7,000	($634.42)	($135,392.62)	
7	**Years**	30			$8,000	($627.60)	($133,936.78)	
8	**Monthly Payment**	($648.07)			$9,000	($620.78)	($132,480.95)	
9	**Total Payments**	($233,304.29)			$10,000	($613.96)	($131,025.11)	
10	**Total Interest**	($138,304.29)						

Figure 15: Data Table Command

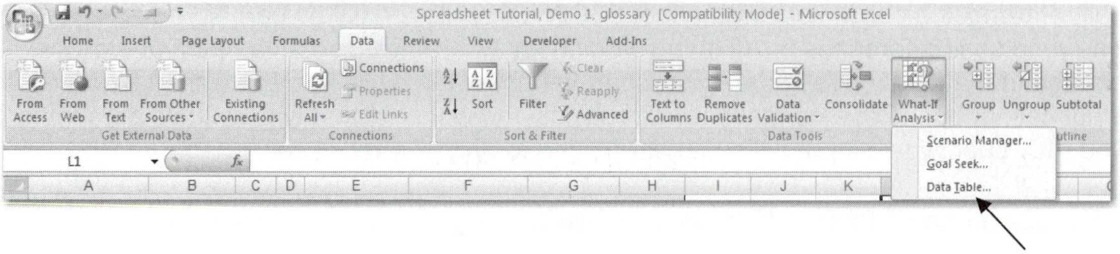

Figure 16: Data Table Dialog Box

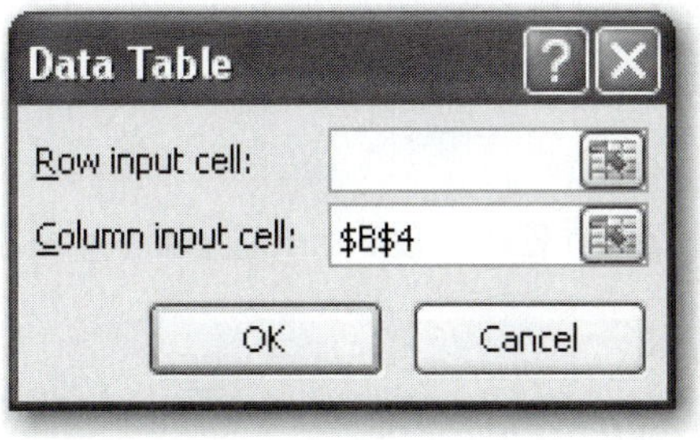

Date Calculations: When working with dates, you must determine whether you need the number of days between two dates or if the calculations should include both the start date and the end date. If you need to know the number of days between two dates, then you can simply subtract the start date from the end date. However, if your calculation should count the start date and the end date, then a more appropriate formula is: **=(EndDate – StartDate) + 1.** Microsoft Excel provides several date functions. You may wish to use your system's online help system to further investigate available date functions.

DAVERAGE Function: When working with an Excel table, the DAVERAGE function is one of several database functions available for use. When you use the Advanced Filter tool to filter a list, you can use the DAVERAGE function to return an average for the visible cells in a particular column. The DAVERAGE function returns an average for the visible values in a specified column and ignores the hidden values in the column. The syntax for the DAVERAGE function is **=DAVERAGE(TableName,"FieldName",criteria)**. (See Excel Table and Advanced Filter.)

DMAX Function: When working with an Excel table, the DMAX function is one of several database functions available for use. When you use the Advanced Filter tool to filter a list, the DMAX function identifies the maximum value from the visible cells in a particular column and ignores the hidden values. The syntax for the DMAX function is **=DMAX(TableName,"FieldName",criteria)**. At this point, consider using your system's online help feature to review database functions. (See Excel Table and Advanced Filter.)

DMIN Function: When working with an Excel table, the DMIN function is one of several database functions available for use. When you use the Advanced Filter tool to filter a list, you may want to identify the minimum value from the visible cells in a particular column. The DMIN function returns the minimum value from the visible values in a specified column and ignores the hidden values. The syntax for the DMIN function is **=DMIN(TableName,"FieldName",criteria)**. At this point, consider using your system's online help feature to review database functions. (See Excel Table and Advanced Filter.)

DSUM Function: When working with an Excel table, the DSUM function is one of several database functions available for use. When you use the Advanced Filter tool to filter a list, you may want to view the sum for the visible cells in a particular column. The DSUM function returns the total for the visible values in a specified column and ignores the hidden values. The syntax for the DSUM function is **=DSUM(TableName,"FieldName",criteria)**. At this point, consider using your system's online help feature to review database functions. (See Excel Table and Advanced Filter.)

<u>Excel List</u>: In Microsoft 2007, an Excel list is now called an Excel Table. (See Excel Table.)

<u>Excel Table:</u> (Previously called an Excel list.) An Excel table is a group of data that have a similar structure. An Excel table consists of rows and columns, with each row representing a record and each column representing a field or data attribute. Generally, the top row of the list consists of the field names. Figure 17 provides an example of an Excel table.

To create an Excel table, you can:

1. Click on any cell in the data range.
2. On the Ribbon, click the Insert tab.
3. From the Tables group, click the Table button. See Figure 18. The Create Table dialog box will appear. If the table range reference is correct, click the OK button.

Figure 17: Excel Table Example

	A	B	C	D	E	F	G	H
1	**College of Business Administration**							
2	**Faculty Information**							
3	**Last Name**	**First Nam**	**Gende**	**Degre**	**Department**	**Hire Dat**	**Salary**	**Rank**
4	Abdul	Mohammed	Male	M.Ed.	General Business	8/1/1999	$ 72,000.00	Assistant
5	Barnes	Fred	Male	MS	Information Systems	8/1/2002	$ 42,000.00	Instructor
6	Chen	Geo	Male	Ed.D.	Information Systems	8/1/1999	$ 62,500.00	Assistant
7	Chiaf	Sally	Female	Ph.D.	Economics	8/1/1994	$ 75,000.00	Associate
8	Friel	Essie	Female	Ph.D.	Economics	8/1/1993	$ 72,000.00	Professor
9	Hulva	Tracy	Male	Ed.D.	Finance	8/1/1992	$ 78,000.00	Associate
10	Jones	Mary	Female	Ph.D.	Marketing	8/1/1992	$ 100,000.00	Professor
11	Lancaster	Zoribel	Male	J.D.	General Business	8/1/1990	$ 51,500.00	Associate
12	Malcom	John	Male	MBA	General Business	8/1/1996	$ 42,000.00	Instructor
13	Mencor	David	Male	J.D.	Finance	8/1/1990	$ 52,000.00	Associate
14	Namiesnoiwoski	Elaine	Female	Ph.D.	Finance	8/1/1994	$ 75,000.00	Associate
15	Nguyen	Stewart	Male	Ph.D.	Marketing	8/1/1996	$ 89,000.00	Associate
16	Peterson	Mike	Male	J.D.	General Business	8/1/1999	$ 55,000.00	Assistant
17	Plagg	Nathan	Male	Ph.D.	Management	8/1/1997	$ 72,000.00	Assistant
18	Porter	Larry	Male	Ph.D.	Information Systems	8/1/1988	$ 125,000.00	Professor
19	Reese	LouAnn	Female	MBA	Accounting	8/1/1998	$ 72,000.00	Assistant
20	Ritzhaupht	Courtney	Female	MBA	Management	8/1/1982	$ 50,000.00	Instructor
21	Uhlenhopp	Kevan	Male	Ed.D.	Management	8/1/1997	$ 72,000.00	Assistant
22	Weiss	Clare	Female	Ph.D.	Accounting	8/1/2001	$ 72,000.00	Assistant
23	Whaley	Dari	Female	Ed.D.	Accounting	8/1/1996	$ 70,000.00	Associate

Figure 18: Table Button

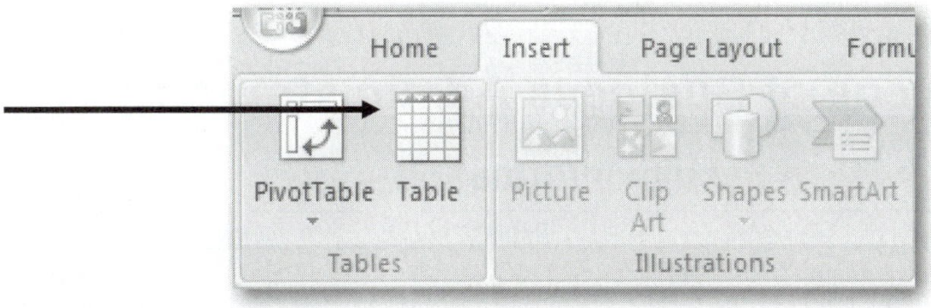

External Cell Reference: An external cell reference references a cell or range of cells from a worksheet located in another workbook. To reference a cell contained in a worksheet in another workbook, you use the following syntax: **=[WorkbookName]WorksheetName!CellAddress**. If the worksheet name or workbook name contains a space in its name, you should enclose the path in single quotations. For instance, you would use the following syntax: **='[Workbook Name]Worksheet Name'!CellAddress**. Use your system's online help feature to learn more about external cell references.

Filter: (Previously called AutoFilter.) The Filter command allows you to select and display records from an Excel table that meet certain criteria. Records that do not meet the criteria are temporarily hidden from view. (See Excel Table.)

To use the Filter command, you can:

1. Place your cell pointer anywhere in the Excel table.

2. On the Ribbon, click the Data tab. From the Sort and Filter group, click the Filter button.

3. At this point, the field names located in the top row of the Excel table have drop-down arrows beside their names. The drop-down arrows allow you to specify the criteria to use when filtering the records. Figure 19 shows the drop-down arrows that have been added to the Excel table. (Note: The Filter button works as a toggle. By clicking the Filter button, you can toggle on or off the drop-down arrows.)

Filter Example: As an example, assume you only want to see the information systems faculty. This request requires you to first click the drop-down arrow beside the Department field name. A drop-down list will appear. See Figure 20. The drop-down list provides several filtering options, including text filters. From the text values list, you would select "Information Systems". Figure 21 shows the results for this example.

Figure 19: Filter Example

A	B	C	D	E	F	G	H
College of Business Administration							
Faculty Information							
Last Name	**First Nam**	**Gende**	**Degre**	**Department**	**Hire Dat**	**Salary**	**Rank**
Abdul	Mohammed	Male	M.Ed.	General Business	8/1/1999	$ 72,000.00	Assistant
Barnes	Fred	Male	MS	Information Systems	8/1/2002	$ 42,000.00	Instructor
Chen	Geo	Male	Ed.D.	Information Systems	8/1/1999	$ 62,500.00	Assistant
Chiaf	Sally	Female	Ph.D.	Economics	8/1/1994	$ 75,000.00	Associate
Friel	Essie	Female	Ph.D.	Economics	8/1/1993	$ 72,000.00	Professor
Hulva	Tracy	Male	Ed.D.	Finance	8/1/1992	$ 78,000.00	Associate
Jones	Mary	Female	Ph.D.	Marketing	8/1/1992	$ 100,000.00	Professor
Lancaster	Zoribel	Male	J.D.	General Business	8/1/1990	$ 51,500.00	Associate
Malcom	John	Male	MBA	General Business	8/1/1996	$ 42,000.00	Instructor
Mencor	David	Male	J.D.	Finance	8/1/1990	$ 52,000.00	Associate
Namiesnoiwoski	Elaine	Female	Ph.D.	Finance	8/1/1994	$ 75,000.00	Associate
Nguyen	Stewart	Male	Ph.D.	Marketing	8/1/1996	$ 89,000.00	Associate
Peterson	Mike	Male	J.D.	General Business	8/1/1999	$ 55,000.00	Assistant
Plagg	Nathan	Male	Ph.D.	Management	8/1/1997	$ 72,000.00	Assistant
Porter	Larry	Male	Ph.D.	Information Systems	8/1/1988	$ 125,000.00	Professor
Reese	LouAnn	Female	MBA	Accounting	8/1/1998	$ 72,000.00	Assistant
Ritzhaupht	Courtney	Female	MBA	Management	8/1/1982	$ 50,000.00	Instructor
Uhlenhopp	Kevan	Male	Ed.D.	Management	8/1/1997	$ 72,000.00	Assistant
Weiss	Clare	Female	Ph.D.	Accounting	8/1/2001	$ 72,000.00	Assistant
Whaley	Dari	Female	Ed.D.	Accounting	8/1/1996	$ 70,000.00	Associate

Figure 20: Filter's Drop-Down List

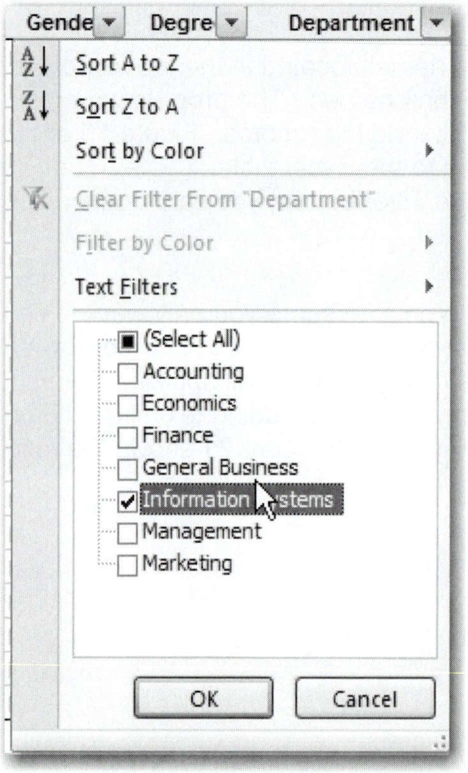

Figure 21: Filter Results

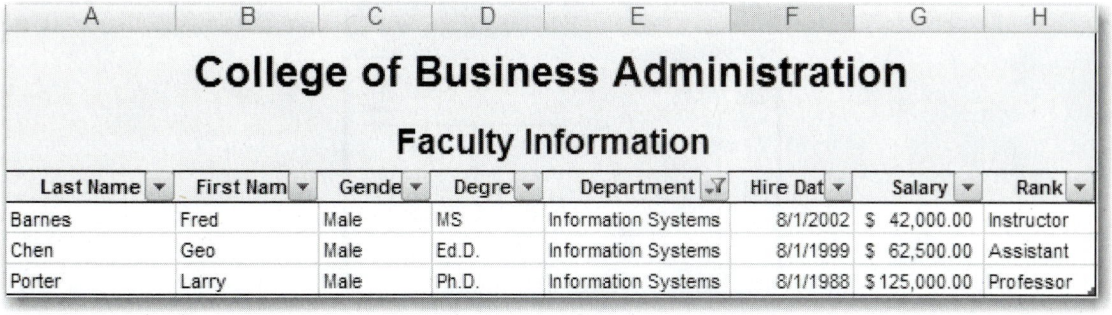

A	B	C	D	E	F	G	H
College of Business Administration							
Faculty Information							
Last Name	First Nam	Gende	Degre	Department	Hire Dat	Salary	Rank
Barnes	Fred	Male	MS	Information Systems	8/1/2002	$ 42,000.00	Instructor
Chen	Geo	Male	Ed.D.	Information Systems	8/1/1999	$ 62,500.00	Assistant
Porter	Larry	Male	Ph.D.	Information Systems	8/1/1988	$ 125,000.00	Professor

Formula: A formula is a mathematical expression that specifies how to calculate data. A formula can be simple or complex and include predefined functions, such as AVERAGE, SUM, or PMT. A formula must begin with an equal sign (=). To view a spreadsheet's formulas, you can simultaneously press the CTRL key and the grave accent key (`).

Get External Data From Access: This command retrieves data from a Microsoft Access query or table. This command is located in the Get External Data group located on the Data tab.

Goal Seek: Goal Seek is a Microsoft Excel command used for performing what-if analysis. Goal Seek asks you to specify a target value for a particular cell, called the Set Cell value. Goal Seek also asks you to indicate which cell contains the value that needs to be changed, called the Changing Cell.

To use Goal Seek, you can:

1. On the Ribbon, click the Data tab.

2. In the Data Tools group, click the What-If Analysis button.

3. Select the Goal Seek command. See Figure 22. The Goal Seek dialog box should appear. Figure 23 shows the Goal Seek dialog box.

Figure 22: Goal Seek Command

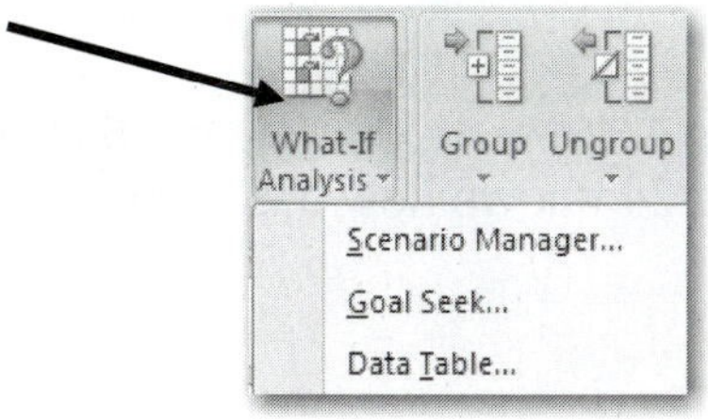

Figure 23: Goal Seek Dialog Box

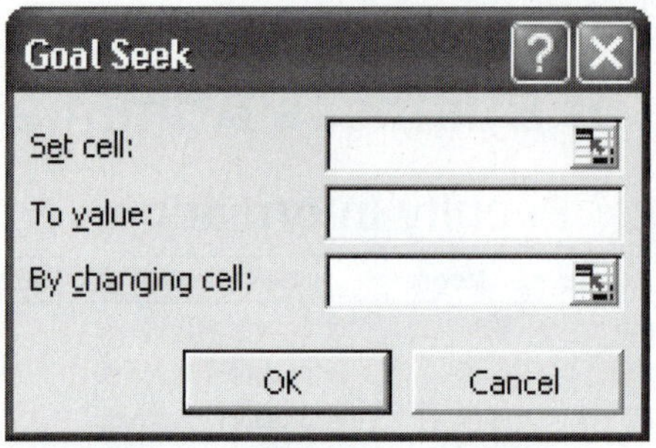

<u>Grouping Worksheets:</u> Occasionally, you may need to work with two or more worksheets at the same time. For instance, you may want the worksheets to use a similar worksheet format. Instead of separately formatting the worksheets, you can group the worksheets and format them as a group. When working with a worksheet group, keep in mind that all changes that you make to one worksheet in the group are made to all worksheets in the group. When you are finished working with the worksheet group, you should ungroup the worksheets.

To group nonadjacent worksheets:

1. Hold down the Ctrl key and click the sheet tab for each worksheet that you want to include as part of the worksheet group.

To group adjacent worksheets:

1. Hold down the Shift key and click the first sheet tab and then click the last sheet tab for the worksheet group.

Ungrouping the worksheets is accomplished by:

1. Right clicking one of the sheet tabs, and then selecting the Ungroup Sheets option from the shortcut menu.

<u>IF Function:</u> The IF function is a logical function that evaluates whether a specified condition is true or false. The syntax for an IF function is: **=IF(condition,value_if_true,value_if_false)**.

<u>IF Function Example:</u> Assume the CSM instructor gives 25 bonus points to each student with zero absences. Figure 24 shows how the IF function can be used.

Figure 24: IF Function Example

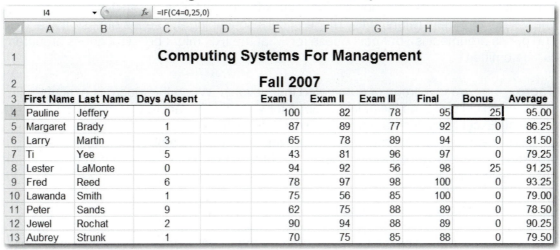

I4 f_x =IF(C4=0,25,0)

	A	B	C	D	E	F	G	H	I	J
1	**Computing Systems For Management**									
2	**Fall 2007**									
3	**First Name**	**Last Name**	**Days Absent**		**Exam I**	**Exam II**	**Exam III**	**Final**	**Bonus**	**Average**
4	Pauline	Jeffery	0		100	82	78	95	25	95.00
5	Margaret	Brady	1		87	89	77	92	0	86.25
6	Larry	Martin	3		65	78	89	94	0	81.50
7	Ti	Yee	5		43	81	96	97	0	79.25
8	Lester	LaMonte	0		94	92	56	98	25	91.25
9	Fred	Reed	6		78	97	98	100	0	93.25
10	Lawanda	Smith	1		75	56	85	100	0	79.00
11	Peter	Sands	9		62	75	88	89	0	78.50
12	Jewel	Rochat	2		90	94	88	89	0	90.25
13	Aubrey	Strunk	1		70	75	85	88	0	79.50

Import External Data: Microsoft Excel enables you to easily import data from other sources into Microsoft Excel.

To import data, you can:

1. On the Ribbon, click the Data tab.

2. In the Get External Data group, select the data source. See Figure 25. For instance, if you want to import data from a text file, click the From Text button. You would then select your file and click the Import button. The Text Import Wizard would, through a series of dialog boxes, walk you through the text import process.

Figure 25: Get External Data Group

Insert Sheet Columns: (Previously called Insert Column command.) Microsoft Excel makes it easy to insert a column in your worksheet. On the Ribbon, click the Home tab. In the Cells group, click the drop-down arrow on the Insert button, and then select the Insert Sheet Columns command.

By default, Microsoft Excel inserts the new column to the immediate left of the selected column. If the active cell is B4 and you issue the Insert Sheet Columns command, Microsoft Excel will shift the current Column B to the right. Column B now becomes Column C, and you have a new Column B.

<u>IRR Function:</u> The IRR function is a financial function that determines the internal rate of return for a series of cash flows. The syntax for this function is: **=IRR(values,guess)**. The values argument refers to the range of cells containing the series of cash flows. The guess argument is your best guess for what the IRR might be. The guess argument can be omitted.

<u>Macro</u>: A macro is a group of automated instructions. When the macro is executed, Microsoft Excel performs these instructions for you. For instance, you may want Microsoft Excel to copy data from one worksheet to another, print a worksheet group, or clear a certain worksheet area. Macros provide you with the ability to custom design procedures for your worksheet or workbook. Microsoft Excel's macro recorder is an easy way to build a macro.

To use the macro recorder, you can:

1. On the Ribbon, click the Developer tab. (If the Developer tab is not showing, you will need to add it to the Ribbon. Use the system's online help system to learn how to add the Developer tab to the Ribbon.)

2. From the Code group, click the Record Macro button. See Figure 26.

Figure 26: Record Macro Button

3. Name the macro; click OK.

4. The macro recorder will now record your actions.

5. When you are finished, click the Stop Recording button. See Figure 27.

Figure 27: Stop Recording Button

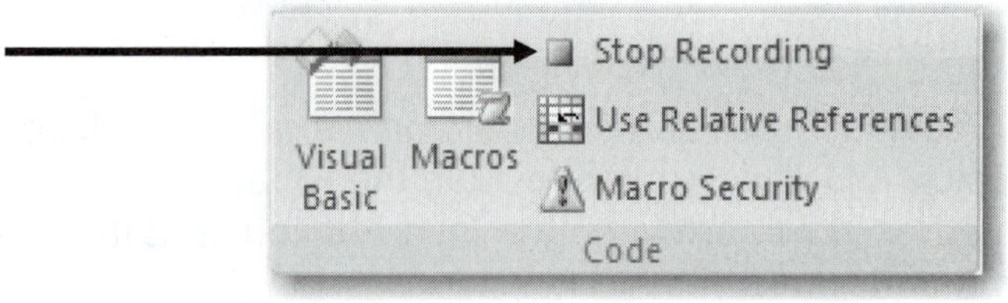

<u>MAX Function:</u> The MAX function returns the highest value from a specified range. The syntax for the MAX function is:
=MAX(BeginningCellAddress:EndingCellAddress).

Median Function: The MEDIAN function determines the median value for a set of numbers. The syntax for the MEDIAN function is: **=Median(BeginningCellAddress:EndingCellAddress)**.

Microsoft Query: Microsoft Query retrieves data from an external source, such as a Microsoft Access database. (Use your system's online help feature to learn more about Microsoft Query and how you can use it to connect to different external sources.)

To access Microsoft Query:

1. On the Ribbon, click the Data tab.

2. From the Get External Data group, click the From Other Sources button. (The following steps assume you will use the Microsoft Query Wizard.)

3. Select the From Microsoft Query option. See Figure 28.

Figure 28: Retrieve External Data Using Microsoft Query

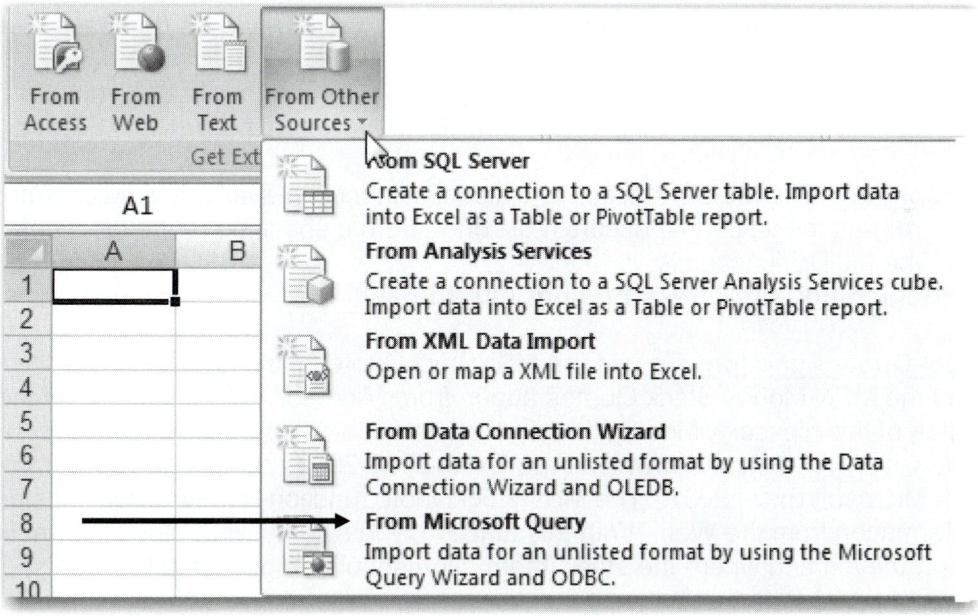

4. At this point, you can invoke the Query Wizard or you can use Microsoft Query without the wizard. The Query Wizard helps you construct the query. To use the Query Wizard, check the Use the Query Wizard to create/edit queries box at the bottom of the Choose Data source dialog box. Figure 29 shows the Choose Data Source dialog box.

Figure 29: Choose Data Source Dialog Box

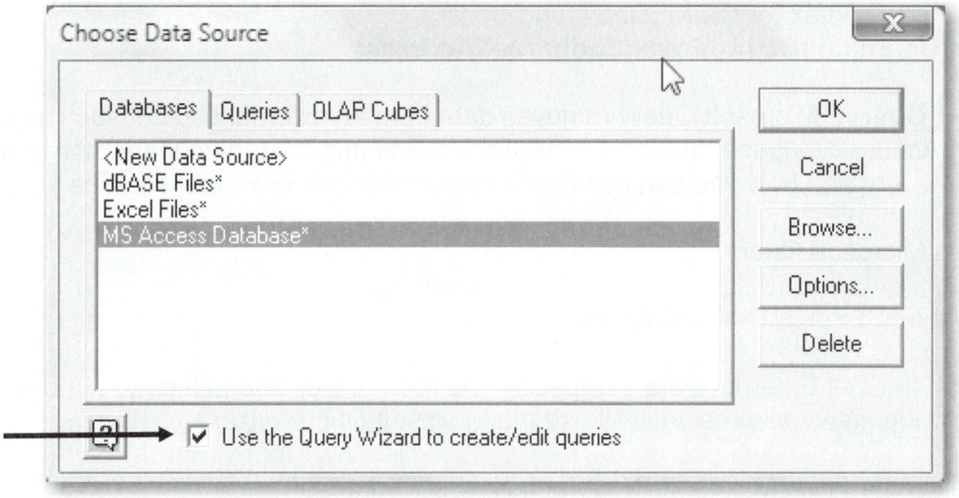

5. Double-click the MS Access Database* option; locate your Microsoft Access database, and then click the OK button. At this point, you will be able to construct a query using the tables and queries from your Microsoft Access database.

MIN Function: The MIN function returns the lowest value from a range of values. The syntax for the MIN function is: **=MIN(BeginningCellAddress:EndingCellAddress)**.

MODE Function: The MODE function is a statistical function available in Microsoft Excel that returns the value that occurs most often from a specified range of values. The syntax for the MODE function is:
=MODE(BeginningCellAddress:EndingCellAddress).

MSNStockQuote Function: To use the MSNStockQuote function, you should download the MSN Money Stock Quotes add-in from Microsoft's Web site. As of the preparation of this glossary, Microsoft had not updated this add-in for Microsoft Excel 2007. However, you can still download the Excel 2003-2002 add-in. This add-in will work with Microsoft Excel 2007. The MSNStockQuote function retrieves current stock quote information from the Web. With this function, you specify what stock information you want retrieved and where the stock information should be placed in the worksheet.

Nesting Functions: A nested function is a function that is included within another function. As an example, assume that an instructor gives bonus points to his students. The bonus points are based on the number of absences that each student has. If a student has no absences, he is given 25 bonus points. If a student has one absence, he is given 10 bonus points. If a student has more than one absence, he is given no bonus points. In this case, you can use the formula **=IF(C4=0,25,IF(C4=1,10,0))** to assign the correct bonus points to the students. Notice the placement of the second IF function.

NOW Function: The NOW function returns the current date and time. The syntax for the NOW function is: **=NOW()**.

Page Break: The Page Break command forces spreadsheet sections to print on separate pages. For instance, you may want the input section to print on page 1, and the results section to print on page 2. You can insert vertical and horizontal page breaks.

To insert a vertical page break, you can:

1. Select the column to the right of where you want to insert the page break.
2. Click the Page Layout tab.
3. From the Page Setup group, click the Breaks button.
4. Select the Insert Page Break command.

To insert a horizontal page break, you can:

1. Select the first row below where you want the page break inserted.
2. Click the Page Layout tab.
3. From the Page Setup group, click the Breaks button.
4. Select the Insert Page Break command.

Pivot Chart: A Pivot Chart report is based on the contents of a Pivot Table. Pivot Chart reports are interactive, allowing the user to dynamically change the appearance of the report.

To create a Pivot Chart report, you can:

1. Place the pointer in one of the Pivot Table cells.
2. On the Ribbon, click the Options tab.
3. In the Tools group, click the Pivot Chart button. See Figure 30.
4. The Insert Chart dialog box will appear. Select your chart, and then click the OK button. See Figure 31.

Figure 30: Pivot Chart Button

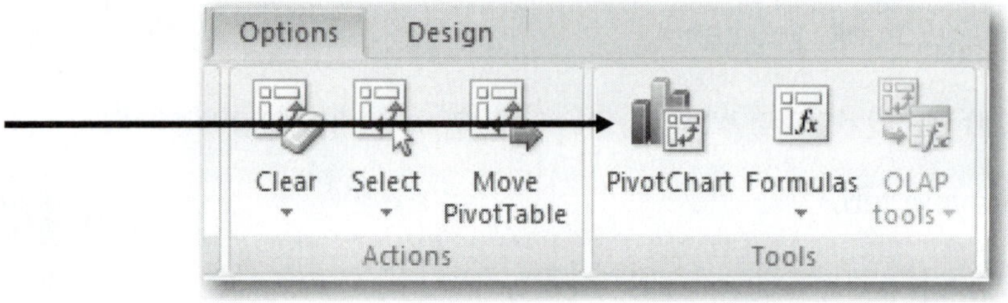

Figure 31: Insert Chart Dialog Box

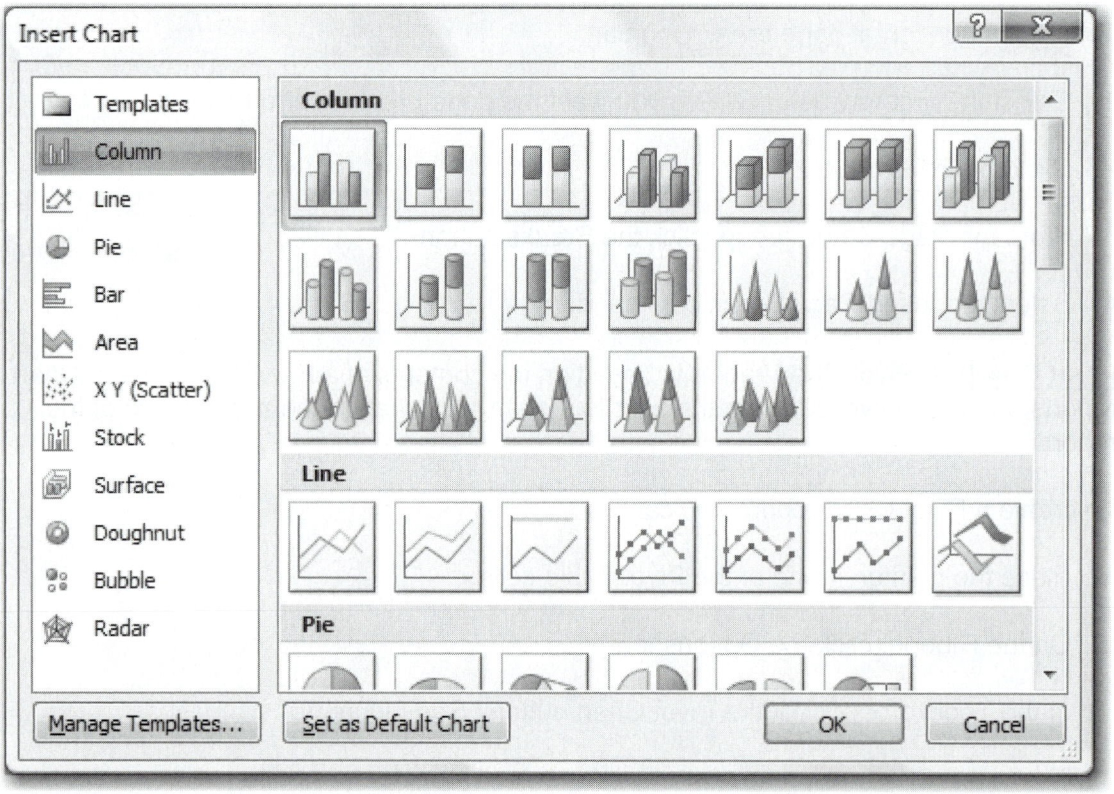

Pivot Table: A pivot table organizes data from an Excel table (or an external data source) into a tabular report. A pivot table allows the user to dynamically view different data dimensions. You can quickly alter the pivot table's layout by specifying different row, column, page, and data fields.

To create a pivot table, you can:

1. Place the pointer in one of the cells in the Excel table.

2. On the Ribbon, click the Insert tab.

3. In the Tables group, click the Pivot Table button. See Figure 32.

Figure 32: Pivot Table Button

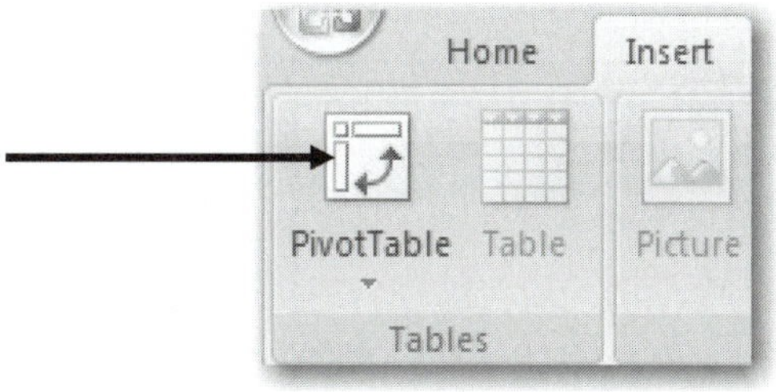

1. The Create Pivot Table dialog box appears. In the Create Pivot Table dialog box, you can specify the data to analyze and where the Pivot Table report should be located. See Figure 33.

Figure 33: Create Pivot Table Dialog Box

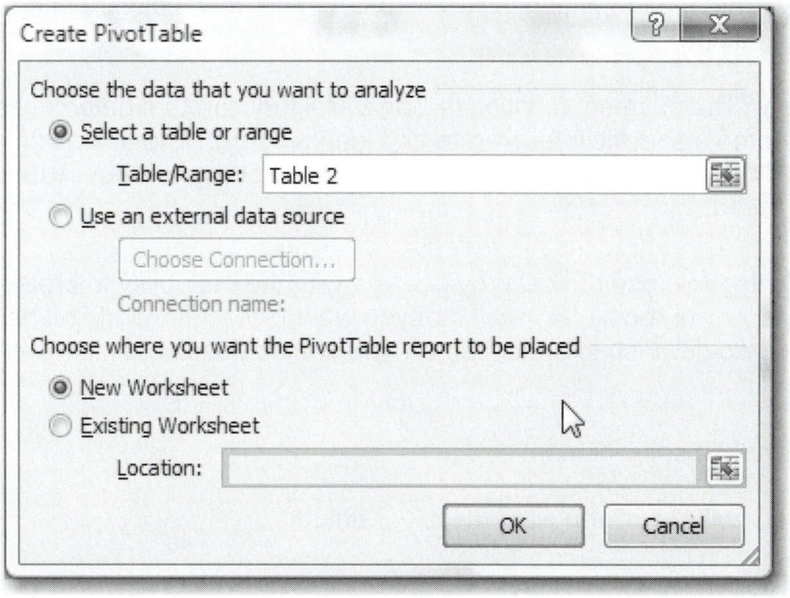

2. After you click the OK button, the Pivot Table Layout Guide appears. See Figure 34. (Note: In Figure 34, the Pivot Table Layout Guide's appearance is the classic view. You can change the layout guide's appearance by changing the display option located in the Pivot Table options.)

Figure 34: Pivot Table Layout Guide

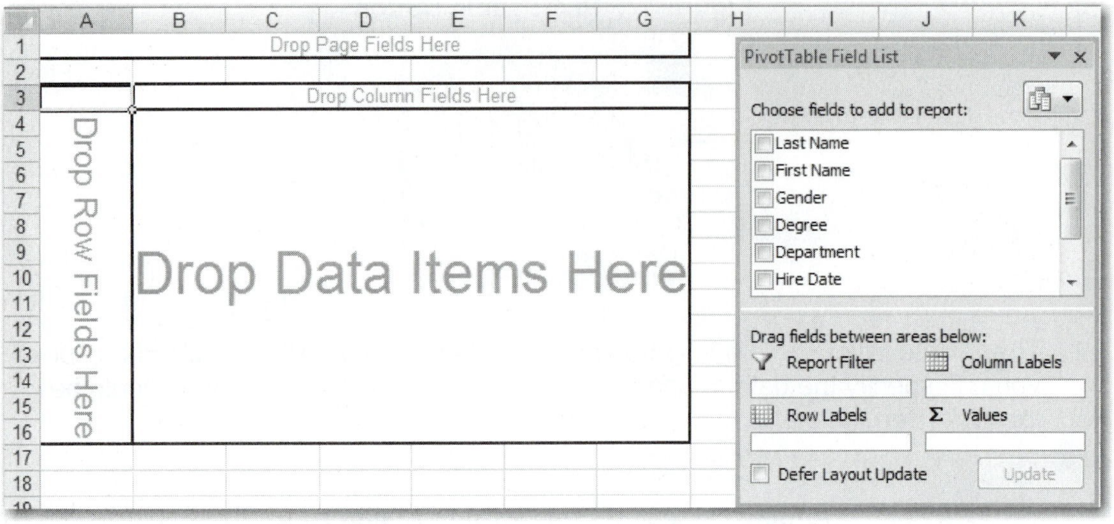

3. You can drag and drop field names onto the page, row, column, and data areas of the layout guide.

PMT Function: The payment function is a financial function that determines a periodic payment based on a specific interest rate and loan amount. The syntax for the PMT function is: **=PMT(rate, number of payment periods, present value, future value, and type)**.

Protecting Cells: Microsoft Excel provides you with the capability to protect a single cell, worksheet, or workbook. Any cell that you want protected must first be locked. Likewise, if you do not wish to protect a cell, you should deselect the locked property for that cell.

To lock (or unlock) a cell, you can:

1. Select the cell(s) that you want to lock or unlock.
2. On the Ribbon, click the Home tab.
3. In the Number group, click the dialog box launcher. See Figure 35. The Format Cells dialog box will open. See Figure 36.
4. Click the Protection tab. At this point, you can either lock or unlock the selected cell(s).

Figure 35: Number Group

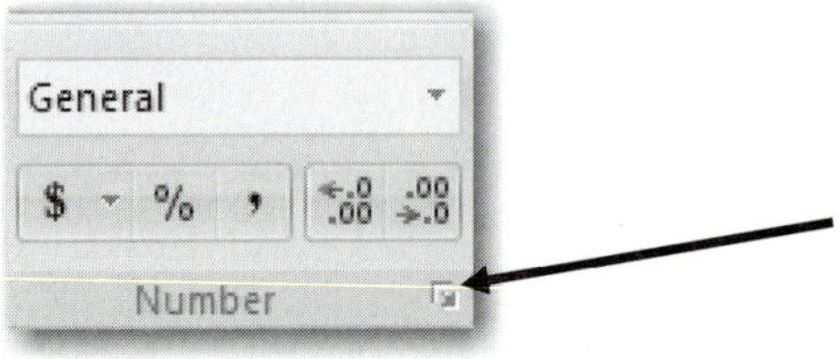

Figure 36: Format Cells Dialog Box

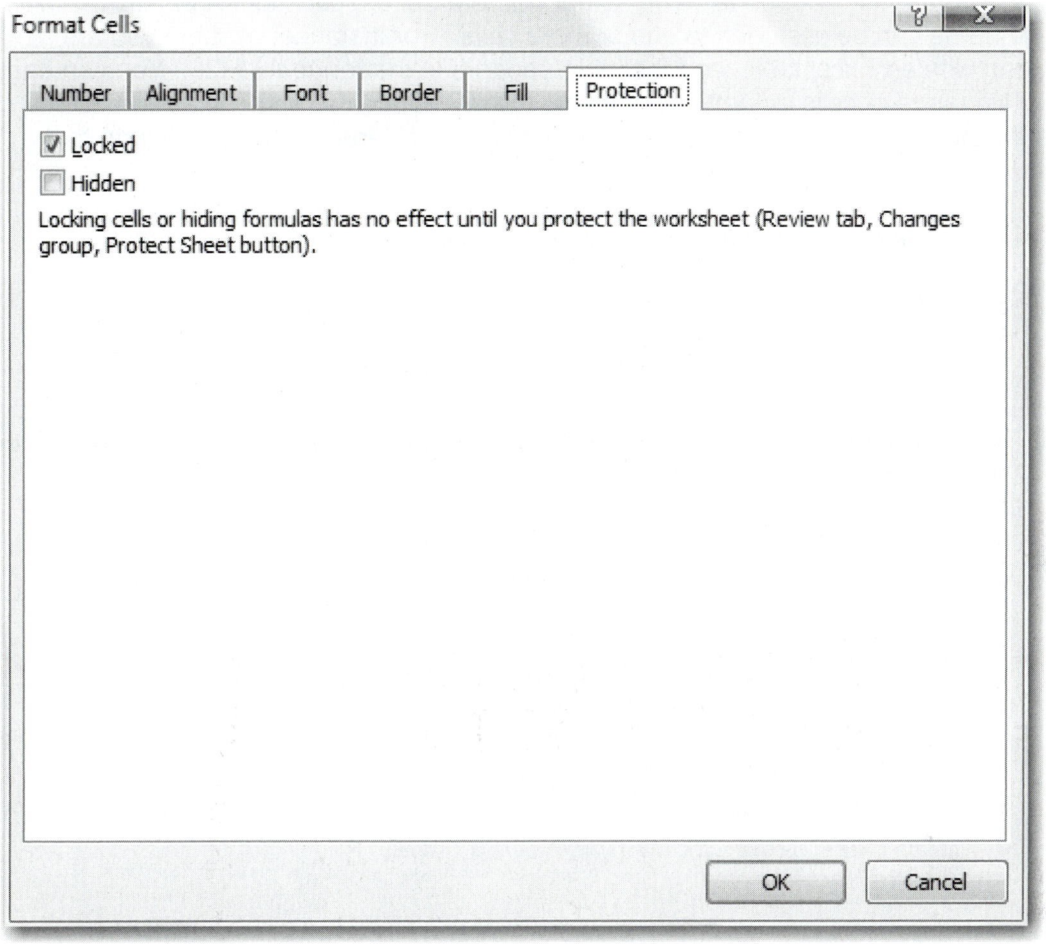

To protect your worksheet:

1. On the Ribbon, click the Review tab.
2. In the Changes group, click the Protect Sheet button, and then click the OK button. See Figure 37.

Figure 37: Protect Sheet

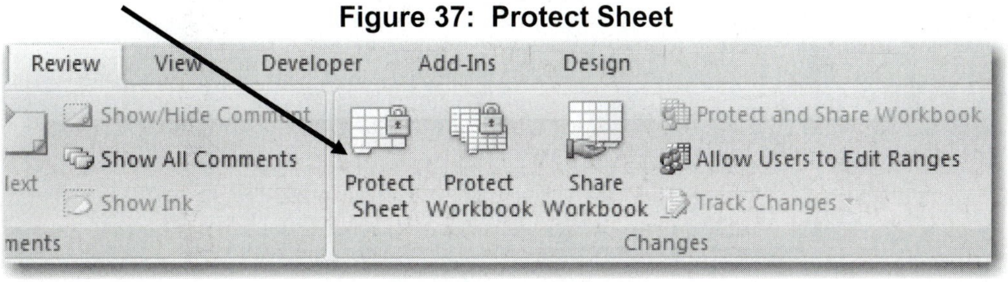

<u>Range Name:</u> When working with cells, it is sometimes easier to assign a cell or cell range a name, as opposed to using actual cell references, such as A4 or A6:H26. A range name can be assigned to one or more cells. For instance, assume you are working with an Excel table, and the table appears in the range A6:H26. You can easily give this range of cells a name, such as database. Once the name is assigned, you can use the range name, as opposed to the actual range reference, when referring to the cells.

To assign a range name to a group of cells, you can:

1. Select the cell range.

2. On the Ribbon, click the Formulas tab.

3. In the Defined Names group, click the Define Name button. See Figure 38. The New Name dialog box will appear.

4. In the New Name dialog box, type a name for the range, and then click the OK button. See Figure 39.

Figure 38: Define Name Button

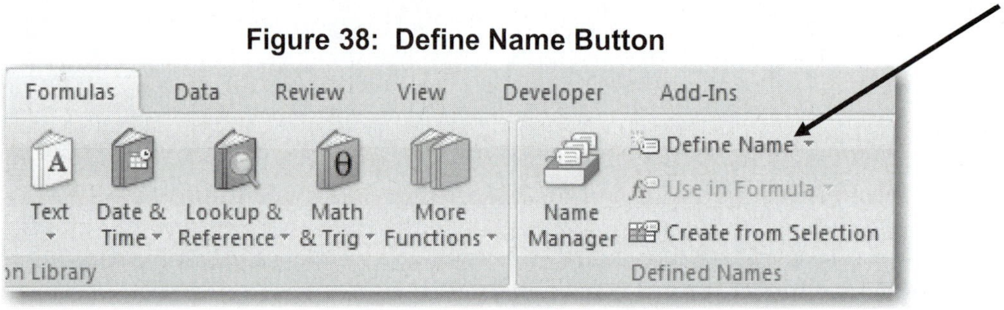

Figure 39: New Name Dialog Box

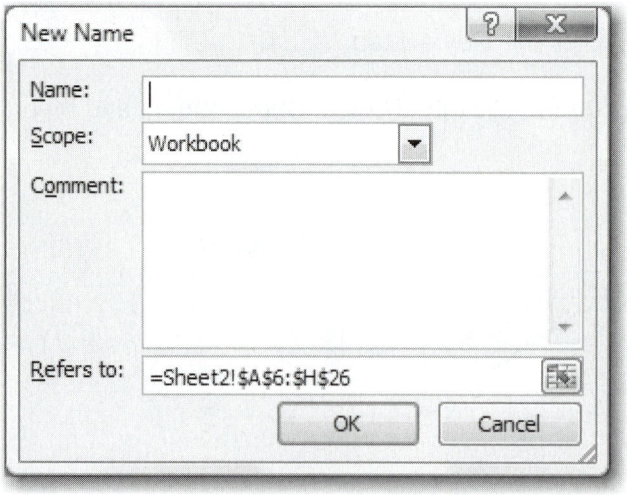

Relative Cell Reference: When a formula is copied to a new cell, a relative cell reference adjusts based on the formula's new location. Assume you type =A8+B8 in cell C8. Next, assume that you copy the formula to cell C9. Since A8 and B8 are relative references, the formula in cell C9 appears as =A9+B9.

Scenario Manager: When performing what-if analysis, you often want to view the results for different situations or scenarios. The Scenario Manager enables you to create, save and compare different scenarios. Also, the Scenario Manager allows you to specify which cells you want to change as part of your analysis. The Scenario Manager dialog box allows you to add, edit, delete, and show different scenarios. By clicking the Summary button, you are able to generate a report.

To access the Scenario Manager dialog box, you can:

1. On the Ribbon, click the Data tab.

2. From the Data Tools group, click the What-If Analysis button. See Figure 40.

3. Select the Scenario Manager command. The Scenario Manager dialog box appears. See Figure 41.

Figure 40: What-If Analysis Button

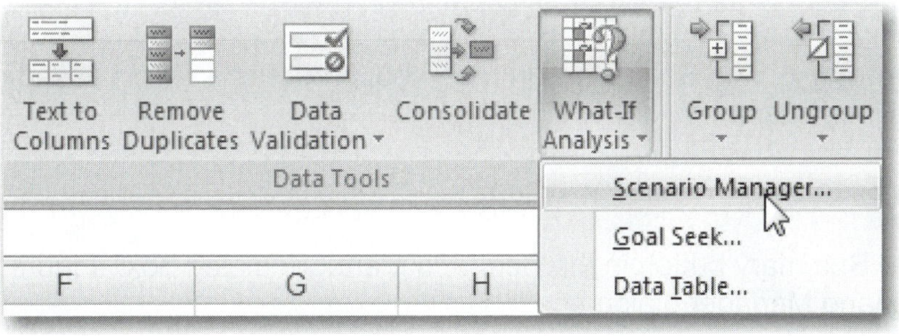

Figure 41: Scenario Manager Dialog Box

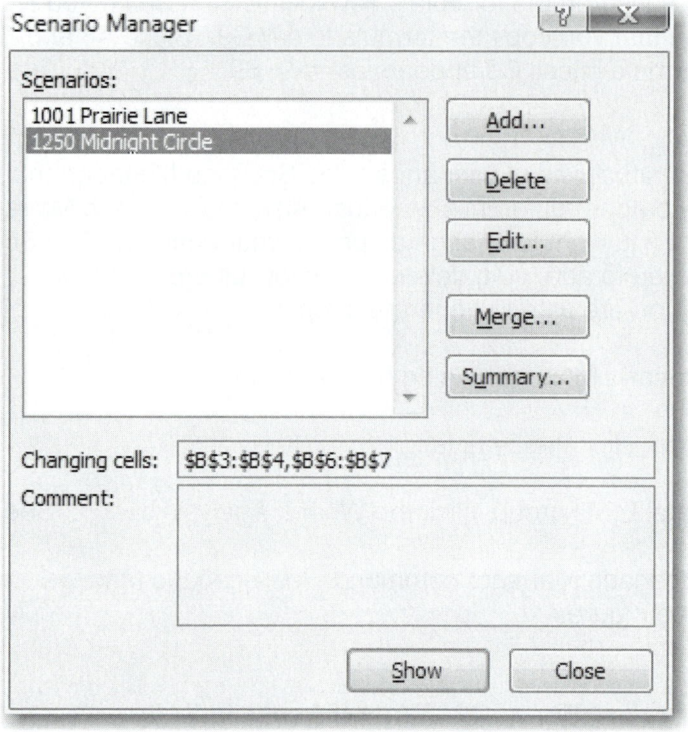

<u>Scenario Summary:</u> The Scenario Summary tool prepares a report based on previously defined scenarios.

To prepare a Scenario Summary, you can:

1. Click the Summary button in the Scenario Manager dialog box. Figure 41 shows the Scenario Manager dialog box.

2. Select a report type, and then click the OK button. Figure 42 shows the Scenario Summary dialog box, and Figure 43 shows a Scenario Summary report based on the two scenarios shown in Figure 41.

Figure 42: Scenario Summary Dialog Box

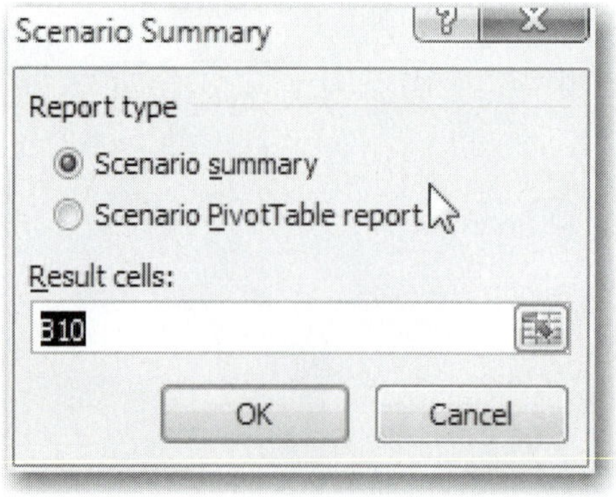

Figure 43: Scenario Summary Report

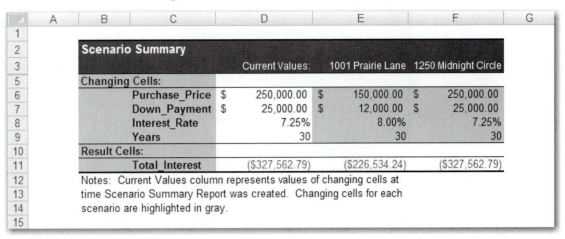

Scenario Summary				
		Current Values:	1001 Prairie Lane	1250 Midnight Circle
Changing Cells:				
	Purchase_Price	$ 250,000.00	$ 150,000.00	$ 250,000.00
	Down_Payment	$ 25,000.00	$ 12,000.00	$ 25,000.00
	Interest_Rate	7.25%	8.00%	7.25%
	Years	30	30	30
Result Cells:				
	Total_Interest	($327,562.79)	($226,534.24)	($327,562.79)

Notes: Current Values column represents values of changing cells at time Scenario Summary Report was created. Changing cells for each scenario are highlighted in gray.

<u>Solver:</u> Microsoft Excel provides a powerful what-if analysis add-in tool called Solver. Solver finds a solution that maximizes a cell's value, minimizes a cell's value, or reaches a specified value. When working with Solver, you must specify a target cell, changing cells, and any constraints. The target cell is the cell that you want to maximize, minimize, or reach a certain value. For instance, you may want to find a solution that maximizes profit, minimizes cost, or results in a specified income of $60,000. The changing cells are cells that Solver will adjust in order to find an optimal solution. For instance, you can ask Solver to adjust the cells that contain your expenses, number of units sold, and the price per unit. Constraints are restrictions that are placed on Solver. (Note: You may need to install the Solver add-in. Please refer to the system's online help system for more information.)

To use Solver, you can:

1. On the Ribbon, click the Data tab.

2. In the Analysis group, click the Solver button. See Figure 44.

3. The Solver Parameters dialog box appears. Figure 45 shows the Solver Parameters dialog box.

4. Enter your parameters, and then click the Solve button.

Figure 44: Solver Button

Figure 45: Solver Parameters Dialog Box

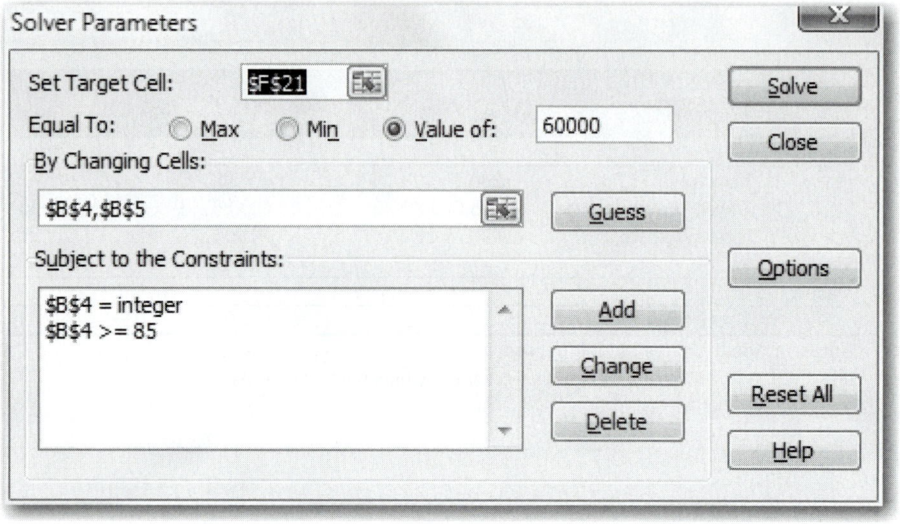

Sort: Microsoft Excel can arrange row data based on the values contained in one or more columns. The data are arranged in ascending or descending order. A quick way to sort involves clicking in the column that you want sorted, and then clicking the Sort and Filter button in the Editing group located on the Home tab. See Figure 46. You can then select either the Sort A to Z command or the Sort Z to A command. If you need to sort the rows based on values contained in two or more columns, you can use the Custom Sort command.

Figure 46: Sort and Filter

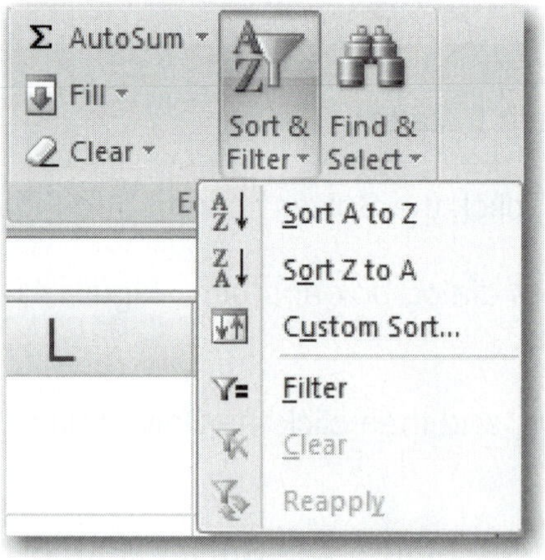

Assume you want the faculty data in Figure 47 sorted based on rank and then based on last name. To sort the data, you can:

1. Click in one of the cells that is part of the table.

2. On the Ribbon, click the Home tab.

3. In the Editing group, click the Sort and Filter button.

4. Select the Custom Sort command. The Sort dialog box appears. See Figure 48.

5. In the Sort dialog box, specify the sort order. To add a level, click the Add Level button. Notice in Figure 48, that Microsoft Excel will first sort by rank (primary sort), and then by last name (secondary sort). Also, notice that you have the option of specifying ascending and descending order for each sort.

6. Click the OK button. Figure 49 shows the results.

Figure 47: Faculty List Before Sort

	A	B	C	D	E	F	G	H
1	**College of Business Administration**							
2	**Faculty Information**							
3	**Last Name**	**First Name**	**Gender**	**Degree**	**Department**	**Hire Date**	**Salary**	**Rank**
4	Abdul	Mohammed	Male	M.Ed.	General Business	8/1/1999	$ 72,000.00	Assistant
5	Barnes	Fred	Male	MS	Information Systems	8/1/2002	$ 42,000.00	Instructor
6	Chen	Geo	Male	Ed.D.	Information Systems	8/1/1999	$ 62,500.00	Assistant
7	Chiaf	Sally	Female	Ph.D.	Economics	8/1/1994	$ 75,000.00	Associate
8	Friel	Essie	Female	Ph.D.	Economics	8/1/1993	$ 72,000.00	Professor
9	Hulva	Tracy	Male	Ed.D.	Finance	8/1/1992	$ 78,000.00	Associate
10	Jones	Mary	Female	Ph.D.	Marketing	8/1/1992	$ 100,000.00	Professor
11	Lancaster	Zoribel	Male	J.D.	General Business	8/1/1990	$ 51,500.00	Associate
12	Malcom	John	Male	MBA	General Business	8/1/1996	$ 42,000.00	Instructor
13	Mencor	David	Male	J.D.	Finance	8/1/1990	$ 52,000.00	Associate
14	Namiesnoiwoski	Elaine	Female	Ph.D.	Finance	8/1/1994	$ 75,000.00	Associate
15	Nguyen	Stewart	Male	Ph.D.	Marketing	8/1/1996	$ 89,000.00	Associate
16	Peterson	Mike	Male	J.D.	General Business	8/1/1999	$ 55,000.00	Assistant
17	Plagg	Nathan	Male	Ph.D.	Management	8/1/1997	$ 72,000.00	Assistant
18	Porter	Larry	Male	Ph.D.	Information Systems	8/1/1988	$ 125,000.00	Professor
19	Reese	LouAnn	Female	MBA	Accounting	8/1/1998	$ 72,000.00	Assistant
20	Ritzhaupht	Courtney	Female	MBA	Management	8/1/1982	$ 50,000.00	Instructor
21	Uhlenhopp	Kevan	Male	Ed.D.	Management	8/1/1997	$ 72,000.00	Assistant
22	Weiss	Clare	Female	Ph.D.	Accounting	8/1/2001	$ 72,000.00	Assistant
23	Whaley	Dari	Female	Ed.D.	Accounting	8/1/1996	$ 70,000.00	Associate

Figure 48: Sort Dialog Box

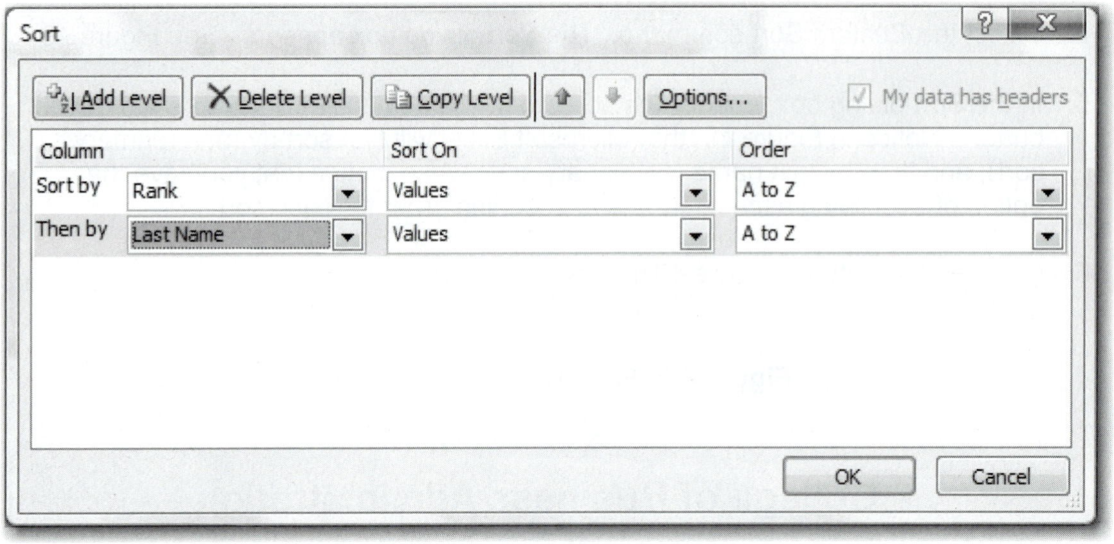

Figure 49: Sort Results

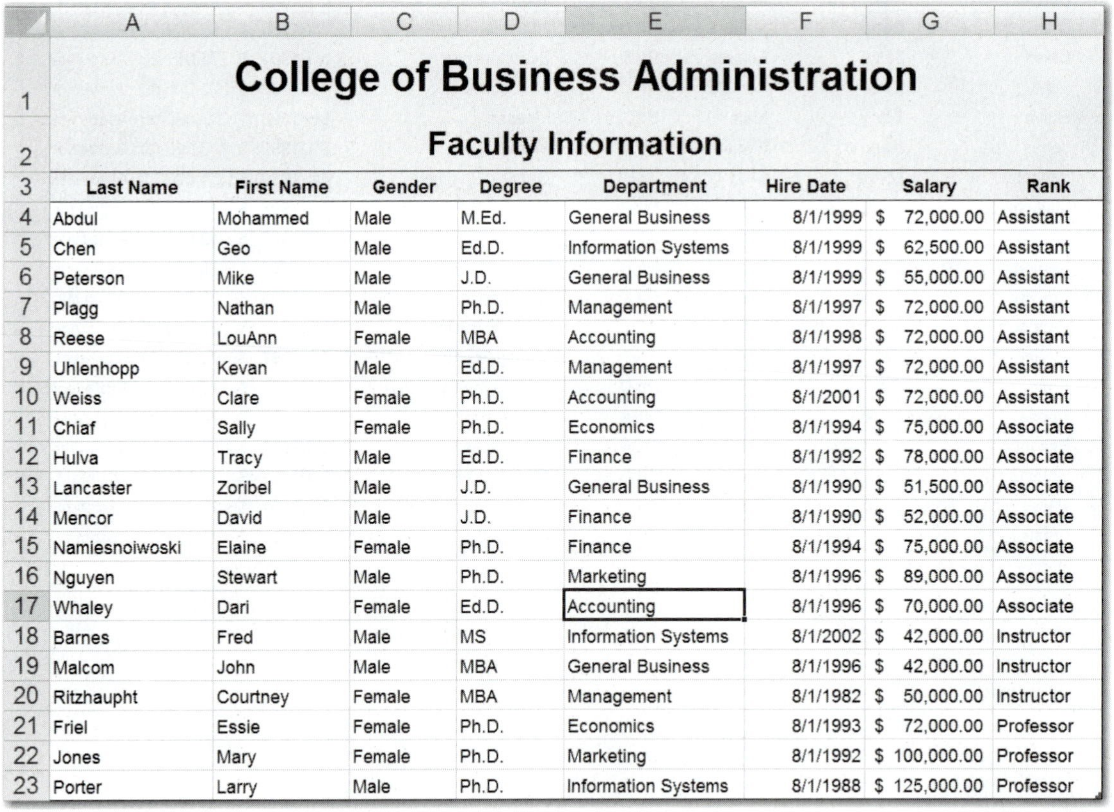

College of Business Administration

Faculty Information

Last Name	First Name	Gender	Degree	Department	Hire Date	Salary	Rank
Abdul	Mohammed	Male	M.Ed.	General Business	8/1/1999	$ 72,000.00	Assistant
Chen	Geo	Male	Ed.D.	Information Systems	8/1/1999	$ 62,500.00	Assistant
Peterson	Mike	Male	J.D.	General Business	8/1/1999	$ 55,000.00	Assistant
Plagg	Nathan	Male	Ph.D.	Management	8/1/1997	$ 72,000.00	Assistant
Reese	LouAnn	Female	MBA	Accounting	8/1/1998	$ 72,000.00	Assistant
Uhlenhopp	Kevan	Male	Ed.D.	Management	8/1/1997	$ 72,000.00	Assistant
Weiss	Clare	Female	Ph.D.	Accounting	8/1/2001	$ 72,000.00	Assistant
Chiaf	Sally	Female	Ph.D.	Economics	8/1/1994	$ 75,000.00	Associate
Hulva	Tracy	Male	Ed.D.	Finance	8/1/1992	$ 78,000.00	Associate
Lancaster	Zoribel	Male	J.D.	General Business	8/1/1990	$ 51,500.00	Associate
Mencor	David	Male	J.D.	Finance	8/1/1990	$ 52,000.00	Associate
Namiesnoiwoski	Elaine	Female	Ph.D.	Finance	8/1/1994	$ 75,000.00	Associate
Nguyen	Stewart	Male	Ph.D.	Marketing	8/1/1996	$ 89,000.00	Associate
Whaley	Dari	Female	Ed.D.	Accounting	8/1/1996	$ 70,000.00	Associate
Barnes	Fred	Male	MS	Information Systems	8/1/2002	$ 42,000.00	Instructor
Malcom	John	Male	MBA	General Business	8/1/1996	$ 42,000.00	Instructor
Ritzhaupt	Courtney	Female	MBA	Management	8/1/1982	$ 50,000.00	Instructor
Friel	Essie	Female	Ph.D.	Economics	8/1/1993	$ 72,000.00	Professor
Jones	Mary	Female	Ph.D.	Marketing	8/1/1992	$ 100,000.00	Professor
Porter	Larry	Male	Ph.D.	Information Systems	8/1/1988	$ 125,000.00	Professor

Subtotal: The Subtotal command provides subtotals and grand totals for an Excel table. When inserting subtotals in your worksheet, make sure your list is sorted in proper order. For instance, if you want to insert subtotals at each department change, then you should sort your Excel table by department.

To insert subtotals, you can:

1. Select the table.

2. On the Ribbon, click the Data tab.

3. In the Outline group, click the Subtotal button. See Figure 50. (The Subtotals dialog box will now appear. At this point, you can specify where to insert subtotals, what function to use, and which fields to subtotal.) See Figure 51. Figure 52 shows a worksheet with subtotals.

Figure 50: Subtotal Button

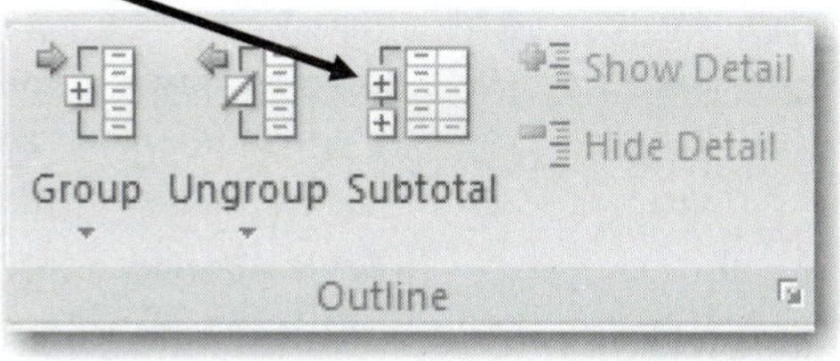

Figure 51: Subtotal Dialog Box

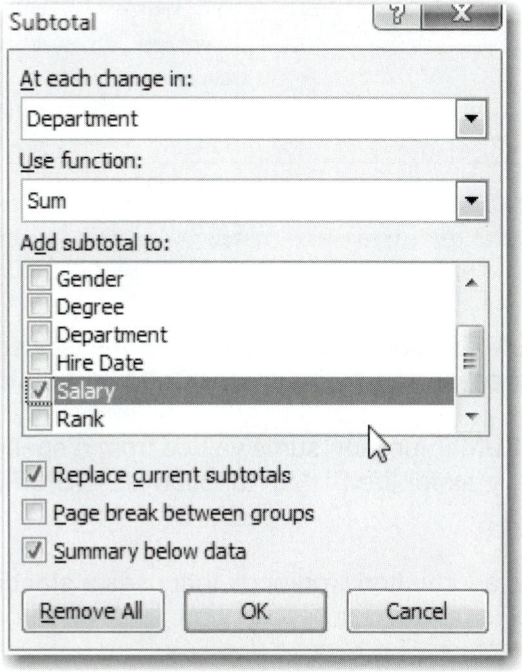

Figure 52: Subtotal Example

	A	B	C	D	E	F	G	H
1	**College of Business Administration**							
2	**Faculty Information**							
3	Last Name	First Name	Gender	Degree	Department	Hire Date	Salary	Rank
4	Reese	LouAnn	Female	MBA	Accounting	8/1/1998	$ 72,000.00	Assistant
5	Weiss	Clare	Female	Ph.D.	Accounting	8/1/2001	$ 72,000.00	Assistant
6	Whaley	Dari	Female	Ed.D.	Accounting	8/1/1996	$ 70,000.00	Associate
7					**Accounting Total**		$ 214,000.00	
8	Chiaf	Sally	Female	Ph.D.	Economics	8/1/1994	$ 75,000.00	Associate
9	Friel	Essie	Female	Ph.D.	Economics	8/1/1993	$ 72,000.00	Professor
10					**Economics Total**		$ 147,000.00	
11	Hulva	Tracy	Male	Ed.D.	Finance	8/1/1992	$ 78,000.00	Associate
12	Mencor	David	Male	J.D.	Finance	8/1/1990	$ 52,000.00	Associate
13	Namiesnoiwoski	Elaine	Female	Ph.D.	Finance	8/1/1994	$ 75,000.00	Associate
14					**Finance Total**		$ 205,000.00	
15	Abdul	Mohammed	Male	M.Ed.	General Business	8/1/1999	$ 72,000.00	Assistant
16	Peterson	Mike	Male	J.D.	General Business	8/1/1999	$ 55,000.00	Assistant
17	Lancaster	Zoribel	Male	J.D.	General Business	8/1/1990	$ 51,500.00	Associate
18	Malcom	John	Male	MBA	General Business	8/1/1996	$ 42,000.00	Instructor
19					**General Business Total**		$ 220,500.00	
20	Chen	Geo	Male	Ed.D.	Information Systems	8/1/1999	$ 62,500.00	Assistant
21	Barnes	Fred	Male	MS	Information Systems	8/1/2002	$ 42,000.00	Instructor
22	Porter	Larry	Male	Ph.D.	Information Systems	8/1/1988	$ 125,000.00	Professor
23					**Information Systems Total**		$ 229,500.00	
24	Plagg	Nathan	Male	Ph.D.	Management	8/1/1997	$ 72,000.00	Assistant
25	Uhlenhopp	Kevan	Male	Ed.D.	Management	8/1/1997	$ 72,000.00	Assistant
26	Ritzhaupht	Courtney	Female	MBA	Management	8/1/1982	$ 50,000.00	Instructor
27					**Management Total**		$ 194,000.00	
28	Nguyen	Stewart	Male	Ph.D.	Marketing	8/1/1996	$ 89,000.00	Associate
29	Jones	Mary	Female	Ph.D.	Marketing	8/1/1992	$ 100,000.00	Professor
30					**Marketing Total**		$ 189,000.00	
31					**Grand Total**		$ 1,399,000.00	

SUM Function: The SUM function provides a total for a specified cell range. The syntax for the SUM function is: **=SUM(BeginningCellAddress:EndingCellAddress)**.

SUMIF Function: The SUMIF function sums values from a specified range based on specified criteria. The syntax for the SUMIF function is: **=SUMIF(range to evaluate, criteria, range to sum)**.

Template: A template is a formatted workbook that uses a standard format. The standard format is useful for a particular application, such as invoice creation or sales tracking.

VLOOKUP Function: The VLOOKUP function retrieves a value from a lookup table based on a specified lookup value. The VLOOKUP function's syntax is **=VLOOKUP(lookup_value,table_array,col_index_number,range_lookup)**. The lookup value is the value that is "looked up" in the lookup table, such as a student's average. The table array specifies the location of the table, such as the range A17:B21. The col_index_number specifies the lookup table column that contains the return value. In Figure 53, the lookup table contains two columns. The first column contains the grading scale, and the second column contains the letter grades. In Figure 53, the VLOOKUP function will find an approximate match for the student's average in the table's first column and then retrieve, from the same row, the corresponding letter grade, which is located in the second column of the lookup table.

Notice that cell J4 contains the following: =VLOOKUP(I4,$A$17:$B$21,2). In this instance, the VLOOKUP function uses cell I4's value as its lookup value. When the VLOOKUP function finds an approximate match in the lookup table, it returns the value from the same row and second column of the lookup table. The range_lookup argument is an optional argument. If it is not specified, VLOOKUP assumes that it is looking for an approximate match, not an exact match.

Figure 53: VLOOKUP Example

J4 | fx | =VLOOKUP(I4,$A$17:$B$21,2)

	A	B	C	D	E	F	G	H	I	J
1	Computing Systems For Management									
2	Fall 2007									
3	**First Name**	**Last Name**	**Days Absent**		**Exam I**	**Exam II**	**Exam III**	**Final**	**Average**	**Letter Grade**
4	Pauline	Jeffery	0		100	82	78	95	88.75	B
5	Margaret	Brady	1		87	89	77	92	86.25	B
6	Larry	Martin	3		65	78	89	94	81.50	B
7	Ti	Yee	5		43	81	96	97	79.25	C
8	Lester	LaMonte	0		94	92	56	98	85.00	B
9	Fred	Reed	6		78	97	98	100	93.25	A
10	Lawanda	Smith	1		75	56	85	100	79.00	C
11	Peter	Sands	9		62	75	88	89	78.50	C
12	Jewel	Rochat	2		90	94	88	89	90.25	A
13	Aubrey	Strunk	1		70	75	85	88	79.50	C
14										
15	**Grade Lookup Table**									
16	**Average**	**Letter Grade**								
17	**0**	**F**								
18	**60**	**D**								
19	**70**	**C**								
20	**80**	**B**								
21	**90**	**A**								

Web Query: Microsoft Excel can retrieve data from a Web page for you, such as recent stock information. Microsoft Excel provides you with the capability to create your own Web query and also to use a saved query. Use your system's online help system to learn more about creating, saving, and editing web queries.

<u>Worksheet Formatting:</u> For each case that you prepare, you should apply good design skills. One method for applying a standard format to your worksheet is to use the Format as Table command.

To use the Format As Table command, you can:

1. Select the worksheet area that you want to format.

2. On the Ribbon, click the Home tab.

3. In the Styles group, click the Format As Table button. A drop-down menu will appear. The drop-down menu provides you with several formatting options. Select the format that you want.

Database Glossary

This database glossary is designed to accompany MIS Cases: Decision Making With Application Software, Fourth Edition, published by Pearson Prentice Hall. When preparing an MIS Cases: Decision Making With Application Software, Fourth Edition database case, several database skills are necessary. Each case's skills check feature identifies the major skills that are required to complete the case. Before preparing the case, you should use the skills check feature to help identify which skills you should review.

This database glossary provides a brief explanation and review for many of the database skills utilized in MIS Cases: Decision Making With Application Software, Fourth Edition. This glossary is designed for Microsoft Access 2007 users. This glossary does not provide detailed explanations for the skills. If you need a detailed explanation on how to use a particular skill, you should use your system's online help feature to learn more about the skill. Your system's online help feature is an excellent way to learn about the skill, as well as obtain a detailed explanation on how to use the skill in a database application.

Database Skills

<u>Advanced Report Design:</u> As this term is used in MIS Cases: Decision Making With Application Software, Fourth Edition, advanced report design means using advanced formatting options to customize a report, rather than relying solely on the Report Wizard to generate the report. When custom designing a report, you have many advanced formatting options available to you, such as the ability to include report, group, and page headers and footers; subtotals and totals; graphics, and the ability to force page breaks. Keep in mind that you can adjust the properties for the entire report, its individual sections, and the controls appearing in the report.

To create a custom report, you can:

1. From the Reports group located on the Create tab, click the Report Wizard button. See Figure 1.

Figure 1: Report Wizard Button

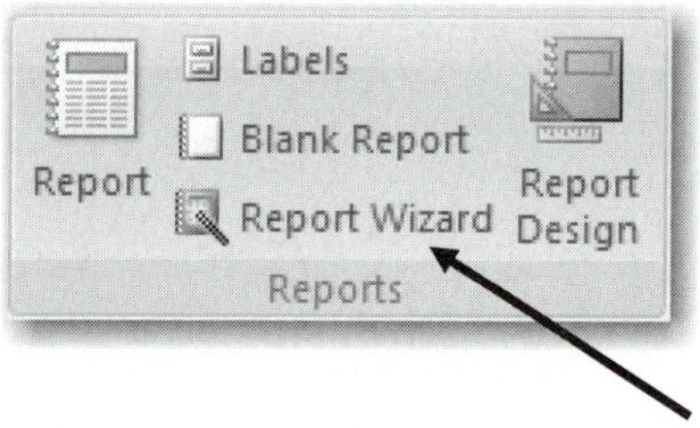

2. In the Report Wizard dialog box, click the drop-down arrow, select the table or query on which to base the report, and then click the Next button. The Report Wizard, through dialog boxes, will ask you a series of questions about your report, and then prepare the report based on your specifications. Figure 2 shows the first Report Wizard dialog box.

3. In the next Report Wizard dialog box, specify any required grouping levels, and then click the Next button.

4. A Report Wizard dialog box will ask you to specify the sort order. Specify the sort order, and then click the Next button.

5. A Report Wizard dialog box will ask you to specify the report layout. Specify the report layout, and then click the Next button.

6. A Report Wizard dialog box will ask you to select a style for the report. Specify the report style, and then click the Next button.

7. A Report Wizard dialog box will ask you to name the report and specify how to preview the report. Name the report, and then select the modify the report's design option. Click the Finish button. See Figure 3.

8. The Report Design view window opens. At this point you can edit the newly created report. Figure 4 shows the Report Design view.

Figure 2: Report Wizard Dialog Box

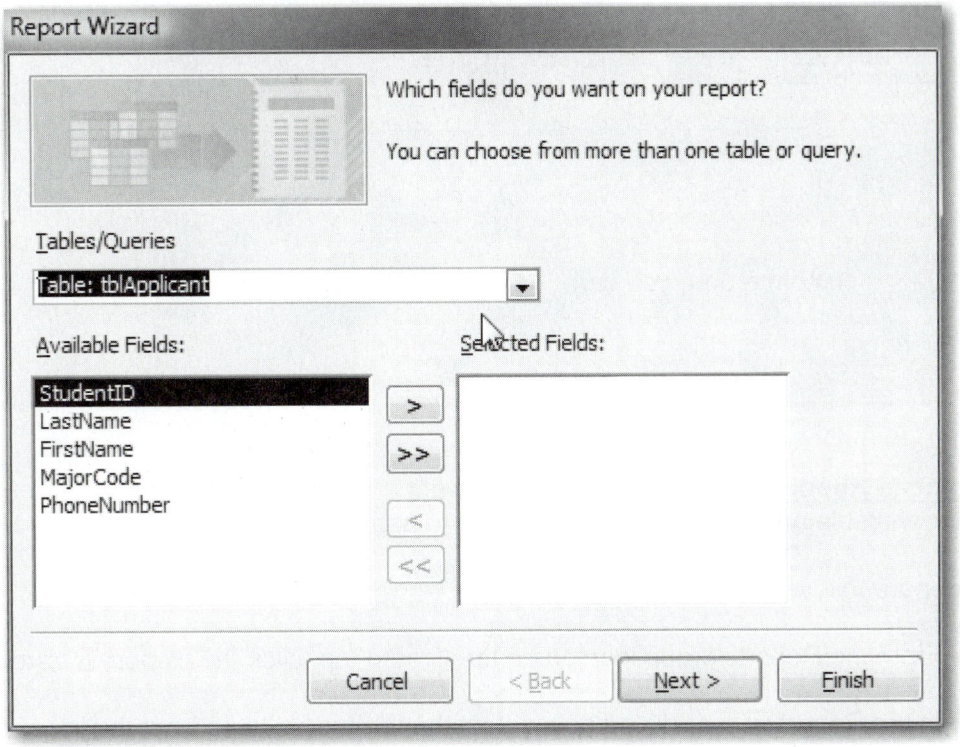

Figure 3: Modify Report's Design Option

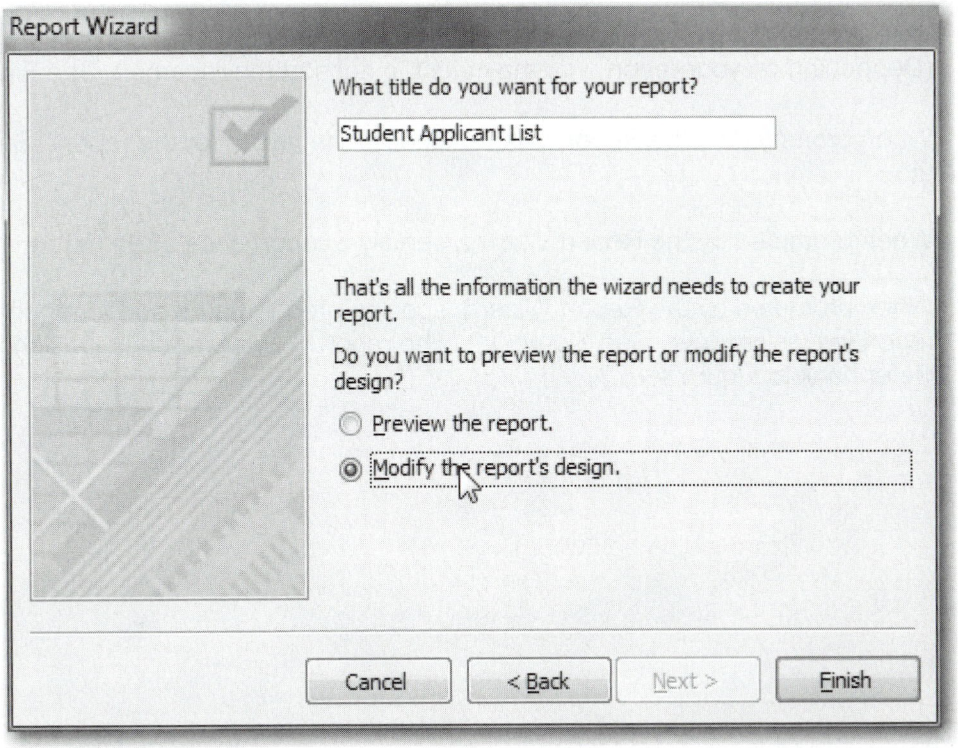

Figure 4: Report Design View

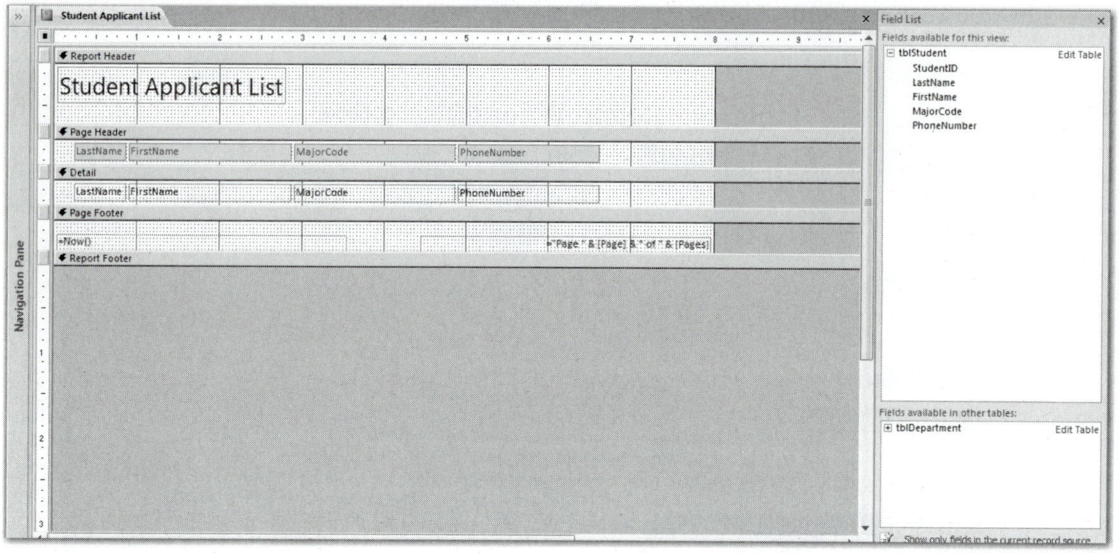

<u>Advanced Report Example:</u> Assume you want a custom report based on the tblStudent table and that you want the report to appear similar to Figure 5.

To prepare this report, you can:

1. From the Reports group located on the Create tab, click the Report Wizard button.

2. In the Report Wizard dialog box, select the tblStudent table from the list of tables and queries box. See Figure 6.

3. When prompted, do not add grouping to the report. See Figure 7.

4. When prompted by the Report Wizard, specify a field to sort and a sort order. (Depending on your report, you may elect to not sort the records.) See Figure 8.

5. When prompted by the Report Wizard, specify the layout for the report. See Figure 9.

6. When prompted by the Report Wizard, specify a report style. See Figure 10.

7. When prompted by the Report Wizard, specify a report name and to modify the report in Design view. See Figure 11. The report will now open in Design view. Refer back to Figure 4.

Figure 5: Student Applicant List Report

Student Applicant List

7/13/2007

Last Name	First Name	Major Code	Phone Number
Grant	Mitchell	44	555-1255
Sasser	Lexina	45	555-6456
Rother	Elwood	45	555-6577
Chen	Shibo	42	555-4789
Elotmani	Damir	46	555-3812
Schoenhals	Eliah	46	555-6058
Erbst	Troy	44	555-1300
Ottinger	Clarissa	46	555-9351
Blochowiak	Edith	46	555-0202
Harley	Sasha	43	555-5931

Figure 6: Report Wizard's Table and Field Selection

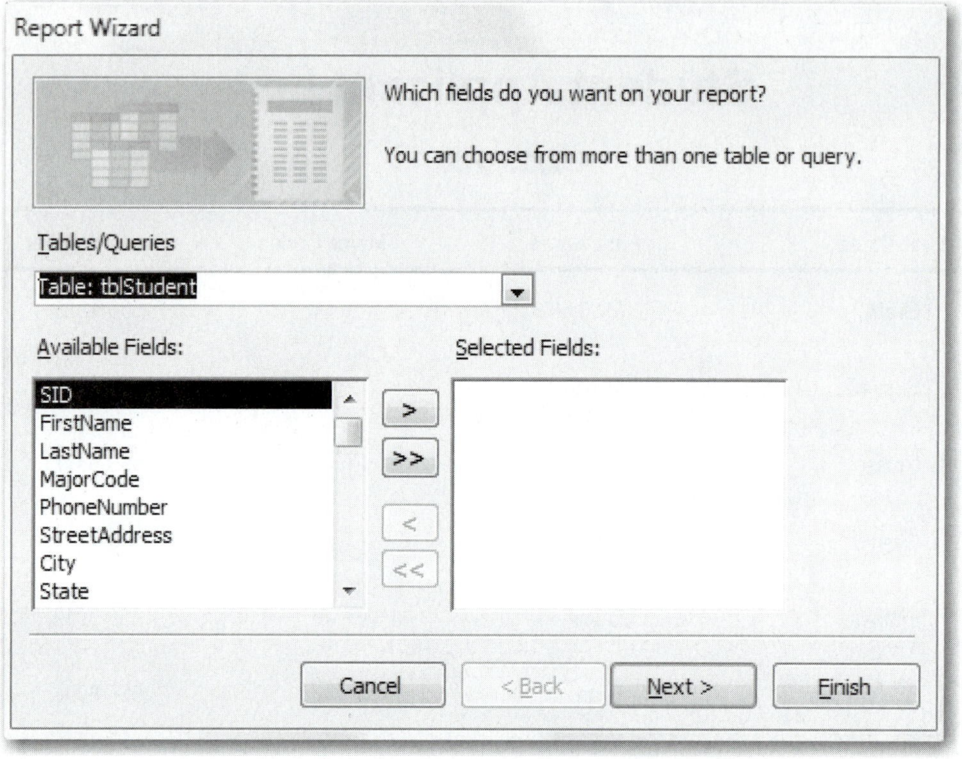

Figure 7: Report Wizard Grouping Dialog Box

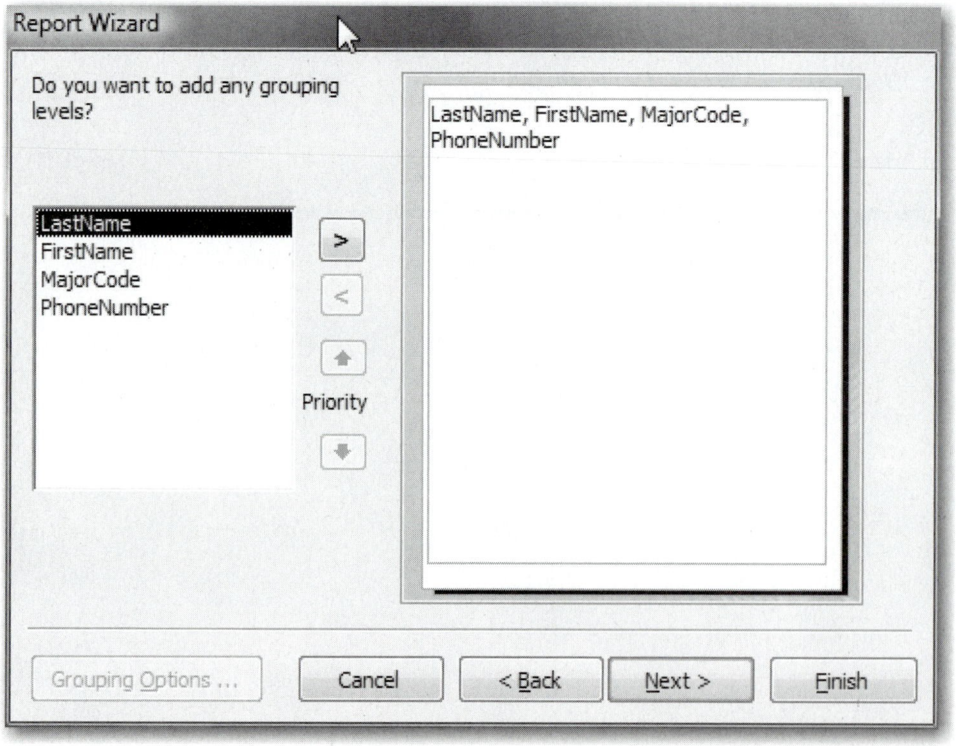

Figure 8: Report Wizard Sort Order Dialog Box

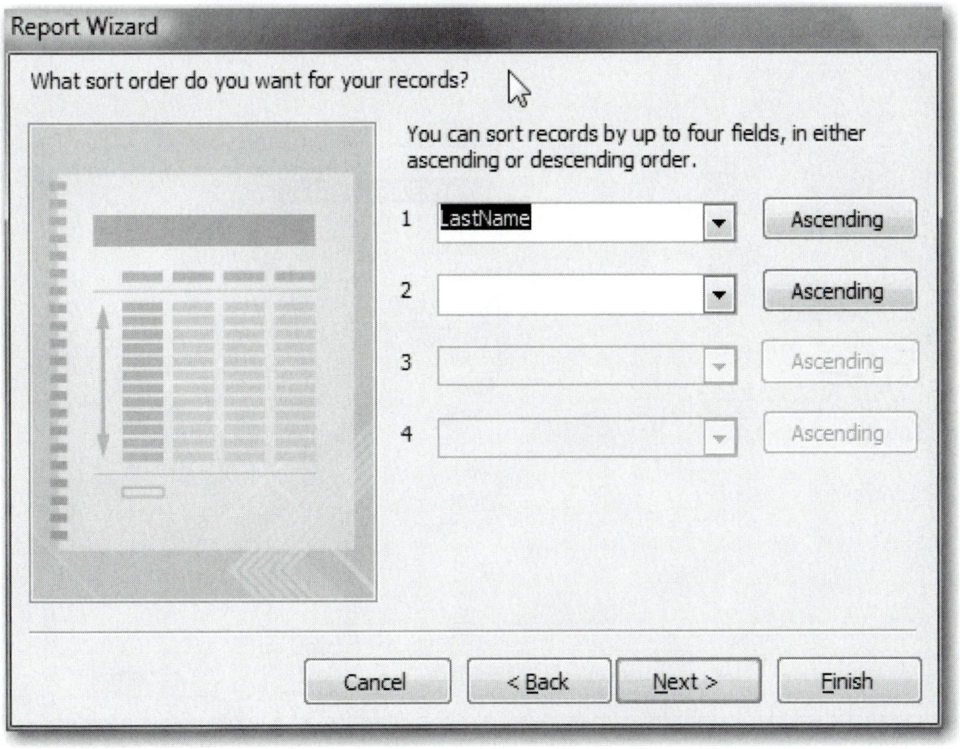

Figure 9: Report Wizard Layout Dialog Box

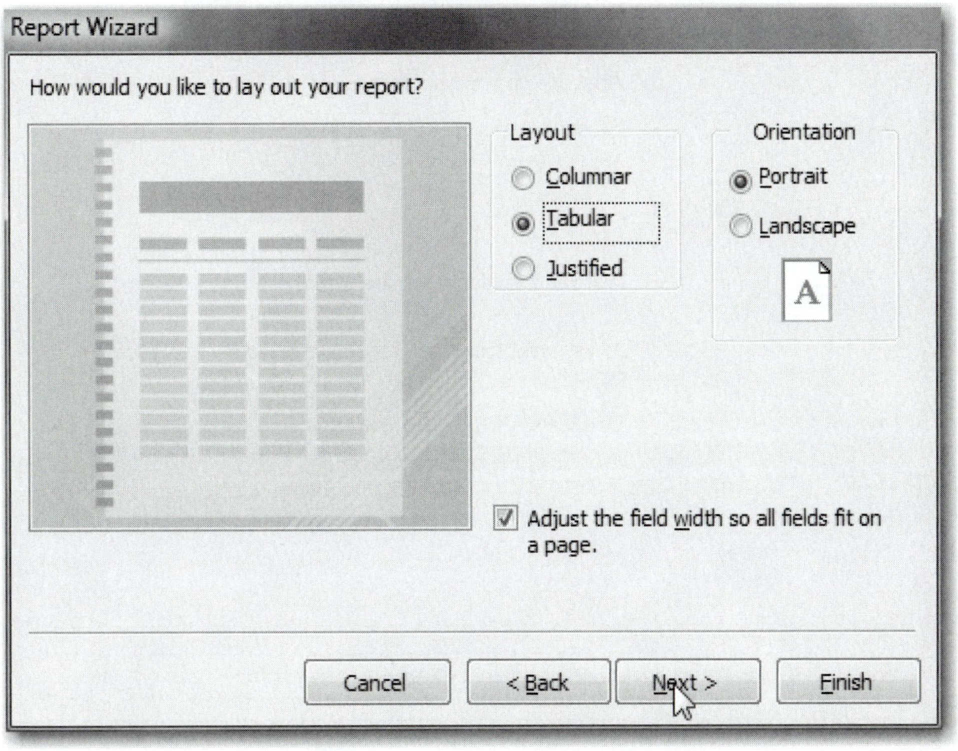

Figure 10: Report Wizard Style Dialog Box

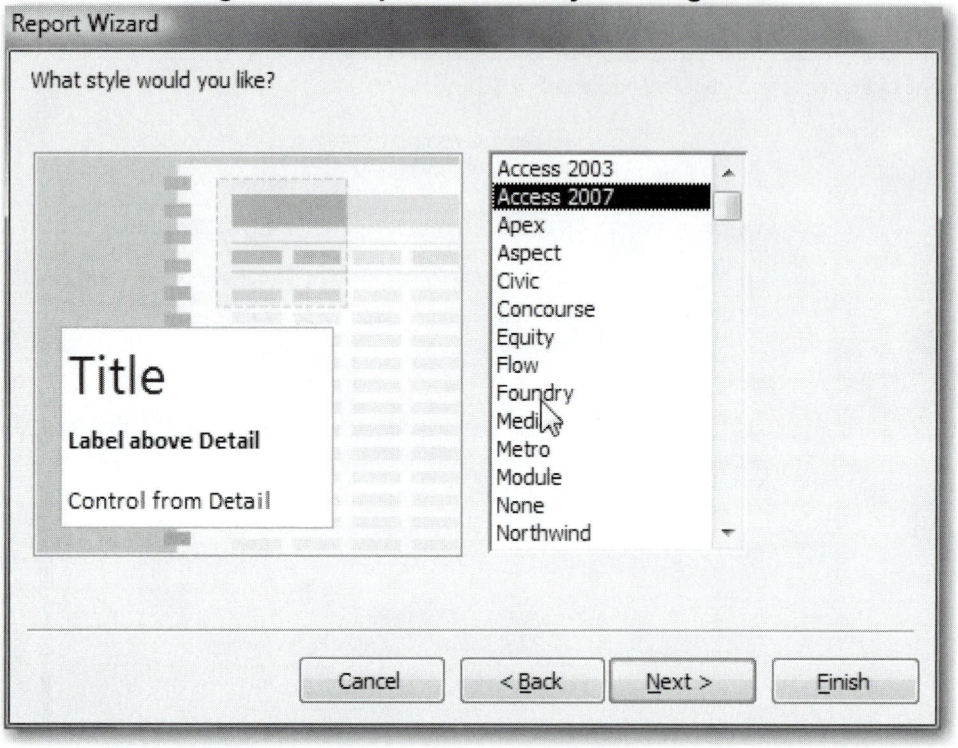

Figure 11: Report Wizard Name Dialog Box

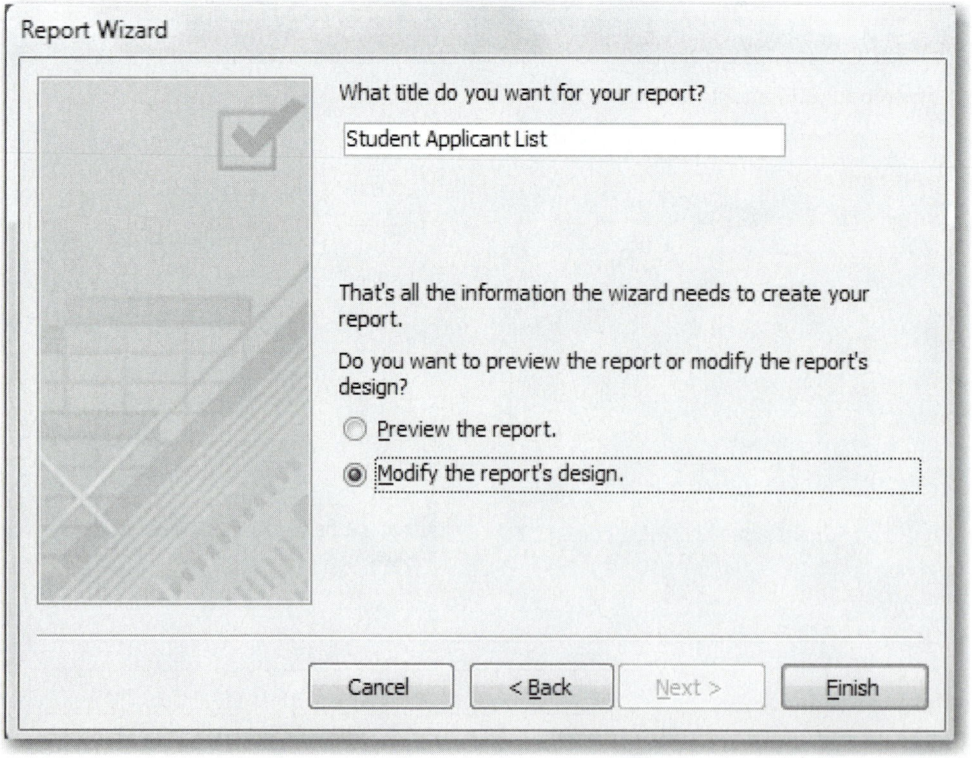

To modify the report header, you can:

1. Click on the control containing the words "Student Applicant List." Sizing handles should appear.
2. Move the pointer to the right side of the control. When the mouse pointer changes to a double-headed arrow, you can resize the control.
3. Use the buttons located in the Font group to center and bold the report title.
4. It may be necessary to resize the page header section. To resize the Page Header section, you can:

   a. Place the mouse pointer on top of the Page Header bar. When the mouse pointer changes to a double-headed arrow with a thick line between the arrow heads, drag downward until the page header section is approximately the size you want it to be.

To place an unbound control on the report, such as the current date, you can:

1. From the Controls group located on the Design tab, click the Text Box button. See Figure 12.

Figure 12: Text Box Button

2. On the report header design grid, position your mouse pointer where you want the control to begin, and then drag until the control is the size that you want. Keep in mind that you can always resize the control.
3. Click inside the control and enter "=NOW()".
4. Select the control and then set its format properties. For instance, you can click the Center button located on the Formatting toolbar to center the contents. You can also change the font color, as well as bold the text. Figure 5 shows the current date centered and bold with a font size of 16.
5. Double-click the control's label, and then press the Delete key.
6. To include a bound control on your report, you can drag and drop the field name from the Field List box to the location on the report where you want the control located. (In this example, the Report Wizard has already placed the bound controls on the report.) You can set the control's properties, as well as resize the

control. In the detail section shown in Figure 4, the LastName, FirstName, MajorCode, and PhoneNumber controls are examples of bound controls. In the Page Header section, the LastName, FirstName, MajorCode, and PhoneNumber controls are examples of unbound controls. Although not shown in Figure 4, calculated controls can also be placed on a report.

To remove a control from a report, you can:

1. Click on the control and then press the delete button. Compare Figures 4 and 5. Notice that Figure 4's Page Footer section controls have been deleted from the report shown in Figure 5.

Aggregate Function: An aggregate function performs a calculation on a group of records. Microsoft Access provides several aggregate functions, including COUNT, SUM, AVG, MIN, and MAX.

Aggregate Function Example: Assume the dean needs counts for the number of student worker positions by department in the college. Figure 13 shows how the COUNT function can be used in a query. Figure 14 shows the query results.

Figure 13: Count Function Used in a Query

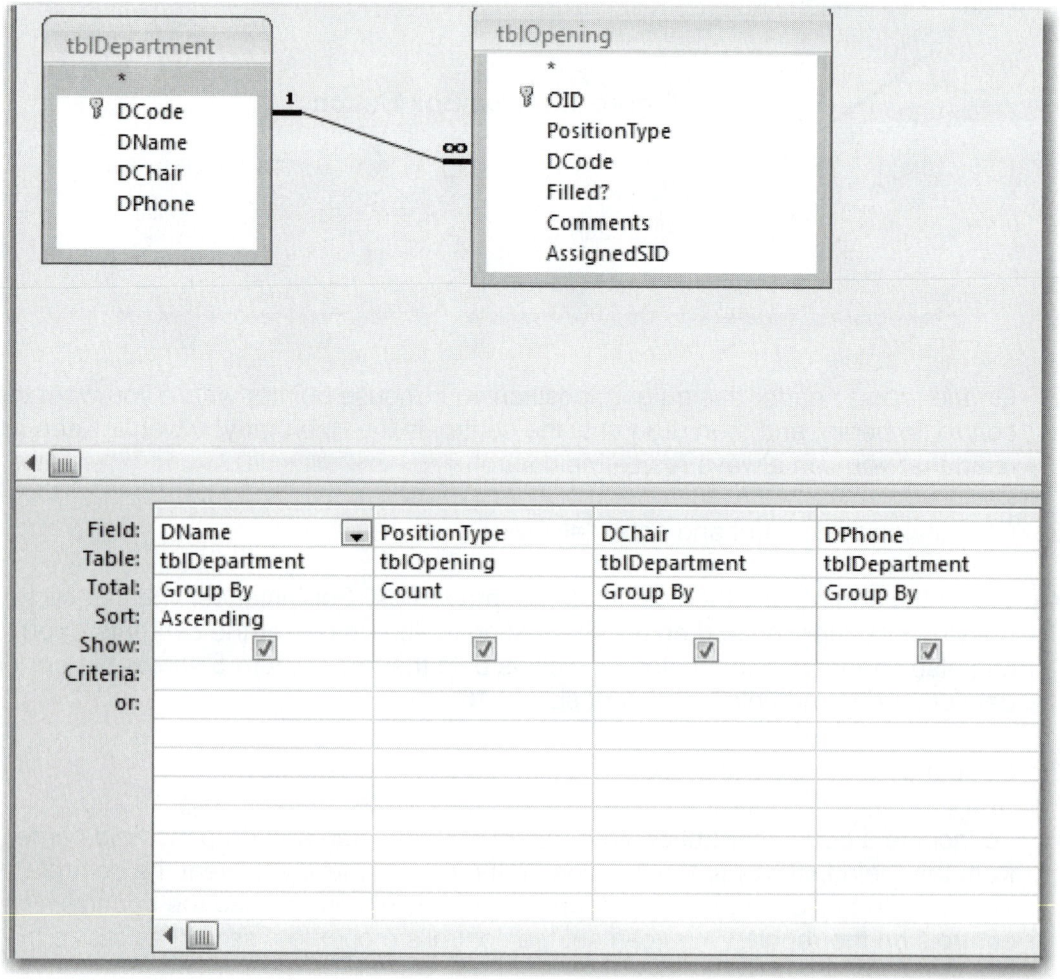

Figure 14: Count Results

qryOpeningsByDepartmentCount

DName	CountOfPositionType	DChair	DPhone
Accounting	3	Dr. Terrell	888-1432
Finance	2	Dr. Ice	888-1434
Information Systems	2	Dr. Miller	888-1435
Management	2	Dr. Tullis	888-1436
Marketing	1	Dr. Gray	888-1437

Analyze It with Microsoft Excel: In Microsoft Access 2007, this command has been customized. (See Export Data to Microsoft Excel.)

AutoFilter (Microsoft Excel): In Microsoft Excel 2007, this command is called Filter. (See Filter in Microsoft Excel.)

AutoLookup Query: An AutoLookup query works with tables that have a one-to-many relationship. The AutoLookup query uses the join field from the table on the many side of the relationship to lookup and automatically provide data from the table on the one-side of the relationship. The AutoLookup query is especially useful when building main forms with subforms.

AutoLookup Query Example: Assume the college dean asks you to design a form that captures data about available positions by department. At the heart of this request is an AutoLookup query. Figure 15 shows the Design view for the qryPositionsByDepartment query. Notice that the tables have a one-to-many relationship. Also, notice that the DCode field in the query design grid is from the tblOpening table, not from the tblDepartment table. After saving this query, you can use the Form Wizard to build a form that will allow the dean to enter and view data for each available position by department. Figure 16 shows a sample form based on the qryPositionsByDepartment query.

Figure 15: AutoLookup Query in Design View

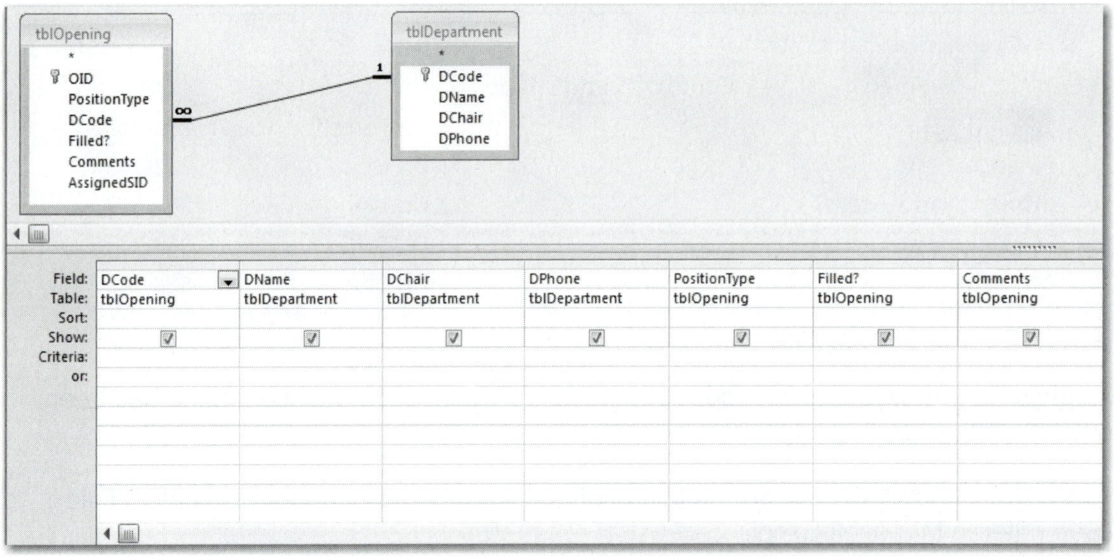

Figure 16: Available Positions Form Based on an AutoLookup Query

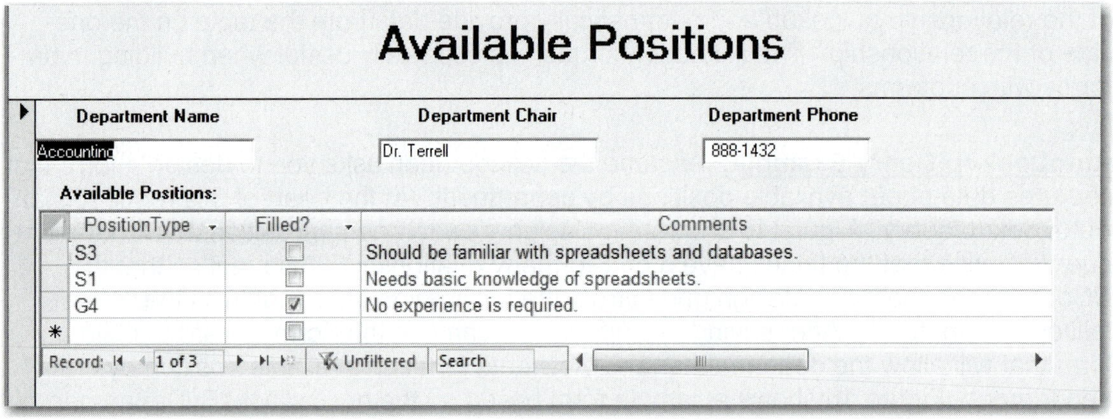

<u>**Calculated Control**</u>: A calculated control displays the results of an expression. An expression may include operators, object names, functions, literal values, and constants. At this point, you should use your system's online help feature to learn more about calculated controls.

To include a calculated control on a form or a report, you can:

1. From the Controls group located on the Design tab, click the Text Box button. See Figure 17.

2. Position the control on the form or report.

3. Click inside the control, and type the expression.

Figure 17: Text Box Button in Controls Group

Calculated Field: A calculated field is used in a query. The calculated field displays the results of a computation, often involving another field or fields. Since a calculated field's values may change, a calculated field is not stored in a table. The calculated field's values are updated each time the query is run, so the calculated field will display accurate data. When using a calculated field, you should precede the expression with a name for the calculated field, followed by a colon. Figure 18 shows the Design view for a query that includes calculated fields. Figure 19 shows the query results.

To include a calculated field in a query, you can:

1. While in the query's Design view, click in an empty field located in the design grid.

2. Type a name for the calculated field followed by a colon. Next, type the expression.

Calculated Field Example: Assume your college has 10 available student worker positions. The pay for each position is based on its classification and the number of hours available. Your college dean needs to know how much money to allocate for each position type. Further assume that each position is for a 15-week period. To provide the dean with this information, you can design a select query that includes calculated fields. See Figures 18 and 19.

Figure 18: Query Design Window with Calculated Field

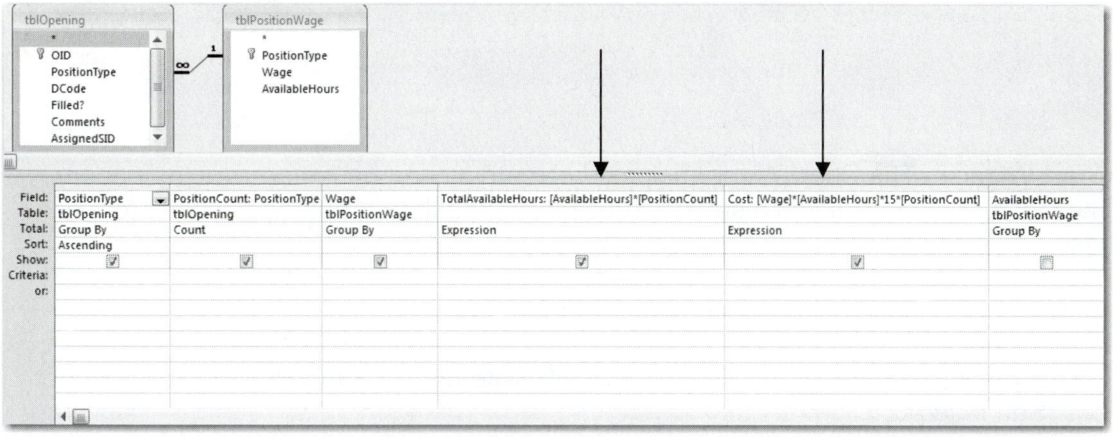

Figure 19: Query Results with Calculated Fields

PositionType	PositionCount	Wage	TotalAvailableHours	Cost
G3	2	$9.50	40	$5,700.00
G4	1	$9.75	40	$5,850.00
S1	3	$8.00	30	$3,600.00
S2	1	$8.50	15	$1,912.50
S3	3	$8.75	60	$7,875.00

Chart (Microsoft Excel): A chart is a graphical representation of selected data contained in a table, query, or spreadsheet. In MIS Cases: Decision Making With Application Software, Fourth Edition, you are asked to prepare charts with Microsoft Access and Microsoft Excel. Several methods are available for chart preparation.

To create a chart using Microsoft Excel, perform the following steps:

1. Export the data from Microsoft Access to Microsoft Excel.
2. In Microsoft Excel, select the data you want represented in the chart.
3. From Microsoft Excel's Charts group located on the Insert tab, click one of the Chart buttons. See Figure 20.

Figure 20: Microsoft Excel's Charts Group

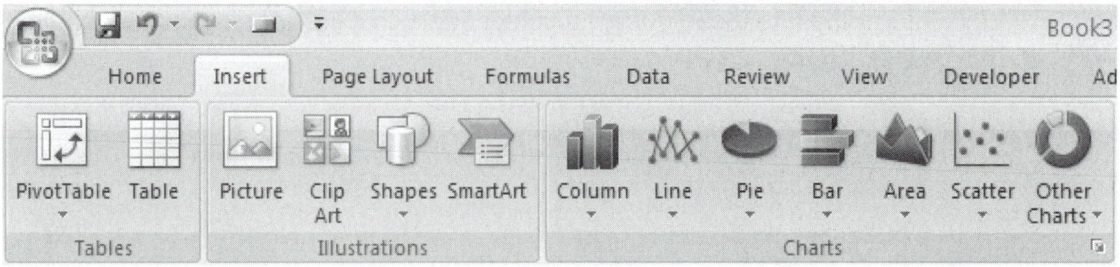

Chart Wizard: The Chart Wizard helps you create a chart based on a table or query. The Chart Wizard asks you a series of questions, and then prepares the chart for you based on your answers.

To create a chart using Microsoft Access, perform the following steps:

1. From the Reports group located on the Create tab, click the Report Design button. See Figure 21.
2. From the Controls group located on the Design tab, click the Insert Chart button. See Figure 22.

3. In the Detail section of the report, drag to size the chart. The first of several Chart Wizard dialog boxes will appear. Figure 23 shows the first of a series of Chart Wizard dialog boxes.

4. Select the table or query to use for the chart and then click the Next button. The Chart Wizard will now ask you questions about which fields you want in the chart, chart type, chart layout, and chart title.

5. To view the chart, click the View button located in the Views group, and then select Report view.

Figure 21: Reports Design Button

Figure 22: Insert Chart Button

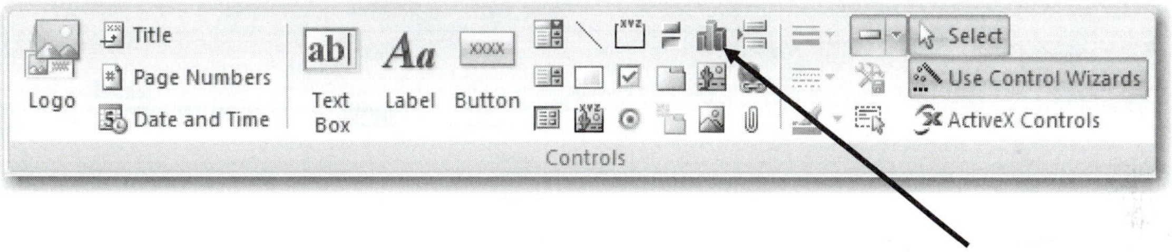

Figure 23: Chart Wizard Dialog Box

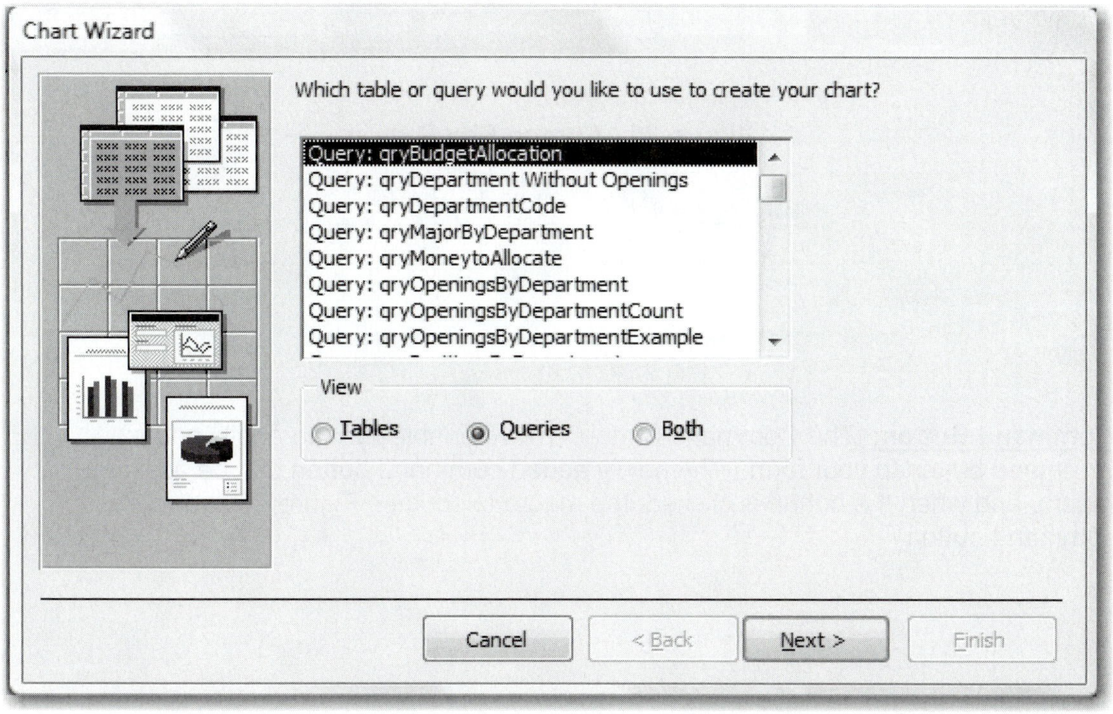

Combo Box: An end user uses a combo box to select a value from a list. The end user clicks the arrow beside the combo box, and then makes a selection from the list of values. In Figure 24, DCode and Assigned Student are examples of combo boxes. The Assigned Student combo box is open, and shows the list of available values. Several methods are available for including a combo box on a form.

To place a combo box on a form, you can:

1. From the Controls group located on the Design tab, click the Combo Box button. See Figure 25.

2. Answer the Combo Box Wizard's questions. These questions ask you to specify how you want the combo box to obtain its values, which table or query provides the values for the combo box, which fields you want included in your combo box, sort order, whether or not to hide the key column, what to do with the selected value, and a name for the combo box.

Figure 24: Form with Combo Boxes

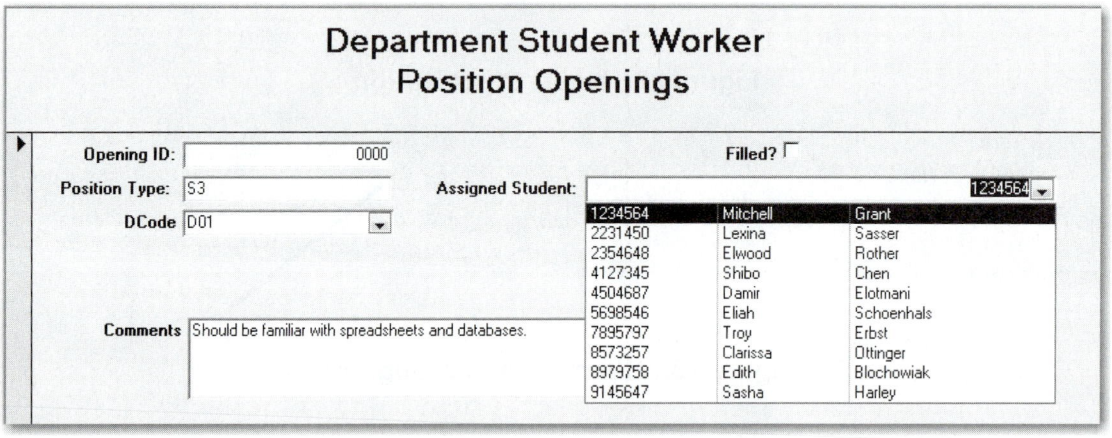

Figure 25: Combo Box Button

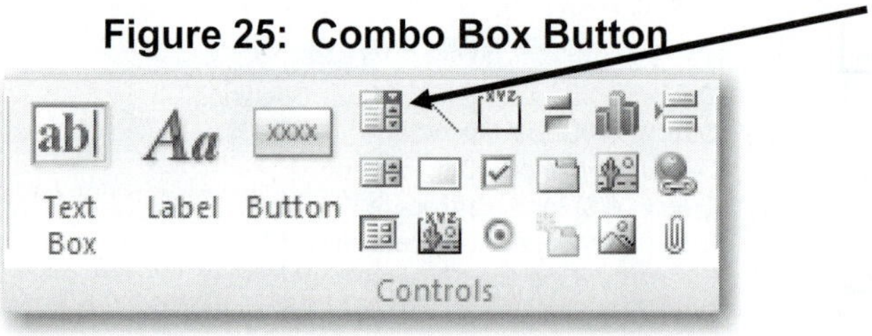

Command Button: The Command Button Wizard enables you to easily add a command button to your form. The newly added command button can be assigned a macro, and when the button is clicked, the macro executes. Figure 26 shows a command button.

Figure 26: Print Record Button

To add a command button to your form, you can:

1. From the Controls group located on the Design tab, click the Button command. See Figure 27.

Figure 27: Button Command

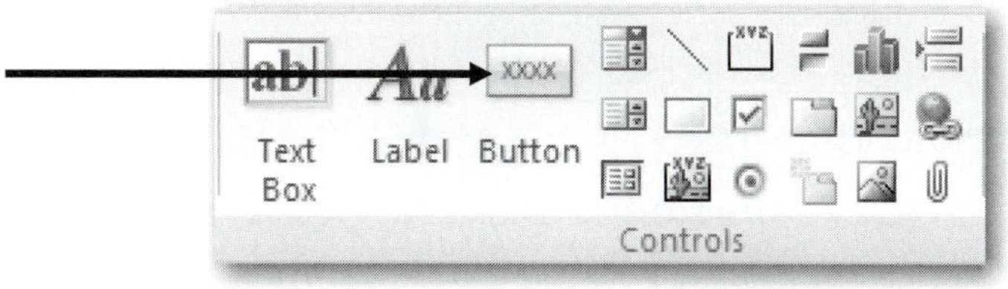

2. Position your mouse pointer on the form's design grid and then drag to indicate the size of the button.

3. Next, answer the Command Button Wizard's questions. Based on your answers, the Command Button Wizard designs a button for the form. The Command Button Wizard asks you what actions should occur when the button is pressed, whether you want text or a picture to appear on the button, and what name you want for the button.

Crosstab Query: A Crosstab query applies an aggregate function to a group of records and displays the results in a spreadsheet-type format. You can create a Crosstab query in Design view or you can use the Crosstab Query Wizard. When creating a Crosstab query, you must identify at least three fields in the design grid. One field serves as the row heading; a second field serves as the column heading, and the third field contains the data values that you want correlated.

To create the Crosstab query in Design view, you can:

1. From the Other group located on the Create tab, click the Query Design button. See Figure 28.

2. In the Show Table dialog box, select either the table or query on which you wish to base the Crosstab query. Click the Close button. See Figure 29.

3. From the Query Type group located on the Design tab, click the Crosstab button. See Figure 30.

4. Add the field that will serve as the Crosstab query's row heading to the design grid. In Figure 31, the field is DName. In the Crosstab row, select Row Heading from the drop-down list.

5. Add the field that will serve as the Crosstab query's column heading to the design grid. In Figure 31 the field is PositionType. In the Crosstab row, select Column Heading from the drop-down list.

6. Add the field that contains the data values that you want summarized. In Figure 31, the field is PositionType. In the Crosstab row, select Value from the drop down list. In the Total row, select the function that you want applied to the values. In Figure 31, the Count function is selected.

7. Run the query. Figure 32 shows the Crosstab query results.

Figure 28: Query Design View Button

Figure 29: Show Table Dialog Box

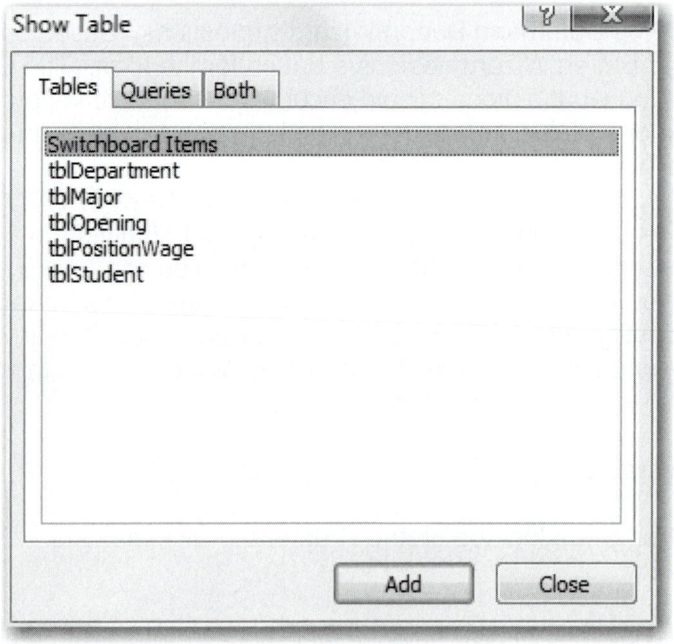

Figure 30: Crosstab Button

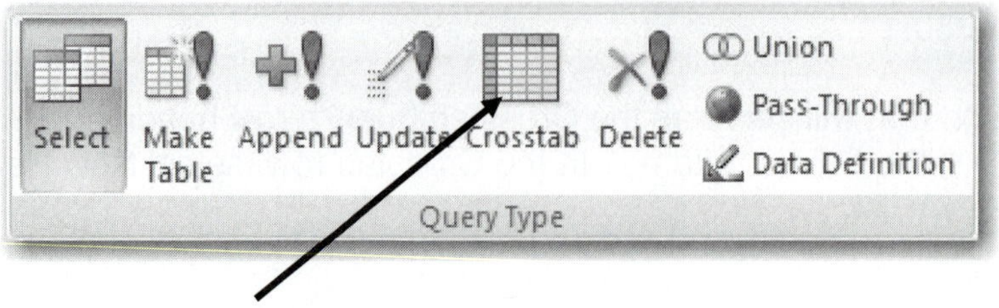

Crosstab Query Example: Assume the college dean wants to view the number and type of available student positions for each department. Figures 31 and 32 show how a Crosstab query can satisfy this information request.

Figure 31: Design View for Crosstab Query

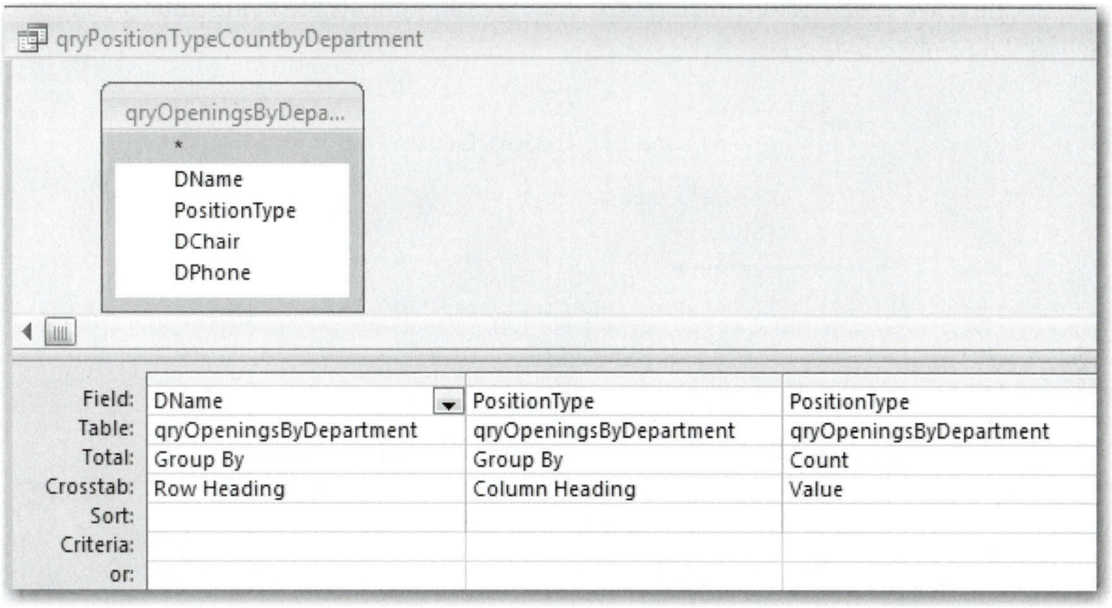

Figure 32: Crosstab Query Results

DName	G3	G4	S1	S2	S3
Accounting		1	1		1
Finance			1	1	
Information Systems	1				1
Management	1		1		
Marketing					1

Data Access Page: Microsoft Access 2007 does not support data access pages. In previous versions of Microsoft Access, a data access page was a Web page that linked to a Microsoft Access database. The data access page was accessible via a Web browser and allowed users to view data at varying levels of detail. Depending on how the data access page was designed, the user could update the data in the database.

Export Data to Microsoft Excel: (Previously called Analyze It with Microsoft Excel.) This feature enables you to export a table, form, or query to Microsoft Excel.

To export a table, form, or query to Microsoft Excel, you can:

1. From the Navigation Pane, click the name of the table, form, or query.

2. From the Export group located on the External Data tab click the Excel button. See Figure 33.

3. In the Export – Excel Spreadsheet dialog box, specify the file name, file format, and export options. Click the OK button. See Figure 34.

4. In the Save Export Steps dialog box, you have the option of saving your export steps. See Figure 35.

Figure 33: Export Group

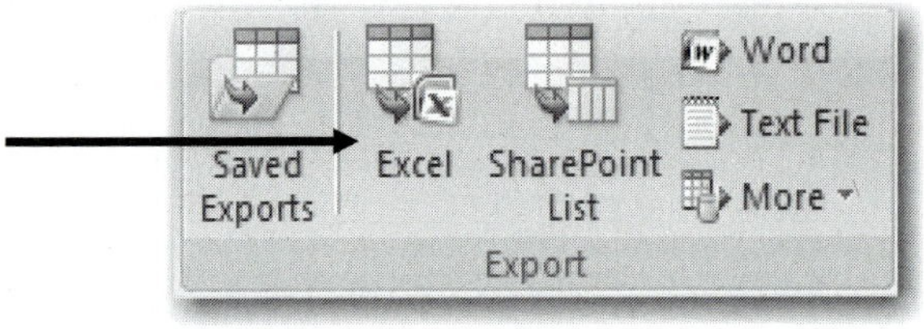

Figure 34: Export – Excel Spreadsheet Dialog Box

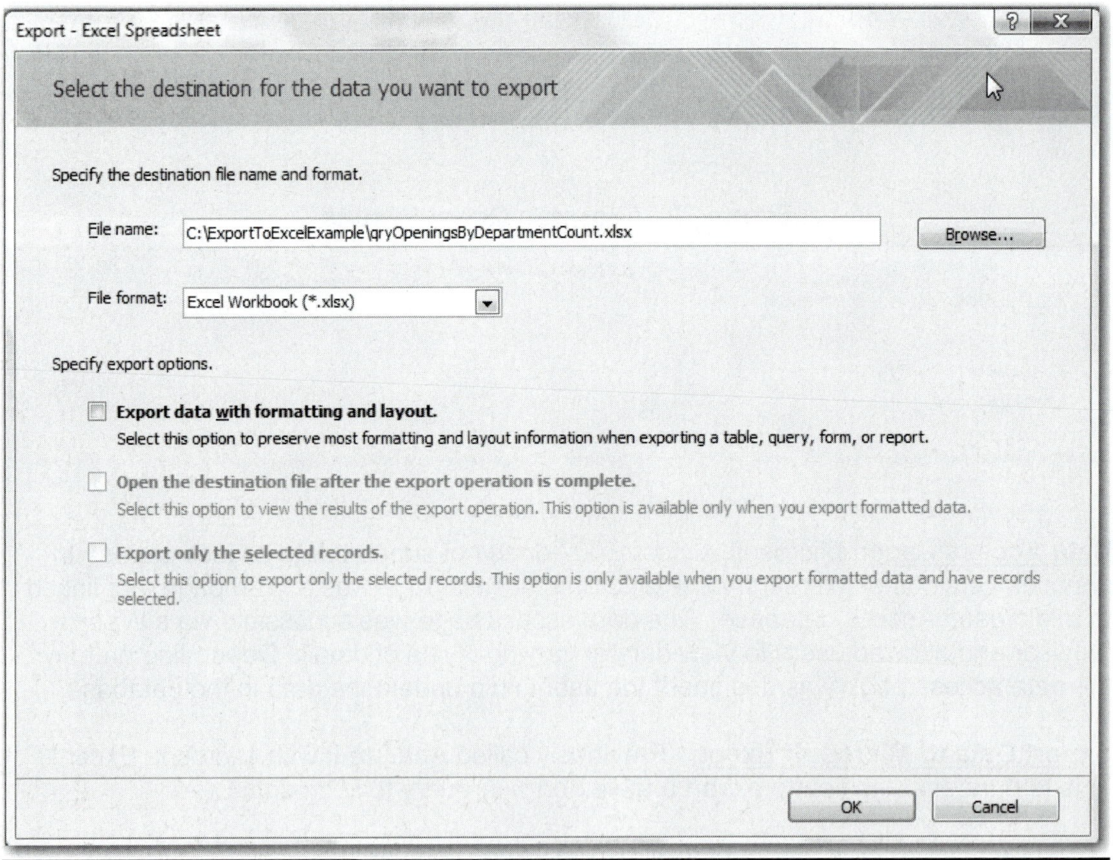

Figure 35: Save Export Steps Dialog Box

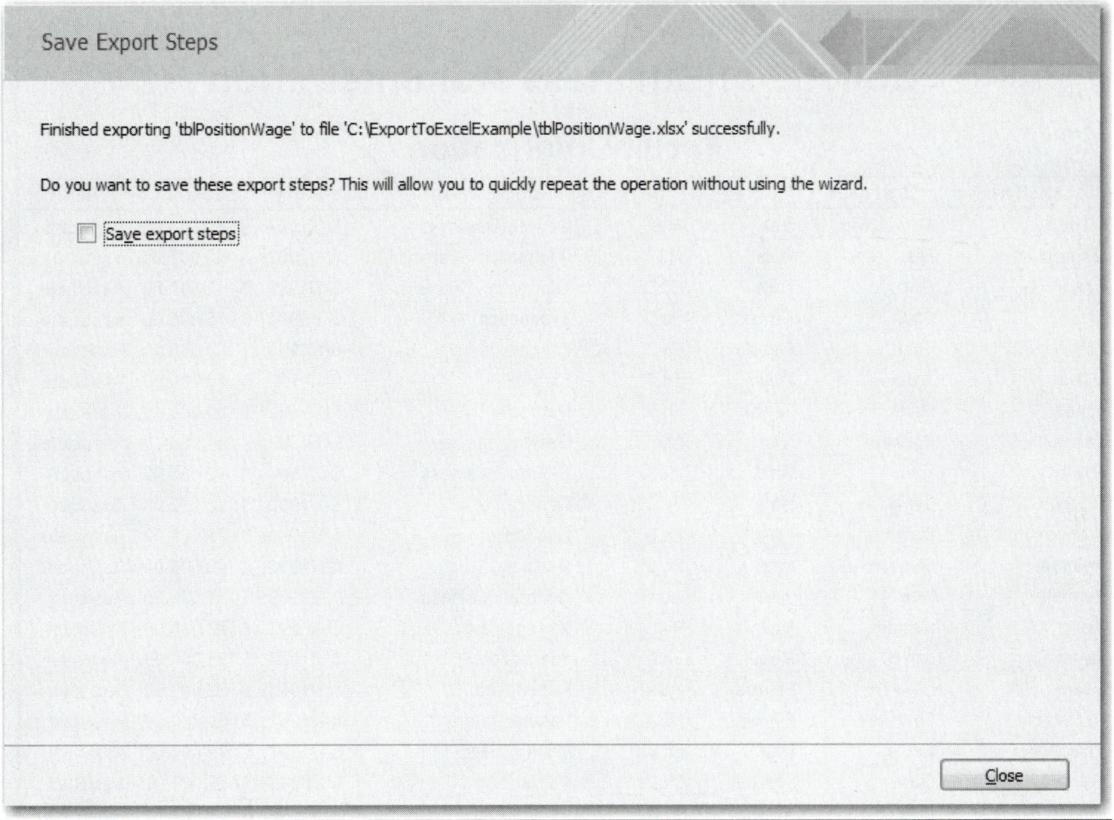

Filter (Microsoft Excel): (Previously called AutoFilter.) The Filter command allows you to select and display records from an Excel table that meet certain criteria. Records that do not meet the criteria are temporarily hidden from view.

To use the Filter command, you can:

1. Place your cell pointer anywhere in the Excel table.

2. From the Sort and Filter group located on the Data tab, click the Filter button.

3. At this point, the field names located in the top row of the Excel table have drop-down arrows beside their names. The drop-down arrows allow you to specify the criteria to use when filtering the records. Figure 36 shows the drop-down arrows that have been added to the Excel table. (Note: The Filter button works as a toggle. By clicking the Filter button, you can toggle on or off the drop-down arrows.)

Filter Example: As an example, assume you only want to see the information systems faculty. This request requires you to first click the drop-down arrow beside the Department field name. A drop-down list will appear. See Figure 37. The drop-down list provides several filtering options, including text filters. From the text values list, you would select "Information Systems". Figure 38 shows the results for this example.

Figure 36: Filter Example

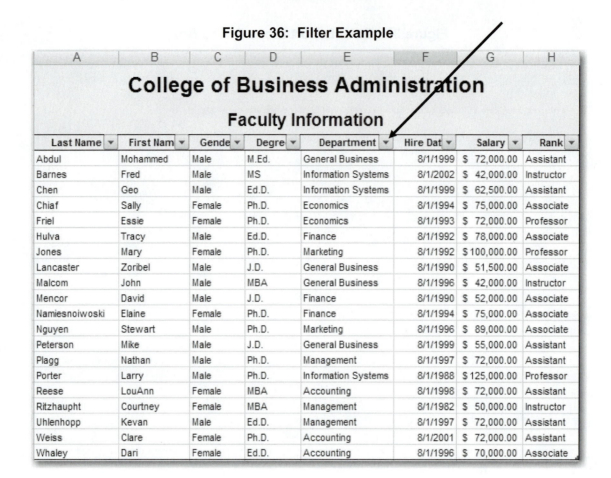

A	B	C	D	E	F	G	H
College of Business Administration							
Faculty Information							
Last Name	**First Nam**	**Gende**	**Degre**	**Department**	**Hire Dat**	**Salary**	**Rank**
Abdul	Mohammed	Male	M.Ed.	General Business	8/1/1999	$ 72,000.00	Assistant
Barnes	Fred	Male	MS	Information Systems	8/1/2002	$ 42,000.00	Instructor
Chen	Geo	Male	Ed.D.	Information Systems	8/1/1999	$ 62,500.00	Assistant
Chiaf	Sally	Female	Ph.D.	Economics	8/1/1994	$ 75,000.00	Associate
Friel	Essie	Female	Ph.D.	Economics	8/1/1993	$ 72,000.00	Professor
Hulva	Tracy	Male	Ed.D.	Finance	8/1/1992	$ 78,000.00	Associate
Jones	Mary	Female	Ph.D.	Marketing	8/1/1992	$ 100,000.00	Professor
Lancaster	Zoribel	Male	J.D.	General Business	8/1/1990	$ 51,500.00	Associate
Malcom	John	Male	MBA	General Business	8/1/1996	$ 42,000.00	Instructor
Mencor	David	Male	J.D.	Finance	8/1/1990	$ 52,000.00	Associate
Namiesnoiwoski	Elaine	Female	Ph.D.	Finance	8/1/1994	$ 75,000.00	Associate
Nguyen	Stewart	Male	Ph.D.	Marketing	8/1/1996	$ 89,000.00	Associate
Peterson	Mike	Male	J.D.	General Business	8/1/1999	$ 55,000.00	Assistant
Plagg	Nathan	Male	Ph.D.	Management	8/1/1997	$ 72,000.00	Assistant
Porter	Larry	Male	Ph.D.	Information Systems	8/1/1988	$ 125,000.00	Professor
Reese	LouAnn	Female	MBA	Accounting	8/1/1998	$ 72,000.00	Assistant
Ritzhaupht	Courtney	Female	MBA	Management	8/1/1982	$ 50,000.00	Instructor
Uhlenhopp	Kevan	Male	Ed.D.	Management	8/1/1997	$ 72,000.00	Assistant
Weiss	Clare	Female	Ph.D.	Accounting	8/1/2001	$ 72,000.00	Assistant
Whaley	Dari	Female	Ed.D.	Accounting	8/1/1996	$ 70,000.00	Associate

Figure 37: Filter's Drop-Down List

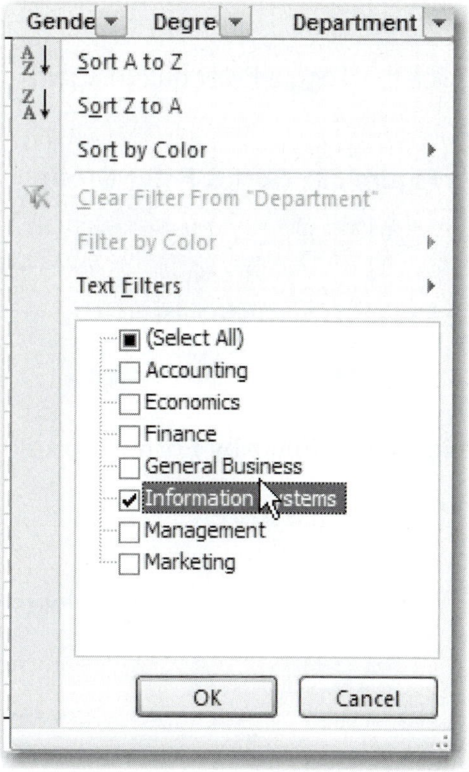

Figure 38: Filter Results

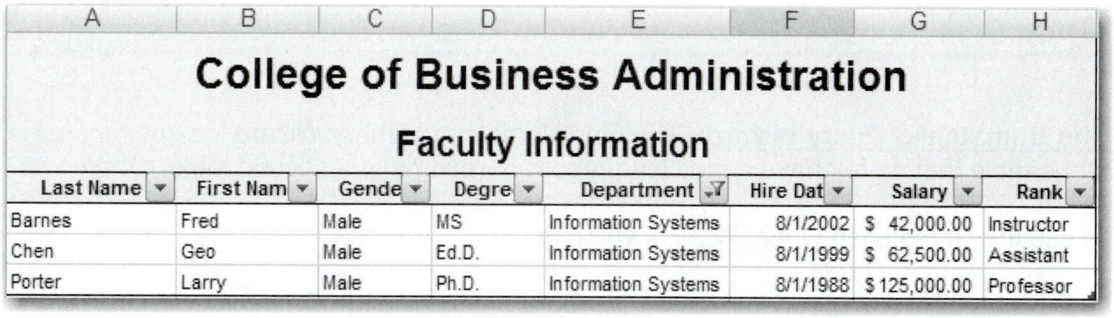

College of Business Administration

Faculty Information

Last Name	First Nam	Gende	Degre	Department	Hire Dat	Salary	Rank
Barnes	Fred	Male	MS	Information Systems	8/1/2002	$ 42,000.00	Instructor
Chen	Geo	Male	Ed.D.	Information Systems	8/1/1999	$ 62,500.00	Assistant
Porter	Larry	Male	Ph.D.	Information Systems	8/1/1988	$ 125,000.00	Professor

<u>Filter by Form</u>: Filter By Form allows you to locate records based on specified criteria. The user uses a form to enter search criteria. The search criteria are entered by clicking drop-down lists beside the field names and selecting search values.

To use the Filter by Form tool, you can:

1. From the Sort & Filter group located on the Home tab, click the Advanced button. See Figure 39.

2. Select the Filter by Form command.

3. Click in the field that you want searched. A drop-down list will appear. For instance, Figure 40 shows the Last Name field as the current search field.

4. From the Sort & Filter group, click the Toggle Filter button. Refer to Figure 39. The results should now display.

5. To remove the filter, click the Toggle Filter button again.

Figure 39: Sort & Filter Group

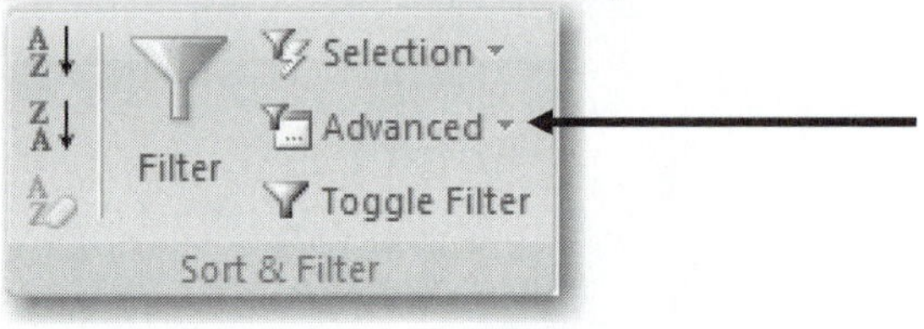

Figure 40: Filter by Form Example

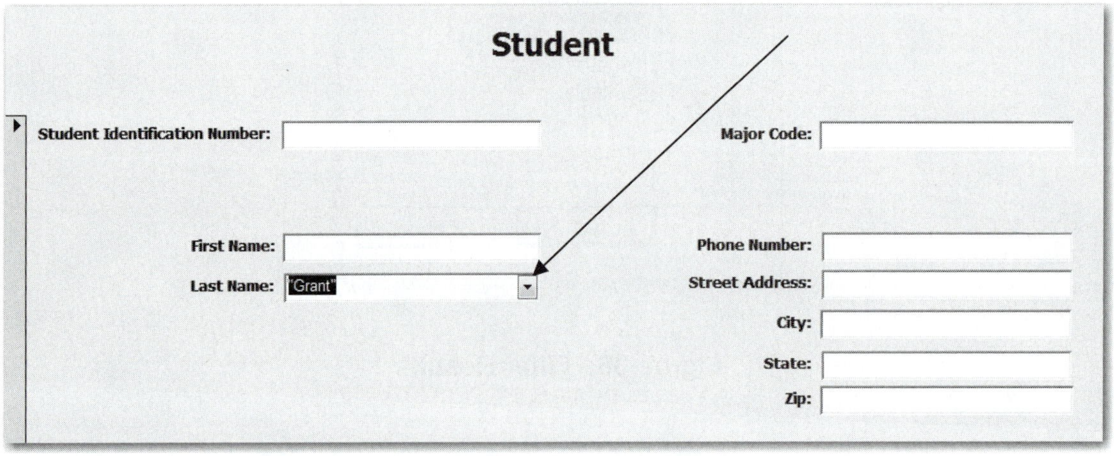

<u>Find Unmatched Query Wizard:</u> The Find Unmatched Query Wizard locates records in one table that do not have a matching record or records in a second table.

To use the Unmatched Query Wizard, you can:

1. From the Other group located on the Create tab, click the Query Wizard button.

2. In the New Query dialog box, select the Find Unmatched Query Wizard option. See Figure 41.

3. Through a series of Find Unmatched Query Wizard dialog boxes, specify the tables or queries that you want compared, designate a matching field, specify the fields that you want to see in the query results, and then name the query.

Figure 41: Find Unmatched Query Wizard

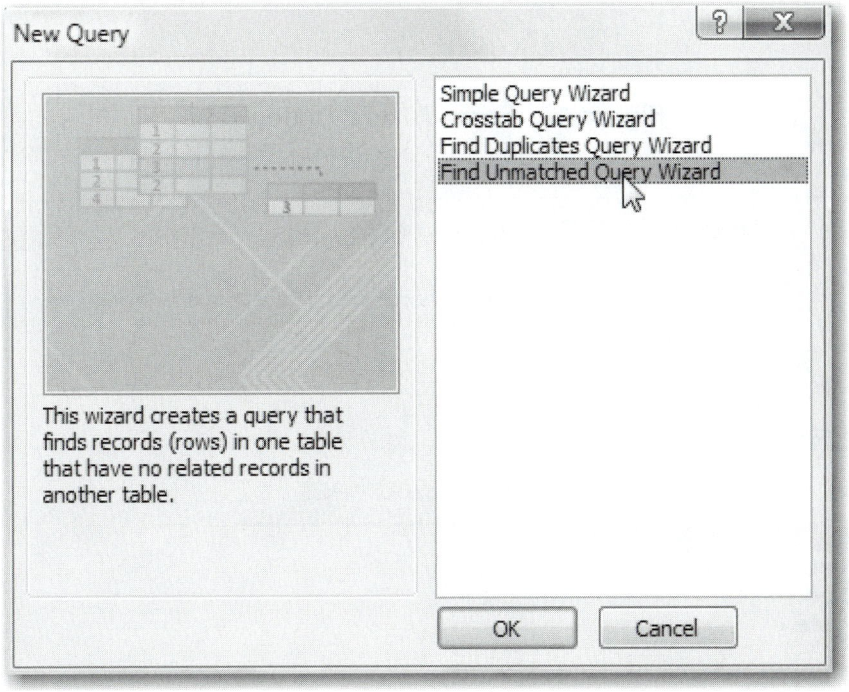

Form Design: As this term is used in MIS Cases: Decision Making With Application Software, Fourth Edition, form design means preparing user-friendly, professional-looking data entry forms. When designing a form, you have several options. See Figure 42. Use your system's online help system to learn more about form design options.

Figure 42: Forms Group

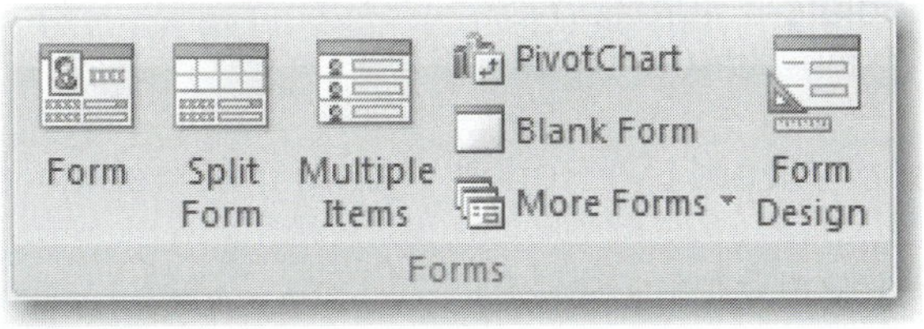

Form Wizard: Microsoft Access provides a Form Wizard to help you quickly design a form. Through a series of dialog boxes, the Form Wizard asks a series of questions about the new form's contents and appearance. The Form Wizard uses your answers to design the form. Once the form is designed, you have the option of modifying the form's contents and appearance.

To use the Form Wizard, you can:

1. From the Forms group located on the Create tab, click the More Forms button.

2. Select the Form Wizard option for the drop-down list. The first of several Form Wizard dialog boxes appears. See Figure 43.

3. In the remaining Form Wizard dialog boxes, specify the form's layout, style and title.

Figure 43: Form Wizard Dialog Box

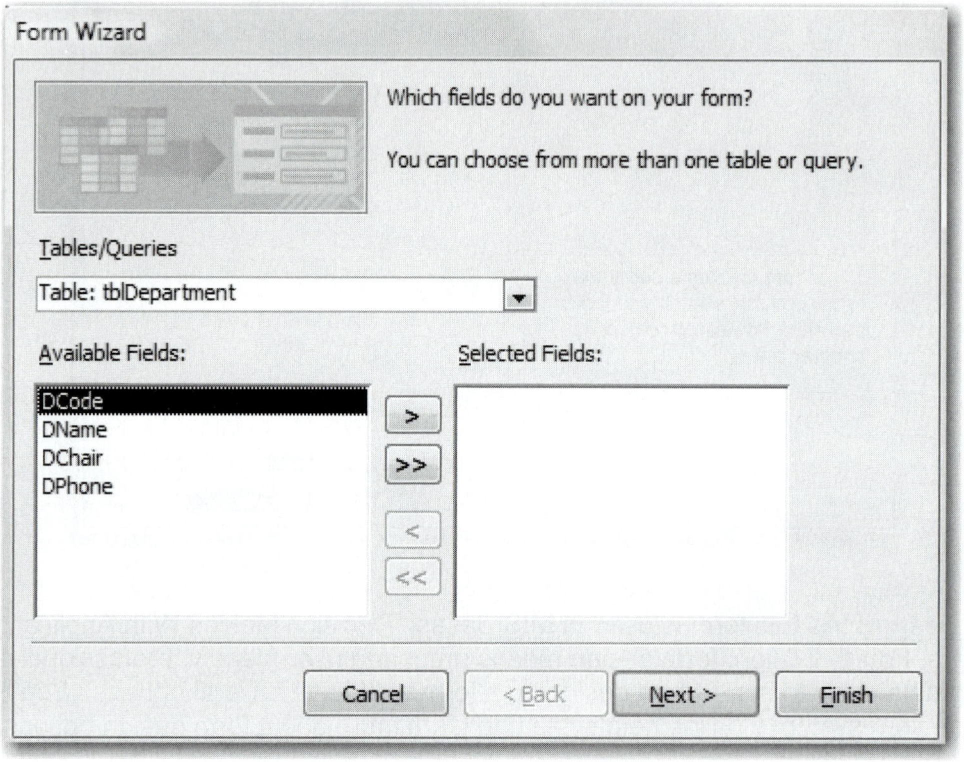

IIF Function: The immediate IF function evaluates a condition as either true or false. The syntax for the immediate IF function is: **=IIF(condition,value_if_true,value_if_false)**.

Label Wizard: The Label Wizard is a Report Wizard that creates mailing labels for you.

To use the Label Wizard, you can:

1. In the navigation pane, click on the table or query that contains the fields you want to use in the labels.

2. From the Reports group located on the Create tab, click the Labels button. See Figure 44.

Figure 44: Labels Button

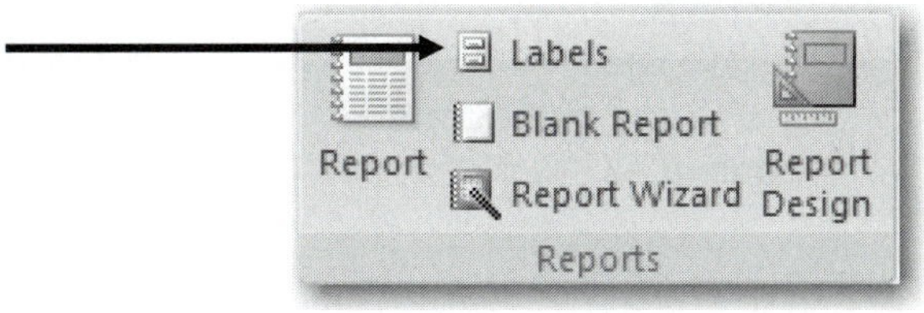

3. The first of several Label Wizard dialog boxes will appear. See Figure 45.

4. The Label Wizard dialog boxes ask you a series of questions, and based on your answers, prepares a set of mailing labels for you. The Label Wizard asks you to specify label size, font and color, fields to include, sort field, and name for the labels. Figure 46 provides an example of mailing labels generated by Microsoft Access's Label Wizard.

Figure 45: Label Wizard Dialog Box

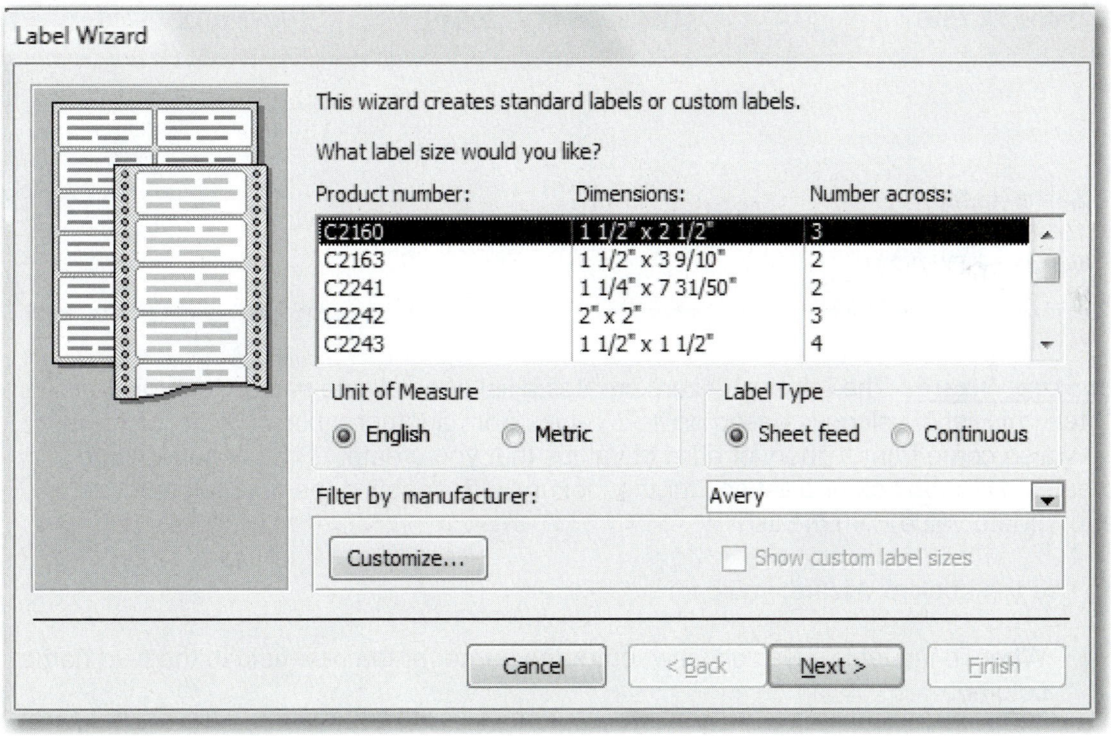

Figure 46: Mailing Labels Generated By the Label Wizard

Mitchell Grant 1010 Boulevard Rd. Dallas,TX 75201	Lexina Sasser 210 Rushing Meadows Garland,TX 75202	Elwood Rother 3001 Ripple Creek Grapevine,TX 75203
Shibo Chen 15712 Tanglewood Road Denton,TX 75204	Damir Elotmani 2121 Hyde Parke Dallas,TX 75205	Eliah Schoenhals 1920 Pine Drive Dallas,TX 75206
Troy Erbst 1780 Glacier Drive Dallas,TX 75207	Clarissa Ottinger 11908 Coltrane Lewisville,TX 75208	Edith Blochowiak 1223 Ridgewood Allen,TX 75210
Sasha Harley 10625 Brighton McKinney,TX 75201		

Lookup Wizard: The Lookup Wizard creates a list of allowable values for a given field. Often, this list of values is based on field values from another table. The list of values may also come from a query or a list of values that you create. The Lookup Wizard creates a combo box or a list box for the lookup field, enabling the user to select an appropriate value from the list.

To use the Lookup Wizard, you can:

1. When in the table's Design view, enter the name for the new field in the field name column.

2. For the new field's data type, click the drop-down list, and then select the Lookup Wizard option. See Figure 47. The Lookup Wizard dialog box now opens. Next, the Lookup Wizard asks you, through a series of dialog boxes, about how it is to obtain its values, the location of the list's values, the fields that contain the values that should appear in the list, sort order, the width of the columns, and a name for the lookup column.

Figure 47: Lookup Wizard Option

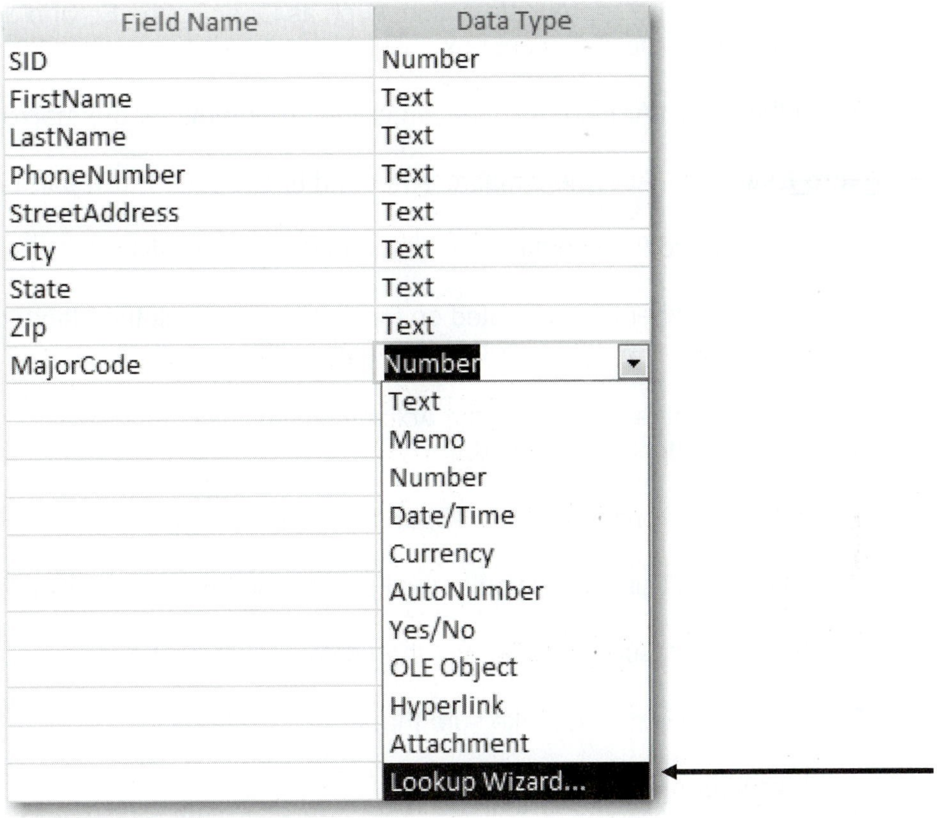

<u>Macro:</u> A macro is a group of automated instructions. When the macro is executed, Microsoft Access performs these instructions for you. For instance, you may want Microsoft Access to print a record or report, open a form or report, find a record, move data between tables, or exit Access. Macros provide you with the ability to custom design procedures for your database. Keep in mind that you can also create macro groups. You should use your system's online help feature to investigate macros.

To create a macro, you can:

1. From the Other group located on the Create tab, click the Macro button. See Figure 48. The Macro Builder window opens. See Figure 49.

Figure 48: Macro Button

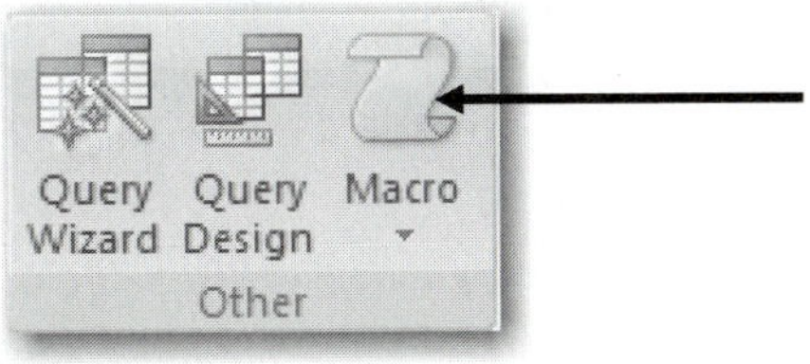

2. In the Action column, click the drop-down list arrow beside the first empty box, and then select the appropriate action, such as OpenForm. Enter a descriptive comment in the Comment box.

3. In the Action Arguments pane, enter the arguments for the macro.

Macro Example: Assume a macro is needed to open the frmDepartment form.

To create a macro to open this form, you can do the following:

1. From the Other group located on the Create tab, click the Macro button. The Macro Builder window opens. See Figure 49.

2. Click the first empty box in the Action column; click the drop-down arrow, and then select the OpenForm action.

3. In the Comments box, enter "Opens frmDepartment".

4. Press F6. (This moves you to the Form Name box in the Action Arguments pane.)

5. Click the drop-down arrow, and then select frmDepartment.

6. In the View text box, make sure that Form is selected.

7. Save your macro.

8. To run your macro, click the Run Macro button located in the Database Tools group.

Figure 49: Open frmDepartment Macro

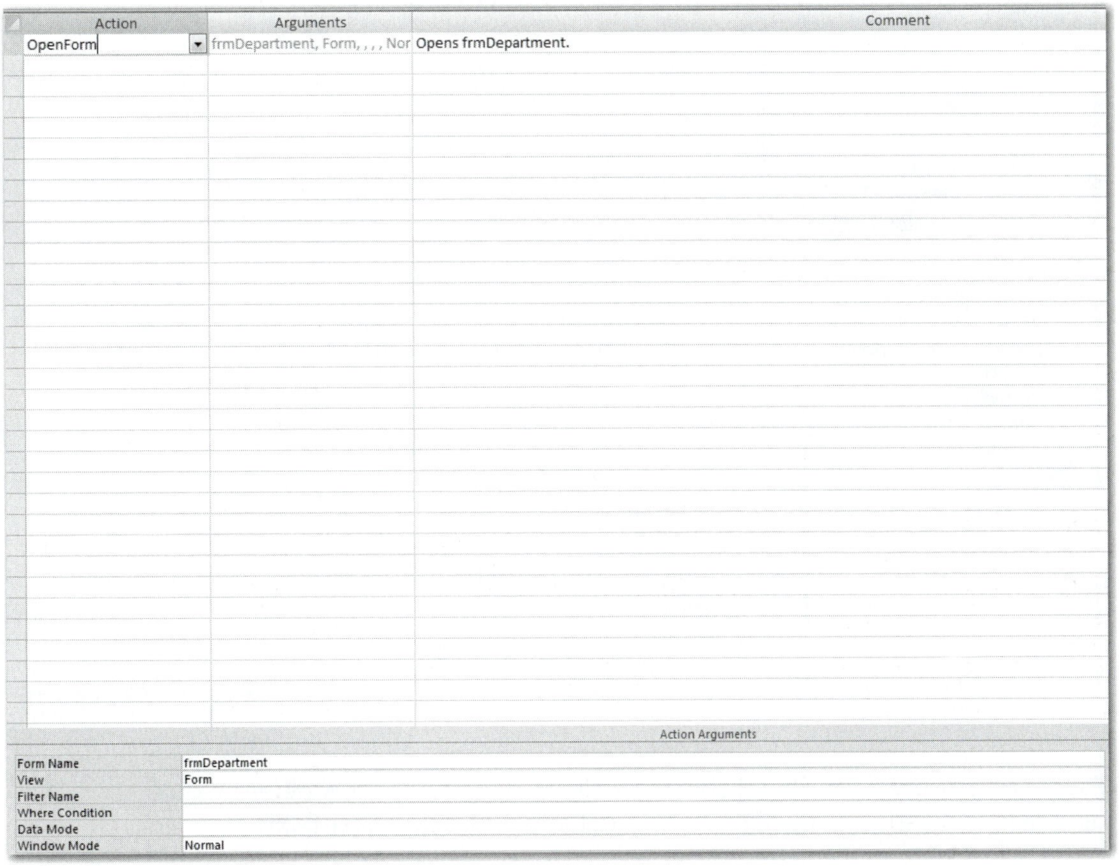

<u>Parameter Query:</u> A parameter query prompts the user for search criteria each time the query is executed. When creating a parameter query, you enter a prompt message in the criteria row. The parameter query will retrieve and display records from the table(s) meeting the entered search criteria. (See Select Query.)

To create a parameter query, you can:

1. Create a select query.

2. In the criteria row, enter a prompt message for the field for which the user should supply a value. The prompt message is contained in brackets. For instance, if the user should supply a department code, the prompt message would appear as [Please Enter Department Code]. See Figure 50.

Figure 50: Parameter Query in Design View

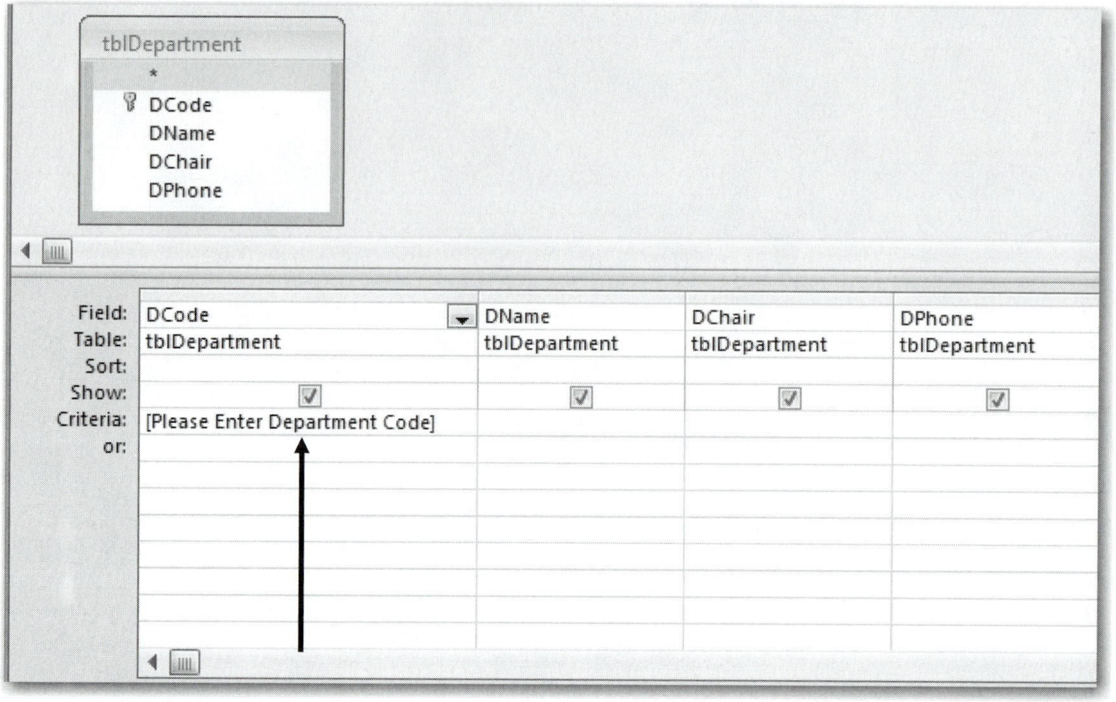

PivotTable View: The PivotTable view allows the user to view different data dimensions by specifying different row, column, data, and filter fields.

To create a PivotTable, you can:

1. Open the query or table that will serve as the source for the PivotTable.

2. From the Views group located on the Design tab, click the drop-down arrow located on the View button. Select PivotTable View. The PivotTable view window should now open.

3. From the PivotTable Field List dialog box, you can drag and drop field names onto the row, column, data, and filter areas of the layout guide.

Relationship: A relationship is an association between two tables. Different types of relationships exist, such as one-to-one, one-to-many, and many-to-many. If you need to associate data in the Department table with data in the Position table, you should define a relationship between the two tables. To define a relationship between two tables, the two tables must have a common column. For instance, the Department table has a DCode field, and the Position table has a DCode field too. (Keep in mind that the field names do not need to be the same.) The two fields should have the same data type. At this point, you should review your system's online help feature to learn more about relationships.

To define a relationship, you can:

1. From the Show/Hide group located on the Database Tools tab, click the Relationships button. See Figure 51. The Relationships window should now open. See Figure 52.

2. If a table is missing from the Relationships window, click the Show Table button located in the Relationships group. See Figure 53. The Relationships group is located on the Design tab. You can double click the table name to add it to the Relationships window.

3. Click the field name in the first table and drag the field name onto the corresponding field name in the second table. (In other words, you can click the primary key in the first table and then drag the primary key field onto the foreign key in the second table.) The Edit Relationship dialog box appears. In the Edit Relationship dialog box, you can enforce referential integrity and specify the join type, as well as make other changes to the relationship.

Figure 51: Relationships Button

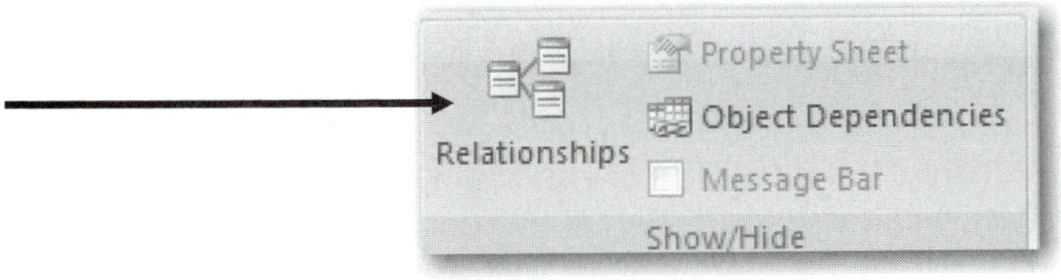

Figure 52: Relationships Window

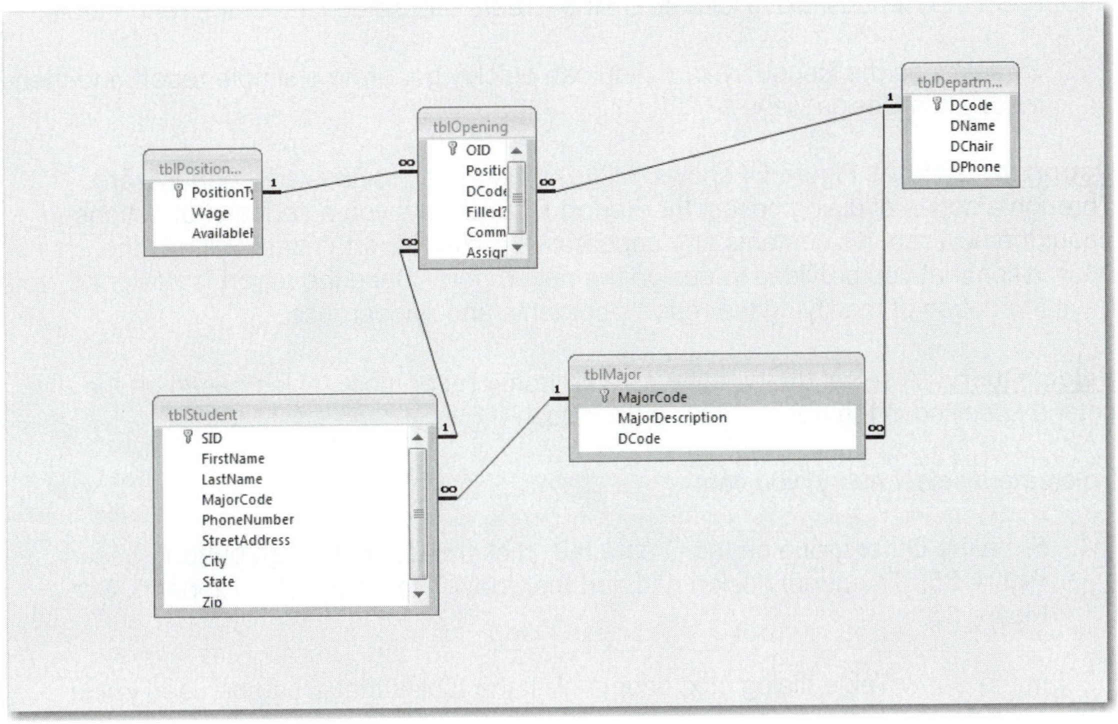

Figure 53: Show Table Button

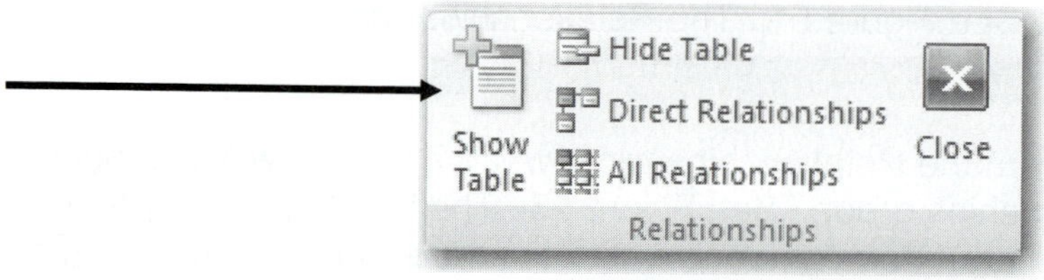

<u>Report Design:</u> As this term is used in <u>MIS Cases: Decision Making With Application Software, Fourth Edition</u>, report design means preparing user-friendly, professional-looking reports. When designing a report, you have several options for creating the report. These options include using a Report Wizard, the Report tool, or the Blank Report tool. See Figure 54.

Figure 54: Reports Group

To design a report, you can:

1. From the Reports group located on the Create tab, select one of the report tools.

2. By selecting the Report Wizard, you can quickly generate a simple report and then modify it in Design view.

<u>Report Wizard:</u> As Figure 54 shows, Microsoft Access provides a Report Wizard. Through a series of dialog boxes, the Report Wizard asks you a series of questions about the new report's contents and appearance. The Report Wizard will use the information that you provided to design the new report. Once the report is designed, you have the option of modifying the report's contents and appearance.

<u>Select Query</u>: A select query retrieves data from one or more tables based on the criteria specified in the design grid's criteria row.

To create a select query, you can:

1. From the Other group on the Create tab, click the Query Design button. See Figure 55. The query design grid and the Show Table dialog box appear. See Figure 56.

2. In the Show Table dialog box, double-click the tables that are to be used in the query.

3. To add a field name to the design grid, double-click its name in the field list.

4. In the criteria row, enter the selection criteria. For instance, to show only the filled position records for the Information Systems Department, you would enter "Information Systems" in the criteria row in the DName column and enter "Yes" in the criteria row in the Filled? column. See Figure 57.

5. From the Results group on the Design tab, click the Run button to execute the query. See Figure 58.

Figure 55: Other Group

Figure 56: Query Design Window

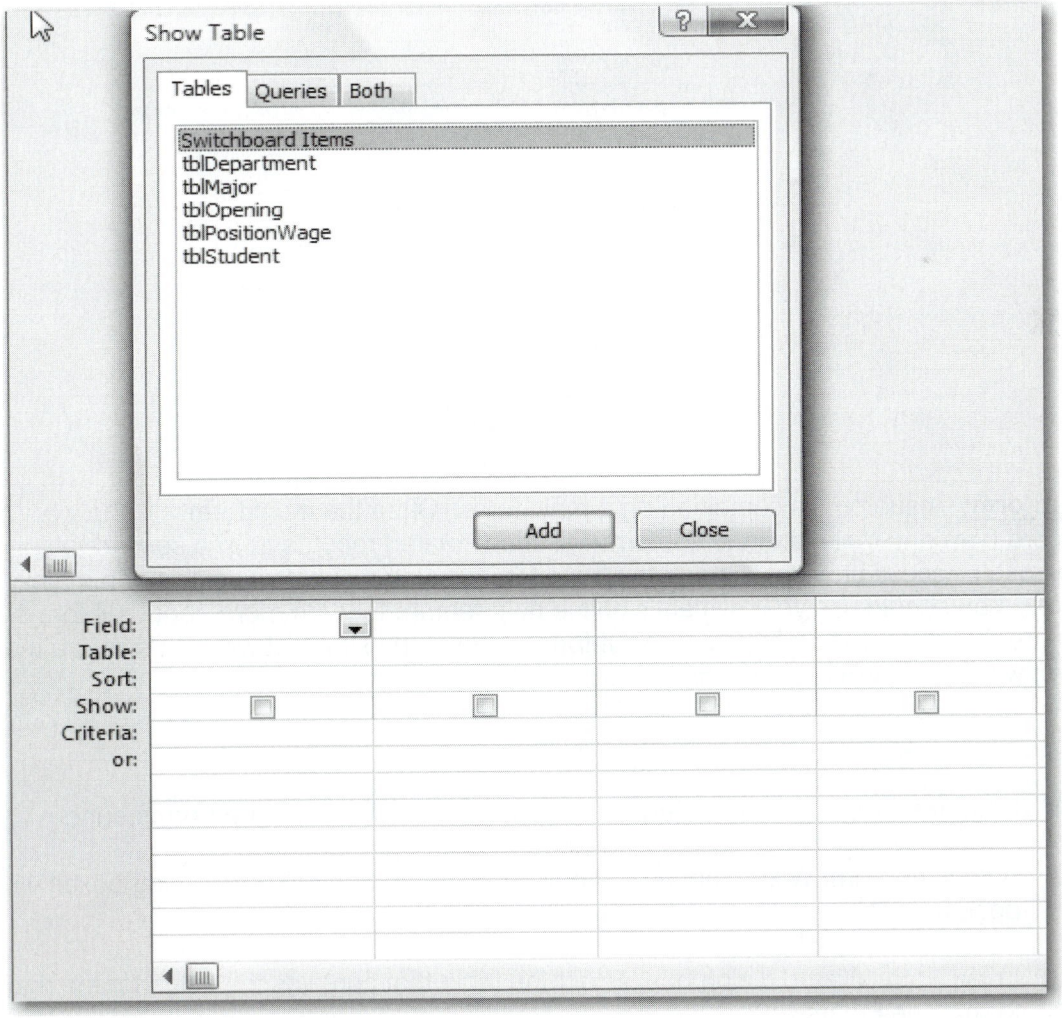

Figure 57: Select Query in Design View

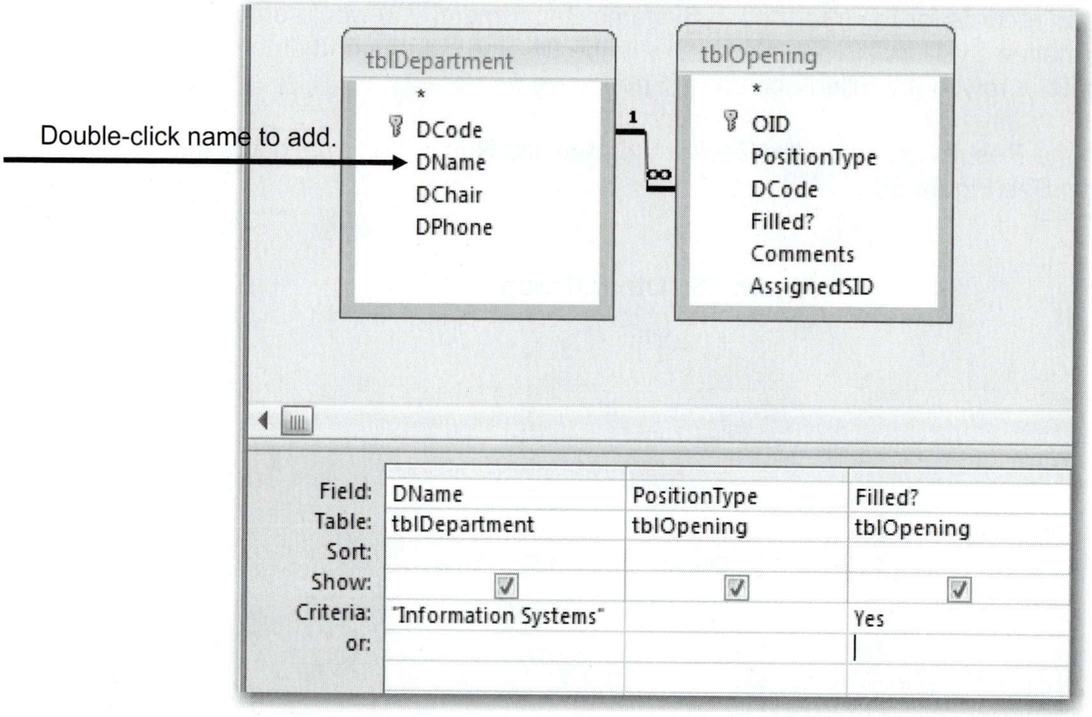

Figure 58: Results Group

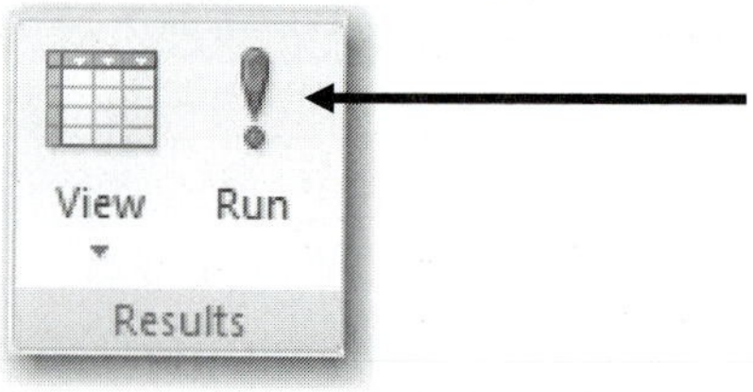

<u>Subform</u>: A subform is contained on a main form. Often the main form will show a record from one table, and the subform will show related records from a second table. Microsoft Access provides several methods for including a subform as part of a main form. You should use your system's online help feature to learn more about subforms. Figure 59 shows a main form with a subform. One of the simplest ways to create a main form with a subform is to use the Form Wizard.

To create a main form with a subform, you can:

1. From the Forms group located on the Create tab, click the More Forms button.

2. Select the Form Wizard option. The first of several Form Wizard dialog boxes will appear.

3. In the Form Wizard dialog box, select the table that contains the fields for the main form. See Figure 60.

4. In the Form Wizard dialog box, select the fields that should appear on the main form. See Figure 60.

5. Before pressing the Next button, select the table that contains the fields for the subform. Select the fields for the subform. Click the Next button.

6. The Form Wizard will ask how you want to view the data. Select the form with subform option, and then click the Next button. See Figure 61.

7. The Form Wizard will ask how to layout the subform data. Select the datasheet option, and then click the Next button.

8. The Form Wizard will ask you to select a style. Select a style, and then click the Next button.

9. The Form Wizard will ask you to name the form and subform. After you have named the form and subform, click the Finish button.

10. Switch to Design view and make any necessary changes to the new form.

Figure 59: Main Form with Subform

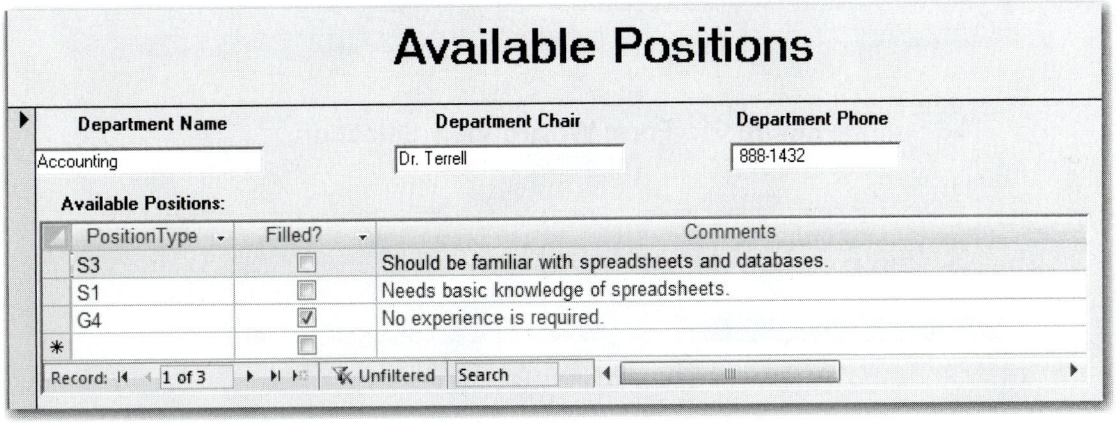

Figure 60: Form Wizard Table and Field Selection

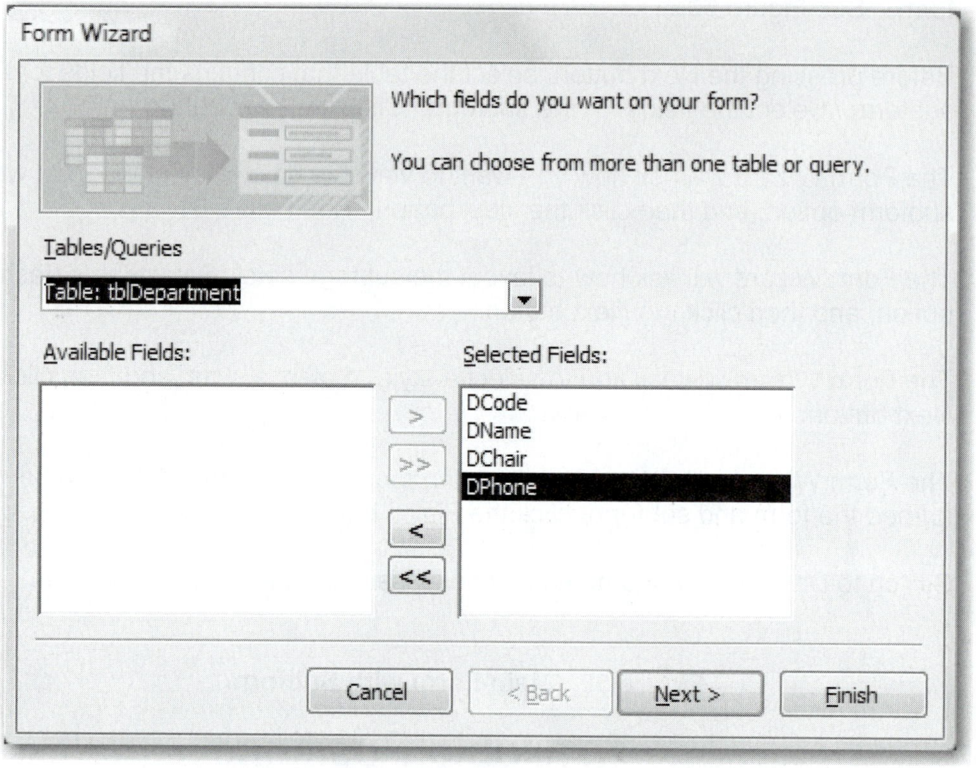

Figure 61: Form Wizard View Selection

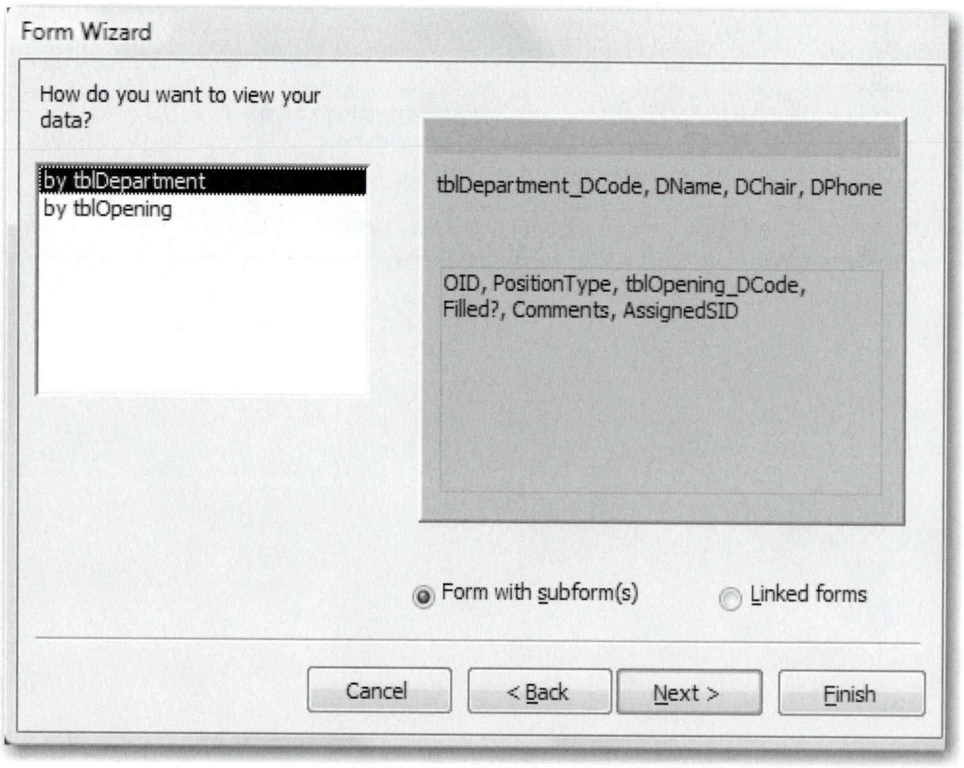

Switchboard: A switchboard provides a menu that a user uses to access various database objects, such as forms, tables, reports, and queries. Figure 62 shows a sample switchboard.

To create a switchboard, you can:

1. From the Database Tools group located on the Database Tools tab, click the Switchboard Manager button. See Figure 63.

2. Click the Yes button when asked if you would like to create a switchboard. The Switchboard Manager dialog box now appears. At this point, you can add switchboard pages and add items to the switchboards. See Figure 64.

Figure 62: Sample Switchboard

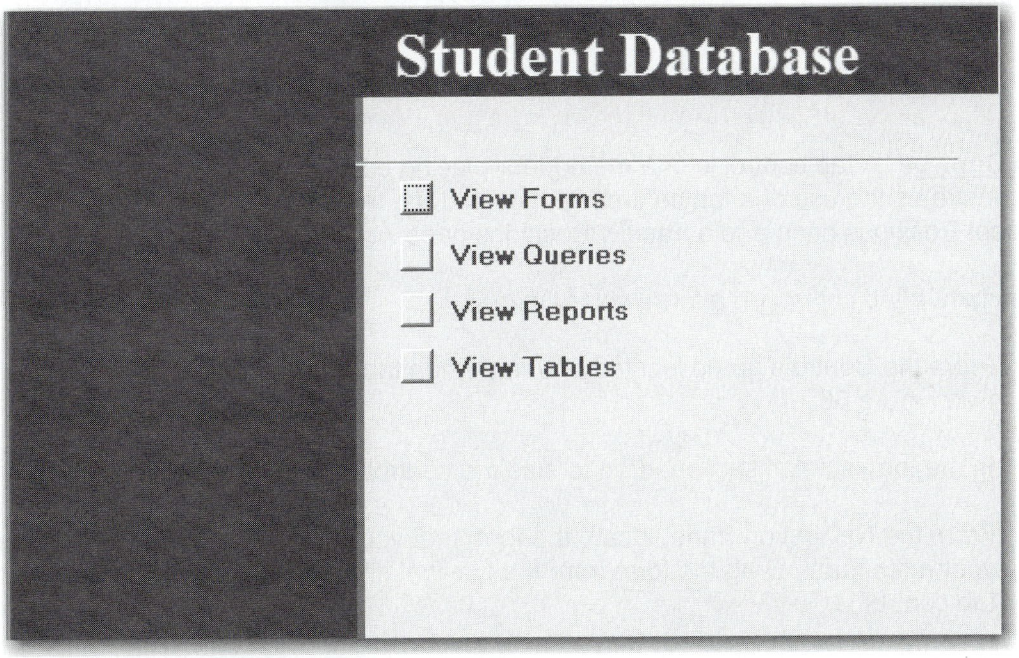

Figure 63: Switchboard Manager Button

Figure 64: Switchboard Manager Dialog Box

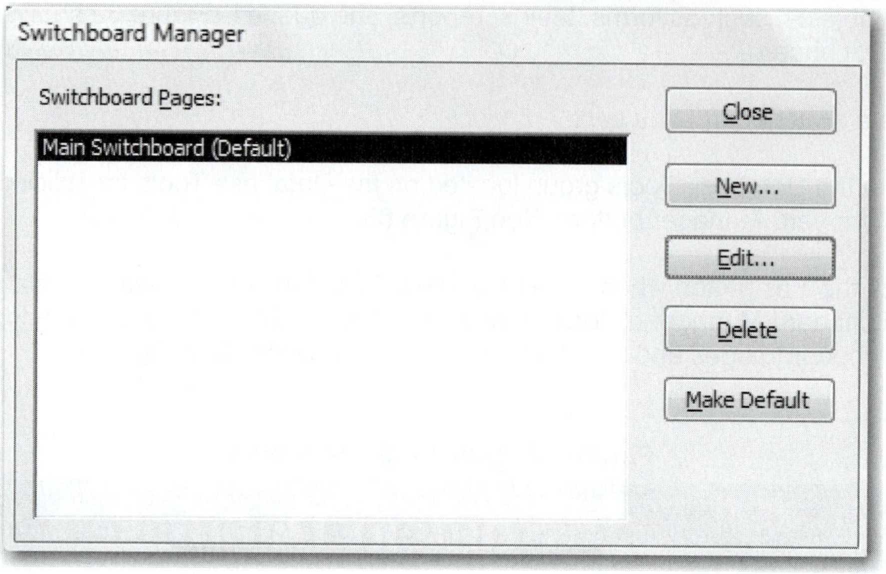

<u>Tab Control:</u> A tab control is one method for placing a subform on a form. Figure 65 demonstrates the use of a tab control. Notice that the tab control has two pages, a Student Positions page and a Faculty Positions page.

To include a tab control on a form, you can:

1. From the Controls group located on the Design tab, click the Tab Control button. See Figure 66.

2. In the form's detail section, drag to size the control. See Figure 67.

3. From the Navigation Pane, locate the form that you wish to use as the subform on your main form. Drag the form from the Navigation Pane onto the newly created tab control.

4. At this point, you may need to reposition the subform's placement on the tab control page.

5. Double click the tab control page's tab. When the property dialog box opens, change the name property.

Figure 65: Tab Control Example

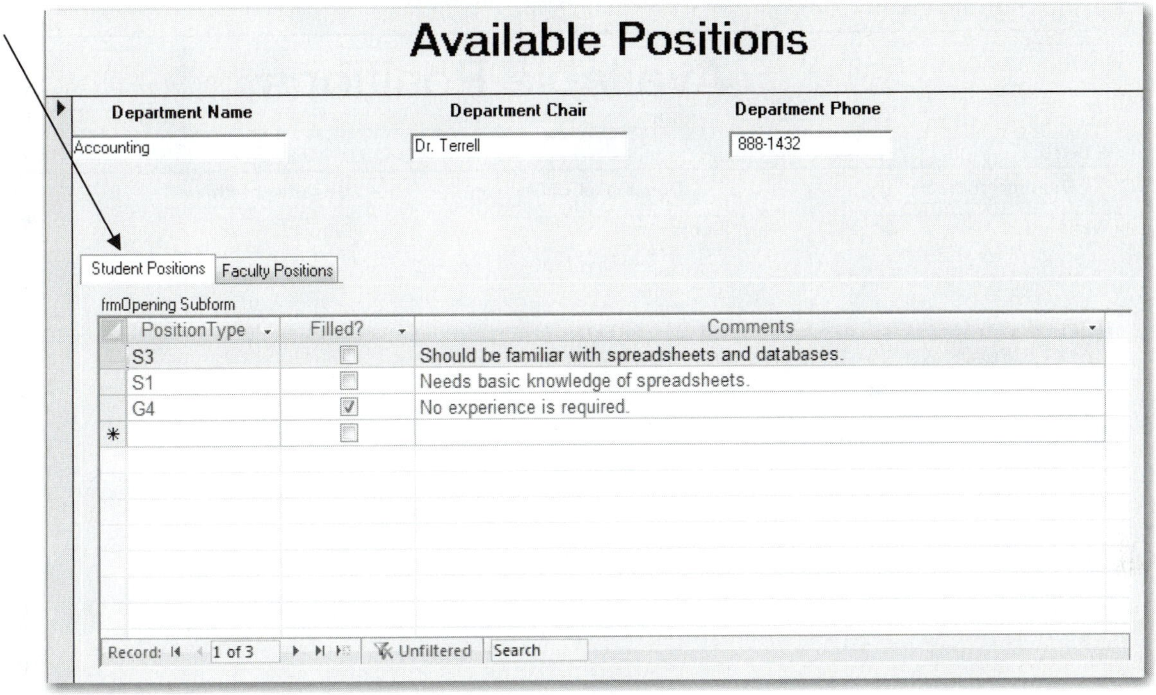

Figure 66: Tab Control Button

Figure 67: Tab Control in Design View

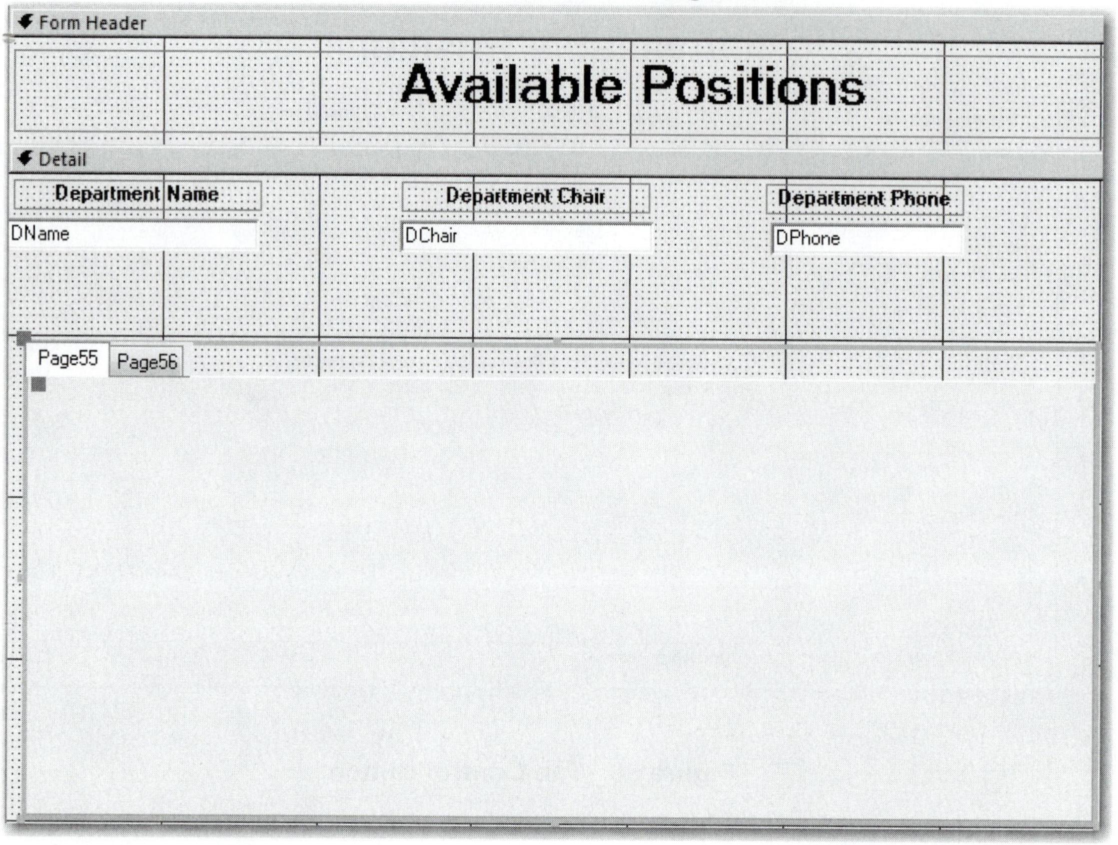

<u>Table Design:</u> As this term is used in <u>MIS Cases: Decision Making With Application Software, Fourth Edition</u>, table design refers to the process of creating tables. Keep in mind that the process of identifying which tables to create and which fields to include in the tables is a more detailed process and covered in database management courses.

To create a table, you can:

1. From the Tables group located on the Create tab, click the Table Design button. See Figure 68.

Figure 68: Table Design

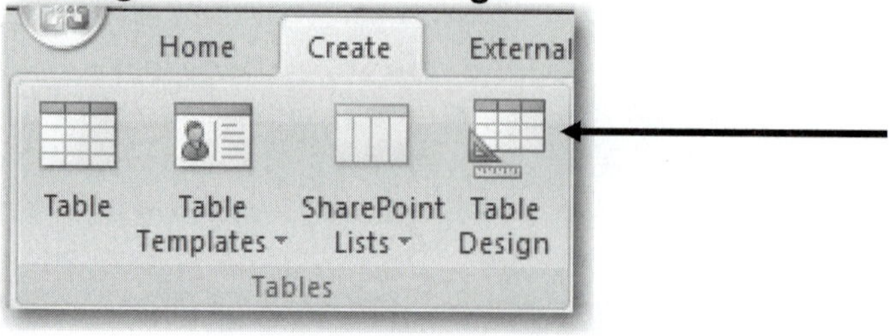

2. For each field, you can specify its name, data type, description, and properties. You should select one field to serve as the primary key. Figure 69 shows the table Design view.

Figure 69: Table Design View

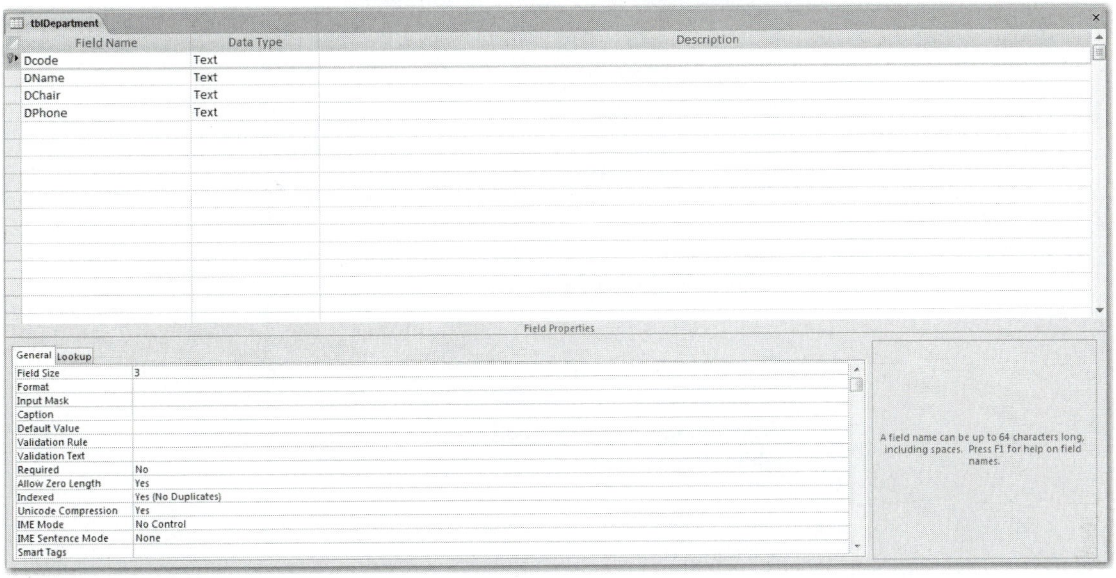

<u>Update Query:</u> An update query makes global changes to a field or fields. For instance, assume that hourly wages paid to student workers will increase by 10 percent. You can create an update query to update the hourly wage field values. Keep in mind that the update query results cannot be reversed.

To create an update query, you can:

1. From the Other group located on the Create tab, click the Query Design button. Click the Close button.

2. Add the table or tables that contain the fields that you want updated.

3. From the Query Type group located on the Design tab, click the Update Query button. See Figure 70.

4. Add the fields that should be updated to the design grid. See Figure 71.

Figure 70: Update Query Button

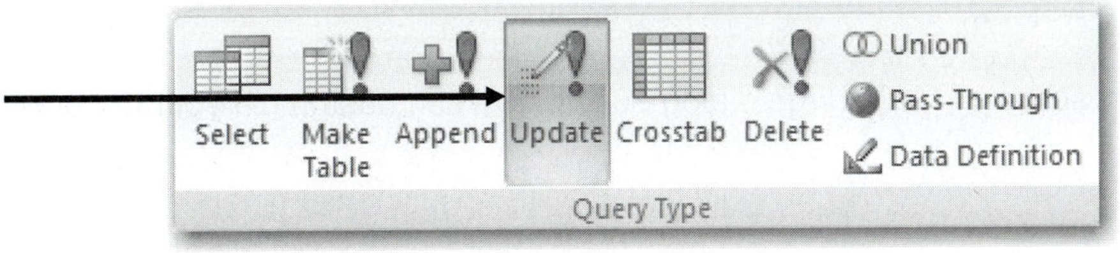

5. In the Update To row in the design grid, enter the expression that the update query should use to update the field's values.

6. Run the query.

Figure 71: Update Query in Design View

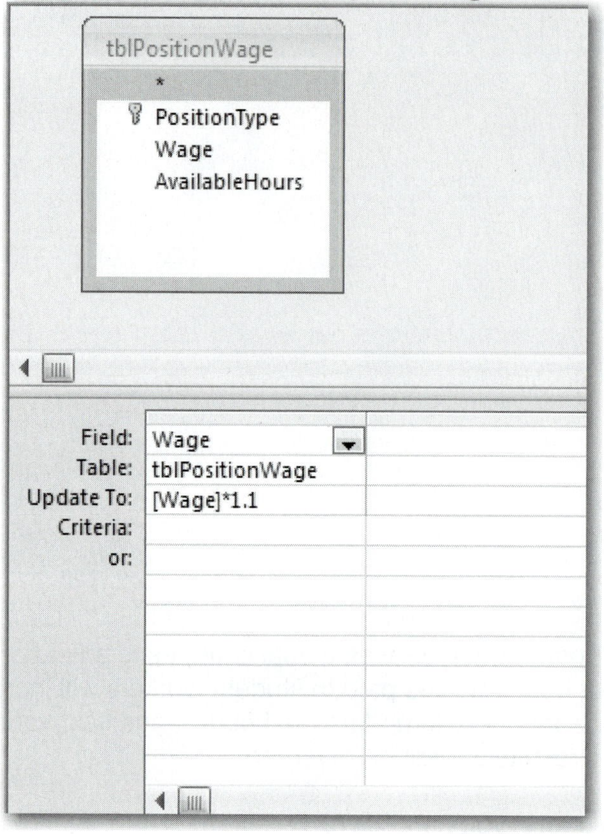

<u>Word Mail Merge Wizard</u>: The Word Mail Merge Wizard allows you to include data from a query or table in a Microsoft Word document.

To include data from a table or query in a Microsoft Word document, you can:

1. From the Export group located on the External Data tab, click the drop-down arrow beside the More button.

2. Select the Merge It with Microsoft Office Word command. The Microsoft Word Mail Merge Wizard appears. Specify whether you want to link to an existing Microsoft Word document or create a new document. Click the OK button. A Microsoft Word document opens, and the Mail Merge dialog box displays on the right hand side of the window.

3. Through a series of Mail Merge dialog boxes, you can customize your document.

Web Page Glossary

This Web page glossary is designed to accompany MIS Cases: Decision Making with Application Software, Fourth Edition, published by Pearson Prentice Hall. When preparing an MIS Cases: Decision Making with Application Software, Fourth Edition case, several Web page skills are necessary. Each case's skills check feature identifies the major skills that are required to complete the case. Before preparing the case, you should use the skills check feature to help identify which skills you should review.

This Web page glossary provides a brief explanation and review of the skills utilized in MIS Cases: Decision Making with Application Software, Fourth Edition. This glossary does not provide detailed explanations for the skills. If you need a detailed explanation on how to use a particular skill, you should use your system's online help feature to learn more about the skill. Your system's online help feature is an excellent way to quickly learn about the skill, as well as obtain a detailed explanation on how to use the skill in a Web page.

Web Page Skills

Basic Web Page Design: As this term is used in MIS Cases: Decision Making with Application Software, Fourth Edition, basic Web page design is the ability to create and develop a basic, simple Web page. When designing a Web page, you make decisions about information placement, fonts, colors, backgrounds, content, titles, links, page length, and images.

Header: Headers label primary and secondary sections of a Web page. Headers provide the Web page visitor with an indication about a section's content, enabling the visitor to determine if she wants to view the information contained in the section. For instance, a work experience section might be labeled "Work Experience". Likewise, if you discuss your family in your Web page, this section might be titled "My Family".

HTML: The Hypertext Markup Language is a language used to create Web pages.

Hyperlink: A hyperlink enables the reader to "jump" to a different location. A hyperlink links to another location in the Web page, another document on the server, or a document on a server thousands of miles away. A word, combination of words, or graphic can serve as a hyperlink.

Image Insertion: Web page editors make the addition of images to your Web page very easy. An image can enhance the presentation of the Web page, and it can serve as a hyperlink. Many Web sites provide free graphics for Web pages.

List: A list is a series of items that are included on a Web page. You can create different types of lists, including bulleted, numbered, definition, directory, and menu lists.

Paragraph: A paragraph is a group of sentences that convey a single idea. Paragraphs are often separated by a blank line. To separate one paragraph from another, a paragraph break is inserted.

Table: A table organizes and presents data as a series of rows and columns.

Text Editing: Text editing is the ability to make changes to previously entered text.

Web Page Editor: A Web page editor is a program used to create professional-looking Web pages.